The War Lo
A Study of Plato's

This new examination of the *Republic* begins with questions ignored by most students of this famous and much-studied dialogue. Why is Plato's most extensive portrait of philosophy pervaded with the language and imagery of war? Why is a discussion supposedly about justice almost entirely about how to educate natural warriors? Why must the philosopher-kings of Kallipolis be first of all 'champions of war'? Why is the supposedly 'feminine drama' of Book Five preoccupied with war? The pursuit of questions such as these brings Craig to an understanding of Plato's teaching about justice, philosophy, and politics that differs radically from what is generally held today.

The search for why the *Republic*'s philosophers come from the ranks of 'war lovers' leads Craig to reassess the relation between the 'city in logos' and timocracy (the regime openly dedicated to war), and this reassessment in turn brings a new perspective on Plato's political thought in general. Similarly, analysis of the timocratic man leads to a deeper understanding of the psychology on which the whole dialogue is based, especially its teaching about justice and its treatment of love. Following the dialogue's hint that language provides the 'tracks' of ideas, Craig compares the four distinct kinds of love that figure in the dialogue, and thereby helps clarify several puzzling issues, not the least of which is the strange kinship between the philosopher and the tyrant. And through examining the peculiar problems posed by what he argues are two distinct kinds of timocrats – exemplified by Glaukon and Adeimantos – Craig illuminates the rationale underlying both educational schemes sketched in the dialogue: the political one of Books Two and Three and the pre-philosophical one of Book Seven.

In bringing the *Republic* vividly to life, Craig shows that Plato's ideas on virtually all questions of permanent interest to human beings provide a corrective to views now in vogue. *The War Lover* is thus as much a commentary on contemporary intellectual and political life as it is a challenging new interpretation of an ancient text.

LEON HAROLD CRAIG teaches in the Department of Political Science at the University of Alberta.

To my family

THE WAR LOVER

A Study of Plato's *Republic*

Leon Harold Craig

UNIVERSITY OF TORONTO PRESS
Toronto Buffalo London

© University of Toronto Press Incorporated 1994
Toronto Buffalo London
Printed in Canada

Reprinted in paperback 1996, 2003

ISBN 0-8020-0586-1 (cloth)
ISBN 0-8020-7942-3 (paper)

Printed on acid-free paper

Canadian Cataloguing in Publication Data

Craig, Leon H., 1941–
The war lover : a study of Plato's Republic

Includes bibliographical references and index.
ISBN 0-8020-0586-1 (bound) ISBN 0-8020-7942-3 (pbk.)

1. Plato. Republic. I. Title.

JC71.P6C73 1994   321'.07   C94-930579-0

University of Toronto Press acknowledges
the financial assistance to its
publishing program of the
Canada Council and the
Ontario Arts Council.

This book has been published
with the help of a grant from the
Canadian Federation for the Humanities,
using funds provided by the
Canada Council.

Contents

Acknowledgments vii

A Notice to the Reader ix

Prologue: On Reading a Platonic Dialogue xiii

1 *War and Peace* 3

2 *A Tale of Two Cities* 22

3 *Sons and Lovers* 42

4 *Heart of Darkness* 58

5 *Crime and Punishment* 112

6 *The Portrait of a Lady* 183

7 *Pride and Prejudice* 245

Epilogue: On Reading Plato's *Republic* 290

Notes 293

Bibliography 427

Index of Names 435

Acknowledgments

When one works on a book for over a dozen years, one is apt to incur more debts than can be readily recalled. But I know the following friends and colleagues deserve mention for having read and criticized parts or all of it at one or another stage of its composition: Leah Bradshaw, Patrick Coby, Laurence Lampert, Pat Malcolmson, Waller Newell, Zdravko Planinc, Tom Pocklington, Jene Porter, Larry Pratt, Gerald Proietti, Tom Swanky, and Fred Vaughan. My good friend Christopher Drummond – an English professor of the old school – read the entire manuscript with an eye towards purging it of my more egregious blunders; he cannot be blamed, of course, for those misusages I have stubbornly retained simply because they sound right to my ear. And very special thanks go to Heidi Studer, who, from first glimmerings to final proofs, so generously contributed every kind of assistance and encouragement a dilatory author could use. I must also express gratitude to the editorial staff of the University of Toronto Press, steadfastly cooperative however cranky my ideas, and in particular to my copy editor, John Parry, whose queries and suggestions caused me to reconsider every third or fourth sentence I had written. Finally, but most importantly, there is my wife to thank, who has endured the prolonged gestation of this book through half of our years together. Had I another life to live, it would not be sufficient to pay back all that I owe her.

A Notice to the Reader

In referring to Plato's texts, I have stayed with the normal practice of citing the subdivided Stephanus page. But in order to lend this a bit more precision without the clutter of line indications (which I have resorted to in only a few instances), I adopt the following conventions. When a relevant piece of text extends more or less throughout adjacent sections, it is indicated with a dash (e.g., 436d–e); a briefer bit of text falling *on* a subdivision is cited without such hyphenation (e.g., 473cd); and so long as no possible confusion could result, I indicate material extending into the next Stephanus page only by citing the subdivision of the concluding page (e.g., 547ea rather than 547e–548a, and 508e–b rather than 508e–509b).

> I believe that Plato actually succeeds in convincing
> those who read and understand his dialogue.
> But here is the difficulty:
> the number of people who read Plato is limited;
> and the number who understand him is still more limited.
>
> Alexandre Kojève
> *Introduction to the Reading of Hegel*

Prologue

On Reading a Platonic Dialogue

I do not know whether the following study of Plato's *Republic* is truly novel. I do suspect, however, that it is strange enough in both form and substance to warrant some comments pertinent to its peculiarities. These remarks derive from my assumptions about the purposes of philosophical scholarship in general, but are directed especially to the reading of and writing about Plato. And while these assumptions are by no means idiosyncratic, neither are they universally subscribed to by scholars today, although I gather they enjoyed a broad consensus until recent times.

Before the nineteenth century, it seems that most educated people, whether knowingly or otherwise, agreed with Plato's assessment of the strengths and weaknesses of written speech as expressed in his *Phaedrus* (274b–278d; cf. *Theaet.* 142c–143c, *7th Ltr* 341c–e). There he has Sokrates criticize the art of writing on several counts. First, it tends to weaken one's memory, given the normal inclination to rely upon written reminders to the prejudice of exercising one's natural mnemonic powers. Moreover, although written speech, like a clever painting, may seem lifelike, it is a static thing, endlessly repeating the very same words. Thus it cannot be questioned for necessary clarification and justification; and yet speech about difficult matters is never perfectly clear, nor can speech alone provide conclusive grounds of its veracity. As a consequence, something written cannot defend itself against criticism, whether just or unjust, without the further intervention of its author. Furthermore, since whatever is written is potentially accessible to anyone who can read, it is inherently imprudent speech, unable to exercise judgment of when to speak and when not.

Prologue

Indifferent to all differences of nurture or nature or fortune, it says the same things to everyone, be they young or old, sensible or foolish, friend or enemy. Finally, because it is available to be read and parroted by one and all, including those who are inadequately instructed or otherwise unfit, writings can allow the unwise to seem wise to the unwise, and first of all to themselves. This often has the consequence of making them dogmatic in their opinions and, accordingly, that much harder to get along with, that much less suited for political life.

Sokrates contrasts the word written on paper with that 'inscribed with knowledge in the soul of the learner, having the power to defend itself, knowing before whom to speak and before whom to remain silent' (276a). Writing is but an image or phantom of this living and breathing speech, which in the very nature of things is superior, more powerful. He observes that anyone who is serious about his ideas treats them as does a sensible farmer his seeds, sowing them only in appropriate soil, which has been properly prepared. There they may germinate and grow, and perhaps even multiply. Such a cultivator of ideas endeavours to plant knowledgeable speech, and only in select souls, where his words will bear fruit to the benefit of both sower and sown.

Aware of its inherent limitations, a serious and prudent person none the less has uses for writing. As a hedge against a failing memory, it provides a means of storing reminders for oneself concerning things one already truly knows. And it may serve likewise for others akin to oneself, those who follow the same path, and in whom one's communicated thoughts may gestate and grow. With such aims in mind, writing can be a refined form of amusement or recreation. However, in treating it as but a pleasant pastime, the writer presumes that an intelligent reader appreciates as well as he that nothing written deserves to be taken with complete seriousness, apt as it is to include much that is playful.

Even so, writing about worthy topics, about just and noble and good things, can itself be a noble as well a good and just thing. But to practise what could rightly be called an *art* of speech – written or otherwise – presumes not only that the speaker knows the truth concerning each particular form of thing about which he speaks, and that he can express precisely what he himself has learned through dialectical analysis and synthesis; it presumes as well that he understands human nature in its full significant diversity and can adapt his mode of expression to the differing requirements of different kinds of people:

Prologue

> For one to know the truth of each form about which he speaks or writes, he must have the power to define it entirely, [and] having defined [it], go back down through the forms until [reaching] the undivided; through the same way, he must discern the nature of a soul, discovering the form [of speech] adapted to each nature, arranging and adorning his speech accordingly, offering complex and fully harmonious speeches to the complex soul, while simple [speeches] to the simple [soul]. Not before [there is this] power will there be a kind of speech practised by art, so far as such can come into being, either for instruction or persuasion. (277b-c)

As Sokrates' speech makes clear enough, not all the problems with writing are peculiar to the written word. Some inhere in communication as such. He expressly extends his criticism to lawgivers and poets and rhetoricians, to rhapsodes and orators – to any speech, whether oral or written, that is intended to be persuasive, but which is expressed under conditions that do not allow adequate opportunity to question what is said. If a person writes knowing the truth, and can support through discussion what he has written, and through his own speech has the power to show the inferiority of writing, then (Sokrates contends) the worth of his name ought *not* to be derived from what he has written, but from the serious pursuit that underlies it. Such a person deserves to be called a 'lover of wisdom' (*philosophos*) or some such thing; to call him 'wise' is too great a name, being fit only for a god (278d; cf. 236de, 238d, 239b).

Of course, one is obliged to reflect upon the fact that the philosopher's criticisms of writing have all been given in writing, in a piece of writing cast as a dialogue, a dialogue in which he acknowledges that wise men and women from old have conveyed some of their wisdom in writing (235b) and confesses that his own love of learning renders him fatally attracted to books (230de), and in which he suggests that a well-wrought discourse – one manifesting 'logographic necessity' (*anagkē logographikē*) – must be organized like a living being in which each part is necessary and proportioned to fit with every other, and all together are sufficient (264bc). Perhaps it *is* possible, then, to invent, or discover, a form of writing that transcends the normal limitations of writing, one which successfully imitates the virtues of living speech.

But in its absence, the person intent upon using speech responsibly is apt to agree with Sokrates that live discourse has several advantages over something written. First and foremost, it allows a speaker to as-

Prologue

sess, directly and continuously, both his audience and the circumstances in which he speaks. Thus he may, within the limitations of his own prudential judgment, tailor his speech according to the practically infinite gradations and combinations of actual conditions in which he finds himself. For example, is he speaking in public, perhaps to "The Public"; or is the setting private, confidential, even intimate? And is he free to say what, and as much as, and only as much as, he wishes; or is he under some sort of compulsion or obligation to say more or less or other than he would prefer? Are those to whom he speaks one, few, or many? Are they children or adults, male or female, familiar or unknown, trustworthy or unreliable, intelligent or foolish, friends or enemies, involved or disinterested, superiors or inferiors, rustic or refined, pious or profane? What is their mood at the time? And are they willing listeners, attentive, sober, and at leisure, or otherwise? We all appreciate that it would be folly to solicit garden tips from an angry man, armed and in a hurry; and that one could surely find a better time to criticize his children. To the extent that his audience is not homogenous, however, the problem confronting a speaker is accordingly more complicated: he may simply choose to speak to some and ignore others; he may speak to its various sectors in turn; or, he may use equivocal language, intending that different auditors understand him differently (as adults do in speaking about delicate matters in the presence of children). In short, given sufficient experience with life, one comes to realize that the human use of speech is governed by more than a concern for the full and frank communication of the whole truth to all and sundry. And so almost everyone, as a reflection of natural politeness, tacitly adapts his oral speech to these other considerations, often without much awareness of doing so. Published writing, in so far as it allows the author no such prudent adaptation, would seem greatly inferior as a means of efficient, precise, and judicious communication.

Second, writing, unlike live discussion, does not allow for questioning.[1] Indeed, precisely because of this, it is the special concern of a serious writer to anticipate questions. But the more heterogeneous his potential readership – which need not be identical with his anticipated readership, to say nothing of his preferred readership – the more difficult this is. As for the kinds of questions human speaking itself gives rise to, there are but two general sorts. One kind concerns *what* is said, and thus seeks further clarification as to what is meant (often by soliciting in turn the speaker's ratification of a certain un-

Prologue

derstanding of what he said). Of course, this is not to presume anything so absurd as that speakers always intend to be clear, even less to suggest that they ought to be; while clarity is a cardinal virtue of thought, *precision* is the first virtue of speech, as skilled diplomats have always known. Nonetheless, in so far as someone's speaking presumes an intention on his part to communicate something in particular to those he addresses, questions of clarification are in order. The other kind of question a given speech may provoke concerns *why* something is said. However, this simple 'why' question is itself amenable to two meanings. It may be interpreted in the childlike manner, as asking why something said should be regarded as true or right, i.e., as seeking its rational justification. Or one may construe it in a way more peculiar to adults, as inquiring into the speaker's motivation for saying what he says. A moment's reflection on political life is sufficient to reveal why an adequate response to the first interpretation is not necessarily so for the second, and again reminds us of the difference between thought and speech. Speaking the truth, the whole truth, and nothing but the truth is surely more fitting at a coroner's inquest than at a funeral service. Because a considerate speaker concerns himself not only with how much truth people desire or deserve, but also with how much they can bear, 'why tell the truth?' is a legitimate question more often than one might care to admit to children. Nor should it be forgotten that the opportunity to question afforded by live discourse is a two-way street. A speaker may be as interested in assuring himself that he has been understood – or understood in a certain way – as is a listener in either the warrant for or the motive behind what is said.

A third advantage of living, breathing speech over something written is that the words expressed can be augmented, qualified, complemented, even negated by the non-verbal features of face-to-face communication: the tone of voice, the volume, the variable pace and rhythm of delivery, the amazing expressiveness of the human face, the scarcely less remarkable eloquence of the hands and arms. The very posture of a speaker, his dress, his entire outward appearance, may enhance (or diminish) his communicative effort. Similarly, what he sees of his effects on his audience may permit him to adjust not only his words but his manners so as to better achieve his intentions. Not that all bodily manifestations favour the purpose of the speaker, of course. Some are as involuntary as a stammer, a lisp, a sneeze, or a blush (cf. *Phaedrus* 237a, 234d, 240d).

Prologue

In fairness to writing, however, one should note as well its special advantages over oral speech. Certain of these are obvious, such as its relative permanence, its exact reproducibility, and (consequently) its potential for reaching a far vaster audience, including all succeeding generations. It has other strengths too, less broadly appreciated perhaps, but no less important. Precisely because a writer cannot so readily determine the actual characteristics of his readership, nor rely on their questions to guide an amplification of his words, nor avail himself of non-verbal means of augmenting those words, he must give more careful consideration to what he says. Accordingly, written speech tends to be more thoughtful, more complete, more precise, more coherent, more restrained – more purely rational – than its oral counterpart. And to the extent that it is, it merits more careful consideration by the reader, who may the more easily give it such in that the words do not expire with the breath that spoke them, lingering on only in a fallible memory. Words fixed in print are there to be consulted, compared, and analyzed, interpreted and reinterpreted, evaluated and reevaluated to one's heart's content.[2]

The human capacity for speech, as Aristotle observed long ago, may itself be regarded as evidence of man's being political by nature (*Politics* 1253a 9–18). No one can seriously doubt the political relevance of speech, nor, consequently, the propriety of treating what is (and is not) said as an important political concern. So far as we know, people always have. But for reasons reflecting both its strengths and its weaknesses, written speech intended for any sort of public distribution is especially apt to interest those who, from whatever motive, concern themselves with protecting or promoting what they conceive to be the right order and advantageous policies of a given political association. And while this potentially includes every adult member of that community, those exercising predominant political power are especially inclined to make the superintending of public speech their business. Nor is it obviously wrong that they do so; indeed, it may be irresponsible of them not to do so. Thus arises censorship, and even persecution, and the first reason why a prudent writer may choose not to express his views on anything with perfect clarity, in terms understandable to one and all, and especially not his views on political matters, nor on what often comes to the same thing, religious matters. Thus he must resort to artful writing if he is to write at all. And thus the art of writing is, whatever else, a political art.[3]

Prologue

Centuries, or rather millennia, of experience have proven that censorship need stifle neither creativity nor communication. Paradoxical as it might seem to those who have never thought about it before, censorship, if applied with some restraint and intelligence, may actually enhance both, cultivating a greater respect for words in readers and writers alike.[4] It should be sobering for us to reflect on the fact that most of the great literature of the world was produced under what today would be regarded as illiberal conditions. And, in contrast, that the contemporary societies which enjoy the broadest base of literacy in human history, and which provide the greatest freedom and the most generous material support for an unprecedented number of writers, have generated so few works of comparable quality. The literary *forte* of such regimes seems to be quantity.

But writers of the past, more constrained by circumstances, proved amazingly resourceful in inventing, and agile in applying, a wealth of literary devices whereby they might speak indirectly about politically sensitive matters. To begin with the most ancient, natural, and familiar, there are parables, fables, and allegories, whose tacit messages may not be what they first seem to be, or what they are expressly interpreted to be. Then again, an author may recount an already familiar myth or story, but with subtle alterations which - if noticed - point to a novel interpretation of its significance.[5] And on the assumption that what has actually happened (and is thus a "proven possibility") carries more weight with most people than what has been merely imagined, one may present what is partly fictitious as if it were altogether historically factual.[6] Or one may use examples that, upon reflection, illustrate something other than that which they are alleged to. Or provide chapter titles that are multiple entendres, or that are misleading as to the actual contents.[7] One may set out the plan of a work, and then silently depart from it for reasons the reader must guess; or even appear to have no plan at all, to be hopelessly disorganized, confusing because confused.[8] One may put forward incomplete or simplistic arguments, possibly with the missing parts or vital qualifications somehow supplied elsewhere in the text, or with the expectation that any intelligent reader will supply them himself. Or play the devil's advocate, advancing powerful arguments ostensibly in order to refute them, and then fail to do so convincingly. (Hence, not be playing after all?) An especially important variant of this technique available to writers of novels, dramas, and such is the voicing of heretical thoughts

Prologue

through the mouths of disreputable, or even mad characters.[9] One may use an idiom or a folk adage in a seemingly idiomatic way, while nonetheless allowing for its being taken literally; or, introduce a subtle variation of it.[10] Or use naturally symbolic terms (such as 'light' and 'dark', 'blood' and 'water'), or language of an acquired fecundity (such as that imparted by Christianity to words like 'meek', 'grace', 'save', and 'faith'), in apparent innocence of their richer meanings. One may profess principles, moral or intellectual or literary, which are unobstrusively but unmistakably qualified, or even contradicted, in the very writing in which they are advocated.[11] And one may be obscure on purpose, but without necessarily making such an intention obvious; there are any number of ways to accomplish this, ranging from the use of monstrous verbiage and convoluted grammar to the employing of arcane mathematics or the technical vocabulary of some abtruse specialty (such as astronomy). Nor should anyone underestimate the utility of being boring: a long stretch of soporific prose may provide the ideal place for concealing unsettling thoughts from all but the most diligent of readers. And there are countless ways of subtly alluding to other texts, standard arguments, famous claims, and familiar doctrines (whether orthodox or infamous).[12] Also, many clever things can be done with numbers.[13] In short, the art of political writing, or rather the political art of writing, entails more than a mastery of the various rational and passionate means of persuasion, more than a talent for crafting beautiful speech, or amusing or informative speech. Its paramount requirement is a mastery of equivocal speech. And, of course, one must have something important to say, something worth the care and effort of both writer and reader.

But if a deference to established political authorities is the first reason for resorting to such artful writing, it is not the only one, nor necessarily the most important. A writer may himself conclude that circumspection is appropriate in discussing certain matters, and measure his speech accordingly. He may believe that most people, whether literate or not, lack either sufficient ability or inclination to pursue difficult and complex questions systematically – with all the thoroughness and rigour and care, the patience and persistence such questions demand – and in any case are too preoccupied with their daily affairs to spare the requisite time and energy. After all, the vast majority of people, literate and illiterate alike, live and die without once subjecting a fundamental question, such as what is justice, to radical examination.[14] This is not itself evidence of a decline in standards of

Prologue

education, for nothing suggests it ever has been or could be otherwise. Hence one should not presume otherwise, but simply accept it like any other fact of life and write accordingly. That is, write for the seriously interested few, yet with an awareness that it may happen to be read by almost anybody. Given sufficient artfulness, however, an author may write so as to seem to say one thing on the surface, intended for the casual, superficial reader (something beneficial, or at least harmless, and more-or-less orthodox, thus unobjectionable to any concerned authorities), while at the same time conveying to the reflective reader something more radical, more challenging, more dangerous.

And to repeat: what the writer regards as too dangerous for popular dissemination may not be confined to that which has been proscribed by particular political authorities. They might object, for example, to any suggestion that their particular conception of justice is seriously flawed, whereas the writer may have doubts about the reality of justice *per se*, and nonetheless be convinced that political life would significantly deteriorate were his skepticism to become widely shared. This, then, may be the sort of view he would wish to insinuate to only those precious few who are governed, not primarily by love of honour and wealth (as are most people), but by a profound love of truth, and who order their entire lives accordingly, and who thus can be trusted not to abuse his confidence in them, appreciating as well as he the propriety of his reserve.

For these reasons, and another still to be discussed, there grew up in the West a tradition of esoteric writing. At first, apparently, the distinction between exoteric and esoteric was used to characterize various written works *in toto*. Aristotle, for instance, refers to things intended for popular dissemination as "exoteric discourses", distinguishing them from teachings reserved for a more select audience.[15] But it was acknowledged early on that skilful writers could use the very same writing to convey more than one teaching simultaneously: something safe and salutary, if necessarily simplistic (or even false) for the superficial reader, and something more radical and demanding for the reflective reader. Some such awareness has been manifest since antiquity in various debates concerning the interpretation of poetry. Indeed, the recognition that a rather conventional exoteric doctrine may serve to mask one or more esoteric teachings – and that such is not merely permissible, but sometimes morally obligatory – became a mark of the well-educated person, and remained so into the nineteenth century.[16] The recent demise of this recognition is something of a mystery, but it is probably in part at least a belated consequence of the Enlightenment and its optimistic assumptions about mankind's capacity for rational rule (of which liberalism so generously partakes). In any case, allusions to the distinction, often in the form of references to different kinds of readers, are common enough to leave no serious reader in doubt but that most of our greatest authors wrote with conscious regard for it. So, whenever any apparently serious and intelligent writer distinguishes – however unobstrusively – classes of readers, or of minds, or kinds of writings, or acknowledges reasons why it may be improper to express certain thoughts publicly, or discusses discretion in speaking and writing, one must give him the benefit of the doubt and assume, at least initially, that he writes with due respect for considerations that he himself thought worthy of notice.[17]

One of the more intriguing discussions of the rationale behind the esoteric-exoteric distinction is comparatively recent, that of Nietzsche in *Beyond Good and Evil* (aph. 30). And although he offers a rather peculiar, not to say unique, perspective on the matter, one should remember that he was a trained and gifted philologist, prodigiously so in fact, and well-read in both ancients and moderns:

> Our highest insights must – and should! – sound like follies and in some cases like crimes when without permission they come to the ears of those who are not predisposed and predestined for them. The exoteric and the esoteric as philosophers formerly distinguished them, among the Indians as among the Greeks, Persians, and Moslems, in short wherever one believed in an order of rank and *not* in equality and equal rights – differ from one another not so much in that the exoteric stands outside, and sees, evaluates, measures, judges from the outside, not the inside: what is more essential is that it sees things from below – but the esoteric sees them *from above*! There are heights of the soul from which even tragedy ceases to look tragic; and rolling together all the woe of the world, who could dare to assert that the sight of it would *have* to seduce and compel us to pity and thus to a doubling of that woe? ... What serves the higher type of man as food or refreshment must be almost poison to a very different and inferior type. The virtues of the common man would perhaps signify vice and weakness in a philosopher; it may be possible that if a high type of man degenerated and perished, he would only then acquire qualities that would require those in the lower world into which he had sunk henceforth to worship him like a saint. There

Prologue

are books which have an opposite value of soul and health depending on whether the lower soul, the lower vitality, or the higher and more powerful turn to them: in the former case they are dangerous, disintegrative books, causing decomposition; in the latter they are herald's calls, challenging the most courageous to *their* courage. Books for everybody are always malodorous books: the smell of petty people clings to them. Where the people eats and drinks, even where it worships, there is usually a stink. One should not go into churches if one wants to breathe pure air. (translation based on R.J. Hollingdale's, Penguin Books)

Needless to say, this apparently exoteric discussion of esotericism is unavoidably reflexive. Hence, it is only prudent to assume that the distinction is exemplified as well as explained. (One might begin by noting that its more radical impiety is not to ordinary religion, but to the martyrdom of "Saint Sokrates".)

So, as Nietzsche intimates, there is a third reason for an art of esoteric writing, this one having less to do with politics and more to do with philosophy. That is, one can write in such a manner as may itself promote philosophy through providing nourishment and inspiration to those who are naturally suited for a life of thought. Why someone might want to do this is a most interesting question which must for now be set aside. So too the question of who specifically are those suited by nature for such a life, what constellation of qualities distinguishes them. Suffice it here to suggest that the occurrence of the requisite conjunction is far from common, and accordingly such people are few in number, far fewer than populate the ranks of the merely very intelligent. For by the *life* of thought is meant that the *activity* of thinking – therefore of questing, observing, interrogating, analysing, refuting, comparing, synthesizing, interpreting, evaluating, and to that extent learning and knowing – is the *dominant* activity of one's life, to which everything else is subordinated so far as humanly possible. This, as I understand it, is the primary meaning of 'philosophy': it refers to a special way of life, a way of life true to the name, a life ruled by the love of wisdom. Seen in this light, the more common usage of the term (as someone's writings, teachings, doctrines, even policies) is a secondary and derivative meaning.

A philosopher, then, can write so as to encourage philosophy in the primary sense of the word. His persuasive exhortations may open the door, affording tantalizing glimpses of the philosophic life. But

Prologue

it is his fascinating puzzles and paradoxes, his intriguing mysteries, engrossing problems, and challenging theories that seduce a natural soulmate to cross the threshold and taste this life for himself. And that which a philosopher writes may incidentally be recognized as 'philosophy' in its secondary meaning, but not necessarily. It could be more popularly known as a poem, a play, a novel, a memoir, or even as a work of dispassionate scholarship. In any case, designed to draw a special kind of person to the philosophic life and perforce away from various other kinds of lives, including all those more overtly political lives, such writing remains a significant political act. Imagine an attractive and talented young man of a wealthy and prominent family, otherwise destined to fill a high corporate or political office, possibly providing vital leadership in war or peace, but being deflected instead to the philosophic life by his reading some book. All those, beginning with his family, who saw themselves, their firm, or their polity impoverished by the transformation of his ambition would certainly concede – indeed, insist – that philosophical literature can have political consequences. And since virtually anything a philosopher might care to write about could have this as well as other political effects, all genuinely philosophical writing is best considered *political* philosophy. And thus there are two meanings to this notion as well. Political philosophy is ordinarily understood to mean philosophizing (whatever that is) about politics (whatever that is). But it can also mean – and this is both a broader and a deeper conception – philosophizing (about anything) in a "politic" or "polite" way (that is, with due regard for the possible political consequences of doing so). As is easily seen, a marriage of the two conceptions results in political philosophy of the highest order, or in the fullest sense, political philosophy *par excellence*, as it were: polite philosophizing about political things.

So, one can discern at least three reasons for the political art of philosophical writing – i.e., for a kind of writing which is intended to have distinct exoteric and esoteric meanings: censorship; a concern for the common good; and a wish to beget philosophy. These reasons are by no means discordant, and the acknowledged masterworks of political philosophy typically show evidence of all three concerns. Perhaps an example that is not at all hypothetical can help demonstrate how such a multiplicity of intentions may be harmonized. Imagine writing about anything bearing on theological matters in a political setting where religious conformity is enforced. There – but not only there – a philosopher might well choose to write in such a manner as to appear to accept the common understanding of the divine powers and their relationship to the human world. He may even go so far as to criticize certain *details* of the conventional understanding (as unclear or inconsistent or incomplete, or as insufficiently noble or moral to be altogether godlike); and inasmuch as such criticism seems to presuppose a *basic acceptance* of the conventional understanding, it may actually serve to enhance the credibility of his own apparent orthodoxy. Thus he establishes a façade that is effective with unsuspecting and less reflective readers, and which should satisfy the authorities' concern for protecting the uncomplicated faith of ordinary believers. Yet throughout he may have scattered observations and conclusions which, when correctly reassembled, suggest to his few more thoughtful readers that the conventional religious account is fundamentally untrue, even if he also indicates why it is salutary to maintain some reformed version of it (and, hence, why his own exoteric account has the character it does). But having provided an esoteric refutation of the commonly accepted view of divinities, he thereby opens the door to a fresh consideration of what, then, *does* rule the kosmos. With respect to this philosophical question of first importance, he may supply what in his view are the essential "ingredients" of an adequate alternative account, yet without himself intending to offer one that will withstand radical scrutiny. He thereby awakens a philosophical reader's curiosity, and leaves it to do its natural work.

But whereas a philosopher writing about, say, space and time, or form and matter, can be reasonably confident that such "metaphysical" topics will attract but a minute readership made up mostly of people interested in understanding such things for their own sake, a philosopher writing about something overtly political cannot presume so narrow an audience. For in addition to that select few with a theoretical interest in the subject, he is apt to attract readers whose interests are primarily practical. Some desire to understand politics better in order to become more politically efficacious; some hope to see more clearly what is right or advantageous for the here and now; some are in search of ammunition or intelligence useful to their own partisan commitments; and some simply take a special interest in monitoring what other people think about political matters – believing with Hobbes that 'the Actions of men proceed from their Opinions: and in the wel governing of Opinions, consisteth the well governing of mens Actions'. Knowing all this and more, the great political philosophers, as a measure of that greatness, wrote about politics (when they did so at all),

Prologue

with the utmost care and precision. But perhaps none wrote with more consummate artistry than the rightful founder of our tradition, Plato ... or as his most equivocal admirer characterized him, "the divine Plato".

Cognizant of the strengths and weaknesses of written speech as few before him or since, Plato crafted a novel literary form which could fully exploit the one while greatly attenuating the other. The Platonic dialogue – a wonderful synthesis of reverent memorial, dramatic poetry, philosophic argument, Aesopian fable, and God only knows what else – manifests, to my mind at least, perfection in the art of writing. If one but learns how to read it properly (which is not all that difficult to do, but does require sensible principles of interpretation as well as some fair amount of practice), one sees that the dialogue form overcomes those limitations of writing so persuasively articulated by the Platonic Sokrates in the *Phaedrus*. It does not weaken the memory, but rather strengthens it, as it does all the other powers of the rational soul. The serious study of a dialogue enhances acuity of observation, exercises one's imagination, expands curiosity, hones analytical skills, matures judgment, and cultivates one's sense of humour. But it also arouses the spirit and invokes the passions, allowing one to better understand them and their relationship to reason, in order that their energy may be harnessed and their unruliness subdued. But most important of all, arriving at an adequate interpretation of a dialogue requires one to think synoptically, synthesizing disparate evidence into a single coherent vision of the whole.[18] And synthetic thought is the *sine qua non* of political philosophy.[19]

Thus one may say that the problem of interpreting a Platonic dialogue replicates the problem of understanding the world, requiring the same set of powers in their same order of importance.[20] And especially so the human world. For these philosophical discussions, all pursuing questions of perennial importance to human beings, are each provided concrete dramatic settings which bear in various ways on what is said ... and not said. Whether the scene is richly described (as it is in *Charmides, Symposium, Protagoras*) or sketched with spartan simplicity (as in *Meno, Alkibiades I, Minos*), the reader's first task is to notice these circumstantial features, and reconstruct in his imagination the conversational environment from the textual clues provided. When does the encounter take place, or does it matter? If one can determine when, it matters. Where does it take place, and is it somewhere more-or-

Prologue

less public, or is it private? And what explains the presence of the particular congregation of people: chance, choice, or some sort of compulsion? Are their spatial relationships specified, what accounts for them, do they change, if so why? Having reconjured the scene, the reader must endeavour to see how its various features somehow illustrate or qualify or complete what is said, and why the setting as a whole was chosen as a peculiarly appropriate one for that particular discussion.

Similarly, the reader must assess the characteristics of each participant – to the extent that these are revealed, that is, an important variable in itself. Begin with their names, if any are provided, for a name may have literal, symbolic, homonymic, or historical importance. There may be a peculiar appropriateness to a certain character being named Aristodemus ('best of the people'), or Polus ('colt'); a nice irony in another being called Euthyphro ('rightminded'), or Agathon ('good'); and the part assigned an Apollodorus ('gift of Apollo') may suit him to a tee. And consider the various implications of portraying the philosopher conversing with someone historically familiar, someone famous and influential (e.g., Parmenides, or Gorgias), or whose political role and fate are well-known (e.g., Nikias, or Kritias), or who will prove instrumental to Sokrates' own fate (e.g., Anytus, Chaerophon) – to say nothing of someone who is all of these things at once (Alkibiades, for example, or Aristophanes). And contrast such confrontations with the studied, almost awkward anonymity that pervades *Lovers* (to cite the extreme case).

But there's more to people than names.[21] In a Platonic dialogue, just as in a live conversation, the age and outward appearance and social class and political status and popular reputation of a person influence how he behaves and how others behave towards him. So, too, do his mental powers, verbal facility, and other strengths and weaknesses of body and soul. As in life, so in these philosophical artworks, participants don't merely argue with each other in the dispassionate manner of idealized mathematicians; they also flatter, boast, abuse, commiserate, swear, threaten, exult, promise, pretend, become embarrassed and discouraged and angry and tired and careless, often revealing more about themselves than they intend. And they *do* things: eat, drink, tug, jostle, whisper, interrupt, exchange glances and places, walk up and down, back and forth, lie on couches and under trees, move furniture, sit, stand, sneeze, arrive late, leave early, and engage in many other actions that to a thoughtful person speak louder than

Prologue

words. Sometimes they learn and thus change as the discussion progresses, and sometimes they don't. But whatever happens must be seen as reflecting the kind of person they are, or have become, precocious or obtuse, haughty or deferential, smugly dogmatic or open-minded, or different things by turns. One must presume there is a reason this character fails to notice something of crucial importance, or that another subsequently forgets it. And beneath the polite veneer of even the most abstract discussion, the attentive reader with an eye for nuance can often detect subtle traces of an interlocutor's hopes and hates, loves and fears, his sympathies and resentments, perhaps the entire range of passions whose presence and order predispose his soul. All this and more may be there to be gleaned by careful, thoughtful, patient reading and re-reading of these astonishingly rich and ingenious texts. On the basis of whatever dialogical evidence one gathers, and in light of all the talents and experience one brings to the gathering, full-blooded, multi-coloured, three-dimensional characters may be reconstituted, and come to life in one's imagination. Given sufficient experience with such revivification, one realizes that it is possible to meet in the dialogues all the important kinds of men one deals with in the world, and that their dialectical interaction is reproduced with an almost prophetic fidelity. In any event, psychoanalysis of this kind is essential for assessing, correcting, completing, and recasting the otherwise inadequate arguments which occupy centre stage.

And one should always remember to ask oneself why a given dialogue has the particular dramatic structure that it has, or how that structure might bear on the speeches and deeds depicted therein. For Plato's basic dialogic form of writing comprises a surprising variety of sub-forms. Seemingly simplest in structure are those that are cast as if they were plays to be performed, with the reader allowed direct access to what each character says (e.g., *Euthyphro, Meno, Sophist, Theages, Gorgias, Laches, Krito*). Next there are those that are completely narrated, with the narrator, then, standing between the reader and the original dialogic action, but also thereby permitted to enlarge upon it (e.g., *Lysis, Charmides, Lovers*). But there are also complicated mixtures of these two simpler forms, with a performed section framing or partially framing a narrated centre (*Euthydemus, Protagoras*); sometimes this primary section is being narrated well after the fact (*Phaedo, Parmenides*), and not even by someone who observed it at first hand (*Symposium*). Some are admitted to be imperfectly remembered, while in others this

Prologue

is left a silent possibility. And there are various sorts of dialogues within dialogues within dialogues, some hypothetical, some supposedly recapitulations of previous discussions. Plato even contrived one (*Theaetetus*) as a performed dialogue within a performed dialogue, the former being read by a slave of the character from the latter who wrote it in stages, allegedly basing it on his recollection of a narrative recounting by Sokrates of an earlier conversation with someone else, and who subjected the text to subsequent revisions after several further consultations with the philosopher over an extended but indefinite period of time! One must presume that Plato constructed these more elaborate dialogical structures with some purpose in mind, and that reflection on them is integral to an understanding of what they contain. This attending to literary form is all the more obligatory in light of the fact that several dialogues themselves contain discussions of literary form (e.g., *Phaedo, Symposium, Phaedrus, Theaetetus*) – discussions which are necessarily reflexive without necessarily being authoritative (as is easily seen by comparing the actual style of *Republic* with the discussion of style it contains, 392c–398b). Suffice it to say, whatever the specific form of a given dialogue, it is worth thinking about.

So, too, is its name. For while we must agree that Plato conceals himself – and especially he conceals his opinions – *in* the dialogues, he inescapably reveals himself in selecting which conversations to depict and in which specific forms and with which casts of characters. But he most directly speaks in his own voice through the titles he chose for them. As Strauss observes, 'While everything said in the Platonic dialogues is said by Plato's characters, Plato himself takes full responsibility for the titles of the dialogues.'[22] Twenty-seven are simply named after particular men. Usually the eponym is a participant in the discussion (*Minos* and *Hipparchus* being exceptions), but – curiously – not always the most prominent or memorable of the philosopher's interlocutors. Why a given dialogue is called *Laches* and not *Nikias*, or *Gorgias* and not *Kallikles*, or *Phaedo* and not *Simmias* or *Kebes* (or *Simmias AND Kebes*) is a puzzle. Only once in the entire corpus do a pair of interlocutors get equal billing (*Lovers*), and that despite a seemingly massive disproportion in their respective contributions. Seven dialogues are simply named after things, most if not all being political things. Only one dialogue has a title compounded of both sorts of names: *Apology of Sokrates*.

These remarks all derive from my subscribing to the judgment that, in reading Plato:

Prologue

> ... one can not take seriously enough the law of logographic necessity. Nothing is accidental in a Platonic dialogue; everything is necessary at the place where it occurs. Everything which would be accidental outside of the dialogue becomes meaningful within the dialogue. In all actual conversations chance plays a considerable role: all Platonic dialogues are radically fictitious. The Platonic dialogue is based on a fundamental falsehood, a beautiful or beautifying falsehood, *viz.* on the denial of chance.
> (Leo Strauss, *The City and Man*, 60)

Plato himself indicated that the dialogues are fictitious in that they portray a 'beautiful' (*i.e.*, beautified) Sokrates, one who has also become 'young' or 'new' (*2nd Ltr* 314c). However one construes their fictionality, this 'law of logographic necessity' is inherent in the judgment that the dialogues are premier works of literary art. Great art mirrors the essential features of nature, which is to say it does not simply mirror nature. Its artfulness, or artificiality, its radical fictitiousness consists precisely in its presenting a purified vision of the nature of things, including human things, a vision ruled by the most rigorous necessity, purged of the trivial, the adventitious, the transient, the inconsequential, the ephemeral – purged of everything spurious in that skein of appearances which, like a fluttering translucent veil, masks the deeper reality one seeks to know. In the greatest works of literature, including the masterpieces of philosophy, every word counts, every piece fits, nothing is wasted, nothing is missing, and truth as well as beauty pervades the whole. For it is its revelatory relationship with a permanent reality, including the permanent reality of human dreams and desires, that imparts enduring, inexhaustible significance – greatness – to a work of art. And can it have this if its maker hasn't first sought and glimpsed that reality? If he is not, that is to say, philosophical?[23] And when a philosophic artist such as Plato, a virtuoso of speech, presents his truth about reality wrapped in a veil of his own making, it must be remembered that this too, whatever its apparent similarity to the veil draping everyday life, is but a part of his art, profoundly fictional in being perfectly – because intentionally – tailored to the shape of his truth, compatible with its colours, harmonized with its tones, its taste, its scent.

Because the dialogues are both radically fictitious and faithful portrayals of Sokrates, they can and must be pervaded with irony. The reader should be prepared to find any and every speech, deed or dramatic feature having an ironic aspect. Precisely what Platonic or

Prologue

Sokratic irony *is*, however, is difficult to express; strictly speaking, it's whatever is manifested in the dialogues. But like so many Platonic ideas, it seems to be a sublimation of a notion in everyday use, and in this case not a particularly flattering one. The original, ordinary meaning of *eironeia* is to dissemble in speech, especially to say less than one thinks and somehow insinuates. As such, it is a more-or-less transparent feigning of ignorance, and often simply in order to provoke someone else. It is related, in both meaning and popularity, to sarcasm. Referring to a man as ironic, then, would not normally convey a compliment. Being *eironikos* is something one might accuse one's opponent of, who in turn could be expected to deny it. Obviously the concept and its connotations have changed some from its original signification, and not least of all because of the character of Sokrates. For he has come down to us as famous for his irony, and this irony, along with his professed ignorance and consequent "humility", are essential to his charm. References to Sokratic irony are plentiful in the literature about the dialogues. This is in marked contrast to such references within the dialogues themselves. The term and its cognates are mentioned only a total of thirteen times in the entire corpus, and but five of these are explicit applications of the term to Sokrates (*Gorgias* 489e; *Symposium* 216e, 218d; *Republic* 337a4, a6). But since they reveal that both admirers and detractors agreed that 'ironical' describes his habitual demeanour (something which Plato has Sokrates confirm with his single reference to himself in connection with irony, *Apology* 38a), it is safe to agree with Alkibiades that Sokrates did indeed spend 'his whole life being ironic and playful toward human beings'.[24] Sokrates also employs the term three times to describe others (*Gorgias* 489e; *Euthydemus* 302b; *Erastai* 133d). From these and its four additional uses (*Cratylus* 384a and *Sophist* 268a, b, c), one gets a glimmer of what irony is for the philosopher: there is a kind of dissembling involved, a use of speech whose meaning isn't altogether clear, or oracular speech requiring interpretation, speech that is intentionally 'duplicitous', saying one thing to this person, something else to another.

With but this much as a basis, let me venture the following remarks about Platonic-Sokratic irony. It is speech that is somehow both true and false, that is comic but none the less serious, frank and yet disingenuous. Even a wary reader risks being seduced by one side of it, thereby slighting the other. Sometimes the sense in which what is said is false or humorous seems uppermost, tempting one to treat it as a more subtle variant of sarcasm, and thus inadvertently over-

Prologue

looking what is serious and true about it. Other times the sober, evidently truthful aspect is more accessible, and one has to work harder to get at what is funny or false. Of course, the truth can be pretty funny, too.[25] In any event, one must be ever aware that Plato treats seriousness and play as sisters – reason enough, perhaps, to reconsider bigamy. And if one agrees that justice involves a recognition of both equality and inequality, Sokratic irony is the *just* mode of speech *par excellence*. For in saying the same thing to one and all it implicitly acknowledges their common humanity, allowing everyone, without personal prejudice, an equal opportunity to make of the words what they will. And yet in intending different messages for different kinds of people, it treats them differently in due recognition of their unequal talents and efforts and character – in effect employing a sort of "labour theory" of intellectual entitlement.

But to refer to Sokratic irony merely as *just* speech may be to understate its virtue. If we are justified in regarding Sokrates' profession of ignorance as the foremost example of his irony, then one must concede that his manner of speaking transcends the requirements of justice. 'Noble' is the name usually reserved for behaviour beyond the call of duty. Thus one may agree with Strauss (*The City and Man* 51) that Plato portrays Sokrates as noble, or magnanimous in the literal sense (i.e., "great-souled"):

> Aristotle ... treats the habit of irony primarily as a vice. Yet irony is the dissembling, not of evil actions or of vices, but rather of good actions or of virtues; the ironic man, in opposition to the boaster, understates his worth. If irony is a vice, it is a graceful vice. Properly used, it is not a vice at all: the magnanimous man – the man who regards himself as worthy of great things while in fact being worthy of them – is truthful and frank because he is in the habit of looking down and yet he is ironical in his intercourse with the many. Irony then is the noble dissimulation of one's worth, of one's superiority. We may say, it is the humanity peculiar to the superior man: he spares the feelings of his inferiors by not displaying his superiority. The highest form of superiority is the superiority in wisdom. Irony in the highest sense will then be the dissimulation of one's wisdom, i.e., the dissimulation of one's wise thoughts.

And if this can be fairly said of Sokrates, how much more so of Plato himself, who was under no obligation to write anything, much less such beautiful and useful games of philosophical discovery and self-

Prologue

discovery, and less still to attribute them so ironically to a Sokrates who through the author's magic touch has been rendered eternally *kalos kai neos*.

But this last observation raises an issue of no small importance concerning the understanding of Plato's dialogues. Because it is evident in each of these artful conversations that one of the characters is playing a leading role, it is naturally tempting to presume that he is a stand-in for the author. This mistake is the more readily made since in all but seven cases, the dialogic leader is Sokrates, and in most of the remaining cases someone who seems essentially like him, either a 'stranger' (or 'guest'; *xenos*) from Elea (*Sophist, Statesman*), or from Athens (*Laws, Epinomis*), or the 'cosmologist' Timaeus of Locri (*Timaeus*). But the companion dialogue of the latter (*Kritias*), not to mention *Kleitophon*, offers sufficient warning against all such facile identifications. As touched upon above, Plato is responsible in each and every case for the whole dialogue: for everything said and done and not said and not done by everyone he chooses to put in it, as well as for the selection of conversations (and their titles) which together constitute the Platonic corpus. So it is only prudent to begin with the assumption that his teaching is in the whole, not in any of the parts, whether the parts be those played by the individual characters in a given dialogue, or the individual dialogues addressing but a part of the given reality. And since Plato never speaks in his own name to tell us what that teaching of the whole is, it is left to the reader's interpretation (cf. *7th Ltr* 341cd). Each character's words and deeds must be interpreted in light of those of the others and the concrete dialogical setting they share. Thus one must assume that the perspective offered by each character is a partial one – if not necessarily because of his own limitations, then because of the limitations of those with whom he converses – and that only the author's perspective is comprehensive, his synoptic view being properly the reader's goal as well. This is not to deny what should be clear to a child: that Plato had an enormous admiration and love for Sokrates (he would hardly have memorialized him in thirty-three dialogues otherwise; cf. *7th Ltr* 324e–325c; *Phaedo* 118b). But the two are not to be identified. To mention only the most obvious difference: one wrote books, the other didn't.

Despite the certainty of his authorship, however, Plato has contrived to write in such a mode as precludes his being directly quoted: one can only quote his various characters – and often to contrary effect! Thus, Plato himself communicates with his reader indirectly, through the medium of interpretation. And whatever light the dialogues may throw on one another, each must be interpreted on its own terms first. Doing so requires bringing all one's rational powers and experience, and even one's natural passions, to bear on every bit of internal evidence supplied by the text. Only through such active engagement can one resuscitate the conversation, restoring the depth and movement and colour of life to the pale, flat, static image of a dialogue embalmed in Plato's written words. For true dialogue is a living thing, and if the conversations Plato orchestrated are to live again, the reader must be the source of that life: they can come to life only in him, in his life, a life which will be elevated and enriched by his silent but active participation in these ennobling discussions. So far as they are understood, that is. And to the extent that one cannot satisfactorily explain *why* anything is said or done, or the *order* in which it is, or why obvious rejoinders are *not* made, or why something is 'repeated' (and despite the hundreds of occasions this apparently happens, I believe there are not but three or four times in the entire corpus when something is exactly repeated; in all other cases, some words have been changed, and one must presume that such changes, however subtle, have significance) – to the extent one cannot explain everything in and about a dialogue, one had best admit that one's interpretation is inadequate, and one's understanding of it incomplete. That is, one has not perfectly recaptured the author's understanding of it, *his* interpretation, which is the only conceivable standard of correct interpretation, elusive though this invariably turns out to be in practice.

No doubt some will find my adherence to "the law of logographic necessity", and the assumption of the dialogues' literary perfection whence it is derived, scarcely credible. Surely, they are apt to think, this is carrying ancestor worship to an absurd extreme, in effect treating Plato as if he were a god. But this is not necessarily the case. For example, his writings may merely be divinely inspired. True enough, a person's life is sure to be salted with many mistakes and accidents, good, bad, and indifferent. But the reasons why this is so need not operate upon that which he writes. Is this not the precise difference between living life and producing literary art: that if he cares enough to do so, an author may return again and again and again to what he has written in an effort to comb out the mistakes; whereas it is in the nature of space, time, and matter that a person lives his life but once, and is pretty much stuck with the results? The fact that in one's own experience no amount of currying ever proves

Prologue

sufficient to yield literary perfection is not itself clear evidence of its impossibility, for we are *per hypothesis* speaking about rare and exceptional writers here. Still, it is said that occasionally even Homer nodded. Very well. Perhaps Plato is superior to Homer. Perhaps he is superior to everyone else who has ever lived, or who ever will. Somebody must be. But in a practical sense, such speculations are beside the point, which is that an assumption of literary perfection is a prudential judgment, and it is not made for the sake of honouring (much less revering) Plato – justifiable though this may be – but rather for the sake of the reader's getting the most for himself, and of himself, out of what Plato wrote. For if one assumes the contrary: that the dialogues are flawed – and a moment's reflection reveals that there's really no intermediate position – one thereby provides oneself an ever-too-ready explanation for anything one does not understand about them, but which one might if one but persisted. Of the only two alternatives, far better for oneself to assume, like a good scientist, that in the Platonic kosmos everything has a cause, and if one does not at first see what it is, one must try, try again ... for the causes of things are often deeply buried. And in the mean time, it is simply prudent to acknowledge one's ignorance.

Because interpretations are as much a reflection of the reader as of the writer, they vary from reader to reader, and from reading to reading. For each serious reading of a dialogue – not to mention other intervening experiences, including acquainting oneself with other interpretations, and studying other dialogues – leaves one changed. On successive readings, one notices things hitherto missed, remembers things hitherto forgotten, imagines possibilities hitherto unconsidered, discovers that this character or that argument has a strength or a weakness not previously recognized; the personalities of the participants alter and deepen, their relations are seen in a somewhat different light, the magnitude and significance of the issues before them grow; the whole thing changes. *Seems to*, that is – for like the reality it mirrors, it hasn't really changed at all; it is only the interpretation that changes, as the reader labours to understand it perfectly, himself changing as a consequence of his endeavour (however vain) to approach the single best or true interpretation: that of its Creator.

No one who appreciates what is entailed in finally understanding a dialogue, and who is accordingly self-conscious about the activity of interpreting, could ever be dogmatic about what Plato taught, nor about any of the important questions he saw fit to explore dialogically.

Prologue

The Platonic dialogue is an inherently anti-dogmatic form of writing. Read with an active intelligence, then, these dialogues are not static images of speech, endlessly repeating the same old thing. They can even be questioned, provided one does so sympathetically, out of a genuine interest in the truth. For if a diligent search is made, one can usually find one's legitimate objections acknowledged and correct speculations confirmed somewhere in the text, though often where one would least notice it prior to having successfully thought the matter through oneself. Nor are the dialogues imprudent writings, conveying an identical message to each and every reader regardless of their natural differences; doubtless these compositions remain essentially silent to some.

Plato's dialogues, then, are so many invitations to enjoy philosophy in the primary sense of the word. They are designed to entice certain kinds of readers to experience for themselves – to the extent they are naturally inclined and otherwise suited to do so – the activity of thinking, of thinking for the sheer fun of it, for the challenge of it, for the personal satisfaction of the learning and knowing that comes of it. And in so far as this is a peculiarly human thing to do, distinguishing the human from all other forms of being, the dialogues invoke one's essential humanity. Their study has a humanizing effect. The dialogues promote philosophy because what they teach primarily are questions, not answers. Knowing the answers to all the important questions makes one wise, with no further need to inquire. One would be to that extent godlike. Whereas knowing the important questions, which entails taking them to heart, makes one philosophical.[26] This is the governing intention of a Platonic dialogue: to assist the reader in becoming thoroughly conversant with an important question, so that he knows both why it is important (its centrality to an understanding of man's world), and why he should regard it as a question (why all the readily available – and hence commonly accepted – answers are variously inadequate). Knowledge of the important questions is not knowledge to be despised, for it is sufficient to determine a whole ordering of life – that lived by one who is properly called a philosopher, and the only one who is.

Plato doubtless gave the important questions much thought: his dialogues provide ample evidence of that. And he quite likely had opinions as to their answers, perhaps some so well-considered that he was practically convinced that they were true. Maybe he even knew they were true, and not mere opinions and convictions. I suspect so. But

Prologue

in any case, no one will ever know. For he wrote nothing that clearly conveys what he thought beyond the thought that philosophy is a worthy way of life for a human being, and that teaching people the important questions effectively promotes that way of life, whereas teaching them sufficient answers tends to foreclose it. Some people none the less think that he teaches answers, and perhaps it is best for them and everyone else that they do so. Nor could it be altogether accidental that they gain this impression. But readers more favoured by nature or nurture will appreciate that the dialogues are designed to lead a certain kind of reader, one more akin to Plato himself, as deeply into the important permanent questions as his own rational powers and desires will carry him. And there the philosopher leaves him, lost in a labyrinth of questions upon questions, to fend for himself as best he can. Thus one can see that the issue of *the* correct interpretation of Plato's dialogues (or the writings of any other great philosopher, for that matter), while of overwhelming practical importance to a student of those writings, is philosophically irrelevant. For even if one somehow knew clearly and completely what Plato thought is true – strictly speaking, a biographical question – one would still be left with the only *philosophical* question that finally matters: is he right? Is *that* the truth? In so far as one's interest is philosophical (rather than historical), one has to face that ultimate, trans-interpretive question sooner or later. Plato chose to write in such a manner as to make it rather sooner than later, and, not at all incidentally, precluded his being treated dogmatically by or towards anyone with intelligence.

Of course, as a practical matter, endeavouring to determine what Plato *probably* thought, or even *must* have thought, given what he wrote, is a natural, perhaps irresistible, ambition. The purpose of studying the dialogues, after all, is to share Plato's best thoughts – or at least the best of those he saw fit to share – on the assumption that one will be able to go further, faster, exploring the questions in his company than one possibly could on one's own, that he will acquaint one with nuances and aspects and perspectives and considerations and refinements that one might not otherwise see in a lifetime of trying. That he will, in short, assist one to think well about things worth thinking about. Thus one wishes to understand the dialogues exactly as their author understood them, this being the best means of gaining for oneself that comprehensive vantage point on reality from which they were written. Thus the adequacy of one's interpretation is practically all-important. And the risk is not so much that of being *mistaken*

Prologue

(although, through careless reading or thinking, one can be just plain wrong), as it is of being *superficial*, of failing to get very far, or very deep – of failing, that is, to make very much good use of the dialogues' vast resources for informing and strengthening one's soul.

In my experience, a dialogue such as the *Republic* is insurmountable, unplumbable, inexhaustible. Even the best interpretation will, by whole orders of magnitude, leave more unsaid than said. It may, however, be worth sharing with others of like mind and purpose – one's natural friends, as it were – if it can help them to gain a more synoptic view of the dialogue, or to delve more deeply into its mysteries, or even just to see it afresh. For an interpretive commentary, if it is to remain faithful to the spirit in which the dialogues were written, really shouldn't try to *prove* anything to anyone, much less to someone who cannot or will not see it for himself. Dialogical scholarship is sufficient if it is sufficiently suggestive. And those who can profit from it may someday, somehow return the favour, if not to the author himself, to someone else who would be equally grateful. It is to such readers, those who agree that a Platonic dialogue is always a wonderful basis for further dialogue, that the following effort is directed, being but an expression of my own gratitude to those from whom I have learned all that I value most.

THE WAR LOVER

A Study of Plato's *Republic*

> The whale, like all things that are mighty,
> wears a false brow to the common world.
>
> *Moby Dick*

> Being a lover of war and a lover of wisdom
> the Goddess chose the place that would bear men most closely
> resembling herself, and there made her first settlement.
>
> *Timaeus 24cd*

> Courageous, carefree, scornful, violent – so wisdom wants us:
> she is a woman and loves always only a warrior.
>
> *Thus Spoke Zarathustra*

> ... for they loved the praise of men more than the praise of God.
>
> *John 12:43*

— 1 —

War and Peace

The story is a familiar one. Having satisfied his curiosity about an innovation in the local religion, a notoriously combative philosopher named Sure Strength (*Sō-krates*) and his blooded squire Gleaming (*Glaukōn*) are retiring towards their acropolis when overtaken by a numerically stronger party of men who threaten their capture. Along with some who remain anonymous, its ranks include another battle-tested young man named Dauntless (*Adeimantos*) and the taciturn son of a famous general, named like his father in honour of Victory (*Nikeratos*, son of *Nikias*). The apparent leader of the group is named War Ruler (*Polem-archos*[1]). Negotiations ensue, and through a mixture of compulsion and persuasion, the opposing forces are melded into one, which thereupon resolves to return to the lower city in pursuit of rations, recreation, and new recruits. Night action is contemplated.

Welcomed most warmly into the home of a wealthy arms merchant named Head (*Kephalos*) – a pious old patriarch whose favourite authorities are renowned generals and martial poets (329b, 329e-a, 331a) – the philosopher engages his host in a conversation about being old and being rich and the bearing of the one on the other. The old man's contribution concerning the first issue is focused primarily on the natural decline with age of men's power to enjoy their own bodies and those of women, and the importance they attach to this. Sure Strength chooses to ignore the many interesting questions one might raise about these matters, and asks instead about the source of his friend's fortune, mentioning two possibilities usually regarded as just. Was it inherited, or was it earned? As politeness would dictate, he naturally remains silent concerning less reputable possibilities. The philosopher's third question solicits Head's opinion as to the greatest good that comes from possessing great wealth, and it is out of the response to this – of all questions – that the night's marathon discussion about justice is born. While much of what he says and does might suggest otherwise, the old oligarch attests that being rich facilitates living the sort of life that allows one to confront Hades without fear. Abstracting from his pious apology for wealth a definition of justice as being "the truth and giving back what one has taken from another", Sure Strength immediately refutes it with a powerful counterexample concerning soundness of mind as the just prerequisite for handling both weapons and the truth.[2]

Thereupon the aged host's son and heir, War Ruler, rushes to his father's relief. Wielding a pithy line of poetry, the young man advances an account of justice that is confined to those one loves (i.e., friends, *philoi*). But when encouraged by the philosopher to do so, he readily expands it to include appropriate conduct towards those one hates (i.e., enemies, *echthroi*, literally, "the hated"). Pressed to indicate more substantially how the just man is "most able to help friends and injure enemies", War Ruler suggests, "In making war and as an ally in battle" (332e). Sure Strength accepts this reply without demur, whereas he will settle for nothing less than perfect specificity with respect to the just man's utility in peacetime. They go on to speak of both guarding and using such things as shields and lyres, as well as of the martial and musical arts that employ them. They agree that the one who is cleverest at landing a blow in boxing, "or in any other kind of battle", is also cleverest at guarding against it, and that "a good guardian of an army is the very same one who can steal the enemy's plans and his other practices" (334a). And upon being brought to see certain consequences of mistaking who his true friends and enemies are, or at least ought to be, War Ruler refines his conceptions accordingly. He also learns to distinguish injuring from causing pain and even death. His conversation with the philosopher concludes with a formal alliance being struck, making explicit his willingness "to do battle in common" in defence of a proper respect for the wise (335e).

The terms of this treaty are no sooner announced than it is put to the test. For now the philosopher is savagely attacked by a wily professional named Bold Fighter (Thrasy-machos), who, events prove, has an ally of his own (cf. 340a–b). Despite his many taunts and feints and boasts, however, it is only after his mercenary nature has been suitably enticed with promises of money and praise that Bold Fighter presents his own laconic definition of justice: "the advantage of the stronger" (338c). Sure Strength withholds the proffered reward on the grounds that he does not know what is meant in this case by "the stronger". And as subsequent discussion shows, understanding who are the *truly* strong *is* a problem of first importance. But Bold Fighter treats the philosopher's professed puzzlement as merely a stratagem whereby to gain an advantage in their battle of words and wits. In the course of his several unsuccessful attempts to explicate and defend what would seem a defensible view, it is established that an internal justness is as essential to the power of an army – or of a band of pirates, for that matter – as it is to that of a city (351ea; cf. 351c). Upon thrice proving himself stronger than this, his most determined opponent (340a, 343a, 350d; cf. 583b), the philosopher thereby establishes himself as both the rightful ruler of the assembled cohort and the very touchstone for what is just, at least according to the perspective of Bold Fighter.

There's to be no resting on laurels, however. For Gleaming, pointedly described as "always most courageous in everything" (357a), and apparently more provoked than intimidated by the fate of Bold Fighter, challenges Sure Strength to prove in no uncertain terms that justice itself is good, and as such inherently more powerful than injustice. Playing – or playing at playing – the devil's advocate, he suggests that justice originates in a conspiracy of the naturally weak many against the naturally strong few. Hence no true man of power and sense would honour justice and thereby facilitate what is in effect a commitment to mediocrity and his own containment. The common praise of its goodness is but part of a pervasive scheme of mutual deception, one which is politely accepted and perpetuated out of a lack of power for committing injustice with impunity. However, the rare individual with the power for the most complete injustice includes as a component of that power a capacity for generally appearing just; but also – "since he is courageous and strong" – for using force when nothing will serve so well as force (361ab). Having thrown down the gauntlet, as it were, Gleaming is cleverly seconded by his brother, Dauntless (cf. 367a). The latter, for his part, drives home the essential point that justice is without either natural or supernatural foundation beyond that reflected in the often confused and contradictory realm of common opinion (which is despised by any man who can think and act for himself). Those willingly just are so out of "lack of courage, or old age, or some other weakness, depreciating injustice because lacking the power to do it" (366cd). And so he too insists on being shown that "justice is stronger than injustice" (367e). Now, while to them Sure Strength pretends that their challenge has perplexed and dispirited him, he admits to his anonymous auditors that it in fact *delighted* him, and further enhanced his long-standing admiration for the nature of these brothers (367e–a). There is, then, a special irony in his reiteration of another lover's praise for their performance in battle. His response to the stand they have here taken differs radically from the character of their challenge, however. First rallying them to his side with a shrewd appeal to their nobility (368bc), he proposes that they embark jointly on an adventure, an adventure of the sort they would naturally find most attractive: the founding of a new city, one true so far as possible to the very idea of justice. Only when its form is fully and finally revealed will its utter novelty be clear, for it is to be a city in which any ruler must be "both warrior and philosopher" (525b).

This revolutionary project is accomplished in four stages. First, they establish the simplest possible city, one concerned primarily with meeting life's basic necessities, which strictly speaking are needs of the body (369d; cf. 341e). Yet even here, in what would otherwise seem a return to Arcadian life, each inhabitant must act with some discretion due to the dangers of destitution and war (372bc). But these may not be the only problems threatening the success of their rustic anarchy. Apparently its unvaried, undemanding, egalitarian way of life, while conducive to bodily health, would not satisfy all, or even most, human beings. Sooner or later the more imaginative and restless spirits would, like Gleaming, reject it in favour of something more to their taste (372d).

So for these and perhaps his own reasons, the philosopher agrees to complicate and luxuriate the city, even though their doing so has one indisputable consequence: they now most definitely must be prepared for war. That no one objects to this development says all that needs saying concerning the natures of those who follow him. In fairness, though, it should be noted that this prospect would almost surely have been forced on them sooner or later by neighbours manifesting the natural human inclination towards unlimited acquisition (373d).[3] For even were they themselves to abstain from all superfluities, outsiders may covet their necessities, or their land, or even their labouring bodies (cf. 422ea). The philosopher expressly reserves judgment as to whether war works bad or good (373e), but observes that their city must now be made "still greater" by the addition of "a whole

War and Peace

army, which will go out and do battle with invaders for all the wealth [*ousia*: literally, "substance"] and other things". And would he not have to agree that often the best defence is a good offence (cf. 422d)? He *did* remind everyone earlier that whoever can most skilfully guard against a blow is the very one who's most skilled in landing it himself, and that generally "of whatever one is a skilful guardian, he is also a skilful thief" (334a) – an ominous observation, one might add, given every polity's need for guardians.

Now, in meeting this need, there are obvious alternatives to a professional standing army. None, however, is considered. But since "[successful] contesting in war seems an art [*technē*]", the triple rationale that establishes the founding principle of their regime – one man, one job (370a–c) – is fully applicable here. For any sane adult but minimally acquainted with nature and history must agree that one shouldn't care more "for the art of shoemaking than the art of war" – indeed, that it is the art of arts in so far as it is of "greatest importance that what has to do with war be done well". Merely picking up "a shield or any other weapon or tool of war" will not render one "an adequate combatant in a battle of hoplites or any other kind of battle in war"; rather, one must practise it full-time "from childhood on" (374b–d). Hence, in this or any other regime that recognizes the priority of these truths, one finds "the shoemaker a shoemaker, and not a pilot along with his shoemaking, and the farmer a farmer, and not a judge along with his farming, and a warrior a warrior, and not a moneymaker along with his warmaking" (397e; cf. 547d).

Having agreed, then, that the guarding of their city will be the responsibility of professional warriors – a dangerous class of men armed with teeth, of "meateaters" who will rule if they have a mind to (cf. 372b–c and 404b–c) – the philosopher focuses the balance of the night's discussion on them, as if all the great problems of political life, including justice in cities and men, turn on this: the proper nurture of those suited by nature to be warriors. Urging his own comrades not to be cowardly in confronting this challenge, he observes that their first task is to determine what in fact are the characteristics of a natural warrior-guardian (374e). Likening them to guard dogs, he suggests that a suitable young man would have keen senses, be swift, and be sufficiently strong of body "to fight it out with what they've caught"; as for his soul, the first and only requirement is that it be courageous because infused with the sort of spirit that makes one "irresistible and invincible" (*amachos ... kai anikētos*), "fearless and indomitable"

The War Lover

(*aphobos ... kai aēttetos*; 375b).[4] After further consideration, Sure Strength and Gleaming conclude that a fitting candidate "will in his nature be philosophic, spirited, swift, and strong" (376c). Perhaps it should be added, since apparently it is easy to overlook, that aptitude and enjoyment usually go together (cf. 370a–c, 455b–c, 486c, 536d–a). Hence it would seem that primary consideration ought to be given to those who love a good fight.

Be that as it may, the qualities upon which they do base their selection make such guardians as dangerous to their fellow citizens and each other as to their enemies; whereas it is imperative that they be gentle towards their own and harsh only towards outsiders. This, then, becomes the fundamental problem: finding, or making, "a disposition at once gentle [or tame; *praos*] and great-spirited [*megalothumos*]". Pursuing its solution so engrosses these inquisitive brothers and comrades that they willingly forgo the food, drink, and wild night on the town they earlier found so enticing. The crux of the puzzle confronting them is how to provide a civilizing nurture for what must be the most problematic gift of nature: spiritedness (cf. 410d–e). The education they devise is aimed not at making warlike men pacific (any more than one would wish guard dogs to be timid), but rather at taming them, rendering them tractable and disciplined, which must in their case mean self-disciplined. Only then will they be capable of making proper discriminations and identifications, and consequently of acting with discretion: aggressive or accommodating as appropriate. In the course of outlining a fitting regime of domestication, their whole city is progressively asceticized, with much of the luxury introduced in the second stage being purged in the third (399e; cf. 421ea).

The foundation of their city's martial culture is determined to be a certain kind of music[5] (376e, 401d–e, 403d, 424d). The philosopher and his subordinates agree that the souls of their warriors must be fed only such tales as will encourage them to "choose death in battles over defeat and slavery" (386b; cf. 387b). And in the interest of promoting, among other things, that all-important fraternal harmony among the guardians of their city, "Above all it must *not* be said that gods make war on gods" (378bc; cf. 383c, 589d, 613ab). Given to neither tears nor laughter (387d–e, 388e), immune to favour and flattery (390d–e; cf. 590b), they must be men of truth and moderation, capable of the strictest obedience (389b–d), and neither experienced nor apt in the art of appearing other than one is (395c, 396d). Time and again, these guardians are referred to as "champions of war" (e.g., 404a, 422b,

521d, 543b), and as such "champions" (or athletes; *athletai*) in the "greatest contest" (*megistos agōn*; 403e; cf. 344e, 578c, 608b). Repeatedly, pedagogic choices are made with explicit reference to that which is suitable for "warlike men" (e.g., 399a, 404a, 467c, 521d), and with one eye on their enemies (e.g., 382c, 415e, 423a, 468a, 469b). They disdain soft and slack musical rhythms in favour of modes that "imitate the sounds and accents of one who is courageous in warlike deeds and every violent work" (399a; cf. 397b). And the "best gymnastic" is akin to this music, "a simple and equitable gymnastic, and especially concerning things of war" (404b; cf. 410b). These two arts – music and gymnastic – rightly mixed, are to produce the disciplined guardian they desire, one whose spirited part is in tune with the philosophic. Sure Strength expressly warns against the danger of too much music softening the spirit with the result that one becomes "a feeble warrior", whereas too little leaves one still savage, "like a wild beast" (411a–412a). He and Gleaming endorse a medical policy attributed to warfaring physicians (407ea; cf. 459c), and a stern but sane law for those who are naturally defective in either body or soul (410a). The only recreations mentioned are the traditional favourites of warriors: the hunt and the chase, athletic contests, horse racing, and dancing (412b).[6] And without so much as a hint that any legitimate considerations counsel otherwise, they agree that those selected to be the supreme rulers of their city – guardians in the precise sense – shall come exclusively from the warrior class.[7] They would choose the sort of older men who command the respect of this class, men who are prudent and powerful, and whose loving care for the city derives from the conviction that its wellbeing is identical with their own, not least because it accords so profoundly with their taste (412c–d; cf. 401d–e).

These guardians are to be billeted with their supporting warriors in a military-style camp, one which has been carefully sited for its strategic advantages. And it is explicitly argued that their housing must be the spartan barracks appropriate for soldiers, not the sumptuous residences of moneymakers, which too often are but citadels of private indulgence (415d–e, 417a; cf. 464c–d, 543b, 548a). Their sustenance will be provided them when and as needed for "moderate and courageous men who are champions of war". They will mess together "like soldiers in a camp and live a life in common", which is to say a life that is uniform, without frills or any means of expressing a vain individuality (416d–b). Their new city being thus established, with its true fortifications those built in music (424d), the philosopher sketches for it a foreign policy that is concerned exclusively with war, and which is premissed on such a city being several times more powerful than mere numbers would suggest (422a–423a; cf. 522d–e).

The story takes a comical[8] as well as a radical turn when, in order to quell a threatening mutiny in the ranks – instigated by War Ruler and Dauntless, but supported by Gleaming and Bold Fighter – Sure Strength is obliged to elaborate on the place of women and children in their new commonwealth. His professed doubts and fears concerning the wisdom of doing so, his likening the task to something mortally risky, are all dismissed, even laughingly disparaged by his companions, and serve only to elicit cavalier assurances of their determination and support (450ab, 450c–a, 453cd). So, with a great show of reluctance, he at last accedes to their desire to hear what he ironically calls "the feminine drama" (451c). It is dominated by the question of whether woman as such is equally suited for the role of guardian. If so, some women too must be taught music and gymnastic "and what has to do with war" (452a). Doing so would require profound departures from what is customary "in gymnastic, in music, and not least in the bearing of arms and riding of horses" (452c).

The issue is admittedly controversial, perhaps incorrigibly so. One may expect all sorts of disputes and disputants concerning "whether female human nature can act in common with that of the male race [*genos*] in all deeds or in none at all, or in some things yes and others no, particularly with respect to war" (453a). Sobered by a pointed reference to the successful, if much less radical innovations of the martial regimes of Crete and Sparta, the philosopher's comrades are admonished to consider without prejudice what would otherwise seem a ridiculous proposal. It is readily conceded that "one woman is apt at medicine and another not, one woman apt at music and another unmusical by nature" (455e). They also agree, though not without a meet trace of skepticism, that one woman "is skilled at gymnastic and war, whereas another is unwarlike[9] and no lover of the gymnastic art". And that there is among women "a lover of wisdom and a hater of wisdom", as well as "one who is spirited and another without spirit". Since similar natural differences were used to select from the class of men those suited to be guardians, they conclude that "one woman is fit for guarding and another not" (456a). One may notice, however, that the philosopher has ensured that any conclusions reached on this point remain hypothetical to an unusual extent, being suspended from some especially dubious 'if's (451e, 454d, 455ab). Here is only the second time in the night's discussion that he expressly leaves open a line of retreat (455a; cf. 453c, 437a). That something is awry soon becomes clear. In the context of discussing their injunction against plundering corpses on the battlefield, Sure Strength suggests that it provides "a pretext for cowards not to advance against the one who is still fighting", characterizing it as "the mark of a womanish and small mind to hold the enemy to be the body of the dead who's flown away and left behind that with which he fought" (469d).

The radical change in the political relationships of the sexes requires an even more radical change in the traditional constitution of the family. The philosopher outlines a communal family arrangement encompassing the entire warrior class of guardians and their auxiliaries. The feature most essential to it seems also the most questionable: the opportunities for sexual reproduction must be strictly rationed and secretly manipulated so as to serve the good of the city (459c-e). More specifically, this means arranging "marriages" so as to produce offspring of the finest quality, and in such quantity as will "most nearly preserve the same number of men, taking into consideration wars, diseases, and everything else of the sort" (460a). With one eye on the particular traits desired in the city's children, and the other on encouraging certain kinds of public service (or at least the virtue requisite to it), "the privilege of more frequent intercourse with the women must be given to those young men who are good in war or elsewhere" (460b). The inherent political dangers of trying to breed pedigreed guardians in the manner of staghounds and gamecocks – but with "a throng of lies and deceptions" substituting for physical control (459a-e) – is highlighted rather than obscured by the philosopher's subsequent emphasis on "keeping the guardian's herd as free as possible from faction" (459e, 464d-e), on promoting the unity of the city (462ab), on its being a community of shared pleasures and pains (464a-b), and on the men of this class living "in peace with one another" (465b).

At the verge of the dialogue's exact centre – and immediately before introducing what turns out to be the keystone of this revolutionary regime, the apparently absurd idea of having a philosopher for a king – the philosopher pauses for a lengthy digression about war (466e-471b). And this despite the fact that he has already responded once to the question of how they will wage war (422a-e). His discussion now, however, is in no way redundant. Could it be that his superior understanding of war and faction, of friends and enemies, of Greeks and barbarians, is meant to be the final proof of his right to be king? He begins in a humorous vein, suggesting that the entire communal family, both male and female guardians along with their children, must do everything together, including going off to war (466d, e). Having the children along on campaign is alleged to be beneficial in three ways, all having directly to do with war: they can observe at first hand the martial craft they will eventually practise themselves; moreover, "they will help out and serve in many things having to do with war", thus augmenting their observations with experience; finally, it is noted that "every animal fights exceptionally hard in the presence of its offspring" (466e–a). It seems fair to add that such direct exposure to war would toughen the souls of children as little else one could imagine – if it doesn't kill them, it should only make them stronger (cf. 537a). But given how prominent fortune can be in the fortunes of war, it may kill them. Fittingly, then, the philosopher's bright partner here raises this obvious objection: "There's no small risk that in defeats, such as are apt to happen in war, they'll lose the children along with themselves and make it impossible for the rest of the city to recover" (467b). This is indeed a grave risk to any polity, the loss of a whole generation of children. One might go so far as to suggest that it is the second-greatest political disaster a city might face, surpassed only by the loss of the mothers.

Sure Strength silently acknowledges the force of these objections by a subtle change in the terms of their discussion. They now agree that since the risk-free life is an idle if not ignoble dream, and that some risks must be run – namely, those which surmounted leave one the better, the stronger for it – they will have "boys who are to become warlike men observe the things concerning war", suitably guided by "fathers" knowledgeable in the dangers of war (467b–c). With their military apprenticeship policy thus sensibly modified, the philosopher turns to the question of the battlefield behaviour expected of their soldiers towards one another as well as towards both real and apparent enemies. They agree, among other things, that any display of cowardice on the battlefield means demotion out of the ruling class, and that anyone allowing himself to be "taken alive by the enemy" shall be abandoned to his fate (468a). Whereas the one who distinguishes himself on campaign will be honoured in all the traditional and some novel ways, including especially ones that "increase his strength" (468d). They also agree to reserve the term 'war' for fighting between those who are truly alien and foreign to each other, and who as such are "enemies by nature". Struggles with "what is one's own and akin", strife among those "by nature friends", is to be called 'faction' (470b–c; cf. 334c–a). Beneath their discussion runs a natural, rather than merely conventional, distinction between Greek and barbarian (470e; cf. 499cd, 533d).

But now his young, and increasingly eager lieutenant, more than convinced that the city they have described would be altogether good and its guardians "irresistible" (471d), is overwhelmed with impatience to learn one thing: "how it is possible for this regime to come into being" (472ab). He openly accuses his leader (a confessed procrastinator; cf. 458a) of employing dilatory tactics in order to put off indefinitely his confronting this paramount challenge. And so Sure Strength is at last compelled to reveal his strategy for conquering all human ills: have "the philosophers rule as kings, or those now called kings and lords genuinely and adequately philosophize" (473cd). This seemingly ridiculous plan is no sooner announced than he is obliged to deploy his forces in anticipation of a mass assault. For there are apt to be many, including some of consequence, who will react with indignation to such a strange and aristocratic idea, and "stripped for action each take hold of whatever weapon falls to him" (474a; cf. 501c, 502d, 497d). Ably assisted by his auxiliaries, however, the philosopher defends himself and his work with an extended *apologia* that rests on distinguishing the few true philosophers from the many various false pretenders who bear primary responsibility for the bad reputation of philosophy (474b–521b; cf. 539b–c). In light of *that* concern, one might suggest that the entire night's discussion amounts to a defence of the philosopher against the all-too-common conception of him as a soft, indolent, pacifistic, irreverent, politically useless, effeminizing corrupter of young men, by example if not by active intent.

Having shown the justness of true philosophers being kings, and the necessity of true kings being philosophers, they turn to considering "in what way such will come into being and how one will lead them up to the light, much as some are said to have gone from Hades up to the gods" (521c; cf. 589d, 590d, 611e, 613ab). Sure Strength outlines an unprecedented curriculum as fitness training for philosophy, repeatedly insisting that whatever is studied "mustn't be useless to warlike men" (521d; cf. 522e, 525b, 527c). And although the subjects studied are familiar enough, the spirit in which they are approached is decidedly untraditional (cf. 376e). Arithmetic, for example, is studied "for war and for ease of turning around the soul itself from Becoming to Truth and Being" (525c). Similarly, it is the military and philosophical applications of geometry that are considered (526d, 527c), as well as those of astronomy (527d).

Suitable recruits come from the ranks of what have been referred to throughout the discussion as "champions of war" (521d), for the kings of this "beautiful city" (*kallipolis*; 527c) must be those "who have proved best in philosophy and war" (543a). Such candidate guardians must be tested so as to determine who is "steadfast in studies, steadfast in war and in other lawful things" (537d). Only those are to be promoted who pass the "greatest test", namely that which reveals them to have "dialectical natures" capable of a "synoptic view", but who also have "orderly and stable natures" such as can be trusted with wielding this profoundly dangerous "power of dialectic" – a power that can compromise philosophy and destroy even the most beautiful and just of cities (537b–539d; cf. 413ea). Once formally educated, these select of the select must also be second to none in the practical experience essential for refining and applying what they know to the ever-changing circumstances of everyday existence. With an eye towards acquiring such prudence, then, they must leave their citadel and go down, again and again, into the more benighted sectors of the city, and "be compelled to rule in the affairs of war and the rulerships which are suitable for young men" (539e; cf. 347a-d).

Setting a sort of example, Sure Strength himself now returns to a consideration of ordinary political life, offering a genealogy of regimes and men, with constant reference to how each stands with respect to war (e.g., 549a, 551d, 552a, 555a, 556e, 556d, 557e, 561d, 566e, 575b, 579d). That done, the philosopher challenges the greatest of the poets to a battle of wisdom, limiting their contest to the four "greatest and fairest things" of which Homer presumes to speak, namely: war, the command of armies, the governance of cities, and the education of a human being (599cd ff.). The dialogue concludes with Sure Strength recounting an old war-story which he attributes to "a strong man", a warrior who died in battle, but who has divinely chosen to observe the workings of the fates and then return to life, a fitting messenger concerning the eternal order of justice (cf. 469a).

Perhaps one of the stranger things about Plato's *Politeia* is its subtle preoccupation with war. Suitably distilled – but apparently not otherwise (and this appearance can hardly be accidental) – his "Republic", both the substance of the discussion and the form of regime depicted therein, reveals itself to be recurrently if not constantly attentive to war. While quantitative considerations are hardly everything, they are something, indeed the first thing (cf. 522c). And so consider: the term 'war' (*polemos*) and its cognates – such as 'waging war' (*polemein*), the 'warrior' (*polemikos*), the 'art of war' (*polemikē*), and 'enemies' (*polemioi*) – occur nearly ten dozen times; 'battle' and it cognates, nearly three dozen. Add to these the frequency of other war-related phenomena, such as the dozens upon dozens of references to courage (*andreia*; literally, "manliness") and cowardice, to various kinds of strength, to disputes and quarrels, strife and struggle (*agōn*), to other terms for and even conceptions of enemy (*echthros*, "the hated", occurs, for example, over three dozen times), and is it not fair to say that this most celebrated portrayal of politics and philosophy, of justice and the rational soul is painted primarily in the colours of war?

Certainly peace (*eirēnē*) enjoys no comparable prominence, being mentioned less than a dozen times. Two of these uses occur in the context of Polemarchos' frustrated effort to specify the utility of the just man in peacetime (332e, 333a). The word is used two more times in exemplifying the absence of compulsion characteristic of the democratic regime, where (according to the philosopher's immoderate "democratic" rhetoric) no one is required "to make war when others are making war, nor to keep the peace when others are keeping it, if one doesn't desire peace" (557e). The only regime that is explicitly acknowledged to provide its inhabitants some prospect of living out their lives in peace is promptly denounced as "a city of pigs" – and perhaps justly so (372d; cf. 372b7–8 with 607a4). In any event, the possibility of its being established and maintained is about as remote as that of the philosopher-king. Another reference concerns the typical behaviour of tyrannical natures in peacetime (575b). And another merely helps distinguish what is presented as the highest regime actually found in political life (cf. 497ab), the one where the rulers are "naturally more directed to war than to peace" (547e).

Only three mentions of peace involve the guardians, but each is doubly interesting. One occurs in a summary judgment about their regime in *logos*: "for a city that is to be governed from on high, women must be common, children and their entire education must be common, and similarly the practices in war and peace must be common, and their kings must be those among them who have proved best

The War Lover

in philosophy and with respect to war" (543a; cf. 499d2). Another – and it is the central of the eleven references to peace – comes in a question about the guardians as a class: "Then will the men, as a result of the laws, live in peace with one another in all respects?" (465b). Glaukon's emphatic affirmation is justified in part, perhaps, by the first mention of peace in conjunction with these natural warriors, this one having to do with their musical education. The philosopher advises that, in addition to the warlike modes, "leave another for one who performs a peaceful deed, one that is not violent but voluntary, either persuading someone of something and making a request – whether a god by prayer or a human being by instruction and exhortation – or, conversely, holding himself in check for someone else who makes a request or instructs him or persuades him to change, and as a result acting intelligently, not being arrogant, but in all things acting moderately and in measure and being content with the consequences" (399bc; cf. 411c-e, 586c, 618bc, also *Laws* 815b-816d).

But perhaps the most interesting reference to peace is the very first one, for it transports the issues of war and peace to an altogether different field of contention. Kephalos, the man who grew old and wealthy manufacturing armaments for other men's use (cf. 601d-e), is responding to the philosopher's initial question to him about what it is like being old. He attests that a majority of his contemporaries lament the lost pleasures of youth – especially those which attend most men's most urgent desire: sex (cf. 390bc, 403a, 458d). Whereas, *he* agrees with the great tragedian Sophocles, that "in every way, old age brings much peace and freedom from such things. When the desires cease to strain and finally relax, then ... we are rid once for all of masters full many and mad" (329cd; cf. 573b-c). So here, at the beginning of a discussion that occupies the philosopher from "yesterday" until "tomorrow", Kephalos reminds everyone that not all struggle and strife, not all faction and war, are among or within polities. A human being can be at odds with *himself*, internally discordant. Perhaps *most* people are. A person might even be his own worst enemy, and consistently act contrary to his own good, the animosity within him more than a match for his self-love. Perhaps the human soul is but another battleground, and life itself but one long war, on the inside as well as the out (cf. 603cd).

Reflecting on the respective priorities of war and peace as manifested in the course of making a just regime in *logos* – and especially on what

War and Peace

determines the regime's character and taste: the nature and nurture of its ruling class – an unprejudiced observer can scarcely avoid concluding that war must be regarded as the fundamental fact of political life, indeed of all life, and that every decision of consequence must be made with that fact in mind. Decent people may prefer to think that war exists for the sake of peace, and perhaps it is salutary that they do so. But those who care more for truth than for decency, or those charged with caring for the city, must understand that in reality the opposite is the case. Seen in that light, the well-ordered regime is but an island of peace and friendship and decency, the better to survive and prosper in a sea of war (cf. 351c, 375c, 378c, 386a, 431d–e, 423a–b, 464d–b). Or, rather, it is like a well-run ship sailing such a sea, with its multifarious personnel all necessary, equal to their tasks, and working in harmony of purpose under the rule of a true pilot – someone who understands both the sea and sailors (cf. 341cd, 346b, 488a–e).[10]

As noted, however, the concerns of war and peace, while writ large in the external political realm, have their analogues in the realm of the soul as well. Apparently the constitution of a human being, his inner *politeia*, is as subject to enmity and faction (442cd, 444b, 589a), to barbarian subjugation (533d), to rebellion and revolution (444b, 518d), to subversion and anarchy and tyranny (560b, 560e), as is that of a city. The unjust man is described as one "powerless to act, because he is at faction and not of one mind with himself, ... an enemy [*echthros*] to himself as well as to just men" (352a), whereas a just man is one who has "become his own friend" (443d; cf. 589b, 621c). There are many subtle allusions to common and chronic conflicts within the soul, as well as enough that are not subtle (e.g., 486c, 537b, 603d). Several arise in the course of discussing the various types of inferior men. The young Timocrat's soul is explained as a precarious balance between fundamentally opposed forces (550b). The Oligarchic soul "wouldn't be free from faction within himself, ... but rather is in some sense two-fold, although for the most part his better desires would master his worse desires" (554de). Nonetheless, "afraid to awaken the spendthrift desires and summon them to an alliance and love of victory, he makes war like an oligarch, with few of his troops, [and so] is defeated most of the time and stays rich" (555a). The soul of the Democrat is perpetually an arena of contention, the principal antagonists being the austere oligarchic elements in him and the profligate tyrannic ones, with first this side and then the other "doing battle and holding

The War Lover

sway" (560d). And with alliances and counter-alliances being struck, "faction and counter-faction arise in him and he does battle with himself" (560a). The Tyrannic soul is portrayed as a barbaric chaos of insatiable desires, ever driven and maddened by their stings, "but especially by love [*erōs*] itself, which guides all the others as though they were its armed guards", intent upon seizing "anything that can be taken by deceit or force" (573e).

Arguably the most memorable reference to psychic conflict, however, is also the most important. It is the story the philosopher tells about a well-named man, Leontios son of Aglaion (i.e., "Lionlike son of Splendor"; cf. 588d), whose experience is cited as crucial evidence that the spirited part of the human soul must not be confused with its desiring part. Sokrates avows that he "trusts" this particular report – and well he might, since his own experience has quite likely ratified it more than once. Leontios, like the philosopher at the beginning of this dialogue, was journeying from the lower to the higher city when he was arrested, not by a party of high-spirited young men, but by a morbid spectacle: fresh handiwork of the public executioner. His reaction is no less curious for its being familiar. He found the sight at once attractive and yet repugnant. "For awhile he battled and covered his face", but finally, much to his disgust, the desire to look "overpowered" him. The philosopher observes, "This *logos* certainly indicates that anger sometimes makes war against the desires as one thing against something else" (439e–a).

While there are, then, quite a number of overt references to both faction and warfare in the soul, one does well to remember that the reigning analogy of this inquiry into justice matches cities with men, and that but a minor portion of the many facets of this analogy are ever made explicit. Thus, one must bear in mind that everything said about conflict among or within cities may have its analogue at the level of the individual human being. And furthermore, what men call justice, defined in terms of its necessary work of "producing unanimity and friendship" (351d; cf. 353a, 477c–d), is thereby confined to such collections of human parts as are by nature capable of maintaining a more-or-less peaceful and harmonious unity. Presumably this includes a single man or woman, as well as polities of appropriate size (423bc, 443de, 462a–d). As for the rest, perhaps all *is* fair in love and war.

No doubt most people would recognize the pertinence of speaking about strife within the soul (cf. 430e–b). The connection between war and philosophy, however, is apt to be a good deal more puzzling. Could any two things be *less* akin, *less* compatible, more *alien* – more downright cacophonous – than the taste for war and the love of wisdom? Are we really to believe that a single person can (indeed *must*) somehow combine, *harmoniously*, in one soul, the qualities of a hardened warrior – coarse, rude, insensitive to the point of cruel, ignorant of everything except what has to do with war, contemptuous of life's refinements and finer pleasures (and of the people who value such things), given to manic fury when crossed – combine *that* with the kindly, gentle, modest, retiring philosopher, distinguished above all by his equanimity? "But these contrasting requirements are like impossibilities", we may be tempted to say, "for surely a gentle nature is opposed to a spirited one!" And given the popular conceptions of both these kinds of men – or the dominant scholarly views of them, for that matter – anyone would have to agree that a more radical contrast could hardly be drawn than that between the *active* life – epitomized by politics and war, pursuits that are necessarily parochial and partisan and timely – and the *passive* life of contemplation known as philosophy, that impartial, disinterested, cosmopolitan search for eternal truth. After all, is this not what is "so paradoxical" about the great "third wave" or "contraction" (*kuma*) that Sokrates comically warns of, a paradox captured in the very name 'philosopher-king' (472a, 473e)? But however strange it seems, from the moment the warriors first make their appearance, to the final discussion of selecting rulers for the regime, philosophy and warfare are conjoined (376bc, 543a). Perhaps the popular view is mistaken. And perhaps even we scholars have something to learn, not only about the warrior, but about the genuine philosopher as well.

Of course, if one agrees that conflict is by nature endemic and ineradicable, both within as well as among cities – and I, for one, know of no clear evidence to the contrary – then the idea that philosophic *rule* requires the virtues of a warrior becomes a good deal more plausible. For actual ruling requires that knowledge be carried into practice, and thus demands not just the prudence whereby general principles are applied to particular cases, but *whatever* virtues are requisite for translating thought into deed. If all men individually were ruled by reason and had enough of it, wisdom would be sufficient for ruling them collectively. But the divine in man must contend with the animal, which is – virtually by definition – *alogos* (cf. 588b–e, 589cd, 590b–e).[11] So there is more to life than to a chess game. Still, the bare fact that

The War Lover

there is a need for something – that, for example, it would be supremely *useful* were the qualities of hero and sage combined in one man – is no guarantee that it is a natural possibility.

There are grounds for suspecting, however, that the relationship between the love of wisdom and a talent for war is more intimate than would be implied by this convenient marriage of the requirements of politics with those of philosophy. Simple fidelity to the dialogue obliges one to consider whether the search for truth – be it something about the searching, or something about the truth itself – does not require the same toughness and tenacity, the same alertness and quickness of response, the steady courage, strength, and stamina for the most strenuous labours, the same absence of sentimentality, the greatness of spirit, indeed all the distinguishing qualities and powers of the "warlike man", most especially his drive to be victorious. For this is no more than what the philosopher seems to teach to those who would inherit his way of life (485a, 503c–d). According to him, the true philosopher is orderly (500d), sharp-sighted (484c), "moderate and in no way a lover of money" or of bodily pleasure (485de); he despises deceit and vanity (485c, 486b, 490a), is untouched by illiberality or pettiness (486a), but rather is endowed with a befitting greatness (486a; cf. 490c, 494b, 536a); not merely is he no coward (486b, 535b), he is positively courageous (487a, 490c, 494b) – indeed, "most courageous" (535a) – and contemptuous of death (486ab); he must be capable of the most intense striving (485d; cf. 494d); he treats challenges and tests as so many battles (534c); and he takes care of his body as it is "growing into manhood [*androutai*], thus securing a helper for philosophy" (498b). The person suited for philosophic studies is "the steadiest and most courageous ... and, in so far as possible, the best looking" (or, "best formed"; *eueidestatos*), with a disposition "noble and stern" (*gennaios kai blosuros*; 535b; cf. 375a). "Won't such a one be first among all in everything, straight from the beginning, especially if his body naturally matches his soul?" (494b; cf. 496c). That very, very few could ever even hope to measure up to such a demanding constellation of qualities is neither here nor there. It is never suggested that true philosophers would be any more common than the most pre-eminent of heroes (cf. 491ab, 503b, d).

It is tempting to regard the philosopher's assimilation of philosophy and war as no more than a tactic of pedagogy, a singularly effective way of capturing the attention and respect of high-spirited young men who are naturally attracted by the excitement and glamour of war.

Men who are first of all concerned with being men do not take readily to a way of life they believe will emasculate them. And one might disarm their suspicions and fears of philosophy by gilding it with the perhaps spurious lustre of that most manly of activities: fighting, waging war, defying death. That the philosopher has such a stratagem in mind seems undeniable. He is confronted from the outset with headstrong young men who are convinced that all the good things in life are to be had through politics if one is but man enough to take them (359b, 366d), whereas they regard the practice of philosophy as *at best* "useless", and more typically degenerative (487d). There is an obvious need, then, for some way to overcome this prejudice if the souls of young men such as these are to be opened to philosophy and a rational consideration of the Good.

But this is an inadequate explanation, not least of all because the curious identification of philosophy and warfare continues to the very end of the discussion – that is to say, well past the point where the pedagogic revolution has been accomplished (518d, 519d). In any case, it begs the more fundamental question: why is the philosopher hunting – or fishing, rather – for his natural heirs and allies, his natural kinfolk, among those naturally attracted to and suited for war? And lest this be thought but a peculiarity of the *Republic*, let it be noted that this same view – that there is a deep relationship between philosophy and war, and that those best suited for the former are to be found among the ranks of those well suited for the latter – seems to pervade the entire Platonic corpus,[12] and that echoes of it recur throughout our philosophic tradition.[13]

— 2 —

A Tale of Two Cities

Given the subtle ambiance of war that pervades the dialogue, perhaps it would be enlightening to examine more closely its account of the city and the man that are explicitly dedicated to war. This city is presented as the highest type historically found in political life, for it is second only to that of the city in *logos* from which it has supposedly decayed (while retaining certain key features of it), and so is actually first in rank by the admitted default of this higher regime (544c, 547d, 583a; cf. 497ab, 520ab, 592ab). The philosopher's "tragical" derivation of the regime of war is ironic, not least because the first version of his and his companions' good city – the Aristocracy described in books Two through Four – itself seems like nothing so much as "an improved Sparta, correcting its worst vices, while preserving its virtues"[1] (and, as such, a sublimation of the regime of war). One would certainly not guess that this Aristocracy ignores the natural distinction between men and women (quite the contrary; cf. 377c, 387ea, 395d–e, 431bc), much less that it is ruled by philosophers. After all, *its* guardians are chosen expressly for their manifesting, through all of life's trials and tribulations, a high-spirited dogmatism and brute preference for the familiar (376a, 412d–e; cf. 429bc, 430a–b, 431de). In a certain sense, the still higher regime of the philosopher-king could also be said to originate in a regime grounded on and dedicated to the fighting spirit, one which has a vague suspicion of its wise men (who are strangely akin to their regime in being "mixed"; cf. 547e with 548c), and which is ruled instead by simpler warrior-kings. For any of a number of reasons, then, this regime that is open and honest in its devotion to war is worth a closer look.

A Tale of Two Cities

We confront it directly when the philosopher at last returns to finish business he was obliged to postpone because of the young men's amusing revolt in the name of justice and women (449c). But as a fortunate consequence of their long "detour" through his speculations about things in the heavens and beneath the earth, he and such dialogical partners as have managed to follow his "daimonic hyperbole" (509c) return with an awareness of the permanent reality whereby they may understand the ever-changing realm of appearances, which is to say, understand the world that we all experience in everyday political life. Sokrates is careful to take up at the very place he left off when diverted from a consideration of ordinary cities by this erotic-thumatic mutiny (cf. 516e). And Glaukon, displaying an enviable stamina as well as a prodigious memory, here assists the philosopher by recalling the place almost precisely: "Concerning the remaining regimes, ... you asserted that there are four forms worth an account of and whose mistakes are worth seeing; and similarly with those [men] who are like these regimes" (544a; cf. 522b). Thus he refers to Sokrates' original suggestion that while there is but one form of virtue, vice (or badness; *kakia*) is boundless, though it can be rendered intelligible in terms of four archetypal forms (445c; cf. 449a). The philosopher had gone on to say, "There are likely to be as many types [*tropoi*] of soul as there are types of regimes having distinct forms [*eidē*]." Altogether, then, five of each, it would seem (445d). But as a consequence of their excursion to heights unknown to merely political men (in the course of which they have the opportunity to unshackle themselves from a reliance on ordinary opinion and language, and learn something about the reality of forms), the question of whether there is only *one* form of good regime is finally brought out into the open. As Glaukon presciently observes, "You were presenting your arguments pretty much as you are doing now, as though you had completed your description of what concerns the city, saying that you would class a city such as you then described, and the man like it, as good. And you did this, as it seems, despite the fact that you had a still finer city and man to tell of" (543c-a). On balance, a fair judgment. For his has been a tale not of one but of *two* cities, presumably somehow akin but none the less distinct.

Perhaps that is why the philosopher mentioned two names by which one might refer to a good regime: 'Aristocracy' (*Aristokratia*) and 'Kingship' (*Basileia*). His explanation for doing so is disingenuous: "If one exceptional [kind of] man was engendered among the rulers

The War Lover

[*eggenomenou ... andros enos en tois archousi diapherontos*], it would be called a kingship, if more, an aristocracy. ... Therefore, I say this is one form. For whether it is many or one who arise, none of the city's laws worth mentioning would be changed, if that rearing and education which we described were used" (445d-e). None changed, perhaps, but a lot added, unless one regards the paradoxical features introduced in Book Five - with such great hesitation and hoopla - as not "worth mentioning". Glaukon can hardly be the only one who concludes that a new and higher conception of "exceptional man" is revealed thereafter. And subsequently an unprecedented educational regimen is outlined, one which is contrasted explicitly with the previous scheme (521d-b; cf. 536d-e). But the most profound difference concerns the perspective of the rulers as regards their ruling the city, with a consequent difference in the "wages" paid them for doing so.

The issue of the appropriate wages of ruling arises early in the dialogue. Sokrates, in opposition to Thrasymachos, contends that a ruler in the precise sense of the word - one who practises an art (*technē*) of rule - rules necessarily in the interest of the ruled, rather than in his own interest. If one concedes that exercising power on that basis is not choiceworthy for its own sake, then "there must be wages for those who are going to be willing to rule: either money [literally, silver; *argyrion*], or honour, or a penalty if one should refuse" (347a). Upon Glaukon's protesting that he doesn't understand 'penalty' as a kind of wage, the philosopher replies, "Then you don't understand the wages of the best, on account of which the most decent rule, when they are willing to rule. Or do you not know that love of honour and love of money [*philargyrion*] are said to be, *and are*, reproaches."

Thus we are subtly reminded that, for wages to matter, they must be paid - or withheld - in a coin one cares about, something one loves. What the city has to distribute are the lesser goods of money (or what it can buy) and honour, as well as assorted "bads" (penalties and punishments, i.e., various pains and losses). Sokrates goes on to observe that since good men are not lovers of honour, "necessity and a penalty must be there in addition", and that "the greatest of penalties is being ruled by someone worse if one is not oneself willing to rule" (347ab, c). Thus it is that the decent rule, when they do, entering into it "as a necessity and because they have no one better than or like themselves to whom to turn it over. For it is likely that if a city of good men came to be, there would be a fight over not ruling, just as there now is over ruling ... " (347cd).

A Tale of Two Cities

When the rulers for the city in *logos* are first chosen – or rather, when the rulers for the first city in *logos* are chosen – they are selected for having shown, among other things, that they love (*philein*) the city as much if not more than themselves, and thus will give it loving care, "*entirely eager [pasē prothymia]* to do what they believe to be advantageous for the city and in no way willing to do what is not" (412d-e). Their wages are a frugal sort of room and board (416c-e, 420a, 543b-c), and the fullest honours the city can bestow, "both while [they are] living and when [they are] dead" (414a). But not for nothing did Sokrates later warn Adeimantos in concluding his apology for making philosophers kings of their city, "that having to do with the rulers [*to tōn archontōn*] must be pursued as it were from the beginning [*ex archēs*]" (502e). For those first rulers, who are pre-eminently "lovers of the city" (*philopolidas*), contrast markedly with the lovers of wisdom who, having once escaped the closed, cave-like confines of political life, "are not willing to mind the business of human beings, but rather their souls are always yearning to spend their time above" (517c; cf. 604bc, 608cd). These latter must be *persuaded and compelled* to "go down again" and "share the labours and honours" of the city (519e-520b). They can be persuaded and compelled only in as much as they acknowledge their educational indebtedness to the city for having given them "the power to participate in both ways [of life]" (520bc; cf. 433a, 397de), and recognize the ruling of it to be one of those burdensome activities necessary for producing justice in the soul (520e; cf. 443e). Moreover – and this would appear to be crucial – it is a burden that can be *shared* with others not inferior to themselves, so that they may be rewarded with the freedom to spend "the greater part of their time with one another in the pure region", and finally retire there, to enjoy without stint that which they love (520d-e; cf. 498bc, 540b).[2]

It seems clear enough, then, that there are two good regimes, two distinct versions of the city in *logos*, however much and for whatever reason the philosopher wishes to blur that fact. His own careful attention to names should alert one to the potential significance of his binominal proposal. As he observes in a different, but not unrelated context, "It appears to me that just as two different names are used, ... so two things also exist and the names apply to differences in these two" (470b; cf. 454b, 509d).[3] Moreover, as Glaukon noted, the two regimes are ranked. Aristocracy – the city described in books Two through Four, with a regime dedicated to civic virtue and ruled by men who most fully exemplify such virtue (cf. 430c, 428cd, 431cd)

– seems a practical, if quite remote possibility. But the peculiar form of Kingship elaborated in books Five through Seven, devoted to the divine virtue of wisdom and incorporating several radical features without precedent in human experience, is riddled with paradoxes (as the philosopher partially admits, 472a, 473e; cf. 501a, 540ea). Men and women are required to turn on and off their sexuality at will, and simply in accordance with the public interest. And if they could do that, what need of the massive doses of "medicinal" lies and deceptions entailed in the rigged breeding lottery (458d, 459c–e)? The biological anonymity required for an artificial communal family of the ruling class would frequently be subverted by the very scheme of genetic inheritance on which its scientific breeding program relies – for children don't inherit just qualities of body and soul useful to the city; they often *look* like their parents. And in any case, the scheme as it is outlined is incompatible with the just assignment of all children, including those known to be of working-class parentage, to their proper natural class (415a–c, 423c–d). Various asymmetries in the reproductive roles of males and females, as well as differences in strengths, preclude the "sexual equality" (understood as sameness in way of life) prescribed for the guardians (cf. 460b). The keystone of the regime – the part-time king/part-time philosopher – violates the fundamental principle of justice in the city: one man, one task.

These are but a few of the more obvious contradictions woven into the fabric of this second city in *logos*, a city that could exist *only* in the purity and plasticity of *logos* (cf. 588d), for it turns human nature (which is *not* pure logos) on its head (cf. 456bc). There may be *another* (even related) kind of true Kingship that *could* possibly evolve or be "engendered" out of an Aristocracy (cf. 424a) – as Sokrates labours manfully to persuade Adeimantos (499b–503b) – but *this* one seems impossible, plain and simple. And yet, it too may be worth understanding, for the practical paradoxes which emerge when the regime is applied to the city may not have analogues when it is employed as an ordering of the soul. Thus, one may still prefer to mould oneself a citizen of this "divine" *kallipolis* which exists purely in *logos*, regardless of the actual regime into which one has been thrown by fate (592a–b). According to the philosopher, this would be some variation or mixture of the four basic kinds of actual, or, as he characterizes them, "human" regimes (497c): Timocracy, Oligarchy, Democracy, and Tyranny.

These four archetypal regimes, and their corresponding dispositions in human beings, are examined in a certain order. Indeed, the phi-

A Tale of Two Cities

losopher makes the proper order of their examination an important question (545a, b–c, 550c–d, 555b, 571a; cf. 449ab, 580b). Nor is this the first time he has done so. The order in which things are discussed (cf. 358c), the order in which things are understood (cf. 354b), and the order in which things are done (cf. 328a) become explicit issues in the dialogue from the moment when Sokrates and Adeimantos begin, like ones "telling tales within a tale", to "educate the men in speech" (376d; cf. 377a). They agree that music must be taken up before gymnastic (377a, 403c; cf. 546d). Their reform of music follows a chosen order: first, what is said; next, how it is said (in what style); next, what melodic accompaniments on what instruments will be allowed; finally, what rhythms should be employed (cf. 377bc, 392c, 398b–c). The natural, or proper, relationship of these four musical components – what ought to follow what, and why – is made a matter of explicit decision (399ea, 400d–e). There apparently is an order to the tests a prospective guardian must pass (413c–e). There definitely is an order to finding the four dimensions of their first good city's goodness (428ab, 429a, 430d–e, 432b–e). The discovery of the form of justice also proceeds in accordance with an intentional order: it is (as planned) found first in the city, then something similar is discerned in the soul, and finally it is compared with the various commonplace views about justice (cf. 368ea, 434d–a, 442d–a). There is a natural order to the paradoxical features introduced into the regime in Book Five (457c, 472a, 473bc), as well as an unnatural order to their manner of consideration (451bc, 450c, 452e, 458ab, 457a, 471c–e). The three parts of Sokrates' apology for the uselessness and bad reputation of philosophy are given in a logical, as well as a psycho-logical order (i.e., one which is rhetorically effective; cf. 489de, 495bc). So are the central images whereby he subsequently explains and justifies the truly philosophical life (509cd, 514a, 516a). The educational curriculum that would prepare one for such a life eventually follows its natural order (cf. 522c, 526c, 530c, 531cd) – but only after Sokrates proves in his own inimitable way that haste does indeed make waste (527d, 528a–b, d–e). Finally, one might note the order to the three proofs whereby the life of the just and kingly man is shown superior to that of the unjust and tyrannical (cf. 580cd, 583b). Suffice it to say, the philosopher treats questions about the right order of things with a studied respect.

Careful attention to his order of examining the regimes, then, is simple prudence. Judging by what is actually done, three principles of order are involved, although only two of them are explicitly discussed. One principle determines the sequence in which the regimes are considered. It apparently is a principle of natural devolution (568cd). The various actual regimes, according to the philosopher, do not come into being and pass away utterly at random, but rather each incorporates an internal source of instability that imparts to it a natural disposition to transform itself into something fundamentally different[4] (cf. 449ab, 546a). As such, the several regimes represent stages in a trajectory of political decay: Timocracy has a natural tendency to decay into Oligarchy ("second in place and second in praise"; 544c), which in turn decays into Democracy, etc.[5]

Given this order, one can discern other regularities, all being but so many dimensions of decadence, of departure from the political health of the best imaginable polity. Each successive regime represents a further decline in the rulers' concern for virtue and the preservation of the polity, and consequently in that of the ruled as well. For in the most profound sense, this is what it means to rule a city: not merely making and enforcing the law, but establishing by word and deed *all* the ethical and other standards for the rest of the citizenry. This entails inculcating the religious beliefs and cultivating the artistic taste of the entire community (377d-e, 378b-c, 427b, 400d-402a).[6] Only to the extent that the inner regime of each citizen harmonizes with the outer one of his city is there unanimity of ruler and ruled, and only then can it be truly said that they constitute one city (cf. 431de, 343b-c, 422e-c). To a considerable degree, however, such harmony and unanimity are reflections of the extent to which the rulers rule primarily in the common interest, rather than primarily – much less exclusively – in their own interest. Thus a decline in the concern for the common good is matched by declines in the internal stability of a regime, in its capacity for self-defence, and in the prudence with which it uses its resources (with a corresponding increase in the baser expressions of selfishness, and in the importance attached to bodily desires and material goods; cf. 550e). All this and more are manifested in the descending order of the philosopher's science of regimes, which is, needless to say, a universal political science applicable equally to Greeks and non-Greeks (cf. 544d).

Another principle determines the order in which the corresponding types of human beings are examined. Although he explicitly raises the possibility of considering all the regimes before the succession of corresponding men (545a), Sokrates leads his partners to reaffirm

A Tale of Two Cities

their earlier arrangement of describing first a city and then the citizen akin to it. The procedure is the more curious in that he had immediately before suggested that the various characters or dispositions (*ēthē*) in human beings are themselves the sources of the kinds of regimes: "Do you know that there are necessarily as many forms of human types as of regimes? Or do you suppose that the regimes are born 'from an oak or from rocks' and not from the dispositions of those in the cities, which, tipping the scale, draw the rest along with them?" (544de; cf. 435e, 445cd).[7] The original rationale for considering the city *before* the man was based on the presumption that the idea of justice would be writ large in the good city, in light of which it would be easier to discern the form of justice in the individual soul (368d–a). Perhaps this reasoning applies equally to the various partial or partisan views of justice that characterize defective polities and people, and to other things as well. But with that in mind, recall also that the philosopher had warned that the city and the man must be meticulously *compared*, "considering them side by side", and "rubbing them together" like firesticks in the hope of thereby bringing to light the justice which informs them both (434d–a; cf. 514b). He is silent as to what one is to do should any notable differences be discovered, but the image of firesticks rubbed together does suggest that a certain amount of mutual adaptation is possible, and may be required.

In any case, similar dialectical comparisons of the inferior cities and men are facilitated by the retention of that original arrangement, with each type of soul being taken up immediately after the civic regime with which it supposedly corresponds. Beyond a doubt, rubbing them together *is* mutually illuminating, and serves to augment, refine, and qualify the explicit accounts given by the philosopher. And since Sokrates warns they are only "outlining a regime's shape [*schēma politeias hypograpsanta*] in *logos*, not working it out precisely" (548cd, cf. 500e–501c), some polishing and detailing of this kind are needed. One might add that it is natural to consider the dispositions of individuals *after* those of the cities inasmuch as the latter normally shape the former. That the philosopher also suggests an opposite line of causation (as quoted above) simply raises for us his political version of the age-old conundrum about the chicken and the egg.

One other principle of order is employed, although it is never explicitly discussed and only once acknowledged (558c). Perhaps it could be said to follow naturally from the first principle. In any event, whether he is discussing a city or a man, the philosopher's procedure is to address first its coming into being (its generation), and then its fulfilled character. (The account of its inevitable decay [cf. 546a] is necessarily interwoven with his depicting the rise of the next, and inferior, form.) As this procedure is surely not militated by the strategic analogy of seeing the man writ large in the city, one may wonder why he chooses to proceed in this way. Does he believe that the nature of something is essentially revealed in its origin? Or, by contrasting inception with maturity, does he thereby intend to show precisely the opposite? True enough, some things, including many human conventions and forms of politeness, can be fully explained only by an historical account tracing them back to their origins. But is this also the case with those things which are by nature? And which kind of thing is a political regime? Is it profoundly conventional in character – as many would argue, including some of no slight ability (cf. 338e–a, 358e–b, 364a) – or is it in some sense natural? As anyone the least familiar with our philosophic tradition is aware, these are questions of first importance. Indeed, philosophy could be said to originate in the recognition of two distinctions: that between Knowledge and Opinion, and that between Nature and Convention.[8]

Recall, the philosopher first proposed that they investigate what justice is like in cities in order to facilitate examining it in individuals. He no sooner secured agreement to this, however, than he subtly changed the project to one which required their watching "a city *coming into being* in *logos*" in order "to see its justice coming into being, and its injustice" (369a; cf. 588cd). But even this is not precisely what is done, for his partners are not allowed to be mere passive observers of such things, but must actively participate in *making* it come into being. And somehow, somewhere along the way, constructing a city in *logos* turns into that of creating *the good* city (427e). Now, apart from possibly revealing the original source or cause of injustice in political life (cf. 372d–e, 373d, 422a), the philosopher's thrice-amended proposal has several other pedagogic advantages. Not the least of these is its impeding, if not altogether precluding, the participants' consciously or unconsciously treating as *the* city some particular city with which they are fondly familiar (probably, but not necessarily, their own; cf. 470e, 499cd, 544d, 563d). As a consequence, they are able to construct a city with which they are well-satisfied, but that is not based on slavery. Something profoundly controversial[9] is thereby proven to them in deed far more effectively than it ever could be through speech. Similarly, they are obliged to reconsider the role of women in political life, not to mention that of philosophy. Constructing a city from the ground up requires them to revise their opinion as to the very basis of the political association (cf. 359b-c), and revolutionizes their attitude towards it (cf. 358e-b with 471c-e). As for the ostensible point of the reigning analogy (i.e., to further one's understanding of the nature and power of justice in the soul of a human being), one is invited to see how justice – and injustice – come to be in men, not simply according to how the guardians are educated, but also by analogizing from the discernible stages through which their city grows. So, for these and no doubt other reasons, whether he is dealing with the regime of a city or that of a soul, the philosopher first examines its origin, then its nature. In every case but one, that is.

The exception? The Timocratic Man.

The philosopher, having just completed his sketch of the timocratic regime, asks Glaukon, "Who then is the man corresponding to this regime? How did he come into being, and what sort is he?" (548d). Glaukon's response is pre-empted, however, by a suggestion from his brother Adeimantos that deflects attention towards an immediate consideration of the *nature* of the timocratic man. Only after discussing "what sort he *is*" do they turn to explaining "how he comes into being" (549c). One must presume that this spontaneous departure from their agreed-upon order has some significance. And as one proceeds to hunt for it, one discovers other features no less curious in the philosopher's account of this kind of man and the city he both rules and reflects.

Sokrates repeatedly characterizes the regime in question as being "in the middle [*en meso*] between aristocracy and oligarchy" (547b, c, d; cf. 619a), and proceeds to identify four features it shares with the former, a like number with the latter, as well as certain features peculiar to it. He agrees with Glaukon's judgment that this regime is "a mixture of bad and good", although we cannot be sure his agreement is based exclusively on the evidence he has just provided Glaukon (and to which I shall return). However that may be, his concluding observation about the regime is of special interest: "due to the dominance of spiritedness [*thumoeides*], one thing alone is most distinctive in it ... " Only in the case of this regime is the "*one* distinctive thing" in fact *a pair*: "love of victories and love of honours" (*philonikiai kai philotimiai*; 548c; cf. 524b-c).

This leads one to consider more closely its name: 'Timocracy'. Responding to Glaukon's desire to learn which four forms of defective

The War Lover

regimes are worth knowing, the philosopher declares they are the very ones "having names" (544c).[10] But whereas the others do indeed have common names – 'Oligarchy', 'Democracy', 'Tyranny' – this first archetype is initially identified by two *proper* names, i.e., two actual and particular instances of it (or "phantoms" of it [*eidōla*], perhaps one should say; cf. 520c). Sokrates refers to it as "the one that is praised by the many, that Cretan and Laconian regime". But thereafter, for some reason (perhaps having to do with the wisdom of its lawgiver or the sex of its country; cf. 599d, 575d), the latter exemplification is apparently given priority in that Sokrates speaks of the individual "who loves victory and loves honour" as being affixed "with the Laconian regime" (545a). In any event, when he finally begins his general discussion of that kind of regime, the philosopher makes an express point of the fact that there is *not* any well-established *common* name for it. Accordingly, he proposes not one but *two* names by which it might properly be called. Given his earlier claim that this regime is distinguished essentially by "love of victories and love of honours", one might now expect him to suggest that it be known as either 'Nikocracy' (after *nikē*, "victory"), or 'Timocracy' (after *timē*, "honour"). But that is not what he recommends. Referring to it for the moment simply as "the regime which loves honour", he contends that "it should be called either 'timocracy' or 'timarchy'" (*e timokratian e timarchian*; 545b). The first name compounds 'honour' and 'strength' (*kratos*), the second 'honour' and 'rule' (*archē*). Each name is subsequently used once: the philosopher suggests they try to tell "how timocracy would arise from aristocracy" (545c), whereas he later speaks of "the transformation from timarchy to oligarchy" (550d). But "the *man* who [supposedly] corresponds to the regime" is always called 'timocratic' (*timokratikos*; 549b, 553a, 580b), never 'timarchic', much less 'nikocratic' or 'nikarchic'.

This identifying of both the city and the man exclusively with honour is all the more curious in light of the fact that Sokrates and Glaukon later distinguish only three "primary classes of human beings" (each identified by its dominant love): "wisdom-loving, victory-loving, gain-loving" (*philosophon, philonikon, philokerdes*; 581c). That is, they do not there acknowledge as one of the basic kinds of men what would seem to be the pre-eminently *political* class, the honour-loving men who naturally gravitate towards ruling office in any regime (cf. 551a, 558bc, 562d, 564d, 475ab, 582c). That certainly seems a mistake. If it is, the reason for it – or the cause of it, rather – would be their basing their discussion on the earlier tripartite analysis of the soul, an admittedly over-simplified account (435cd, 504ab), and which is summarily referred to here (" ... just as a city is divided into three forms, so the soul of every one [man] also is divided in three ... "; 580d). With each part of the soul having a single kind of pleasure peculiar to it, associated with a single ruling desire and a single dominant love, it would seem the human race could comprise only three classes: those ruled by the calculating part of the soul; those ruled by their spirit; and – by far the most numerous class – those ruled by their manifold appetitive part (but who may be spoken of as 'money-loving' or 'gain-loving', given the practical connection between money and appetitive satisfaction). Yet in introducing the regime devoted to war and dominated by spiritedness, the philosopher immediately associated it with *two* loves, thus with two kinds of desire, and two kinds of pleasure: that which attends victory, and that which comes from honour. So, it would seem that either the various parts of the soul can have more than one kind of desire and pleasure (and if that is the case, mightn't they also be suited for more than one kind of work?). Or, the spirit is not simple, and one must tell of *two* kinds of cities, each dominated in its own peculiar way by spiritedness.

As a final curiosity of this regime, it seems upon reflection that there is something amiss with the account given of its coming into being. In fact, if the second version of the city in *logos*, that of the philosopher-king, is practically impossible – as must be conceded, and virtually is (592a–b) – then there is *no* explicit account of the arising of Timocracy. And, consequently, the entire cycle of regimes has no origin. Instead of that pleasing and persuasive tale – so plausible, so neatly symmetrical, so complete, so *poetic*: political life rising by stages from primitive beginnings to its zenith whereat wisdom rules, and from which it subsequently declines in stages to the nadir of tyranny – instead of that, we are left with an adventure that begins on earth and ascends into heaven, and which is radically discontinuous with what is supposed to follow. The actual beginning of all the defective forms of regime remains a mystery, cloaked in a myth not essentially different from that which has Thebans arise from dragon's teeth sown in the earth by Kadmos, bringer of the written word and wedder of Harmonia, daughter of Ares and Aphrodite (cf. 414d–e).

The "tragedy" Sokrates concocts to account for the genesis of the warlike regime is plainly admitted to be so much child's play (545de). But while it is, as a whole, false, there may be some important truth in it even so. For it concerns the guardians' inevitable failure to reduce their own reproduction to a geometrically exact science (546a–e). This has the eventual if not immediate consequence that those chosen to be guardians in their turn won't be pure, but will instead be a mixture of precious and base metal, the one sort drawing the regime towards virtue in accordance with its original constitution, the other towards money-making and material possessions (547b–c). Of course, it is well known that alloys are often stronger than their separate constituents. This is true, for example, of the bronze compounded of tin and copper.[11] Whereas the precious metals in their purity, and particularly gold, are too soft for use as anything but ornamentation (cf. 373a, 417a). Be that as it may, and despite (or is it, rather, because of?) Sparta's great reputation for stability, the philosopher portrays Timocracy as resulting from such a mixing of the precious and the base – a compromise regime poised between two contrary tendencies, the one inclining it towards virtue and the other towards wealth, while of itself loving both victory and honour (cf. 550e).

Now, it may be possible to *adapt* the philosopher's playful "tragedy" so as to connect up with the account of Aristocracy given in books Two through Four. But as he leaves things, Timocracy in effect comes out of nowhere, an autochthonous regime. This happens to match in a curious way the discussion of the timocratic man, whose nature is described before any attempt is made to account for *his* generation. Perhaps the most noteworthy fact about such a man is his very conspicuousness. The rare individual who rises to any challenge, who enjoys risking himself, who will not accept defeat, who craves distinction and demands respect – such a strong soul stands out above the crowd, and naturally thinks of himself (and is thought of by others) as a leader. More often than not, however, his lineage is nothing remarkable; he seems a spontaneous production of nature, his origin a mystery. Similarly, his regime may be thought of as springing up naturally and directly from apolitical nature, where only the strong survive and the rule of superior force and cunning holds sway (cf. 411de, 586c).[12]

But when one stops to think of it, the dialogue *does* provide an account of such a regime coming directly from nature, of a city arising from men responding naturally to the world as they find it. This account begins with the observation that "a city ... comes into being because each of us is not self-sufficient [*autarchēs*] but is in need of much" (369b). The subsequent discussion of its naturally growing from the minimal, "most necessitous", grouping of "four or five men" to that of a sizeable "throng" (*suchnos*; 370d) stresses "need" (or, "use"; *chreia*) and "necessity" (*anagkē*), and implies that such needfulness is met by a rational division of labour. But if the variety of man's bodily needs (for food, shelter, clothing, and perhaps shoes; 369d) is all that is meant by his lacking self-sufficiency, then a man does not need several other men; he merely needs several arts. The philosopher explicitly presents this as an option (369e-a). And while a single man may not be so proficient or efficient practising several arts as he would be practising one, proficiency and efficiency are not the issues: self-sufficiency is. Of course, if men must gather together for some *other* reason - if their real lack of self-sufficiency is *not* a matter of each being unable to develop sufficiently the variety of skills required to feed and clothe himself - then the philosopher's several arguments for basing their necessary association on a rational division of labour are each and all quite compelling (370a-c), and this rational arrangement rightly constitutes the essential difference between a city and a mere herd or pack of gregarious animals.[13] As for what this other reason might be, physical security, especially from other men, should come immediately to mind; and if it doesn't, we are soon provided a reminder (cf. 373d-e).[14] A particular group of men agreeing to work together in a city is not in the world alone. It may have to contend with those who prefer to take what they want from others, rather than labour to produce these things themselves.

As for the simple city in *logos*, not yet big but no longer little, it soon abandons its barter economy in favour of one that uses money, thereby opening up new possibilities for good and evil (371b). And producing more than is strictly necessary for mere life, its citizens can imagine and afford a better, more luxurious life, involving commercial and quite probably other sorts of relations with neighbouring cities (370e-a). And before they know it, rulers in the form of warriors arise in, or otherwise enter, the city (374a-d; cf. 569b). Despising dirt farmers and mechanics, to say nothing of shopkeepers (cf. 371c, 372d, 549a), these manliest of men, high-spirited and physically advantaged, become a class unto themselves, organized with one eye towards external enemies that might threaten their livelihood, and the other towards keeping the producing class that supports them in some kind of bondage (cf. 415de, 431cd, 442a, 434a-b, 547c). These warriors are not attached to their way of life because it is easy - quite the contrary: it is filled with dangers and the most strenuous exertions. They must exercise constantly for war, and give thought to little else.

The War Lover

But they love it because it's a man's life, and one must be a man among men to live it. Respecting only each other, and craving that respect; priding themselves on their discipline and self-discipline, on their courage and endurance, on martial prowess and cunning – and yet strangely susceptible to the blandishments of women (548ab, 549cd, 550d; cf. 373bc, 404d, 420a) – they are not without all appreciation for the finer things in life. They enjoy those they can taste without debilitation. Hunting, for example, and some forms of music (although most have little musical talent themselves, 548e; cf. 394e–b). But because they have been nurtured primarily through physical exercise and force, with little effort made to cultivate a true respect for, much less facility in, the gentler arts of speech and thought (547e, 548bc, 549b; cf. 554d, 560b) – and so not being rationally and thereby thoroughly convinced of the inherent superiority of the ascetic way of life as such – they remain deeply, if secretly and ashamedly, attracted by its polar opposite: the life of luxury and ease and sensual delight (548a–b, 549ab, 550d–e; cf. 563ea).

Such a regime is liable to degenerate in just the way the philosopher describes, and history is replete with examples of martial societies' being corrupted by their own success in subduing other, more luxurious and effeminate societies. They eventually succumb to the safe and pleasant life that the animal in all of us craves. And insofar as the regime is well-named, being on balance truly a Timocracy in that the rulers' love of *honour* is indeed their ruling passion, then a decay towards oligarchy is most apt to be its eventual fate. For things other than warlike virtue and guile can be honoured, and "always what is honoured is practised, and what is unhonoured is neglected" (551a; cf. 582c). Wealth, especially, has a well-nigh universal appeal – not only for the pleasure it will buy, but for the power it represents (cf. 565a, 580d–a) – and most timocrats will sooner or later have cause to seek its consolations (cf. 553ab). They, like all men, live in anticipation of the future, and in their case it is with an awareness that the means of garnering battlefield honours will slip inexorably from their grasp, while the very strenuousness of the warfaring life becomes increasingly hard to bear.

As the philosopher's treatment of the other defective regimes makes clear enough, love of wealth is not peculiar to Oligarchy[15] (cf. 548a, 561d, 565a, 566a, 568d); it is a nemesis common to all "human" regimes. This comes out clearly in tracing the particularly close, and reciprocating, relationship that Democracy has with Oligarchy – something hinted at upon their first being introduced: "oligarchy, ... and this one's adversary, ... democracy" (544c). The oligarchic city is described as "not being one, but of necessity two, the city of the poor and the city of the rich, dwelling together in the same place, ever plotting against each other" (551d; cf. 556e, 554de), and replacing each other by turns (556e; cf. 561ab, d, 559e-a). Earlier, however, we were told that this debilitating complexity pertains to virtually *all* cities: "The others must be called something bigger, ... for each of them is very many cities, but not *a* city, as [say] those who play. Two, at least, enemies to each other, one of the poor and the other of the rich. And within each of these, there are very many ... " (422ea). Though not in the same way or for the same reasons, both Oligarchy and Democracy encourage licentiousness (555c-d, 560c-b), and both breed a dangerous class of drones, a "disease growing naturally in oligarchy and democracy alike" (564ab; cf. 552a-e). What typically distinguishes the "natural" oligarch from the vast majority of democrats is not any difference in their dominant personal concerns in life – which for him as for them is money – but, rather, his superior abilities for pursuing it successfully. His obsessive concern with profit imparts an industrious austerity and efficient order to his life (553d, 554a). And while the agreement among the parts of his soul as to which will rule is somewhat forced, the fact remains that he is for the most part a moderate, temperate man, with the plain grace that comes from being so (554d-e). As Sokrates observes in the course of discussing the decline of Democracy, "Presumably, when all are engaged in money-making, those most orderly by nature become, for the most part, richest" (564e; cf. 330ab).

It is true that from one important perspective, Oligarchy and Democracy are qualitatively distinct regimes, the former being openly dedicated to the accumulation of wealth and the latter to a certain conception of freedom (562bc; cf. 553d, 554a, 555b and 557b, 560e, 562cd). But from another, perhaps equally important perspective, they are only "quantitatively" different, being but variable points on a single continuum. For as the philosopher is careful to point out, a regime can be made more oligarchic or less; *how* few "the few" are depends on the size of the property assessment established for enjoying full civic rights (551ab). While it would do some violence to the language, the property requirement could be established so low that the regime was practically democratic. Having added, then, the average democrat's preoccupation with wealth to the typical timocrat's secret fascination

The War Lover

with wealth and the definitive tyrant's obsession with seizing everyone's wealth for himself (568d–c), one can discern the warp on which the philosopher has woven his science of regimes.

The woof is honour. Much as the hunger for wealth is not a monopoly of Oligarchy, the attraction and effects of honour are not unique to Timocracy. The wealthy man is not merely wealthy, but also honoured for being so (551a, 553d, 555c). And the most dangerous "drones" among the dispossessed of his regime are those who feel their disgrace more than their debts (555d; cf. 564b). However, the drone class is far fiercer in a democracy than in an oligarchy, where "not being held in honour but being driven from the ruling offices, it is without exercise and isn't vigorous" (564d). We are reminded that a democracy also distributes political honours, but exclusively to those who profess to be "well-disposed towards the multitude" (558c); and that "it praises and honours – both in private and in public – rulers who are like the ruled and the ruled who are like the rulers" (562d). In Sokrates' description of the battle for the soul of the young Democrat, the issue turns largely on which traits of character are extolled, and which dishonoured (560c–e). And what finally distinguishes the true or natural democrat is not primarily a commitment to freedom, but rather a steadfast refusal to admit "that some pleasures are of noble and good desires, whereas some are of wretched ones, and that the former must be practised and honoured and the latter pruned [or checked, punished; *kolazein*] and enslaved". Instead, the democratic man maintains that all desires are of like status, and lets himself be ruled by whichever happens to be at the time most insistent, "dishonouring none but fostering them all on the basis of equality" (561b–c). The only distinction he makes among the desires is "quantitative" – i.e., their relative intensity – by means of which they order themselves, moment by moment, person by person. Freedom for him means at bottom no more than this equal lack of external restraint on desires, the licence to do whatever one feels like doing, and to live in whatever manner one finds attractive, but only for so long as it remains so (557b, e–a, 561c–d). If he were to rank desires and pleasures by some external standard, he would also have to rank human beings in accordance with their respective dominant desires. But as it is, he feels free, even obliged, to treat everyone as equals, thus equally deserving of freedom (558b–c, 563b). And insofar as pleasure is the touchstone of his life, he cannot in good conscience deny extending the "law of equality and freedom" to beasts as well as to beastly people – after all, they, like him, are simply ruled by their desires, and ought to be free to enjoy the good of pleasure (563c; cf. 505b). He learns only the hard way that not everyone is equally pleased by his regime of equal honours and pleasures for all, and thus does not genuinely honour tolerance and equality (569ab). Whereas the democrat is content to live and let live, some men's desires are not so modest and respectful of others as are his (567a-c). More tyrannically inclined, they desire to have everything for themselves and have no compunction as to how they get it. Ruthlessly consistent in their recognition of pleasure as the only good – hence, the bedrock of all judgment and evaluation – force or fraud, fair means or foul, are equally honourable to them (565e; cf. 344a-c). They regard the typical democrat, confiding in his tissue of congenial assumptions, as a gull easily corrupted (565a), duped (565bc, 566de), and then exploited (567ab). Explicit reference to honour is conspicuous by its near-absence in Sokrates' account of a city under Tyranny, however. Its sole occurrence is in connection with poetry; we are reminded that it is the tragedians who "extol tyranny as equal to a god", and who accordingly "are honoured most of all by tyrants" (568b-c).[16]

Reflection on the philosopher's science of regimes teaches one to see that wealth and honour are, like the two foci of an ellipse, the points about which virtually all political life revolves. To vary the image, they are the constituents common to all regimes, and the means whereby one regime can be transformed into another. And this in no way slights the power of Aphrodite. It is in this deeper sense that the various regimes, one and all, reflect the nature of their composing human beings, nearly all of whom are ruled by some combination of love of honour and love of the pleasures brought by wealth. That such an understanding lies concealed beneath what seems to be a quite different account featuring several qualitatively distinct regimes – an account which does not conflict with this understanding, but is complementary to it – need not disconcert anyone. After all, why should we be surprised to find that almost nothing is as it seems in the very dialogue which teaches that the most important distinction for philosophy is that between Appearance and Reality (509d)?

Insofar, then, as a timocracy tends to transform itself over time, it most likely will degenerate into an oligarchy. But it is not strictly necessary that it do so. There is another direction in which it might evolve, given some rare good fortune. If enough of the rulers, or even one of enormous influence, truly cared less for honour than for victory

The War Lover

in "the greatest contest" (cf. 403e, 608b), it might be possible to accomplish the *reverse* of what the philosopher describes in his tragic myth; that is, the regime might be directed up towards virtue, away from and against its normal inclination to veer downwards towards wealth. For one thing this regime shares with the Aristocracy in *logos* is the honour it pays its rulers (547d), and there is no honour higher than willing obedience (cf. 549a), unless it is admiring imitation (cf. 561d). That the warriors of Timocracy also keep themselves apart from the rest of the city, eating and training together as in Aristocracy, further enhances the power of leaders who are honoured. It would take, however, one or more truly exceptional men – masters of that which rules virtually everyone else: those insatiable desires for honour and wealth – to lead their city in such an ascent. But one could never hope for more than a very few of such, certainly not enough to constitute an entire warrior class. Necessarily, then, the bulk of this class would still be high-spirited, prideful, honour-loving men.

The typical timocrat is subject to degeneracy because he is not a simple man, loving only honour and satisfied with being honoured. He also secretly, if only secondarily, loves wealth, and his regime gives him some licence to enjoy it privately, thereby strengthening its appeal (548b). From this insidious complexity, this "mixture", flow his vices, his liability to decay, and his inability or unwillingness to rule in the common good (cf. 519c). But if he were better educated: not merely repressing his desires by a spirit toughened through gymnastics, but one charmed and made more tractable by music, and thus respectful of powers other than brute force; with his mind rationally persuaded of the value of prudence and justice and especially moderation, and with such convictions grounded in a sufficient understanding of himself; and if one could expunge from him so far as possible all respect and hankering for wealth, and deny him any opportunity to indulge what remains; and if he could be raised in an environment of austere beauty and grace in which the only things glorified were virtue and dedication to the common good – if all these things could be arranged, then he might be elevated to the highest kind of honour-loving man, one who wishes to be honoured simply for his virtue, and who does willingly, even eagerly, whatever is required to be so, and who is truly content to live out his life as an honourable man.

Now, is this not the project to which the philosopher and his followers are dedicated from the moment the class of warriors first enters their city? Inasmuch as the principal wage of the ruling class is honour, and hardly anything else (414a; cf. 468c–e) – and certainly not "food alone", as Sokrates insists when rubbing a little painful but beneficial salt into Adeimantos' wounded pride (420a) – such a regime might be called a 'Timocracy', but it is a clear improvement over the regime of that name which the philosopher expressly outlines. One might avoid some of the confusion by calling the latter regime 'Timarchy', thereby acknowledging that there are two cities ruled by honour-loving men, a higher and a lower one, akin and yet distinct. But since the first is the ultimate in what could reasonably be expected by way of public-spirited rule – the best that one could hope for in this world, men still being men – it might as well be called 'Aristocracy', the regime in which the Best are the Strongest. Being a gentler, more refined, more peaceful regime, it would not be misleading to regard it as somewhat feminized, its masculinity moderated by a reasonable femininity. It is more like the Cretan than the Laconian regime in one respect: its people refer to their homeland as a "mother", rather than as a fatherland (414e, 575d; cf. 470d). One should bear in mind that Crete also had a great lawgiver, Minos,[17] whose achievement perhaps exceeded that of Lykourgos (599d; cf. *Minos* 318c–d). Of course, what can go up can come back down, and doubtless eventually will. If the rulers of an Aristocracy should ever fail to replace themselves with men as good as themselves, lovers of victory and virtue, or at least pure lovers of the honour of virtue, promoting into their ranks instead secret lovers of wealth, men with too much bronze or iron in their souls, the resulting factionalism of the ruling class will compromise the regime, and its decline will begin (415c, 546d–c).

— 3 —

Sons and Lovers

According to the philosopher's account, the city dominated by spiritedness, and thus distinguished most by its citizenry's love of victories and honours, is naturally preoccupied with war. The features of government that it shares with Aristocracy all bear on war: the honour it pays its rulers; the strict segregation of "its war-making part from farming and the manual arts and the rest of money-making"; its common messing arrangement; and its "caring for gymnastics and the contests of war" (547d). And everything said to be peculiar to this regime pertains directly to war: its preferring as rulers spirited men "naturally more inclined to war than to peace"; its "holding the wiles and stratagems of war in honour"; and its "always spending its time making war" (547e–a).

The nature of "the *man* corresponding to this regime", however, is discussed primarily in terms of his *loves* (548d-b). For it turns out that the timocratic man is distinguished not merely by a pair of loves but by a goodly number. First mentioned is his love of victory (*philonikia*), followed by a love of music (*philomousia*), love of listening (*philēkoia*; i.e., "attentiveness"), love of ruling (*philarchia*), love of honour (*philotimia*), love of gymnastics (or athletics; *philogymnasia*), and finally, love of hunting (*philothēria*). Understanding the natural Timocrat, then, would seem to be primarily a matter of comprehending this constellation of loves: what each one is, and its consequences for both city and soul; but especially, how and why they naturally go together (to the extent that they do). For were these loves not themselves somehow ordered, his life would be a chaos, more erratic and manifold than Sokrates' caricature of the Democrat (561c–e). But this is manifestly not the case. In fact, the warrior seems every bit as single-minded as the Oligarch obsessed with money. Judging from outward appearances, he is a comparatively simple man (cf. 547e, 550b). And yet, it is not obvious that any of his loves is simply the logical implication of another – which is not to deny any and all manner of *psycho*-logical connections (for the *psyche* may well have a 'logic' all its own). Nor in practice are the various loves and his other natural characteristics always found together in fixed proportions. This Sokrates makes clear in commenting on Adeimantos' judgment that the Timocrat would be like his brother Glaukon "so far as love of victory goes": "Equally [*Isōs*] in that", the philosopher replies, "but in these other respects his nature in my opinion does not correspond [to Glaukon's]. ... He must be more stubborn, and less musical, although he is a lover of music ... " (548d–e; cf. 398e).

In fact, the lack of any necessary concurrence among these seven loves was tacitly established earlier. In discussing with Glaukon the kind of person whose nature is genuinely suited for philosophy, Sokrates warned: "First, the one who is to take it up must not be lame in his love of labour [*philoponia*], one half loving labour, the other half lazy. This is the case when one is a lover of gymnastic and a lover of the hunt and loves all the labour done with the body, but is not a lover of learning, nor a lover of listening nor an inquirer, but hates the labour involved in all of that. Lame also is the one whose love of labour is the reverse of this" (535d).

It is fair to assume, then, that understanding the Timocratic Man is an exercise in dialectical thinking, involving both the proper "division" or differentiation of his loves – of victory, music, listening, ruling, honour, gymnastics, hunting – and their "collection" into a single synoptic view (cf. 537b–c). But an adequate synopsis must also integrate the other characteristics the philosopher attributes to him: his stubbornness (or wilfulness, obstinacy; *authadeia*, cf. 590ab); his limited musical aptitude (cf. 393d); his taciturn nature and lack of rhetorical skill; his "arrogance" or "haughtiness" (*hypsilophrōn*; literally, "highmindedness"; 550b); and his tending to be harsh with inferiors, civil towards equals, and "to rulers most obedient" (548ea). His presumption that prowess in war establishes one's right to rule is perhaps the least mysterious thing about him.

But there is a still further complication to his nature, and it involves yet another love: he has an inherent tendency to be transformed with age from a despiser of money into a lover of money (*philochrēmatos*;

The War Lover

549ab). This, coupled with the presumption that normally the more senior, "philochrematic" timocrats would rule a timarchy, perhaps explains why such a regime would manifest some features of the oligarchy towards which it tends to decay: that despite the principles to which their regime is dedicated, some if not most of its citizens will none the less come to desire money, and in the darkness of privacy will honour it "savagely" (or "wildly", "fiercely"; *agriōs*). Thus, they will possess private storehouses and treasuries where they can hoard wealth, and private homes where they and their wives can escape public scrutiny and indulge their desire for the pleasures wealth buys (548a). And because liberality cannot be openly expressed and thereby cultivated in such a regime, they will be stingy with their own money as well as inconspicuous in consuming it, while being "lovers of spending what belongs to others" (*philanalōtai allotriōn*; 548b; cf. 462c). All of these oligarchic tendencies the philosopher attributes to an education that relies excessively on force, neglecting the persuasive powers of music and *logos*.

So this apparently simple man whom the philosopher calls 'timocratic' is at heart strangely complex – indeed, it turns out, even more so than his heptophilia would suggest. For, as we shall see, the tendrils of these loves intertwine with still others. And while it is only prudent to assume that each and all of them must be understood as the means of understanding him, it must also be conceded that the relevant dialogical evidence is scattered far and wide. What must first be appreciated, however, is how absolutely crucial it is that one understand this particular archetype of human nature. Indeed, it is no exaggeration to say that all hope of resolving certain of its deeper mysteries (including its most puzzling dramatical features), and thus of comprehending the dialogue as a whole, rests on an analysis of this particular kind of *psychē*. Simply put, the Timocratic Man is the key to understanding both Glaukon and Adeimantos, those "sons of Ariston" (literally, "of the Best"), whose singular nature so filled the philosopher with admiration and delight when they jointly challenged him to prove the superiority of the just life (367e). Incidentally, this is the only occasion in the dialogue when the brothers are identified together as offspring of Ariston (elsewhere in the discussion, they are so referred to individually – Glaukon twice [327a, 580b], and Adeimantos once [427cd]). Having been pointedly described as *sons* of the Best, they are each *prima facie* candidates for the status of second best, according to the devolutionary scheme of cities and men outlined in Book Eight.

Sons and Lovers

They would seem to be, that is, the dialogue's exemplification of timocratic men. Seeing them as such, one may note that the philosopher, this natural aristocrat or kingly man – having already discussed justice with an old oligarch, a young democrat, and a tyrant in his prime – conducts the balance of this seminal investigation, fully nine-tenths of it, with two timocrats, two young men who are already battle-tested (368a), who are openly contemptuous of their inferiors (i.e., almost everyone), and who are all the prouder for the dangerous ambitions they harbour. Can one avoid supposing that the crux of the problem of justice in cities and souls – and whatever else is at issue in this dialogue – is somehow bound up with understanding the kind of human being who is distinguished by the strength of his spirit, the kind the philosopher calls *timokratikos*? What else *can* one think, given the fact that after its stirring "prelude" (as the discussions in Book One are called; 357a), this dialogue entitled *Politeia* is almost exclusively a conversation between the philosopher and these two brothers.

But why are there two of them, *two* timocrats sharing the role of principal interlocutor? And why are they cast as *brothers*?[1] And why is the work of responding to the philosopher divided between them precisely as it is? Now, there *are* other dialogues which feature some such division of labour between a pair of young men (e.g., *Lysis*, *Phaedo*, *Erastai*), but only *Politeia* features two blood brothers in the main supporting roles. Both are indeed "sons of Ariston": begotten by the same father, born of the same mother, and raised in the same household; they played in the same neighbourhood, were educated in the same schools, were subjected to the same laws, and fought in the same wars, ... and yet, they seem no more alike than Comedy and Tragedy. Whatever else, they serve as ever-present reminders of the unpredictable variability naturally involved in breeding human beings (cf. 415a–c, 459a–e, 546a–d).

Sokrates conducts twice as much dialogical investigation with Glaukon as with Adeimantos. But beyond the quantitative distribution of the "workload" (by no means an insignificant fact), one may discern an even more important qualitative distinction in the kind of "work" each prefers to do. When life's more familiar, everyday matters are being discussed, the respondent is Adeimantos, who can be counted upon to represent intelligently and passionately the concerns and perspective of responsible (albeit more ordinary) human beings and citizens. Glaukon, in contrast, is the philosopher's partner for the more radical and difficult portions of the inquiry, whenever the essential nature of something is being plumbed.[2] And it is imperative to notice that this pattern is set by the brothers themselves, and can therefore be presumed to reflect their respective interests, hopes, desires, and fears. It begins with what each contributes to their two-pronged challenge – Glaukon appealing directly to Nature, Adeimantos surveying what other men say, the realm of Opinion – and continues to the dialogue's conclusion.[3] The philosopher *never* directs the conversation from one to the other. This is not to preclude, of course, his subtly manipulating it according to his understanding of their divergent strengths and weaknesses. But to all outward appearances, the brothers pass the role of philosopher's helpmeet back and forth as their own spirits move them, and to that extent take up the work for which each is naturally most suited. Given that, as sons of the Best, *both* somehow represent men ruled by the spirited part of the soul, each bears careful watching. Together they illuminate the multifaceted nature of the Timocrat, this man whose peculiar constellation of loves inclines him to war.

If anything pervades the dialogue like the spirit of war, it is love. Perhaps this is only fitting.[4] The philosopher's sole reference to the God of War reminds us of His traditional association with the Goddess of Love (390c). The naturalness of this conjunction receives a kind of confirmation by Sokrates' sole reference to Helen of Troy, for love of whom was fought the most celebrated war in Antiquity. Nor should it be forgotten that this war inspired the poetry that educated the Greeks (586c; cf. 600a–e, 606e). It is true that Sokrates censors the story of how the clever but deformed Artisan God bound together his passionate wife and her lover of choice. But this censoring is apparently for reasons having to do with inculcating moderation in the guardians, given the hazards and ridicule to which the sexually immoderate are vulnerable.[5] And perhaps men of high spirit are especially prone to immoderation in their loves.[6] Be that as it may, if one follows the philosopher's suggestion to treat linguistic usage as the "tracks" of ideas (430e; cf. 432e, 435a, 454b, 470b, 505c, 507b, 509d, 533de, 560e), one discovers that he distinguishes four kinds of love. They are not all evaluated in the same way. And while one supposes his own usage to be both precise and refined, one may also assume –

at least provisionally – that it takes its departure from certain distinctions in popular use, which (in turn) reflect already acknowledged nuances of difference in normal human experience.

One kind of love, *storgē*, can be understood as the sort of affection which exists between dog and master, and between ruler and ruled. But it is especially used in ordinary discourse to refer to that cherishing of children by their parents and of parents by their children. Thus it is used by the Athenian Stranger, for example, in Plato's *Laws*: " ... much as a child, even if he is likely to be at odds with them in the future, in the present needfulness [*aporia*] of childhood cherishes his parents and is cherished by them [*stergei te kai stergetai hypo tōn*], and always flees to his necessary kindred and finds only in them his allies [*symmachoi*] ... " (754b). It is worth noting that Sokrates never uses this term – nor mentions any other kind of love – in describing the relationships he suggests would exist within the communal family of the ruling class. And this despite wondering aloud whether their kinship would be in name only (463cd; cf. 465ab). Apparently the correct answer is 'yes'. The philosopher's few uses of *stergein* are always in other contexts (and only this verbal, never the nounal form [*storgē*], is used). He observes, for example, that those with truly philosophical natures "are completely unwilling to accept the false, but hate it [*misein*], cherishing [*stergein*] the truth" (485c). And he asks Glaukon, "do you expect anyone would ever sufficiently cherish [*sterxai*] something that, when he does it, he does painfully, accomplishing little with much effort?" (486c; cf. 455b).

Another division of love, *agapē*, refers to the mature, mutual affection between husband and wife; it also refers to the presumed fondness of gods for humans, and to humans' fondness for gods as well as for each other (such as the "brotherly love" manifested in charity, or in the Christian injunction to love thy neighbour as thyself). *Agapē*, like *storgē*, can also refer to parents' love for their children. In much everyday use, its meaning trails off towards "liking" and "being content with". The philosopher employs *agapē* fairly often. His ironic judgment that Kephalos "didn't seem overly fond" [*agapan*] of money is his first reference in the dialogue to any kind of love (Kephalos himself had used the term mere seconds before; 330b). It is immediately followed by an observation that supposedly contrasts Kephalos' attitude with that which is more typical of those who have made their money themselves: "For just as poets are fond [*agaposi*] of their poems and fathers of their children, so money-makers too are serious about money –

as their own product" (330c). Shortly thereafter, he partially instantiates the point in his reference to Homer's being fond (*agapa*) of his portrayal of Autolykos (334b). And this is the sort of love Sokrates speaks of in his invidious comparison of Homer as Educator with other famous teachers, such as Pythagoras and certain sophists (600b-c). And after Glaukon, as a preliminary to his "reviving Thrasymachos' argument", presents a tripartite classification of goods, including centrally "a kind we like [*agapōmen*] both for its own sake and for what comes out of it" (357c), the philosopher supposes justice to be of this class of good things: " ... that it belongs to the finest, which one who is to be blessed should like [*agapēteon*] both for itself and for what comes out of it" (358a). By contrast, Glaukon opines that justice is a sorry mean between what is best (doing injustice with impunity) and what is worst (suffering injustice without the power to avenge oneself), and consequently is "liked [*agapasthai*] not because it is good, but honoured due to want of vigour in doing injustice" (359a).

This kind of love is the only one referred to in connection with justice. The closest any other kind comes is the one time Sokrates testifies that the philosophical nature is "a friend and kinsman [*philos kai xyggenēs*] of truth, justice, courage, and moderation" (487a). Fully half of the uses of *agapē* shade towards the mildest kinds of loving: being "content" or "satisfied with". For example, Glaukon avows they will be content (*agapēton*) for the present with an abbreviated account of the soul (435d). And Sokrates asks, "But if we find out what justice is like, will we also insist that the just man must not differ at all from justice itself but in every way be such as it is? Or will we be content [*agapēsomen*] if he is nearest to it, and participates in it more than the others?" (472bc). And later, speaking of a true philosopher living in one of the inferior kinds of cities, he observes, "Seeing others filled with lawlessness, he is content [*agapa*] if somehow he himself can live his life here pure of injustice and unholy deeds, and take his leave from it graciously and cheerfully with fair hope" (496d; cf. also 399c, 473b, 583d). *Agapē* is last mentioned by the philosopher in recounting his tale of the warrior Er, who was divinely informed, "Even for the one who comes forward last, if he chooses intelligently and lives earnestly, a likable life [*bios agapētos*] is reserved, not a bad one" (619b; cf. 620c).

Still a third dimension of love is *erōs*.[7] This ordinarily refers to the intensely passionate – and profoundly selfish – sort of love whose most familiar manifestation is sexual desire (*aphrodisia*). Thus, one would not go terribly wrong in equating it with lust. Like so many other important themes of the dialogue, it first surfaces in that surprisingly rich conversation with old Kephalos, who professes to welcome the decay of sexual passion that normally comes with advancing years.[8] He endorses the judgment of an aged tragedian that he has thereby "escaped a sort of frenzied and mad master" (329c). This view, that erotic love is a despotic ruler of the soul and as such the greatest threat to a moderate and just life, also seems to be the perspective on *erōs* actively propagated by the philosopher, at least through the balance of *this* dialogue.[9] After inviting Glaukon to attest that "excessive" pleasure is incompatible with moderation or any other virtue, Sokrates asks, "Can you tell of a greater or keener pleasure than that connected with sex?" Glaukon, in tune with the discussion and presumably speaking from experience, concedes he cannot, and volunteers, " ... nor a madder one either" (403a; cf. 583a). They subsequently agree that "erotic necessities" are more forceful in persuading most people than are those necessities of Reason epitomized in geometry (458d; cf. 493c). Erotic love is repeatedly classed with inebriation, madness, sickness, and irrationality (e.g., 395e, 396d, 439d, 573b-c, 578a, 586c). It also is directly implicated in the philosopher's indictment of a certain kind of poetry, whose dangerous charm can subvert even a good regime (607c-b; cf. 368a, 398a-b).

Now, anyone familiar with it might agree that erotic love is a power that can dominate a person body and soul, drowning other passions and overturning judgment. Hence, characterizing it as tyrannical would not seem wildly hyperbolic. Doing so presumes, of course, that one already has some separate and distinct notion of *tyranny*, conceiving it (say) as the exercise of absolute power without regard for any considerations that do not originate within the tyrant. But the philosopher as much as identifies the tyrannic inclination in human beings – the will to tyranny *per se* – with unbridled *erōs*, contending that the tyrant is himself tyrannized, "maddened by desires and loves" (578a), infested by a love (*erōta*) that is a "great winged drone" (572ea; cf. 552c-e, 474d, 360b-d). This has strange and perplexing implications. "Is it for this reason", he wonders, "that *Erōs* has from antiquity been called a tyrant?" (573b). It is worth noting that all six references to a deified *Erōs* appear in the midst of the philosopher's description of the tyrannical nature, which he in effect treats as a case of daemonic – if not downright diabolic – possession (573d, 574d-a; cf. 617de). The problem would seem to call for an exorcist.

The War Lover

However, in describing the goal aimed at in the musical education of the guardians, Sokrates implies that *erōs* might not be as utterly incorrigible as he makes it seem in his perhaps extravagant condemnation of tyranny. For he speaks of a "naturally correct love [*orthos erōs pephyke*]", namely, that of "loving [*eran*] moderately and musically what is ordered and noble" (or "ordered and beautiful", *kosmiou kai kalou*; 403a). Roughly a fourth of the dialogue's forty-odd mentions of *erōs* and its cognates occur in the context of discussing this "naturally correct love", exactly as many (eleven) as are used in the discussion of the tyrannical nature. Glaukon agrees that "nothing mad or akin to licentiousness must approach an *orthos erōs*", and consequently that sexual pleasure must play no part in the relationship between "lover and beloveds" (*erastēs kai paidikois*). On that high but narrow basis, Glaukon assumes responsibility for making it a law of their city in *logos* that "a lover may kiss [*philein*] and be with and touch a beloved as though he were a son, for the sake of noble things, if he persuades him". Such sons and lovers must always conduct themselves so that nothing more is even so much as rumoured (403bc; but cf. 468bc).[10] Thus the warrior-guardians' musical regimen does conclude where, according to the philosopher, it ought to conclude: "Surely musical matters [*mousika*] should end in love matters [*erōtika*] of the beautiful [or, noble; *kalos*]" (403c). Subsequently, however, the adequacy of music's power for taming erotic love is cast in doubt – great doubt, actually – by the fact that the rulers of their city have to resort to "a throng of lies and deceptions" (not to mention more material drugs) in their comical effort to make work an unworkable scheme for the selective breeding of guardians (459c–b, 546d).

The fourth species of love, *philia*, would normally be regarded as the antistrophe of that profoundly selfish and self-seeking, lustful kind of love called *erōs*. For *philia* is what animates friendship; hence, it is ordinarily understood as the most selfless and communal of loves. According to proverbial wisdom, friends so far as possible have all things in common (as Sokrates reminds Adeimantos; 424a). The dialogue is fairly steeped in *philia*. For apart from the seven references to friendship itself – such as the philosopher's claim that it is produced by justice (351d), and that the self-mastery implicit in moderation is due to a friendship among the parts of one's soul (442c), and that the tyrannical nature never tastes true friendship (576a; cf. 580a) – this species of the genus *love* is present in the dozens of references that are made to friends and other things dear (*philos*), and in the dozens upon dozens of references to various special manifestations of *philia*, including over a hundred mentions of the lovers and the loving of wisdom (*philosophos, philosophia*). In fact, the dialogue includes some thirty-one varieties of *philia* apparently worthy of individual denomination. In addition to the seven loves that define the timocrat, there are several associated with the lover of money (*philochrēmatos*) towards which he tends to decay: the lover of gain (*philokerdēs*, 581a–583a), the lover of spending what belongs to others (*philoanalotēs allotriōn*, 548b), the lover of money-making (*philochrematistēs*, 551a), and the lover of silver (*philargyron*, 347b). Most, if not all, of the specific breeds of loves and lovers have some sort of pertinent relationship with the highest kind of lover, the philosopher. Several have a natural kinship with him, e.g., the lover of learning (*philomathēs*), 376b-c, 581b, 499e), the lover of rational speech (*philologos*, 582e), the lover of sights (*philotheamonas*, 475d-e, 476b; cf. 402d), and the lover of labour (or, of toil, work; *philoponēs*, 535c-d; cf. 494d, 619d). Others provide a significant contrast or opposition, and must be clearly distinguished from philosophy in order that its essential nature be grasped – for example, love of quarreling (*philapechthēmosynē*, 500b), love of meddling (*philopragmosynē*, 549c), the lover of the technical arts (*philotechnos*, 476a), the lover of opinion (*philodoxos*, 480a), the lover of gain (*philokerdēs*, 582b), and the lover of honour (*philotimos*, 582c; cf. 347b). One would naturally presume that the lover of wisdom is radically distinguished from the lover of falsehood (*philopseudē*[11]) had Sokrates not raised some question about it (485d; cf. 382c-d, 414bc, 459c). Other loves mentioned also bear on philosophy or philosophers, albeit in less obvious ways, such as the lover of Greeks (*philhellēnes*, 470e), the lover of the city (i.e., the patriot; *philopolis*, 503a), the lover of laughter (*philogelōs*, 388e; cf. 606c, 451a-b, 506d), the lover of boys (*philopais*, 474d – as distinct from the *paid-erastēs*), the lover of play (or of jesting, "kidding"; *philopaismōn*, 452e), the lover of poetry (*philopoietēs*, 607d; cf. 568b-c), perhaps even the lovers of food (*philositos*, 475c; cf. 354a-b) and wine (*philoinos*, 475a). In dramatic contrast with his general treatment of *erōs*, the philosopher has nary a disparaging word for *philia* as such, despite his plain contempt for several expressions of it (cf., e.g., 391c, 485e, 500b, 548b, 549c). Apparently there is no danger that *philia* (much less *agapē* or *storgē*) will tyrannize a soul or a city.

It is worth emphasizing, I suspect, that these four species of love, however distinct in the philosopher's speech and analysis, are often indistinct in everyday speech and practice. Also, that a given love relationship can be a synthesis of more than one kind of love, to say nothing of other, even contrary, passions. Experience suggests that this is the rule, not the exception. It may be that one or all kinds of love are capable of transmutation into something else – stronger or weaker, higher or lower, even something opposite – as children become parents, students become teachers, subjects become rulers, friends become lovers (and vice versa). Time passes, and people learn, and change, and forget, and change. Perhaps no human relationship, however, undergoes such a radical inversion as erotic love turned sour, unless it is a friendship betrayed. But again, what experience suggests is that there are no strict and invariable laws of generation and decay to be found here; at most, there are tendencies. "Universal laws of human behaviour" rarely come to more than this, no doubt in part at least because of the uncertain alchemy of human loves. That said, one may none the less venture to suggest that over the course of this long night of conversation, some of the philosopher's companions experience a metamorphosis of love with regard to wisdom, and consequently in their feelings about other things as well. In fact, there are grounds for suspecting that this is the dialogue's ruling intention.

At least one special love is conspicuous by its absence, and not merely from this dialogue, but from the entire Platonic corpus: love of truth (*philalēthia*). As noted above, however, the philosopher does describe his nature as "cherishing [*stergein*] the truth" (while positively *hating* everything false; 485c; cf. 535d–e, 490b, 485d, 413a).[12] This may serve as a reminder that dividing love into its naturally distinct kinds is only half of the task of dialectical reasoning. One must establish as well that all of these modes of engagement are in fact related to each other – that strands of commonality run through them – such that they are properly collected into a single family of phenomena (537c; cf. *Phaedrus* 266b–c; also 265b). And here as before, it is perhaps best to follow the tracks of the philosopher's own usage, paying special attention to those occasions when he refers to two or more kinds of love in conjunction. Much of the "synagogical" work is practically done for us in the context of the philosopher's (exceedingly strange!) discussion of the kind of love by which he is identified, *philia*. This is the only type of love for which he offers anything approaching a definition, and in the course of doing so he mentions all three others. He immediately links *philein* and *stergein* in suggesting "that when we say one loves [*philein*] something, if it is rightly said of him, he mustn't show a love [*philounta*] for one part of it and not another, but must cherish [*stergonta*] all of it" (474c). He thereupon exemplifies what he means by referring to the "boylover and eroticist" (*philopaida kai erōtikon*) who is stung and aroused by *all* boys in the bloom of youth (474d). Apparently we are to understand that with respect to wisdom the philosopher is more like an indiscriminate philanderer than a faithful monogamist, more like a wino than a connoisseur (475a), more like a gourmand than a gourmet (475c; cf. 354b). Be that as it may, *agapē* and *philia* are similarly associated in the philosopher's observation about those who could truly be called whole-hearted lovers of honour (*philotimous*): "if they can't be honoured by the greater and more august, are content (*agapōsi*) to be honoured by the lesser and more paltry" (475ab). Both the affiliation and rank order of these two modes of loving are later confirmed in the philosopher's contrasting an hypothesized failure of Homer to be "honoured and liked" (*etimato kai ēgapato*) by those he educated, with the "vehement love" (*sphodra philountai*) shown certain sophists (600c-d). *Agapē* and *erōs*, in turn are linked in the claim that it is "entirely necessary that one who is by nature erotically disposed [*erōtikos*] be fond [*agapan*] of everything related and akin to his beloved" (485c). For whatever it's worth, *agapē* and *stergein* are never affiliated this directly anywhere in the dialogue.

As for the inter-penetration of *erōs* and *philia*, which seem beyond doubt the two most important kinds of love, there is a wealth of dialogical evidence, including their interesting association at the conclusion of the philosophical critique of poetry in Book Ten (complementing the political critique in books Two and Three). There reference is made both to "friendly" lovers of poetry (*philopoiētai*, 607d) and to the "lustful", erotic love of it (*erōta poiēseōs*, 607e). And special note should be taken of Sokrates' discussion with "erotic" Glaukon (474d; cf. 475a) concerning who are meant when reference is made to those with a truly philosophic nature. Here, at the dialogue's centre, he suggests that "they are always in love [*erōsi*] with that learning which discloses to them something of the Being that always *is*, and that does not wander about [*planōmenēs*], driven by generation and decay" (485ab). Shortly thereafter, obliged by Adeimantos to apologize for philosophy's unsavoury reputation, he expands on the point: " ... it is the nature of the real lover of learning [*philomathēs*] to strive for what *is*, and he does not tarry by the many things opined to be but proceeds, his love [*erōtos*] neither blunted nor ceasing, until he grasps with the appropriate part of the soul the nature itself of each thing that is. ... And once near and coupled with what really is, having begotten knowledge and truth, he knows and lives truly, is nourished, and so ceases from his labour pains, but not before" (490a–b; cf. 506c–e, 511d–e). The philosopher's private apology, which includes the essentials of a public apology (cf. 498c–a, 499d–b), also includes what may be the most significant of the many variations on the dialogue's central teaching: " ... that neither a city nor a regime, nor similarly a man, will become perfect [*teleos*] until some chance necessity compels those few philosophers who aren't vicious, those now called useless, to take charge of a city, whether they want to or not, and the city to obey; or a true love [*alethinos erōs*] for true love of wisdom [*alēthinēs philosophias*] flows from some divine inspiration into the sons of those who hold power or kingship, or into the fathers themselves" (499b–c; cf. 473cd, 474bc; cf. also *7th Ltr* 335d).

But what is especially provocative throughout Sokrates' intersecting references to what would otherwise seem to be radically *diverging* kinds of love are the repeated hints that *philia* for *sophia* entails – and may even essentially *be* – a *sublimation* of *erōs*. This seems implicit, for example, in his asking Adeimantos whether those so instinctively and violently opposed to the very idea of making a philosopher their king would not be persuaded by his explaining what kind of person a philosopher truly is: "For how will they be able to dispute it? Will they say the lovers of wisdom [*philosophoi*] are not lovers [*erastai*] of that which *is* and of truth?" (501d). Ignoring his ironic naïveté for the moment (since it's irrelevant to the point at issue), notice that the philosopher's choice of *terms* for expressing the character of his love for reality and truth is reinforced by the erotic *imagery* he subsequently uses in portraying the higher reaches of philosophical activity (506c ff). Are we – or whoever, like Adeimantos, has the capacity to fly back and forth among "*all* the things that are said" (*panta ta legomena*), and "inferring" (*syllogisasthai*) from such a synopsis their real import (365ab) – are we to conclude that the philosopher's closest kin is not some sort of saint, but rather the Tyrant (cf. 572a–b)? That beneath the appearance of a selfless, impersonal, benign if somewhat eccentric love for the sort of "abstract truths" most people don't even know exist (much less care enough about to quarrel over), there is a driving, intensely selfish and personal lust to possess and dominate all of reality like a god? Could it be Plato who first intimates what one of his great-grandsons will in more jaded times teach openly, that the motive force of philosophy is a desire not so much to *know* the world, as to "*create* the world in its own image*"*, that it "*cannot* do otherwise", that "philosophy *is* this tyrannical drive itself, the most spiritual will to power, to the 'creation of the world', to the *causa prima*".[13] There *is* a disturbing similarity between Sokrates' description of the tyrannical individual (who can be competently judged only by someone who has the power through thought to enter and clothe himself in this man's disposition! 577a) and his earlier description of a young man introduced prematurely to dialectics (cf. 572d–574e, 537e–539c). Both are characterized as mad (573a–c, 539c).

Of course, in reaching a conclusion on this or any other serious question, one cannot rely exclusively on linguistic conjunctions and other patterns of usage. Language merely provides a diligent hunter with the "tracks" of ideas; for a variety of reasons, tracking is not always successful, and in any case there is more involved in mastering something than merely being led into its presence. It should be noted, however, that while a proposal to explain the philosopher's erotic imagery and terminology as "merely pedagogic" might be said to beg the question, accepting this explanation would in fact be to answer it.

Just as a discussion of war would be incomplete without a consideration of peace, so must an examination of love include some attention to hate. And much as the dialogue contains over ten times as many mentions of war as of peace, a comparable disproportion exists between its hundreds of references to the several species of love, and the scant dozens to any kind of hate. That the second proportion is the inverse of what one might have expected, given the first, must surely count as one of the more bemusing – and amusing – ironies of this ever-surprising book. Moreover, of the available range of everyday terms for hating and loathing, the philosopher declines to use several (e.g., *stygein, apoptiein, echthairein*) and restricts himself to two families of words.

One term for hatred, *echthra*, appears most frequently as a kind of enemy (*echthros*). In fact, there are more references to *echthroi* (thirty-eight) than to *polemioi* (the term for 'enemies' derived from the word for 'war', *polemos*, and employed twenty-three times). Otherwise, *echthra* is used sparingly, no more than six times. Three of these are in the course of distinguishing war from faction: "Now, the name 'faction' is applied to the hatred [*echthra*] of one's own, 'war' to that of the

The War Lover

alien. ... Then when Greeks battle barbarians, and barbarians Greeks, we'll say they are warring and are enemies [*polemious*] by nature, and this hatred [*echthran*] must be called 'war'. Whereas when Greeks do any such thing to Greeks, being by nature friends, Greece then is sick and factious, and this hatred [*echthran*] must be called 'faction'" (470b–d; cf. 547a). The philosopher is silent as to what one should call the fighting that arises out of mutual hatred amongst barbarians. The verbal form of *echthra* (*echthrein*) is never used, although a verb based upon it (*apechthanesthai* – literally, "rouse to hatred"; "cause ill-will", "irritate") is used occasionally (cf. 343e, 378c, 567a).

The various cognates of his other term for hatred, *misos*, figure a bit more prominently, but only a bit, and with surprising selectivity. Its verbal form (*misein*, "to hate") is employed a total of seventeen times. A third of these have to do with its being "injustice that produces factions, hatings [*misē*], and quarrels" (351d, 351e, 417b, 555d, 567d, 568a). Another third have to do with hating the lie (382b, 382c, 485c, 490b, 490c, 535e), although the philosopher is careful to point out three of the various circumstances in which lies are "useful, and thus *not* deserving of hatred [*misous*]" (382c–d; cf. 413c). Other mentions include that of coming to hate oneself because of the unsuitability of one's pursuits (486c), and the hating of the shameful or the ugly (402a; cf. 606c). Orpheus' choosing to return as a swan "out of hating [*misei*] the race of women" (620a) is in provocative contrast to Agamemnon's choosing to return as an eagle "out of hatred [*echthra*] of the race of human beings" (620b). And much as the philosopher linguistically distinguishes some thirty-one special varieties of *philia*, he also recognizes four special kinds of hatred worthy of names. Once again, all have something to do with philosophy: hatred of argument (or, of rational speech; *misologos*, 411d; cf. 582e), hatred of wisdom (*misosophia*, 456a), hatred of labour (*misoponia*, 535d), and hatred of the people (or, of democracy; *misodēmia*, 566c; cf. 499d–e, 558bc).

The two families of terms are conjoined only once. Conversing with the now docile Thrasymachos, Sokrates for some reason singles out the case of injustice arising between two, and asks, "Will they not differ [or, distinguish themselves, i.e., discriminate; *dioisontai*] and hate [*misēsousin*] and be enemies [*echthroi*] to each other and to the just [men]?" (351e; cf. 466d).

With this much evidence before us – and it is most of what there is – a synoptic observation seems justified. Bearing in mind the plenitude of hate towards people one can find in this world, of which Polemarchos reminds us with the very first mention of hate (334c), there is curiously little reference to it in the dialogue. And when it is mentioned, it is all attributed either to injustice or to a natural antagonism between what is "one's own and akin" (*oikeion kai suggenes*) and what is "alien and foreign" (*allotrion kai othneion*) – exemplified by the natural animosity between "Greeks" and "barbarians" (470b). One can only wonder why no mention is made of hatred arising out of the rivalries of love (cf. 521a–b).

— 4 —

Heart of Darkness

Better informed concerning the philosopher's views on love and hate, we may return to the Timocratic Man, that high-spirited individual whose regime and nature alike would more than justify his being called *Ho Philopolemos*, "The War Lover", although for some strange reason the name is never uttered in this dialogue (cf. 583a; *Timaeus* 24cd; *Iliad* XVI, 65 and 90; *Anabasis*, II.6.6).

Perhaps it would be best to begin the longer, fuller consideration of his generation and nature with a reminder of the seven loves that animate his soul: of victory, of music and of listening, of ruling and of honour, of gymnastic and of hunting. As noted above, such a plurality of interests might suggest a kaleidoscopic life not unlike that of a fashion-ridden democrat who, treating all desires as equal, moves with the promptings of the moment (561a–e). However, bearing in mind the traditional view of the warrior (on pain of irrelevancy), one must instead presume the opposite: that this pleiad of loves somehow results in an apparent integrity and single-mindedness nearly as conspicuous as his courage. Still, compared with the majestic simplicity of a kingly man – who, as we shall see, also enjoys a surprising multiplicity of loves (including most of the very same loves!) – the heart of the timocrat conceals a potentially debilitating complexity. For beneath that natural pairing of loves by which he is conveniently identified, *philonikia kai philotimia*, there is a latent fault, a spiritual fissure that can result in profoundly divergent inclinations. Nor is that all. One mustn't forget those three "oligarchic" loves hovering on his horizon: of money, and of money-making, and of spending what belongs to others.

Heart of Darkness

Suffice it to say, he presents a more challenging problem of psychoanalysis than is generally realized, for the insinuating tendrils of all these various loves, entwining with still other loves, infiltrate the furthest reaches of the discussion, just as they do the world it mirrors. As a consequence, tracking down the *totality* of evidence that might bear on his case becomes a task virtually coterminous with comprehending the entire dialogue. After all, one could hardly expect to understand the love of something apart from any knowledge of the thing itself. Thus, one must attend not merely to any speeches about, for example, the *love* of music (which, as a matter of fact, is mentioned just this once, in describing the nature of the timocratic man); one must consider as well everything said about music itself, and any manifestations of this love "in deed". Given, then, the magnitude of the challenge he presents to even a dedicated searcher of souls, one ought not be surprised should the nether depths of his heart, like the genesis of love itself, remain shrouded in darkness. Perhaps, however, his nature – and thus human nature – can be illumined at least to the point where one can see why, in turning over the rule of himself to that within him which "loves victory and is spirited", he typically becomes "a haughty-minded man who loves honour".

'Man' should be emphasized, for the central issue in the account given of his coming into being is *manliness*: the reality of it, common opinions about it, the reputation for it, the honour owed it. The account of the timocratic nature begins with Sokrates asking Glaukon, "Who, then, is the man [*anēr*] corresponding to this regime [*politeia*]?" (548d). It ends with Adeimantos agreeing unqualifiedly, on the basis of the description provided him, that the "timocratic youth [or, young man; *neanias*] is like such a city [*polis*]" (549b). It is a good deal easier for us than for Adeimantos to "rub together" the city and the man and see for ourselves whether or not he is right.

In making such a comparison, several things come to light. For example, the honouring of the rulers in the city is "zealous" (even "excessive"; *sphodra*) "submission" (literally, "hearkening"; *hypokoos*) in the man. And from the fact that the man's attitude towards money is transformed with age, one may surmise that the oligarchical features of governance attributed to the city similarly emerge over time. The privatization of property and enslavement of the producing class, which mark the culmination of the mythical transition from Aristocracy to Timocracy (547bc), are necessary but not themselves sufficient conditions for the surreptitious luxuriating of the city. The philosopher

The War Lover

places the principal onus for hankering after wealth, in the case of both the city and the man, on a defective education: the citizens depart from their own laws because of their " ... having been educated not by persuasion but by force, through neglect of the true Muse accompanying arguments [*logoi*] and philosophy, giving more distinguished honour to gymnastics over music" (548bc). Whereas, the man is "not pure with respect to virtue through having been abandoned by the best guardian", namely, "argument [*logos*] mixed with music, ... only it being a saviour of virtue throughout life" (549b; cf. 560b). But surely the most puzzling and thus arresting detail in the philosopher's presentation of things timocratic is his claim that the first feature peculiar to the city's mode of governance is its "being afraid to bring the wise to the ruling offices, because the men of that kind it possesses are no longer simple and earnest, but mixed ... " (547e; cf. 519c). Whether they are "mixed" in the same way the regime is "mixed", or why else they would be suspect, is not clear (548c; cf. 547a). One is also left wondering whether men who *are* simply and earnestly wise – were there to be such – *could* rise to rulership of this regime. Apparently the only hope for clarifying such matters lies in a better understanding of "the man corresponding to this regime".

But if comparing the descriptions of the timocrat's nature with that of his city can further illuminate both, a similar rubbing together of the accounts of each one's generation seems bewildering, if not outright impossible. They do both culminate in kinds of factionalism. But what, in heaven's name, could possibly correspond to that mystifying, mock-tragical calculus of harmonious geometrical astronomy which allegedly governs "better and worse begettings"?[1] For it is the guardians' ignorance of this "nuptial number" that supposedly results in the arising of a timocratic city. The philosopher's account of how a single timocratic *man* comes into being seems literally prosaic by comparison.

We're told, "Sometimes he is the young son of a good father living in a city that is not governed by a good regime, who flees the honours and offices and lawsuits and everything which goes with love of meddling [*philopragmosynē*], and is willing to have less [*elattousthai*] so as not to be bothered" (549c). (One probably should not, without further thought, conflate 'son of the *good*', *agathon*, with 'son of the *best*', *ariston*; cf. 460c; 506e, 508b.) But as the young man hears and sees for himself, his good father's attitude contrasts radically with most everyone else's, beginning with that of the mother. She complains about the father's disinterest in political power, money, and her. Finding him too easy-tempered (*rathymōs*) and always self-absorbed, she contends he is a slackard and lacking in manliness (*anandros*), and nags on in a similar vein as women are wont to do in such cases (549d). It is not clear which aspect of her diminished status pains her more, the personal, the social, or the financial. The wife's perspective on her husband is partially shared by other members of the household, who confidentially urge the son to resolve that when he becomes a man he will become a real one: more assertive, more protective of what is rightfully his, more demanding of respect – in short, "to be more of a man than is his father". This view is further reinforced by what the youth hears and sees throughout the city (and, one should remember, he is by nature attentive, *philēkoos*, like Adeimantos, a careful listener of what others say). He learns that men such as his father, who are content to mind their own business, are regarded as simpletons and are spoken of slightingly; whereas the opposite sort are "honoured and praised". As a result, the young man is divided. Part of him admires what he sees at first hand of his father's behaviour and understands of his reasoning. But another part of him is enticed by the direct appeal made by everyone else to his desires, and especially to his sense of manly pride. And so, though not having a bad man's nature, yet having kept some less-than-good company, and finding himself tugged at from opposite directions, he settles on a middle course, turning over rule in himself to his middle part, that which "loves victory and is spirited", and thus becomes an arrogant and honour-loving man (550b).

Whether or not Adeimantos is correct in giving complete approval to this account, his enthusiasm for it suggests that he believes it squares with experience. Perhaps it also squares in some unobvious way with the philosopher's obscure, not to say obscurantist, description of the regime's genesis. It would be fair to suppose that the "ruling class" of the home in which the timocratic son is raised *is* factionalized, and that he is himself a mixture of noble and base races. Quite *why* the father and mother are not better matched in their natures is not expressly addressed. The truth may simply be that individuals, even good ones, have no better luck finding suitable mates than would the guardians of philosophical kingship in applying that divine science of breeding their own replacements. In some if not most cases, the true qualities or "metals" of souls can be a long time a-showing. We are also left wondering whether a similarly timocratic son would result from a "good mother" and an inferior father. The pregnant "Some-

The War Lover

times" with which the philosopher begins his account leaves open that as well as other possibilities (cf. 415b–c), but the precise aetiology would *have* to be somewhat different.

Nor does the particular kind of factionalism manifested by the parents, and mirrored in the son, seem to be the same as that manifested by the city. The timocratic regime settles on some point intermediate between Aristocracy and Oligarchy (547c) because one part of its ruling class pulls it towards money-making and private property, while the souls of those already "rich by nature" draw it towards virtue and the "original establishment" (*archaia katastasis*; 547b). It makes at least superficial sense to describe the resulting balance or compromise as something in between the two types of regimes that would result from a total domination of one faction or the other, and it accounts for its manifesting some elements of each of those types. And it is only slightly less obvious why it also has the specific features of its governance that are said to be peculiar to it, and which make it pre-eminently the regime devoted to war. If one set out to design a regime that aimed at promoting *both* wealth accumulation *and* virtue, what better way than through ordering it for war? Success in war (victory) yields and protects the spoils of war, the wealth. And virtue – courage, prudence, and the self-discipline of moderation – produces the success. And the just distribution of honour, including the highest honour of ruling, encourages the virtue.

But the tensions to which the young Timocrat's soul is exposed do not seem to be of the same sort; we're not told that his father draws him towards virtue, while his mother and everyone else incite him to money-making. Rather, the latter faction repeatedly appeals to his manliness, to his sense of pride and shame, to what is respected and praised *in a man*, as opposed to what is derided and despised. (It is doubtful, to say the least, whether the same paradigm of exhortation would produce a timocratic *woman*.) That is, they appeal mainly, *and directly*, to his spirit, manifested as manly pride and its demand for recognition, for respect, for *honour*. And they do so, it seems, with complete success. Perhaps this is because the naturally better kind of young man, one who is well-bred and gifted, is precisely the one who is naturally ruled by a strong spirit in any case. Their blandishments merely silence, or neutralize, such rational reservations about allowing one's spirit free rein as he may have acquired from the speeches and example of his father.

Heart of Darkness

If this is so, then Sokrates gave a more substantial and illuminating account of the making of a timocrat earlier, when in the course of apologizing for philosophy's motley reputation, he analysed the corruption of the best natures, the ones most suited for philosophy (490e–495b). There he began with the observation that those with the requisite natural qualities – "manliness [or, courage; *andreia*], befitting greatness [i.e., magnificence, grandeur; *megaloprepia*], facility in learning [*eumathia*], memory" (490c; cf. 487a) – are but infrequently born among human beings (491ab; cf. 503b, d). Whereas the sources of their corruption are great and many, beginning with the very excellences themselves. Because these qualities allow a young man to be universally victorious – "to be first among all in everything, straight from the beginning, especially if his body matches his soul" (494b) – everyone in the city, anticipating his later usefulness for their own affairs, supplicates and flatters him in order to gain access to the power they expect will be his. Such a youth, and especially if his natural gifts of soul are complemented by physical beauty and stature, and supplemented by the political and economic advantages of a well-placed family, is most apt to acquire a greatly inflated estimate of his ability and worth, and to "exalt himself to the heights, mindlessly full of pretention and empty conceit" (494d). This certainly sounds like someone justly described as "haughty-minded" or "arrogant". In all probability, he will not listen readily to a lone and contrary voice preaching the truth: "that he has no intelligence in him, although he needs it, and that it is not to be acquired except by slaving for its acquisition." Exposed to what the vast majority of people praise and blame with so much pomp and exaggeration, "What do you suppose is the state of the young man's heart," Sokrates asks Adeimantos, "or what kind of private education will hold out for him, and not be swept away by such praise and blame, bearing him off on its current wherever it tends, so that he'll say the same things are noble and base that they do, practise what they practise, and be such as they are?" (492b–c; cf. 365a). Adeimantos agrees that in such circumstances no private arguments are likely to prevail (492e). The philosopher himself restricts their conclusion to the human realm of endeavour, expressly excluding cases of divine intervention (492e; cf. 494de, 380c).

If true goodness in a man were easily recognized, the example and arguments of a good father might be sufficient. But it isn't. In fact, the contrary is more the case: what virtue truly is, how it comes to be, and its relationship to happiness have been central questions of political life for so long as people have reflected on it. As the dialogue itself proves, this is the kind of knowledge one must toil to obtain. Moreover, it has been long and widely recognized that a son's relationship with his father is not a simple one; affection and admiration and gratitude and attraction are apt to be co-mingled with more than a trace of repulsion and fear and resentment, and sometimes even a sovereign contempt (cf. 553ab, 562e). Perhaps there is good reason why such a complex of passions animates a son, and it may even have some counterpart in his father. In any event, the natural rebelliousness through which most youths must pass - and the more spirited they are, the more intense and extreme this recalcitrance can be - predisposes them to turn a ready ear to contrary voices. And since a father virtually never enjoys complete control over the environment of his son, if his standards are not suitably reflected in the rest of the family, nor ratified and reinforced throughout the rest of the city, chances are the son will - for better or worse - part with the ways of his father, even if only temporarily. Should the son be an inferior offspring of an inferior father, of a miserly oligarch say, he may be moved by an appeal to his baser desires for pleasure and ease (cf. 558c ff). But the well-born youth is distinguished by, more than anything else, the quality of his spirit (375a). It will rule him regardless, at least initially, and thus it is to his spirit, to the natural loves and hates of his spirit, that one must make one's appeal if one hopes to influence him. So, why does he love what he loves, and why do those loves make him become what he is?

Virtually by definition, spiritedness is that basic something which makes a person courageous, aggressive, strong-willed, competitive (a "lover of victory"), tenacious, impervious to fear and bodily pain, but also inordinately sensitive to status. More exactly what this something is, and why, and how it relates to the other phenomena of one's life, are admittedly vexing questions for anyone who would unriddle the human soul. But much as the first requirement of an acceptable theory of the heavens is that it "save the appearances" - *all* of the appearances, including especially those troublesome apparitions known as "Wanderers" (*planetai*) - so must an adequate psychology square not only with the perceptible regularities characteristic of the broad generality of human beings, but also with the significant exceptions to the norm. One must start from, as well as finally return to, whatever can be confidently observed. Among these everyday facts of common sense and experience is the primary evidence for this something that traditionally has been called the spirit.

It is readily seen, for example, that "spiritedness" is a variable quality in human beings and other higher animals, much as we acknowledge it to be, generally speaking, more evident in males than in females. Anger, including indignation and vengefulness, is the passion especially associated with spiritedness, so much so that it is natural to speak of anger – and in many different languages – as a "show of the spirit". Suffused with anger, one is more apt to be aggressive, to overcome one's fears, ignore pain, and be courageous to the point of recklessness. And one's spirit tends to be provoked, made angry, by anything that frustrates one's desires, obstructs one's will, or violates one's sense of propriety – but especially by affronts to one's pride. Insults and blame, then, and often even fair and well-intended criticism, pain the spirit; whereas praise and flattery, admiration, "popularity", and honour (including that implicit in others' envy) placate the spirit and give it pleasure.

It takes no more than this everyday assessment of untutored common sense to see why the timocratic nature would be readily identified with *both* a love of victory *and* a love of honour, or why the cultivation and expression of courage would be especially associated with the high-spirited man (cf. 582e). Honour typically attends victory, whether the success comes in athletics, war, art, making money, or any other competitive endeavour that is publicly regarded as significant. And these public estimates of importance, manifested in what a polity treats as honourable, tend to channel people's energies; which is to say that the distribution of honour is a generally effective means of ruling people, especially men (cf. 551a). It is often difficult to determine, even in one's own case, whether victory is pursued more for the self-satisfaction of achievement, or for the honours others bestow in their recognition of one's excelling. It is presumed that victory bespeaks the virtue of the victor, and thus his right to honour. Hence we would say approvingly, "to the victor goes the glory".

Physical courage, the willingness to expose one's body to pain and mortal harm, is naturally the most visible of the virtues, and as a rule commands the most honour (cf. 582c). Doubtless this reflects the fact that so many people feel self-preservation to be the most basic and urgent passion of life, and thus the most difficult to overrule. While being honoured for almost anything can be gratifying (cf. 475ab), virtually all *men* would rather be honoured for being courageous than for anything else, as this is seen as being honoured for manliness as such: for having that greater spiritedness that naturally distinguishes the male, for having thus proven oneself a true man. The field of battle, where success or failure seems to carry the greatest consequences for city and man alike, has long been recognized as the greatest test of such courage, and accordingly holds forth the promise of the greatest honours. Thus, the man who is dominated by an intense love of victory and honour is fatally attracted to war, the milieu in which a man can shine the brightest. In most ages, the political utility of courage in both war and peace has been obvious enough to make its promotion a generally acknowledged element of the common good, and this partially accounts for the public recognition it has received throughout history. But also, most people being painfully aware of their own fears, they cannot help but admire (if only grudgingly) what they recognize to be outstanding displays of courage. They therefore honour, but they also envy, and doubtless some even resent, the courageous man who, having conquered his fears, seems so much the freer, so much more the master of self and circumstance.[2]

Surveying the evidence of everyday life also reveals a conspicuous minority of people who seem especially driven to excel, to develop their natural powers to the fullest. Almost everyone finds such a prospect attractive, but only a few attempt to pursue it with any constant determination, and fewer still do so with little or no external encouragement. Thus, these few who just naturally aspire to outdo everyone else, who are so competitive they seem almost incapable of resisting a challenge, stand out from the rest. It is not surprising to find that they are prominent among those attracted to athletic activities, most of which are ordered around competition. Nor can one ignore what has so often been noticed: that most competitive sports – by accident or design – have much in common with war; not only is the physical training similar, but a fair number of sports simply are stylized warfare, or kinds of combat. Combat can take many forms, requiring various kinds of strengths and skills. Similarly, athletics has always included a broad range of activities suited to a variety of physiques. If one athletic contest (*agōn*) places a premium on strength and quickness, another favours the swift, or the daring, or the dextrous, or the crafty, or the one with the greatest stamina, or balance, or coordination, or special skills won through long practice. A man can usually find an athletic endeavour that suits him – or more to the point, that he can make himself suit (and thus excel in) – if his spirit is strong enough to sustain the labour involved. It is because some appreciable athletic excellence *is* within the potential of nearly every man (were he to strive for it with sufficient tenacity), and because it is an achievement almost any man can understand and judge and vicariously experience, that athletics commands the popular honour it does (620b).

But neither the glamour surrounding athletics nor the excitement of contesting (*agōnia*) completely accounts for its appeal. Apparently a few people truly love athletic labour itself, and so could be said to be "lovers of gymnastic" in the strictest sense. By contrast, most of us would readily agree with Glaukon's placement of physical training in that *third* class of good things, something liked only for its beneficial consequences (e.g., the health, strength, beauty – and admiration – that come from being physically fit and skilled), but which in itself is drudgery (357c). Nonetheless, a few people, and they are not identical with that small class of premier athletes, genuinely *enjoy* the strenuous training of body and soul that is entailed in preparing for serious athletic competition. Perhaps they approach it as a test of self-overcoming, where the challenge is provided by whatever in oneself is resistant to the absolute control of the will. And the enjoyment they experience would be the peculiar exultation that comes from achievement through sheer will power, the joy of self-mastery.

But for most of us, the judgments we reach about this matter are bound to remain speculative, lacking direct access to the relevant experience. Let this serve as a reminder that there may be natural limitations on any given person's ability to understand the full gamut of human life (cf. 581e-d). And that with respect to matters of far greater importance than athletics, there may be no substitute for experience. This is not to say, of course, that to experience something is thereby to understand it, but only that an experiential basis for judgment is sometimes a prerequisite of knowing. For this and other reasons, much about one's fellows (and even about oneself) may be fated to remain mysterious, permanently consigned to the realm of speculation. To be sure, speculation is no sin – quite the contrary: intelligent speculation plays an essential part in pursuing wisdom, and may even constitute the highest employment of the rational imagination. But for all that, it is not to be confused with certain knowledge. An all-knowing god would have no use for speculation. One needs neither speculation nor revelation, however, for the point at hand. There is a variety of evidence, much of it grounded in quite common experience, testifying to the existence of substantial practical relationships between love of athletics and love of both honour and victory, thereby supporting the view that all three loves are typical expressions of an especially competitive spirit.

The naturalness of the timocrat's love of listening and love of music, on the other hand, is by no means so transparent. The two loves' association with each other is seen easily enough: a serious love of most types of "music" – history, melody, the various kinds of poetry – presumes that one is a careful, attentive "listener" of sure memory. The Muse of Astronomy, however, is one that would seem to appeal more to a "lover of sights" (or, "of spectacles"; *philotheamon*), than to a lover of listening (cf. 530d, 475d). The Muse of Dance perhaps draws equally on both loves, but in any case it is the least problematic with respect to its association with the warlike, timocratic nature. The War Dance (*pyrrichē*), danced by men and boys in armour (an integral part of military training in Sparta; cf. 399ab, 412b), is not something peculiar to Greek culture; it is a feature common to almost all societies with a martial tradition. One thinks of the Kurds and the Cossacks, the Zulus and Watusi, the Scots and Gurkhas and Tahitians, and the majority of Indian peoples inhabiting North and South America.[3] Some warriors dance in preparation for battle, some in celebration of a victorious return, some do both. Their dances may be sombre and pious in character, but more typically they are as vigorous and boisterous and athletic as combat itself. In fact, stylization of warfare seems to be one of the two principal sources of "folk-dancing" in general, the other being the rituals of courtship.

Still, of all the loves in the war lover's psychic constellation, the one that is apt to remain most puzzling is his love of music, and especially of poetry. One might be tempted to regard it as a spurious attribution were not the love of poetry (and of elegant, concise speech in general) as characteristic of martial societies as their love of dance. So far as we can tell, poetry originated, and no doubt remained especially at home in, "oral" communities, those in which the history and traditions were heard over and over again, memorized, and orally transmitted from one generation to the next. As the schoolyard doggerel of children reminds us, rhythm, rhyme, and tune are first of all mnemonic devices (cf. 601ab). But a reliance on oral tradition imposes a great economy on a culture. Only the richest, most important,

Heart of Darkness

most beautiful and pleasing stories can be preserved in living memory. The prospect of being among the precious few so memorialized must be very attractive to a lover of honour (cf. 368a). It might seem no great wonder, then, that the poetry which finds favour among admirers of manly virtue includes all those inspiring *mythoi* of heroism: the epics of Achaeans and Trojans, the *sagen* of Vikings and ballades of Knights Errant, tales of Samurai and Conquistadors, of Dog Soldiers and Troubadours.

It is a *bit* puzzling if one thinks about it, however. Why would a poetry honouring *others* be pleasing rather than painful to a lover of honour? Is it because, as is sometimes said, he feels little or no need to compete with the dead (cf. 414a, 468e-b)? One suspects that there would be many sons of illustrious fathers who would testify otherwise (cf. *Laches*, 179b-d). True enough, there is an inner logic to honour which dictates that he who would be honoured by others must be willing himself to bestow honour on those who are by the same criteria deserving of it. Still, he would not be a timocrat were his thought and action ruled exclusively by logic. Of course, all poetry honouring martial virtue implicitly ratifies the propriety of honouring martial virtue, and perhaps this is sufficient explanation in itself, as every warrior thereby enjoys a kind of honour by association. But it may also be the case that what it is in him that desires honour is not precisely the same as that which is gratified by beautiful tales of manly excellence.

In any event, the poetic taste of martial men is not confined to heroic epics and odes. There are the panegyrics to the gods, the lyrics of love and courtship, the pithy epigrams of the Spartans, the equally "laconic" *haiku* (cf. 607a). Such versifying manifests an appreciation of other things – of life's basic truths and insoluble mysteries, and of love's power for good and evil – all beautifully and thus the more memorably expressed. Might the timocrat's notable affection for music reveal his spirit's taste for beauty? Indeed, perhaps the primary appeal of beauty is to the spirit, or to the human spirit, rather; for animals have spirit, but seem indifferent to beauty as such. And does a conspicuous desire for beauty, then, or a special sensitivity to beauty – and, consequently, the power for creating beauty – presume extraordinary spiritedness? And is this why music must be the basis of an education that would tame the spirit: because beauty truly *charms* the spirit, such that it peacefully accepts a *logos* initially alien to it, provided that *logos* is wrapped in an appropriate beauty (cf. 411b, 441ea)?

The War Lover

Paradoxical though it seems at first, tragedy may be especially attractive to a high-spirited man precisely because it so beautifully portrays an heroic nature that ultimately fails or falls, and thereby beautifies that failure or falling. He can sympathize, for deep inside every victory-lover is the dark foreboding that it could happen to him, and eventually *will* happen to him if he continues to test himself, to pursue ever-escalating challenges, taking ever-greater risks, tempting fate. Sooner or later, he too will find – must find – the mountain he cannot climb, the dragon he cannot slay, the storm he cannot weather. Indeed, the failure to find something that bests him may be the most damning failure of all, for it raises the suspicion that he was not sufficiently willing – or not sufficiently driven, one might rather say – to test himself to the uttermost. There is only one way to prove that he didn't play it safe, nor hedge his bet, and that is to perish in the struggle. His idea of a man is one who prefers to die with his boots on, as it were, one who seeks "a good day to die". For in the final accounting, it is not the *accomplishments* of striving (which sometimes can be brought about without great effort or sacrifice), but only *the striving itself* that has value.[4]

Whatever the mysteries concerning the timocrat's love of music, some of his love of ruling can be explained easily enough: rulers are honoured (especially in a Timocracy); being selected to rule is itself an honour (and especially in a Timocracy); and being obeyed is an honour (most especially when that obedience is freely rendered by warriors). Describing the nature of the *timokratikos*, the philosopher mentions in one breath that he is a lover of ruling and a lover of honour, and that he in effect treats rulership as the appropriate means of recognizing valorous conduct in war (549a). Political rule would seem the pinnacle of achievement to a timocrat, offering at once the greatest challenge and the greatest honour, perhaps even immortal fame. For the desire to rule need not terminate at the boundaries of one's own polity. Conquest offers practically unlimited possibilities (cf. 351ab). Nothing less than ruling the entire world need satisfy the man who combines love of rule with largeness of soul (cf. *Alkibiades I* 105a–c; *Alkibiades II* 150c).

But for all the wealth of connections one finds in practice between love of honour and love of ruling, the latter is certainly not a mere derivative of the former. We occasionally hear rumours of "grey eminences", of there being a "power behind the throne", of ones who in truth rule but without the normal public acknowledgement. In fact,

Heart of Darkness

there is no shortage of evidence that ruling, the sheer experience of wielding power, is something that can be loved for its own sake as well as for its consequences. That there is a love of rule *per se* is mentioned only once in the entire dialogue, being the central of the timocrat's seven loves. More precisely stated, this "friendly" lover of ruling (*philarchos*) is mentioned but once. For, presumably, he is to be distinguished from the "lustful" lover of ruling (*erastēs tou archein*) whom the philosopher persistently condemns (521b; cf. 488b–e, 496c–d). But this explicit recognition that ruling can be its own reward, at least for someone who loves power more than anything else, would seem to throw a rather different-coloured light on the philosopher's various discussions about the wages of rule (346e–d, 414a, 420a, 520a–521a). As for his account of tyranny, suffice it to say that one is obliged to reconsider *that* from beginning to end.

In thinking about ruling, however, one is reminded that the entire constellation of loves that defines the timocratic nature has some direct involvement with philosophy, beginning with *philarchia*. For *archē* doesn't refer only to 'ruling office'. It can also mean 'origin', 'first cause', 'fundamental principle', or 'element'. The relevance to philosophy of this whole family of meanings surely needs no comment.

But to illustrate more substantially the strange similarity between the philosopher's portrait of the War Lover and that of himself, consider in detail another love they share, the love of hunting (*philothēria*; 535d, 549a). First, however, it should be noted that the philosopher speaks of two kinds of hunting: one with dogs (*kynēgesia*, from *kyōn*, 'dog'; cf. 375a, 404a, 416a, 537a, 440d, 469de, 539b), and the other without (*thēra*). Still, the specific word for hunting dog (*thēreutikos*), the sort that Glaukon keeps (459a), reminds us that the two ways of hunting are related. In any event, the warrior class of the city in *logos* would be expected to participate in both kinds (412b).[5] The timocrat is identified simply as a lover of hunting as such (of *thēra*). It is worth noting that this hunter (*thēreutēs*) initially enters the city in *logos* when it is luxuriated in response to Glaukon's rejection of the first, and vegetarian, version of it; indeed, the hunter is the first "unnecessary" kind of "artisan" to do so (373b). But later, when their city has been again asceticized (this time to Glaukon's satisfaction, if not altogether to Adeimantos's; cf. 404d, 419a), and they proceed to what is ostensibly their main philosophical business – searching for justice in it – Sokrates suggests, "now we must, like hunters, station ourselves around the thicket and pay attention so that justice doesn't slip through somewhere and disappear into obscurity, [since] the place really appears to be hard-going and steeped in shadows, ... dark and difficult to explore". Here, the hunter referred to is the one with dogs, *kynēgetēs* (432b). That is, Sokrates likens he and his fellow discussants, to a hunter and his dogs quartering the thicket in search of justice.

The same episode reminds us of the natural connection between hunting and tracking (432d). In fact, all seven references to tracks or tracking (*ichnos, ichneuein*) would ordinarily be called metaphoric, and each has a direct relevance to political philosophizing. Adeimantos is the first to use the term, insisting that "if we are to be happy, we must go where the tracks of the arguments [*ichnē tōn logōn*] lead" (365d). Only those can be craftsmen in their city whose own natures sufficiently enable them to "track down the nature of what is fine [*kalos*] and graceful" (401c). The central reference to tracks is the philosopher's suggestion that one treat linguistic usage as the tracks of ideas (430e). He subsequently raises some question as to whether or not their political project in *logos* "harmonizes with the track of the good" (462a). The requirement that the truly musical man must "pursue [*diokōn*] a gymnastic by the same tracks" (410b) introduces still a third hunt-related word, *diōkein* ('to pursue', 'chase', 'follow closely', 'seek after'; it can also mean 'to prosecute', cf. 405b). It is the most frequently employed term in the philosopher's hunting vocabulary, over half of its uses having to do with the pursuit of virtue (399e, 400e, 410b, 545b), or the pursuit of truth (454a, 490a), or the pursuit of the Good (359c, 505d).

What one finds with respect to hunting is also true with respect to *gymnastikē* (i.e., 'the art of athletic training or exercise'; from *gymnos*, 'naked', that being the condition in which such *gymnasia* was practised; cf. 452c). Judging from the philosopher's references to it, strenuous exercise seems as relevant to the lover of wisdom as it is to the lover of war, if not more so. And the significance of gymnastics for philosophy is not confined to its admittedly important - indeed, crucial - role in cultivating the necessary accord between the calculating and spirited part of the soul. Nor is it merely a collateral aspect of the requirement that a philosophic nature must be a lover of all kinds of labour - although the philosopher is unusually emphatic about this, insisting that a suitable candidate for philosophy mustn't be a "cripple" in his love of labour, loving only the labour of the body, or only that of the soul (535b-d; cf. 504cd, 619d). No doubt this warning serves as a salutary corrective to the popular notion of the philosopher, that he is lazy and loves an easy-going life, ever day-dreaming and prattling in lieu of doing something useful.[6]

But philosophy's involvement with gymnastic goes beyond all this, and even beyond the concern that the soul be disciplined in courage and moderation through a rigorous gymnastic of the body. For as the philosopher intimates, bodily gymnastic is needed not only to arouse the spirit, but to toughen the mind (410e, 441e). The point is well worth the emphasis Sokrates gives it. There is, for reasons not too difficult to uncover, a natural tendency to presume that what is rational (e.g., in political arrangements and policies) is that which is painless, or which minimizes pain. This, however, is more a reflection of man's hope than it is of reality. And as anyone who has ever done anything to be ashamed of knows, thinking about painful experiences can itself be painful. Often what people find "unthinkable" is nothing more than what they find too painful to contemplate. And yet the world comes with no assurance that the truth is always pretty and pleasant. But if the Good is not simply pleasure (cf. 505b–d), then neither is pain to be equated with the Bad. Some painful things may be good. Gaining the capacity to consider painful thoughts dispassionately may be among them. If a philosophic nature is one that desires *all* the truth (as we are repeatedly told, e.g., 475b–c, 485a–d, 501d), it must be able to *bear* all the truth, the painful as well as the pleasant. Gymnastic of the body trains one to endure and even despise physical suffering, and this carries over to other kinds of pain as well, diminishing its significance in oneself and to oneself.

Beyond even this, however, the philosopher refers to a gymnastic *of the soul*. He speaks of the soul being "exercised [*gymnazein*] in many studies" to see whether it has the "power for the greatest studies [*ta megista mathēmata dynatē*]" (503e). He recommends that when "the soul begins to reach maturity, it ought to be subjected to a more intense gymnastic" (498b). Presumably, the curriculum he outlines in Book Seven constitutes such a philosophical gymnastic. Practice in arithmetic, for example, is referred to expressly as a gymnastic that can strengthen and quicken the mind (526b). He treats an unwillingness to stand up to the strain of intense studies as a kind of cowardice (535b; cf. 374e, 504a). The recommended regimen apparently culminates in a "continual and strenuous participation in arguments, exclusive of other practices, exercising [*gymnazomenō*] in the antistrophe of bodily gymnastic" (539d).

As for the relationship between philosophy and the timocrat's love

The War Lover

of music, one might begin by observing that it is in the very context of discussing Timocracy that one finds the only reference to a "true Muse", namely, that which should accompany philosophy and *logos* (548bc; cf. 591d). Nonetheless – and surprising as it might seem – the philosopher places greater emphasis and fewer qualifications on philosophy's kinship with gymnastic than on its kinship with music. He avows that some god gave music and gymnastic to human beings, "not for soul and body except incidentally", but for the sake of harmonizing the spirited and philosophic parts of the soul (411ea; cf. 441e). Here, the philosophic part is paired with gymnastic, music with the spirit. It seems that music's principal benefit to philosophy comes less from what it does for rationality than from its making spiritedness tractable, so that the full power of the spirit is reliably at the disposal of reason.

But this very capacity of beautiful music to charm regardless of truth or goodness makes it as much a threat to the pursuit of truth as it is to wholesome politics. There is no shortage of evidence in this world that lies can be charming (cf. 377a, 377d, 378bc). The philosopher speaks knowingly of there being an old quarrel between philosophy and poetry (607b). Hence the political desirability of a comprehensive censorship of all music and art (401b-d), and hence the natural inferiority and proper subordination of poetry and rhetoric to philosophy (595a-b, 607c, 608b). Still, the right kind of musical education – and this is a philosophical, not a musical, question – may facilitate the subsequent introduction of philosophy:

> "So, Glaukon", I said, "isn't this why the rearing in music is most sovereign? Because rhythm and harmony most of all insinuate themselves into the inmost part of the soul and vigorously lay hold of it, bringing grace with them; and they make one graceful if correctly reared, if not, the opposite. Furthermore, [it is sovereign] because the one properly reared on rhythm and harmony would have the sharpest sense for what has been left out, and what is not of fine [or noble, beautiful; *kalos*] workmanship or not of fine nature. And having the right kind of dislikes, he would praise the fine things; and, taking delight in them, receive them into his soul and become a gentleman [*kalos k'agathos*; literally, 'noble and good']. He would blame and hate the ugly things [or, 'the shameful things'; *ta aischra*] in the right way while he is still young, before he has the power to grasp *logos*. And when *logos* comes, the one who is so reared would welcome it, recognizing it as being especially akin." (401d-a)

This description of how good taste is cultivated in the young is richer than it might first seem. It stresses the "negating" character of good taste: that by virtue of exposure to the harmonious integrity or wholeness of good music, one is made sensitive to the *absence* of such wholeness, to what is *missing*, to what is *not* well-made, to what is *not* beautiful or noble. Such cultivation of the spirit's instinct for beauty is of special importance to political philosophy because of its bearing on synoptic judgment in general (since the most difficult aspect of reaching a sound comprehensive judgment is recognizing whether everything relevant has been included); and on understanding justice in particular (which also proceeds in this "negative" way: we recognize more readily what is *not* just, than what is; cf., e.g., 331c–d, 334d, 335cd, 336a).

The timocrat is a lover of listening. By no means are all such lovers truly philosophical (cf. 328d); some are merely "like [*homoious*] philosophers" (475e) in being a kind of "lover of opinion" (*philodoxos*; 480a), much as are the typical "lover of sights" (*philotheamonēs*) and the "lover of the arts" (*philotechnos*; 476a). Nonetheless, a philosophical nature *is* one that loves the labour of careful, attentive listening (535d), as well as being a lover of the sight of the truth (475e).

It is with respect to the timocrat's most conspicuous pair of loves, however – his love of victory and his love of honour – that one can see a clear distinction between him and the philosopher. For the philosopher endorses one of these loves almost without qualification, whereas he is decidedly cool towards the other. He uses the lover of honour as an illustration of his claim that whoever is called a lover of something, if it is correctly said of him, loves the whole of it, indiscriminately (475ab). Whereas honours are things about which an intelligent person *does* discriminate: "he would willingly partake of and taste those that he believes will make him better, while those that would overturn his established habit he will flee, in private and in public" (592a). Good men, the philosopher says flatly, are no more willing to rule for the sake of honour than for the sake of money, "for they are *not* lovers of honour". He asks Glaukon, "don't you know that love of honour and love of silver [*philargyron*] are said to be, *and are*, reproaches?" Glaukon emphatically assures him that he does (347b).

The love of honour often manifests itself simply as a yearning for popularity, which like all reputation is but a kind of common opinion. As often as otherwise, this opinion is not an accurate reflection of an individual's nature, character, behaviour, and achievements, nor

The War Lover

does it even pretend to be. Nonetheless, the man who loves honour – as the tacit price of valuing that honour – tends to subordinate his own judgment to these public estimates of importance, and accordingly shows an excessive regard for those of high social status, and an abusive disdain for those of low. This indiscriminate love of honour is something one might hope to be cured of by sufficient experience (cf. 620c). For sooner or later, an intelligent person learns to trim his respect for the judgment of those who do the honouring, and the value of their honours diminishes accordingly. Most people's judgment may be tolerably sound with respect to, say, athletic excellence, or strength and beauty of the body. But what about when they are judging judgment itself, excellence of mind? If being famous for wisdom is more than slightly paradoxical, then a concern for such fame is doubly so (cf. 582c-d, 598c-a, 600e-a, 602ab). Thus, it is not surprising that philosopher-guardians would despise the petty honours of the Cave, and partake of them only under some sort of compulsion (cf. 519d). However, insofar as true philosophy is not honoured (489ab, 528b-c, 494a; cf. 495c-d), the honour-loving man cannot be truly captivated by it. He regards "the pleasure of learning – whatever learning doesn't bring honour – to be smoke and drivel" (581d). In fact, love of honour first surfaces in this dialogue as a power that tends to corrupt dialogue (336c), and dialogue is the philosopher's special tool (cf. 582d). His depreciation of honour is of a piece with his depreciation of politics (e.g., 496c-b). This is not to say that a political philosopher is indifferent to all questions of honour, since he must be concerned with both the reputation of philosophy (489a, 495a-496a, 535c, 536c, 539c-d; cf. 528b-c, 521b, 582c, 592a), and the proper rank order of things (508a, 509a, 511a, 595c, 528b-c, 537b-d, 494c). But his attention to it is for the sake of the city and philosophy, not for the sake of honour itself.

The philosopher's attitude towards *victory*, however, contrasts noticeably with his attitude towards honour. Nowhere in the dialogue is victory or love of victory ever disparaged. The only reservation is the warning that a spiritedness pursuing victory "without calculation and intelligence" is too readily disposed to use force (586cd; cf. 411de). The Guardians are described as victors more blessed than even Olympic victors (465d). And with respect to the issue that could be said to cause this dialogue – whether it is better to be just or unjust – the just man is acknowledged thrice victorious over the unjust man, once again in the Olympic style (583b). The philosopher's concluding words are in praise of victors (621cd).

As the philosopher's discriminating treatment of victory and honour should remind us, then, neither these two things themselves nor the desires for them are strictly coincidental. Despite the manifold affiliations between love of victory and love of honour that one normally finds in everyday practice, and for all the many occasions when victory (success, achievement, attainment) brings honour, there is no strict necessity conjoining them. There are victories that can be enjoyed in solitude, as anyone knows who has ever solved a puzzle just for the joy of it. Whereas other things are honoured besides victory and noble effort, notably beauty (cf. 591b). What is most important to recognize, however, is that these two loves of a timocrat can *conflict*, and those occasions when they clash reveal which love is uppermost in him. For example, there are some timocrats who would cheat to win, rather than go without the honour. But there are some who would not, being more shamed than pleased at receiving credit not really due them. One usually knows in one's heart whether an apparent victory is a true victory, and thus – whatever other gratifications it may bring – whether it fully satisfies one's love of *victory*. This intrinsic connection between love of victory and natural justice should not be overlooked. Also, there is an asymmetry between the two loves worth remarking: whereas one may pursue victory for its own sake as well as for the sake of such honours as may attend it, one cannot pursue honour for the sake of victory. That is to say, victory belongs to the central class of Glaukon's tripartite classification of good things (357b–d), those which (like thought and sight and health) are desirable both for themselves and for their consequences. This is the class the philosopher, when placing justice in it also, calls "the finest" (*kallistos*; 358a).

There are, then, *two distinguishable kinds of timocrats*, depending upon which of these two characteristic loves – of victory (*philonikia*), or of honour (*philotimia*) – is uppermost. Only one of these kinds of men is rightly called 'timocratic', for love of honour is indeed the strongest and thus the ruling love of his soul. The other kind, often scarcely distinguishable in appearance, is only incidentally a timocrat. While almost surely not indifferent to honour (which, after all, is something almost everyone finds gratifying), he none the less loves victory most, and treats honour as appropriate but incidental to winning. To the extent his victories are achievements known and appreciated by others (as, chances are, they're apt to be), he expects honour as a matter of course, being no more than his just deserts. To speak of the victory-lover as a 'timocrat' rather than a 'nikocrat' is to adopt the common –

The War Lover

but mistaken – presumption as to what primarily moves him. This mistake is the more likely in that love of honour, manifested in the concern for popularity, distinction, reputation, respect, status, fame, and such is far stronger in most people than is the love of victory *per se*, hence more commonly encountered, hence more apt to strike people as a plausible motivation for achievements that bring honour.

No doubt many nikocrats, just like most timocrats, share this misunderstanding of themselves and each other. Yet the difference between them is crucial. For the man in whom love of victory is uppermost is open to be detached from the opinions of others, as the man who most loves honour can never be. The lover of honour is constantly being drawn back towards those who bestow it. He can never completely sever himself from what they think. But since their honours are never his permanent possession, he lives with a mounting dread that, sooner or later, the good he most craves will go to others, leaving him in galling obscurity. As a hedge against that approaching eventuality, he finds a less vulnerable, less ephemeral, less perishable good increasingly attractive: wealth. The fact that the oligarchic man loves not only money, but the challenge and honour of *money-making* (cf. 550e), reveals the lingering trace of his timocratic heritage. Alternatively expressed, the successful oligarch is often among the more spirited few of the great many money-lovers.

In all these respects, the lover of victory differs profoundly. He enjoys a kind of self-sufficiency insofar as he is the judge of his own accomplishments; his self-satisfaction in his successes and valiant attempts cannot be taken from him by others; and the good he seeks does not necessarily wed him to the crowd (cf. 528a). Loving victory for its own sake, he is free to pursue whatever challenges attract *him* (which doubtless will depend somewhat on his stage and station of life), without regard for what most people think. Indeed, withstanding popular ridicule may constitute one of the finer tests of his courage (cf. 451a, 452b, 474a, 517d).

Reflecting upon the philosopher's discussion of the timocratic man and his loves, as well as upon his treatment of the two young timocrats he spends most of a day and night talking with, one can scarce avoid concluding that it is from the ranks of this kind of nature that the most promising prospects for the philosophical life are to be found: that it is among timocratic youth that the philosopher goes hunting (or fishing, rather) for his natural heirs and kinfolk – just as in the city in *logos* the "complete" and thus true guardians are a select few chosen from among those making up the warrior class. No one, notice, is immediately assigned to the uppermost class. The ones regarded as being of the Golden race live most of their lives with, or as, men of Silver. We are told that gold in the soul is revealed only through (or might it be transmuted by?) the most rigorous of tests (413de). Perhaps the majority of timocratic natures are best thought of as having electrum in their souls, and are distinguished among themselves by which of the two precious constituents is proportionally greater and by how much. If that is the case, they may be amenable to a refinement process. Alternatively, perhaps there is an alchemy of souls whereby one can sublimate gold out of silver.

For some lovers of victory can be transformed into lovers of wisdom upon their coming to see the pursuit of wisdom as the greatest challenge of all, one calling for the finest virtues and greatest exertions. And they may recognize it to be an ideal challenge precisely because it is an endless challenge, this contest with ignorance, in which no one entirely succeeds, no matter how strenuously he tries or how blessed by nature; yet neither does one entirely fail, for he "celebrates a triumph with every conclusion", as another philosopher puts it. And if there is some deeper connection between philosophy and warfare – as the entire dialogue seems to suggest – perhaps the ones *best* suited for philosophy are *not* those who are *gentle* by *nature* (however omnivorous their curiosity, however clever their calculating part), but rather those whose great spiritedness makes them passionate lovers of victory; those who, as well as having a quick, agile, tough, supple mind and reliable memory, have the strength and energy and boldness and stamina of spirit for confronting the supreme challenge, the contest of contests; those who are driven to *become* the *best*, and have only to learn what truly *is* the best; those who want the most out of life, who in fact want it *all*, and who realize for themselves that the only way to have it all is to *know* it all, and reign supreme over all that one knows, a kingdom that grows in richness and expanse with each new exploration and conquest.

As for someone with a genuinely timocratic nature, of which the finest embodiment is he who wishes to be honoured for his virtue, he can be made into a true gentleman by his coming to respect philosophy, and to honour wisdom as the highest virtue. He needs only be assured that philosophy is manly, that it is not corrupting if pursued in the right way by those who are naturally suited for it, and that it can be beneficial to the polity that supports it. Such a gentleman

The War Lover

is a valuable – indeed, peerless – intermediary between the philosopher and the city in which the philosopher remains essentially a "stranger" or "guest-friend" (*xenos*; cf. *Apology* 17d).

Left in his natural state, the timocratic man, by virtue of his spiritedness, is both a lover of victory and a lover of honour. As should now be clear, however, these are *not* simply two sides of the same coin. In a sense, he, like his regime, is actually Janus-faced, a mixture of two natures: one faces up towards the best, the really and truly best, and thus implicitly towards the permanent realm of Truth and Reality that determines the best; the other faces down towards the many, towards what appears best to them in their dusky political realm of familiar, parochial, transient opinion. So long as his loves remain harnessed together – and the many practical, everyday connections between victory and honour tend to keep them so – his seems a nature distinctive unto itself: courageous, competitive, willing to take risks, self-assertive and energetic, resolute, prideful, sensitive to slights, capable of vehement anger, perpetually poised for contention with his fellow man even to the point of war. And although the psychic mixture that defines him is normally a stable one, imparting to him an outward integrity of character and consistency of behaviour, it is not as solid as it seems. For there is a fissure in his foundation that poses a peculiar threat to him, to his apparent integrity and steadfastness – a division, potentially profound, within the human spirit itself. And while the recognition of this spiritual fissure is pertinent to an understanding of each and every one of us, it is of paramount importance for anyone whose spirit is the dominant part of his soul.

Here one might recall that, before the dialogue is half over, the philosopher demonstrates that the soul has three distinguishable parts: an appetitive, a rational, and a spirited part (435c–441c). His labouring to demonstrate that the soul has these three parts contrasts dramatically with his somehow divining that there are four parts to their city's goodness (428a). Speaking more precisely, he shows that the soul has *at least* three parts. And far from proving that it has *only* three parts, he explicitly leaves open the possibility of its having *more* parts, more divisions. He speaks of justice in the soul of an individual as the power which harmonizes the three parts, like so many musical notes, adding: "And if there are some other parts in between, he binds

Heart of Darkness

them together [as well] and becomes entirely one from many, moderate and harmonized" (443de).

For any of a number of reasons, the philosopher's introduction to psychology is worth reviewing. Not only must its limitations be clearly understood, it has a good deal more merit than seems to be generally appreciated.[7] Its beginning, moreover, has several intriguing features. First, there is the explicit warning that its validity *is* limited, and that one cannot get a *precise* (*akribēs*) understanding of the soul from the methods (*methodoi*) about to be employed. The analysis is intended to be sufficient for the immediate purpose: showing whether or not the soul has three forms in it corresponding to the natures of the three classes of the city in *logos*, such that the account of justice and the other virtues discovered through examining that city (with each of its three parts doing its own natural work well, manifesting its own virtue, and not meddling with the others) might also be applicable to the soul. We along with Glaukon are advised that there is also a "longer and fuller way" (*makrotera kai pleiōn hodos*), leading to a superior account of the soul as such (435cd; cf. 504b-d).

Second, Sokrates asks whether it isn't "altogether necessary" [*pollē anagkē*] to agree that the very same forms [*eidē*] and dispositions [*ēthē*] as are in the city are in each of us? Surely they didn't get there from somewhere else? (435e). Since this would seem to be the very point at issue, the philosopher's seeking immediate agreement to it ought to strike one as questionable, to say the least. Whether all the observable qualities that one could correctly ascribe to a city are reducible to the qualities of the composing individuals – and conversely, whether all the qualities an individual can manifest, a city can as well – are surely questions too serious and complex to be decided by a rhetorical appeal to untutored intuition. For example, one might call a city "well-counselled" because it employs cleverly designed deliberative institutions that tend to ensure that all proposed policies and laws will be thoroughly considered, perhaps on several successive occasions, or by separate deliberative bodies, with all relevant sources of information consulted, and purged of the influence of thoughtless passion (cf. 428b–e). This would be a characteristic of the regime itself, and not necessarily of a majority of its citizens, or even of those staffing its institutions. Put the same individuals in poorly designed institutions, and the regime would be poorly counselled, and thus poorly governed (regardless of the integrity of its officers). But the philosopher's own examples both clarify the question, and narrow it to the sorts of distinctly human qualities as could impart a basic character to an entire regime (cf. 544de). He suggests it would be ridiculous to think that spiritedness (*thumoeidēs*), or love of learning (*philomathēs*), or love of money (*philochrēmatos*) didn't originate with private individuals. And strictly speaking, one must agree: individual people, not cities, are spirited and loving; to attribute such qualities to a city can be regarded only as an elliptical way of speaking about the individuals (or succession of individuals) within it, and especially about the ones that count the most, those in the ruling class. Still, regimes can be variously structured so as to promote or dampen these qualities in their citizens, which is a principal reason why differences among regimes matter, and why it is practical to ascribe such qualities to the regimes themselves. Notice, however, a curious asymmetry in the philosopher's examples: spiritedness is not represented by either or both of its most characteristic loves, as are the other parts of the soul. There may be a reason for this.

Third, the philosopher follows something he assures us is *not* hard to know with something that *is*: "Do we learn with one, become spirited with another of the parts within us, and desire the pleasures of nourishment and generation and all their brethren with some third; or do we act with the whole soul in each, once we are started?" (436ab). It is a particularly difficult question because – somehow – both alternatives seem true to our experience of ourselves. On the one hand, learning and being angry and being thirsty seem to be radically different kinds of things; it's hard to conceive of such disparate experiences being manifestations of the very same element within us. On the other hand, each of us experiences himself as a single consciousness, as one person (barring pathology) – it is the same "I" who learns, becomes angry, or is thirsty. If the soul does have parts in some sense, with a different part responsible for each kind of experience, then what is it that *unifies* the consciousness, such that each of us naturally thinks of himself as one person? Certainly not the body, for it clearly has parts, some of which are dispensable, others of which are replaceable. One must presume that the living soul pervading a body is what unifies *it*, such that whatever happens to any part of it can be sensibly said to happen to one and the same person, and not simply to an assembly of contiguous, interchangeable parts (cf. 353d, 462cd, 572a, 577e, 579e, 609e–b, 611b–a).

But the most curious feature prefacing his short course on the soul is the elaborate lengths to which the philosopher goes in order to clarify a logical point that might otherwise lead to linguistic confusions and spurious disagreements – only to fail in achieving the analytical clarity at which he would have us aim. The logical point at issue is nothing more nor less than what we accept as the basic law of all reasoning, the insistence that two contradictory claims can't both be true (cf. 454a). Sokrates gives a peculiarly "psychological" version of it: "It's plain that the same thing won't be willing at the same time to do or to suffer opposites with respect to the same part and in relation to the same thing. So, if ever we find that happening in these things, we'll know it was not the same thing, but a plurality" (436bc; cf. 602e–a, 604b). Aside from a perhaps too ready presumption as to the clarity and reality of opposites (cf. 437b, 583c), there would seem to be little to quarrel with here.

But the philosopher apparently sees some point in pursuing greater analytical precision with respect to motion, asking first the quite general question as to whether it is possible for the same thing at the same time both to stand still *and* to move with respect to the same thing. Despite Glaukon's emphatic assurance that it is not, Sokrates none the less presents the example of a human being "standing still" while simultaneously moving his head and hands. After securing Glaukon's agreement as to how this would be correctly analysed and reported, the philosopher considers what he implies is a more "subtle" (or "refined") case, that of a top spinning on its axis, "or anything else going in a circle around the same spot" (cf. 424a, 546a, 616c–b), comparing the situation when its axis remains steady to that when the axis itself inclines or rotates as the top spins. He concludes his elaboration with a return to something similar to, but even more general than, the formulation with which he began, saying that they needn't be frightened by such semantic tricks, nor persuaded that the same thing at the same time, with respect to the same part and in relation to the same thing, could ever suffer, be, or do opposites (436ea). Despite all of his efforts, however, it seems that even this is not good enough, for he explicitly recommends that it be treated as an assumption, and that all reasoning based on it be subject to radical reconsideration should they find grounds for suspecting things might be otherwise.

Apart from the fact (noted above) that this logico-linguistic digression never gets the job done – rather conspicuously failing to consider the case of something at rest *on* something else which is moving, such as an entranced man on a sailing ship (cf. 488a–e, *Timaeus* 19b–c, *Laws* 789c–d) – it raises other questions. First, why does the philosopher choose *this* occasion, of all moments and topics, to clarify a basic principle of logic that would be germane to every argument in the dialogue, beginning with his refutation of Kephalos' view of justice? Is it because this is the most important thing to know about the human soul: the basic rule governing its employment of *logos*? Or is it because the human mind is the very thing that *can* hold contradictory positions simultaneously, if only unwittingly (and thus, one may wish to say, unwillingly; it is a special virtue of dialogue, and so of a soul with the capacity for it, that it can bring to light these contradictions as a precondition of their being exorcized)? Or is it because no strictly logical account of the human soul *can* do justice to its being at once a unity *and* a plurality? Second, why does the philosopher choose these particular examples: any "same thing", both at rest and in motion; a human being standing still yet moving his head and hands, as might an orator (cf. 514a); finally, a top rotating on an axis that can itself be either restrained, or allowed to wander as it will (might the soul have an "axis" that unifies its parts, and about which it "revolves"? – cf. 330e, 518d, 526e)? Third, why do these suggestive examples deal with *bodily* motion, when the point at issue will be the incorporeal motions of the soul, the motions and "emotions" felt within the consciousness?

Thinking about these questions does provide one with more than just a salutary warning about the ambiguity pervading ordinary language. One is reminded, for example, that nothing in the perceptible world is ever totally at rest or totally in motion; the solidest granite is steadily decaying in accordance with its nature, and yet we also wish – on pain of incoherence – to attribute such changing to some unchanging "it". Thus the perplexity the mind experiences in grappling with the problem of Being: is fundamental Nature Motion, or is it Rest, or is it somehow both at once (cf. 477a, 478c–d, 479b)? If the last is the case, and yet this violates what we take to be the fundamental law of all coherent thought – if one cannot think about Being, much less speak about it, without falsifying it – serious doubt is raised as to the natural compatibility between mind and reality, and thus about the reasonableness of the philosophic life (cf. 511d–e). And one is further reminded that, with respect to the human form of being, being alive presumes a multiplicity of active motions; and similarly, being conscious of being alive entails an awareness of motions in both body and soul (as is most clearly evident, perhaps, when one consciously attempts to be "perfectly at rest").

But what is most immediately important to notice about the philosopher's elaborate yet incomplete logical clarification is that he uses *physical* examples to elucidate *psychical* phenomena. Thus we are reminded of the – seemingly inescapable – necessity of our speaking and thinking of intelligible but insensible things in terms of the perceptible realm (cf. 611c–d). The words and concepts we use for dealing with invisible things, such as regimes and souls and virtues and powers, typically originate in language invented for communicating about the sensible realm of matter in motion, ... and yet we understand its application to this radically different realm without any difficulty whatsoever! We speak, quite naturally and coherently, about political things in physical terms: imperial expansion, balance of power, straddling an issue, separation of church and state, cultural decay, social stratification, economic growth, the collapse of a coalition, a gap between promise and performance, and so forth. In discussing our own and other people's inner experience, we readily resort to the language of bodily sensation, and refer to being grief-stricken, or light-hearted, or stung by criticism, to having wounded pride, a burden of guilt, or a dirty mind, to being hot-tempered (as opposed to cool, calm, and collected), to displaying a colourful imagination, or dark suspicions, a short memory, or large appetites; we easily distinguish between someone who is bubbling with enthusiasm and another who is boiling mad. Such figures of speech are so natural and commonplace (virtual clichés) that we scarcely notice that originally they were, one and all, metaphoric. The growth and adaptation of language through our amazing facility for employing it metaphorically are central to the mystery of how language works (for none of the apparent explanations of how it works really works). And, in turn, the uniquely human use of rational speech for both thinking and communicating is central to the problem of understanding human nature. Thus, these metaphors grounded in perceptible images point to a truly wondrous power of the rational soul – this perplexing, perplexable thing each of us is, and hence intimately familiar with, while understanding it hardly at all.

But our so readily resorting to metaphors may also betray a serious limitation of that soul. For perception depends on organs of the body, and these organs seem designed (or, to have evolved) primarily to serve the basic needs of the body, not the higher desires of the soul. To be permanently confined to speaking and thinking about intelligible but imperceptible things in the imagistic language of the perceptible realm may entail an incorrigible falsification in one's thinking about reality. But is it within the capacity of the human soul to know this? Or to do anything about it if so? Perhaps. For the philosopher himself subsequently refers to the need for a purely formal account of things and their relationships, "making no use of anything sensed in any way" (511c; cf. 510b).

"Know thyself" is doubtless good advice, but as Glaukon begins to realize, it's devilishly hard to follow (435c). For one desires to know that which one shares with others, the basic form of being that is common to us all – ironically named *homo sapiens* – but also what it is that differentiates oneself and others. Different bodies, obviously, but there's more to it than that: no two of us are as alike as peas in a pod. Thus, a comprehensive psychology, one that illuminates significant human diversity as well as commonality, must account for the discernible natural classes of people (such as those institutionally recognized in the city in *logos*); and observable differences in age cohorts (329a; cf. 561a); and any differences among the races (cf. 435ea); and especially what has traditionally been regarded as the greatest natural difference to be found among human beings, that which differentiates male and female (cf. 453c, 454d). With respect to this particularly challenging problem of dialectics, the dividing and collecting of human souls, the philosopher's introductory analysis dividing the soul into its three main parts focuses primarily on showing what humans have in common. But it is laced with hints as to why we are as different as we are.

Sokrates begins, appropriately enough, with that within us which wants or longs for anything; this entails as well a consideration of rejecting and not wanting. The basic longings and repulsions arise spontaneously, intruding without invitation into our awareness, and just as automatically recede when satisfied. He provisionally groups together thirst and hunger and the other *desires* (which cause the soul to long for and embrace something it wants to become its own), with *willing* (whereby the soul, as though having posed a question to itself, nods assent and attempts to fulfil that which is willed; 437c). This conflation of desire and will seems a mistake, and for the best of reasons: it *is* a mistake. But it is a revealing one. In fact, it is such a common mistake (Glaukon repeats it shortly thereafter; 439e) that we are tacitly being invited to see the reason for it. Comparing the philosopher's description of each provides a clue: willing is more deliberate, and deliberative; it is somewhat like responding to a question. But it has a close working relationship with the desires in much everyday practice, for it is the desires that urge the "questions", and in all animals and many people to desire something is practically tantamount to willing it. The philosopher's subsequent analysis is all about desire and nothing about will; moreover, it concludes with a reminder that the will does *not* always say 'yes' to a desire (439c). Similar remarks apply to the conflation of their opposites, "not wanting and not willing and not desiring", as if these were all the same sort of thing: the soul's thrusting away and driving out. However, we are meant to see that this problem is even more complicated, since it involves (apart from will) both the *temporary* rejections resulting from satiated desires, and the *constant*, positive, specific aversions and repulsions (which Sokrates does not – but the reader easily can – analyse by adapting the provided paradigm of positive, specific appetites).

The basic problem with understanding desire in the soul is less one of *distinguishing* among the various desires than it is that of showing why they are to be *collected together*, referred to by a common name, and attributed collectively to one discrete part of the soul (much as one must try to see why such an heterogeneous collection of craftsmen – from farmers and smiths to physicians and merchants – are regarded by the philosopher as belonging to the same natural political class). According to his analysis, all desires share a common *form* (and thus he seems to speak interchangeably of the soul's "parts" or "forms"): they are a longing for something more-or-less specific, and they are unintelligible apart from that for which they are a desire. The desire and its object are, as we might say, 'conceptually related'. This is most clearly revealed by analysing the simplest, most urgent, and most distinct desires, thirst and hunger. Thirst is the desire for drink, and hunger is the desire for food; these desires are as qualitatively distinct as are their objects. The philosopher chooses thirst for paradigmatic analysis. He contends that thirst *per se* is simple; if one feels a desire for some more specific kind of drink, this is due to additional bodily conditions acting in conjunction (e.g., the desire for a *cold* drink is due to being *hot* as well as thirsty). So long as one defines thirst as being the *body's* craving for water to replenish its liquids, and does not confuse *being thirsty* with the various reasons a *soul* might desire, say, wine (cf. 475a), this analysis seems sound enough.

The War Lover

But then the philosopher himself clouds the issue by raising the plausible objection that no one simply desires food and drink, but rather desires "beneficial" (*chrēstos*) food and drink, "for everyone, after all, desires good things" (*tōn agathōn;* 438a; cf. 359c, 505de). Thus, all the desires would seem to carry this tacit qualification: that something be "beneficial". The point having been raised, one wants immediately to "clarify" it by agreeing that everyone desires good things *for themselves;* or (better still) what they *believe* to be good things (as this might dispel one's uneasiness about denominating *all* desires as being for something truly *beneficial*, as opposed to merely pleasant). In any case, the obvious rejoinder to this reasonable objection is that the simple food and drink which one desires simply for sustenance *are* beneficial; that is *why* one has these desires. And the fact that the philosopher does not promptly dispose of the objection in such a straightforward manner is the more curious, given that later in the dialogue he makes this very point himself.

There, in order to show both what it is that truly distinguishes the natural Oligarch from the natural Democrat, and why the latter is mistaken in treating all desires as equal, Sokrates presents a more discriminating analysis of desires. He distinguishes between the few "necessary" desires, and the many "unnecessary" ones. The former are those that "we are by nature *compelled* to long for"; and these are actually of two quite distinct kinds, involving rather different (albeit related) ideas of 'necessity': the desires one simply cannot suppress; and those whose satisfaction is advantageous to us (558de; cf. 493bc). Whereas the "unnecessary" desires are those a person could rid himself of ("if he were to practise from youth on"), and whose presence does no good, "and sometimes does even the opposite" (559a). The example he uses to illustrate *both* sorts is the desire for food, with the desire for a simple, nutritious food such as bread being "necessary" on both counts (ineradicable, and helpful), whereas the desire for rich and palate-pleasing foods is "unnecessary" (559b–c; cf. 404c–d). Thus we see, incidentally, that often the particular things we long for involve a synthesis of various desires.

Of course, introducing into the analysis of desire such complexities as arise out of the interaction of the body's needs and the soul's preferences would subvert the intended simplicity of this preliminary account of the soul, an account undertaken (ostensibly) only for the more limited purpose of showing the pertinence to the individual soul of a certain idea of justice. The deeper investigation of desire (pursued still further in Book Nine and elsewhere) is doubtless part of that "longer and fuller way" the philosopher referred to initially, one which would lead to a more precise understanding of the soul. So, instead of the more complicated account of desire, he here engages in a complicated and somewhat bewildering digression about what might be called 'quantitative relations', or 'correlatives', or 'variable qualities'; and – stranger still – about distinguishing kinds of knowledge. When he at last returns to the supposedly simple matter of understanding thirst (439a), it is by no means obvious that he has clarified, much less resolved, the objection that presumably prompted all of this: that no one desires simply drink, but rather beneficial, or good drink. But since it was he, and not Glaukon, who raised the issue in the first place, one should not assume that this digression is nothing more than an obfuscating diversion which tests the young man's ability to endure distractions. It is more prudent to assume that it does somehow contribute to a better understanding of the question, and on that basis proceed to try to see quite how.

The entire discussion is about the various ways things may relate to other things. Whereas thirst is qualitatively distinct from hunger and other desires (to the extent that it is) by virtue of the *object* to which it is related – drink – being qualitatively distinct from food and other things (to the extent that *it* is; and the existence of soup is sufficient reminder that such distinctions are far from absolute); other things are related only among things of like kind, as "the greater" is to "the less", and "the much greater" to "the much less". Such correlatives are applied to other things in order to express variable or relative properties of these things, such that one can speak of a large drink or a small one, of more drink or less, answering to much thirst or little. The implication seems to be that good and bad, or beneficial and harmful, when applied to the various objects of one's desires, are "relative" in this same way. A given portion of a given kind of food at a given time for a given person is more-or-less beneficial, or a given drink more-or-less harmful, just as it is more-or-less large or small. None of these particular objects of desire is purely and absolutely good, just as none of them is absolutely large. And much as suitably similar kinds of things can be ranked according to relative size, they can be ranked according to relative goodness or beneficiality. Whether and how one can rank dissimilar things – and say, for example, which is greater or better, a city or a man (cf. 368e) – is less clear. Much less clear, actually.

The War Lover

The various special bodies of knowledge are also differentiated in a way analogous to that by which the desires are. Carpentry, for example, is a particular *kind* of knowledge because of its relationship to houses, being the skills and principles whereby they are built. This serves to remind us that most of the special kinds of knowledge are "arts" (*technai*), kinds of productive powers that exist primarily to secure the objects of our desires. And it is an especially poignant reminder that something may be the object of a congruence – or a conflict – of desires (as a house may be desired both as shelter for the body and as privacy for the soul). But the character of this defining relationship between a kind of knowledge and its object differs from the relationship between a desire and its object. A knowledge of carpentry is necessarily a knowledge of both good and bad houses (i.e., well or poorly constructed, in light of the purpose for which they are intended); a knowledge of medicine is necessarily knowledge of both sickness and health. But the knowledges themselves are not thereby both good *and* bad, sick *and* healthy. By contrast, desires themselves must somehow be evaluated as good or bad, sick or healthy. The distinguishing of desires in terms of "necessary" and "unnecessary", as referred to above, presumes just such an evaluation. The full complexity of this issue is perhaps made more vivid through a careful consideration of the other bodily desire the philosopher regularly associates with hunger and thirst, namely, sex (cf. 389e, 426a, 436a, 571c–d, 580e, 586ab; also 403a, 585ab). Moreover, the problem of evaluating the desires points to another kind of knowledge, essential to both the correct practical employment of the productive arts and to an adequate theoretical understanding of reality: knowledge of the Good (cf. 505a-b, 506a). It remains to be seen how this relates to the superintending kind of general knowledge the philosopher here displays in the course of referring to it: knowledge of knowledge and learning (involving still another way something can relate to something of like kind, but not as "greater" does to "lesser"). Similarly unclear at this point is precisely how the *desire* for *knowledge* of the Good relates to the Good itself, and whether desire for the good is a pervasive, superintending desire ruling a hierarchy of desires (accounting for, among other things, the desire to have only healthy and good, "necessary" desires).

Sokrates and Glaukon expressly agree, however, that thirst can be understood only in relation to drink, and that thirst *per se* is simple, being simply an impulse for drink, and not for any particular kind or quality or amount of drink. Whatever its merits as an analysis of thirst, as a *general* account of desire it seems to have some serious limitations. To be sure, there are obvious ways in which it can be extended. The desire for shelter, for example, may account well enough for the existence of the knowledge of carpentry, being the desire behind the desire for such knowledge. But what about one's desire to understand the human soul? This, indeed all desire for theoretical knowledge, does not answer to some desire that comes and goes in the manner of thirst, nor is the intensity of it roughly proportionate to the extent of deprivation (cf. 585a-c). Curiosity, while typically activated by wondering about something in particular, is distinguished precisely by its catholicity, by its *not* being a desire to know some particular kind of thing, but any and every thing (cf. 475b-c). And although people vary greatly with respect to the range and strength of it, virtually no one is without some trace of this "idle" curiosity. Or, consider the desire for honour, or for justice, for beauty, for victory, for revenge – all of which seem to have an especially close association with the spirit. While it remains true that these desires can be understood only in conjunction with their "objects", the formal and relatively non-specific, or even comprehensive character of these objects raises problems that have no counterpart in the contemplating of a glass of water.

Reflecting on such desires as these, one is led to conclude that what the philosopher has presented is a tolerably good analysis – not of desire as such – but of appetites, the *bodily* desires. And that what has first been discerned is that part of the total economy of the soul which represents the needs and yearnings of the body for food and drink, sex and sleep.[8] This, in fact, fits much better with its analogue in the city, the money-making or producing class, whose various arts and crafts serve first of all the wants of the body, and whose members are themselves motivated primarily by the money that provides the usual means of catering to the wants of their own bodies (cf. 580d-a). But they are certainly not the only ones in the city who are moved by desire. They are distinguished, rather, by the particular *class* of desires whence they derive their own *primary* (but not sole) motivation. To say that someone is motivated primarily by money or bodily desire is not to say that he is indifferent to honour, nor that he never does anything to satisfy his curiosity. Were that the case, we would not be speaking of different *classes* of human beings, but of different *species* of animals, as opaque to each other as are dogs and men. But the tacit acknowledgement that the other parts of the soul also assert themselves through characteristic desires or loves suggests that something common runs through the entire soul, a desirous core, as it were, or an erotic axis rather.

These reservations are confirmed, and other issues amplified if not altogether clarified, as the dialogue approaches what would seem to be its consummation: proving the superiority of the just and kingly life to that of the unjust and tyrannical. The philosopher offers three proofs for his thesis, which taken together purport to show that living in perfect accordance with natural justice – which is apparently identical with the philosophic life (cf. 619c–e) – is both freer and more pleasant. And he begins the central of these arguments with the reminder that "just as the city is divided into three forms", so too is the soul of an individual. This is followed by explicit acknowledgment that there seems to be a division of pleasures corresponding to the soul's parts, and similarly with respect to desires and ruling principles (580d). He does not expressly correlate this soul-related taxonomy of desires with their earlier classification into "necessary" and "unnecessary" (the latter being further subdivided into "law-abiding" and "lawless"; 571a–572b), but there is no incompatability between the two schemes. Any or all parts of the soul might have both necessary and unnecessary desires. He does, however, persist in calling one part of the soul *the* "desiring part" (*epithumētikon*) because of "what is biggest and strongest in it", those intense desires for food, drink, sex, and all their accompaniments. Because these desires for nutrition and procreation, which bulk so large in most people's lives, are the most familiar manifestations of *erōs*, it is natural to think of them as located in that "desiring" part of the soul. And, consequently, to think of the soul's three distinguishable motors (*logos*, *thumos*, and *erōs*) as each being located in distinct parts. But it is as important to recognize the limitations on this oversimplified analysis as it is to see its utility.

So, might all conflicting motions and tensions one feels in the soul be no more than a clash of appetites – one tugging towards this object, another towards that – or is there some different kind of thing in the soul, whose effects we experience but which cannot be accounted for in anything like the manner of hunger and thirst? The philosopher suggests that one way we could tell is if we ever feel conflicting urges towards the very same object, such as being thirsty, and thus feeling bidden to drink, but simultaneously something in us forbids us to drink, and so we are "not willing to drink" (439c; cf. 437c). It can't be an ambivalence in the desire itself (thirst), which *per hypothesis* is simple. The philosopher suggests that what forbids such immediate gratification of desire comes from calculation. Thus, it would not be "irrational" (*alogos*) to conclude that there is a second part in the soul, "the rational part" (*logistikon*), distinct from "the part with which it loves [*era*], hungers, thirsts, and is agitated by the other desires". This latter can be referred to as "the irrational [*alogiston*] and desiring part, companion of certain replenishments and pleasures" (439d).

It may not be irrational to conclude this, but it does seem a bit premature. After all, one might be thirsty, but find the smell of the available water repugnant (having an aversion, say, to its sulphurous odour). But thinking about situations like this actually strengthens the philosopher's analysis in two ways. First, such specific aversions can be treated as somewhat like negative counterparts to the appetites, analysed using the same paradigm, and assigned to the same irrational part of the soul, that of the bodily (or animalistic) appetites and aversions. Second, no one can mistake the experience of being thirsty but finding the water itself (or its container, or whatever) repugnant to one's senses with that of being thirsty and yet *unwilling* to drink for some *reason* (ranging from having grounds for distrusting the quality of the water, to purposely wishing *not* to drink at that time, e.g., in the midst of athletic training). Of course, the fact that the rational part can oppose the appetites shouldn't overshadow the fact that it can also serve the appetites, and does in most people most of the time, only opposing one appetite in the name of another – as when they pass up bread now in order to buy wine later (such denial of immediate gratification being something, so far as we can tell, animals never do). In many people, their reason seems but a slave of their appetites, employed mainly in finding an expeditious way of satisfying them to the maximum extent (cf. 553d). And virtually the sole evidence of reason's natural *ruling* role available to such people is provided by those occasions when it is deliberately summoned to adjudicate among conflicting appetites.

Now, while this much is sufficient for revealing that there *is* a second distinct part to the soul, it is far from an adequate understanding of that part. For as the philosopher subtly reminds us, our reason is at work this moment in trying to understand our soul – attempting to distinguish its parts, to see in what respects the various desires are the same and in what different – and its doing so bears scant resemblance to any adjudication among the appetites. Moreover, we have

The War Lover

been provided precious little insight as to the power this rational part has at its disposal. Glaukon is doubtless correct in observing that "erotic necessities" are more persuasive and compelling with the vast majority of people than are the logical necessities of geometry (458d). Still, as his observation concedes, the inherent power of reason in the rational soul of a human being is *not* negligible; clear reasoning *is* persuasive, and geometric proofs, once understood, *are* compelling – one cannot easily (*if at all*) believe other than what they show. Of course, such conclusions are "unopposed", as it were, the irrational parts of the soul being utterly indifferent to geometry.[9] And Glaukon's observation implicitly acknowledges another important point: rational considerations are more compelling with some people than with others. What could account for this besides disparities in the proportional strength of the various parts of their respective souls, which implies that each part does have a characteristic strength (perhaps derived from its characteristic desires or loves)?

The analysis carried just this far, however, is far enough to throw some additional light on a brief and powerful argument the philosopher presented earlier, in the course of explaining the sense in which their city in *logos* could be called "moderate". There, he began by making this observation:

> Moderation [*sophrosynē*] is order [*kosmos*] of a certain kind, and control [*egkrateia*] of certain pleasures and desires, as they say when they use – I don't know in what way – the expression 'stronger than himself' [or, 'master of himself'; *kreittō hautou*] and some others of the sort which are, as it were, its tracks. ... Isn't the phrase 'stronger than himself' ridiculous though? For, of course, the one who is stronger than himself would also be weaker than himself, and the weaker stronger; the same 'himself' is referred to in all of them. ... But this speech [*logos*] appears to me as if it wishes to say that, with respect to the soul, in the same human being there is something better and something worse, and when that which is by nature better controls that which is worse, one says 'stronger than himself'. At least it is praise. And when, from bad rearing or some association, the smaller and better part is dominated by the worse multitude, then this, as though it were reproachable, is blamed, and such a person is called weaker than himself, and licentious. (430e-b; cf. 389de)

Paradoxical as Sokrates pretends to find them, expressions such as 'self-restraint' and 'self-mastery' and 'self-control' are ones we all use quite naturally and sensibly. We explain someone's accident or mistake as due to his becoming so angry he lost control of himself; or characterize a grief-stricken (or embarrassed, or enamoured) person as having to struggle to retain, or recover, control of himself; the glutton, we say, has no self-restraint.

As the philosopher observes, these linguistic "tracks" reveal at least three very important facts about our tacit self-understanding: first, that we already implicitly recognize that our souls do, in some sense, have more than one part (or facet, or dimension, or some such thing); second, that these parts have a natural hierarchical order, with one part being better than the other(s) in that it is naturally *better suited to rule* one's whole self; and third, that we each of us "identify" more closely with that naturally better part – that this is one's "essential" or "true" self: only when *this* part is *in fact* ruling am "I" in control. One may *excuse* oneself or others for doing something foolish or destructive or immoral on the grounds of an "understandable" loss of self-control (resulting from extreme provocation or temptation, say); whereas one never *praises* oneself or others for such a loss of control, even should something good come of it (in which case, we're more apt to say, "Luckily, however, ... "). Sometimes, though, we speak more precisely about our experience of the irrational side of ourselves, and, for example, account for our failure to carry through what we have decided as being due to "weakness of will"; or we discriminate between someone's being "overcome by desire" and his being "overcome with emotion", or from having "lost his temper". Do not such figures of speech point to still another division in the soul, and the existence of another part?

And so, with "two forms [*eidē*] in the soul distinguished", the philosopher asks about that with which they have been especially preoccupied in educating their warrior-guardians: the spirit. Incidentally, for whatever it's worth, the first reference to a lover of wisdom is in conjunction with the fourth mention of spiritedness (375e), and the first mention of spiritedness is in conjunction with the fourth reference to courage (375ab). Its natural connection with victory (*nikē*) is observed there as well: "Then will a horse or dog, or any animal whatsoever, be willing to be courageous if it is not spirited? Have you not noticed how irresistible and invincible [*a-nikētos*] spirit is, so that its presence makes every soul fearless and indomitable in the face of everything?"

The War Lover

This encomium with which spiritedness is first introduced certainly seems inflated, but perhaps there is good reason for it. In any case, extraordinary spiritedness is the first quality of soul specified as essential to a potential guardian. Indeed, initially it is the *only* one ("And as for the soul's – that he must be spirited"; 375b). This is consonant with the fact that there is a far greater emphasis on the spirit in the *Republic* than in any other dialogue except the *Laws*. Well over four-fifths of Plato's explicit references to the spirit occur in these two dialogues. But there is an interesting difference in the terminology the philosopher uses in these, his two most important exemplifications of political philosophizing. Whereas in *Nomoi* the main term used to refer to spirit is the ordinary one (*thumos*; it occurs 49, or 7 × 7, times), this is *not* the case in *Politeia*. In the latter dialogue, *thumos* is mentioned but thirteen times, and instead the philosopher relies primarily on a term that scarcely occurs elsewhere in his writings, *thumoeidēs*, usually best translated by 'spirited' or 'spiritedness', but its literal meaning is 'spirit-formed'. He uses it exactly twenty-eight (i.e., 4 × 7) times. There may be more than one reason for this philological peculiarity, but surely its occurrence in a dialogue that would have us understand philosophy and almost everything else of importance in terms of forms (*eidē*) is not accidental.[10]

About this "spiritedness", then, is it owing to a third distinct part of the soul, "or would it have the same nature [*homophyes*] as one of the others?" Glaukon suggests it might be the same as the desiring part (439e). And this would probably be most people's guess. No one is apt to regard anger as an expression of reason, and most people simply distinguish between the rational part of themselves (with which they more closely identify), and the irrational. This is satisfactory so far as it goes, but it does not go far enough to be adequate as even a basic understanding of one's soul. For it indiscriminately lumps together the *desires* (those feelings intelligible only in relationship to some more-or-less specific object) with the *emotions*. These latter kinds of feelings – such as grief, pity, fear, love, hate, joy, honour, indignation, and especially anger – are *not* naturally keyed to some particular kind of thing, as thirst is to drink. One may find all sorts of things amusing or sad, fearful or pitiful; one can get angry at anything from a national policy to a balky drawer; and the range of particular objects one may love and hate seems as big as the world.

Sokrates responds to Glaukon's hypothesis with a three-part rebuttal that does considerably more than establish a clear distinction between spiritedness and desire. First, he recounts an intriguing anecdote about a spirited man, Leontios son of Aglaion. His avowal that he "trusts" the story is an incidental reminder that this is one more aspect of the rational soul to be accounted for: trust. Is there no more to it in a man than in a well-treated dog? Perhaps the tale itself will throw some light on this question, since there would be little point in telling it were it not self-evidently trustworthy. Leontios, apparently making the same journey as that which the philosopher recounts at the dialogue's beginning, was arrested along the way by a gruesome spectacle: the corpses of recently executed men. He desired to look but was also disgusted with himself for having such a desire. Probably most of us have had a comparable experience, finding some morbid sight (or story) both fascinating and repulsive; it can be a peculiarly intense and unsettling, even uncanny, experience. For a while Leontios battled with himself, covering his face. But at last, "overcome by the desire", he opened wide his eyes and ran towards the corpses, saying, "Look, damned wretches [*kakodaimones*], take your fill of the fair sight". The philosopher suggests that such experiences clearly indicate "that anger [*orgē*] sometimes makes war against the desires as one thing against another" (440a). On the assumption that anger is the most prominent and characteristic expression of the spirit – and this is true virtually by definition: the spirit is, whatever else, the seat of anger – this would seem sufficient for the immediate purpose of distinguishing the spirited or "angering" part from the desiring.

But the philosopher follows this argument with another that, for all its simple brevity, is even more powerful and revealing. We commonly get angry and reproach ourselves for giving in to our desires, acting contrary to what our rational part determines would be best. Here, it seems, our spirit clearly reveals itself to be the natural "ally of *logos*". Whereas we hardly ever have the opposite experience: getting angry at ourselves for being ruled by reason (440a–b). In the struggle between reason and appetite, the will does not weigh in on the side of the latter; rather, we *will* one thing (that which we deliberately choose), while *desiring* something else. We may get angry or resentful in a general sort of way when things turn out such that we could have said 'yes' to our desires without suffering ill consequences. And we may regret miscalculations, and even reproach ourselves for being poor or careless reasoners (the implication being to put one's rational faculties to *better* use, *not* worse). And even in the extreme case where repeated failures of his best-laid plans tempt a person to trust his

The War Lover

instincts rather than rational analysis – perhaps vowing, like Macbeth, "From this moment on, the very firstlings of my heart shall be the firstlings of my hand" – this disenchantment with reason still concedes the natural rule of reason inasmuch as such a resolution is presumed to be rationally justified by an analysis of actual experience. But we do not normally get angry at ourselves and reproach ourselves, or feel disappointed in ourselves, for following reason rather than the appetites. And this would seem to be a fact of profound importance, pertinent both to the distinction between the appetitive part and the spirit, and to the contention that there is a natural affiliation between reason and spirit. This latter aspect receives further support from the philosopher's providing still a third argument for regarding the spirit as distinct from the soul's desiring part.

He asks Glaukon to consider the difference between a person's reaction to his suffering justly and that of his suffering unjustly. Not that we are always so objective when judging in our own case. No doubt this is why he suggests that the "nobler" (*gennaioteros*) a person is, the more pronounced the difference would be. The nobler a person is, "the less is he capable of anger" at someone who is justly inflicting hunger, cold, or other bodily discomfort on him, and "his spirit would not be willing to rouse itself" against the one who's causing the discomfort. Something similar would apply, it seems, in all cases where a person recognizes his suffering to be in his own or the common good (e.g., in military training). Whereas, when someone believes he's been done an injustice, does not his spirit "boil and become harsh and ally for battle with what seems just?" It will then willingly endure those very same discomforts – hunger and cold and whatever – so as to stand firm and be victorious, not ceasing in its "noble efforts [*tōn gennaiōn*]" until it has either succeeded, or met its end, or, like a dog called back by a shepherd, it is gentled by *logos* (440cd). One might add that this discriminating reaction according to whether one believes suffering to be just or unjust is even more readily apparent when one is a "disinterested spectator", and not personally involved on the side of either sufferer or perpetrator. One does not have to be endowed with an especially noble nature to react with great indignation (even long after the fact) to the unjust punishment of a total stranger; whereas there is a sense of satisfaction (even if tinged with some sadness or regret) in seeing justice done through the well-deserved punishing of someone equally unknown.

Correct as this reasoning seems to be, one might still wonder how it serves to show that the spirited part differs from the desiring. Presumably, the point is that were the spirit either akin to the appetites, or naturally allied to them, it *would* be roused in support of the desires for food and bodily comfort, regardless of the supposed justness or unjustness of one's being deprived of these things. The desires themselves do not discriminate; one is no less cold or hungry for being justly so. But the philosopher may be hinting as well that the desires are the root cause of injustice, whereas the human spirit – as revealed in the uniquely human passion of indignation, and as displayed most clearly, if not most powerfully, in cases where one's own interests are not involved – is indeed the natural ally of *justice*, much as it is the natural ally of *logos* (which may itself indicate something important about true justice). This latter point is further confirmed here in that the spirit is utterly reliant upon reason to distinguish between just and unjust suffering (as it is in the case of all other emotional reactions: it is only by virtue of reason that one can discern when something is pitiful or sad or loathsome or threatening, rather than joyous or funny or reassuring). There is, of course, no guarantee that the rational part will do its allotted work well; yet neither is there much evidence that righteous indignation is any the weaker for the opinions guiding it being dead wrong. In fact, the less examined one's opinions about justice, the more adamant the spirit is apt to be. For it is only through coming to see justice as a difficult *question* that one begins to moderate one's passionate reactions to the various practices of this world, filled as it seems to be with injustices of all imaginable kinds and degrees.

Glaukon completes the effort of both distinguishing spiritedness from desire and showing it to be the natural ally of reason by observing that this conclusion corresponds nicely to their city, in that the guardians were likened to the true herdsmen of the city and the auxiliary warrior class to their obedient dogs (440d). This, of course, implies that those of the money-making, producing class are like sheep or cattle. And we earlier were reminded that the essential difference between the useful dog and the dangerous wolf it is set to guard against is a civilizing nurture (416a; cf. 334a, 343b, 345b–d). On the assumption that the philosopher and his two young timocratic auxiliaries exemplify the relationship between herdsman and dogs, one might give special consideration to those instances when they are insistent in their pursuit of what they believe to be just, but he whistles them back and restores calm to their souls (e.g., 419a–421c, 519d–520e).

However, the surprising evidence that the spirit is especially related to reason raises the possibility that it might actually be an aspect of that part after all, with the consequence "that there are not three forms in the soul but two, the rational and the desiring" (440e). The pointed references to the city in *logos*, made here separately by both the philosopher and his auxiliary, could be seen as heightening this possibility, given that the guardians all originate in the spirited warrior class. And so they turn to this question, only to dispose of it in remarkably short order, quickly finding three pieces of evidence that seem to imply a clear distinction between spirit and reason. First, Glaukon, attesting that the difference is easy to see, cites the example of small children, some of whom are born chock full of spiritedness but all of whom are devoid of reason, which makes its appearance only later, in most cases much later – and in some cases never, he adds with pardonable exaggeration. Sokrates swears in appreciation of such a fine, swift insight, adding that one could make the same point using the example of spirited but irrational beasts. And as a final piece of evidence, he calls upon Homer to testify that the rational part can rebuke "that which is irrationally spirited, as though it were a different part" (441b–c). The line he quotes here, about Odysseus' smiting his breast and reproaching his heart with speech, he had approvingly cited earlier as well (390d). One presumes such employments of poetry exemplify the proper relationship between it and philosophy. Be this as it may, the philosopher now concludes that, for all the difficulties of negotiating these deep and dark waters, they have reached agreement "that the same classes [*genē*] as are in the city are in the soul" (441c). And the way is at last clear to discern the same form of justice in both.

But a pause here seems appropriate. True enough, the quality that has dominated attention thus far in the dialogue, spiritedness, has been shown to reside in a third distinct part of the soul. But further reflection on the evidence supplied for this conclusion raises some disturbing questions for the philosopher's additional claim that the spirit is the natural, but subordinate ally of the rational part in its struggle to rule the appetites. For example, the vignette about Leontios and the corpses is worth further pondering. His turbulent reaction – while hardly surprising, but (on the contrary) both normal and appropriate – turns out to be quite perplexing when one tries to account for it. For beyond the strange attraction-repulsion most people feel regarding scenes of death and destruction and acute suffering (puzzling enough, to be sure), there are several potentially complicating factors in this case, not the least being one's passionate reaction to the stern exaction of justice, mingled perhaps with an awareness of human fallibility and vulnerability. Thus, it is easy to see why the necessity of providing a clear, coherent, fully convincing explanation of Leontios' psychic experience might well bring to an abrupt halt anyone's ascent to self-knowledge.

In any event, one can scarce avoid suspecting that the powerful desire which so maddened Leontios, and to which he finally succumbed, somehow involves *curiosity* – granted, what we rush to qualify as *morbid* curiosity – but curiosity none the less: the desire to know what and why and how, moving one to inquire and explore and observe new things. And curiosity, along with the desires for clarity and coherence and truth, seems to belong to the rational part of the soul (certainly not to the naturally lower, appetitive part), being essential to its acquiring the understanding of things whence is derived its competence and thereby its right to rule. But the spirit's reaction in this kind of case is surely peculiar. After all, we do not typically become furious with ourselves for seeking to satisfy the rational desire to know, and to see for ourselves. Usually, as noted above, our inner struggles are between irrational desire and a will to follow reason (603cd). Still, a milder version of Leontios' reaction is perhaps experienced in the self-disgust and shame one may feel for being attracted by the sight of freaks and monstrosities and deformities, or even to prurient gossip (eternally popular though it be).

Why *is* the spirit aroused in such cases? Is the rational part itself divided? Is there a reason *not* to look, or not to listen, with which the spirit might be siding? This is a possibility. If curiosity is a simple, catholic desire to know, mustn't it be some other part of reason (perhaps even some other desire of reason) that interests us in discriminating between what is worth knowing and what is not, and thus be naturally responsible for superintending curiosity? One mustn't forget that just such discrimination distinguishes a lover of wisdom from the various lovers of opinion, and should distinguish an adult from a child (475e–477b, 475bc). But a preference for not wasting one's time on trivia would hardly account for the vehemence and uncanniness of one's reactions to so-called morbid attractions.

Might Leontios' revulsion, then, be due (or partly due) to something inherent in the spirit itself? Perhaps each part of the soul has its characteristic aversions as well as desires. Is there, for example, an atavistic aversion to death and decay rooted in the spirit (as the natural complement of a brute fondness for life), something which is instinctively aroused in such cases, an irrational reaction akin to pity? If so, the spirit has a complexity not recognized thus far in Sokrates' psychology, since it is precisely spirited men who are presumed most capable of fighting and killing, doing so with Macbethean gusto even, "Nothing afeard of what thyself didst make, Strange images of death." Or might there be an aversion to what is instinctively recognized as ugly or shameful, a natural complement to the spirit's love of beauty and nobility? Either of these possibilities seems to argue for there being something in the spirit that is *not* readily subservient to the rule of one's reason – indeed, it may be profoundly recalcitrant to such rule. But what is most unsettling for the philosopher's analysis thus far is the fact that, in this instance at least, Leontios seems to identify with *his spirit*: torn between whatever in him *wants* to look, and his will *not* to look, he sides with the latter, blaming his *eyes* for leading the real *him* astray (cf. 507c–508d, 518c–d). And is not his the normal reaction?

Further reflection on the spirit's possible reactions when its own desires conflict with reason reveals a second cause for hesitation in agreeing that these two parts are natural allies. Presuming that the appeal of beauty is to the spirit, how then is it possible to enlist its support in the rational censorship of poetry and other kinds of beautiful music? The philosopher never suggests that his rational standard of noble beauty (the Good; or, rather, what prudence determines to be good; 452de) is that which almost everyone naturally subscribes to – quite the contrary: it is as alien to popular conceptions as is his idea of the truly comic. The comprehensive supervision of the arts is required precisely because the beauty that pleases most men is, as often as not, only skin deep, and attracts irrespective of its benefit or harm to either city or man. Still, as he later remarks, occasionally a man *will* force himself to reject something he finds beautiful, and to which (hence) he is attracted – be it a person or a poem – renouncing it on the basis of a rational judgment that loving it is not beneficial (607d–e). How is this possible if the spirit is both the source of power enforcing reason's rejection *and* the element in the soul being attracted?

Similar remarks apply to honour. The desire for honour, like other desires, supposedly has a simplicity to it. It is simply the desire for honour *per se*, and – since limited bodily capacities are not involved – for as much as can be got (reflected in the philosopher's using it as an example of how a true lover of something loves the whole of it;

475ab). But if love of honour is one of the most characteristic expressions of the spirit, how can its power be marshalled in support of a rational discrimination amongst honours, being content to partake of only those that reason determines will make one better, rejecting any not deemed harmonious with promoting and maintaining a rational and just regime within (591b–a)?

Still a third ground for reservation concerns the evidence cited in distinguishing spirit from reason. The very mention of spiritedness in small children and other animals should remind us that, in cases such as these where reason is virtually non-existent, the spirit is clearly an ally or servant of the appetites. There is a difference worth noting, however, between a child's angry fit brought on by frustrated desire, and those occasional bouts of what seems to be sheer wilfulness (which are apt to make their initial appearance upon a child's first learning to say 'no'). Strength of spirit can manifest itself – and not only in small children – as a kind of brute obstinacy that not only is no ally of reason, but often seems directly contrary to it (thus some people are spoken of as "just plain contrary"). In the interest of maintaining self-mastery and freedom, the spirit is unwilling to accept the inferiority implicit in being led by the reasoning of others, even should its own reason recognize the suitability of doing so. The reference to Odysseus' berating his own heart raises a different kind of complication, however. The hero has returned home incognito, and witnessed some of the women of his household freely cohabiting with the insolent suitors of his wife and estate, who have been exploiting the hospitality of his house during his absence. He was made angry at the sight, and filled with a lust for revenge. As Homer tells it (*Odyssey* XX, 1–25), this warrior's heart growled within him as does a bitch with whelps at the sight of some man she doesn't know. Despite being hopelessly outnumbered, he felt an urge to attempt dispatching them all, then and there. But he found the will-power to resist such a suicidal effort by reminding himself that he had already proven capable of enduring worse provocation before (when the Cyclops was devouring his comrades), and by applying his mind to how he *could* accomplish successfully what his heart so fervently desired. The incident seems to show, whatever else, that the spirit can be exerted against itself, and perhaps even turn on itself, as when one is angry at oneself for being carried away by anger.

The War Lover

These apparent contradictions and other complications may dissolve, however, in light of the recognition that the spirit itself has two parts. There is a lower half, more akin to that found in animals; it is an instinctively selfish part, in which is seated a love of one's own and the familiar, and a hostility to the strange. And there is a higher, more distinctly human half, that takes pleasure from order and beauty and power and harmony as such, irrespective of their further bearing upon one's own immediate welfare. Only this higher, more educable half of the spirit is by nature a reliable ally of reason; for, as most of us know from experience, even one's sense of beauty is capable of being elevated and refined through rational instruction. One might think of the human spirit as a more-or-less ill-matched team of horses yoked together in the soul. One is noble and light and well-behaved, receptive to the inducements of the driver, and obedient to his commands. The other is dark and unruly, more responsive to the weight of the chariot than to the directions of the charioteer. In most people, the dark horse seems the stronger, though neither is especially strong. Only a blessed few have a strong team in which the light horse leads. But as neither horse – much less the driver – can go anywhere without the other, one's spirit as a whole is strongest when, for whatever reasons, the team works in coordination, and one experiences a unity of will and feelings. Such is the case, for example, when one pursues victory in things that bring honour. Or when defending oneself or one's own against perceived injustice. In any event, virtually all expressions of the spirit manifest the efforts – for or against – of both members of its team. So, in one sense, the soul has three parts: chariot, driver, and team. Seeing this much is sufficient for an introductory psychology. But a more refined and fuller analysis requires recognizing that in another, and at least equally important, sense, the soul has *four* parts. For certain phenomena of human experience are unintelligible unless one distinguishes the two horses, seeing them as related (they are both horses) but none the less significantly different elements of the spirit (as different as the natures of two horses can be).[11]

This *division in the spirit* is revealed in many ways, but perhaps never so clearly – or ironically – as in our equivocal attitude towards victory, ... someone else's victory, that is. Not always, to be sure, but often enough, we both admire another's achievement *and* resent it, enjoy it and yet regret it. Feeling grateful for the nobility of the performance, we are moved to a generous praise of the performer; but at the same time envying him, we may feel resentment or spite. What accounts for such opposing inclinations towards the very same thing? As none of these feelings seems a direct manifestation of either calculation or appetite, where is one to look but *within* the spirit? Is it not the noble half of the spirit that swells in exhilaration at the beautiful sight of excellence displayed in victory, whereas it is the base element of the spirit that feels the pain of envy, and resents the cause of it? Of all the kinds of inner factiousness to which we humans are prone, *this* may be the most dangerous and discouraging, the ugliest disharmony, and the most debilitating sickness we suffer from: *our equivocal attitude towards human excellence*. Part of us admires it, identifies with it, is inspired and uplifted by the very sight of it. But part of us profoundly resents it, feeling humiliated and disadvantaged and depressed by it; confronted with one's inferiority, one wishes, if only momentarily, there were no differences of rank among us, and no need to strive to excel.

As wise men and women have long recognized, this human form of soul we share is flawed, compounded as it is out of varying proportions of beast and god, not altogether at home in the material world but with only episodic access to another. What more precisely the psychological root of the problem is, however, has been a perennial source of dispute. The "longer and fuller" account of the soul, synthesized from evidence and arguments dispersed throughout the dialogue, suggests that flaw is a fissure in the spirit, a cleavage in that part of the soul which must mediate between the low and the high, between the demands of the body and the aspirations of the mind. One side speaks for what is divine and masterful and aristocratic in us, the other for what is brutish and slavish and egalitarian, that within us which is resentful of all rank, privilege, and surpassing excellence. If such is our nature, then no one is born free of this germ of evil, this taint of original sin. There is a malicious numen glowering in the darkness of every human heart. What none the less distinguishes the noble few from the vulgar many – the natural difference between Greeks and barbarians, one might say – is that the former not only despise this baseness in others, but also recognize it in themselves, are ashamed of it, and resolve to master it, to overcome it, if possible to root it out. Whereas the others too happily indulge it.

As has been often noted, the passion most readily and closely identified with the spirit is anger. And as manifested in that peculiarly human form we call indignation, anger has a special pertinence to this dialogue. First, there is its necessary connection with the will to justice (cf. 440c–d, 536c). That there is a different kind of necessary connection between justice and *truth*, and thus between a passion for justice and a love of truth, is perhaps more easily seen. Beyond the purely formal agreement that by 'justice' we mean 'the right way to do things', we are all reasonably confident that being just involves – whatever else – dealing fairly and honestly with one's fellows, or at least with one's political partners. And that it generally requires speaking the truth to them, though with tacit allowance made for adapting it to the relevant conventions of politeness. And that it sometimes requires some of us exerting ourselves to discover or report the truth about what people say and do, or have said and done, and the consequences thereof. And, not to be forgotten, justice presumes that there is a truth about justice itself.

However, the spirit's involvement with justice is no less crucial than reason's. As noted before, there are plausible grounds for believing that the spirit – or a part of it – has an intrinsic appreciation for beauty and order, for health and strength, with a complementary disdain for what is ugly or chaotic, and an outright repugnance for disease and decay. To what besides the spirit can we attribute such responses? But if the evidence for this conclusion remains problematic to some extent, there need be no comparable reservation as to the spirit's evincing an instinctive sense of propriety, as manifested most clearly in righteous indignation on behalf of others. What else is being displayed when one's temper burns at the thought of public authorities punishing someone they know to be guiltless, or of some innocent and helpless person being tortured for the perverse amusement of his tormentors, or even of wanton and pointless destruction of anything beautiful or useful? Add to this the spirit's desire for revenge – which is both unique to human beings, and its satisfaction uniquely sweet; and which, operating in conjunction with the rational part's desire for truth, constitutes the synthetic desire that wrongdoers get their just deserts (something distinct from but complementary to the concerns for deterrence, restitution, and reformation) – and one begins to see that the spirit's contribution to justice is equally vital with that of reason. Spirit without reason lacks rectitude, proportion, and impartiality; reason without spirit lacks energy and commitment for either prosecution or execution.

Yet, as hinted above, this division of labour within the soul poses problems of its own. However refined one's judgment, weakness of spirit results in a feeble championship of justice: it will not generally be pursued with sufficient vigour, nor will the soul be firm in its determination to punish wrongdoers with sufficient severity (cf. *Laws* 730d). Often the prevalence of injustice in political life is due more to the softness of otherwise good men than to the evil ambitions of bad men. Such softness can itself incline one to a kind of blindness. Whereas the failure of the rational part to do its work well may result not only in true justice miscarrying in many particular cases, but in a fanaticism about what is believed to be just. For the work of the rational part includes more than seeking the truth concerning what is perfectly just (which in practice entails appreciating the extent to which one's *knowledge* of it remains *im*perfect). It must also determine the "just" place of justice among other important human concerns (such as freedom and survival). And it must make a prudent assessment of the extent to which everyday life can be expected to manifest justice (men being men and not angels, or even supermen). And it must recognize the destructive consequences of a single-minded insistence on perfect justice, even presuming someone knew what it is.

Precisely because the human spirit can be so powerfully aroused in the name of justice, it can become the single greatest threat to the very decency in political life it aspires to promote. Political decency presumes moderation, and not least of all in one's expectations of a polity's justness (cf. 549c, 562b-c). This moderation, in turn, grows primarily out of realistic assessments of practical possibilities. Whereas no passion – certainly not joy, nor pity, nor grief, not even erotic love (cf. 474d-e) – can so *distort* one's judgment as can righteous indignation (cf. 419a). But this means that an ill-disciplined or ill-led spirit can be as great a threat to the *pursuit of wisdom* as it is to wholesome *politics*. Hence, there is a double reason for becoming aware of one's ignorance about justice: an appreciation of the *questionableness* of justice is of paramount importance for *both* the practical *and* the theoretical concerns of one's life. As for the latter, justice is not only a worthy problem in its own right, calling for the greatest power of synoptic judgment – a philosophical challenge of the first order. But beyond that, unself-conscious ignorance about justice can distort one's perspective on everything human.

Thus it is the equivocal nature of the human spirit that provides the key to understanding why the dialogue ostensibly devoted to an examination of *justice* is also its author's fullest explication of *philosophy*.

And so, while the potentially noble manifestations of the spirit necessarily have a greater prominence in this dialogue, the philosopher reminds us before it is over that there is an emotional dark side to the spirit, too. For it – or part of it – is also the seat of feelings that have little or no redeeming value in a human being, notably envy and resentment and spite. These base expressions of spiritedness are the emotional counterparts of the unnecessary desires, introducing still more needless and useless (and usually destructive) hostility into human affairs. Their very existence alongside indignation and generosity and compassion seems to point to the spirit's Janus-like nature, suggesting that it must have a base, dark, ugly facet, as well as a noble, light, beautiful one.

Envy (or, grudgefulness; *phthonos*) is explicitly associated with the love of honour (586c), and it's no great mystery why. This is the side of brutish self-centredness, which is not merely preoccupied with one's own well-being most narrowly conceived, but can be positively hostile to that of others (captured in our epitomizing spite as a "dog-in-the-manger" attitude). Evolutionary biologists can readily account for the presence of such a disposition in the psychic economy of an animal by showing that its inclination to behave in certain ways prejudicial to the well-being of its competitors often has long-run 'survival value' for itself or its offspring. But being ruled exclusively by such a survival concern is precisely the mark of animality. It should go without saying (but given the presuppositions prevalent in our time, it probably doesn't), envy is something of which a genuine philosopher is free, one more respect in which he is akin to the divine (500b–c; cf. 476e, 500a, 528a; *Phaedrus* 247a). Or, alternatively stated, it is something of which anyone who aspires to become philosophical must free himself. Envy is expressly associated with a tyrannical nature, or with the tyrannical inclination in human nature (579bc, 580a).

But if envy may occasionally have some constructive result (e.g., moving a person to better himself), there is nothing to be said for resentment, common though it be. If made to choose between all having none and some having more than others, resentment prefers the former: *that* is its essential structure, and to the extent that a person is resentful, his perspective on justice is distorted by spite. Sad to say, much of the egalitarian impulse in modern life seems fuelled by resentment rooted in the baser, irrational side of the spirit, and deserves to be distinguished from whatever yearning for equality might result from an overflowing generosity of spirit. But if resentment is invariably ugly, that ugliness is compounded when it is the response to benefits received. Nor is such a response unusual. Whereas gratitude is arguably the most fundamental expression of natural justice (being the minimal repayment of one's debts, and sometimes the only possible kind of repayment; cf. 331d, 338b, 520a–b), resentment of one's benefactors is not merely unjust, but in going beyond ingratitude's neglect of justice, it is gratuitously offensive (if a play on words might be permitted here). Indeed, there may be no surer sign of ignobility, nor clearer evidence of a lack of natural grace, than such resentment.[12]

This analysis of the spirit receives a subtle confirmation, as well as a rather interesting amplification, in the discussion comparing the tyrant's soul with that of the kingly man (580a–592b). While reaffirming that there are three basic forms embraced within the architectonic form of the rational soul (580d), the philosopher also makes plain that there can be subordinate forms or parts within the form of a given part: "One part ... was that with which a human being learns, and another that with which he becomes spirited; as for the third, because of its many forms [*polyeidia*], we had no specific name to call it by, but we named it for what is biggest and strongest in it", i.e., the "desiring" part (consequently the "money-loving" and "gain-loving" part, for it is the source of greed within us – that which for ever wants more "means", to the point that acquisition seems desirable in itself; 580d–a). To this evidence can be added that found in the geometrical centre of the dialogue where, coordinate with a basic ontology, are presented certain subdivisions of the rational part (i.e., the powers of imagination, of trust, of analysis and calculation, and of synthetic intuition; 511d ff).

The human soul, then, may be understood as forms nested within forms within a form, much as the dialogue itself is a story comprising stories within stories (cf. 376d). The subdivisions of the most crucial part, however, the spirit, are never made explicit. Presumably, the philosopher has left them for the reader to discover for himself, and in himself. But he has left no shortage of clues. For example, after suggesting that there is a single kind of pleasure and desire and ruling principle peculiar to each part (580d), he goes on to ask two leading questions about the spirit that together manifest an interesting asymmetry: "Don't we say that the spirited part is always wholly set on mastery [or, being strong; *kratein*] and victory and good reputation [*eudokimein*]? ... If we were to designate it victory-loving and honour-loving, would that strike the right note?" (581ab; cf. 443d). One is

The War Lover

hereby invited to ask, what about calling it 'mastery-loving' (or, 'strength-loving'; cf. 338c)? Something must account for a noble human being's love of freedom and independence and self-control – and for love of the *power* these things presuppose (cf. 431a, 577de, 579c). And while often in practice – indeed, probably most times – the desires for and the pleasures of mastery and victory and honour are experienced as a single synthetic desire.or pleasure, analysis of other experiences reveals them to be distinct, does it not?

Thus, one cannot accept unreservedly the results of the contest over which way of life is most pleasant (581e; cf. 588a), since the philosopher reduces the contestants to the wisdom-lover, the honour-lover, and the gain-lover (582a–583a). And this despite having just asserted that "the three primary classes [*ta prōta tritta genē*] of human beings are ... wisdom-loving, *victory*-loving, gain-loving" (581c). The pleasures of victory as such (i.e., the personal satisfactions of success and achievement, of proven mastery and power, of doing one's best, perhaps being the best) are never considered, much less the sheer joy of being strong and free and master of oneself. And within the parameters of what *is* compared, he leaves it to us to determine from our own experience whether "the pleasure that comes from knowing" comes more from the *knowing itself*, or from the successful *pursuit* of knowledge – is it more from the "hunt", the "chase", the "capture", or from the "possession"?

This central of the three "proofs" purporting to show that the fully just and kingly life is superior to the most unjust, tyrannical life tacitly appeals to one's own experience of various kinds of pleasure, and invites one to rank them as to their pleasantness. The third such proof offers an explanation of sorts as to *why* certain pleasures yield a purer and more lasting satisfaction, if not necessarily a more intense enjoyment in every case. It requires our acknowledging the fact that much of what we regard as pleasure is but relief from pain, a returning of the soul to some intermediate condition of repose. And similarly – but, it would seem, less plausibly – that much of what we regard as painful is but the cessation of pleasure (583c–a). Thus we are to distinguish true, pure, and absolute pleasure (and pain), from their mere phantoms and shadows, those relative and mixed, so-called pleasures (and pains). The philosopher argues that pleasures of the mind are the finest examples of the former, whereas the most and greatest of the bodily pleasures epitomize the latter (584c, 585a–586c). And while he speaks of the typical expressions of *frustrated* spiritedness

(586cd), its surrogate satisfactions as it were, he does not explicitly categorize the various pleasures one's spirit may enjoy. That is to say, he leaves it for us to judge for ourselves which pleasures of the spirit are more like the ephemeral pleasures of the body, and which more solid and lasting, more akin to the pleasures of knowing and of exercising virtue. Of course, with only rare exceptions, fame is notoriously fleeting. Moreover, as a hundred generations of athletes can attest, being honoured is the one kind of pleasure whose cessation feels like pain. This is not necessarily so with victory. Whatever honour attends it may be quickly dissipated, but the victory itself is for ever. And seen in that light, it can be a source of lasting satisfaction, savoured for as long as the victor values his achievement. Most satisfying are those victories with constructive consequences, and ones that something more can be built upon. In short, there are ample grounds for rationally preferring a life founded on the love of victory to that of a lover of honour, whose life rests on sand.

The philosopher completes his comparison of perfectly just and unjust men by "moulding in *logos* an image of the soul", representing the desiring part by a "multi-coloured, multi-headed beast" (including heads of both "tame and savage beasts"), the rational part by a human being, and the spirit by the "single idea of a lion" – but all enclosed within the appearance of a human being (588b–e). However, in employing this composite image to compare different states of soul, and having already explained why licentiousness is blameworthy (it fattens and strengthens the "terrible, big, and many-formed beast" in us), he asks, most strangely, "And aren't stubbornness and bad temper blamed when they inharmoniously foster and exert the lionlike *and the snakelike* part?" (590ab). Suddenly, for some reason, there are *two* beasts representing the spirit, and of radically different symbolic stature. The only other mention of the snake is in Glaukon's characterization of that high-spirited rhetorician, Thrasymachos, who, he suggests, was "like a snake, charmed more quickly than he should have been" (358b). Lions are tamed, snakes are charmed. Music charms (411b), as does pleasure in general (413c). Poetry has special charms (601b, 607c), and the philosopher's own critique of it tacitly presumes a division in the spirit (cf. 604c–d, 606a–c). But there are few charms more effective with most spirits than well-crafted flattery, which we are warned can make even a lion behave like an ape (590b; cf. 620c).

— 5 —

Crime and Punishment

Having distinguished two kinds of timocrats – one who is predominantly victory-loving by virtue of the nobler side of his spirit being stronger, that which is attracted to beauty and challenge and excellence; and another in whom the love of honour is stronger because that part of the spirit dedicated to utility and the self and one's own tends to dominate – we can now better understand the characters of Glaukon and Adeimantos and their respective roles in the dialogue. Both are "sons of Ariston, a renowned man whose race is divine". Both have earned celebrity as warriors, and show themselves bold in other respects as well. Both are obviously intelligent, with quick, agile minds, active imaginations, and sound memories. And both reveal traces of the entire constellation of loves that defines the timocratic nature. If one has more of an eye for beauty, the other has more of an ear for it (compare 357c with 367cd; cf. 475d). Neither brother – nor anyone else, for that matter – is influenced exclusively by one side of the spirit. Most expressions of spiritedness evidence, to varying degrees, the contributions of both parts, the two halves themselves being, as it were, brothers. Both young men, in short, are blessed with precious metals in their souls, and in ranking them there is a risk of unjustly exaggerating the strengths of one and the weaknesses of the other. But perhaps this is forgivable in the interests of clarity.

Begin with the fact that Adeimantos precipitates the discussion of the timocrat's nature with the observation, "I suppose that he'd be rather near to Glaukon here so far as love of victory goes" (548d). Adeimantos' rivalry with his brother, evident in his subtle attempt to relegate Glaukon to the category of second best, invites one to add that so far as love of honour goes, the timocrat is nearer to Adeimantos. There is a pattern of evidence suggesting that he is truly *timo*-cratic in that honour (broadly construed) is his foremost concern. But this same evidence suggests that he tends towards the highest kind of honour-loving man, one who regards virtue and public-spiritedness as the most honourable things, and thus the qualities for which he wishes to be honoured himself.[1] Less impressed by the plastic givens of nature, he stresses the importance of their particular fixation through proper nurture. It is he who intervenes to assure the philosopher, most emphatically, that a consideration of rearing and education is an important part of seeing how justice and injustice come to be in a city (376d). His perspective on life is profoundly political. When asked whether a city is greater [*meizon*] than one man, he answers without hesitation that it is (368e). That Glaukon would agree is by no means certain.

While not indifferent to honour (cf. 361c, 577c), Glaukon is only incidentally timocratic, and would be better described as a nikocrat. Every aspect and nuance of his character – assertive, brash, self-possessed, ambitious, decisive, demanding, arrogant – justifies his brother's characterization of him: he exudes that basic confidence so essential to success, and thus so fundamental to a natural lover of victory.[2] One might have guessed that this competitive young man would be the first person in the dialogue to mention contests (362b). This natural self-confidence, like the natural courage to which it is related, is more easily tempered where it's found than created where it isn't (cf. 596a). And inasmuch as the victories gained solely through one's own efforts are among the most personally satisfying, he inclines towards an individualistic perspective. He finds the idea of self-sufficiency profoundly attractive, and so tends to overestimate the extent to which he is a "self-made man", one who is blessed by a self-perfecting nature and who thus owes little to nurture or chance. Because he is willing to confront any challenge that *he* regards as intrinsically worthwhile, irrespective of whether or not it is popularly honoured, he is open to the philosophical life should he become convinced that it is the most select and demanding, the most enhancing, the most free and independent, and (hence) the most satisfying life. In short, that it is a way of life worthy of his talents, offering rewards commensurate with his efforts. Not surprisingly, he is the philosopher's favourite companion from the dialogue's beginning to its end (cf. 500c): the story opens with him alone accompanying the philosopher on an ascent from the lower to the higher city (whereas Adeimantos is instrumental in causing their return to the lower city); on several occasions Sokrates expresses his wish that Glaukon's curiosity be gratified (430de, 472e, 509c; cf. 338a); the story concludes with a tale of cosmic significance directed especially at Glaukon (cf. 618b, 621b).

By contrast, we meet Adeimantos in company with several others, both named and unnamed. And at a crucial juncture, we see him drawn back towards this party, briefly confer with its original leader, decide among alternatives presented him, and then step forward as its spokesman (449a–d). This is a role for which he seems especially well-suited: as an intermediary between the highest authority and the rest of the political community (both the distinguished few at the forefront and the anonymous many beyond). At various times in the course of the dialogue, he takes it upon himself to speak for the more intelligent and responsible sector of public opinion. Skeptical, critically astute, not easily awed, he several times stubbornly refuses to accept developments that seem contrary to common sense and experience. Indeed, his spirited defence of his most precious opinions – his reluctance to surrender any of them – shows why stubbornness to a point is a good thing. It adds ballast, a sense of gravity absent in those who are too-easily persuaded and who are (consequently) for ever tossing on the waves of fashionable opinion. More than once he requires the philosopher to "apologize", to defend himself and his work against sensible objections (419a, 422a, 487b–e). But whereas he is bold enough to advance these challenges, he is also cautious enough, or prudent enough, to cloak himself as an anonymous "someone" or a political "we" while doing so.

Such polite devices are not for Glaukon. As the philosopher himself testifies in his only narrative observation on the young men's respective characters, Glaukon "happens to be always most courageous in everything" (357a; cf. 535a). "*Always ... most* courageous ... in *everything*"! As an endorsement regarding the cardinal virtue of the spirit, it would be difficult to improve on that. And it is the first mention of courage in the dialogue. Glaukon certainly does seem the bolder of the two. Whereas most men are courageous only by default, and overcome other fears out of the greater fear of shame inherent in the spirit's honour-loving, utilitarian part (this being what "political courage" typically rests upon; cf. 430b–c), Glaukon is courageous by a positive inclination rooted in the victory-loving side of his spirit.[3]

It is he who initiates the challenge to the philosopher, offering a stronger version of Thrasymachos' position. Only after Glaukon has taken the lead does Adeimantos second him, insisting that what most needed to be said had not yet been said. When Glaukon objects or interrupts, be it about something he doesn't like (372c, 372d) or something he wishes better to understand (347a, 506d), he does so openly and in his own name (cf. 378e). He makes dialogical decisions expressly to suit himself (348b, 430d), and is further encouraged by the philosopher to do so (527d-a).

In addition to his brother's assurance that Glaukon exemplifies love of victory, and the philosopher's judgment that he is unqualifiedly most courageous, we are told that he is musical (398e), more so than is typical for a timocrat (as he is *less* stubborn, 548e). One can fairly say that his claim to musicality is borne out by the poetic inventiveness incorporated in his challenge to the philosopher, of which his clever adaptation of the Herodotean (or pre-Herodotean) story of Gyges is the main but not the only evidence (359c-360b; cf. 361d). It is Glaukon who cares enough and knows enough about the melodic side of music to want its reformation discussed (398c; cf. 522a). And it is he who is the true lover of poetry, accepting its "exile" only with regret, and after having been shown its possible danger to something he has come to regard as more beautiful still (cf. 607b-608b, 509a). Adeimantos' attitude towards poetry is more equivocal. On the one hand, his familiarity with its shows that he is drawn to its beauty; but his cogent analysis of certain poetry's morally corrupting influence leaves him leery of its power. Inclined as he is to want to place civic responsibility ahead of selfish pleasure, he readily becomes a compliant – not to say enthusiastic – participant in the virtual banishment of the most enjoyable forms of poetry (398a-b). Whereas, it would seem to be Glaukon's lingering affection for poetry that causes Book Ten, the only one of the dialogue's many "beginnings" in no way imposed upon the philosopher, and which, given the conclusion of Book Nine, seems otherwise gratuitous. So one might have guessed without being told that Glaukon is also "an erotic man" (474d-a), and perhaps even one who, as he himself implies, cares more for beauty of soul than of body (402de). Be *that* as it may, we can safely presume that his testimony as to "erotic necessities" being more intrusive than geometric ones is based on personal experience (458d), and that it accounts for the single occasion when he seems to side against the philosopher (450a). And since he is a keeper of hunting dogs (459a), we can also

The War Lover

assume that he is himself a lover of the hunt. Quite what is implied by his also keeping well-bred birds, presumably fighting cocks, is less clear. Perhaps it is further evidence of his natural competitiveness and love of contests; or perhaps it simply expresses his appreciation of beautiful or noble, albeit useless, things.

The philosopher discusses the spirit almost exclusively with Glaukon (cf. 375a–b, 410b–412a, 435e, 439e–441c, 456a, 465a, 580d–c, 586c–e, 590a–c, 603c–606d). The only exception is rather revealing: he discusses the origin, nature, and decay of the timocratic man with Adeimantos (548d–553d). Glaukon laughs, and can even laugh at himself (398c, 451b, 509c). His natural sense of the comic gives him a greater capacity for irony. Only he participates with the philosopher in the satire of Book Five, his role apparently that of the straight man (but cf. 461cd). It is a comedy which Adeimantos' mock indignation begins (449c) and real indignation threatens to end (487b–d). Adeimantos speaks of laughing (366c), but never actually laughs himself. And even the laughter he speaks of is that which comes not from joy, but from scorn (cf. 337a). The philosopher expressly attributes to him the injunction against allowing their warrior-guardians to be lovers of laughter (389a). More infected with the tragic view of life, his spirit's most characteristic passion is indignation (cf. 363c–e, 377e–b, 390c, 419a, 426b–e). One of his few substantial contributions to the construction of the city in *logos* concerns the subtle dangers of a "creeping lawlessness" caused by people's tendency to regard as play something that is inherently serious[4] (424d–e, 425d–a).

Judging from his own speeches as well as by the philosopher's manner of dealing with him, Adeimantos is no great lover of labour. As noted above, he does only half as much work in the dialogue, and it is generally easier work. He favours a leisurely life over one of great striving, and will settle for less than the best if the best seems too demanding. While he would naturally prefer to be rich, he would be content to live frugally as a gentleman, provided there was no stigma attached to possessing only modest means. The central point in his speech seconding the challenge to the philosopher (all of it being based on what others praise and blame) concerns the reputed *difficulty* of being just and moderate, and the comparative *ease* of intemperance and injustice (364a–d; cf. 365cd). In all probability, his peculiar sensitivity to the normal human inclination to take the easy way derives from self-awareness (cf. 449c, 504c). Apparently he was satisfied with the simple and easy life of the first city in *logos* so long as everyone else was. The fact that it allowed for no distinction in terms of honour, power, or property, and thus provided nothing to strive for; that it demanded no special courage; presented no alternative to being moderate (how many barley cakes can a man eat?); and left little scope and no motive for being unjust – all this was acceptable to him. His spirit openly revolts only at the prospect of inferiority; it can be persuaded to settle for equality.

Glaukon, on the other hand, took one quick look at that simple, healthy city's humdrum way of life, and brusquely rejected it as fit only for pigs. His spirit rebelled in the name of luxury (fine food, vintage wine, comfortable furniture, and everything else that makes up the conventional notion of the good life). But his subsequent acceptance of a far more rigorous asceticism (cf. 404d) makes it clear that his real objection went deeper: there was neither need nor scope for excellence, for the qualities of a real man. He is perfectly willing to be an ascetic warrior-ruler; he is *not* willing to be an ascetic dirt-farmer or shopkeeper. By contrast, Adeimantos, though he initially accepted an ascetic way of life, subsequently objected to that imposed on their ruling class (419a). But it is first and foremost his sense of justice that protests: those who are contributing less to the city, sacrificing less for it, are getting more from it. And those who are most deserving are being treated as inferiors, mere hirelings. He's mollified when the philosopher also takes away most of the producing class's wealth on the grounds of its being incompatible with their remaining industrious and politically content (421d–a; cf. 442a–b). And to further reconcile him to the austere Aristocracy in *logos* (which evolved from the low simplicity of the first city through a stage of luxury to this higher simplicity; 399e), Sokrates assures him that the demands made on the ruling class are not really all that onerous (423c–e; cf. 435c). His repressed hankering after the easy life leaves him secretly longing for wealth (419a–b), and overly respectful of the power of wealth (422a), as does the fact that luxury and privilege are typically signs of high status. And his suspicion of argument (367b, 367e, 487b–d) – stemming *not* from an uncivil ignorance of it, and a consequent habitual reliance on force (411de), but quite the opposite – leaves him vulnerable to becoming a hater of argument (although he is by no means that now). The truly philosophic nature, however, is not only a lover of wisdom and lover of learning (475b–c, 581b), but also a lover of rational argument (*philologos*, 582e).

Glaukon, for his part, seems positively to enjoy argument. As the

The War Lover

philosopher tells it, he thought that he was freed from argument upon the capitulation of Thrasymachos (who was soundly thrashed and knew it), but that "always most courageous" Glaukon volunteered to reopen the whole issue again, confident that he could succeed where the professional teacher of powerful speaking had repeatedly failed. He expresses a preference for dialogue over rhetoric (348a-b), and (unlike Adeimantos) is prepared to reach conclusions simply on the basis of argument (358cd). He avows, "For those with intelligence, the whole life is the [proper] measure of listening to such discussions" (i.e., as they've been having; 450b; cf. 358d and 532a). Some evidence for the sincerity of this profession is provided by his display of prior acquaintance with theoretical problems (e.g., 525e, 528b, 531ab, 531e, 597a). All of the philosopher's more theoretical investigation is done with Glaukon (cf. 475e, 511d), who prefaces his own challenge with a set of theoretical distinctions concerning the Good (357b-d). He is the first to mention both 'nature' (*physis*; 359b) and 'form' (*eidos*; 357c); he regards knowledge as the most vigorous of all powers (477d); and he speaks longingly (if not altogether knowingly) of "how sweet is the pleasure of learning the natures of the things that are" (582b). The nature of philosophy is discussed with him, whereas the *reputation* of philosophy is discussed with Adeimantos (explicitly characterized as "sensibly apologizing"; 490a). Pursuant to his cultivation as a gentleman intermediary between the philosopher and the non-philosophic many (499d-500e; cf. 425de), Adeimantos is pointedly warned that "it is not easy for the best practice to enjoy a good reputation with those who practise the opposite" (489c).

With these remarks as a background, one might attempt a more detailed psycho-analysis of the brothers, using as a basis each one's major speech in the dialogue: their respective contributions to the challenge they jointly pose the philosopher (358a-362c and 362d-367e). This may well stand as the most powerful one-two punch in the history of political philosophy. For first bold, musical, erotic Glaukon - appealing directly to nature - delivers a positive attack on the just life and eulogizes the unjust life. Then Adeimantos - that most careful, thoughtful, skeptical listener of what other men say - rips to shreds the conventional defence of the just life. The first glorifies crime; the second casts serious doubt on punishment. One cannot begin to appreciate the brilliance of the philosopher's response, a truly revolutionary pedagogical strategy, without understanding *why* he tells us that although he "had always been full of wonder at the nature of Glaukon and Adeimantos", this time he was "particularly delighted" (367ea). Why? What have they just revealed about themselves?

Glaukon thinks of himself as a more natural man, and he probably is. Less affected by formal education, he endorses living in accordance with the natural truth of things, something he distinguishes from opinion (362a). Injustice comes naturally because it's naturally good, "having more" being "what any nature naturally pursues as good" (359c). Whereas justice is in one sense unnatural, since it is an artificial restraint contrived by men; yet, in another sense it too is natural, for it is naturally attractive to the many weak individuals who lack the *power* to get more, and so are content to settle for an equal share. These individually weak many, through the artifice of what might be called a social contract, become collectively strong. It is in this sense that justice is, as Thrasymachos so confusedly argued, "the advantage of the stronger". It is the advantage of the artificially strong (but naturally weak) many; and in seeking to regulate a peaceful competition for life's good things, it is tacitly weighted against the naturally strong few, those who would prosper "disproportionately" in an unregulated competition. From the perspective of these latter, justice is indeed "the other person's good" (as Thrasymachos *also* claimed).

Thus, the root of the problem is the natural inequality of men, and their necessarily differing perspectives on life. If *all* men were like *most* men, then this artificial scheme called justice would be, on balance, good for everyone (presuming it could be adequately policed – a separate, and at least very important *practical* problem). But as things actually are, justice is *not*, on balance, a good deal for the naturally best – and most dangerous – individuals, those who can commit injustice without having to suffer it. And in fact, it is primarily against *them* that the whole artifice is directed, denominating as a crime the strong man's natural effort to get more. But men don't differ in their reasoning, nor in the selfishness of their desires; they differ only as to their power. Thus so-called just people have no claim to moral superiority. And thus a *real* man – brave, assertive, intelligent, toughminded – needn't feel honour-bound by the rules of a partnership so clearly prejudicial to his own interests, one that in effect requires *him*, the finest example of fulfilled human nature, to put the welfare of his natural inferiors, the weak and misbegotten, ahead of his own. With the clearest conscience in the world, then, he can merely *appear* to go along with the conventions of political life, and selectively depart

The War Lover

from them whenever he sees an opportunity to do so undetected. And should he occasionally be "compromised", he can always extricate himself through some combination of persuasion and a manly show of force. He can thereby rise to rule the city, arrange whatever marriages and partnerships he likes, win whatever private and public contests he cares to engage in, and through it all get the better of everyone (Thrasymachos' concern), do good to his friends and harm to his enemies (Polemarchos' concern), and even win the favour of the gods with the magnificence of his offerings (Kephalos' concern). Thus speaks the natural man.

By comparison, Adeimantos is a more "artificial", a more domesticated or civilized man. He speaks at length about the true implications of the education youths receive at the hands of parents, teachers, politicians, and priests, and of the actual rank order of what people value as revealed in what they praise and blame. As later revealed in his reaction to the first city in *logos* (and elsewhere), he would be willing to settle for an equal, modest share if others truly would. But he knows they won't, and that consequently life is a rat-race. For behind that veneer of "respectability", and apparent support for equal justice, everyone is still trying to get ahead, by fair means or foul – so far as their courage and wits will take them, that is. Adeimantos, in contrast to Glaukon, is a sophisticated calculator of profits and losses (notice how many of his substantial contributions to the discussion concern economics, about which he's obviously given more than a little thought; e.g., 371cd, 422a, 565a, 568d-e, 424de, 425c-e). And so he naturally concentrates on the comparative "wages" of the just and the unjust life, in this world and any other (cf. 363cd).

Glaukon has a keen eye for opportunities, and a blind eye for practical difficulties. He is of the "damn the torpedoes – full speed ahead" school of thought. Insensitive to whatever might obstruct his achieving his ambitions, he is poised to pursue anything and everything he finds attractive (which, in his untutored state, is a fairly conventional catalogue of goods; 360bc, 362b-c). His thinking reflects an animal boldness that can be tamed and tempered by education, but not created by it. Glaukon tends to see things in black and white. Single-minded, and obtuse to complicating factors, he exists in a kind of blissful stupidity, supremely confident of himself because he is oblivious to so much else.

Adeimantos seems to have given matters more thought; for him there are only shades of grey. He has the kind of sophistication that

Crime and Punishment

tends to vitiate ambition and paralyse action.[5] By virtue of having listened carefully and critically to what all kinds of men say, he has considered the various pros and cons from a practical perspective, and consequently is much more impressed with the difficulties than the opportunities. As he sees things, there is (regrettably) no easy way, no clear, unproblematic choice between living justly or unjustly. Both involve difficulties. Everyone seems to agree that practising justice and moderation is difficult, and that doing injustice is the easier way, thus the naturally tempting way. Except that getting away with it is *not* easy ("nothing great is easy," he half laments; 365cd). He is aware, as Glaukon clearly isn't, that "in real life" for a single *individual* to succeed in living unjustly on a grand scale (which entails virtually always appearing to be just – and surely this *is* the height of injustice: exploiting the reputation for being a pillar of the community in order to be its greatest criminal; 361a), would involve an enormous effort, requiring him to be constantly on guard, especially over *himself*, ever aware of the distinction between outer seeming and inner being (365c; cf. 409c-d). Consequently, he could never relax, never "take it easy", never simply "be himself" and act naturally. He would have to be analysing and calculating and dissembling all of the time.

Hence the value of *partners* one can confide in, co-conspirators that one can trust. But not trust implicitly, because of course similar reasoning is equally available to other men. And they too know that everyone bears watching, but especially the more intelligent and bold (367a). They, like Adeimantos, well appreciate why in actual political life, where the intentional manipulation of appearances is raised to an art, the overriding necessity is that of distinguishing appearance from reality. This prudent mutual suspiciousness further aggravates the difficulties of getting away with injustice, but also increases the potential rewards for successfully doing so. In sum, either alternative, the just or the unjust life, poses difficulties. But the latter offers much greater pay-offs. So even if it involves somewhat greater difficulties, it is still – unfortunately, sadly, tragically – the rational choice.

Both brothers distinguish nature from convention, from opinion, and from artifice. But Adeimantos, as a measure of his greater sophistication, presses the analysis further and deeper, making explicit the tension between what is praised as *good* (including justice), and what is commonly acknowledged to be *pleasant* (and easy). Or to express the point somewhat differently, he reveals the tension between justice and happiness: that justice regularly requires putting the happiness

The War Lover

of others ahead of one's own. Which would be all right if others always reciprocated, but they don't, being men, not angels. And Adeimantos explicitly links justice and moderation, something that Glaukon was silent about (of course, the very idea of it contradicts what he accepts as the fundamental law of nature, "having more"). Adeimantos appreciates the similar difficulties inherent in the practice of each of these virtues, justice and moderation. But beyond that he sees the deeper link between them, something the philosopher's subsequent analysis makes manifest: people who, for whatever reason, have moderate desires, also have minimal difficulties both in practising justice and in ruling themselves (cf. 410a). Whether by nature less ambitious, or by education more pessimistic, Adeimantos seems to have, or at least wishes to have, more moderate desires. Not surprisingly, it is he whom the philosopher later asks, "Do you wish, so that we not discuss in the dark, that we first distinguish the necessary desires from those that aren't?" (558d). And it is with and for him that the philosopher further distinguishes the "law-abiding" from the "lawless" desires (571a-572b).

Whereas Glaukon shows himself more imaginative and creative, using poetry for inspiration, Adeimantos is more analytical and critical. He displays a scholar's thorough familiarity with the canon of classical poetry, and a teacher's sensitivity to its pedagogic effects on those who, like himself, are "good natured", having the capacity to put two and two together and not short-change themselves (365a). Were they boxers, Glaukon would be the puncher, Adeimantos the counter-puncher – one better at landing a blow, the other at guarding against a blow's being landed. Glaukon is instinctively an attacker; Adeimantos would retreat to high ground where, having taken his stand, he would prove a stout and stubborn defender: his spirit is of the "over-my-dead-body" persuasion. Thus, Glaukon is an initiator, Adeimantos a responder to other men's initiatives, and often a refiner and improver of them. He intervenes on the grounds that the argument has not been adequately stated by his brother (who had subtly taunted him; 360b5; cf. 474ab), and explains his contribution to their challenge as necessary "so that what Glaukon wants will be clearer" (362d-e). There is a logical subordination here – akin to that between a maker and a critic of poetry – which needn't always imply a practical subordination. There is no practical danger that all men will cease initiating, any more than that they'll cease making poetry, or trying to be the first to land a blow.

Glaukon is more individualistic, more drawn to the Homeric image of the hero (notice the density of 'first-person, singular' locutions outlining what *he* will do, and what *he* wants done in return; 358b–d; cf. 509c). He portrays the unjust man as a kind of heroic individual who, like a clever artisan, not only is an astute judge of his own powers and possibilities, but is capable of correcting his own infrequent mistakes (360e–b). Adeimantos, however, thinks politically. His unjust man is a clever conspirator, for whom it would be imprudent to attempt being "perfectly" or "completely" unjust lest the conspiracy fail; he recognizes that there must be some partial, if only temporary, justness among the partners for any joint enterprise to have any prospect of succeeding (cf. 351c–d, 352b–c). And so he must be a clever persuader, capable of employing deliberative as well as forensic rhetoric (whereas Glaukon alluded only to the latter; 365d, 361b; cf. 327c–a).

Glaukon's completely unjust man, this heroic *solus criminalis*, is a practical impossibility, as he could easily see for himself were he to give the matter more thought – or rather, were he inclined to think like Adeimantos. For to pull it off *as a way of life*, this "ideally" unjust man must aspire never to say or do *anything* recognizably unjust, not even in the privacy of his own home, in front of wife or children or servants (cf. 549c–e, 577a–b). Thus his entire practice would habituate him to conventional justness. Moreover, he has to be able to speak *for* justice, and to retain credibility he must do so convincingly, against all comers (e.g., he would have to be able to refute Thrasymachos and Adeimantos, or at least credibly appear to). Thus he must be thoroughly conversant with the very best arguments for justice, indeed lead those arguments (cf. 368ab). And if our practices, our thoughts and speeches and deeds do not shape us, what does? Similarly, Glaukon's perfectly just man who always appears totally unjust is also a practical impossibility (cf. 612c–d, 613c). No one, in the very nature of things, could ever suffer the fate Glaukon paints for him (361b–a), and thus the philosopher needn't show that such a man is nevertheless somehow happy merely because he is just. For in actually being just, he is normally law-abiding, fulfils his duties towards the common good, is generally respectful of others' property – so he *cannot* appear totally unjust. Moreover, he's under no obligation not to defend himself by all decent means. As for the persecution of good men in tyrannical regimes, it has nothing to do with their appearing unjust, nor does anyone really believe that it does (cf. 567a–c). The fate of Sokrates may be as near as one can get to approximating the case of Glaukon's really-just-but-

The War Lover

seemingly-unjust man, ... and that was a close vote, even after an outrageously provocative non-apology. But Glaukon's rhetoric is so ingenious, so powerful, so vivid and captivating, that almost no one notices the utter impracticality of his presentation. Sokrates praises his artistry, likening him to a maker of man-like statues (361d; cf. 501a–c, 514c, 420c), a compliment the young man later returns (540c).

After Glaukon has completed his revival of "Thrasymachos' argument", Adeimantos – no doubt moved as much by sibling rivalry as by any true sense of fraternity – steps forward to help accomplish "what Glaukon wants" (cf. 367a), insisting that what most needs saying has not yet been said. Perhaps he is right. His portion of the challenge strengthens considerably the case for injustice. As already noted, he associates justice with "unnatural" moderation, has a more practical conception of the supremely unjust man, and brings to the surface the apparent tension between the good and the pleasant, or between justice and happiness. But these are not his most important contributions. For it is he who reveals that beneath the unsettling disagreement between the praisers and blamers of justice, there is a far more disturbing *agreement*, namely, that reputation – or *appearance* – is all that matters in this world, and possibly in the other too, ... if there is an other (cf. 363a, 365b, 365d-e).

For that is a second, most important respect in which his half of the challenge surpasses Glaukon's: he expands the scope of the issue to the cosmic level, speaking extensively about the gods that his brother barely mentioned as an afterthought (362c). In fact, Adeimantos' portion is almost all about the gods (363a-d, 364b-a, 365d-b); he makes no less than twenty-three direct references to the gods, as well as speaking of sundry other things holy or divine. The judgment of the gods, whom we presume are not fooled by appearances, is typically the last refuge of those who defend the superiority of living justly. But if there are no gods, or if they are indifferent to human affairs, one needn't concern oneself with them. If, on the other hand, one is persuaded of their existence by those authorities who testify to it (primarily the great poets), these same authorities assure us that the gods can be propitiated by prayers and sacrificial gifts. So, for a clear-eyed, hard-nosed calculator of profits and losses, the rational course is evident: commit injustice, and out of the proceeds offer the gods those "magnificent sacrifices" Glaukon spoke of, just to cover your bet (365d-b; cf. 331b). Gods or no gods, then, the *kosmos* seems indifferent to the *reality* of justice. One need not fear any punishment but that of men, which can be evaded if one is a clever conspirator and a persuasive dissembler, for punishment in *this* world proceeds strictly on the basis of appearances.

Thirdly, Adeimantos recognizes two distinct possibilities of there being truly just men who are of *higher* quality than the unjust (whereas Glaukon, like Thrasymachos, acknowledged only the pitiful simpleton; 348cd, 360d). But Adeimantos gives this recognition a malicious twist: of all people, these superior just men, being fair in their judgments, must sympathize with intelligent, "conscientious" practitioners of injustice. For if those of higher wisdom *know* – whether by their own natural efforts, or by divine revelation – that living justly is the best way, they also can appreciate that this truth is far from obvious, and that being just is contrary to some powerful inclinations of human nature. And if the gods themselves are just, then perhaps they, too, would forgive injustice after all (366c–d). Be *that* as it may, such reasoning could well explain the philosopher's patient indulgence of these young men.

Finally, in insisting that Sokrates show not *only by argument* that justice is stronger than injustice (367b, 367e; cf. 487b–c), Adeimantos casts doubt on the power of *logos* to reveal the truth, thereby raising the suspicion that all "rationality" is but a veneer, and in the final analysis is derivative from, if not utterly irrelevant to, that which fundamentally causes human actions: a deep, unteachable, a-rational substratum of one's given nature, one's spiritual *fatum*, as it were.

In sum, Adeimantos has a far more sophisticated perspective on the problem. All the more remarkable, then, that it is Glaukon's portion that naturally commands the lion's share of attention. Why is that? Is it not because he has the poet's gift for creating memorable images, which makes Adeimantos' critical and analytical ability seem arid and pale by comparison? The most memorable part of their entire challenge is his centrepiece: his variation on the "Ring of Gyges" story. It is worth a closer look.

In Glaukon's version of what he implies is a familiar folk tale,[6] Gyges, "ancestor of *the* Lydian" (i.e., the fabulously rich Kroesos), began life as a humble shepherd toiling in the service of the ruler of Lydia (cf. 343b, 345c–d, 440d). One day, a great thunderstorm and earthquake struck where he happened to be pasturing his flock, and a gaping chasm opened down into the earth (cf. 621b, 414de). Unusually curious and brave, he descended into this cave-like rift in the earth where

The War Lover

he beheld, among other wonders about which other men tell other tales (cf. 377a), a hollow bronze horse pierced by windows. Peering in, he beheld an apparently Titanic corpse, naked except for a gold ring. Taking this, he ascended back to the surface (cf. 469d). Subsequently, upon the occasion of all the king's shepherds gathering to render accounts to their master, he came wearing the ring. Idly fumbling with it, perhaps while awaiting his call to report, he chanced to revolve the ring on his finger, turning towards the inside of his hand the decorative collet that would normally face outwards. Whereupon he became invisible to other people, as he realized from the fact that they spoke about him as though he were absent. Wondering at this, just as he had at the chasm and the things he saw in it, he revolved the ring back to its normal position, whereupon he once again became visible. He tested the ring in this manner until he was assured that it did indeed have the power it first seemed to. Satisfied as to that, he promptly contrived somehow to be sent as a messenger to the king, whom he slew in order to seize the throne for himself, but only after first seducing the queen to his purpose. Quite how the power of invisibility facilitated killing his lawful ruler is left to our imagination, as is the means whereby he corrupted the trusty queen.

The point of the story, according to Glaukon, is that it can assist us in a mental experiment proving that *no one* not an utter simpleton is *willingly* just, and that the only thing distinguishing the so-called just from the unjust is *power*. Give any man the power to do as he wants, and he will reveal his true, and common, nature in acting to get more for himself – a nature which is perverted by the law that compels everyone to honour equality, or at least pretend to. So, assume there were two such rings as Gyges found, and give one to a "just" man and the other to an "unjust" man, and imagine what would happen. Once confident of this power to appear and disappear at will, nobody would be so "adamant" (*adamantinos*), so "Adeimantos-like", as to stick to justice and refrain from helping himself to "what belongs to others". Anyone not a wretched fool would take whatever he wants of those things sold in markets, would sleep with whomever he wants, kill or liberate whomever he wants, and altogether act as a god among humans (cf. 380d–381e; 614b7).

Of course, Glaukon did not have to tell this particular story merely in order to convey what he means by a magical ring with the power to make one selectively invisible. And it is worth asking why he, or anyone, would not want to use it to remain *permanently* invisible. Nor does he give much indication as to precisely how its power is so practically advantageous; apparently he believes this is self-evident, despite the fact that someone chose to bury the ring. The actual point of the story is to illustrate what he doubtless regards as the optimum rational *use* of the ring. It implies that one could enjoy everything worth having if one wielded tyrannical power in a large and prosperous polity. One could even achieve a kind of immortality akin to that of Gyges, who established a ruling dynasty so successfully that one of his descendants became proverbial for wealth and magnificence, the envy of the world.

The rhetorical effect of this story is amazing. It simultaneously taps two dreams that probably every human being has had at least once: what if I could become invisible whenever I willed it? and what if I were absolute dictator of the richest and most powerful state in the world? If you have ever wished for such things, is that not sufficient to ratify Glaukon's (and Thrasymachos') basic point? For why would we want such power; what would we do with it? Wouldn't we occasionally "invade the privacy" of others (if only out of curiosity about what people say behind our backs)? Mightn't we penalize, even "extinguish", some of those we dislike, and benefit those we like – and do so, moreover, with a clear conscience (cf. 334bc)?

But the primary issue is *not* whether a person might use such power to do "evil" rather than "good". The primary issue is whether this tyrannical impulse is not in everyone. And second to that, were someone *not* inclined to use such power "selfishly", *why* not? Could he give compelling rational grounds for not at least sometimes favouring himself? If he couldn't, his reluctance to exploit this power suggests he is just another soft and sentimental fool. That is not something to be especially proud of. And if a person is willing to be a little unjust, why not a lot? If he is *willing* to be unjust at all (as opposed to believing himself somehow "compelled" to be; cf. 331ab), there seems no reason for stopping short of being as unjust as he can imagine, provided he can get away with it. In everyday life many settle for being "imperfectly unjust" out of fear, or weakness, or lack of ambition, or inability to think big. But as for the person who *wants* to be only "moderately unjust", ... well, the kindest thing one can say is that he is confused. Thus, it seems that nothing less than an unqualified rejection of the least injustice will suffice as a repudiation of the most self-indulgent tyranny.

The War Lover

Reflecting on the two sides of the timocratic nature – incarnate in the brothers Glaukon and Adeimantos – one sees the advantages to a philosopher in having both sets of qualities. Can there be a sophistication that does not vitiate manliness, a clear, cool, refined understanding of the world that does not sap the will to strive? Sokrates seems to manifest that very synthesis of Glaukon's cheerful courage, creativity, aggressive curiosity, unfailing confidence, ambition, and unfettered imagination, with Adeimantos' restraint, sobriety, patience, gravity, attentiveness, perceptivity, insight, subtlety, and social sensitivity. How does such a synthesis come to be? What is due to nature and what to nurture? The philosopher himself emphasizes that "the parts of the nature" required for "the most precise guardians" are "rarely willing to grow together in the same place" (503b). As he explains it to Adeimantos:

> "You know that natures that are good at learning, have memories, are shrewd and quick and everything else that goes along with these qualities, and are as well full of youthful fire and magnificence – such natures don't willingly grow together with understandings that choose orderly lives which are quiet and steady. Rather, those who possess them are carried away by their quickness wherever chance leads and all steadiness goes out of them. ... Whereas those steady, not easily changeable dispositions, which one would be inclined to count on as trustworthy and which in war are hard to move in the face of fears, act the same way in the face of studies. They are hard to move and hard to teach, as if they had become numb; and they are filled with sleep and yawning when they must work through anything of the sort."

And yet, the philosophic nature "must participate in *both* well and nobly, or not be given a share in the most precise education, nor in honour, nor in rule" (503c-d; cf. 375c). Hence the further importance of understanding the two sides of the timocratic nature, and the sort of nurture or nurtures that would so far as possible amalgamate the virtues of both.

To crystallize the difference between the brothers, these two divergent kinds of timocrats, Adeimantos seems better suited for serving as a guardian of the first good regime in *logos*, Glaukon of the second. In the Aristocracy described in books Two through Four, where education is but a means to political virtue, the rulers are moderate, steady, civic-minded elders who lead a refined but spartan life, whose principal reward is honour, and whose claim to rule rests on their proven ability to retain certain salutary convictions and opinions in the face of all experience (412d-e, 413c-e; cf. 429c, 431c, 433a). The philosopher expressly refers to it as Adeimantos' city (427cd; cf. 371e). By contrast, Glaukon is a more promising candidate for Philosophical Kingship, the regime in which knowledge is treated as an end in itself, being both the requisite and the reward of self-rule in accordance with a divine pattern (cf. 461e). A careful consideration of his strengths and weaknesses in light of the various discussions about the nature suited for philosophy suggests that he, the victory-loving kind of timocrat, is blessed with the better natural basis for pursuing wisdom, that his nature is amenable to being *nurtured* to manifest the other desirable qualities, those that come more naturally to Adeimantos. Suffice it simply to notice that it is he who emphatically agrees that "a man must not be honoured before the truth" (595c).

In light of the brother's challenge, it seems fair to say that this dialogue in no way minimizes the problem of justice. Book One surveys the three most plausible (and thus quite common) conceptions of justice, and finds that each represents considerations important to a full understanding of justice, but that all are none the less inadequate as fundamental ideas of it. From the brief conversation with Kephalos, we are reminded of the conceptual connections between justice and such things as honesty, reciprocity, gratitude, equity, and the distinction between what is one's own (on any of several valid grounds) and what belongs to others. And we are also reminded of there being at least a practical connection between justice and piety, in the support the latter can lend the former; yet we see at the same time the natural limitations on that support: it's not enough that only old men with a belated concern for the afterlife be just. But surpassing in importance all these very important considerations is our being shown that justice itself cannot be a set of practical rules, clear and categorical commandments or laws – e.g., "always tell the truth" and "always return what you have been given" – since such substantial rules of practice invariably admit of exceptions. But the recognition that a particular case is a legitimate exception to a generally valid rule of conduct presupposes that justice itself is something still more basic, in light of which one recognizes both the normal validity of the rule and the occasional legitimate exception to it. And this more basic something cannot be yet another substantial rule (to which there is an exception, and so on).

The War Lover

The discussion with Polemarchos, who is as preoccupied with human affairs as his father is with divine, reminds us that we presume justice to be a good thing; that the practice of it is intended to improve matters and people; that it involves discrimination, in that some people have a right to expect more of us than do others, especially our friends and partners and allies of one kind or another; that it requires a dedication to the common good of such friendships, partnerships, and alliances; and that one must stand by one's commitments, be they explicit or implied. But also, we're shown that behaving accordingly entails being able to distinguish in substantial terms good from bad, and friends from enemies (or at least non-friends). Moreover, if justice is the virtue regulating dealings among more-or-less restricted groups (e.g., one's fellow citizens, those accidental friends and partners and allies in life), one is left with the question of how to deal with the rest of mankind, some of whom may themselves be good people, indeed better than many of one's friends and partners, and to that extent perhaps more naturally *deserving* of preferential treatment.

The arguments with Thrasymachos remind us of the practical connection, as well as the theoretical distinction, between justice and legality, and similarly between justice and political power. But we are simultaneously obliged to concede that knowledge of justice alone, presuming it were available, is not sufficient for carrying theory into practice, not even if it is supported by good will, as often enough it isn't. The reality of justice also requires strength, but what kind of strength? What is the strongest kind of strength among human beings, who are physically weaker than horses but none the less rule them in order to garner the advantages of equine strength. Thus we are subtly shown the need for, as well as the difficulty of, distinguishing political strength (that which comes from controlling the polity, typically expressed in the rulers' being able to draft and apply laws to their own advantage), from some pre- or trans-political strength such as would allow one to *become* politically strong in the first place. Presuming, that is, the possessor of this other kind of strength chooses to use it to pursue political rule, which further presumes his having nothing more attractive or pressing to do with his life. Thrasymachos, like Glaukon and most everyone else, is unaware of anything more attractive, and so he simply assumes that anyone would rule who could. He thereby unwittingly conflates the two kinds of strength, with the result that his tough-minded, "realistic", "empirical" account of political life actually explains little, and least of all why there are different *kinds* of regimes (such as those he himself refers to). Why aren't the pre-politically strong everywhere the same, with the consequence that they everywhere institute the same kind of regime? Or do they? And he treats as similarly unproblematic the presumption that whoever rules invariably does so to his own advantage. Never having met King Solomon, he discounts without thinking the possibility that one's idea and practice of justice could itself be a source of strength. Still, to acknowledge the possibility is not to understand how or why.

Upon recognizing that an adequate understanding of justice cannot be had by reducing it to a finite set of substantial rules of conduct (regardless of how fondly familiar, "intuitively self-evident", or devoutly believed); nor by basing it upon purely formal distinctions; nor by simply equating it to either legality or the factual distribution of power behind the law – upon recognizing the inadequacy of all such common views, one is raised to the level of self-conscious ignorance about justice.

But one's mind is no sooner purged of unjustified confidence in any and all available answers to this vital question than one is confronted in the starkest possible terms with the possibility that what people are in the habit of calling justice is contrary to human nature; that its faithful practice would be prejudicial to the well-being of the naturally best people; that it exists only as mere convention, a frail artifice founded on the false premise of approximate human equality, and sustained as much by wholesale public hypocrisy as by sincere acceptance; that it is irremediably reliant on appearances, and so while enjoining honesty and fair-dealing actually invites dishonesty and duplicity in human affairs (people being the naturally selfish creatures the very need for justice presupposes them to be); and that it is without a shred of natural or supernatural support. In short, justice is paradoxical to the point of incoherence, a superficially attractive idea that founders on the radical inequality of human beings and the consequent incommensurability of their perspectives. And "crime", then, is no more substantial than table manners, a mutable and partisan concept haphazardly sustained by an evadable and corruptible scheme of human punishment. And exhortations to be just are more intelligently interpreted as exhortations to *seem* just, the better to get away with being *un*just.

Both brothers profess not to believe the position they so persuasively argue for. Both claim that they are attacking the just life and praising injustice in such brazen and ruthless terms in order to provoke the strongest possible defence of justice (358c–d, 367ab). In the course of doing so, however, they necessarily reveal what they are capable of thinking, and thus give anyone who hears them grounds for mistrusting them. Their pose as Devil's Advocates is the merest fig leaf and hardly adequate for covering their naked ambitions; still, it's the only guise consonant with their immediate purpose. But as the philosopher observes, something divine indeed must have happened to them if they can argue so powerfully for injustice and remain unpersuaded themselves (368a). And yet, he goes on to say, "You do not seem to me to be truly persuaded". He says he infers this from the rest of their characters. We can infer it from a simple fact. As they each indicate in their respective parts of the challenge, they realize full well that the best way to facilitate getting away with injustice is always to appear just to others. They appreciate the paradoxical situation Thrasymachos got himself caught in, a professional teacher of skills whose main and great value (as he sees it) is that they enable one to get the better of everyone else; but in advertising that fact, he has to violate the fundamental principle of the approach to life that he's selling: pretence, stealth, misleading appearance. The point is to be a wolf in sheep's clothing – not to groom one's fur (much less polish one's fangs) in public. And from this perspective, it makes even less sense to be trying to convert sheep into wolves, the more effectively to compete with oneself. So, if the brothers were utterly and finally convinced of their own position (and capable of ruling themselves in accordance with it), not only would they refrain from attempting to present an even stronger version of it than did Thrasymachos, they would have joined in condemning him, or even tried to convert him themselves. After all, the more *other* people believe in justice, the easier it is to prey upon them (cf. 347ea). At the very least, they would have let the matter drop when the sophist did. So, why didn't they? What divine thing accounts for their *not* being fully and "truly persuaded" of the position they articulate so well?

It is certainly not the arguments the philosopher has presented thus far, which (as they see clearly) have shown only that the *appearance* of justice has good consequences, introducing harmony and cooperation into any group engaged in a joint enterprise, be it a city, an army, or a band of thieves (351a–352a). And while sometimes only the reality of justice can sustain the appearance, this is not *invariably* the case. As for his claim that, analogously, an individual needs justice in his own soul (where appearance cannot substitute for reality) so that it not be weakened and paralysed by internal faction and enmity (352a-b), that would presume what the philosopher himself later insists must be shown: that the soul has parts, and moreover that they are not always automatically in harmony. Besides, he might himself be merely appearing to be just – and trying to persuade them to be really so – for his own advantage (cf. 357ab). So, what divine blessing causes them to doubt their own reasoning?

Is it not Sokrates himself? They have only to behold the man. It is obvious that he is no timid, weak-minded simpleton – they just witnessed his demolishing Thrasymachos on the sophist's home ground: powerful *logos*. And yet, as they are sufficiently acquainted with his ways to know (cf. 358d, 367de, 487e, 504ea), he is virtually indifferent to what they, like most people, treat as the greatest goods in life. Could it be that the philosopher really *does* know something they don't – something truly *important*, that is. Slender as the possibility may be, they *must* find out, even if it does require revealing more about themselves than they would prefer. For they realize, or have been led to realize, that the question is not about some theoretical abstraction, but is of vital personal significance to each and all: how one answers it determines one's entire approach to life (344de; cf. 578c, 608b, 403e). And *that* is not something any intelligent youth, intent on being clear-eyed and hard-nosed about his prospects, can afford to take unnecessary chances on. It is this will to get the most out of the only life they are sure of that makes them pause before the philosopher. They *have* to ask him.

The situation confronting Sokrates is of permanent political significance, for it is one that perennially recurs. He is dealing with talented youths who would like to pride themselves on being "realistic", not "idealistic", about the world. (That such an "ideal" is probably one of the least "realistic" they might entertain, given the scope of their ignorance, is just one more of life's plentiful ironies.) Oblivious to their own limitations, they are not in awe of established views and ways, but rather inclined towards rebellion. Since this posture tacitly asserts the need to radically reconsider fundamental questions, they are in fact somewhat more open to actually doing so. They find wealth attractive, but tend to take it for granted, and so are not (yet) obsessed with making money, and are even inclined to contemn a narrow preoccupation with making money. And their very capacity for conceiving great crime is the same as also makes them capable of great good (cf. 491d-e, 495b).

The War Lover

Whatever their pretensions, however, they have only commonplace notions about the practice of justice, about what the good things in life are, and about how politics "really" works. They regard the demands that their polity makes on them in the name of justice and the common good as alien impositions; it's not their regime, they neither made it nor control it. Being young, they have little access to its political heights, and – being young – they are short of patience. Moreover, for all their willingness to play seriously with big questions, they none the less have a rather vulgar conception of philosophy, and an utterly unacceptable view of the gods: if the powers ruling the universe are as they conceive them to be, it would indeed be impossible to defend the superiority of the just life. Thus, Sokrates need not and does not accept the young men's challenge on their terms, but on his own terms, which will become theirs before he is through (cf. 612b–614a). He will answer their question, not exactly the way they asked it, but the way they will subsequently agree they should have asked it. The truth is, he knows what they want better than they do.

But for the moment, confronted with such opinions and attitudes, what can the philosopher do? Presuming, that is, he regards them as would a friend or relative, and given that he believes them to be profoundly (however understandably) mistaken – his own way of life testifies to that – but given also their equivocal attitude towards speech: Glaukon has a healthy distrust of rhetoric (he knows what *he* uses it for, and has no intention of being duped himself); Adeimantos suspects that dialectic serves the interest of sophistry as readily as it does that of the truth. The philosopher could, of course, subject them to a cross-examination of their premises, revealing that they do not know what their challenge presumes they do about justice, politics, the good life, nature, virtue, the gods, or anything else of importance. But what would that really accomplish besides leaving Glaukon momentarily perplexed and Adeimantos further convinced that – yes, indeed – some people sure are clever at argument?

What the philosopher confronts is a pedagogical challenge of the highest order. And it is this problem of education, or rather of re-education, that dictates the course of the remainder of the dialogue. How the philosopher meets this pedagogical challenge is of central importance to his teaching about politics, for in the final analysis the pedagogical problem and the political problem are simply different facets of the same problem. Notice, the dialogue turns out to be almost

Crime and Punishment

entirely about education and mis-education: about how men and women are properly educated to be good human beings and citizens, and how various kinds of inferior regimes, and people more deficient than they need be, are the result of mistaken and unsuccessful efforts in education.[7]

All political associations with any claim to our interest concern themselves to some extent with educating their young to be good citizens, or at least acquiescent subjects of their respective regimes. Of course, some regimes do so much more vigorously and tenaciously – and effectively – than do others. They recognize that education is the most rational form of political activity. Since people act on the basis of what they believe to be true, if one can govern what people think, one governs people. The most secure regime is that which can educate its citizenry to be enthusiastic supporters of their political community and its ruling principles, and especially its conception of justice. There is some reason to believe, however, that the sounder – the more rationally defensible – those principles truly are, and the closer the actual practice of a regime is seen to conform to the principles it preaches, the more easily and solidly can people be educated to support it. And so, in the course of constructing an imaginary city in *logos*, those who participate in the project learn the reasons why its regime would be a good one. And they also learn how it would go about educating children from earliest childhood to be good citizens of it, citizens who could be counted upon to do their part in making it an harmonious whole. Special attention is given to the education of the most important class, the rulers, so that they are both willing and able to rule for the good of all (for Thrasymachos is right about this at least: it is the ruling class that imparts a specific character to the entire regime; cf. 421a).

One should notice, however, that in becoming Guardians, those so chosen are not allowed to follow a course of development analogous to that of the city in *logos*, which, upon being liberated from simple innocence, passes through a stage of feverish and dissolute luxuriousness, which in turn requires that it undergo a rigorous purgation before finally realizing its austere, virtuous beauty. In dramatic contrast to this, every effort is made to insulate the city's youth from corrupting influences, to the point where a serious question arises as to whether the city can find competent judges who have any understanding at all of vice (408c–409e; cf. 577a–b). This raises a further question about the strength and depth of (what Milton would surely disparage as)

The War Lover

"a fugitive and cloistered virtue, unexercised and unbreathed, that never sallies out and sees her adversary". Would such virtue bear comparison with virtue in the face of all temptations (cf. 619cd)? Despite this reservation, there is doubtless much of value to learn from this explicit account of how one could, starting from scratch, form people through education to be responsible citizens of a good regime.

But the far more challenging problem, from both the theoretical and the practical perspective, is how one can re-form people's political beliefs and habits, how one can re-educate people who already firmly believe certain things about politics and justice and the good life; and who, moreover, are not altogether open to argument for any of several reasons, including a healthy suspicion of human reasoning. We are not explicitly told how one might cope with *this* pedagogical challenge, the re-educating of mis-educated *adults* – a problem far more difficult than that of properly educating children, who have no beliefs to displace, who are altogether open and eager to learn, who haven't yet acquired a distrust of human authority, and who have no awareness of interests at cross-purposes with the truth. But this re-education of adults *is* the key to practical political reform, is it not? And for whatever it's worth, this is in fact a closer educational analogue to the dialogue's depiction of reforming their partially corrupted city in *logos*.

Normally, the most important educational influences in a child's life are its parents. It will first of all learn what its parents believe, then what is believed by such other adults as it encounters (especially teachers and priests). Children mature into adults themselves largely through imitating the adult world as they see it; most of their play is this imitating of adults, and again, first of all of their parents. Thus is established a recurring cycle of education and mis-education. If it is practically impossible to take children from their parents immediately after birth so as to educate them "properly" (cf. 540e–a) – and in fact not desirable for a host of reasons, beginning with the comprehensive importance of parental love for healthy maturation – then the only way to break into this circle of education so as significantly to change it would be by re-educating adults, perhaps before they become parents in their turn (cf. 534d). We are not told how to do that. Rather, we are *shown* how to do it. The most important pedagogical-political lesson this dialogue has to teach is never explicitly discussed, but it is quite beautifully *demonstrated*. It is on display throughout the course of the night's discussion and, if one is fortunate, in the course of one's own study of that discussion.

So the philosopher is confronting the most challenging of pedagogical problems, and as noted before it is one that perennially recurs: how to re-educate intelligent, high-spirited, opinionated young men who are rebellious against the respectable views and authorities of the polity that nurtured them, but who remain none the less profoundly under their sway. Now, what does he have at his disposal besides argument, which has but a limited effect on most people, and then only if one can somehow get them to listen (cf. 327c)?

First and foremost, he has himself as an example, and, as a way of teaching others how to live, action does indeed speak many times louder than "mere" words (cf. 473a1-3). These young men trust the man more than they do his *logos*, for they have only to trust their own senses, what they can see for themselves. He's no fool, but neither is he any part of the established order of things, living as most people do, pursuing what they pursue. They are not sure why. He is something of a mystery to them. He arouses their curiosity, first of all about him, and then about that which interests him. And he, in turn, is sympathetic to them, and seems to take them seriously, as if they and their concerns and opinions matter to him. They are flattered. Being initially attracted to the man, perhaps even becoming strangely infatuated with him, they will listen to him, giving him the opportunity to demonstrate his own superior understanding of things, and thereby establish his intellectual authority over them. And so they may be gradually led to trust his *logos*, and finally to trust *logos* as such. Thus, what begins as a highly personal form of leadership by the philosopher may prepare the way for these young men learning to lead themselves by the same beacon as guides him: the utterly impersonal rule of educated reason.[8]

Second, the philosopher has his special wisdom, his knowledge of *erōtika*, and thus of human nature, especially the nature of youth. Inasmuch as a love of teaching, of helping others to learn, goes hand in hand with one's own love of learning, the philosopher spends what no doubt to many adults seems a disproportionate amount of his time with young people, who being less mired in everyday affairs have a keener interest in the great permanent questions than do most of their elders. For it is one of the sad facts of life that this distinctly human quality of our nature tends to bloom with youth, only to fade with neglect more quickly than beauty (498ab). The philosopher, however, by spending so much time with the young, comes to know them well, and is regularly reminded what it is to be young. And because their enthusiasm is infectious, he retains an eternal youthfulness and beauty of soul, and is thereby repaid for his efforts on their behalf. By knowing what young men think and feel, what their current interests are, what they most desire, how they typically act and react – by knowing all this, he can capture their attention and hold it while he introduces them to other points of view and new interests, awakens new desires even, which may in time supplant the old ones entirely. Because he understands the developmental trajectory of the human soul in all its archetypical incarnations, the philosopher can practise a noble kind of rhetoric, persuasive speech in the service of a noble end: educating human beings.

Third, the philosopher knows a bit about politics, too, and it's surprising how impressive that is to certain kinds of people, this ability to make sense out of what is arguably the most bewildering complexity that a human being can turn his attention to – astrophysics seems simple by comparison, calculus dull, and neurosurgery merely a mechanical trade.

How, then, does the political philosopher choose to meet this pedagogic challenge that confronts him? His strategy is most ingenious, positively inspired. First, he professes himself somewhat at a loss, unequal to their challenge, but none the less willing to try his best (368b–c). Thus he solicits their sympathy and encouragement, thereby softening their adversarial stance. But the masterstroke is his suggesting that they jointly conduct a mental experiment, one that the sort of young men he is dealing with would naturally find most attractive: they will attempt to describe a basic city; better still, build one in *logos* themselves from the ground up in order to see what makes it work, and how justice and injustice arise in it. This is the first step in revolutionizing their perspective. It will be *their* city, and they will be doubly attached to it: first, simply because it is *theirs*; and second, because they *made* it, it is their own offspring, a product of their own procreative efforts (cf. 330c). For reasons deserving of long reflection, the project will now naturally transform itself into that of making a good city, a happy city, a beautiful city, the perfect city, the city of their dreams. They can imagine themselves founding a city that will exemplify through the ages the very idea of what every city should be, one in which everyone leads secure, wholesome, virtuous, graceful, productive – and, consequently, gratifying – lives, unmarred by chronic bickering, not to mention more serious kinds of internal strife.

They may even fall so in love with their own brainchild as to wish more than anything to see it actualized (cf. 466d, 471c–e). Imagine being the founder and ruler of such a regime! Imagine the lasting fame that would accrue to him, living on in people's memories larger than life. It is a peculiar fact of human nature that most people wish to be well-remembered after they are dead (and presumably past all awareness of their reputation). The thought of dying in utter obscurity, it seems, can call into question the significance of having lived at all; for some unhealthy souls, even infamy is better than that. But it is an ironic fact that one of the grandest manifestations of man's selfish love of fame – the desire to be honoured through subsequent ages as a great political statesman or founder or reformer – typically requires the extreme of selfless dedication to the common good. Anyone aspiring to the exalted status of founding father must put the success of his project ahead of all other considerations, and be prepared to set the example for personal self-sacrifice. Thus, as they enter into the spirit of this adventure, they take still another step in the revolution of their perspective on politics. They must stop thinking exclusively of themselves, and take responsibility for the welfare of the whole city, this city that will be built to their specifications, designed to prosper, and endure, and to protect itself from all harm – not only as might come from external enemies, but also from clever, cynical, ruthless men who would seek to exploit it for their own selfish advantage; and even from the many merely incompetent men who are not fit to play any part in ruling it (cf. 412c, 421a, 434a–b). Largely without realizing it, they have become tacit partisans of justice.[9]

And they have also become a good deal more interested in the rest of the truth about politics, desirous of all that might constitute a true *science* of politics. Their old grab-bag of ill-considered opinions, which presumed the city to be a going concern, will no longer do. They shall want to know, because *now* they *need* to know, the principles upon which a good regime can be founded, and why there is such a variety of ever-changing, defective regimes (with which their city shall have to deal). They may even discover that such problems have a certain intrinsic charm of their own.

And so, taking part in this imaginary political adventure – seriously taking part, determined to think the problems through as realistically as possible – can initiate the transformation from rebellious youth to responsible citizen. Learning that there are no simple answers, that constructing a coherent and harmonious regime requires substantial sacrifices (cf. 398a, 399e, 403ab), and that aiming at perfection requires enormous sacrifices (cf. 416d–417b) – unacceptable ones, to speak the truth (cf. 457cd) – should enhance one's respect for the difficulties of establishing and maintaining decency in political life. And the fact that this experiment takes place in *logos*, and not in political actuality, facilitates this reversal of perspective. For not only is doing it in one's imagination easier, it is also more pure. There is neither the hard work, nor the frustrations and disappointments of failures and partial successes that can vitiate enthusiasm from the outset. In *logos* (where things are no sooner said than done; cf. 588d), their regime can be as perfect as reason allows – something actual political life never is. Nor is one attracted by the selfish temptations with which actual political life abounds; because a city in all the purity of *logos* provides no possibility for gratifying the lower desires of the soul, the project brings forth the best in a person: one's noble side holds sway unopposed, perhaps clearly revealing itself for the first time. Moreover, there is twenty-four centuries of testimony that establishing one's city "merely" in *logos* is no bar to its founder gaining immortal fame (cf. 599a–e).

And is this not a legitimate way to discover what justice is, or at least what political justice is? One endeavours to describe the best regime one can imagine, on the assumption that a truly good regime will be a just regime, at least in the sense uncovered with Thrasymachos: that it will be at the peak of its strength because united, and united because it is an harmonious arrangement, with all of its parts working cooperatively (justice being whatever it is that produces this social harmony, whereas injustice, formally defined, is whatever introduces "factions, hatreds, and quarrels" among the citizenry; 351a–d). Admittedly, these young men (like the rest of us) want to know about justice in the individual human being, what it *is* and what *power* it has, thus what it *does* in and for and to the individual. But presumably there is *some* sort of connection between the justness of the city and the justness of the man – there must be some reason we use the same term in connection with both (368e, 435ab). Now, it may be only as Glaukon suggested, that the notion of a just man is derivative from that artificial thing called justice in the city, being someone who takes to heart and more-or-less willingly abides by these conventions, and who thus is publicly praised (but often privately despised) as "just". Then again, if justice in political life is *not* the artificial, conventional thing Glaukon and many others today believe it to be, there may be some other explanation. Sokrates' proposed experiment leaves all possibilities open.

But anticipating for the moment the actual results of the experiment the better to assess it, notice: the account of natural justice that the philosopher ultimately provides is *radically individualistic*. It should more than satisfy the demands of Glaukon's own heroic individualism. And this must be one of the more ironic features of the dialogue – that despite the "collectivist" character of the regime they construct, despite its making strenuous and exacting demands on everyone but especially on its ruling class, the philosopher's teaching about justice at all levels remains thoroughly individualistic, rooted in that least social of everyday maxims, "mind your own business". It tacitly concedes that Thrasymachos and Glaukon and Adeimantos are correct in regarding self-interest to be the fundamental law of nature (cf. 347d) – that all things by nature seek their good – and that any standards of considerate behaviour towards others not grounded first of all in the self-interest of the individual are at odds with nature. It teaches that their mistake, however, resulting in their failure to discern any such standards, is a consequence of their inadequate albeit quite ordinary understanding of the self and its interests, and especially of the loves of the self. They have not seen that love can be utterly selfless and yet remain profoundly selfish, and that sometimes only by being the former can it be fully the latter. Because they do not know themselves, because they do not know the heights and depths and breadths of the human soul, nor what makes it move, nor what makes it healthy and strong and beautiful, they lack what is most needed for serving one's own true interests. The philosopher provides them the opportunity to make good this deficiency in the course of presenting them a most powerful account of natural justice. And so far as I can judge, it is essentially true.

It is an admittedly strange account, and at first blush rather unpromising as a comprehensive resolution of the entire spectrum of problems people normally think of in connection with the term 'justice'. In fact, it seems (at best) only tangentially related to many, if not *most* of them. The suggestion that the essential truth about a just polity boils down to each citizen's devoting the best years of his life to doing well one, and only one, of the tasks that needs doing in the city, namely that for which his body and soul are naturally best suited, and be appropriately rewarded for it, and refrain from meddling in work naturally better suited to others – the suggestion that *this* principle ought to put an end to the heretofore endless quarrels over justice is apt to be met with a healthy skepticism, if not outright incredulity. It hardly seems equal to the task, to say the least.

In fairness to the account, however, one must constantly remember what one is looking for, and what kind of answer is possible, and what necessarily would be involved in recognizing it. One is asking, in effect, whether a dispassionate examination of nature (including human nature) reveals any principles, or any guidance whatsoever, upon which to base a mutually beneficial, permanent association of human beings, given that the arrangement must be one that each should accept as being in his own best interest. Whether each *would* accept it as such (were he to become adequately acquainted with it), and for ever and always agree to it, and regularly act in accordance with it, is philosophically irrelevant to there being a truth about natural justice. It is *not*, of course, philosophically irrelevant to the truth about *politics*. It may be the case, as Aristotle argues, that human beings in their diversities of natures and circumstances – to say nothing of their normal tendency to remember more readily grievances than benefactions, and their greater inclination to blame than to praise[10] – will never permanently agree about justice. And so he may be right in concluding that political life will always contain within it the germs of sedition, and thus will always need to be policed (cf. *Politics* 1301a–1302a).

There are any number of reasons why many people of almost all kinds might not accept even a demonstrably true account of natural justice, beginning with the fact that knowing and living in accordance with the truth of things are hardly their foremost concerns. Nor are they necessarily capable of grasping this truth, whatever their degree of concern. And of all things, learning the truth about justice presumes, first of all, a greater-than-average willingness to do so. Moreover, one must appreciate at the outset the architectonic character of the question, and the encyclopaedic range of potential evidence to be considered, and the demands it might make on one's power of synthetic judgment. One is obliged, it seems, "to take everything pertinent into account", but with only a dim and vague antecedent awareness of what this might be. Such an intuition or premonition about justice comes primarily from the various common opinions about it, including especially those embodied in the laws of apparently decent regimes (cf. 538d-e, 589cd, 590de), opinions that, for all their confusion and disagreement, presumably point to the perennial matters of concern and conflict. In short, to ask what is just by nature is not much like asking how many stomachs a cow has.

But even bearing all this in mind, what the philosopher discovers "rolling around at his feet" (432d; cf. 479d, 388b) — or did he have it concealed "in his hand" from the beginning? — seems obviously inadequate. His discussion focuses almost exclusively on the burdens of political life, on the distribution of duties and responsibilities and consequently of powers; he says comparatively little about the distribution of benefits. Alternatively expressed, he seems to treat political justice as a matter primarily of the production rather than the consumption of beneficial things, as if the whole of justice were practically equivalent to a rational division of labour.

Of course, this is not a serious deficiency if the most *important* benefits of political justice in fact are, contrary to popular estimation, *common* goods, things not needing distribution. And true enough, his basic principle does dictate that every able-bodied person benefiting from the communal life of the city make a useful contribution to it, that he "do his part", and that seems only fair. Moreover, it provides some guidance as to what makes this "part" rather than another "his" (370a-b; cf. 455b-c, 486c). And insofar as one believes that other people ought to respect an adult's "right" to manage what are acknowledged to be his own affairs, and offer criticism or assistance or advice only if and when asked — and virtually everyone has asserted as much on his own behalf at least once — this principle, reciprocally enjoining everyone to mind his own business and not meddle in that of others, seems on balance attractive (433ab; cf. 370a). And the fact that, were a political community willing and able to order its practices according to this principle, everyone's basic need for food, shelter, and safety would be met so far as practical; and all would enjoy the blessings of the art of good government (cf. 346d-e); and otherwise be left free to pursue the pleasures of family and friendship — these are not inconsiderable accomplishments with which to credit a conception of justice.

But it raises its own kind of questions. For example, what ensures a natural harmony, not merely between the diversity of natural abilities

The War Lover

and the variety of politically useful tasks, but in approximately congruent proportions (cf. 371a, 428de)? And *how far* is one to carry the rational division of labour? to the point that there are those who specialize in affixing heads onto stick pins (cf. 370cd, 374a–b, 395b)? In answering these and other practical questions, we seem reliant upon what passes for common sense, which is often little more than a reflection of familiar practices. But if this were generally adequate, justice would not present the theoretical problem that a world of divergent practices suggests that it does.

Perhaps some reliance on common sense is unavoidable, however. After all, justice is problematic only for those possessed of a rational soul, and it seems fair enough that the means used to pose the question be equally available to solve it. Still, put the most generous construction possible on this "having and doing of one's own" (433ea), it none the less seems to provide no guidance at all regarding whole other sectors of what is ordinarily acknowledged as belonging to the "problem terrain" of justice, and precious little substance or specificity concerning matters to which it does pertain. Looking to this formal principle alone, what would one say ought to fall within the scope of private property – what kinds of things, and in what amounts? And what would constitute a just distribution of it, and what limits if any ought there to be on the disposing of it through inheritance (cf. 330a–b, 331de), gifts (cf. 390e, 420a, 614a), or sale (cf. 556a). Should usury be allowed (cf. 555c, 506ea)? Should gambling? Is there to be no protection at all for the fool who would be too soon parted from his money? There may be a rough justice in that, but it often has dire consequences for others besides the fool (cf. 555d).

And what about the various sorts of contracts? The extensive role that promises and contracts play in civil life, and their centrality to everyday concerns of justice, are conceded, even subtly emphasized in the dialogue. Contracts are the first things that come to Polemarchos' mind when he is asked to specify the utility of justice under conditions of peace (333a; cf. 554c). According to Adeimantos, it is somehow via contracts that creeping lawlessness moves from individuals to a subversion of the entire public regime (424de), a judgment the philosopher himself seems to agree with (426e; cf. 443e). And in considering remedies for the regime-destroying evil endemic to Oligarchy: the increasing concentration of wealth into the hands of a decreasing number of citizens – his second-best proposal (after the entailment of property) is one that would enhance the value of virtue by prescribing that most voluntary contracts be made at the contractors' own risk (i.e., *not* enforced by the regime; 556ab). Are we to understand that this is a generally adequate policy regarding contracts so far as a public system of justice goes? Are questions about, for example, the fair allocation of assets and liabilities upon the dissolution of partnerships, or about obligations to third parties, simply not worth worrying about?

And what about prices and wages? Are they to be established solely by the market (cf. 371b), without regard to intrinsic worth, or to distortions resulting from contrived monopolies or natural disasters? What is a fair system of taxation? Revolutions have been fought in the name of issues such as these. Compared with the considerable specificity one finds in his *Laws*, to say nothing of Aristotle's *Nichomachean Ethics* or *Politics*, the philosopher in this dialogue seems to treat such practical matters with a studied indifference. Issues over which men have quarrelled ferociously, and which are often seen as distinguishing whole regimes, are apparently finessed with the observation that they're easily resolved by gentlemen who have been adequately educated (425b–e, 427a).

If one presumes that the Aristocracy in *logos* exemplifies the correct or best practical interpretation of this basic principle of justice, some matters are clarified, but at the price of an even greater perplexity. Again, consider for example the distribution of private property: the ruling class of Guardians and their auxiliaries has none (416c–b, 419a–420a, 464bc), the individuals of the producing class have all there is (although no indication is given us regarding what proportion of the city's property is thusly held, as opposed to remaining communally owned; cf. 547c). Now, are we seriously meant to believe that this is *just*? That in a just regime, those with gold and silver in their souls should be content with this psychic wealth, provided their barest physical needs are met, and expect nothing more from a political association to which they devote their lives? Of course, one may suppose that they all "volunteer" for their jobs on that basis, entering into this monastic brotherhood of public service with their eyes wide open, as it were (although it is not clear that such is the case: 415b–c, 519ea, 423c–d). And while this, if true, would not be irrelevant to the justness of the scheme (nor is the fact that they enjoy, perhaps by way of compensation, a near monopoly of honour; cf. 414a, 415a, 434b), neither does it seem an adequate defence of the inherent justness of what seems a grossly lopsided distribution of private property (and perhaps of honour as well).

If, however, there's any truth to the claim that "virtue is in tension with wealth" (550e; cf. 555cd), that a pursuit of one is at odds with a concern for the other, then one cannot speak of a just distribution of property in isolation from this other thing a human being should value incomparably more: the enjoyment of his own natural excellence. And it would be dangerous, perhaps even paradoxical, to think, as many do, that one is the appropriate reward of the other, rather than virtue's being its own reward (and perhaps the prerequisite of anything else being truly good). So one should bear in mind that as a consequence of the city in *logos* being just in the way that it is, each member of the ruling class does receive the fullest measure of all virtue of which he is capable (433b, 442b-d) – and, one should add, the opportunity for a lifetime of friendship with others worthy of friendship (cf. 334c). Perhaps they're not being short-changed after all (cf. 420b, 466a–b, 521a).

But what, then, would constitute a just distribution of property *within* the money-making, property-owning, producing class? This would seem to be much more relevant to the world with which we are familiar. But beyond being warned that they should not be allowed to become either rich or poor (421e–a) – and how this is to be arranged is left wholly to our imagination; presumably it would require some perpetual system of wealth redistribution or confiscation – this issue remains steeped in the shadows of that place one can only traverse with great pain and difficulty (*dusbatos ... topos ... kai episkios*; 432c). Is it not as important to the truth about natural justice as most people suppose it to be (cf. 329de), and as the philosopher himself might seem to affirm it to be in making the whole discussion of justice arise out of one concerning the principal benefit of wealth?

And what, according to this principle of justice, should be done with those who *refuse* to mind their own business, those who rob and steal and embezzle and extort from their fellow citizens, who defraud and blackmail and slander them, who bear false witness against them, who assault and rape and enslave and even kill them? Or with those who commit crimes against the whole political community, stealing or wilfully damaging public property, blaspheming or desecrating or otherwise dishonouring what the rest of the community reveres, or who treasonously betray it, or attempt to subvert it? Or with those of

Crime and Punishment

smaller spirit who are incorrigibly lazy, who default on their debts, prostitute themselves, violate the sanctity of marriage, or neglect familial responsibilities? And what about incest? Various passages in the dialogue imply that these are, by both nature and common consent, rightly regarded as crimes (cf., e.g., 442e-a, 451b, 458e, 461b-e, 565b-567e, 569b-c, 574a-575b). But the entire practical business of crime and punishment is left in the dark, except for whatever fitful light is thrown by the tacit suggestion that an individual who commits injustice ought to be punished in order that he might be made better (591ab; there is no allusion to the public's interest in punishing for the sake of deterrence, retribution, and restitution). Or by their concluding that it is foolish to try legislating all the details of correct behaviour right down to manners and sumptuary practices (425b). Or by the dictum that those judged to have incurably bad natures ought to be put to death (410a; cf. 610d).

But as for any practical *procedures* whereby these and all other criminal judgments can be justly made – procedures that guard so far as possible against personal bias and honest mistakes, incorrigible ignorance and the manifold difficulties in distinguishing appearance from reality – procedures which do all this, but without paralysing the human administration of justice – with respect to this practical matter of rightly great concern, the principle of 'doing and thus having what is one's own' seems utterly mute. And this despite the prominence given to the corruption of judicial proceedings in the philosopher's own account of the arising of tyranny (565a-c). Ought one to be regarded as innocent until proven guilty? Or have the right to a speedy (but not too speedy) trial? Or to confront one's accusers? Or to cross-examine witnesses? And to speak in one's own defence, but only if one chooses to; or to allow or require others to do so (cf. *Apology* 18a-19a, 24d, 27a-b, 33d-b, 37ab)? Is all hearsay testimony, and any given under duress, inadmissible? There is no suggestion that natural justice entitles one to be judged by a jury of one's peers, and some indication to the contrary (409b) – although the acceptances of this and other of the principles referred to above are widely regarded as landmarks in the emergence of truly just trial procedures, and other philosophers have argued that some at least are natural laws, being the clear dictates of reason.[11]

In short, anyone familiar with the myriad questions that have arisen in political life concerning the right way to do things is apt to be perplexed by the apparent sparseness of the account of justice given in the philosopher's major dialogue supposedly devoted to it. Barely a hundredth part of the entire discussion is recognizably an explicit discussion of what justice *is*, or *why* this and not something else is *just*, or how a just man properly behaves in various concrete situations and what makes that the just way. There is vastly more explicit discussion of philosophy, or of poetry for that matter, than of justice. However, if one assumes that the dialogue's teaching about justice is not confined to these conspicuously brief and few explications of it, but is *exemplified* throughout – and first and foremost in the character of Sokrates – it is possible to discern something far richer, and to my taste profoundly satisfying. Admittedly, to expand the scope of one's attention to the farthest reaches of the dialogue, and to consider every feature with an eye for what it might reveal of the philosopher's perspective on justice, may be to embark on the labour of a lifetime. Of course, this is a liability only for those who have something better to do. For one who hasn't, let me suggest that it is particularly helpful, by way of beginning: first, to hypothesize that the important truths about political justice are reflected not only in the essential features of the philosopher's cities in *logos* but in his account of the inferior regimes, and why their conceptions of justice are defective; second, to observe how he treats the other characters in the dialogue; third, to attend to how he actually uses the term 'justice' (for though his explanations of it are thrifty, his employment of its various cognates is liberal – lavish, in fact); and fourth, to reflect on how he spends his time (cf. 358d).

Not that doing even this much is an easy task. Consider, for example, the third recommendation, that of examining the philosopher's own usage of the family of terms by which we speak of things just and unjust. Justice itself (*dikaiosynē*) is mentioned 130 times, the just (*dikaios*) 230, the unjust (*adikos*) 105, injustice (*adikia*) 78, doing injustice (*adikein*) 64, penalty (*dikē*) 30, and so on. However, roughly three-fourths of the some seven hundred uses of these words and their cognates are concentrated in four places. Not surprisingly, Book One is permeated with references to this thing everyone has opinions about but which no one seems quite able to capture in words. So, too, is the brothers' challenge to the philosopher to prove the inherent superiority of the just life over that of the unjust. And, of course, there are Book Four's explicit discussions of justice and injustice in both the city and the man. Finally, there is that curious "proof" of the soul's immortality, which pivots on whether or not an existent soul can be destroyed by anything, but in particular by its special nemesis, injustice (608e–614a). The bad news is, it's the *other* uses scattered throughout the rest of the dialogue which are, in my opinion, more revealing, often by first of all being more puzzling. One is hard pressed to see an obvious connection between justice as each part doing its own work well and, for example, the philosopher's being guilty of an injustice should he fail to affirm that the soul is immortal (608d), or decline to gratify Glaukon's desire to be shown the moderation in their city (430de); or why it is "just" that they all be perplexed by the apparently contradictory requirements they have specified for the nature of a good Guardian (375d), or why certain kinds of desires can "justly" (*dikaiōs*) be called 'necessary' (whereas certain others could "fairly" [*kalōs*] be called 'unnecessary'; 558d–a), or why those who speak the equivalent of pointless prayers are "justly" laughed at (499c).

Believing as I none the less do that the dialogue conveys a teaching about natural justice that is both powerful and true, I feel obliged to indicate some of my reasons for thinking so (cf. 506bc). But I am equally bound to warn at the outset that I do not pretend to have done adequately everything I suspect needs doing well in order to speak with authority concerning the dialogue's complete teaching about justice (cf. 450d–b). Nor should the following be regarded as an attempt to *prove* anything to anybody; at most, it calls attention to considerations a serious and open-minded seeker after the truth about justice might wish to consider in order to prove something to himself.

I shall begin with what it seems the dialogue would have us recognize as the essential truths about political justice. The inherent limitations on the justness one finds to be possible in even the best of cities, however, highlight in several ways the still greater importance of discovering a complementary kind of justice of the individual person, something that provides (whatever else) standards of right behaviour towards others with which it is naturally beneficial for him to comply. The philosopher's revelation that there is indeed natural justice of this kind, a just way of living that is in the self-interest of each and every human being to practise for the sake of his own greatest power and happiness, seems to me a more than adequate response to the radical challenge posed by those clever and dangerous "sons of Ariston". Having spoken about it and its relationship to some of the more commonplace opinions about justice, I shall discuss some of the puzzles which remain, and some of the dialogic evidence that, in conjunction with one's own experience, might help resolve them.[12]

Whereas wisdom, courage, and moderation are easily seen to be virtues of the individual human being – dimensions of human excellence whose reality, not merely whose appearance, is inherently valuable to their possessor (and which would be so even were man not naturally political) – it is not obvious that one can say as much for justice. Rather, justice is thought of, first and foremost (if not exclusively), as a *social* virtue. Indeed, justice is generally regarded as *the* social virtue, supposedly governing people's dealings *with each other*, and reflective of their being by nature political animals, living in communities that are more – and usually much, much more – than mere herds or packs or flocks. As such, justice is the cardinal virtue of political regimes. In distributing the duties, responsibilities, rights, and powers necessary to sustain a common political life, as well as some of the benefits it makes possible, its *de facto* conception of justice is what virtually *defines* a regime. But since there are many different distributions of such things that can be made to function more-or-less well – and thus different types of regimes, with differing allocations of burdens and benefits for the constituent individuals (or kinds of individuals) – the question naturally arises: which is best? People being people, even those of good will tend to see as a better regime one in which people such as themselves enjoy a more generous share of benefits – usually justified (in their own eyes, at least) by their making a more important contribution, if not exactly bearing more burdens. Thus, there are serious differences of opinion as to which regime, if any, is *truly* the best. Is there any objective answer to this question, any hope of knowledge that might replace these warring opinions?

To see what there might be to see, we should probably begin as the philosopher begins, by asking why humans live in political communities. After all, if one can discern the purpose for something, or a coherent complex of complementary purposes, one thereby has a natural standard for judging it: how well does it fulfil the purpose for which it is intended (or stated in practical terms, how well compared with available alternatives)? The adequacy of a mirror, for example, is judged by its purpose of faithfully reflecting how things look, and eyes by how well they see (cf. 352e–c, 507c–b, 527e). However, if something is expected to serve several not altogether, or not always, harmonious purposes – to say nothing of directly conflicting purposes

– the problem of judging it is compounded, perhaps to the point of insolubility. People's *not agreeing* as to the proper purpose of something has a similar practical consequence.

As to whether or not people *ought* to agree, that depends on whether or not there is a correct account, and that in turn may depend on whether the thing is natural or artificial. Something that exists by nature presumably has a natural purpose (*telos*), if none other than to exist in accordance with its specific nature (which may require a specific environment that can also, then, be regarded as natural). Whereas, in the case of something artificial, its purpose is whatever its artificer intended for it to be (which ultimately, of course, must be somehow a reflection of *his* nature; in this sense, the mirror reflects much more than the look of a person). If, however, there is a multiplicity of artificers, *agreement* among them as to the purpose of what they make would constitute the only conceivable standard for properly judging either it, or the use to which it is put. But if they simply do not and will not agree on its purpose, there is no ground for concluding that some are right and others wrong. Their conflict not being rationally resolvable, it will be settled on some other basis.

By way of attempting to show both the naturalness and the true purpose or purposes of the *polis*, the philosopher suggests that each of us is "not self-sufficient, but in need of much" (369b). And it seems obvious that a political community is potentially more self-sufficient than is any single person (whereas an individual is potentially a more unified whole than any city can ever hope to be; cf. 462b-d). Still, it would be useful to have a clearer understanding as to the nature of this human needfulness supposedly at the basis of the political association. Beasts need food and shelter, and might even find shoes and clothing (not to mention doctors) useful sometimes, but this needfulness is not sufficient to their forming cities.

The philosopher's elaboration on how the *city* (as a common settlement of "partners and helpers"; 369c) overcomes individual human needfulness leads one to think of the city as a community of interdependent artisans bound together by the mutual necessity implicit in the rational division of labour. What *begins* as a counsel of *efficiency* to an assortment of needy individuals, each free to do what he thinks is best for himself (369c, 369e-c), is transformed by stages into the fundamental *dictate* – "one man, one job" – of a well-ordered regime (374a-d, 397e, 423d, 433a, 443c). This development, moreover, sets the seal on a most radical and inescapable interdependence, transparent to all but the meanest intelligence (cf. 371de). It is evidently *desirable* that their sharing of a common fate be obvious to everyone in the city, the high as well as the low, thereby imparting to each a sincere because self-interested regard for the common good. Beyond a doubt, such a shared recognition would itself contribute to the greater justness of the regime.

But this salutary political interpretation conceals certain truths as important as those it reveals. The fact that each human being has specific bodily needs of varying urgency, beginning with the need for food and water and some protection against the elements, does not itself imply that he needs other human beings to help him supply them. As noted before, it implies at most that he needs minimal skills in several arts. There is, however, another bodily need not explicitly mentioned, but which makes joining with *trustworthy* "partners and helpers" much more compelling: one needs a safe place to sleep (cf. 578d). Why this need is not acknowledged at the outset is the first question posed by the philosopher's account. Mutual security, especially against other men (who, possessed of reason and thus capable of foresightful planning, are the most dangerous competitors), is a much more pressing reason for a multitude to gather together in a common settlement. However, *this* does *not* imply a division of labour; quite the contrary: it would be in the common interest that everyone develop to the fullest a capability of contributing to the common defence, the safety of the whole community being the first and most obvious dimension of the common good (cf. 373ea, 471d).

But given that this common practical necessity for security enjoins a communal way of life (cf. 493c), a rational division of all *other* productive labour would seem sensible for the reasons given: everything else needed would be produced in greater quantity, better quality, and with less effort and more satisfaction if each man specialized in one of the other arts comprised by the city (370c). And since most work is not fun, men are not indifferent to the efficiency of their labour. Thus one can see that the individual's need for physical safety, his need to protect "mere life", does not adequately explain the city; it doubtless helps explain the *origin* of the city, but it is far from satisfactory as an explanation of what a city *is*. A group of animals gathered together for mutual security is a herd, not a political community. The essence of the truly *political* community is its rational division of labour, and the radical interdependence implicit in it. And the extensive reliance each member has on the others to supply his most urgent needs and wants, a fact evident to everyone, gives some grounds for mutual trust.

But in the case of cities, just as with individuals, this concern for maximizing technical efficiency runs counter to the concern for self-sufficiency, and leads cities to specialize in the production of certain "goods" for the sake of engaging in trade with other cities having complementary specialties (370e–a). Thus the city, supposedly a remedy for the individual's lack of self-sufficiency, becomes a reflection of it. And while the city in *logos* is subsequently purged of most of the luxuries earlier introduced (cf. 373a–b, 399e, 404d), and may in fact be left with a self-sufficient way of life (cf. 422d, but also 425cd), the stated grounds for that being done are never self-sufficiency. The only "import" *expressly* disallowed is a certain kind of music (398a).

That the philosopher permits his young partners to lose sight so quickly of what is supposedly the natural *telos* of the political association – self-sufficiency in meeting men's bodily needs – suggests that he views that *telos* quite differently. Only in the city can man cultivate his rational nature to the fullest, for only there may men employ and thus develop their reason dialectically: in perfecting the arts (cf. 350a, 405c–406a, 601d–e), in ordering and governing the whole, in enjoying whatever may come from sharing a common *logos* (which is everything from tragedy and comedy to friendship and religion), and in systematically pursuing an understanding of things for its own sake. In short, the city exists not because humans are needful (so are the beasts), but because humans are rational. Alternatively expressed, the city is needed not because it is the only means of meeting man's bodily needs, but because it provides the only environment sufficient for man's cultivation of his rational soul, and thus the only environment in which he can live as a human being. *This* is the natural purpose of the *polis*, and this is the end to which one must look in order to determine what is the naturally best, naturally just arrangement of it.

Given that the city is grounded in necessity, however, and that in order for it to survive and prosper a certain amount of necessary work must be done, the question remains how best to organize it: how best to distribute both the burdens of making it work, and whatever benefits that come from its working well need distributing. On this matter, then, is there any guidance to be found in the nature of things (men included)? And thus one returns to the fundamental principle of political justice as enucleated in the discussions of it in Book Four, as exemplified in the cities in *logos*, as revealed in the philosopher's own use of language throughout the dialogue, and as contravened in varying degrees and ways by the archetypically defective regimes. Why should one accept that each man doing well one – and only one – politically useful job is the fundamental truth upon which to base a regime, such that it will be naturally just so far as possible?

In order to reach a judgment on the question, one needs to have a clear understanding of all its consequences and other implications. Does it get done the essential work of political justice (353b), reflected in the fact that the members of the polity would be basically satisfied with it and each other, living in peace and friendship, free so far as possible from those "factions, hatreds, and quarrels" that are due to injustice (351d)? And is it adequate as the architectonic virtue of a polity, making it well-ordered as a whole, never detracting from but promoting and sustaining to the utmost the *other* aspects of political goodness? (This, notice, is why the philosopher says *he* infers that "the practice of minding one's own business, when it comes into being a certain way", is probably justice; 433b–c). And while it is doubtful that these other dimensions of a city's goodness are best described as wisdom, courage, and moderation (427e), in actually applying them to the city the philosopher gives each of these human virtues a decidedly political interpretation.

The first city in *logos* is *called* "wise" in that it is "well-counselled" (*euboulos*) with respect to dealing with itself and other cities (428b–d). And this despite its architects having provided it no deliberative institutions. True, nothing they have done precludes such institutions, but the fact that no particular set is specified suggests that formal criteria alone are insufficient for determining one set to be universally best. There may be, then, a variety of structural and procedural and consultative arrangements that facilitate sound political judgment (and hence are more-or-less equally just), with no way of determining apart from concrete political experience which kind is naturally best for a particular time and place. But this conspicuous absence may also be meant to suggest that there is no adequate *institutional* substitute for flesh-and-blood prudence, courage, good will, moderation, and love of the polity (cf. 412cd). Rule by human beings manifesting these qualities is always in accord with natural justice. How one brings such men to positions of rule is a difficult question of immense practical importance, and there may be ways other than the one depicted in the city in *logos* (cf. 473a). But that practical difficulty does not affect the naturally best, naturally just answer to the question of *who* ought to rule. Such rulers could be trusted if anyone can to devise for a given polity adequate deliberative institutions and procedures, a fair system of imposts and taxes, regulations to facilitate public and private business, a useful system of weights and measures and currency, and so on (cf. 425c-e). There is, of course, no answer in the nature of things as to how much ought to constitute a pound, but it is basic to both peaceful political cooperation and natural justice that those who deal with each other use the same measures, and get what they presume they are paying for.

Such rulers can also be relied upon to understand why certain acts must be treated as crimes, being incompatible with sustaining an harmonious community as the environment in which human beings can safely live rational lives. Among acts that qualify are those (mentioned above) which the philosopher tacitly treats as crimes. But other acts are not naturally crimes in this strict sense, although they become such by law (it being a first principle of justice that all the laws of a decent political community be generally obeyed; cf. *Crito* 50ab, 53b-c). Whether kinds of usury should be permitted, or land entailed, or the distribution of inheritance regulated, or all types of gambling prohibited are questions to which there may not be universally correct answers. What is best for a given political community would require an assessment of the character of the citizenry and their concrete circumstances, looking off towards the goal of keeping the polity unified and free of chronic discord (423bc, 462a-b; cf. 500d-c) - the prerequisite of its being a beautiful environment for rationality. This requires guarding especially against the emergence of great disparities in wealth (421e-a), or anything to obstruct the opportunities for people to do what useful work they can naturally do best (and reaping the fitting reward for it; 423cd), or anything to corrupt the basic civic education in the virtues of honesty and moderation, piety, and an appropriate courage.

Similar remarks apply to what constitutes a just schedule of punishments. Whereas certain acts are crimes by nature, their fitting punishment by political authorities may not be set by nature alone, but only in conjunction with a dispassionate assessment of political conditions. The severity that may be required to first instil order in primitive circumstances, or to restore it in decadent ones, would be out of place in a well-established, decent regime.[13] Thus, what may be justly needed by Drako could become "draconian" by virtue of its success.

The War Lover

In bygone days of the Old Wild West, they hanged horse thieves, and given what leaving a man afoot in a hostile environment could mean, it's not clear to me that they were mistaken in doing so, ... although I would not usually regard horse-stealing to be a capital offence, and suspect Plato wouldn't either. It certainly would not always be proof-positive of someone's having the sort of incorrigibly bad, tyrannical nature portrayed at the beginning of Book Nine.

As for just criminal trial procedures, the matter seems similar to that of establishing sensible deliberative institutions. The philosopher's raising the problem of having good judges while remaining silent about fair judicial procedures may be interpreted as implying that there are no means within human command – or even any *clearly best* approximation – of ensuring *both* that those who are innocent always are acquitted *and* that those who are guilty always pay the just penalty. But there are grounds for concluding that natural justice requires its political application to be weighted on the side of "over-protecting" the innocent (since – for reasons still to be discussed – the guilty *never* really get away scot-free). In any event, no purely procedural rules can ever substitute for having astute judges, who should be chosen from among the most upright and knowledgeable of a community's elders (409a–e), since the judging of disputes ("civil" as well as criminal) is one of the most important functions of ruling a polity, being the direct manifestation of the regime's conception and practice of justice (433e).

Their city is called "courageous" because it is stoutly defended – and known to be – by hand-picked professionals who maintain themselves at the peak of proficiency, are rigorously disciplined, are available any time of day or season, and are as thoroughly imbued as humanly possible with the ethos that death is preferable to defeat and slavery (386a–b, 429a–430b). So long as the soldiers "preserve" that opinion in themselves, they will be the most effective "preservers" of the city as a whole. The existence of a professional army would not itself preclude the other men (and even the women) assisting in the defence of the city *in extremis* (cf. 429b, 471d). But it does acknowledge several important facts of political life: that, *ceteris paribus*, no polygenous part-time citizen army is a match for serious full-time professionals selected (or self-selected) for their natural fighting qualities of body and soul (374c–d); that these are the sort of men who would tend to dominate a citizen army in any case; that such professional soldiers being more than a match for several times their own number of the other kind (422c) means, among other things, that they are capable of enforcing their rule over the vast majority of their fellows, and sooner or later are likely to do so.

Thus, this especially dangerous class of men is the greatest practical threat to the just governing of *any* regime – one can't do without them, nor do away with them even if one could. Nor should one want to, for without their balancing influence a polity would soon become too peace-loving for its own good. History, both long past and recent, is saturated with evidence that such men must be made a party to the just rule of the polity lest they enslave it (cf. 547c). Hence, one must find – or make – a place in the regime whereby these men's natural talents can be harnessed to the public interest, and that will satisfy their own longings for special recognition. Then every effort must be made to nurture them tamely to accept that place, and to despise anything incompatible with it.

But since every polity wishes to be defended and every polity must be policed, every polity has useful work for which especially manly men are naturally suited. To turn this task over to inferior people, out of either contempt for the tasks or fear of their being performed "too well", is a poor bargain. In a practical sense, the justice within a regime is often no better than the quality of its police (which, properly speaking, includes everyone responsible for ensuring that the rulers and their laws are obeyed). When they are corrupt or incompetent or unreliable, the inherent justness of the laws and the rulers who make them is beside the point. Moreover, the continued existence of any regime, including an internally just one, is no surer than the quality of those who defend it.

But if these vital tasks – indeed, practically sovereign tasks – are to be done well, those selected to do them should receive, preferably while still youths, a special kind of education aimed at making them self-disciplined, honest, plain-speaking men, proud to be what they are and having no wish to seem otherwise (cf. 389b–d, 395b–396b). And it especially requires establishing a *tradition* of the strictest obedience to one's lawful superiors (which is the easier both to establish and to maintain if they are recognizably one's *natural* superiors), such that these men take the greatest pride – not in that Achilles-like wilfulness to which men are so naturally inclined – but in having the adamant self-control to follow orders without question. But all this is not merely bowing to political necessity. It is also *just*: by virtue of their

The War Lover

nature thus nurtured, such men *deserve* the share of rule assigned them; and given both what they do and what they are – exemplars of political virtue – they naturally deserve the lion's share of honour. A regime that denies it to them, or has men in these roles that do not in fact merit such honour (as it is most likely to have should these tasks not be properly honoured), is to that extent unjust. And given the consequences that flow from it, the just distribution of *honour* is more important, more fundamental, than the just distribution of property (cf. 551a).

Their city's being "courageous" in this sense is the basis for further claiming that it ought to be designated "stronger than pleasures, desires, and itself", and thus "moderate", if any city can be rightly so-called. For in it there would be practical unanimity of opinion as to who should rule, including whose *taste* should rule that entire diversity of "desires, pleasures, and pains" one finds in the heterogeneous collection of people making up a normal political community (431b-e). The citizens are moderate, first of all, in being obedient to the law, knowing they will be made to obey should they not do so willingly (414b, 415de). Everyone thereby acquires the degree of self-restraint that law-abidingness demands. But it is worth noting, then, that "the city's" moderation is unlike "its" wisdom and courage, since these latter are a direct consequence of its principle of political justice (i.e., each part of the city doing its appropriate work). Whereas it is the warrior class doing its appropriate work of policing the community that indirectly promotes in the citizenry at large the more ordinary notion of moderation (the self-restraining of the bodily appetites and other irrational desires; 389de). Of course, being thus obliged to moderate such desires, each citizen thereby experiences at first hand the benefits of moderation, which more than anything promotes the willingness to be moderate.

The philosopher further suggests, however, that what makes *any* regime moderate to the extent that it can be is *agreement* throughout the city as to the criteria entitling one to rule it (the relevant pre- or proto-political "strength", whether this be conceived as sheer numbers, lineage, martial prowess, prudence, comprehensive virtue, piety, wealth, or whatever; cf. 432a). Political moderation entails especially, then, the restraint of *the desire to rule* on the part of those who do not meet the agreed-upon criteria. That reaching and sustaining such an agreement is itself of pivotal importance for moderation in general points to the centrality of this issue – who is to rule – to any more comprehensive harmony in political life. Moreover, the fact that it is accordingly difficult to see a difference between a city's being *moderate* in this sense and its being *just* (manifest in its enjoying unanimity and friendship, free of factions, hatreds and quarrels) is not adventitious. The similar resistance that people experience to being either moderate or just, as noted by Adeimantos (363e–364a), is grounded in the natural relationship between the two virtues, at the political as well as the individual level. Cities in which people have moderated their selfish desires should not find the practice of justice especially laborious.

But while the very difficulty one has in grasping the distinction in the philosopher's account of the two virtues emphasizes the practical importance of there being political moderation in order for there to be political justice, it also emphasizes the theoretical importance of the dialogue's account of justice. The dialogue *does* purport to *answer* this central question of political life: "who *ought* to rule, and *why*?" There *is* a naturally best answer to this question, an answer that everyone *ought* to agree upon, whether one construes the question with regard for what is "politically acceptable" (given the limitations on most people's willingness and ability even to appreciate, much less manifest true virtue; cf. 498d–a, 518de) or construes it in the strictest sense. The latter interpretation is answered by Philosophical Kingship. But the world as we know it is not ready for a regime of this kind (cf. 502d). The human race would have to transcend itself, and many become what only the very few very best are now (and hence prove to be humanly possible; cf. 459ab), before mankind could and would acknowledge and submit to strictly just rule. Thus, it is only the former interpretation of the question that is of any practical interest, and it is answered by who rules in the first city in *logos* (Aristocracy): older men of experience and proven political virtue, who are powerful in that they naturally command the respect and thus the obedience of those charged with carrying out their decisions, and whose entire lives bespeak their identifying their own well-being with that of the whole city (412c–414b). That they be powerful in this practical sense virtually necessitates that they enjoy the allegiance of the natural warrior class, and the *surest* way to do that – perhaps the *only sure* way – is by their having proven themselves exemplary in courage and self-mastery and military cunning (cf. 333ea).

Offensive as this may be to modern sensibilities and the treasured doctrine of distinguishing civil from military rule in order to subordinate absolutely the latter to the former, the dialogue teaches in every conceivable way that achieving truly just rule involves a package deal. There is a special relationship between a select class of those who would be the naturally best rulers (prudent, tough-minded, public-spirited, and scrupulously fair) and those who are naturally the best suited to serve as soldiers and police. And it is not simply a matter of how such rulers are most effectively nurtured into being. Nor of how to assure them the allegiance of those with the means to enforce the rule of whomsoever they prefer – though these are weighty concerns too often ignored in discussions of political justice, hidden in clouds of congenial assumptions. This special relationship reflects as well, and perhaps most important of all, the fact that members of a properly nurtured warrior class are the *only* ones that can be counted on, through thick and thin, to support rulers of this kind. While members of the "working class" (i.e., all those who do their productive labour primarily for the sake of the money they earn thereby) could be expected to *acquiesce* without any difficulty in being so ruled – bearing in mind that access to ruling-class status is perfectly open to anyone of the requisite natural abilities who is willing to pursue the job on the terms offered – working-class people can *not* be counted on, even had they experienced such rule, to so appreciate its superior justness as always to *choose* (e.g., "elect") such rulers for themselves (cf. 434ab, 562b–563e, 564c–e). Only natural warriors, properly nurtured, could be relied upon to stick by prudent, courageous, moderate, and therefore just rulers (cf. 431c), and the entire dialogue is a meditation on why this is so. If the massive scale and other qualities of modern political life render impractical any arrangement along these lines, so much the worse for its justness.

But while it's not so difficult to see why a regime in which each natural class of citizens did its appropriate work well would manifest the political virtues the philosopher attributes to it (all of which, according to his own account, remain grounded in *opinion* – presumably, *correct* opinion – but in any case, *not* knowledge; cf. 412e, 428ab, 429cd, 430b, 431c, 431de, 432b, 432e, 433b, 433c, 434a–b), other implications of his teaching about political justice are less obvious, though not obviously less important. Several of these have to do with the money-making, producing class, which it is fair to say is treated slightingly. And that is the first thing to notice: it gets only so much attention, compared to the other classes, as in the philosopher's opinion it deserves. But this is a bit more than first appears. For example, Book One is, among other things, a discourse on "working-class justice". Still, such guidance as the dialogue provides does take some assembling, and much is left to be surmised.

A second point: what is vital in applying this principle of justice to a city is not so much that one get a perfect natural fit between each individual and the various specific occupations, but that virtually all individuals end up in the proper natural *class*, as determined by what it is that primarily motivates them (i.e., money, honour, or virtue). As the philosopher explicitly observes, a natural carpenter and a natural shoemaker "exchanging tools or honours", or even a single person trying to do both tasks, are no great concern to the justness of the *city*. Rather, what is essential to the city's being just is that the right kind of people be its rulers, and those whose first concern in life is wealth (and what it will do for them and theirs) are *not* the right kind of people (434a-b; cf. 415b-c, 423cd, 546d-c). They can never be trusted to rule in the common good without materially favouring themselves, and without imparting to the entire regime an exaggerated regard for wealth, with a consequent neglect of virtue. And they are the ones who least appreciate education beyond that which is strictly utilitarian (581d).

Thirdly, given that a just regime is one that generally accepts the view that he who can but does not work shall not eat (cf. 498bc), pursuing a single useful occupation for which one has a natural talent is the first (and usually the most important) practical step an individual can take by way of establishing an harmonious life for himself (423d). One normally gets the most satisfaction out of work one does well, and that is work for which one has natural abilities that training can build upon (cf. 352e, 455b, 486c, 491a, 536e). Hence, a regime ought to ensure that it creates no artificial obstacles to each citizen's pursuing some worthwhile and naturally suitable task, but instead guarantees so far as possible equality of such opportunity. Moreover, each true art (*technē*) has a principle of just practice implicit in what defines it (342c-e, 346d). Cobbling is, by definition, the skill whereby one makes good shoes (i.e., shoes that best serve the purpose for which people buy and have shoes; cf. 353a); otherwise, anything could count as cobbling (or as shoes, for that matter). Similarly, medicine is necessarily defined as the knowledge whereby one restores and preserves health (there being an infinitude of ways to make people sick; cf. 341e). Thus, insofar as people form a political community in order to share the proceeds of the refined skills made possible by a rational division of labour, thereby gaining ready access to all the various products and services available in a city, the nature of such skills provides a standard for people's dealing justly with each other: let each artisan simply remain true to the defining mission of his art, and practise it to the best of his ability for the sake of that person who entrusts himself to the artisan's technical expertise. That is, do your best to give the customer (or employer) what he's paying for. In fact, presuming a city to be "wise, courageous, and moderate" in the ways discussed, it might seem that all its also being "just" adds to its goodness (or all of "perfect goodness" that would be "left over"; 428a) is this very thing: that everyone actually *does* his allotted work *well* – meaning, in accordance with what are regarded then and there to be the best standards intrinsic to each art – or at least as well as he can.

But this natural standard of "just workmanship", while important, is inadequate for resolving all the issues posed by the idea that the *polis* is a community of artisans. One set of problems results from the fact that such a standard is not comprehensive. For example, it cannot of itself determine which of all possible arts ought to be admitted. Surely not every skill which produces something useful or pleasing ought necessarily to be a *profession* (cf. 373b–c). Is there any real need for, say, professional athletes and dancers, or even for professional barbers and cosmeticians? (Or were the old Republican orators right to complain that the decline of Rome began when men started leaving home to have their hair cut?) Second, it gives no indication as to *how many* practitioners of each useful art there ought to be. How many doctors and lawyers, for example, does a just, wholesome regime really need (cf. 405a)? Third, the standard of just practice implicit in the arts themselves gives no guidance as to how each art is best employed. Is an expert cobbler well-employed making dozens upon dozens of fine pairs of shoes for a single patron? Or is it an intelligent use of a doctor's skill to assist some ancient shell of a man to cling uselessly to life, although he may well be able to do it (cf. 406a–e)? Finally, it does not prescribe what the artisan should be paid for faithfully labouring on behalf of his client or employer, nor what share of "profit" should go to those "middlemen" called 'merchants' and 'traders' (cf. 371a–d). Now, a regime may decide to allow some or all of these matters to be settled by a "free market" operating in accordance with the so-called laws of supply and demand (cf. 371b), but the justness of doing so – in light of all the foreseeable consequences of doing so – needs separate, and very careful, consideration. And thus one needs more than the "tectonic" justice implicit in the various *technae* if a city is to be ruled well; one needs an architectonic conception, a justice of the whole, not merely of the parts.

Beyond these issues, however, there is a different order of problems that results from the fact that the justice implicit in good craftsmanship *per se* most obviously serves "the other person's good", rather than the craftsman's good. As such, it epitomizes the problematic character of justice as ordinarily conceived. With all due respect for the satisfaction that comes from a job well done, what primarily serves the artisan's own good are the *wages* for doing it, by means of which he must meet his own needs and wants (cf. 346d). Thus, there is an inherent "conflict of interest" built into the artisan-client relationship. The consumer wants the best possible product or service at the lowest possible price, whereas the producer wants the greatest amount of payment for the least amount of work. And there is a special complication here that must be appreciated, as it leaves the non-expert consumer at a disadvantage, thus undercutting mutual trust: while each true art has a standard of *correct* use implicit in what defines it, the technical power itself is neutral, and can be used for good or ill. Moreover, technical skill often carries with it the ability to accomplish whatever the artisan wishes *stealthily*, without danger of detection. Or as the philosopher so provocatively puts it, "of whatever one is a clever guardian, he is also a clever thief" (334a).

Because this is true, it is often the case that an unscrupulous but clever craftsman can see ways to further his own monetary interest at the expense of his client; and insofar as he is ruled by a love of money, he will be inclined to do so. A builder can use shoddy material in places where it will not show and pocket the savings; a doctor can order expensive treatment his patient does not really need. Admittedly, there are many practical maxims and measures that mitigate the abusive potential inherent in the otherwise rational division of expert labour, but their very existence testifies to the problem. So, we are well warned as "buyers" generally to "beware", and that "you only get what you pay for" (or, at least, that "you don't get what you don't pay for"). And in comparatively small, stable communities, the importance of maintaining a reputation for good workmanship and fair dealing tempers unjust temptations considerably, as does recourse to laws against any sort of provable fraud or breach of contract. The fact remains, however, that there is no adequate substitute for dealing with people who are inherently just and who wish to stay that way, nor any infallible safeguard against those who aren't or don't (cf. 333a–e). Thus, if it cannot be shown that just practice is inherently beneficial to the practitioner, the prospect of there being even "in *logos*" a just polity – one where all the members live in peace and friendship, harmoniously cooperating with each other – remains threatened by the challenge of Glaukon and Adeimantos, and justly so.

As a fourth point: it should be noticed that there is no discussion of any virtue peculiar to the money-making producing class. With his having located a part of the city's goodness in each of the other two classes, one would expect the philosopher to turn next to the producing class and attribute to it industriousness, say, or that and thrift. But he doesn't. Instead, he speaks of moderation, and expressly calls attention to the fact that "it is *not* like courage and wisdom, each being in a separate part", but stretches throughout the whole (431d–a). Now, one might be tempted to explain this as his letting the discussion be tacitly ruled by his reigning analogy: since he would not want to have to attribute an unintelligible "industriousness" (much less "thrift") to the appetitive part of the soul, he ignores it in the city despite its "obviously" being a desirable attribute of this portion of the citizenry. But apart from this explanation's being based on the false assumption that the philosopher never intends to say anything about either city or man that a careful comparison wouldn't show to be equally applicable to the other, it in effect dismisses as a serious teaching the entire discussion and exemplification of justice in the city. Surely one ought to think twice, however, and even twice again before doing that.

And if one does so, one can see that encouraging an unqualified industriousness in this class – popular as such a policy is alleged to be with Protestants – may be at odds with its remaining moderate and just. Love of labour is potentially a most valuable quality of soul, but it is not itself a virtue – an ambitious, industrious criminal is not to that extent less vicious, but more so (cf. 491e, 495b, 518ea). And since what is produced has to be somehow consumed, either by those who themselves produce it or by those to whom they sell it (for, in contrast to what has been so common in history, the ruling class of the city in *logos* does not live a life of luxury supported by the surplus productivity of those who toil), unrestricted industry will eventually make the producing class either rich in things, or rich in money. And if this industriousness is not more-or-less evenly spread throughout the class, but some become much richer than others, the problem of maintaining justice in the city is further aggravated (cf. 564e, 422ea, 421e–a, 551d). It is difficult in practice, if not practically impossible, to sustain over the long run a distinction between honouring industriousness and honouring accumulation of wealth – with all that means for the neglect of true virtue (cf. 550ea). One must, however, encourage industry to some extent if the necessary work is to be done well, or even done at all (421e–a). Perhaps, then, restricting the work schedule of the producers so that it is sufficient for maintaining only a moderate general prosperity, and encouraging them to pursue wholesome leisure-time activities with friends and family, are in the best interest of maintaining a just polity (cf. 372a–b).[14]

Moreover, given the normal human inclination to exaggerate one's own importance and competence, as well as the justness of one's own perspective and feelings (cf. *Apology* 22de), the more successful those of the producing class are in their own work, the more they will imagine themselves competent to rule (good government being among the easiest things to take for granted by those without experience of anything else; cf. 619cd). And were they given access to arms, and any training in using them, this could only increase both their boldness and their discontent at being denied any part in ruling. But while people's being discontented with their role in political life can be a serious problem for stable rule, it is *not* a reliable indication of the comparative justness of that rule (563d), much less of their own competence to rule instead. Thus, the philosopher expressly warns against the danger of someone "by nature a craftsman or some other kind of money-maker, inflated by wealth, multitude, strength, or some other such thing" trying to join the class of warriors and rulers (434ab; cf. 442a–b).

Granting some voice in government to those who naturally belong to the money-motivated, property-loving, working class (and, recall, this includes everyone from common labourers to neurosurgeons) may often be expedient, even unavoidable. But so far as one can tell from this dialogue, there is no reason whatsoever for regarding it to be an inherent requirement of justice (in marked contrast to the popular modern view that sees political obligation arising only from the consent of the governed). That said, it is doubtless true there are many political situations in which granting this class more power (and training in arms, for that matter) would be not only prudent, but a step towards

The War Lover

greater justness (various kinds of tyrannies and oligarchies come to mind). And there can also be no doubt that some ways of making government more responsive to the wishes of this class are better than others, being more conducive to political moderation if not to justice. And because Democracy – though necessarily dominated by people of this class (since they are everywhere the majority), and hence inclined to vulgarity (*apeirokalia*; cf. 403c, 405b), and vulnerable to demagogical subversion (565cd) – because Democracy none the less offers each individual the freedom to make of himself something better than a democrat (557d), it is by no means the worst regime (cf. 561d), and may often be the best that actual circumstances allow. In which case, natural justice requires that it be defended in whatever way this is most effectively accomplished (cf. 618c). But all those who are convinced that political justice requires every adult of even the meanest capacity and character be accorded an equal voice in the governing of his polity meet in this dialogue a powerful critique of their view (cf. 561b-c, 562c-e, 590c-d). And there may never have been a time when a radical re-examination of that conviction was more urgently needed than now.

Reflection on the dialogue as a whole suggests that the key issues with respect to political justice are, first and foremost, who ought to rule (and in doing so, decide a host of lesser issues) – this is the question that receives the most attention (notice, it underlies the philosopher's entire taxonomy of regimes, both just and unjust), and about which the answer provided by the dialogue is most explicit. Second, how one should deal with the most dangerous class of men, doing justice both to them and everyone else (alternatively expressed, who should and who should not bear arms). Third, how education should be managed in order that citizens become so far as possible capable of living moderately and justly. And fourth, how one should distribute all the burdens and benefits of political life such that they best correspond to the diversity of people's kinds of, and capacities for, happiness (cf. 420b, 421b-c). With respect to all these issues, the dialogue teaches that sufficient – not complete and perfectly exact, but *sufficient* – guidance is to be found in a correct understanding of the natures of cities and men.

None the less, the philosopher himself characterizes the political justness manifest in the city in *logos* (both by its individual citizens, and by the city itself) as but a kind of "phantom [*eidōlon*] of justice", thereby distinguishing it from the simple truth of justice (443c; cf. 432c, 520c). A city, being at best a "just thing", cannot be perfectly just, but must in certain respects be unjust as well (cf. 479a). If this is true of even a city in all the purity of *logos* – that it is at best a just thing, a just thought perhaps, its "making" a just deed, but not the very form of justice – how much more so for those found in actual political life (473a)? Of all the truths about politics, it would seem most important that a person come to terms with this one, lest he (despite, or rather precisely because of, good intentions) do more actual harm than good. Even the best of rulers are not gods, but remain human beings, fallible in their judgments, ignorant of many things of permanent importance and of all the future, dependent upon imperfect executors of their will, and obliged to strike a balance among many legitimate but not wholly reconcilable objectives (e.g., perfect equality of opportunity *versus* inequality of nurture within the loving care of private families). The last point is epitomized, perhaps even summarized in a way, by the apparently irresolvable conflict between ordering a regime so as to bring forth the greatest virtue in the most people, and ordering it so as to promote the greatest virtue of the very best people. These two worthy objectives are reconciled as well as they can be in Aristocracy, the first city in *logos*.[15] The manifold paradoxes displayed in the city of Philosophical Kingship show why they can never be perfectly reconciled.

But, to repeat, the overriding problem with political justice is *not* that there is a lack of adequate guidance as to what truly is just in the arrangement of regimes. It is, rather, that even the best account of *political* justice provides insufficient motivation for each and every individual citizen to wish to *be* just, rather than merely *appear* to be. That is the deeper problem posed by the brothers Glaukon and Adeimantos: not whether there is truth enough to be found about justice, but whether there is reason enough to care about living in accordance with it, such that any person to the extent he was rational would sincerely wish to be just himself. For if there is not a natural justice of the individual – if it is not truly right *for him, good* for him, whoever he be, to mind his own proper business – there is insufficient *will* to justice in the city. (And notice, the problem bears with greatest force on those naturally best suited to rule the city: the most rational, knowledgeable, self-mastered – the very ones most apt to be aware of these facts, and able to rule themselves accordingly.) There would still be obvious advantages to living in a well-ordered regime, but additional advantages in exploiting it unjustly whenever one could get away with it undetected (thus neither being punished oneself, nor undercutting the general respect and support of others for such a regime). Hence, the inadequacies in the nature of political justice can be made good only if there is a complementary natural justice applicable within the man. Fortunately for partisans of civility, there is.

For everyone gets the soul he deserves, the soul he himself has earned with his practice – with his actual thoughts and choices and speeches and deeds – and what could be more just than that? Is not the natural order fundamentally just if with respect to the most important thing of all, one's basic "self" (the goodness of which alone makes truly beneficial whatever other so-called goods come one's way), one gets just what one deserves? If what one becomes, if what one essentially *is* – self-mastered and thus free, or enslaved by lower self and circumstance – depends primarily on how one chooses to live? And if one acts in a way that disfigures one's soul, making it uglier and weaker and smaller than it need be, than it could be, does any amount of fame and fortune gained thereby truly compensate? The fact that almost anyone would pause and recoil at the prospect of what he somehow was sure entailed his own significant diminution suggests that man is more than a beast ruled by pleasure, and that it is the germ of nobility in the human spirit – in the distinctly human, or perhaps divine, side of the spirit – to which the consequences of natural justice appeal. And thus the greater a person's pride in himself, married with a proportionate regard for the truth (especially about himself), the more susceptible is he to this appeal. Presumably, one would find its attraction at a maximum with the likes of Glaukon and Adeimantos, perhaps diminishing to insignificance as one ranges down the broadening human spectrum to its lowest reaches. But it is *real* for everyone. We are each of us neither more nor less than we can justly claim to deserve to be.

The justice administered by men may be more-or-less crude and evadable, and divine justice dubitable, but this natural justice has a near perfection of sanction, in both kind and proportion. A craftsman may debase his art, a tradesman cheat his customers, a doctor may betray the trust of his patients, a banker that of his depositors, a soldier may desert his comrades, a policeman abuse his powers and prerogatives in a thousand ways, a judge may indulge his preferences and even prostitute his judgments, a general may forsake his awful responsibilities, a ruler sacrifice the common good for partisan purposes, a teacher corrupt or exploit those entrusted to his care, a scholar subordinate pursuit of truth to his love of fame, a father neglect his familial responsibilities, a poet may eulogize tyranny – all such individuals and others still worse may occasionally, even regularly, escape the just punishment of other men. But not one of them escapes the just punishments of nature, for each and all have the souls to show for it, being lesser men by a natural standard of excellence (and consequent self-satisfaction) than they would otherwise be. If one regularly cheats and lies and steals and philanders, that is precisely what one becomes, and regardless of any appearances to the contrary: in reality a cheater, a liar, a thief, or a libertine. A man may amass great wealth and influence using every foul means human ingenuity can devise – fraud, extortion, theft, arson, assault, even murder – and many may envy him his apparent success, and secretly long to trade places with him (cf. 344bc, 364ab). What most fail to appreciate, however, is that it's a package deal: there is a soul that goes along with the glitter and glamour (cf. 577a–b, 619bc). While many might envy the riches, anyone with sense would think his longest and hardest before accepting the consequence of having to *be* the person who acquired them in the manner he did. For it's a worse than Faustian bargain. And what matters the judgment of those without sense?

That the truth of all this will be regarded as compelling and personally relevant only by those with some taste for nobility and beauty is neither here nor there with respect to its being true. A person's unawareness of his ranking lower in the natural order of humanity no more affects his actually being lower than does a frog's lack of awareness that it partakes of a lower form of life than does a man. Rather, that lack of awareness is itself evidence of being lower. So the issue by no means turns on whether or not those who commit injustice are, as Kephalos seems to be, tormented by a "guilty conscience"; indeed, "whoever despises himself can still respect himself as one who despises", and is to that extent not beyond redemption. The fact, however, that most humans have something they call a conscience (or sense of shame), and that they tend to be troubled by it when they do something they believe to be wrong, or even just suspect may be, is hardly irrelevant to an understanding of human nature, and of what Nature prescribes as being the best way to live. To the extent that doing wrong makes one ashamed of oneself, this natural punishment tends to make one better (cf. 350d).

But, doubtless, there are many who regularly practise injustice and are proud of it, thinking themselves stronger and cleverer for doing so (while despising the "simplemindedness" of all those who believe in acting justly), and who take pleasure in the fruits of their vice and even in the deeds themselves, and who will leave this world none the wiser (cf. 349b-c, 409cd, 519a). They may be, for all practical purposes, incorrigible. This in no way affects the fact of what they are, which is neither more nor less than they have made of themselves, and that they pay a higher price for their pleasures than they are worth, indeed a much higher price than any pleasures could possibly be worth (584a-586e). That they don't know any better says all that needs saying. There is an ancient rhetorical question which beautifully expresses the most important synoptic judgment to be made about human life: "For what shall it profit a man, if he gain the whole world, and lose his own soul?" And the fact that not everyone treats the question as rhetorical is beside the main point. Whether or not a person recognizes the confirmation of its truth in the totality of his own experience (should he care to consult it) is a separate matter, though admittedly one with its own potent political consequences. Were it not only true, but universally *believed* to be true, everyone would be the more eager to acquire the wherewithal to act in accordance with it, and the problems with political justice would be three-quarters solved. Thus, any decent means of fostering such belief would seem deserving of respect.

The philosopher's summary statement of what justice is and does in the individual is worth reviewing. It comes immediately after his characterizing the "political justice" of the city in *logos* as "a kind of *phantom*" (*eidōlon*) of justice (which is to say, the justice of the city is something which may cast shadows on other things, or facets of it be reflected in other things - speeches, deeds, laws, policies, manners, and so on - but which itself stands as only a kind of shadow or reflection of the very form of justice; 443c; cf. 510a, 520c).

> And the truth was, as it seems, that justice is something of this sort; however, not with respect to one's minding his external business [*exō praxin*], but with respect to what is within, with respect to what truly concerns him and his own, not letting each part in him mind the business of others, nor the classes in the soul meddle with each other; but really disposing his own house well, he rules himself, and orders himself, and becomes his own friend, and harmonizes the three parts, exactly like three notes in an harmonic scale, lowest, highest, and middle; and if there

happen to be some other parts in between, he binds them together and becomes entirely one from many, moderate and harmonized. Then, and only then, he acts, if he does act in some way – either concerning the acquisition of money, or the care of the body, or something political, or concerning private contracts – in all these, believing and naming a just and fine action one that preserves and helps to produce this condition, and wisdom the knowledge that supervises this action; while [believing and naming] an unjust action one that always undoes this condition, and lack of learning, in its turn, the opinion that supervises this.

Although this much may be true, the philosopher's own observation about it suggests that it is not the whole truth (444a). Presumably, the remaining six books of the dialogue are not irrelevant to a fuller, deeper understanding of justice. In any case, his further discussion of *injustice* makes clear that the key issue is which part of the soul rules (444b; cf. 444d). There seems no real danger of the rational part trying to do the natural work of the spirited or appetitive part, nor of those two parts attempting to usurp the tasks of each other. The "faction" and "meddling" and "interference" and "rebellion" he speaks of all concern the natural assertiveness of what should be the subordinate parts of a human soul (but which rule unchecked in beasts). Only slightly less important, however, is the necessity that each and every part of the soul actually *does well* the work naturally suited to it, such that in being just, one fully manifests complete human excellence.

By virtue of being just, then, with each part making a fair contribution to the economy of the whole and therefore manifesting the virtue especially associated with it, a man will also be prudent, courageous, and moderate. Reciprocally, he *must* be all these other things in order to be truly and unfailingly just, requiring as this does tractable appetites, subtle judgment, and a *strong* as well as disciplined spirit. Whereas a weak spirit, however obedient to reason, will *not* do "a fine job" of either restraining the appetites as reason directs, nor of "guarding against external enemies on behalf of the entire soul and body, ... making war, and by its courage fulfilling what has been decided" (442a-b; cf. 611bc). Nor will the whole man be well served if the rational part ruling his soul is ill-educated, ever so confident of being both wise and rigorously rational, but not in fact knowing what is beneficial for each of the parts and for the whole community of body and soul (442c). Or, alternatively expressed, if the mind does not counsel well on how the man would best deal with himself and

The War Lover

other men (cf. 428cd). Nor should it be forgotten that the appetitive part of the soul also has important work to do, concerned mainly with sustaining self and species, and that there are legitimate satisfactions that attend its doing that work well (cf. 586de).

In order further to explain justice and the other virtues, and in particular how they are instilled, the philosopher momentarily shifts away from the analogy between the city and the man, and suggests instead one between body and soul. We are to think of justice in the individual as a comprehensive health of the soul. Or, inasmuch as the body exists for the sake of the soul (cf. 407b-e), and a well-ordered soul cares best for the body in which it must dwell, making it as good as possible (403d; cf. 611bc), justice, then, can be thought of as the comprehensive health of the entire man. Or, since being truly just entails all the virtues, justice is "a certain health, beauty, and good condition of the soul, and vice a sickness, ugliness, and weakness" (444de). Symmetry suggests that "good condition" (*euexia*) is properly interpreted as "strength" of soul. In this sense, then, Thrasymachos is correct: justice *is* "the advantage of the stronger", much as Polemarchos is also correct that justice renders to each what is truly its due (cf. 586de).

Given this understanding of justice in the man, just *practices* may be formally defined and substantially identified in the same way that healthy practices are. We describe as 'healthy' anything which tends to promote or sustain that naturally best physical condition called 'health', the moving image of life, when all of the parts and thus the whole are functioning as they should, and one is at the peak of one's powers and hence most fully alive (cf. 353b-d). But we have to *discover*, largely through reflection on extensive and varied experience, precisely what these healthy practices *are* (although on the basis of what we have so far discovered, it seems we are to some extent instinctively inclined towards some of them at least, and away from some others that endanger health). Similarly, then, just practices are formally defined as whatever introduces this harmonious, active, and competent – and thereby powerful and beautiful – regime into the human soul, and maintains it there, such that one desires only what and as much as is truly good for oneself, feels only the passions that are truly appropriate, has a strong will in an obedient spirit, and reason rightly rules for the good of the whole man.

As for how one recognizes this condition of robust oneness for what it is, and establishes that it is indeed a good thing, the problem is analogous with that of recognizing the existence and goodness of physical health: it is more conspicuous by its absence, and it is a rare individual who has never experienced its absence and thereby learned its value (cf. 583c–d). By virtue of his inner justness, such a person is truly kingly in being a king over himself, able to choose the best from the possibilities confronting him, and free to pursue his choice to the utmost of his natural powers (cf. 618b–e). And whoever can make this of himself deserves to be it. The first step, however, is to *want* it – or, rather, to want it more than anything else – and to be willing to work as hard as it takes, or as hard as one can, to get it.

The second step is to discover what practices, what activities and ways of behaving towards others, substantially conform to the formal definition of just practices: those which – by moderating while refining the appetites, taming while heightening the spirit, strengthening while informing the reason – would promote an harmonious, strong, and self-mastered soul. Distinct from these are all the ways of living which undermine such a psychic regime. The philosopher nowhere presents a comprehensive catalogue of what these just and unjust practices are. And, judging from his analogy of bodily health, one should be prepared to acknowledge a certain amount of class and even individual variation; while there are generally applicable rules of good health, the very same diet and regimen of exercise and rest are not optimal for everyone in every stage and condition of life. But the philosopher does confirm that many of the practices and rules various people have discovered over the ages do in fact have some relevance to making one truly just, or reflect and reinforce the fact that one is such, whereas others do not (cf. 425ab). Educating children in some mixture of wholesome music and gymnastic facilitates the taming and toughening of the spirit and the mind, and the harmonizing of them to each other. Whereas persuading and compelling everyone to obey the sorts of laws commonly found in polities encourage them to discipline their desires, and refrain from doing a variety of things people's appetites or spirits often tempt them to do (and that animals do as a matter of course), and to do other things which require them to overcome sloth and some of the baser promptings of selfishness, and to endure certain kinds of discomfort. From a practical, everyday perspective, what people normally think of as being just consists mainly in *not* being *un*just (cf. 486b). But the deeper significance for the individual who acts "justly" in this negative way lies in its implications for his own self-discipline, the first requisite of self-rule.

This is reflected in the third step of the philosopher's argument as to why one should regard the principle found to underlie the well-ordering of both a city and a soul to be the basic truth about justice (442d–b). He suggests we can confirm it to be that elusive thing people are tacitly seeking in their various arguments and investigations if we recognize that this same principle *also* underlies the more commonplace opinions as to what is just, accounting for both their limited validity and their inadequacies as complete and fundamental conceptions (why, for example, they sometimes admit of exceptions; cf. 331c–d). If we could imagine a man whose soul was ordered as the philosopher has described, and were we required to come to some definite speculation as to whether it was likely that he would do any of the sorts of things commonly thought of as unjust – embezzle money, steal from public facilities or private individuals, betray one's comrades or country, default on one's agreements and debts, philander, neglect one's familial responsibilities, defile what is holy, or any other such thing that is likely to occur to us – what would we decide? In order to reach a conclusion as to how he is likely to behave compared with those whose souls are otherwise, we are obliged to ask ourselves why each of these kinds of things is usually done. How much of what is ugly in the thought and conduct of individuals derives from greed, from cowardice, from envy and resentment and jealousy, or from vanity? And how much from sheer stupidity? It is in light of such a survey that one must judge the plausibility of the claim that someone with a well-ordered soul (and thus moderate appetites, disciplined passions, a strong will, who is sensible, and concerned first of all to stay this way) would not normally do any of these things.

Moreover, personal experience and observation of others confirm in the only way it can be confirmed that the philosopher is correct about something else as well: indulging the appetites and emotions never really satiates them but rather strengthens them, while denying them satisfaction is what tempers them (cf. 442a, 571b–573b, 588e–589e). One may wish it were otherwise, but this seems to be the truth of our nature. *Logos* is sufficient to persuade one's reason of the benefits of courage and moderation, but it is not sufficient for instilling these virtues in the rest of the soul; and yet one's irrational parts must also be educated. Virtue *is* knowledge, but the whole man has to "know" it, not merely his reason. Educating the soul's lower parts is often more like training the body – that is, it requires exercise and practice to the point where something becomes "second nature" (cf. 518de).

This is not to deny the more fundamental importance of thought. Virtue must be understood, of course, if it is to be consciously pursued; nor is it fully manifested if it is not fully understood and appreciated for what it is. However, *speaking* about virtue makes a worthy beginning. For doing so not only facilitates this clearer understanding and appreciation, it also promotes the practices which instil it throughout the soul. Professing one's concern for virtue, and endorsing particular behaviour as being a suitable expression of it, engage one's pride, thereby implicitly committing oneself to practise what everyone regards as being all too easy to preach (cf. 358d; *Apology* 38a). And an awareness that such a harmony between speech and deed is the most effective way of encouraging similar virtue in others may not be irrelevant to encouraging it even further in oneself, as the experience of responsible parents would confirm.

And so it turns out that many if not most just *deeds* still appear to be (as they always have) "the other person's good". But in reality, they are like physical exercise. Glaukon, it should be recalled, placed such exercise in his third category of good things (357c), and observed that this is also where most people would place justice: i.e., among those things that have beneficial consequences for the doer but are in themselves toilsome – the problem being, as he saw it at least, that all those beneficial consequences come solely from appearing to be just, none from really being so. But as he comes to realize, on this point he was profoundly mistaken. Merely appearing to be just (while secretly scheming to be otherwise at every opportunity) will not confer the all-important benefit of a well-ordered soul, any more than merely appearing to exercise will confer physical health and strength.

Reflection on the "vulgar [or, commonplace; *phortika*] standards" by means of which we can "entirely reassure ourselves" that we have indeed found the correct conception of justice also serves, then, as a starting point in one's efforts to discover which practices substantially promote that health and strength and beauty of soul that come from living in the naturally right way. Further guidance is scattered throughout the dialogue: in the analyses of the strengths and weaknesses of the various kinds of regimes and men; in the details of the Guardians' education; in the philosopher's "incidentally" denominating various speeches and deeds and policies and outcomes as just or unjust (e.g., at 461a, 463d, 464e, 466b, 496b, 497a, 520ab, 599d, 605a, 607d, and 620d); and in subsequent discussions about the nature of the soul and its desires and pleasures.

The War Lover

But two points are perhaps worthy of special emphasis. First, woven into the entire dialogue is a subtle emphasis on cultivating the soul's taste for truth. This is in no way qualified by the fact that the philosopher acknowledges the political utility and even necessity of lies (382c–d, 389b, 414bc, 459cd; cf. 331cd, 377a), although it may well indicate an important limitation on the justness of political life. Second, the philosopher chooses to conclude his comparison between the kingly man and the tyrannical one with a particularly important discussion on the psychic effects of certain familiar practices (586a–592b). This discussion is too rich to be done justice by any summary; suffice it to say that, conjoined with the previous analyses of the human soul, one is given sufficient indication as to the inner consequences of indulging envy and anger and stubbornness and a proclivity for violence, of giving in to minor irritations, of greed and licentiousness and illiberality, of a taste for luxury and comfort, or for fame and flattery, and much else besides. Of course, it remains – as it must – for the reader to complete and confirm the entire account in light of his own experience. For my own part, scarcely a day goes by without my seeing its basic truth freshly corroborated. Beyond the shadow of a doubt, there is natural justice, allotting to each of us the soul we deserve, a soul that has been given its determinate order and inclinations by our respective practices.

Now, there is an obvious objection one might raise to this account of natural justice, and it concerns the distribution of natures and nurtures. It might seem that only if every person were equally blessed by nature and circumstance – or (better still?) free to choose his own nature: money-loving, honour-loving, or wisdom-loving; male or female; physically strong, healthy, and beautiful, or the reverse; and the family and regime in which one was to be nurtured – only then could it be truly said that Nature is just. For surely kinds of natures and political nurtures are ordered with respect to their intrinsic goodness and the quality of happiness they offer – does not this truth pervade the dialogue like nothing else? And surely "material circumstances" count for something! Surely one needs the minimal wherewithal to live if he is to make anything of himself, just or unjust. "First food, then virtue", has an intuitive, not to say seductive, appeal (cf. 407a). The very fact that the philosopher chooses to conclude the dialogue as he does with the so-called Myth of Er would seem to concede the basic validity of these objections. And thus, if one is not convinced that the essential features of that heavenly or hellish interlude between sojourns here on earth are truly as they are reported to be – with each soul being repaid ten times over for his prior mortal life (615a-e), and actually choosing its own pattern of future life (617d-e), with almost everyone over an eternity experiencing his or her fair share of both goods and evils (619d, 620bc) – if these things are not so, in the final analysis, Nature is *not* just. Yet, the philosopher himself treats this tale as extraneous to what is offered as an already sufficient demonstration that there is a natural justice in this world that should command the adherence of even the most heroic individual (cf. 612a-c). This is not to say, of course, that the "story" (*apologos*) he attributes to the fallen warrior Er is irrelevant to a better understanding of natural justice, nor to deny that it is a useful, perhaps even essential, practical supplement to it.[16]

But this is the point at which to begin addressing what – for all of its natural psychological appeal – turns out to be an impertinent objection. For the issue is not whether Nature is just (whatever, if anything, that might mean), but whether there is natural justice. That is, the objection does not focus on whether, in the nature of things, there is given a standard of the right way to act, complete with sanctions and rewards, such that it is on balance more beneficial for an individual really to behave justly (rather than merely appear to); nor on whether, by living a truly just life, he lives as well as it is possible for him to live insofar as his own choices have anything to do with the matter. But this is the concrete – and practically all-important – question facing each and every one of us. The issue is *not* that of whether, if one does the best one can, one will live the best life that has ever been lived in the history of the universe. Why should anyone think that *this* is what he deserves? Or, for that matter, that anyone *deserves* anything at all merely by virtue of existing?

Much less is it a question of whether the Kosmos is ordered in the best possible manner. (Although there seems to be no shortage of people in this world who, like Alfonso the Wise, are sure that had they been present at the Creation they could have given God good advice.) By what trans-kosmic standard one might presume to judge the entire natural order is a mystery to me. Everything we learn about the natural world suggests that it is a rigorously unified edifice, and that no part of it could be altered without altering the whole, no principle (or "natural law") of its functioning changed that would not reverberate throughout the entire web of such principles. And the sup-

The War Lover

position that there *are*, in fact or in theory, *other* such coherent wholes, much less that there are *better* ones, is but the blindest speculation, and gives no warrant whatsoever for judging the only one we know of. Moreover it presumes that one somehow knows – and without any recourse to the given natural order being judged and found wanting (and are not man and all his faculties part and product of that order?) – precisely what is at issue in this dialogue: the truth about justice?

One might claim to know this by divine revelation, if one is prepared to assume about God what one is not prepared to concede about Nature: that He is just, and therefore no deceiver (cf. 380d ff, *Genesis* 22:1-12). Yet if one imagines that God is just, mustn't one further assume that He does not have anything directly to do with the natural world – since any intervention by Him would not only impart that much justness to it, it would raise disturbing questions as to why He, being just and hence a partisan of justice, didn't intervene more (cf. 379c, 380a-c)? And so it is accordingly difficult to see sufficient rational grounds for any trust in divine revelation. More likely, God simply Is.

Of course, what various people imagine would be a better world usually turns out upon closer examination to be a highly selective reformulation of this world, concocted of some fact and much fancy, misinterpreted implication, partisan prejudice, and wishful thinking – and the whole of it corresponding to only a minuscule portion of the actual universe, and without any convincing demonstration that it would work at all (rather than immediately disintegrate), much less work better (cf. 457d-a). In particular, the assumption that the world would be a better or juster place if everyone were born with equal natures (licensing as a second-best world one in which they are somehow artificially equalized) is a modern prejudice for which, so far as I know, there is nary a shred of evidence, and quite a few reasons against. But many moderns tacitly, if not altogether wittingly, simply presume that the entire burden of proof rests on those who would argue for some non-egalitarian arrangement as being best, and that in the absence of a positive demonstration to that effect, egalitarianism is the rational "default" position. Suffice it to reply, this is not as "intuitively obvious" to the few Glaukons that arise among us as it is to the many Walter Mittys. In any case, blithe assumptions of this kind beg all the important questions, and so whatever their political utility within a given regime, they will never satisfy serious questioners.

It goes without saying that most of us would prefer to be born in a just regime, one ruled for the common good, and in which each person is reasonably safe, free to pursue some useful work for which he is naturally suited, is fairly rewarded for performing it well, and otherwise encouraged to mind his own business (which may, of course, include much communal and cooperative activity). That considerable benefits accrue to citizens of a just regime is why it is worth working and fighting for. And we may agree that a person is fortunate should he be born into such a regime. Or into a wholesome family that gives every encouragement to his developing self-mastery, and in which there is a solid understanding of what all this entails. But why should anyone think that he *deserves*, that it is his "natural right", to be born *fortunate* (or as fortunate as anyone else), and that otherwise he can justly complain, "Nature is unjust", or, "There is no justice in life"? Precisely because we humans have an unhappy tendency to conflate what we desire with what we deserve, when we do not realize our fondest dreams we are apt to believe we've not received our just desserts. One needs to distinguish the political implications of this tendency (which are considerable) from its philosophical implications (which are nil). One might also note here that common inclination of people to blame whatever discontent they experience on anyone or anything other than themselves (cf. 619c), and that this too is something that must be consciously guarded against in the interest of cultivating one's own justness.

For that matter, is it so clear which circumstances truly are "fortunate" for a given nature (cf. 491c, 604bc)? And is there any way for a soul to acquire the strength requisite for meeting life's vicissitudes except by overcoming obstacles and enduring hardships? Merely reflecting on what most people mean by 'fortunate' makes one wonder whether they're not truly fortunate much more often than they realize. In any case, the natural justice in the individual soul of which the philosopher speaks is not, in the final analysis, dependent upon such matters. It is not operative or applicable only in fortunate circumstances, such that should one find oneself in an unjust regime (as to varying degrees virtually all of us do; cf. 496c-e, 497ab), there is no natural motive to be just oneself, and that one would be truly better off behaving unjustly. However, it should perhaps be emphasized that prudential judgment is required to determine what *substantially* just behaviour consists of in any given situation. By the standard of what it does to the soul (which involves bearing in mind why one does it), lying is normally unjust, as is the failure to return what one has borrowed – but not always (331c, 331e–332c). Similarly, to be willing to work but left to starve in the midst of plenty may justify stealing from illiberal hoarders that have ample, whereas it would not justify doing so from those who have little more than oneself. Be such things as they may, whatever one contemplates saying or doing, the judgment of its rightness or wrongness is to be made in light of its effect on the regime of the soul. It would be supremely useful were one given, or able to contrive, some "demonic sign" whereby one could recognize instinctively and infallibly when one was about to do something harmful to oneself (cf. 496c, 617de, *Apology* 31cd, 40a–c). In its absence, however, one must use one's own experience (and whatever can be gleaned by careful observation of others) in order to make these judgments as well, and first of all as honestly, as one can, since of necessity one lives with the consequences. "Know thyself" – advice as good as it is old and hard.

We are each given a nature along with the gift of life – the inheritances of one's body and soul, as it were, neither earned nor stolen – and challenged to make the most of them in the particular familio-political circumstances in which we happen to find ourselves. There is no doubt in my mind that, judged from a transcendent perspective, some natures, *if brought to perfection*, provide the basis of better lives. But that 'if' introduces an enormous caveat: greater potential requires greater effort to actualize it, is exposed to greater corrupting influences and temptations, consequently is less likely to approach its natural fulfilment, and its failure is more abject (cf. 491b–495a). A more modest and ordinary potential has a higher probability of success, because success comes easier and entails fewer risks. It's not clear that these trade-offs are grossly unjust. Moreover, each kind of nature, if fulfilled, provides its own kind as well as its own share of happiness (cf. 421c, 581cd). And with respect to a given nature, its own kind of happiness *is* best. What is practically important for one's own happiness is that one lead the life that suits the nature one has, that one make the most of *it*, that one not toil without profit and consequently without satisfaction. For someone naturally suited for manual arts to be made to try to live like a philosopher or a priest might be more akin to torture than happiness. In all cases, however, having a soul as well-ordered as one's nature allows, a naturally just, harmonious, self-mastered soul, provides the foundation for the greatest happiness, and some version of such a psychic regime is within the capacity of almost everyone (cf. 590c–a).

We cannot justly be called deserving of anything in particular before the fact, but are given the opportunity to prove ourselves worthy *a posteriori* by putting to good use whatever natural talents and political or familial advantages come our way. It may well be, contrary to the report of our warrior-messenger, that we played no part at all in selecting such things, but that is not what is most important about his tale. For as he tells it, it was "a sight worth seeing, how each of the several souls chose a life, something pitiful and laughable and wonderful to see" (619ea). His story merely reminds us of what we should already know: that there as well as here, only a true philosopher would be *competent* to choose, and he would of course choose such competence ahead of anything else. Thus, the philosophic life is the only absolutely choiceworthy life, being the life that gives one "the power and the knowledge to distinguish the beneficial from the wretched life, thus everywhere and always choosing the best from among those within one's power" (618c, 619c–d, 620a).

But that is not a life that is simply bestowed on anyone; if it holds forth the promise of the greatest power and satisfaction, it also entails the greatest labours and the greatest risks and the greatest loneliness. The few who succeed are the rare of the rare (503b). It has little popular appeal. Most people, given an opportunity to choose what kind of life to live, would bungle it miserably, for unlike the wily Odysseus, who learned better the hard way (620c), they would choose to be rich and famous, and the odds are overwhelming that becoming so would be their ruination (cf. 619bc). An already virtuous person may not be corrupted by coming into possession of these things, but as a rule they are actively pursued at the expense of virtue, not in company with it (550e). For this is a second point to notice in the tale: whether or not one will be virtuous is not determined by the nature one is born with nor by the circumstances one is born into (617e). The choice to honour virtue, and pursue it oneself, is made in the course of living; the order or disorder of one's soul is not established at birth, but necessarily follows from how one chooses to live (618b). And everyone has ample opportunity – and usually ample encouragement – to make the right choice, and the evidential basis for doing so is all around us and accessible to any person who cares to consult it. Most people who are unjust are so not because they have nary a clue as to how to be just, but because they don't really *want* to be just. And so they get their wish. If it entails certain consequences they did not foresee: their ending up with disorderly and diminished souls – sicker, weaker, uglier, enslaved even – they can hardly complain that Nature has dealt with them unfairly. For this is no more than to say that they thought they could get away with being unjust, but it turns out they can't. A burglar might as well complain about the guard dogs he was unaware of in planning his unsuccessful heist. Men, in their humanity, may accept ignorance of natural law as grounds for dealing gently with their fellows, who may thus be thought of as "unwillingly unjust" (cf. 366cd, 589c); and in a spirit of mercy they may place rehabilitation of such "unfortunate" fellows ahead of retribution. Some, out of nobility or philanthropy or overflowing generosity or whatever, may even try to dispel the dangerous ignorance. Mother Nature, however – rich enough to waste myriads in getting one right, and indifferent to human sentiments – is made of sterner stuff: commit what is by nature a crime, and one will suffer the natural punishment.

6

The Portrait of a Lady

Ah, but is there justice for *women*? In defending his opinion that justice in the city is based on each individual's doing only that which he could do best, not meddling in what is more suitably the business of others – that this is a dimension of the city's goodness on a par with its moderation, courage, and prudence, indeed the very "power whereby these others come into being" (433b) – the philosopher expressly applies this idea to, among others, women (433d). But one is left wondering what, more precisely and substantially, *is* a woman's business so far as the city is concerned. Are we here to be guided, as in the case of religion, by traditional practices (427bc)? Is the political role of a woman rightly confined to bearing and nurturing children, seeing that her family is well-clothed and well-fed, and altogether managing the household and herself in the way most pleasing to her husband? Would living in such a manner best contribute to instilling a harmonious regime – the defining consequence of *just* practices – in the female soul, at least so far as this is possible?

Several of the few allusions to women prior to the discovery of justice in Book Four suggest as much, and little else (cf. 377c, 381e, 414e). There is nary a hint that women might engage in *any* of the useful work traditionally done by men. This squares with the fact that, judging from what had been said thus far, men and women must be regarded as importantly, if not radically, different. Moreover, one is left with the impression, subtle but significant, that in at least *some* respects women typically are inferior to men. In the reformation of traditional music, for example, we are advised to take out "the wailings of renowned men and give them to women – and not to serious ones at that" (387ea; cf. 605de). And the Lydian melodic modes are excluded as being "useless for women who are to be equitable [*epieikeis*[1]], let alone for men" (398e). Women are more apt to be ruled by their emotions, and tend to be preoccupied with appearances, especially their own (cf. 373bc). And one finds an immoderate diversity of desires, pleasures, and pains especially in women (along with children and those suited for domestic service; 431bc).

Perhaps the most important indication, however, comes in the context of the philosopher's soliciting Adeimantos' agreement that the guardians must not become skilled imitators of anything inappropriate to them: "We won't allow those whom we claim to care about, and who must themselves become good men, to imitate women – since they are men – either a young woman [*nean*] or an elderly woman [*presbyteran*], or one abusing her husband [literally, her man; *andri*], or one striving with the gods, or boasting (thinking herself happy), or one grieving and wailing in misfortune; much less will we need one who is sick or in love or in labour" (395de). And it's only natural to suppose that something similar would apply to women: that those we "care about", wishing them to become good women, must not imitate *men* (since they are women). In any case, there would seem to be little point to this injunction – a curiously detailed and suggestive injunction – were there not important differences in the natures of men and women as such, differences all the more pronounced in prime examples of each.

That said, however, we must remind ourselves that we've been provided a far more substantial conception of the one than of the other. We have been shown the portrait of a gentleman. But what about a lady? The philosopher and his all-too-manly young helpers discussed at considerable length the natural qualities that distinguish a well-bred male, and how he is rightly nurtured so as to make of him something noble and good, a man who manifests that constellation of virtues – that consummate health, beauty, and strength of body and soul – requisite to self-rule. But in the course of their doing so, as noted above, we are given reasons for doubting that the very same account is applicable in all respects to women. Moreover, if we are still pretty much in the dark as to female nature (and thus feminine virtue), ought we to be altogether confident of what we seem to have learned about male nature (and thus about masculine virtue)? Do not the sexes *mutually* determine *each other* to precisely the extent that the sexes *per se* are distinct? Much as one appreciates day only so far as one knows

The Portrait of a Lady

night, or understands matter in light of form, and motion in comparison with rest, is it not true that the specifically male or masculine can only be understood in contradistinction to what is female or feminine, and vice versa?

Of all the differences encompassed by human nature, the division of the species into male and female "tribes" surely seems the most obvious. Now, it is conceivable that this sexual differentiation is of minor importance, both politically and psychologically. But the vast majority of human beings throughout history have not treated it as such - quite the contrary: it has typically been regarded, by both men and women, as the most consequential difference of all, touching virtually every human practice, even colouring one's entire perspective on life. As should go without saying, this common or popular view may be mistaken; but surely its near universality is itself evidence of *something*. Doing justice to the male-female distinction, then, may well be the most difficult challenge confronting a science of either cities or souls. And one can hardly imagine a road to wisdom that did not traverse those two 'problem terrains,' if indeed they are two. Thus one can begin to see why the discussion must take the course that it does, why a lengthy detour or digression is needed, one which permits a review of ground already covered in order to judge the progress so far and make good any oversights that might have occurred - why, indeed, one must go back and, as it were, begin again (cf. 543c).

Book Five is a new beginning, the third such, and unmistakably reminiscent of the first. For just as the genesis of this whole day-and-night-long conversation would seem to have occurred "under duress", so too this fresh beginning. As before, Sokrates is playfully arrested in the midst of his proceeding and made to return to where he had been earlier, despite a seeming reluctance on his part to do so. In both instances, the decision reached is treated in political terms (328b, 450a), with Adeimantos serving in a mediating role and Glaukon agreeing with the majority (though perhaps having his own reasons for doing so). But here, as throughout the dialogue, the compulsion to which the philosopher yields is more apparent than real, and testifies to his pedagogic skill and mastery of indirect rule. For much as he had incited Glaukon's challenge (and thus the dialogue's second beginning) with his passing claim of being not persuaded by Thrasymachos that injustice - "even if one lets it be and does not hinder its doing what it will"! - is more profitable than justice (345a), so had he sown the seeds of the present revolt in his expressed intention to "leave out" certain matters which "well-educated, sensible men" can "easily" see for themselves. One can scarce believe that the sole example mentioned was chosen at random: "that the possession of women, marriage, and procreation of children must be made so far as possible according to the proverb that all things of friends are common" (423ea). Whether too readily beguiled by the philosopher's rhetoric, or diverted by his emphasis on guarding against innovation in the musical foundation of education (424a–d), Adeimantos had agreed at the time that this would be "the most correct way". But apparently this proposal struck a responsive chord in Polemarchos, who has been reverberating with fascination ever since.

Still earlier in the conversation, Adeimantos had been subtly chastened for objecting – quite sensibly, one would think – to the extreme asceticism of the life Sokrates had outlined for the rulers of their city (419a). In seeming to deny them all private gratifications as the necessary price of making them utterly and reliably public-spirited men, it is inevitable that the question would arise: what's in it for them? Why would anyone in his right mind be willing to rule, "and get mixed up with straightening out other people's troubles" (346e), if he is to be denied the rewards that others enjoy for a job well done? Moreover, the philosopher's immediate response to this objection multiplied rather than diminished its force (420a ff). But now, with this tantalizing allusion to the rulers' sharing all the women, Polemarchos sees a ray – nay – a veritable sunrise of hope (one can almost hear him murmuring to himself, "Might he mean what I pray he means?"). It is doubtful whether he concentrates all that well on matters subsequently discussed. Not that he's apt to have considered how he would react to this idea were he himself *not* one of the rulers.

Be that as it may, when it becomes clear that Sokrates has completed his sketch of the just regime, but without elaborating upon that which anyone with blood in his veins would regard as the best thing about it, and that he now intends to begin comparing it with – "*how* many was it? ... four? – *four* kinds of *unjust* regimes? – how long is *that* likely to take? We'll be here all night! Not that it isn't a reasonable step, I suppose. One could hardly claim to have a sufficient understanding of justice without paying comparable attention to injustice – not merely some abstract definition of it, mind you, but real insight into what *causes* it. And sure, what forms it typically takes in cities, and in various kinds of people ... as Glaukon pointed out, even the

The Portrait of a Lady

best regime needs good judges as well as good doctors. And that means men familiar with *all sorts* of natures, vicious as well as virtuous ... especially the vicious, come to think of it. But as Herakleitos always insisted, 'first things first' – and surely this notion of the rulers' sharing all the women is some kind of 'first'."

Thus Polemarchos' curiosity finally gets the better of him. He has already come to recognize that he does not clearly understand his own views (334b, e; 335b, d), much less those of the philosopher. He wants clarification of this one for sure, but no doubt would prefer *not* being the only one having to admit he isn't "well-educated" enough to see its "sensibleness" for himself (to say nothing of what else his raising the point might insinuate). And since it *was* Adeimantos who had agreed to this novel idea, no doubt without realizing what he was saying, it is only fair that *he* should initiate a return to the topic. Besides, he prides himself in being skilled at covering up his mistakes.

So Polemarchos draws Adeimantos into his quandary. In that barely polite semi-privacy whispering provides, the two comrades briefly conspire. Whereupon Ariston's second son announces his belated discovery: they have been robbed!! But this time the clever thief has been caught in the act – caught trying to cheat his own partners and helpers out of a "whole form of the argument" – as if this friendly sharing of women and children were a minor concern, its merit plain to anyone with sense. True enough, Adeimantos had agreed that *some* such arrangement would be "correct", but one can imagine *many* ways of arranging these matters, and it could make a big difference – indeed, all the difference in the world – as to which particular way the philosopher has in mind. Polemarchos, for example, wonders whether it's the same as what *he* has in mind. So here they've been patiently waiting for Sokrates to get down to the specifics of this child-begetting business – indeed about the whole community of women and children he mentioned – but instead he's proposing to move on and consider some altogether different regimes. Seriously? No, they are resolved not to release him until he's made clear his plans for *their* regime. By now Glaukon is sufficiently intrigued by the challenge to join in this demand, as does a no-doubt-smiling Thrasymachos. He suggests, with good reason, that Sokrates may presume the resolution to be unanimous (450a).

The philosopher protests his innocence, contending that his reticence simply reflected his wish to keep them all out of trouble. They don't know what they're asking, "how much argument about the regime

[they] are again setting in motion from the beginning as it were [or, 'from the foundation'; *ex archēs*]." One might recall here his previous observation that the beginning of every work is the greatest thing – a prudential maxim shortly to be echoed and amplified (377a; 453a). In any event, what a scarce hour ago he had suggested was virtually self-evident, at least to any well-educated and sensible person, he now admits entails no less than a "swarm [*hesmos*] of arguments". And when this "waspish" warning only moves both Glaukon and Thrasymachos to outdo each other in insisting they are indefatigable when it comes to arguments, Sokrates reveals that what he has in mind is not merely difficult and arguable, but *doubtful*, indeed that it raises "*many* doubts" (*pollas apistias*). One may doubt (or distrust; *apistein*) whether it is possible *at all*, much less that it is the *best* possible arrangement (450c).

Perhaps there is good reason for the philosopher's doubt, but he can scarcely be unaware that such protestations only arouse everyone's curiosity the more.[2] Glaukon assures him that his auditors will be neither distrustful (i.e., doubting; *apistoi*) nor lacking in judgment, nor otherwise ill-disposed (450d). Sokrates replies that he does not find such encouragement encouraging. Perhaps he would feel less anxious if they *were* distrustful. It would be different, of course, if he were confident (or, trustful; *pisteuontos*), both that he knew what he was talking about, and that those he was speaking to were as prudent as they are dear. But to have to make arguments even as one seeks, and despite being dubious oneself … well, that's just a slippery, scary business. He insists that it's not so much a childish fear of being laughed at that concerns him,[3] as it is the fear of unintentionally deceiving and thereby corrupting his younger friends about what would make for truly noble, good, and just laws. For in slipping from the truth himself, he might drag the whole company down into blasphemy and error. And he regards *that* as even more grave than involuntary manslaughter! He might as well fall down at once and beg indulgence of Adrasteia, punisher of arrogant behaviour and rash utterances.

The philosopher's apparent hyperbole causes Glaukon to laugh out loud. He responds in like spirit with a comprehensive waiver of responsibility should they be affected "in some discordant way by the argument" (451b). "Be bold and speak", he urges. Sokrates agrees that such a waiver would probably reduce his own culpability, at least in the eyes of the law (much as acting under duress mitigates guilt, one may add). And so only after this fairly extensive foreplay does he at last agree to "go back again and say what perhaps should have been

The Portrait of a Lady

said then" – though, on second thought, perhaps *this* is the correct way: "after having completely gone through the masculine drama, to finish the feminine" (451c). Take note, however, Sokrates does not immediately address the issue that caused his arrest: the provocative (not to say scandalous) suggestion that biologically based families be replaced by some sort of grand communal arrangement. And note as well that the other interlocutors never showed any special curiosity about female nature as such, nor expressed any dissatisfaction with the account of who would rule their regime or why. They are solely but most keenly curious about, in Glaukon's words, "what the community of children and women will be among the guardians, and their rearing when still young in the time between birth and education, which is believed to be the most trying" (450c). The next thing they know, women *are themselves* "among the guardians". As for the latter half of Glaukon's question dealing with the trials of early childhood – that period of nurture which traditionally has been an almost exclusive responsibility of women – this issue is *never* addressed. And "misinterpreting" the question about "their rearing" as if it were about the rearing of *women*, Sokrates (ever light on his feet) requires only a few quick steps to transform *that* into a question of whether the women of the guardians are to be reared the same as the men. The pivotal step is: "If we *use* the women for the *same things* as the men ... "

But wait. In order to assess more fittingly the – what shall we say? strange and "revolutionary"? – character of this so-called feminine drama, trying to imagine what Polemarchos must be thinking as its successive provisions are revealed might be more helpful than scholarly commentary. After all, we have this brash, forceful, skeptical, but sensible and fair-minded (albeit somewhat conventional) young heir to his own particular father's private fortune to thank for it. But to do him justice, we must bear in mind what Sokrates tells us elsewhere about Polemarchos, that eventually he turned to philosophy (*Phaedrus* 257b). Presumably, then, he is the sort of young man who, according to this dialogue (and in contradistinction to popular notions), is naturally suited for the philosophical life – even if for now his taste and perspective would seem more akin to that of Aristophanes than Sokrates. So, as the philosopher was saying to Glaukon, "If we use the women for the same things as the men ... "

"Leaping lizards, where did he get *that* idea? *I* presumed we were going to 'use' women for something entirely different than we 'use' men

– let's hope he's not also suggesting that we use men the way we use women!

"Seriously, though, aren't the men first of all *warriors*? hand-picked for their *strength*? accustomed to *violence*? skilled in the arts of *fighting*, and with using force to defend and police the city? Why would it even occur to anyone to use women for *that*, of all jobs? What would be the point?

"I have serious doubts about this dog analogy that Sokrates swears by. It's one thing to use a female dog to herd *sheep*, but the working-class folk being guarded aren't some different species of animal. I know a couple of pretty imposing blacksmiths, for example – big bruisers, strong as oxen – I'd sure rather march into battle alongside one of them than *any* woman!

"And what's hunting got to do with this whole business? So what if female dogs *hunt* with as well as guard the things that the males guard – and do everything else together, too, for that matter. We're talking about guarding here, and males are a *lot* better as guard dogs, for pretty obvious reasons: usually bigger, stronger, faster, and *fiercer*.

"However, so far as hunting goes, for whatever it's worth, females are often just as good as males – sometimes better, or at least keener. They seem more instinctive somehow, take to it more readily ... almost as readily as males take to fighting.

"But I wouldn't make so little of a female's preoccupation with her litter. A nursing bitch isn't much use for anything besides tending her pups. Now if you want to see really *dedicated guarding*! Though only of what's her own, of course. She won't care for the young of another unless you fool her into thinking they're hers. Not that that's hard to do, since dogs can't count. Rub a bit of her own milk on most anything and she'll think it's hers. Would that fooling women were that easy.

"But haven't our two canophiliacs here forgotten the one enormous qualification to their 'they do everything in common' thesis? You don't bring a bitch in heat around a pack of males unless you want to see real pandaimonium. And kiss goodbye to any guarding *or* hunting you're not prepared to do yourself – you'll sooner train gnats to hum in the Phrygian mode. I wouldn't trust Kerberos himself around a flirting female. Can't say I'm surprised the ever-cerebral Sokrates overlooked something so basic to the ways of the flesh, but what's Glaukon's excuse? After all, he raises the dumb brutes.

The Portrait of a Lady

"Actually, I have to admit being partial to dogs myself. I like how they look up to you, how they fawn over you as if you were important. Keep them tolerably well-fed and they're loyal to a fault. And they're *honest* – don't hide their feelings. Contrast favourably with most people, I must say.

"Now, where are we? that the women must be taught the same things as the men? Ah, yes: music and gymnastic. Why not? I can see the advantages of a man's wife sharing his general point of view. And I've always believed that Lykourgos was right in requiring physical exercise of the women, that it made them healthier mothers of healthier children.

"' ... *and* what has to do with war'? Blessed Miltiades! If *that* was a sound policy, you can bet the Spartans would have adopted it long ago. Make women as fit as you like, you can no more turn them into hoplites than you can chimpanzees into charioteers! Why, the weight of armour and shield alone ... (And, by Hephaistos, I ought to know – the family's been trying to devise lighter-weight models since Father took over the business. The new zinc-alloy line is selling well, but I wouldn't trust it to take a real pounding ... great for dancing, though. Hey! Imagine *women* doing a war-dance. Wouldn't *that* be comical? ... stomping around naked except for helmet and shield, shaking their spears in the air ... droll thought.)

"Anyhow, bodily strength is merely one of a long list of objections, headed, *surely*, by fighting spirit. Mix a few women into the ranks and a Spartan phalanx would carve through our line like a cleaver through cheese. Why persist in this nonsense? And Glaukon agreeing with everything he says, like some portionless son humouring his rich uncle. You'd think neither of them had ever been on a battlefield before.

"Oh, *finally*, he admits that such a policy would make us look ridiculous. But, no, the *most* ridiculous thing about it would *not* be the sight of old as well as young women exercising naked with the men ... though I'll admit that *does* give rise to amusing possibilities! Imagine: you're all worked up from ogling the maids when some wrinkled old crone comes jogging along – wouldn't that make even a starved spirit droop? Truly, a scene worthy of Aristophanes. For that matter, *young* women exercising naked would look pretty comical when they're several months pregnant. And what about wrestling? Hey, wait a minute! Maybe this proposal has more merit than I realized!

"Of course, if one were serious, there are a couple of obvious solutions to these sorts of problems. Why have everyone exercise together? Why not have separate gymnasia for men and women? Or why do they have to be naked? Why not exercise clothed, the way Greeks used to, and barbarians still do? And there Sokrates sits, Innocence himself, speaking of clothing as if it were simply a matter of custom and climate – as optional as he finds sandals, ... and sleep, too, from what I've heard. Strange bird.

"Well, so much for the specifics of the women's gymnastical education! ... though I'm not sure he said even this much about the men's. Unless I missed something, all we established was that our athletic regimen would have to be 'subtler' than the ordinary one, that it would have to be 'simple and equitable'. We ought to sweep the games at Olympia with a shrewd scheme like that. Hasn't Sokrates learned anything practical in all those years of hanging around gymnasia and wrestling schools? What's he been doing there if not pursuing knowledge ... or dare one ask?

"When you think about it, isn't it rather queer that we've spent so little time – none, actually – discussing the best exercises and training routines for developing speed and strength and fighting skills? And nothing whatever has been said about the military arts themselves. For example, what are his views concerning the duties of a cavalry commander? (excuse me, *'our* views') And should everyone be trained to serve in both infantry and cavalry, or is this precluded by our 'one man, one job' policy? And what about that new weapon people are talking about – some sort of combination spear and scythe – should this kind of innovation be encouraged in our city? What if the Spartans were to come up with really *good* lightweight armour? Or – Zeus forbid – some barbarians!

"Now I suppose we'll spend an hour or two discussing what reforms must be made in music so that it also provides proper models of *feminine* virtue. I shouldn't think that the guidelines for *how* things are to be said would be any different, ... and *perhaps* not those for proper rhythms and melodies either. But obviously we will have to lay down some additional patterns for *what* is to be said. I'm curious, is our philosopher friend as high on Penelope as he seems to be on Odysseus? For what my opinion is worth, *there* was a real lady – at least as Homer has portrayed her: beautiful, intelligent, faithful, obedient, graceful, ... and a terribly clever weaver! ... made all of her own clothes. No doubt a marvellous cook, too. Why else would The Wily One have been so reluctant to leave her, and so insistent about returning? *Had*

The Portrait of a Lady

to be her wicked lamb casserole (heh, heh). Helen, on the other hand, ... well, if I've understood *anything* that we've done so far, there'll be some changes made in *her* story!

"What's that? The only thing truly laughable is the sight of the foolish and the bad? ... and that the only serious standard of beauty one should establish is the good? Well might *he* think so. A two-legged reminder of what Aesop said about the camel (or was it the frog?): 'A face that only a mother could love.'

"Alright, 'seriously' then, isn't *beauty* something that just *is*, by nature? It's not something we can 'establish' in whatever way we find useful, is it? like coinage, or weights and measures? Consider, for example, my jogging crone: she may be a woman of surpassing excellence in all *other* respects, but *beautiful* ... ? Let's not bet the preservation of our city on it.

"Oh, *now* we're going to consider whether any of this is possible after all. Like old Parmenides always said, 'Better late than never'. At least he's conceding that it's *controversial* as to what work – if any – females can perform in common with the males. Fair enough. But 'particularly with respect to war'?! Oh, come now, Daimonic one, life with Xanthippe has given you a warped view of womankind.

"Why don't we begin by comparing how they *look* – that would settle it for most people. Okay, we'll do it your way (as usual). Yes, our city is founded on each person's doing what he is suited for by nature. And yes, it's scarcely credible that a woman doesn't differ in her nature from a man. Now stop me if I'm going too fast here, Sokrates, but doesn't that imply that women are suited for *different* work? Obviously, then, the next step is to analyse woman's nature. That done, we'll simply ask ourselves what things that need doing in the city such a nature *is* suited for. (And I give you my word as the son of an honest arms dealer, it will *not* be war!)

"Ah, that's *not* the next step. He's right though – we should first clarify what we mean by 'nature'. And he's right again: this could lead into deep water. (I was over my head just trying to define friend and enemy!) Now 'Eristics'? 'Dialectics'? ... here, dolphin!

"True, we *didn't* stop to consider what form of different and same nature we meant, and with reference to what, when we assigned different pursuits to different natures. I guess we were just relying on common sense for an understanding of both natures and tasks. But since now we're tossing common sense out the door with pitchforks. ...

The War Lover

"However, if you insist on getting technical, the issue of distinguishing same and different natures doesn't seem equivalent to explicating a given nature itself. Wouldn't this be like determining somehow that two words were (or weren't) synonymous, but not knowing what the words themselves *mean*? Or is *that* the point? That the power to distinguish same and different requires a more basic power whereby one grasps a given nature's form first? Or is it rather the reverse, that only through *comparing* can the unique characteristics of each nature be discovered? ... I seem to be swimming in circles. And no dolphins in sight – just the sleek and slippery Sokrates, gambolling in his native element.

"Take his example. There is *some* natural difference between the bald and the hairy, but who wouldn't agree with Glaukon that it's ridiculous to regard *that* difference as relevant to anyone's suitability for cobbling? We have not the slightest doubt about this. Now, why not?

"Come to think of it, there doesn't seem to be *any* occupation for which *that* natural difference is relevant ... unless it involves looking good. It would be tedious to be a bald barber, though ... the same dumb jokes day after day.

"Which reminds me: why is it that you almost never see bald *women*? Imagine now – a *bald* jogging crone! Instant impotence! Why is it that only men go bald? Hardly seems fair. Of course, they've usually got more hair everywhere *else* on their bodies, beginning with their faces. That's probably why women remove what little they do have ... enhances *la différence*, makes them seem more feminine, more alluring ... though I've heard some barbarian women don't. What a thought! ... it's a wonder they reproduce at all.

"Bald or not, a man simply looks more ferocious with a great bushy beard, doesn't he? Make that a bald-but-slightly-bearded jogging crone ... in fact, think of her as sort of fuzzy all over ... Get a grip on yourself, Polemarchos, you're drifting. ...

"Let's see now, maybe we *could* judge the relevant same and different in light of our understanding of what the pursuit itself entails. But wait a minute! 'For example, the soul of a male doctor and a female doctor *have the same nature*'! What? And Glaukon, you agree?! Don't be absurd – that *can't* be *all* we mean by a person's nature: his or her aptitude for some job, ... or even for *all* jobs. It's good enough, maybe, for differentiating among kinds of men, your doctor and your carpenter, say. But it's ridiculous to suggest that the difference between a male doctor and female doctor is no more significant than that be-

The Portrait of a Lady

tween a bald cobbler and a hairy one – though now that you speak of it, I've never even heard of a female doctor. But say there were such a thing. Now, *think*, Glaukon! Imagine yourself their patient. Say you've been away on campaign and picked up some 'social disease'. Both doctors, equally competent, but one's a man and the other a woman – and you'd regard them as essentially *the same*? (Of course, you'd rather be treated by a woman doctor than have your most precious member fall off – who wouldn't? – but that's a whole different issue.) The very same *nature*? I'd wager that a male doctor and one of those blacksmiths I mentioned would understand each other better than either of them understands his own wife. I wonder whether Sokrates knows the difference between a hen and a rooster. Got a hen who's loud in the morning? That's because it has the same nature as a rooster! He's probably mystified why cockfights are always between cocks. Hearing him speak, you'd think he was a disciple of Anaxagoras ("it's-all-in-the-mind") Clazomenae. As if a person's soul had nothing whatever to do with his or her body. But give Empedokles his due and think about bodies – especially hers. Thinking *can* be fun. ... uplifting, even (... crude, Polemarchos, crude! – you're just another crude materialist).

"Anyhow, the doctor example is pretty remote from the issue at hand. As we noted earlier, doctors treat bodies with their souls, the point being that skill in medicine is entirely a matter of rational understanding. But we're talking about guardians here, right? And the only way to get to be one of those is to be first of all a warrior, right? And you'd have to have a pretty strange notion of *war* to think it's fought with just your soul. That's *not* why physicians accompany armies – to patch up bleeding souls and set broken minds. It's not putrid passions or severed appetites that get amputated and cauterized. And my father didn't multiply the family fortune selling shields for the fighting spirit. Female doctors ... strange, but conceivable, I suppose. But female *hoplites*? Not even Daidalos could make that pig fly. Sokrates himself keeps referring to the essential quality here: *strength*. How many times has he noted that women are *weaker* than men? Admittedly, there's more than one kind of strength, yet bodily strength *is* a kind, and call me the son of a female cynic, but I find it hard – *very* hard – to imagine a city that could be governed without its playing any role whatsoever.

"Still, now that he's raised the issue, it's a lot more difficult to *explain* the differences between men and women than I would have ever

The War Lover

guessed it could be. We *experience* it all the time, but what's the 'it' we experience? Obviously it's *not* merely that 'the female bears and the male mounts', but most of the differences we perceive *do* seem *somehow* related to the sexes' differing roles in the procreating business – which, shall we say, 'bulks larger' in the woman's case than the man's ... though his 'bulks larger' *first* (heh, heh) – straighten up, Polemarchos (whoops! must be daimonically inspired: I can't stop! ... take a deep breath and think about Being).

"There has to be more to it than just strength of body, though. Do the differences involve other kinds of strength? Something has to explain why it is that, generally speaking, men *are* better than women at most *everything*, not just at war and whatever requires a strong body. There are plenty of individual exceptions, of course, like Glaukon says. But as a class, men do seem to be better at most everything. Why, even the best chefs are men! Even the best *hairdressers* are men!! ... In a medical sense, anyhow. Are men really stronger in *all* respects, or are they just naturally more competitive? Or is *that* also a kind of strength?

"The only reservation that occurs to me is with regard to anything and everything involving small children ... women's patience with those little beggars is a marvel. For my part, I'd rather spend my life cleaning latrines than working in a nursery.

"Glaukon's supposed to be pretty sharp, but so far as I can tell, he's hardly given a right answer since Sokrates mentioned dogs. Do you believe it? – we're about to be stuck with women governors! As if there's no difference between managing a household and managing a city. Talk about being seduced by words. ...

"So, *the* 'rational' regime has female soldiers, female judges, female doctors, female blacksmiths I suppose, female tanners and stonemasons ... female hangmen (why not?) ... a whole assembly of women artisans. Next they'll be rowing our war galleys. Won't that strike fear in the hearts of our enemies! It sure does in mine. ...

"The way this discussion is progressing, I can predict what's coming up next just as surely as ducks waddle and go barefoot. See: 'one's musical, one's not' – 'one's apt at gymnastic, another isn't' – 'this one's skilled at war, that one's unwarlike' (... with words, maybe; the point is, how do they compare with working-class *men*) – 'this one loves wisdom, that one hates it' (*hates* it? hates *wisdom*? ah, yes, one mustn't overlook spite and envy ...) – 'this one is spirited, that one isn't' – this one has cauliflower ears but can hurl a javelin two stadia, that one made up like a doll can only embroider negligees. ... And *guess* which kind we're going to choose to share as good friends should! Methinks we've solved the problem of jealousy, among the guardians at least. But this is *not* going to help recruiting. ...

"Hey, Sokrates, speaking of gymnastic-loving, horseback-riding, bull-throttling women, did you hear the one about the two Spartans? One Spartan says to the other, 'Who was that lady I saw you with last night?' The second one replies, '*That* was no lady! That was my *wife*!' ... sweet Pallas Athena, I see the point. Oh Glaukon, and for this you gave up our spicy little Corinthian maids. You'd better hope they all *do* look alike in the dark. ...

"Sure, we wanted 'the best women' to cohabit with our best men, but we didn't mean the women most *like* those men. I must admit, though, the thought of *these* women exercising naked with men isn't nearly as funny as when the idea was first suggested.

"And he's not through yet? The next 'wave' of argument is even *greater* than the one he's just 'escaped'? Sure, *he* escaped, and left the rest of us floundering in The Sea of Absurdity. Very amusing. *Now* it's every man for himself. Thrasymachos is right: Sokrates *does* take a kind of perverse pleasure in making monkeys out of people.

"I confess, though, I *am* curious as to what could top this overturning of all political life as hitherto known and enjoyed. Ah, it's that 'All these women are to belong to all these men in common'; and 'none shall live together privately with any'; and 'their children will be common, and neither will a parent know its own offspring nor a child its parent'. Well, except for that last twist, at least *this* is something we actually asked about ... though I'm heartily sorry I brought the whole thing up ... I much preferred *my* phantasies.

"Incidentally, it's a hard day's ride from obvious quite how *this* arrangement 'follows' from his previous craziness. When he first mentioned it, he implied it followed from the very idea of *friendship*. Though Glaukon is right for a change: putting it into practice would involve an even greater disturbance to established ways than his 'let's-be-ruled-by-the-most-mannish-women-we-can-manufacture' suggestion. For obviously this does away with any meaningful notion of family and household.

"But I don't see how it's even possible. If we simply had some sort of sharing of the women by the men, it's easy enough to see why *fathers* often wouldn't know their own children. In fact, I suspect *that* situation isn't entirely without precedent. If it weren't for chastity in

The War Lover

women, would *any* of us know for sure who our fathers are? But by the two goddesses, how is it even conceivable that *mothers* not know their own children? I shouldn't think we need worry much about whether such a paradoxical arrangement would be most *beneficial* for either mothers or children, seeing as how (fortunately!) it just isn't possible.

"Ah, the fox proposes to make it easy on himself, putting off showing its possibility until *after* having shown its supposed advantages. This reverses the procedure he used in trying to peddle his earlier brain-child. But it doesn't seem a very *practical* way to go about this business. Why debate the merits of something that might not even be possible? I wonder what he's really up to, approaching this matter backwards as he is – not for a minute crediting his sudden fit of lazy-mindedness.

"Still, it occurs to me there are two senses of the word 'possible' that are relevant to even sane political proposals. One is whether an arrangement is workable at all – period – starting with a clean slate (presuming there ever could be such a situation – Zeus only knows how). The other is whether it's possible to change to it from whatever one has at a given moment. The latter seems a more variable kind of possibility. That is, presumably people who were pretty much satisfied with their way of life would not willingly overturn it for a change that promised only slight improvement. But if they were somehow convinced that their life could be tremendously improved, putting an end to all human ills, virtually re-creating the Isles of the Blessed – wouldn't people exert themselves more, and sacrifice more, to accomplish it? You can bet your grapes on it (as old Thales was so fond of saying). So might not our wily veteran here wish to paint this communal family arrangement in such glowing colours that he can finesse the possibility issue?

"In fact, I'm coming to suspect his every move bears watching – he does a good imitation of the fumbling, bumbling innocent, but it's all an act: 'Oh, dear me, what *shall* I do! You're *making* me argue even though I'm in doubt and still seeking.' ... yeah, and I'm a Persian belly dancer (... now unemployed, sad to say).

"For instance: notice his fresh emphasis on discipline and law-abidingness, how because *our* rulers are truly 'worthy of their names', they'll willingly rule along whatever lines *we* lay down, and their auxiliaries of course do anything and everything the rulers command. Watch now. He'll rely on *that* – iron discipline – to solve all the problems that would naturally arise from so paradoxical an idea. The rulers will

The Portrait of a Lady

simply *command* their men to mount whatever women 'the city' needs mounted. Simply *command* these women to forget their own kids. And just *order* the children not to wonder who their parents are. And everyone will regard themselves as surpassingly happy, the envy of mankind, by *fiat*.

"So, we're to consider whether these men and women, always eating and training and bathing and housing together, may be led 'by a necessity of inner nature' to 'mix' with one another ... Ah, yes, I'd put my drachmas on erotic necessities over Pythagorean rationalities anytime. So, presuming we can find some way of keeping our soldier-boys off our working-class girls, it's probable that sooner or later they will find even their female comrades attractive – stranger things have happened, I suppose. Deprivation breeds desperation. Think of all those rustic jokes about shepherds being left alone too long with their sheep.

"And so – *finally!* – we get to the long-awaited sharing of at least *some* of the city's women ... hardly my idea of the *crème de la crème*, but women of a sort none the less ... praise Zeus for even small favours.

"Wait! There's to be no unhallowed 'disorderly intercourse'? (Why do I have a bad premonition about this?) They've got to be 'married'? We must legitimize their intercourse by the 'most sacred' of all possible marriages? ... meaning, 'the most beneficial'? ... to whom? ... for what? Is that what 'sacred' means? True, we did agree to regard all good things as coming from the gods. Fair enough. I shouldn't think a little marrying could really hurt anybody under these circumstances: do you, Glaukon, and you Adeimantos, and you Lysias, and you Nikeratos, and you Euthydemos, and even you Kleitophon (and so on) take Kalonike and Myrrine and Praxagora and Lysistrata and Lampito and Ismenia (and so on) to be your lawfully wedded wives, to have and to hold and to have and to hold and to have and to. ...

"Excuse me, why are we talking about dogs again? One moment it's the most sacred marriages and what is holy, and in the next breath it's the matings of dogs and birds! Zeus knows (probably), I enjoy a bit of irreverent humour as well as the next man, but out of respect to my thankfully absent father (who lawfully wedded my mother in the old-fashioned way), should I not protest?

"But of course! We *have* been speaking in terms of what is in accord with *nature*, as distinct from ancestral customs. Perhaps the most *truly* sacred marriages *would* be like the natural marriages of animals ... that

The War Lover

uncoerced free-for-all, each mating with whomever as opportunity and their own spirits move them. The rule of pristine passion, untrammelled by old-fashioned, artificial, merely conventional restraints. Sounds promising. The *natural* religion – that's for me!

"*Holy Aphrodisiacs!* Wrong again! Is he really suggesting that we model our 'naturally best marriages' on the *the art of selectively breeding pedigreed animals*? Sweet Mother of Apollo! What does the poet say? 'Whom the gods would destroy they first make mad'? (... glad I'm not sitting too close to this guy – wouldn't want to get accidentally fried by a bolt Zeus intended for the gentle Sokrates). One doesn't have to be Cassandra to foresee some problems here, even given the most obedient soldiers that ever strapped on greaves. ...

"Ah, we're going to use *drugs*! I thought all morally dubious arts like that had long since been run out of town. Ah, he means big doses of those 'medicinal' lies and deceptions that can be so useful in dealing with madmen and fools. Speaking of which ... For consider the basic set-up: we want the best to mate as often as possible with the best, and the reverse for the poorer, more ordinary stock; the offspring of the former will be reared, but not that of the latter; and all this has to transpire without anyone other than the rulers knowing what's happening, lest the guardians' 'herd' be disrupted by faction! So how are our trusty rulers going to manage this, we wonder? Well, they manipulate a rigged marriage lottery such that it just happens to award the preponderance of breeding rights to those young men who prove best in war or whatever. With everyone being so cleverly deceived, the poor saps who never seem to win a chance to get laid will curse Fortune rather than their all-wise, so-just, too-courageous, utterly shameless rulers. I'll bet they *do* come to suspect that justice is the other man's good, however. ... I must remember never to play dice with this guy ... at least not using his dice!

"And I'm frankly skeptical about the warrior class remaining faction-free for very long. Won't it soon become self-evident (especially at the gymnasium) that there are two groups, the 'lucky limps' and the 'ill-starred stiffs'? A piece of friendly advice, Sokrates: you'd best stock up on the other kind of drugs, too, for it's going to take more than cold showers to make this scheme work. Though some enterprising soul will doubtless see the opportunity here for a brisk business in ... what shall we call them? ... 'aphrodisial substitutes'? Of course, we mustn't allow such things to be *privately owned* ... maybe they could be checked out from a public facility ... administered by special 'manikin-dildo' stewards (who, needless to add, would be male or female), ... with a loss of lending privileges for late returnees (can't *fine* them, obviously, since they haven't a drachma to their names ... presuming they even get private names).

"As for how to implement what the tender-hearted might worry is an overly severe policy concerning the rearing and not-rearing of children, well, there will be these perfectly implacable birthing monitors – and be assured they too could be either women or men – who immediately take the babies away from their mothers as soon as they're born. And the ones the monitors determine to be 'the offspring of the good' disappear into day-and-night nurseries, whereas the rest disappear into the great unknown whence they came (just drown 'em like puppies, eh, Sokrates? I wonder what sort of nature would be suited for *this* job. Somehow, I doubt it would improve the regime of *my* soul ...).

"None of the mothers will be the wiser, however, since we'll use every known device and invent new ones to prevent their being able to recognize which babes are their own. I wonder, though, once the word gets out, whether the ingenuity of mothers wouldn't prove more than a match for even baskets full of philosophers. As the wise Aristides so justly observed, invention is the necessity of mothers (and vice versa) – and everyone admits we're dealing with a kind of necessity here that's more rigorous than logic, at least with normal people. That's definitely *not* you, O Daimonic One.

"Hey! Maybe *that* is why we want some female rulers: we need someone who's wise to all of women's tricks. They are such cunning, devious creatures ... utterly unscrupulous ... ought to fit right in.

"But seriously, Sokrates, if a person had arrived late in this conversation – missed the first four or five hours, say – I'll bet you'd have the very devil of a time convincing him now that *this* was the just and altogether good regime! Aren't *we* the lucky ones ...

"Of course, we still have to determine eligibility rules for the breeding lottery. As is only fair, it's to be restricted to those in their *prime*. Prime for *what*, I foolishly ask. Why for 'bearing and begetting for the city', what else? Would such a public-spirited clan even dream of so much as touching one another for any *other* reason? Unimaginable! Incredible! Inconceivable! Illegal!

"So, women are to do their duty from age twenty to forty, men from twenty-five to fifty-five. This disproportion probably isn't fair, but I'm no longer sure to whom. And as should be obvious to any sensible, well-educated person, everyone no longer capable of reproducing will be left free to have intercourse with whomsoever they please (so long as they're not related to each other in the usually forbidden ways). Oh, so there *is* some other reason a person might want to have sex besides making babies for the city. I was beginning to think I was depraved (and not just deprived). However, you might recall, Sokrates, this whole wonderful, marvellous, and, let me say, truly phantastic conversation began with my father's admitting that he's *glad* he doesn't even *feel* the sexual urge anymore. So in the just city, the rational city, the city ordered according to nature, *he* gets free sex and *I* get zilch! What a world. We *are* just the playthings of the gods ... and of ourselves, of course. To think I voluntarily allied myself with this emissary from cloud-cuckoo land! Looks like that slug Kleitophon will have the last laugh after all.

"But I am becoming confused. What happens when a man who has finally achieved sexual liberation, and so can have sex with 'whomsoever', wants a woman of child-bearing age who's only allowed to be mounted by a duly authorized child-begetter? Or what if one of these now sexually liberated women is hot to get laid by some under-aged young man, who (as I understand it – and please, *please*, correct me if I'm wrong about this) is not allowed to have sex *at all*? Add to that the problem Glaukon raises about determining which relationships would be incestuous ones (and so far as I can tell, Sokrates, your mathematical anti-incest formula either just plain doesn't work, or it works so well that *everyone* is related to *everyone else*), and I begin to suspect that there's no one left for the sexually liberated to have sex with. Ah well, Zeus giveth and Zeus taketh away.

"So we're now to be shown that 'the community of women and children for the guardians' is both consistent with the rest of the regime, and by far the best deal imaginable. Well, the matter of its consistency with our previous provisions having been raised, I must say I don't see how concealing actual genealogy within the ruling class is compatible with assigning every child of the city, regardless of the class of its parents, to its own natural class. And as I recall our 'well-bred lie', this was the rulers' foremost responsibility. But by the time one could detect gold or silver in the soul of a kid from the working class, it would be well-known to him, his parents, and everyone else who his real parents were. Then there's the fact that sometimes children just naturally *look* like one of their parents. Say, for example, kids *you* happened to father, Sokrates – who could mistake those bulging eyes, that pug nose, those thick lips, that peculiar gait? See, if you spent more time thinking through practicalities (and less on trying to figure out how to measure the privates of fleas, or whatever it is they say you wonder about), you would see for yourself that your boat won't float.

"And even were we to agree that there's no greater good for a city than unity nor greater evil than disunity – and I'd want to give at least passing consideration to inconveniences like famine and plague – I'm not as sure as Glaukon seems to be that unifying our city is best done by attempting to establish a 'community of pleasure and pain'. Wasn't our city *founded* on everyone's mutual *need* of each other, united by the obvious interdependence and value of everyone? Whereas there are some fairly clear limits to the sharing of pleasures and pains. It's a lot more feasible with respect to those of the soul than those of the body – the closest approximation to the latter kind is *simultaneous* pleasure or pain ... an orgy, say – but no, you had to insist on that phoney breeding lottery, with some rejoicing over their fortune while others grieve over theirs ... unless you'd have them be voyeurs, you naughty man.

"Seriously, though, it's no doubt true that rejoicing at the same births and grieving over the same deaths *does* have a unifying effect. But if *now* you're suggesting that the *whole city* become one big happy family (and not merely our carefully selected, cleverly manipulated, iron-disciplined, thick-as-a-brick few), you've shed your last fig leaf of credibility. The Naked Philosopher, all set for his coed gym class. On the other hand, the more successfully one unifies only the ruling class that way, the more deeply divided they would be from the rest of the citizens, who experience their joys and griefs in private families, like normal people. It would be tantamount to having a city within a city.

"Presuming, that is, this communal family notion would work for the ruling class, which it won't. You can prescribe by law what titles to *call* people – father, wife, uncle, son, sister, grandmother, whatever – but unless you believe that certain words have magical powers, that will no more create the reality of familial relations than calling me Pharaoh would make me the ruler of Aegyptos.

"Glaukon's right: it *would* be ridiculous to merely mouth the names of kinship without the accompanying deeds. But the ridiculous is just what we'd be left with, since these people have been denied any bases for developing familial *feelings*, the *loving* of particular individuals by other individuals, simply because they're one's own, or because

The War Lover

one finds them beautiful, or because one is grateful to them, or maybe just because one has lived with them in privacy and apart from everyone else ... you must have at least *heard* of such a thing!

"Is the city we've founded Greek, you ask. Try Martian. It *started out* Greek, but somewhere along the way we must have gotten launched into the heavens. Some people – *not me*, you understand – but some would say this is the very sort of thing one should expect to happen were a philosopher put in charge of designing a city. It's been fun, Sokrates, a truly unique experience, but methinks I hear the music and laughter of the all-night festival calling. Now why don't we go out and test Glaukon's hypothesis about erotic necessities? ... or at least get a bite to eat – I've been dying for one of those scrumptious Attic cakes ever since you made them illegal."

As these perhaps vulgar, but surely not impertinent, imagined musings of Polemarchos remind us, no sane and sober human being can regard the ideas put forward in Book Five as a serious *political* proposal. Glaukon observed at the end of Book Four that it looked to him as though their inquiry had reached a point where it was becoming ridiculous to proceed any further (445a). In agreeing, Sokrates flatly declared it ridiculous. Bearing in mind that the entire dialogue is the philosopher's narrative recapitulation of an earlier conversation, one may be justified in attributing a retrospective irony to his characterization. No judgment need rest on that, however; Book Five itself is awash, as it were, in allusions to laughter, the laughable, the comic, and to the past master of political comedy, Aristophanes. But if the novel political arrangements introduced in Book Five are *not* meant to constitute a serious revolutionary alternative to all previous regimes, including the dialogue's own Aristocracy in *logos*, the question naturally arises: what *is* Book Five really intended to accomplish? What purpose or purposes *are* served by this almost palpably ridiculous "feminine drama"?

Doing full justice to that question could very well, I suspect, require a book unto itself. But one can begin by noting that, in rejecting as ridiculous the three or four features put forward in Book Five, one needn't conclude that this portion of the dialogue is without *any* political significance, nor that the serious consideration of these comical proposals in no way leads to a finer articulation of the just city. For despite their paradoxicality, they *do* serve indirectly as both a further test and an elaboration of the teaching about justice (and injustice)

The Portrait of a Lady

with which Book Four concludes. Whereas Sokrates specifies only three steps in their procedure – discover the form of justice writ large in the city (368d-a); see whether something similar can be discerned in the individual soul (434d); then test that formal account by comparing it with various commonplace conceptions in order to see whether it adequately explains their limited validity (442de) – there is in addition this unacknowledged fourth step. The reader who emerges from Book Four satisfied with the account of justice he has been provided (and of virtue generally), an account generated without any explicit regard for women and with but (usually) slighting reference to them, is immediately confronted in Book Five with a concrete test of his newly gained understanding. What *does* political justice require to and from women? If Sokrates' proposed arrangement is ridiculous, then what one isn't?

Similar remarks pertain to the application of the formal account to the individual female soul. Does the just woman manifest the very same constellation of virtues – or dimensions of virtue, or facets of virtue – that are somehow both the effects and the constituents of that complete virtue which the philosopher calls 'justice'? Is she too, then, fully capable of self-rule, fully capable of a self-conscious and self-sufficient and self-mastered existence? That is to say, is female nature every bit as capable of this rare, and rarefied, perfection of existence as male nature is, with no obstacle to its attainment inherent in woman as such? For it would seem to be fully within the capacity of very, *very* few actual men. The question is, then, whether it is similarly within the capacity of at least a few women – whether, in short, there can be a philosopher-queen. Or, on the contrary, is there something about female nature itself that – for better or worse – precludes the kind of simplification of life philosophical rule presupposes, and which can result only from a complete subordination of every other concern to an almost maniacal love of wisdom? Might there be an irreducible complexity to the female soul that would obviate such a singular dedication of all its power? In particular, can woman as such utterly subordinate her bodily child-bearing potential, with its complementary child-nurturing yearnings in the soul – as can Sokrates his body's power for child-begetting – and do so without suffering as a consequence any ill effects? Or is true simplicity of soul possible only for the woman who commits herself unequivocally to the welfare of her children and whatever that entails?[4]

Or might sheer *strength* of soul be the basic issue? Philosophical rule

205

would seem to require enormous strength of both the rational and the spirited parts of one's soul, strength beyond that of almost all men – indeed, one may presume that most everybody, male and female alike, will live and die without even so much as setting sight on such monstrous strength, genuine philosophers being (as Sokrates insists) so very rare. And whereas it is obvious that women are typically weaker in body than men, it is by no means so obvious that they are typically weaker in soul. But even if as a rule they are, there would seem to be no reason in the very nature of things why in some rare case a woman couldn't be as strong of soul as the strongest-souled man (just as it would seem at least possible that some monstrously large woman could be born with a body potentially as strong as that of the strongest man, or even stronger). So, if the prime determinant of the philosophical nature is the respective strengths of a soul's various parts, then the possibility of a woman philosopher must be left an open question. Here, however, one needs to bear in mind especially the virtue of a strong soul's spirited part, what we translate as 'courage' ("heartedness"), but which the Greeks called 'manliness' (*andreia*). Most emphatically, we must not allow our thinking to be ruled by language, whether ours or someone else's. Yet neither should the evidence of common experience imbedded in language be ignored; words are the tracks of *something*, and possibly of something important.

And even if one is persuaded that the same catalogue of virtues is pertinent to man and woman alike – that the fully just woman, like her masculine counterpart, is prudent, courageous, and moderate – need this mean that their respective manifestations are substantially the same? Presuming for the moment that 'courage' rightly names the virtue of the spirited part of the female soul, is it properly and primarily manifested on the same sorts of occasions as is the courage of a man, requiring a mastery over the same spectrum of fears and pains? Or is it rather the case that, while certain fears are common (fear of death being an obvious example), other fears and pains – of either body or soul – are peculiar to each sex? I'm told that women these days live much of their adult lives in mortal dread of breast cancer. I don't. Whereas, and good Dr. Johnson to the contrary notwithstanding, I believe that the prospect of castration more forcefully concentrates the masculine mind than even the thought of hanging, and that women have only a pale and remote appreciation of the spectre to which it gives rise in a man's soul. And even with respect to those fears apparently common to men and women, are they felt – feared – to the same degree? Or do men typically find it easier to risk death, for example? Whereas male pride is more tender, more vulnerable, than that of the female, and its wounding a matter of greater consequence to men?

Similar remarks might be made with respect to moderation: is it a mastery in both men and women of exactly the same array of appetites and desires, experienced to exactly the same degree? Answering 'no' to any of these questions would seem to carry the corollary that only by sheer coincidence would the *nurturing* of such formally similar but substantially different virtues be exactly the same for men and women. If patience (presumably a kind of stamina of spirit) comes easy for a woman but bravery comes hard, and the reverse for a man, it is difficult to imagine their being successfully cultivated in both by the very same regimen.

As noted above, Book Five *does* begin with allegations of injustice, ... but not to *women*. The young men protest that *they* have been treated unjustly, in that they have been robbed of "a whole form of the argument". And perhaps they have, even if they've not correctly identified what it is they're missing. As should be emphasized now, however, it is never suggested that the provisions subsequently introduced are themselves required by *justice*. "Sexual equality" or sameness of treatment for men and women – more precisely, for *some*, comparatively *few* men and women – is not advanced because "equal justice" demands it. Nor is familial communism argued for because "equality of opportunity" is obviously just, and this is the only way one can eliminate the "unfair" advantages and disadvantages which accrue to individuals by virtue of the families into which they happen to be born. When first mentioned, the suggestion seemed to be that this common sharing of their women and children is nothing more nor less than the natural, logical – but quite incidental – consequence of the total friendship of the male guardians.

In this respect, their city's "reformation" in Book Five is of a piece with everything that has gone before. The philosopher never introduces *any* of his political proposals on the ground that they are inherently just; he never claims that anything about justice is intuitively obvious (which, of course, needn't mean that nothing is). Rather, the argument is always that this or that feature or policy is required the better to fulfil the reason, or reasons, or apparent reasons for which men and women need cities. His strategy tacitly accentuates the importance of determining what *is* the true purpose of the city. And that question, in turn, can be answered only in light of an adequate understanding of human nature. As has been hinted, however, there are grounds for suspecting that such understanding is not to be had from an inquiry focused exclusively on men. For how is one to determine what about men is due to their being *human*, and what to their being *men*?

I observed in the preceding chapter that the philosopher's oblique approach to the problem of political justice – his silently dismissing any attempt to describe a completed dream city, but rather generating a city step by deliberate step, almost literally from the ground up, with each step a response to some perceived need – that this approach precludes the young men adopting wholesale certain familiar arrangements and practices, thereby doing little more than institutionalizing their unexamined prejudices and calling that good. Challenged to build a *workable* city *from scratch*, they are obliged to undertake a more radical consideration of certain issues basic to political life. Behind the bizarre surface of Book Five, this same pedagogic strategy continues, albeit now with more explicit encouragement to their becoming self-conscious about what they are doing. For the philosopher speaks repeatedly of what is natural in contradistinction to what is merely familiar custom or convention (while blithely violating nearly every commonsense notion of what things do come naturally to human beings). Thus, in the very course of our rejecting his proposals as outrageous and unworkable and ridiculous, we are necessarily led to examine the naturalness of monogamy, of lifelong commitments to families based on biological kinship, of prohibiting incest, the naturalness of heterosexuality even, not to mention things still more disturbing. And we are required to think again about superior strength, and the ability to wage war, as being at least part of the basis of one's natural claim to rule.

In doing so, we may very well discover the arbitrariness or folly of certain familiar, traditional ways. But we may also rediscover the special merit of some traditional ways (cf. 425a), and of the value of tradition itself (cf. 427b–c). One might suggest that more self-consciousness is called for at this point precisely because in dealing with sexual and familial relations, we are necessarily examining the erotic foundation or core of human nature and thus of political life. But the very fact that the human form of being, in common with all but the lowest forms of life, is divided into male and female versions is what makes the problem of understanding human nature so peculiarly challenging. For the "self" that becomes self-conscious can *not* confidently assume that he (or she) *fully* manifests *human* nature – much less, *only* human nature – as opposed to a one-sided view of human nature. Of all the things that we become self-conscious about, this awareness of the possible limitations imposed by one's particular kind of sexuality may be the most important. It is crystallized in the question most everyone puts to himself sooner or later: what of that which I think, desire, loathe, fear, admire, prefer, or ignore is the result of my being – not simply a human being – but a male (or a female), and one moreover who has been nurtured in a particular political society which imparts to its members, among other things, certain views of what manhood and womanhood properly consist of?

And this very possibility: that one's perspective on life is radically, and perhaps incorrigibly, limited by "virtue" of one's particular form of sexuality, raises a problem of truly comprehensive significance about this (and every other) Platonic dialogue ... for, after all, it *is* a conversation exclusively among men, and (moreover) created by a man.[5] Might not this simple fact compromise, most profoundly, whatever conclusions the discussion gives rise to? Mustn't one wonder whether this entire dialogue about – of all things – *justice* is not itself "unjust" precisely because it is uninformed by the perspective common to half of mankind? Several different responses to such a challenge are imaginable.[6] One might argue that this is not in fact the case because women are incomplete or inferior versions of men, and in particular inferior reasoners; as such, they could make no contributions to this conversation that couldn't be made as well or better by some man. We, of course, are confident that this position is ridiculous, although for some reason it has been widely subscribed to over the ages and in many different religious and political traditions (and not exclusively, though no doubt more enthusiastically, by men). *Or*, one might insist that women as such are not necessarily inferior to men, and in particular not inferior reasoners, but that they are none the less different, with typically (and properly) a different set of interests and experiences, one which would ill-prepare them for making a constructive contribution to any general discussion about political matters. Thus their absence from this conversation about justice in no way compromises *it*; were the topic addressed a different one, household management, say, or the care and feeding of small children, or persuasion, or love even, a different judgment might well be warranted. Modern readers can be pretty well counted upon to reject this alternative also, although it too is a view that has enjoyed wide respect historically. A third ground on which one might defend the adequacy of the dialogue as written would probably be more to modern tastes, for it is based upon the presumption that men and women are substantially alike, that the differences between the sexes are merely ones of body, and of little – not to say trivial – significance. Thus, nothing important would be added by the presence of a woman at this conversation, nor is anything important lost by her absence.[7] Finally, one might contend that the dialogue's account of justice *is* suspect precisely because there *is* a distinctly feminine perspective on life which is pertinent yet absent from the discussion, and that the curious "feminine drama" of Book Five, far from rectifying its inadequacies, simply confirms them. Inasmuch as I believe this position merits more extended consideration, I shall return to it shortly. But for now, let me offer a caution: however much the conversation as portrayed might reveal that various of its participants suffer from limitations of feelings and experience, and consequent narrowness of perspective, one need not and therefore should not presume that these are simply reflections of the author's own limitations. The dialogue as a whole may very well manifest an all-encompassing perspective, the recovery of which requires the reader first of all to recognize the participants' limitations for what they are.

So Book Five brings us face to face with this fundamental problem of human nature, and thus tests our understanding of it, beginning with the account of the soul presented in Book Four (which, it should not be forgotten, was provided as a basis for judging the intrinsic goodness of justice for the individual). If all humans are rightly said to share that tripartite form of soul as the common ground of their humanity, then what explains their observable differences? One can at least *begin* to explain at least *some* differences in light of that basic psychology. The extent to which a person is competitive, for example, or more liberal than stingy, or motivated primarily by love of money rather than by love of honour or of knowledge, may be seen as a consequence of the proportional strengths of the various parts of his soul. But how are we to explain the seemingly most comprehensive and important difference of all, that between male and female?

The analytic techniques used in Book Four and elsewhere in the dialogue are all based upon introspection. We ratify that our soul has at least three discernible parts by our own inner experience of the clash between appetite and calculation, or between anger and desire. Similarly, the more refined analysis of pleasures and desires presupposes immediate experience of, for example, the comparative pleasantness of good food and good talk. But unless one has enjoyed the bisexual experience of Teiresias,[8] such introspective appeals beg all the essential questions raised by the male-female distinction. What alternative means do we have, then? Presumably, any understanding that is available to us requires a synoptic judgment based to some considerable extent on indirect evidence, as doubtless people's everyday views of both masculinity and femininity normally do. The problem with the everyday views – in so many matters, but immeasurably compounded in this one – is that along with valid evidence is synthesized an indeterminate but probably large admixture of prejudice, misinformation, mere convention mistaken for nature, wishes both pious and not, fears, resentments, and God knows what else – all alloyed together under the pressure, not of an overpowering divine love of truth, but of an all-too-human love of self. Thus, any hope for discovering this so-elusive truth about sexuality rests first of all on its being a person's foremost desire, in which all love of self is submerged. This can be so only to the extent one is, or can become, philosophical. For in that case, and that case alone, love of truth expresses the very self one loves.

Approaching the problem with a genuine will to truth, however, is but a prerequisite. One must still decide what to look at and where to find it. Since all observable human beings are *nurtured* instances of what they are, there is precious little evidence available to us of pure, pristine, *natural* masculinity and femininity. But one might carefully attend the behaviour of very small children who have not yet received much intentional nurturing in any sexually specific way, paying special attention to their free play (cf. 537a). Hence it would seem that supervisors of nurseries, for example, have a golden opportunity to gather evidence of this kind. But there are severe limitations on what can be learned from such immature, which is to say incomplete, examples of male and female human beings.

Meditation on the dialogue as a whole, and Book Five especially, suggests that the crux of the problem is well expressed in the poetic wisdom that human beings are more than beasts but less than gods (cf. 611d–a). That is, while the proportions may vary, we are each of a mixed nature, determined partly by divine reason but still sharing through our bodies an extensive kinship with the animals. Reason as such seems sexless; the classes of men and women may differ in their reasoning abilities,[9] but there's no evidence that men understand geometrical proofs any differently than do women. So one might hypothesize, by way of the merest beginning of an analysis, that the souls of men and women are the same to the extent that they are rational, and different to the extent that they are wedded to different types of bodies. Those bodily differences, in turn, and the complementary differences in the emotional and appetitive parts of the soul, are reflections primarily of the sexes' differing procreative roles. Reason, of course, cannot be understood as something simply layered on top of an animal foundation, like so much frosting on a cake. Nor as an especially useful appendage, like an opposable thumb, given us perhaps in compensation for our lacking other organs or powers, such as hooves and horns or an ability to change colours. Reason, rather, penetrates or permeates virtually every expression of our existence, down to the most basic "animalistic" functions (as Book Five so effectively reminds us). The rational and the animal in our nature are far more intimately intertwined than is the flesh and the bone of our bodies. Both constituents of our composite nature can be understood only through long investigations of a most challenging kind. Understanding the rational element is perhaps practically equivalent to understanding the very idea of a philosopher (cf. 611b-e). As for how one can best understand the animal heritage incorporated in one's being, there is little that can be done besides studying animals, although that is plenty. Perhaps those capable of domestication or taming would be especially revealing – beasts such as horses and cows and sheep (cf. 586ab); and surely not to be overlooked is the pig. Of course, one naturally wishes to know all that can be known about those animals most resembling human beings in outward form, the various great apes, who so frequently seem to us "almost human" in their behaviour (cf. 590b, 620c). Since, however, their very appearance tempts one to an excessive "anthropomorphization", it would probably be best to begin with dogs.

But to return to the "feminine drama" itself, it is illuminating – indeed, essential – to contrast its actual constitution with what one might reasonably have anticipated on the basis of either one's own experience or earlier discussion in the dialogue. However, it should be expressly noted that, before the philosopher so referred to it, we were given precious little encouragement to regard the preceding as a distinctly "*masculine* drama" ... although, truly and ironically, it was. For in the strict sense of what was said, their city in *logos* was founded without women.[10] Treating a political community as the rational means of meeting certain elementary needs of the body, Sokrates suggests that the minimal city "would be made up of four or five *men*" (*tettarōn ē pente andrōn*) – a farmer to provide the food, a builder the shelter, a weaver clothing, perhaps a cobbler for shoes (369d). Then, having established strict occupational specialization as the basic principle of their regime, their own particular city in *logos* initially grows in size – not by natural mechanisms of sexual reproduction but by more specialized craftsmen being added in speech as a need for them is recognized (e.g., carpenters, smiths, herdsmen, tanners), until they have assembled what could be described as a "throng" (*suchnos*; 370d). And upon abandoning self-sufficiency as a governing concern (370e), it grows still more (and in the same non-erotic way) with the addition of all the various specialists involved in trade with other cities (e.g., merchants, drovers, sailors, pilots), as well as by increasing the numbers of producers already represented so that their city can produce a surplus for trade. But nowhere in the course of its growth to that point where Sokrates turns to Adeimantos, asking, "Then has our city grown to completeness ... ?" (371e), are women ever mentioned. The young man's equivocal answer ("perhaps") is apparently caused not by his noticing that something important definitely *is* missing, but by his not on the spur of the moment knowing for sure whether all occupations essential to a city *are* present. He, like most everyone else from then to now, overlooks their failure to provide explicitly for women. Doubtless presuming that their presence is implied, he simply takes women for granted (an old story). His oversight is less culpable than ours, however, for he had not heard that instructive story (not quite so old) about the founding of Rome at the expense of the Sabines. So when the philosopher concludes his brief description of their citizenry's way of life with a tacit warning against their not producing children beyond their means (372b), Adeimantos still does not realize that this could not possibly be a problem for his city – indeed, that his city's most urgent danger is altogether the opposite: its inability to survive beyond the first generation of inhabitants (cf. 467b).

Or is his presuming an implied presence of women legitimate? This question demands an emphatic 'No' for the following reason. The philosopher's attractive portrait of rustic anarchy – of an Arcadian polity wherein people live simple, healthful, happy lives in perpetual peace and harmony with each other, with no need for laws, for rulers, for coercion of any kind – rests on the assumption that all significant sources of conflict would be absent, and that the liberation of desire (with its resulting competition, conflict, and need for government backed by force) is exclusively a consequence of *luxuriating* the city. The barest mention of women would have marred such an idyll.[11] Men have fought over women throughout the human record, both as individuals (recall Achilles' quarrel with Agamemnon), and as groups.[12] No less an authority on *erōs* than Sokrates himself observes that leaving sexual relations unregulated is incompatible with people living happily and peacefully with each other (458d), and that no decent familial relations can be sustained in the face of the tyrannical demands levied by unbridled sexual desire (571cd, 574bc).

In fact, it is scarcely an exaggeration to say that all the radical innovations of Book Five are in response to the profound problems posed for political life by its need to manage or somehow accommodate human eroticism, from its most basic to its most sublime expressions. And that the entirety of the discussion in this book is a belated recognition of the fact that man brings not only his material poverty or needfulness or insufficiency to the city, he brings his sexual insufficiency or incompleteness, his sexual "needs" as well. And while we are accustomed to regard the sexual appetite as a bodily need, its true status – both with respect to its being bodily, and to its being a need – seems ambiguous. (Sokrates himself raises the question as to its necessity; 458d.) Nor is its status necessarily the same in all respects for men as for women. Do not men tend to treat sexual gratification as an end in itself, whereas women regard it more as a means?

Its ambiguity, moreover, seems central to the larger ambiguity in human nature, manifest in the tension between public or political and private or personal, between the common good and the good of the individual. Clearly, the sexual desire does not represent an individual bodily need in the strictest sense, comparable in stringency to the need for food and water, for air and sleep; nor is it similar even to the body's need for clothing and shelter. In short, sexual gratification is not necessary to the individual's continued existence (to his "mere life"). As for its being essential to one's psychic health, and thus to a good life, the evidence is equivocal (contemporary views to the contrary notwithstanding). Many people have lived their entire lives without experiencing sexual intercourse, and it is scarcely credible that without exception this has been for the worse. It would seem, however, that the lack of such experience would at the very least impede one's effort to understand human nature, both its broad commonality and its significant diversity.

But if sexual gratification is not strictly necessary to an individual's merely living, and perhaps not even to his living well, it *is* essential to the continued existence of a polity that a sufficient number of its citizens satisfy their erotic desires in procreating children. Moreover, if the quality of the way of life the polity offers is to be maintained at a high level, its best people must do so. While this is not usually something that has to be mandated (much less made an occupational specialty), many regimes over the centuries have adopted policies indirectly aimed at manipulating both the quality and proportionate quantity of its constituting population. Presumably, an altogether adequate account of political justice would be one which provides sufficient guidance for assessing such policies, as well as for the regulating of sexual activity generally. Do men and women typically see eye-to-eye on these matters?

So, having by his own admission "completely gone through the masculine drama [*andreion drama*]," Sokrates at last agrees "to finish the feminine". It would be misleading, however, to title what he thereupon provides as "The Story of Woman", and for at least two rather different reasons. First of all, the philosopher does not take up the question of the true nature and best nurture of the female human being on its own terms, as a problem in its own right. He does not ask, for example, whether women are distinguished by any special needs or wants; nor does he begin with a consideration of whether women have any special aptitudes or strengths. And he steadfastly avoids raising the question that would lead directly to the heart of matters: why *are* there women? (Which, of course, immediately translates itself into the question of why the human race consists of both men and women.) Rather, his "feminine drama" turns out to be an analysis of whether the "masculine drama" is *exclusively* masculine, after all (cf. 452ea).

Second, the only substantial generalization established about women beyond their being "the weaker sex" is that they *are* like men in one, and perhaps most important, respect: they *differ* among themselves with respect to matters of apparently great consequence (i.e., in aptitude for medicine and music, gymnastic and war; in spiritedness and regard

The War Lover

for wisdom; and, thus, in suitability for "guarding", and presumably much else besides; 455e–a). Indeed, it is suggested that they differ so much that certain kinds of women would seem to have more in common with certain kinds of men than they would with other kinds of women (cf. 454cd). So unless he and Glaukon have overlooked some even more consequential basis of commonality, these radical differences among the tribe of women – radical *inequalities*, to be more precise (456d–e) – would seem to preclude there being a female perspective *per se*, and any single account of "woman as such". Or *is* there such a basis in the two qualities that *are* acknowledged to distinguish the female: that she bears the offspring (whereas the male begets; 454de), and that generally she is weaker than the male (451e, 455e, 456a, 457a; cf. 471d, 469de)? Certainly one would want to give long and careful consideration to the differences between human and canine procreation before concluding that the one carries no broader implications than the other (cf. 451d). Similarly with regard to their respective nurtures; suffice it to recall that dogs are indifferent to music, but not to strength (cf. 375a, 377c).

According to the Sokrates-inspired "feminine drama" – which is focused not so much on women as on the "natural community" of the male and the female with each other (466d; cf. 351e), and which culminates in his strange satire on what has traditionally been the woman's arena of primary concern: the family – some select minority of women ought to cohabit as full partners with the minority of men who are chosen for guardian service, "since they are sufficient and akin to them in their nature" (456b). What way of life is suitable for the *majority* of women, whether they should likewise share in all or some or none of the work done by the rest of the men in the city (cf. 453a), is never made as clear as it easily could have been. For while it is suggested that the *class* (or "tribe"; *genos*) of men surpasses that of women in virtually everything practised by human beings, including even certain domestic activities normally reserved for women, it is explicitly noted that "many women are better than many men in many things" (455cd). And yet the belated explication provided here as to *how* we may "distinguish between one who has a good nature for something and one who has no nature [for it]" (cf. 370ab), and thus practically *apply* the principle of justice that is based upon such a distinction, seems both incomplete and misleading.

Incomplete, because the three criteria specified (the ease with which one learns whatever is related to an activity, and extends and preserves what one has learned, and that "the things of the body adequately serve one's thought", 455b; cf. 371c–e) ignore not only the desiring part of the soul (and thus one's moral suitability for certain jobs), but the part that has been and remains in every sense central to this account: the spirit. Surely temperament, one's emotional suitability, can be every bit as important as mental capacity in determining both how well one does a given job and what personal satisfaction one derives from it. Indeed, what is it that's of *primary* importance in determining who is a suitable kindergarten teacher, as opposed to a suitable firefighter, or pastry chef, or bush pilot, or mortician, or car salesman, steel-worker, bus driver, nurse, barber, jewel cutter, bank examiner, or lighthouse keeper? And is it not reasonable to suggest that it's with respect to the desiring and spirited parts of the soul that men and women typically differ (as has been both the ordinary and the learned view since time out of mind)?

Misleading, because Sokrates does *not* go back to the beginning of their city in *logos* and start over, this time constructing it with women explicitly present (which would naturally result in a city composed of families[13]), but instead takes up the question of women in the context of the already art-filled city of his completed "masculine drama". Thus, his peculiar approach to the problem of the sexes and their respective roles in the city, while true to the actual practice of (usually much less radical) political *reform*, has the ironic consequence that the possibility of understanding *anything* as distinctly "feminine" (or "masculine"!) – be it a drama, a nature, or a law – is simply analysed away, dissolving into a multitude of art-related traits (such as those constituting an aptitude for cobbling), while disregarding all traits (such as bald or hairy) which seem irrelevant to the acquisition or practice of the arts. And to compound the irony, this strategy results in making the very conception of the *natural* radically dependent on the *artificial*! In the absence of the arts, we then could not speak significantly of anyone's having "a nature" of any kind. Whereas in the presence of the arts, we cannot distinguish a feminine nature as such, nor a masculine one, nor even a *human* nature, but only the nature of a cobbler, a doctor, a carpenter, a guardian, and so on (454d). How has Sokrates managed to lead Glaukon and the others to this comical result? And why has he done so?

Although he begins with the observation that the basic problem is that of distinguishing correctly the *forms* about which we speak (454a), he in effect confines attention to a comparative *analysis* of certain

The War Lover

natural kinds of things, an analysis conducted, moreover, solely in terms of discrete traits or qualities of *individuals* who are antecedently recognized to be "instances" of the kind in question (and it could as well be a species, such as dog, cat, human; or, as in this case, types within species: male and female). And although he himself is careful *not* to restrict consideration to "differences that show [themselves] with respect to some art" – in fact he expressly adds, "or other pursuit" (*epitēdeuma*; 455d) – his rhetoric and the context in which the issue is raised none the less have that effect. Upon noticing that many if not most such distinguishable traits *vary* among actual incarnations of the kinds being compared (actual dogs and cats, or actual men and women), and moreover vary to such an extent that not all instances of one kind have more of that trait than all instances of the other (e.g., not all dogs are bigger than all cats, not all men are more hairy than all women), they are tempted to conclude that no such variable trait belongs any more to one kind than to the other. Proceeding in this "nominalistic" way (as we moderns would call it), proportional distributions of traits among kinds seem irrelevant to their essential natures (after all, no large cat is more dog than cat by virtue of most dogs being larger than most cats). Whereas, should they find one or more traits to be *exclusive* to a given kind or "nature", its essential identity is reduced to just such exclusive traits. They thereby overlook the possibility that a certain *constellation* of predominant traits (perhaps along with some exclusive ones) naturally tends to *cohere*. And having overlooked it, they cannot then consider *why* that should be. Consequently, they are left no natural basis for the specific identity of what we all in our "unenlightened" state somehow dimly recognize as a *naturally* occurring *kind* of thing – although it is precisely this sort of antecedent recognition that their mode of analysis inescapably relies upon.

To illustrate with the problem primarily at issue in the "feminine drama". If the capacity to bear (or beget) a particular species of thing is regarded as simply one more trait among many (one which, paradoxically, requires us to ignore for the moment the very problem at hand: how we can identify *anything* "specifically"!), and of neither more nor less intrinsic importance than some variable trait (such as amount of hair); then one may all too easily conclude that femaleness (or maleness) reduces to just that exclusive trait (454de), overlooking the possibility that complementing the division of procreative labour are natural *sets* of traits that normally, and properly, belong predominantly to one sex or the other. One overlooks general *patterns* of proportional distribution, intelligible patterns of behavioural and temperamental traits that complement the more obvious morphic ones (upon which our immediate recognition of a natural kind of thing is usually based, i.e., its "look"), patterns that perhaps can themselves be seen as parts of a single grand pattern centred upon procreation – which is to say, centred upon what seems to be Nature's primary if not exclusive business: that of endlessly reproducing itself, sustaining the order of Being through a self-perpetuating stream of Becoming.

As to *why* Sokrates chooses to pursue an understanding of natures and Nature in the fruitless manner he does at the beginning of Book Five, one may suggest that he hereby provides the dialogue's most persuasive illustration of the potential *political* importance of that which, as he will subsequently teach, distinguishes a genuine philosopher: dialectical thinking (531d–534e, 537cd, 539cd). In reaching a dialectical understanding of any naturally distinct form – be it genus, species, class, type, relation, structure, pattern, shape, whatever – analysis into distinct parts or traits or qualities is but a necessary first step; synthetic judgment must complete the task. A "synoptic" view is needed to reconstitute, to synthesize, the analytically distinguished parts back into coherent, and now clearly understood, wholes. The problem of human sexuality is a compound one, of course, requiring that the results of the analysis and synthesis whereby one gains a clear idea of the species *human* (a form which apparently comprises natural subdivisions, natural classes, epitomized by archetypal individuals) be integrated with that which clarifies *male* and *female* (types which cut across the natural taxonomy of all higher animal species). If one's thinking is restricted to analysis, breaking things down into ever finer parts (a procedure that terminates in the ultimate constituents of matter, whatever they be), the hierarchy of distinctive natures that constitute Nature will for ever elude one. Not that any of this critique would surprise Sokrates. For we should notice both the emphatic hypotheticalness that pervades the "conclusions" he and Glaukon reach (452e–a, 453cd, 454d–b), and the fact that he continues to speak of men and women as distinct kinds of beings (e.g., 456de, 458c, 460a, 469d, 579b) – indeed, so distinct that they have different "primes" (460d–e).

Returning from these theoretical foothills to the actual "feminine drama" of the *Republic*, one can see it as a depiction of what would be required *if* women were to be treated as the "equals" of men, mean-

The War Lover

ing that they are to have equal access to the highest echelons of political life on the condition that they live the same way as do the men, so far as this is humanly possible (note 464e).[14] To repeat, it depicts *what* would be required; it leaves the reader to see for himself *why*. Suffice it to note, women as such cannot enjoy *full* political equality (nor can they in justice demand it) if they are not able to fill the highest political roles and discharge the most important civic duties, including those of war, in the finest possible way – and do so, moreover, while *also* doing for the polity that which *only* women *can* do: bear children. Recognizing that the procreative contribution of men, child begetting, is (and by whole orders of magnitude) a less consuming activity in almost every sense of the word, and infinitely easier to reconcile with the entire hierarchy of political responsibilities, is very much to the point. And this is but one of several significant asymmetries in the nature of sexual reproduction. For example, I presume no one is either puzzled or offended by the fact that stockbreeders have hundreds of cows but only one or two bulls, a single rooster for a whole barnyard of hens, or but a few rams for vast flocks of ewes (cf. 468c, 460a). Make childbearing as easy as humanly possible (460d), it cannot be truly "equalized", for this is but one aspect of the problem (if that's the word for it).

But supposing one were somehow preternaturally convinced that justice demands full political equality between the sexes (which, as we've seen, need not imply full political equality *within* the sexes; e.g., one might have a tripartite class structure applied equally to both sexes), then the philosopher's "feminine drama" shows what would be required in order to approximate this so far as possible – and, perhaps more important, shows how far it *is* possible. It entails the abolition of the natural family, and acceptance of polygamy, incest, and infanticide. (Incidentally, *do* men and women find these practices equally attractive or repugnant?) It entails eliminating the very ideas of adultery and marital fidelity, and renders vacuous the ideas of mother, father, son, daughter, husband, and wife. It entails the overcoming of all shame regarding the body, and all concern for bodily privacy, the constant and most rigorous training and toughening of the body, and the surrender of all say in determining when and with whom the procreative powers of one's body are to be employed. It entails forgoing all opportunity to love and nurture the fruit of one's own womb – more, it presumes the eradication of all discriminating love. No woman of the higher classes in the city in *logos* is to have home, hearth, husband, or children of her own.

Now, we are to ask ourselves, in light of all experience with life and love, is it likely that *this* would introduce harmony into the feminine soul; that living thus would produce in a woman (any woman, much less all women) that consummate "health, beauty, and good condition of soul" which Sokrates identifies with complete justice in a human being (444de); that she would thereby enjoy inner tranquility, and the full share of happiness assigned to her by nature (cf. 421c); that this uncompromising regimen of self-sacrifice would make of her a gentlewoman, a *lady*, as something similar but hardly so unprecedented was earlier said to produce gentlemen? It all seems pretty doubtful (just as Sokrates ironically warned that it would; 450c) – or, at least it does in light of all *my* experience. I rather suspect that most women would find the philosopher's "feminine legislation" (457b), taken seriously, to be a recipe for misery, prescribing a way of life divested of its greatest meaning.[15]

What (if anything serious) are we to make, then, of Sokrates' contention that a regime with such provisions is "according to nature" (456bc)? In fact, has he not tacitly abandoned Nature as the standard of what is right and wrong? For if the men and women of the ruling class are to be regarded as the best of their kind (456de), and they are to be brought to the very same perfection in the very same way, not just formally (analogously) the same but substantially as well (456cd) – to the point where, for all practical purposes, they can be "used" interchangeably (cf. 451e) – then must one not conclude that Nature itself is radically defective in its manifesting a sexual distinction in the first place? Do not the philosopher's "feminine laws" imply that there *is not* any good reason, or good enough reason, why the human race consists of both men and women (to answer that earlier question he never asked). Presumably, the sexual division of labour which Nature has imposed with respect to procreation is nothing more than an unfortunate limitation of the bodies with which we are all encumbered, a defect inherent in the material or bestial mode of being (cf. 611bc, 518de, 589cd) – rather as the inherent mutual subjection of all matter to gravitational attraction limits one's ability to take flight at will.[16] Seen in that light, the sexual distinction is something to be minimized, not emphasized, much less idealized; it is to be overcome, so far as possible, and not mirrored more broadly in political life than strictly necessary (cf. 460d).

But if Nature *is* radically defective in *this* way – employing a means of reproducing itself that is prejudicial to the more important concerns of life, or of certain individuals' lives rather – it cannot be the *final* standard of rectitude or perfection for *anything*. Since even if it is sometimes (even most times) proper to accept or reject things in light of what is or isn't "natural", one must none the less look to something still higher whereby one determines when and when not to look to Nature. As to how such *super*-natural power and authority are themselves to be conceived (and that authority could not be a higher one were it without any power whatsoever), and how one is to understand its relationship to the more familiar natural world and especially to that most peculiar product of natural procreation, man, who must strive to gain access to supernatural guidance *via* his own suspect natural powers ... well, suffice it to observe that over two millennia of philosophy and theology since Sokrates testify to the myriad puzzles – not to say, incoherencies and absurdities – that result from conceiving there to be a *radical* disjunction, or discrepancy, between the Natural and the Supernatural or Divine.[17]

Or does the philosopher's apparent inconsistency with respect to Nature, his endeavouring to overcome it in the name of abiding by it, not only oblige us to reconsider and clarify what he (and we) must mean by 'Nature' (to do so, that is, in a much more complete – and credible! – manner than that which he begins for us at 454b); but oblige us also to recognize that the abandonment of a unified natural perspective (supplying both one's epistemological and ethical standards) risks if not ensures incorrigible bewilderment, and leaves political life to the contention between prophets and sophists? Whereas, if one expands one's conception of Nature to include not only the familiar perceptible world of sights and sounds, motion and rest, generation and decay, but also the occult (yet perhaps intelligible) unchanging powers that *cause* it – such that 'Nature' signifies *all* that truly *is*, in whatever mode and to any degree (cf. 477a, 478d); and if in place of a mystifying distinction between the Natural and the Supernatural, one recognizes an explicable distinction between Becoming and Being – then one may truly conceive of a *uni*-verse, and a standard of "the natural" that transcends anything one could directly abstract from the ever-changing everyday realm. Or rather, one gains a coherently related *hierarchy* of natural standards (and senses of the word), ranging from the merely normal to the singularly perfect, and from the strictly necessary to the unqualifiedly beneficial (such that to know it is to want it; cf. 558de). In light of this hierarchical articulation of Nature, one may then understand *both* the degrees of natural attachment most all people, all "normal" people, have to what they regard as their own (be it their own opinions or manners, children or products, country or religion, skill or sex), *and* the naturalness of the wish of a few to transcend the limitations of such attachments. Only by virtue of this broader, richer conception of Nature can one fully appreciate what the task of designing a regime "according to nature", including natural justice, entails. For one must endeavour to satisfy the entire natural spectrum of legitimate expectations, and to reconcile the practically irrepressible natural passions and wants of the great majority of people (and felt to some degree by virtually everyone) with the desire to provide the utmost encouragement to the striving for natural human perfection.

One must doubt whether the city in *logos* as modified in Book Five actually does this, given what makes it truly funny: the various inescapable paradoxes that attend its three "waves" (or "contractions", or "foetuses"; *kuma*) – for Sokrates' "escape" (or "acquittal"; *ekfeugō*) is merely verbal, and the result mainly of an incompetent or complicitous "prosecution" (472a; cf. 450a, 461c-e, 473e-a). But Book Five may none the less show us, in its comical but impractical way, what in justice to women should be "added" to the Aristocracy as depicted in the "masculine drama" (i.e., what should be made more explicit). However, precisely because the philosopher's treatment of these matters has been so oblique, any explication of these additional provisions involves more than the usual amount of speculation. Doubtless there are various ways the main issues could be construed and expressed. In that sense, then, these are but some of *my* "truths" concerning political justice for women which I have garnered from the dialogue.

First, that women *not* be "taken for granted", but that (rather) there be a general recognition that the woman's contribution to the *polis* in the bearing of children and in seeing to their earliest nurture (which, as Glaukon noted, may be the most important and difficult stage; 450c) is of "equal" importance to the productive and defensive labour of men. And, as a necessary corollary, a recognition that the highest *political* roles and the most important *civic* duties are not necessarily the highest and most important roles and duties simply, and that public activities do not *always* have greater intrinsic importance than those of private life – even if it is inevitable that the distribution of public *honour* favour the public realm.

Second, that women too be educated, not necessarily in every way identical to men (which implicitly denies there to be any significant differences between the sexes), but in whatever "gymnastic and music" *are* suited for attuning the parts of the distinctively feminine soul (cf. 416bc). And precisely because the earliest nurture of all the city's children is best left in their hands, it is imperative that the women share with the men – not an identical way of living – but a similar understanding of their common life, and of the complementary contributions properly expected of each sex.

Third, that women in general not suffer undue restrictions (such as excessive confinement to the home) simply as a way of coping with men's inadequate nurture in self-control, but that both sexes be educated to something stronger than "cloistered virtue" (cf. 390bc, 457a, 579bc).

Fourth, that it be recognized that women – like men – are *not* all the same, and that significant injustice results to an important few when they are treated as if they were. So whereas the normal expectation may well be that a girl will grow into a woman whose talents and interests are centred on home and family (and whose deepest satisfactions will be derived therefrom), some allowance should be made for that determined minority who wish to live less conventional lives, especially lives that reflect the higher longings of the soul's rational part (and which often enough need not result in conspicuous eccentricity). And with respect to that (vast?) majority of women who wish to marry and have children, there should be no socio-political obstacles to their marrying someone of their own *natural* class – and especially none obstructing the better-natured woman's opportunity to marry with her masculine counterpart – as this is in the best interest of both the polity and the persons involved (cf. 456e).

Doubtless there is more worth saying about these matters, but this is enough to show the deeper potentiality of the philosopher's comic "feminine drama", how it does test one's understanding of justice in both cities and souls, and how it deepens one's appreciation of both the theoretical and the practical problems – truly fundamental problems – posed by the male-female distinction. This does not exhaust the value of reflecting on Book Five, however. For in addition, it would seem to be an allegory (or begin an allegory) of the relationship between politics and philosophy, an allegory bearing within it, moreover, the portrait of another lady. If, as seems clear enough, the "outer" books of the dialogue depicting the "masculine drama" of actual political life are ruled by Sokrates' explicit analogy between the City and Man (first expressed at 368e-a, but foreshadowed in the confrontation with Thrasymachos: cf. 351ab and 351e-a; and returned to at 543c), the three interior books are governed by his implicit analogy likening Philosophy to Woman.

In fact, this latter analogy isn't left altogether implicit. For example, in Sokrates' apology to Adeimantos for the bad reputation of philosophy among politically responsible people (who too often are of the opinion that most who continue with philosophy beyond youth become queer if not utterly depraved, and even the ones who seem decent are none the less useless to the community), he explains why "those for whom philosophy *is* most fitting go into exile and leave her abandoned and unconsummated [literally, incomplete, not brought to a natural end: *atelē*]. They themselves live a life that is not fitting or true, while others who are unworthy come to her – like to an orphan girl bereft of kin – and disgrace her, attaching to her reproaches such as you also say her reproachers do: that of those who have intercourse with her, whereas some are negligible [*oudenos*], many are worthy of many evils" (495bc; cf. 554c). A moment later, Sokrates likens philosophy to the daughter of an impoverished master who is obliged by her straited circumstances to marry a little bald tinker with a bit of silver, who's been but recently emancipated and has artificially beautified himself for the occasion. The philosopher goes on to suggest that one shouldn't be surprised if the offspring of such a marriage are puny and illegitimate (495e). But while these similes associate philosophy with only unfortunate females, the first line of the dialogue suggests that philosophy is properly regarded as a *goddess*. Often – but not always (cf. 451a) – the devotees of goddesses are themselves women. And it must be conceded that philosophers are not uncommonly perceived as effeminate (when not downright childish), especially by men who regard themselves as being real men (cf. 343a, 350e). Of course, this perception is apt to be coloured by the very reputation Sokrates is at pains to explain for Adeimantos, insisting that it is not a fair representation of the very few who *do* "consort with philosophy in a worthy way" (496a-c).

However, regarding politics as masculine and philosophy as feminine is helpful in understanding these two activities, and the proper relationship between them, only if one has *knowledge* of what masculinity and femininity in the full sense naturally consist of – which, ironically, one could not have on the basis of the explicit conclusions reached in the "feminine drama", as they imply there are no important differences between man and woman.[18] Translated allegorically, the "best politics" and the "best philosophy" would, then, naturally be the same – at least "with respect to guarding the city" – except that the latter is "weaker" than the former; and they are both (allegedly) produced by the same "education" (456a, cd), though perhaps only if they exercise naked together. But even confining one's interpretation to such observations about the sexes as are openly expressed, the allegory yields some surprising implications concerning the natural relationship between political life and the pursuit of wisdom, ... although perhaps they ought not be surprising if the deeper teaching of this dialogue is what I have attempted partially to explicate in my preceding chapters.

Given that the primary business of the city is to sustain and defend a common good life for all its citizens, the comparative "weakness" of women poses a threat to any city in which they have a share in political activities, and especially to one that would use them as rulers and guards. Sokrates copes with this to the extent he can by selecting only the most "mannish" women (i.e., high-spirited, aggressive, athletic), and prescribing for them the most physically demanding regimen of training, one which would toughen them in both body and soul (452bc). Although he is explicit that they, like the men, are to be educated in music as well as gymnastic (456b), he studiously avoids saying anything the least bit substantial about the former (note 457ab, 458d) – which is in direct contrast to the education he prescribed for the male guardians, where he spoke at great length about their music (while saying next to nothing about their gymnastic). This contrasting emphasis might suggest, then, that much as the nature of a man – and thus *politics* – is improved by being tamed, moderated, softened (411ab), and to that extent "effeminized" by music (culminating not in the eradication of war, but in a moderation of its barbarity; 471a-b); so a woman (read *philosophy*), if she is to make a beneficial contribution to the public business, must be strengthened, hardened, toughened. Politics needs more of the right kind of music; the highest form of music is, or is attended by, philosophy (499d, 548b; cf. *Phaedo* 61a); but genuine philosophy – that which is being taught in this dialogue – comes to be only through the most strenuous of gymnastic (539d). So far, so good.

However, the participation of women in public affairs (and by implication, that of philosophy as well) still has to be justified in the first place. Given the weakness of women (which is admitted to persist to some degree despite the most masculinizing nurture; 457a), and in the absence of any indication that their employment brings compensating advantages (which is not to say that there are none), we are left to speculate as to the real reason why the philosopher has introduced them into the guardian class. Now, as noted above, if a city is to persist, at least some of its citizens must bow to "erotic necessities" and have children. And if a city is to prosper, its best people must have children: its best men must beget them, and preferably its best women (whoever these *really* are) bear them (456e, 458e). In any workable scheme, this involves some, usually considerable, cohabitation, and thus necessarily exposes men to the "persuasion" of women; indeed, the more a man is both high-spirited and a gentleman, the more he is apt to be amenable to the influence of a lady (cf. 420a, 548ab). Therefore, by means of their private relations with men, women typically have some – again, usually considerable – *indirect* influence on public affairs, regardless of their public standing. Nor should one forget their involvement, usually extensive, in the early education of children; there may be at least a measure of truth in the old-fashioned view that the hand which rocks the cradle rules the nation. Because this is so – because there cannot be a city without women, and because men typically wish to please women (and even to become what they imagine "a woman wants in a man") – it is best to address this problem directly by ensuring that women receive a proper education, so that what they want in a man is just what a man ought naturally to be.[19]

Can one say something comparable about philosophy, and its relationship with politics and the city? At first blush, it would not seem so. Whereas women are absolutely necessary to the survival of a polity, probably most polities have existed without true philosophy. But they have probably also existed without true *ladies* either – instances of feminine nature brought near to its natural perfection. And, correspondingly, they likely *have* had some lesser kinds of thinking about nature and politics, bastard substitutes for philosophy, producing thought which (as a practical inevitability) *has* had its influence – for better or worse – on political practice. In the nature of things, there would seem to be no practical way to prevent all possibility of incipient forms of philosophy and philosophy-like pursuits arising (cf. 475e–b), no sure way to nip it in the bud as it were, nor totally to neutralize or isolate it once arisen. Only the rule of true philosophy could provide *sure* protection against the hazards of defective "philosophizing".

The War Lover

The philosopher himself insists that the hazards are real and great. He offers to show city-loving Adeimantos "how a *city* can take up philosophy *and not be destroyed* [*dioleitai*]" (497d)! Nor should one overlook what for some strange reason is so easily overlooked in the dialogue's central teaching: that there will be no rest from our ills, that there will be neither public nor private happiness, "unless philosophers rule as kings, or those said to be kings and lords legitimately and adequately philosophize, and there is a conjunction of political power and philosophy, while the many natures now traversing to *either* apart from *the other* are *by necessity excluded*" (473c–e). This double-edged prescription is immediately confirmed when Sokrates prepares to defend it by specifying what *he* means by a philosopher (as opposed to the popular conception). He promises that in light of his idea of philosophers, one can show that "it is by nature fitting for them *both* to engage in philosophy *and* to lead a city, and for the others *not* to engage in it but to follow their leading" (474bc; cf. 519bc).

The natural tension in the relationship between politics and philosophy (epitomized in the fate of Sokrates) does not arise, then, from one side only – that is, from just the dogmatic, intolerant partiality of political life, from its necessarily being to some extent closed, shackled by its sacred past, and accordingly suspicious of the new, the strange, the unfamiliar; nor from its preoccupation with the useful, its utilitarian perspective (cf. 398ab, 401b–d, 406a ff, 424a–d, 427b–d). There are antipathies and mischiefs that typically attend philosophy also – or at least what is commonly mistaken for philosophy, what Sokrates treats as bastardizations of philosophy: weak, puny imitations that are *not* fit consorts of politics. The problem would seem to be that many, probably most, of those attracted by a life of thought tend to be by nature timorous, pacifistic, tender-minded, and excessively rationalistic (although they are no more likely to be familiar with rigorous, thorough thinking than with strenuous athletics). Thus they also tend to be both impractical, and contemptuous of the "arbitrary" manners and other conventions of political life – which often seem arbitrary only because the reasons for them are so deeply buried (cf. 425a–b) – and contemptuous especially of other people's "vulgar" selfishness and greater concern with property (failings they attribute primarily to defective nurture, and thus see as corrigible by education and rational enlightenment). Their contempt for these normal ways of thinking and living is the natural manifestation of their *own* ruling passion: not truth, but vanity. They have a special relationship with knowledge, but it is derivative, not primary, being a consequence of their vanity (cf. 495cd). For what they pride themselves *on* is their intellectual, aesthetic, and moral superiority to the unenlightened, non-progressive majority. As a result of their character, coupled with a special fondness for indulging their own imaginations, they are persistently utopian in their judgments about politics, unwitting but inveterate day-dreamers and "idealists". A chronic weakness of unrigorous and unsystematic, thus superficial thinking is its inclination towards a materialistic account of things, especially with respect to causation (cf. 469de). Ironically, the appeal of this materialism is its supposed "realism"; whereas, pushed to its logical conclusion (which its advocates never do), it explains almost nothing, and least of all the nature and causal efficacy of matter. It does, however, have grave political consequences in its implications for justice, virtue, and religion.[20]

Moreover, many – again, probably most – intellectually inclined people tend also to pride themselves on *not* being ("overly") partial to the regime in which they were born and bred (and whose actual or supposed faults and limitations they see close-up, at first hand, and continuously). And in having instead a special sympathy for other ways of life, supposedly actual but actually imagined. Yet because they do spend a greater portion of their time in speaking and arguing about what they think and imagine and feel, they typically are better-than-average articulators of their views. To the extent their greater persuasiveness influences other sectors of the citizenry, and especially the young, their alienation and utopianism infect the entire polity, more often than not with debilitating results. And so committed partisans of the established order often regard such "sophists" or "intellectuals" as breeders of decadence (cf. 487b-d).

Sokrates would seem to agree. He treats utopian thinking as a fit subject for comedy, and those who engage in it as soft, idle, self-indulgent lotus-eaters who, in their detachment from the practicalities of the everyday life that supports them (but which they take for granted and do not truly understand), live as if they imagined they could be denizens of the Blessed Isles (458a, 519c). And he offers instead an altogether different portrait of philosophy. As he paints him – or sculpts him, rather (cf. 501b-c, 540c, 420cd) – a worthy candidate for philosophy is distinguished first of all by a great, strong, and bold spirit, and second by qualities of mind, that together constitute a nature capable of becoming a paragon of super-masculine excellence. Virtually by definition, a genuine philosopher is *not* impractical, naïve, soft, or sentimental in this thinking about political life. He must not only understand the congenial and attractive truths about politics, but be able to bear the hard and ugly ones as well – the whole truth that is imbedded in the cities in *logos* and in the archetypes of defective regimes. He must understand human nature in all of its significant diversity, its vices as well as virtues, the various strengths of which it is capable and the weaknesses to which it is prone (409a–e, 445c). And precisely because he has an "insider's view" of even the most extreme manifestations of the tyrannical longings that pervade human life, including those which typically animate utopian political thought (576e–b), and because he appreciates the power of the lower, *alogos* parts of people's souls, he does *not* have overly rationalistic expectations about what can be accomplished through politics, including common education. And comprehending the radical difference between himself and most other people, knowing how few like him truly are suited to pursue wisdom with any degree of seriousness, he understands the need for the greatest discretion in his own doing so. In short, the conception Sokrates advances in the dialogue is one in all respects deserving of the title *political* philosopher.

It is the dramatic *contrast* between Sokrates' portrayal of the philosopher (487a) and the image Adeimantos holds based on prior experience with those lesser sorts he has met with in actual life (487cd) – a contrast Sokrates himself immediately confirms and subsequently amplifies – that gives rise to his extended apology for philosophy's bad reputation. For there is much to explain: why the few genuine philosophers seem politically useless but really aren't; why those best suited to be philosophers are typically diverted and corrupted by premature involvement in public life; how the role comes to be filled by men unworthy of it (but who then provide the basis for its controversial reputation; cf. 500b); how a few worthy candidates are none the less saved for philosophy, and why they tend to avoid politics (488e–496e; cf. 536a–b). As a result of all this, one can see that only if the intellectual high ground in the city is actually occupied by its *rightful* possessor, one who by properly nurtured nature is *stronger* than all pretenders and usurpers; *and* only if the polity itself is somehow designed to recognize, receive, and honour the contribution a political philosopher could provide it – only then would the public perception of philosophy approach an accurate reflection of the reality of it, and all those (but only those) best suited for it actually choose to pursue it (cf. 499ea). The tragedy of political life is that these conditions can never be sustained, even if by some rare accident they should temporarily come to pass; that even a city established in all the purity of *logos* can but imperfectly reconcile the requirements of philosophy with those of wholesome political life, and thus is fated to fail (546a).

And so, as the "feminine drama" is recognizably a comedy, the "masculine drama" depicting actual political life in all the human, all-too-human regimes (497bc) is a tragedy – something the philosopher himself hints at when he first speaks of the inevitable decay of their Aristocracy in *logos* by way of providing a mythical beginning for his devolutionary hierarchy of regimes (which spans all the various kinds in which people actually live; 544cd). He offers to speak "tragically", though only in play of course (545e; cf. 393d, 413b), for with his feminine wisdom he cannot take anything human seriously enough to regard it as tragic. Or, as a later incarnation of the philosopher puts it, "there are heights of the soul from which even tragedy ceases to be tragic". And as still others have observed, Sokrates was known to have laughed but never to have cried (nor to have blushed for that matter). The tragic hint may be seen as confirmed by the philosopher's description of that "human" or worldly kind of regime which on a purely political scale ranks highest: Timocracy. For it is precisely *that* regime which is openly suspicious of "the wise", and will not admit them to its ruling offices (547e; cf. 397d, 398a). Whereas, by contrast, it is the colourful, novelty-loving regime, the one which despises the unchanging principles upon which the "divine" city in *logos* is founded (558b), the regime perched precariously but a rung above Tyranny – Democracy – that openly allows philosophy to anyone who has but a passing fancy for it.

But the "tragic" tension between politics and philosophy does not derive simply from the practical "imperfections" inherent in political life as such, those limitations and contradictions and harsh necessities affecting any and all earthly regimes. It runs much deeper. For even a toughened, hardened, strengthened philosophy – a philosophy that is *fit* to come back down into the city and make a beneficial contribution – remains *essentially* feminine in its nature, and accordingly "weaker" than politics in a most significant respect. The ideas that it brings forth, however alien they may seem, will have been begotten by the political life with which it consorts – for the germs of all the great questions are to be found there. But there is a kind of patient acceptance, a "conservative" passivity, that results from the recognition that nothing men accomplish has much intrinsic importance in the grand scheme of things (cf. 486a, 500bc, 604bc, 608cd), and that even the best they do falls short of the truth (473a), and that the one thing needful is to make oneself conform with that which ever truly is (cf. 486d, 490b, 498e, 500c). Whereas action, production, conquest, defence, change, reform, revolution – the whole masculine realm of creation and destruction – depend on a kind of blindness or stupidity with respect to the value of what one's best efforts can achieve. If anything is to be accomplished in this world, there must come a point when men say, "Enough talk – it's time to act. Let's do it and be damned!" But the very presence of philosophy in the city, even provided the best insulation human discretion can devise, poses a constant threat to that necessary blindness and stupidity and over-valuation of what men can make and do.

Moreover, given the unpredictability inherent in erotic matters, not even the best in human wisdom can render judgments about people with mathematical certainty, and thereby ensure that all those who are introduced to philosophy will stand by her to the end and thus become what they by nature ought to be, to the credit of both philosophy and themselves. However promising an initiate may seem, there is always the risk that dialectics will destroy his old ground without enabling him to provide himself with something better, and thus he returns to political life with the skills of a sophist and the character of a nihilist, "filled with lawlessness [*paranomias*]" (537e ff; cf. 467b). Whether a young Glaukon will become another Critias or another Alkibiades, or like Theages and Polemarchos be somehow saved for philosophy (496bc, *Phaedrus* 257b), is known to none but the gods.

The essentially female character of philosophy (or is it of wisdom?[21]) in itself settles nothing, however, as to who most suitably pursues it. For one needs to know in addition which is the operative ruling principle: the "philiastic" one of 'like to like' (329a), or the erotic one of 'opposites attract' (329c). If it is the latter, then philosophy would be inherently attractive to real men and mannish women; if it is the former, then to women and effeminate men. Of course, nothing precludes both principles being at work in this world; indeed I believe there is ample evidence that this is so. But then one wonders which basis of attraction provides philosophy its worthiest devotees. And here, to borrow a tactic as well as some words from Hobbes, "it is not fit, nor needfull for me to say ... : for any man that sees what I am doing, may easily perceive what I think."

There remains one further dimension of interpretation with respect to Book Five, and it may well be the most important – and difficult – of all: what do its three "waves" imply for the regime of a just soul? Recall, having apparently found justice and the other human virtues in a regime he calls Aristocracy, Sokrates warned Glaukon against concluding anything simply on the basis of their political handiwork, and reminded him of the original premises behind their constructing as best they could a city in *logos*. It was to facilitate seeing what justice is in a single human individual by having first discerned its form in some larger thing, presumably a city, "knowing full well that justice would be in a good one at least." If they saw that the same form worked perfectly for each, fine and good. But if something different turned up in the one, they would go back to the other and test it there too, so that by considering them side by side and rubbing them together like sticks, they could perhaps "make justice burst into flame, and with its thus having come to light, confirm it for [themselves]" (434d–a). This requirement is what launches their investigation into the nature of the human soul, with the particular concern to determine whether it, like the city, has distinguishable parts needing harmonious ordering (435bc). Only after that basic psychology has been sketched do they undertake anything like a side-by-side comparison of a city and a man (441c–442d), the outcome of which allows the philosopher to conclude that "justice is something of this sort" – each thing doing only that which only it can do best.

But all of this transpires before the introduction in Book Five (with such well-advertised fear, doubt, and hesitancy) of those three radical, paradoxical changes in cities' customary ways of doing things – innovations unprecedented in human experience (at least outside of comedy) – that transform a practical if unlikely regime into one that is not only impractical several times over, but naturally impossible. Because what results in Book Five is a regime quite different from that outlined in the "masculine drama", they are obliged by their own method to reconsider its applicability to the individual soul (cf. 435a). But this is never done. Which is only to say, it's left for us to do. It is left for the serious student of the dialogue to interpret for himself what is meant by "sexual equality", "familial communism", and "philosophical kingship" at the level of the *psychē*. To that end, the following comments might be helpful.

There would seem to be no point worth making in combining both masculine and feminine elements in a single ruling "class" or "part" were these elements not both distinctive and complementary for the jobs of governing and guarding, ... or, as Sokrates rather more enigmatically construes their common task: "both when remaining in the city and going forth to war, they must guard together [*xumphulattein*] and *hunt* together [*xunthēreuein*] ... " (466c; cf. 451d; whereas we are given sufficient clues for discovering the sense in which philosophy entails hunting, we are left pretty much in the dark as to what hunting has to do with political rule). But whether the job be hunting or governing or guarding or whatever, the "feminine drama", as we have noted, doesn't provide much indication of what the distinctly *feminine* elements (or by contrast, masculine ones) truly *are*, being dedicated instead to the greatest possible diminution of the sexual distinction, or so it would seem. We know it culminates in the conception of a philosopher-king, which is introduced (ostensibly) in order to explain how a city with such a "regime" could most expeditiously be brought into being (a problem we, in turn, are obliged to address at the level of the soul). Sokrates expressly exempts himself from following the pattern of development whereby their own city in *logos*, including the individuals of its guardian class, came into being. Instead, he concentrates on the minimal changes that would be required in order to transform an already existing city (read, 'individual') into one that was *governed* in a way most closely approximating that which they described (473a-b). He claims that one change would do it, but concedes that it's neither a small nor an easy change but none the less a possible one, and yet so seemingly preposterous and paradoxical that he expects to be drowned in a wave of laughter and derision merely for suggesting it (473c).

Thus is introduced the central and most famous teaching of this most famous and fundamental dialogue: that the answer to all human problems, both public and private, is philosophical kingship, a coalescing of politics and philosophy – political philosophy – which we are invited to interpret as something essentially masculine (political rule) being wedded with something essentially feminine (the love of wisdom), the differences between them having been moderated and harmonized by a common nurture. But it is the fact that the philosopher explicitly allows for two alternative ways that such a coalescence might come about which is of special interest here: there is the possibility of a king's becoming truly philosophical (i.e., of something masculine becoming also feminine), or conversely, that of a philosopher's becoming a king (i.e., something feminine being subsequently synthesized with masculinity). A further distinct alternative is subsequently suggested, that of the *sons* (*huieis*) of those who hold power or the office of king becoming divinely inspired "by a true *erōs* for true philosophy" (499bc). Given this third possibility, I shouldn't think it would take a philosopher to imagine still a fourth.

In any event, applying at the level of the soul the "sexual equality" of the city – which, we should not forget, is explicitly legislated only for its upper classes, those to which correspond the rational and spirited parts of the soul – suggests that the finest psychic regime is beyond either simple masculinity or femininity. It is one that constitutes a soul "bisexual" in its relations with *others* (capable of loving both men and women, which is not against nature so long as it is a love of beautiful souls, not bodies: cf. 402d, 403bc), and that imparts to *it* a transsexual, composite perspective on life, a synoptic view that does justice to the entire diversity of perspectives comprised by human nature (cf. 582a–e). What might this mean? That the highest, most complete regimen of nurture is one which results in a soul that is aggressive in tracking down the truth of things, yet compliant in conforming with the truth it finds? One that is equally adept at both analysis and synthesis? A soul both courageous and moderate, its vengeful pride tempered by compassion, assertive or patient as required, inclined neither to violence nor to envy, preferring persuasion to force but capable of both?[22]

If in the fully just soul – one in which the rational part and its natural ally, the spirit, keep a careful watch over the bodily desires, and do "the finest guarding against external enemies on behalf of the entire soul and its body, the one deliberating, the other making war, following the ruler, and with its courage fulfilling that which has been decided" (442a–b) – if in such a soul, masculine and feminine elements share equally in its rule, one needs to know, first, *what* these are, and second, *how* such synthesis is brought about. Presumably, in knowing the "what", one would readily understand *why*. But the same difficulty one faced in interpreting the "allegory of political philosophy" limits one here as well: conspicuously little assistance is provided us in arriving at a substantial understanding of what is distinctive about either sexual mode. All that Sokrates expressly ratifies are the two least-problematic facts about the sexes: females bear, whereas males beget (at least during their primes, cf. 460de); and normally females are weaker than males. With respect to the broader problem, then, it would seem that each of us is thrown back onto his or her own suspect resources.

However, we may have an investigatory strategy suggested to us in the fact that the men and women who are being groomed for guardian status are to "exercise" naked together (457a), and the "gymnastic" with which their education concludes is five years of continual and strenuous "exercise" *in dialectical arguments* (539de). Perhaps the truth is that even the most careful, thoughtful, and extensive *observation* of life is inadequate for penetrating to that single reality that one presumes lies behind the many conflicting opinions about the sexes encountered in the various ways of political life. Perhaps one can learn the deeper truth about the other sex and its perspective on the world only through extensive dialogue with people who are well experienced with living in that mode. Should this be so, one *needs* then dialogical partners of *both* sexes, ones who are themselves intelligent observers of life, self-confident and self-knowing, and who in the mutual trust of friendship will bare their souls, revealing how they truly think and feel.

Moreover, there is reason to believe that the same dialectical means whereby one could learn the truth about the other sexuality is also the means of transcending one's own, and that any success in the former endeavour is only proportional to that in the latter. Earnest participation in dialogical exchanges of this sort, giving back the equivalent of what one takes from another – bearing in mind what both the making and receiving of such naked disclosures can demand of oneself – may be what is required to develop the synthetic perspective, or synoptic view, that distinguishes the true dialectician. Would it be going too far to suggest that this is the higher purpose of the sexual distinction: as an obstacle to be overcome, a test, a challenge whereby one gains in strength and self-knowledge, the better to address the still greater problems of Truth and Being?

What then about "familial communism"? What are we to surmise about the best and most just soul – a naturally royal soul (580c) – from the philosopher's requirement that "all these women are to belong to all these men in common, and none shall live together privately with any; and their children moreover [shall be] common, and neither will a parent know its own offspring nor a child its parent" (457cd)? Much as Glaukon declares this political proposal to be a *lot* more dubious than the preceding one, with respect to both its possibility and its alleged benefits, so the psychological interpretation of it would seem to pose an even greater challenge than that of sexual equality. What are the "offspring" that are to be held in common and whose parentage is to remain indeterminate? And what is the real issue here? It would seem to focus primarily on the latter half of the proposal, in that it would seem to be this desire for parental anonymity with respect to children which dictates the communal sharing of wives and husbands, and the desire that the children be regarded as common property which in turn dictates parental anonymity.

Let us begin with a consideration of what one might conceive to be the "offspring" begotten by the masculine power of a well-ordered soul and born by its, or someone's, feminine power. This latter may be understood as a latent potential for developing, for "feeding and nurturing" to the point of viability, whatever particular something it is that ought to be regarded as communal property; but it is a potential that requires an initiating germ from the former to activate it. So, what products "purely" of soul (as opposed to items of consciousness, "feelings" say, that clearly involve the body) might be seen as corresponding to those products of bodies we call children. For lack of a better name, let us call such "brain-children", these offspring of minds, *ideas*. What, then, is *the problem*, such that elaborate efforts have to be undertaken in order to ensure that these ideas are judged solely in terms of their inherent natural worth – distinguishing the best (and most beautiful; 452e) from those that are merely productive or otherwise useful, while ruthlessly discarding ugly, paltry, and defective ones (460c; cf. 496a, 461b, c). Isn't it simply common sense to judge ideas solely on their merits? Doesn't everyone know that?

Maybe ... but they certainly do not always *act* as if they did. For most people most of the time treat the "parentage" of ideas as of great, even overwhelming, importance (cf. 500a–b). And with respect to most ideas about most things, things they have not thought much about themselves nor even could if they wanted to, this is unavoidable and (one suspects) generally beneficial. They probably should bow to *valid* intellectual authority in some matters more than they do (cf. 489b). The main reason they do not is what seems to be the primary focus of concern when one traces out the psychological implications of the philosopher's central proposal. For the obstacle here is an especially troubling manifestation of the love of one's own, that natural predisposition pervading virtually all of life, and which operates with redoubled power regarding things that one has in any sense "made" oneself. This is the "ancient quarrel" in each of us between poetry (*poiēsis*) and philosophy (607b) – between "making" (*poiein*: to make, do, cause, beget, create, invent, compose), and pursuing wisdom – experienced as the tension between an attachment to one's own opinions (especially those one fancies as being "original") and one's respect for the truth (implicit in virtually everyone's ranking knowledge higher than mere opinion; cf. 475d). Even a person's acknowledgment of an intellectual authority typically reflects in one or more ways a judgment tainted by the preference for "one's own" (cf. 329c).

The *essential* distinction between the poet, the "maker" *par excellence*, and the philosopher is *not* that the one uses various "poetic" devices (meter, rhythm, rhyme) that add a possibly spurious charm to the ideas he expresses, making what may be pedestrian views seem grand and persuasive (601a); that he artificially *beautifies* his speech, whereas the philosopher speaks plainly (cf. 393d) – the dialogue is itself a sufficient refutation of that view. Nor is the poet adequately defined by the parts of the soul to which he makes his primary appeal (602c; cf. 603bc), nor by any special subject matter (604e; cf. 599cd). Nor is it very helpful in practice, even were it so, to understand a poet as an imitator thrice removed from nature and the truth (597e) – for unless one is a philosopher in immediate contact with reality, one would not be competent to make the requisite judgment (cf. 598e–a). Rather, it seems that what essentially defines a poet (and hence underlies the considerable trace of poetic essence incarnate in each of us) is that he is more in love with himself, his own "subjectivity", his "unique personality", and thus with his *subjective view* of the truth (expressed in his offspring, his "makings", his poems), than he is with *truth itself*. That is, the tendency which is full-blown and glorified in what we moderns call a *romantic* poet Plato apparently regards as of the very essence of *all* poetry. The poet – insofar as he is first and foremost a *poet* – does *not* measure all the offspring of whatever souls simply in terms of their intrinsic merit; but like any normal parent, he has a prejudice in favour of his own. The offspring of others are always to some extent rivals of his own. And whatever popular acclaim his poems bring him ratifies and reinforces the worth he attaches to this "unique subjectivity" that his poems express. But this yearning for ratifying acclaim, little as he may care to admit it, shackles him to the popular taste (cf. 602b, 568c).

In this one all-important respect, the philosophical nature is radically different. Much as the ruling class of the city in *logos* must suppress – and to the extent this is impossible, somehow circumvent, or cleverly "outwit" (459c–a, 460cd) – natural parental feelings in the interest of a just appraisal of all the city's children (for superior children are sometimes born of ordinary parents, and ordinary children of superior parents; 415c); so must anyone who is serious about wisdom somehow subordinate his natural preference for his "own" ideas to his love of the *best* ideas (which occasionally may come from inferior minds; 595c–a). Since most child-begetting and all child-bearing are done by the Auxiliaries (compare 460e7 with 540a3–4; thus 464b5–6), this would seem to be primarily a matter of disciplining, and when necessary "deceiving", the spirited part of one's soul (and, most especially, the lower, selfish, honour-loving half of the spirit). For only if the spirit remains content and thus obedient to reason will the entire regime of the soul be preserved (cf. 465d–a). The paramount concern for one who is genuinely philosophical must be to make the *best* ideas *his* ideas, regardless of whose masculine power "first" sparked them, or whose feminine power nourished them to the point of viable expression. And this will be the paramount concern only if the higher part of one's spirit, that which loves beauty and excellence and success for their own sakes, is the stronger half. Originality, authorship, creativity – pre-eminent concerns for the poet (398a, 424bc) – are without philosophical relevance; only the truth has relevance, and truth is by nature the communal property of all who have the rational power to appropriate it. Being perfectly shareable without loss, it is the paradigmatic common good. With respect to the questions of importance to him, the philosopher recognizes no authority beyond that of his own reason, duly refined and informed through dialectical inquiry with a few of that select company who, like him, belong to a single great and noble family, a natural family founded on kinship of soul rather than body. "Someone else's" ideas become *his* in the only way that matters when, and only when, ratified by his own reason and accepted by his own spirit. And in becoming part of what informs him, of what makes him what he is, they become more than just his: they become *him* (cf. 500c).

One can find sufficient confirmation of this interpretation, linking familial communism in the city with the subordinating of poetry to philosophy in the soul (the common obstacle to achieving either being love of one's own), at the very beginning of the dialogue. Explaining to Kephalos why he had inquired about the source of the family's wealth – which was the second and central of the questions the philosopher addressed to the old man – Sokrates observes (ironically, to be sure): "the reason I asked is that you do not seem overly fond of money. This is the way with most of those who do not make it themselves; those who do make it are twice as attached to it as the others. For just as *poets are fond of their own poems* and *fathers of their own children*, so money-makers are serious about their money – as being their own product [*ergon*] – along with [its being] useful, as others regard it" (330bc). The parent in each of us has a special attachment to the produce of one's body simply because it is one's own, an extension of the self one loves; and similarly, the poet in us prefers what one's soul recognizes to be its own. And much as the former partiality compromises a citizen's commitment to be ruled by strict justice in his dealings with all his fellows, the latter presses upon an individual's judgment of the truth, to the prejudice of his instilling a just regime within his own soul.

In light of this interpretation, certain other features of the "feminine drama" can be more readily understood. For example, one can see a clearer – or at least, a different – set of relationships among its three waves. It is difficult to understand at the political level quite *why* "sexual equality" must precede "familial communism". And it is only the latter, the "begetting and rearing of children" and "that whole community of women and children", that the philosopher's auxiliaries insist on being further informed about (449d). Why responding to this demand should require that he *first* establish that some women have a nature like that of some men (only "weaker"), and thus are equally suited for being guardians, is a mystery about their city in *logos* that usually goes unnoticed. But we can easily see its implications at the psychological level. A person, man or woman, is not fully prepared to consider "without prejudice" the dialogical contributions of women, the "offspring" of their souls, if not antecedently open to the possibility that at least sometimes some women may be the intellectual equals of even the best men. Or, alternatively expressed, that a feminine perspective on the world may be equally worthy of consideration.

And once one understands in terms of ideas the communal sharing of "children" and assessing their qualities with complete disregard for actual parentage, one readily acknowledges it to be "beyond dispute" that this would result in the greatest common good. But one may none the less remain quite dubious (knowing people) as to its actual *possibility* (457d), and thus be all the more eager to set other questions aside in order to know *how* it could be possible (466d, 471c-e). Also, we must agree it is at least *likely* that, were the masculine and the feminine perspectives to exercise naked together, it would "by a necessity of inner nature" result in a certain "mixing" that would be reflected in whatever ideas such intercourse produces (458d), and that certain things follow from this recognition, including perhaps a deeper understanding of what by nature is truly sacred (458e). One may even come to see such idea-generating dialogue as a genuinely *erotic* activity, even the *highest* kind of erotic activity inasmuch as the mutual satisfactions it affords are the most lasting (cf. 585b-e). And if the best ideas are most often produced by dialectical intercourse between properly matched partners, we can see the advantages of having older, wiser "match-makers" and "midwives" superintend and select the opportunities for intercourse afforded their more fruitful, younger kinfolk. And even see the benefits of arranging these matters in such a way as to preserve the illusion that whoever produces whatever is all due to chance; that with respect to good ideas it's a question not of who gets the credit for having "just happened" to bear or beget them, but simply of whether or not they're good (460a). However, it is only fitting that those who are themselves older and wiser be free to have intercourse with each other whenever and as often as they please (461bc).

Not that there aren't an abundance of interpretive puzzles that remain. Why, for example, is the masculine prime for begetting ideas later and more extended than the feminine prime for bearing them (460e)? Or, why are certain ideas of "unauthorized" dialogical liaisons to be regarded as "unconsecrated bastards" (461b; cf. 496a)? Or what about the whole nursery business (460c-d)? And those bewildering kinship formulae (461de)? And there would seem to be inexhaustible food for thought in the communal family's policies for waging war (466e-471b).

As for "philosophical kingship" - "the greatest and most difficult, third wave", conceded to be so very paradoxical when applied to a city (472a) - it seems comparatively straightforward in its application to a single man, at least given an adequate interpretation of the two preceding

The War Lover

waves. For the root of the paradox, the profound conflict between the common good of the city and the private good of the philosopher, obviously does not exist at the level of an individual soul. In the city, ruling and philosophizing, while to some extent overlapping, none the less remain two quite different kinds of activities, and both are full-time occupations if they are to be done as well as they can be. Ruling a city requires that one neglect one's own concerns in order to attend to other people's problems (346e), while philosophy – "a life better than ruling" (520ea) – serves as the *reward* for ruling in the second and higher city in *logos*. As a consequence, the best man in that city is the least just by its own standard of justice, his life divided between two jobs, compelled to rule part-time in return for being allowed to philosophize part-time (520d).

But in the regime of a single soul, philosophical kingship entails no such conflict of interest, for all the ruling of one's life is done solely with an eye towards whatever best facilitates one's philosophizing. In fact, the natural community of interests among one's "parts" which is served by this arrangement is so little problematic that it provides the (impossible) model for the unity prescribed for the city in *logos* (462cd). Even at this individual level, however, we are still speaking of *political* philosophy, in that wisdom must be pursued with a full awareness of the political implications of doing so – of both the prerequisites practically necessary for philosophy, and its potential political consequences – which requires first of all a profound understanding of political life. And that is not something to be had from just contemplating one's navel. It requires, paradoxical as this sounds, a kind of "detached immersion" in political life, the sort of posture exemplified by the Platonic Sokrates.[23] Notice, the philosopher – using his special tool, dialectical argument (582d) – introduces the young men to the fundamentals of good politics *before* attempting to correct their misconceptions about philosophy. For only if one first understands the "dogmatic" basis of all a good city's virtues (cf. 412e, 429bc, 431de, 432e) can one appreciate from the outset the need for the greatest delicacy in searching for the truth behind these and all other opinions. So, they learn explicitly about politics "in rational speech" ("in *logos*") while implicitly learning about philosophy "in deed" through the dialogical experience of it. Strange though it may seem, they learn 'What is *political* philosophy?' before they learn 'What is philosophy?'

Given sufficient time to reflect, they may see the deeper truth embedded in the night's conversation. That philosophy *can* make a beneficial contribution to the polity, not by directly ruling it – for that results in both a distortion of political life (e.g., denying the honour-loving class of men their fair share of the good) and a diminution of the philosophical life – but (rather) by influencing it in a private, more "feminine" way, behind the scenes, as it were (cf. *Apology* 36c). Through dialogue with carefully selected men (such as Adeimantos) whose hearts remain attached to a city they but imperfectly understand, who honour virtue and wish to be honoured for their own virtue, and yet are ignorant of the highest virtue, a kind of virtue that is beyond appreciation by the many but not by the few such as themselves (cf. 489cd), the philosopher can affect the city in a way that is both moderating and elevating. And using the same tool, dialogue, he can confer another benefit on the city through restraining head-strong, irresponsible young men such as Glaukon – who because of surpassing natural gifts have the greatest capacity for both good and evil (491e, 495b) – putting them and keeping them "in their place" by the only means they respect: a display of superior strength. And the kind of strength they respect the most in others is the same as they are most proud of in themselves: strength of mind and spirit (cf. *Apology* 39d). But throughout his private attempts to benefit the city and thereby discharge his debt to it (cf. 520b and *Crito* 50d), he must not take unworthy risks, ones which threaten the very environment that makes philosophy possible, namely, the polity upon which the philosopher remains dependent for security, sustenance, and dialogical partners; *nor* ones which needlessly endanger the philosopher himself (cf. 467b).

So, while the two levels of the regime's application, the political and the psychological, could be said to *meet* in this "third wave" (since in order for there to be philosophical rule of a city there must first be a philosopher – that is, someone who has ordered his own soul, indeed his entire life, in accordance with the pursuit of wisdom), they are by no means as harmonious in practice as they are depicted to be on the surface of the "feminine drama". This is subtly confirmed when later in the dialogue Sokrates compares the prospects for happiness of "the best and most just" with that of "the worst and most unjust" (i.e., the tyrant). His pronouncement of Glaukon's verdict has a curious asymmetry: whereas the most wretched is he who, being most tyrannical, is most a tyrant of himself *and the city*; the happiest is he who, being most kingly, is king of himself. There is no mention of the city (580bc).

The War Lover

But one can have a substantial appreciation of such philosophical kingship only insofar as one has a true understanding of what philosophy is, and can thus distinguish a genuine philosopher from all those with whom he is popularly confused. From the moment the idea of philosophers' becoming kings (or kings, philosophers) is introduced, the dialogue is dominated by the Sokratic question that would seem to be the key to everything: 'What is philosophy?' Only in light of an adequate answer to this question – and the attempt to provide one occupies the next two books, the heart of the dialogue, to put it in human terms, or its geometrical centre, speaking mathematically – an attempt which requires leaving the familiar confines of both public and private life in order to speculate about things in the heavens as well as investigate things beneath the earth – only after one has gained a glimpse of the higher truth of philosophy can one return to actual political life with any hope of truly understanding it, because capable at last of seeing it in its larger natural context.

— 7 —

Pride and Prejudice

If the worthiest candidates for the Wisdom-Loving life come from the ranks of the War Lovers – if, that is, the most promising recruits for philosophy are a subset of the Timocratic class – or more precisely, a small subset of that misnamed minority of timocrats whose primary motivation is a love *not* of honour but of *victory* (cf. 428e) – then there must be a way to transform their eristical nature into one that is dialectical. For by virtue of their competitive spirit, they are naturally predisposed to treat dialogical arguments as contests with opponents, battles to be won, rather than to regard them as the means whereby partners and allies make common cause against ignorance and error. So the dialogical vices, which to some extent infect virtually everyone, are hypertrophied in the "nikocratic" timocrat. To disagree with him is to challenge him, calling into question not just his opinions but his mind's ability and spirit's willingness to defend them. With his pride thus engaged, his status on the line, he takes as his primary aim the vindication of his views and thereby himself. To be shown wrong is to suffer defeat and shame, whereas to be conceded right is to win victory and honour.[1] And to the extent he is himself a skilled, clever, forceful arguer who *enjoys* battles of words and wits (and thus wins them more often than not), he is the more loath to pass up any opportunity to contradict and refute someone else, especially someone reputed strong in debate. With his argumentative disposition and taste for controversy, occasionally he may even "go looking for a fight", as we say, bent on provoking some excuse to exert and display his strength (cf. 499e). His prejudice in favour of his own opinions, coupled with his pride in his own powers and the pleasure he takes in winning – all these spirit-grounded phenomena being magnified in him by virtue of the very thing that distinguishes him: greater spiritedness – requires that he undergo a major psychic revolution before his love of strife and struggle, and thus of war, can be sublimated into a love of wisdom.

The frequent, even typical, disjunction between dialogue and truth is expressly noted by that sophisticated young timocrat, Adeimantos, who in seconding Glaukon's challenge had already shown himself an especially attentive listener to what others say. Reflecting on his experience as both participant and auditor of conversations, he has concluded that arguments are often little more than verbal chess matches, with victory going not to him who has the greater portion of truth on his side, but to him who is more clever and experienced in arguing. One must be especially wary of dialogical chess-masters such as Sokrates, who can mislead a small step at a time, the cumulative effect being a single great "slip" (or "disaster", "defeat": *sphalma*, 487b; cf. 451a). With his first-hand appreciation of the actual psychic priorities people bring to conversations – thus keenly aware that the timocrat in everyone prefers winning an argument (and saving face) to learning the truth at the expense of appearing stupid, ignorant, or weak – and with his special sensitivity to the dependence of political life on maintaining the grounds of cooperation and amicability, Adeimantos has become adept in certain techniques of *polite* argumentation. Thus, for example, he often resorts to a hypothetical persona (that anonymous "someone") whenever he wishes to venture an objection to something that has been said (367a, 419a, 487c; cf. 329de, 378e). This technique both mutes the challenge that a direct contradiction would present and insulates him from the loss of standing that would result from the rebuttal of a view with which he had more personally identified himself. Concerned first and foremost to be – and to be seen to be – always the gentleman, he presents a refined spiritedness. It is highly unlikely he would ever behave in the rude and almost savage way that Thrasymachos does upon first entering this conversation.

For according to the philosopher's narrative gloss, Bold Fighter, a professional teacher of powerful speaking, lunged into their midst like a wild beast. And with a great display of indignation, he began berating everyone not only for the "drivel" they had been speaking but for their truckling manner of doing so (336bc). What he subsequently says and does serves as a dramatic illustration of how someone with a large measure of spiritedness is apt to regard dialogical argument. Aware that simply adopting a dictatorial manner may allow one to set the terms of debate (336d, 337c, e); that ridicule can sometimes wither opposition (337a); that often victories in verbal confrontations are more easily extorted by a show of strength and passion than fairly won by superior reasoning on known facts – aware of all this and more, Thrasymachos is ready and willing to exploit the normal preferences for maintaining civility and avoiding the discomfiture that the success of such bullying tactics is premised upon. Priding himself on his realism (which is tacitly a pride in his superior rationality), he presumes that regardless of what they say, everyone, just as he, subordinates the concern for truth to their concern for themselves. Unaware of the paradoxes inherent in his position – for the priority of truth is implicit in every sophistical device aimed at persuading others as to what is true – he views Sokrates' questioning as merely a slick way of creating opportunities to display a shallow superiority, invariably refuting *whatever* his respondents answer, and thereby gratifying his love of honour (336c; cf. 338a, c). In argument, as in other fields of endeavour, one benefits oneself at the price of doing harm to one's competitors (341a). And insofar as it's only a contest for the admiration and praise of others, there is no point in conceding defeat while there remains any manoeuvre that will avoid or mitigate the appearance of defeat (thus 340c-e, 343a, 344d, 350d-e, 352b; cf. 341b, 345b, 351c). But it is Thrasymachos' stubborn pride that in the end does him in, specifically his pride in being a superior knower and reasoner. When the philosopher finally sweats an admission out of him that the kind of person he eulogizes – one who attempts to get the better of everyone – behaves *not* like someone who is wise, but (rather) like an ignoramus, he blushes with shame (350c-d). He's boxed whichever way he turns. For either the argument is valid, and he stands a confessed enthusiast of those who are "bad and unlearned"; or it is invalid, and yet he agreed to every move, every little step, that led to this conclusion. Checkmate.[2]

With the wolf tamed, this belligerent critic reduced to nodding assent (350e, 354a), Sokrates tells us that he now presumed he was freed from argument. But the three discussions recounted in Book One prove to be only a prelude to the song itself (357a; cf. 531d). For Glaukon – that universally "most courageous" Glaukon – would not accept Thrasymachos' abandonment of his position. Nor, as it turns out, would Adeimantos. Once, that is, his brother had offered to "renew" it, and thereby taken primary responsibility for a position

The War Lover

that it is both imprudent and impolite to advocate openly. The philosopher's distinctive ways of dealing with each of these three men (who, for all their differences, are naturally akin by virtue of their spirited natures; cf. 368a, 450a) provide concrete illustrations of both the special difficulties and the unique potentials presented by all those blessed and cursed with an extraordinary spiritedness. And in assessing the philosopher's intentions and accomplishments, it should not be forgotten that Thrasymachos voluntarily stays for the entire discussion although earlier he was only forcibly restrained from leaving (344d); that he even adds his voice to those demanding an *expanded* treatment of certain questions (450a, b); and that Sokrates speaks explicitly of their having become friends, despite their never having been enemies (498cd).

The basic problem, so far as it concerns the philosophical life, is noted at the beginning of the "feminine drama". Its resolution, however, does not come fully into sight until the three-book "detour" initiated there is nearly at an end (cf. 543c, 435d). Tacit reference had been made to it before (cf. 405bc), but the spectre of eristics first overtly arises when Sokrates and Glaukon are confronting the apparent contradiction entailed in maintaining that men and women must have the same occupations despite conceding that they have different natures:

"Oh, Glaukon," I said, "noble [*gennaia*] is the power [*dynamis*] of the contradicting art [*antilogikē technēs*]."
"Why so?"
"Because," I said, "it seems to me that many fall into it even unwillingly [or, unconsciously; *akontes*], and suppose that they are not quarrelling [*erizein*], but discussing [*dialegesthai*], through not being able [or, empowered; *dynasthai*] by differentiating [or, dividing; *diairoumenoi*] among forms [*eidē*] to consider [properly] what is said. They pursue opposition [*enantiōsin*] according to the name [only] of what is said, using eristic [*eridi*], not dialectic [*dialektō*], towards one another."
"This is so," he said, "about what happens to many; but does this apply to us at present?"
"Entirely so," I said. "At least we risk unwillingly being engaged with contradictions [*antilogias*]."
"How?"
"That an other nature not have the same occupations we altogether courageously [or, mannishly; *andreiō*] and eristically [*eristikōs*] are pursuing

according to the name [only], not considering in any way what form [*eidos*] of different and same nature we were defining [or, demarking; *hōrizometha*], and with reference to what, when we were assigning other occupations to an other nature, and the same ones to the same." (454a–b)

Thus is the eristical disposition introduced: linked in the same breath with the primary virtue of the spirit ("altogether courageously and eristically"), hence perhaps more prevalent among men than women; characterized by an inability to distinguish forms, and hence by an undue reliance on merely verbal distinctions; and in contrast to a truly dialectical approach.

The natural connection between spiritedness and an eristical attitude may be something the philosopher has particularly in mind when he later warns Adeimantos that even the most praiseworthy elements in a person's nature can actually destroy a soul and tear it away from philosophy (491b). Someone who is animated by a love of victories, and has the courage to pursue them, is naturally drawn to "strife" (*eris*), including that which takes place in speech. But intentionally to engage in verbal wrangling with no greater concern than that of winning an argument is characteristic of sophistry, not philosophy (509d; cf. 499a, 533de). We are provided a vivid illustration of this by Thrasymachos when, in order to wriggle free from the dialectical clutches of Sokrates, he claims he has been misunderstood because of his using ordinary rather than precise speech (340c–e). And there is no question but that imprecise speech *can* be a source of spurious disagreements. Indeed, precision is the paramount virtue of speech *per se*, even though various degrees of imprecise speech serve most everyday needs well enough.[3] The basic problem may go beyond speech, however, be it ever so precise. As Sokrates perhaps means to warn Glaukon, one can be *unintentionally* caught up in eristical disputes through an unconscious reliance on language as such. For there is no guarantee that the conceptions and distinctions of *any* established or establishable language, however useful for sustaining everyday life, accurately represent the world they refer to.

Upon due thought, this much is clear: what most people regard as reality (i.e., the familiar world disclosed by the senses) is not at all a self-subsistent realm, complete and intelligible on its own terms. And yet, this murky, partially self-circumscribed, ever-fluctuating portion of the perceptible realm is what provides language its first referents (and what is even more troubling, provides the very distinction between appearance and reality). If one lacks the basic dialectical power[4] of "dividing" (differentiating, discriminating, distinguishing; *diairesis*) and "collecting" (recognizing similarity, generalizing; *synagōgē*) – not just language – but the natural reality itself, thereby providing a standard against which to measure the basic fidelity of language as well as the truthfulness of opinions expressed in it – if one lacks the intellectual vision to "carve *nature* at the joints" – then one is fated to remain a captive of a realm ruled by eristics. And it is in attempting to depict the prospects of escaping that realm (what one must imagine the world to be like if escape is to be possible; and how one cultivates and sublimates the psychic power to make the escape) that the philosopher claims to have the most difficulty expressing his thoughts (cf. 506d–a, 509c, 510bc, 511c, 515a, 523a, 524d, 528a, 533a).

Accordingly, the central teachings of the dialogue – conveyed through a set of images known familiarly as The Divided Line, The Sun-Good Analogy, and The Allegory of the Cave, accompanied by a very strange, seemingly insubstantial description of the education that would revolutionize the souls of a select few warriors, transmuting their normally eristical dispositions into those of dialectical philosophers – are generally conceded to be its most obscure, puzzling, and contentious offerings. And while it is fair to doubt whether the bulk of the controversy which now surrounds them has a dialectical (as opposed to an eristical) origin, even exemplary students of "Plato's Republic" may admit to being highly perplexed by these teachings: "The doctrine of ideas which Sokrates expounds to his interlocutors is very hard to understand; to begin with, it is utterly incredible, not to say that it appears to be fantastic."[5] Of course, the "doctrine" in question suggests that it is appearances themselves that are but a kind of fantasy. In any event, let no one suppose that I presume to have seen clearly that I readily agree is so difficult to see. I do none the less have some observations and conjectures that bear on the guiding thesis of this study, and that strike me as worth sharing.

Let me begin by reviewing the dramatic context in which these abstruse matters arise, as it includes a number of features that would seem especially pertinent to their proper interpretation.

Aroused or provoked by the philosopher's extended description of how their city would make war with both Greeks and barbarians, Glaukon impatiently interrupts, insisting that now they put all other questions aside in order to try to persuade themselves that it is somehow possible for such a regime to come into being (471c–e). Sokrates excuses his hesitancy in addressing this issue on the grounds that what he has to say is "so paradoxical" (*houtō paradoxan*; literally, "so against opinion", hence contrary to expectation, incredible, or marvellous; 472a; cf. 473e). As this warning merely inflames Glaukon's curiosity the more, the philosopher next proceeds to depreciate the importance of the whole issue of its possibility, reminding his young partner that their city in *logos* arose only because they were seeking knowledge about justice and injustice, hoping to find in their city a pattern (*paradeigmatos*) whereby to recognize justice itself and "the perfectly just man [*andra ton teleōs dikaion*] if he were to come into being", and similarly with respect to injustice and he who was most unjust, and how each relates to unhappiness (472c). He asks whether a painter who provides a pattern of "the fairest human being" (*ho kallistos anthrōpos*) is any less good for not being able to prove that it is possible for "such a man to come into being" (472d). Glaukon's emphatic denial, while in character, hardly seem justified. For there are important questions here concerning the standards of excellence by which painters (and all other "imitative" artists) are rightly judged (cf. 420cd, 596e), to say nothing of those standards of beauty or nobility pertinent to human beings in general (cf. 500d–c). And beneath these issues is one still more fundamental concerning the relationship between apparent or perceptible ("paintable") human beauty and something more substantial whose appeal is to the mind rather than the eye (cf. 402de, 444e1, 452e, 491c2, 494b6). And this, in turn, may be but one especially troublesome facet of an all-encompassing problem concerning Appearance and Reality (cf. 597de, 601bc, 602a–b).

Having discounted the importance of whether or not the fairest human one can envision is a practical possibility, Glaukon the more readily concedes something similar with respect to their city in *logos*, and further agrees (as many would not) that it's in the nature of things that one can come closer to truth in speech than in practice (472e–a). Whereupon the philosopher offers to show, not how they could replicate in deed their city's coming into being in speech, but how a city could be "governed" (*oikēseien*) in a way most closely approximating theirs, and suggests that this should count as showing that it is possible for such a regime to come into being (473ab). This requires finding and demonstrating what is badly done in cities that keeps them from being so governed; and what would be the minimal change (*metabalontos*) needed to rectify these defects. Nothing more is said here about the former requirement (cf. 520c, 521a), all attention being diverted to the one admittedly not small or easy change – in fact, the philosopher concedes it would seem a ridiculous if not outrageous change (473c); it is certainly a comprehensive change – namely: that cities be governed by philosophers. Almost invisible in the requirement that "political power and philosophy coincide" is the prohibition that those who are *not* capable of properly exercising political power *also not philosophize*, and that their exclusion is part of the philosopher's solution for alleviating human ills (cf. 519bc).

Sokrates no sooner pronounces his "very paradoxical" (*polu para doxan*; 473e) solution to mankind's problems, than Glaukon erupts with a warning that the proposal is sure to provoke an immediate and most violent attack by many people, including some not inconsiderable ones. He does not explain why; he, like Sokrates, treats the likelihood of such a reaction as self-evident. It will be left to Adeimantos to make more explicit the reasons most people, including sensible ones such as himself, would find the very idea preposterous (487b-d). And what he (like others) finds objectionable is *not* that certain politically incompetent people would be denied the opportunity to philosophize. Indeed, one suspects that all those who regard philosophy as a corrupting influence would heartily *endorse* this "submerged" side of Sokrates' proposal.

The philosopher's defence of himself and his radical idea consists of distinguishing what *he* means by a philosopher, as opposed to what most people would *suppose* that he means. Everything turns on re-educating mankind about what it truly means to *love wisdom*. And the difficulty is *not* simply that of making clear what is meant by *wisdom* – as one might naturally presume – but also, and first of all, what it is *to love (philein)*. Don Juan is the model lover: he is to women what a philosopher is to wisdom. According to Sokrates, one is rightly said to love something – be it boys, wine, honour, or food – only if one cherishes *all* of it; a lover of something may prefer the finer parts, but he despises none of it (474c-b). Hence, a genuine philosopher, desiring the whole of wisdom, is not finicky about what he learns, at least when he is young and lacks any basis for judgment, but (rather) is insatiable with respect to learning. Whereas one who *is* finicky about what he feeds his soul, a "bad eater" as it were, is no lover of learning or of wisdom[6] (475bc; cf. 354b). If upon reflection one still finds strange this likening of a genuine philosopher to a gluttonous alcoholic libertine, one might consider whether Sokrates is not more concerned with the submerged side of his proposal – that those who are not themselves truly dominated by a monstrous, insatiable, *erotic* love of knowledge not dabble in philosophy – than he is with its overtly political side.

Given only what has been said thus far, however, a philosopher would be indistinguishable from those who enjoy observing the inexhaustible multiplicity of sights and sounds, all the makings and doings and comings and goings of this world, and who could therefore also be said to be lovers of learning, but who are not on that account to be taken seriously (much of what occupies them being transitory minutiae). In order to differentiate the philosopher from these and other "learners" who are *like* him in certain respects, Sokrates now proceeds to distinguish *knowledge* from *opinion*. He identified the former with truth (475e), and singular forms (476a), with what entirely *is* (and is so unchangingly; 479e; cf. 484b, 485ab), and thus is entirely knowable (477a); and the latter with a sort of dream-like realm (476c) filled with a practically infinite multiplicity of particular things (476b; cf. 533b) that are ever-changing (cf. 484b), and in that sense neither strictly *are* nor *are not* (477a, 479c), and consequently are not strictly knowable but only opinable (478d). Partly because of the radically differing ontological status attributed to the objects being addressed, he further contends that the *power* whereby one *knows* is to be distinguished from that whereby one *opines* (477b–480a; cf. 511de), although powers as such – including the power to recognize and differentiate powers – share a common form (477c–d; cf. 438c–e, 352e–d). It is not necessarily an objection to any of this to note that it is quite abstract, and one might even say hypothetical. Unless or until one has a more substantial account of complete and unchanging Being and its unchanging relationship to the continual flux of Becoming, one has nothing to which a permanent truth can correspond. Hence the real possibility of knowledge, much less of wisdom, will not have been established, nor any differences worth remarking among the various lovers of learning, nor any need to distinguish the power whereby one opines from that of knowing.

But having distinguished, at least in formal terms, the relatively common *philodoxoi* ("lovers of opinion" who, e.g., delight in the many beautiful sights and sounds and shapes and stories, but who lack sufficient power of thought to see and delight in beauty itself) from the comparatively rare *philosophoi* (who *per* hypothesis *do* have such power; 476b), Sokrates returns to the question of who would make the most capable guardian of the laws and practices of cities. Should it be the philosopher who sees clearly and thus understands things as they are, or the non-philosopher who lacking such knowledge might be regarded as scarcely better than blind (484b–c)? Given such a choice, Glaukon cannot but agree that the former must be preferred, provided also (as Sokrates has added) that they "neither lack experience nor fall short of the others in any part of virtue" (484d). Hence, the philosopher turns to showing how these important provisos would be met.

He suggests that they proceed as they did when the subject of guardians initially arose, and so endeavour first to understand thoroughly (*katamathein*) their nature (485a; cf. 374e). Having done that, they could consider the proper nurture of the guardians, how they would be "perfected by education and age" (487a; cf. 376c). But whereas on the earlier occasion Sokrates and Glaukon had focused on what natural qualities the task of guarding itself required (375a), here they focus on what qualities would likely be manifested by a certain kind of candidate for that task, namely someone with a philosophical nature. And whereas before they had specified several requirements of body and only one of soul (that it be spirited, or spirit-formed; *thumoeidē*, 375b),[7] now nothing is said about the body except that a lover of learning would be contemptuous of its pleasures (485d), the entire discussion being about qualities of soul. Sokrates would have Glaukon believe that simply by virtue of a philosophical nature's channelling all of its power towards learning the whole truth about what always is, it would be moderate and no lover of money, liberal and magnificent (*megaloprepēs*), fearless of death and at least to that extent no coward, just and gentle, graceful, with a sure sense of proportion (485d–486d) – in sum, that an adequate practitioner of the philosophical life is "by nature of sound memory, a good learner, magnificent, gracious [*eucharis*], a friend and kinsman of truth, justice, courage, and moderation" (487a). Conspicuous by its absence is any reference to piety (cf. 327a, 368bc, 607c, 615bc).

Having apparently guaranteed fulfilment of the first proviso – that a truly philosophical nature would be second to none in all real virtue – Sokrates seems prepared to address the second: how it would gain the requisite experience for ruling political life. But now Adeimantos intervenes. He has listened with growing incredulity to the philosopher's defence of his "very paradoxical" proposal whereby their city in *logos* might be actualized, and out of respect for the truth as he sees it, he cannot let the philosopher's claims pass unchallenged. Unlike Glaukon, Adeimantos would not so readily agree that it makes no difference at all in judging a painter's excellence whether what he paints be a real possibility or not. By what standard is his *skill* to be judged, then, if not by the fidelity with which he reproduces the look of whatever he paints (cf. 377e)? It's one thing for a portrait painter to ignore his subject's warts – not that he is a better *painter* for doing so, although he may well be a more pleasing (and judicious!) one – but it's something else entirely to portray an ugly old woman as if she were a virile young man. And this is rather like what Sokrates seems to have done. Even making due allowance for things never turning out as well in practice as they can be depicted in the purity of speech, he has provided a portrait of the philosopher that, so far as Adeimantos can see, has no correspondence whatsoever with reality. Thus, the notion of philosophers ruling as kings still seems every bit as ridiculous as it did when first enunciated. And, consequently, their own city in *logos* has no real pertinence to political life as we actually experience it. Once one discredits what is supposedly the most efficient means of achieving even an approximation of it, its practical possibility remains as remote as ever. Say whatever fine things you will for artistic creativity, as a guide for choosing how to live it must be subordinate to the practicalities inherent in things as they *are*, not as they are imagined to be.

Adeimantos being Adeimantos, he doesn't come right out and accuse Sokrates of practising sophistry. For that matter, perhaps the philosopher is misleading himself as well as others *unintentionally* – an "eristical" possibility he had earlier warned them of (454a; cf. 450d-a). But in any event, the outcome of a verbal chess game such as he and Glaukon have been engaging in doesn't affect the real truth of things, as the case in point proves. For while someone might concede that he can't contradict any particular thing Sokrates has said, he sees for himself "in deed" that of all those who persist in philosophy past youth, "most become quite abnormal [*panu allokotos*], not to say completely vicious [*pamponērous*], while those who seem most decent [or, 'most equitable'; *epieikestatous*] do nevertheless, as a consequence of the practice [being praised], become useless to the cities" (487cd). Anyone familiar with Aristophanes' portrayal of philosophers in his *Clouds* would readily grasp Adeimantos' point. His skepticism does not arise from his having confused the philosopher with the various lovers of sights and sounds and arts and practices. He needs, first of all, to have the genuine philosophers distinguished from sophists and other false or incompetent pretenders, as well as from their own reputation (i.e., the popular conception of philosophers). And he needs to be convinced that it is possible for these true philosophers to exist. And to be shown that whatever they know actually has some utility for political life. And that there is some way to overcome their bad reputation, so as to render them politically acceptable as rulers. Only then will he agree that the proposal to have philosophers become kings, or kings philosophers, is both possible and best.

Sokrates' immediate response to the protest of this more practically minded, status-sensitive brother concedes the essential truth of what his "someone" says about the so-called philosophers encountered in actual life: that most of them are wretches or rogues, and that even the best of the lot are politically useless. The admission leaves Adeimantos perplexed. How, then, can it be good for cities to be *ruled* by those who are agreed to be *useless* to them? The philosopher allows that the claim would be "hard to prove" (*dysapodeikton*), and that he can answer only through an "image" (*eikones*; 487ea). Since this is the term he subsequently uses to denominate one of the two basic ontological categories pertaining to the perceptible realm, it is of interest to note that his use of the term may not be confined to visible "shadows" (*skias*) and such "appearances" (*phantasmata*) as we see reflected in water and mirrors (509ea; cf. 375d) – that is, images cast by actual, perceptible objects.

The image he uses here – an extraordinarily rich one, likening a *polis* to a ship (488a–489a) – is meant to allay Adeimantos' most urgent concerns: the apparent inutility of even the best philosophers, and their not generally being held in high esteem. Prior to providing it, however, Sokrates employs another image to indicate the status of his own image-making: because there is nothing analogous to the situation of decent philosophers in actual cities, he must do his "image-making and apologizing on their behalf" as do painters who mix together elements from various sources into a single, synthetic but not naturally occurring thing (such as a "goatstag"; 488a). However, the picture he paints of this ship – with its strong but ignorant shipowner, its fractious sailors fighting over the role of pilot (while vehemently denying that there is an *art* of piloting), the one competent pilot dismissed as a babbling, useless stargazer, and so on – requires no suspension of one's beliefs about the kinds of beings which populate the natural world. And so it is not immediately clear *why* it is to be regarded as an artificial composite analogous to centaurs and satyrs and sileni.

But in any case, the image, while otherwise worthy of detailed explication, seems to beg Adeimantos' basic question. For that a true pilot possesses knowledge essential to safe navigation and proper ship management is not in doubt, nor that he is as a consequence the proper ruler of a ship. Owner, passengers, sailors, each concerned for his own well-being and all committed to a common destination, look to him for guidance and willingly bow to his expertise. Because there *is* a generally recognized pilot's art possessed by only the few who have laboured to acquire it, one does not expect to find on board a ship such pandaemonium as Sokrates describes (which comports with what he himself claimed: that the decent philosopher's situation is *unique*, and thus artistic licence if required if one is to portray it). But that a philosopher – and only a philosopher – possesses all the knowledge essential for safely and surely guiding a ship of state is precisely what is *in doubt*, and this calls into question the entire analogy.

The other problems – that the need for and existence of such knowledge as he has are not generally *recognized*; that the very idea of there being such knowledge arouses violent opposition; that there is already in place an altogether different conception of political skill and knowledge and utility – are strictly subsidiary. True enough, they would be very important dimensions of the whole political problem *given the overall validity of the image*, as would the facts that those who quarrel and fight over ruling are not agreed on why or where they are sailing, and that each wants to use the ship for his own ends. It should be noted, however, that taking these latter details of the image into account means that a philosopher, if he is truly the most fitting governor of a *polis* – a political pilot in the fullest sense – must know more than some analogue to the art of navigation. He must also know how to rule men: how to quell their quarrels over power and privilege, how to get his authority recognized, how to make himself obeyed, how to introduce harmony into all dimensions of political life, and how to cultivate the necessary respect for the common good (cf. 341d). This points to the need for a profound and comprehensive psychology, one providing knowledge of human nature in all its tropical diversity. And the task of political piloting is further complicated, of course, by the fact that there are many ships on the sea (cf. 488a8), not all of them friendly. One must be able to fight one's ship as well as sail it.

Only if somehow convinced that *"true* philosophers" are necessarily *political* philosophers, understanding politics from top to bottom, as it were; and that by virtue of what they *know* would be not merely useful to cities, but supremely useful – only then should one agree

The War Lover

(as Adeimantos does; 489a) that Sokrates' image accurately portrays their situation. As for its also explaining why "philosophers are not *honoured* in the cities", this too only arouses wonder on the assumption that there is some reason why they should be. Thus, lacking assurance that a genuine philosopher is potentially to politics what a skilled and otherwise good pilot is to a ship at sea, the issues of who's to *blame* for decent philosophers' not actually being used as they allegedly could and ought to be, and who ought to solicit whom (489b-c), are beside the point. In any event, that most so-called philosophers are regarded not merely as useless but as "altogether vicious" *does* need explaining regardless, and no light seems shed on *that* by Sokrates' Ship-of-State image.

But perhaps Sokrates' image-making does provide some assurance of his political utility. For it's not as if the philosopher has so far supplied no evidence whatsoever that he *is* knowledgable about political things – quite the contrary. In the course of constructing their city in *logos*, Sokrates had probed to the very basis of political life, and given a plausible account of how one might constitute an harmonious regime in which all the citizens could be virtuous and happy, the rulers respected and obeyed, and the whole city secure – the crucial factor being the character and allegiance of the warrior class. And that character and allegiance, in turn, depend partly on how the warriors are selected and educated (about which the philosopher proved to have extensive and well-considered ideas), and partly on who is set over them as rulers: that they be those whom the warriors themselves recognize as being the best of the good. And here one might remember that Adeimantos is a young warrior, a distinguished one in fact, as is his brother (368a); and one must presume that he knows Sokrates is also a warrior as well as a philosopher (cf. *Apology* 28d-e, *Charmides* 153a-c), one whom other famous warriors praise (*Laches* 181b, *Symposium* 220d-c).

Through it all, the philosopher had shown a high-minded view of politics – excessively high-minded, one might say. But perhaps for that very reason one should suspect he is not in sufficiently close touch with the actual practices of political life. Without denying the perspicacity he revealed in designing their city, even in this case one wasn't always sure that his proposals were quite realistic, given the various limitations people commonly display (cf. 419a). By both nature and belief, Adeimantos needs little persuading that political life *should* be like a well-run ship at sea, and that those best suited to rule it should *not* have to pander to a vulgar, ignorant majority for the opportunity of exercising their abilities (any more than a doctor should have to beg to serve the sick, much less compete with quacks for the privilege; cf. 489bc). But there's a world of difference between how political life should be, and how it in fact *is* – rather like the difference between Sokrates' shining portrait of a philosopher and all those be-warted rogues and dwarfs one actually meets. And so the very contrast one sees between the harmonious politics of their city in *logos* and the perpetual political strife of actual cities (cf. 422ea) leads one to suspect that the philosopher may spend too much time dreaming about the heights of politics to have a sufficient appreciation of its depths, and how vast the distance is between the two.

Now, however, his image of the ship shows otherwise. With this one creative stroke, he reveals that he understands better than Adeimantos that politics (at least as typically practised in a democracy) is little more than a vulgar and vulgarizing power struggle, which sufficiently explains his own avoidance of it. Thus he tacitly confirms that Thrasymachos is more right than wrong about those who actually rule in the cities (343b, 345e). And if it's fair to say – and apparently it seems so to Adeimantos – that in actual practice the notion of political utility is centred upon whatever contributes to the gaining and holding of power (that even policy proposals and debates are usually but means to this end), then perhaps the alleged "uselessness" of decent philosophers is more praiseworthy than blameworthy.

Beyond this, however, the image itself, and even more the making of it, display a commanding view of the political problem, a synoptic view which allows one to see much more than just the "distance" between how things should be and how they typically are (which is but one dimension of the problem – or, rather, a one-dimensional conception of the problem). Reflecting on the rational ordering of a well-run ship gives some indication as to the grounds of the "should", and so helps one to see *why* the political life Adeimantos has observed and experienced contrasts so markedly with the philosopher-led politics of their city in *logos*. At the same time, it tacitly suggests what would be required if the latter were ever to supersede the former. And because the philosopher-pilot has attended to things in the heavens, he better understands how they bear on things of the earth (and perhaps beneath it as well). Thus he sees not only political life in its broader natural context of time and tide, but also why doing so is itself of political importance.

The War Lover

Previously, Sokrates had shown a kind of knowledge *about* politics, even providing insight as to why true utility is the natural political standard (cf. 369b ff). But he had not shown that such knowledge itself *meets* this natural political standard, that it is itself politically useful, much less the one thing most needful. Thus Adeimantos could still doubt the wisdom of philosophers actually ruling. But this most recent display of Sokrates' image-making ability does show this, though only by first enlarging Adeimantos' conception of political utility. The very fact that it is a *persuasive* view - both of why ordinarily politics is debased, and of the need for a perspective on politics that does not partake of that debasement but instead takes its bearings from things that transcend partisan politics - tacitly confirms what the image explicitly teaches: knowledge, or rather its widespread lack and what people believe in its stead, is the root of the political problem. And thus it also tacitly suggests that the solution to the problem is some sort of public education, or re-education - not a general "enlightenment" aimed at making everyone pilots, or even competent judges of pilots, but the inculcation of salutary opinions in keeping with the image.

Having made this image (which manages to disparage "the politicians now ruling" while largely exonerating the bulk of the citizenry who follow them), and having taught it to public-spirited Adeimantos with the exhortation that he, in turn, teach it to others (489ab), the philosopher has begun to demonstrate his own political utility: he is the consummate educator, the educator of educators, of "gentlemen" who both "listen *and* speak" and thus can mediate between the confused Many and the one true political pilot (489e). Notice, the balance of their conversation is all about education and miseducation - right up to the point where Sokrates introduces his famous images of the Sun and Line and Cave in order to speak of "the most precise education" (*paideias tēs akribestatēs*; 503d) and "the greatest studies" (*ta megista mathē mata*; 503e), requisite to those who would be true philosophers and true kings - at which point Glaukon takes over as respondent. Woven into this critique of education is an apology for philosophy's bespattered reputation, along with rhetorical guidance as to how the public misconception of both philosophy and politics might be rectified. But it also includes several crucial observations pertinent to the opposition between eristics and dialectics.

Sokrates begins his instruction on how "moderately [or modestly, sensibly; *metriōs*] to apologize" for philosophy by reminding Adeimantos what sort of nature constitutes a "real lover of learning" (*ontōs philo-*

mathēs), that is, one who does not tarry by the many things opined to be, but whose love (*erōs*) is satisfied only by his grasping with the appropriate part of his soul the nature itself of each thing that simply and completely is (490ab). The philosopher's language is overtly erotic: "having approached and coupled with what really *is*, [thereby] begetting intelligence and truth, he knows and lives truly, is nourished, and therefore ceases from his labour pains." Natures capable of this task are rare in any case, but are made still rarer because, despite their aptitude for learning and other excellences, they seldom actualize their true potential. This is due to their being surprisingly susceptible to corruption. What is most surprising is that their very virtues – such as Glaukon's courage and Adeimantos' moderation – can play a part in diverting them from philosophy (491b). Hence, these best natures (*euphuestatas*), with a capacity for the greatest achievements of both good and evil, turn out exceptionally bad if they chance to get bad instruction (*kakos paidogōgias*; 491e). Whereas, if by chance or divine favour such a nature happens upon a suitable course of learning (*mathēdeōs*), it will necessarily attain all of virtue (492a).

The former outcome is a good deal more likely, however, for sophistry is far more prevalent than true education. But the threat is not so much from individual sophists privately corrupting the youth – in fact, those who say this are the biggest sophists of all, the ones who "educate most completely" *everyone*, young and old, male and female (492ab). Through the various public fora that provide it media of expression, and by means of excessive praise and blame – or, when persuasion fails, with punishments – this collective public sophistry quite overwhelms any contrary kind of private education. Barring divine assistance, that is (492ea; cf. 496c). Actually, what individual sophists offer privately is little more than a variation on the convictions (*dogmata*) conveyed by this great sophist, Public Opinion. Having an empirical familiarity with what pleases and vexes this large, strong creature they are nurturing, and thus knowing how to manipulate its humours, the private sophists organize all this into an art, call it wisdom, and turn to teaching (493a-b; cf. 516cd). Neither knowing nor caring what is *truly* noble or just, to say nothing of what is truly *good*, they simply rely on the names, using them according to the great animal's opinions, which in turn reflect what please and pain it (493bc; cf. 505b). Thus reliant upon everyday language and opinion, they are of necessity mired in eristics (cf. 454a-b). They have no basis for arguing that something is just and noble other than so-called political necessity (including the necessity of bowing to popular hedonism), "neither having seen nor being able to show to another how much the nature of the necessary and the good really differ" (493c). We may presume, then, that the philosopher, unlike the sophist, *has* seen this radical difference between the Good and all the various degrees of necessity. Consequently he can – among some other very important things – *judge* which pleasures (and the desires for them) are simply good, and which ones are otherwise necessary (558de), as distinct from those desires and pleasures that are useless and *un*necessary (559a, 561a), even bad (505c, 561bc). Indeed, having seen the Good in its relation to Truth and all modes of existence, he knows what *real* pleasure is, distinguishing true and pure pleasures from those that are but a kind of "shadow-painting" of pleasure (583b ff). But can he show this, teach this, to someone else? Perhaps each reader had best judge that for himself.

As for anyone who has *not* seen the true nature of Necessity and its relationship to the Good, and who therefore cannot teach it to others, Sokrates asks. "By Zeus, in your opinion would not such be a strange educator?"[8] Adeimantos emphatically agrees, whereupon the philosopher extends the indictment to include all those – painters, musicians, politicians, poets, and other craftsmen – whose makings and doings express and ratify, and thus further inculcate and reinforce, the public taste which rules them (493d; cf. 514b–a, 401b–d). Whether or not they realize it – and probably most do not – these various practitioners are themselves emmeshed in the web they help spin. With all this being so, with the multitude of people being unphilosophical and even antiphilosophical (494a), there would seem little chance of a natural philosopher's sticking by his pursuit through to its completion (*telos*).

But beyond the public depreciation of philosophy in favour of fostering familiar pleasing opinions and common dogmas, the very qualities that constitute the philosophical nature attract flattering assessments and inducements from others bent on using such a person for their own purposes. As a result, he's apt to be filled with a greatly inflated sense of his own importance and competence, and accordingly deaf to anyone who, like a good father (cf. 550ab), might try to acquaint him with his own intellectual needs and the laborious means whereby they may be met (494b–d). And in the remote chance that someone *were* successful in persuading a good-natured youth to pursue philosophy despite the prejudice against it, one could expect the flatterers and sophists to use all means, public and private, in opposing that someone (494de; cf. 517a). Hence it is that such natures, rare enough in any case, are usually misdirected and corrupted by a bad rearing, and end up doing the greatest harm to polities, rather than the greatest good. So, with its most suitable practitioner thus "exiled" (suggesting that some could be "recalled"?), the practice of philosophy is taken up by those "unworthy of education", whose cramped and maimed souls produce only vacuous sophisms, nothing genuine or partaking of true prudence. Full of pretensions that far outstrip both their abilities and achievements, such manikins bring disgrace upon the activity, further reinforcing the general prejudice against it (495b–a).

Having accounted for the wretchedness of most so-called philosophers, those who bear major responsibility for the ridicule and notoriety attached to the activity, Sokrates turns to explaining how, despite all odds, the few genuine and decent (but still reputedly useless) ones come to exist. Sokrates briefly describes four natural ways whereby someone who *is* worthy of consorting with philosophy might escape the more usual fate of such natures. He adds that his own case, depending as it seems on some superhuman agency (*ta daimonion sēmeion*), is probably not worth mentioning, since it may well be unique (496b–c). Be that as it may, these blessed few, having (on the one hand) tasted the sweetness of the philosophic life and (on the other) having seen the madness of the many and that no one engaged in their politics does anything healthy, and that there are no allies with whom a philosopher could make common cause in aid of justice – these few keep quiet and mind their own business, avoiding the arena of public politics much as they would a gathering of savage beasts (496d). They know their efforts would be of no use to either city or friends, and of no profit to themselves or anyone else. This might start Adeimantos wondering. What if there *were* allies: not themselves philosophers, but public-spirited gentlemen who recognize the need for such wisdom as the philosopher possesses, and who would willingly be guided by it (cf. 335e, 474b)?

So concludes the philosopher's moderate, modest, sensible apology for philosophy, showing that it is unjustly slandered. But it has culminated in a scathing indictment of conventional politics,[9] while none the less contending that were a philosopher to chance upon a *"suitable* regime", he would himself grow to full stature and save the common things along with the private (497a). Not very surprisingly, this assertion prompts Adeimantos to ask further about this suitable regime: which

The War Lover

of those now existing is it? The philosopher answers that no current regime qualifies (497b). One might have predicted this answer from the moment he introduced the very idea of philosophical rule, for it was touted as the one neither small nor easy change aimed at correcting "what is badly done in cities today", i.e., all cities (473b). And while he had left the impression that *any* regime could thereby be transformed into something that would approximate their city in *logos*, it would still be a legitimate variation of Adeimantos' question to ask which of the current regimes would be most amenable to such a change.

The philosopher, however, ignores this rather obvious practical question, and instead now speaks – not expressly of a suitable regime, nor of their city in *logos* – but of *"the* best regime", one virtually divine, by comparison with which all actual regimes are only too human (497c). Yet the numerous subsequent references to "the Many" (*hoi polloi*) and the problem of persuading them suggests that, within the general or theoretical exposition of how true philosophy might be made to serve political life, both Sokrates and Adeimantos are tacitly addressing the more particular practical question of how a *democracy* might come to accept some sort of philosophical rule. This suspicion might be seen as confirmed by Sokrates' later suggesting to Adeimantos that for anyone wishing to organize a *polis*, "as we have now been doing", there is likely to be a necessity of going to a democratic city (557d). The fact that only freedom-loving democracies openly tolerate philosophers rising among them is doubtless an important consideration (561d; cf. 520ab). And equally doubtless, the philosopher appreciates that Adeimantos, and all civic-minded people like him, will never be finally won over until persuaded that philosophical rule is somehow a practical possibility.

As this is the first time the philosopher has spoken of the simply "best regime", however, the young man wonders whether it is the same as that which they have just described in speech. A reader might find both his question and Sokrates' response to it somewhat puzzling. Here, however, one must see things from within the conversation as it originally unfolded, and remember that the Aristocracy in *logos* was characterized as "perfectly good" (*telōs agathēn*) only on the *hypothesis* that it had been "correctly founded" (*orthōs ōkistai*; 427e; cf. 510c). As for the goodness of the provisions subsequently specified in Book Five, they were attended by a conspicuous throng of rather "iffy" suppositions (e.g., 451e, 452ea, 454de, 456e3-4, 462c-d, 464b, 466cd). But even more to the point, it was never made clear that *their* city was to be ruled by philosopher-kings; Sokrates had originally described the "altogether complete guardians" (*phylakes panteleis*) in seemingly quite different terms (i.e., that they were to be the elder warriors of greatest competence in guarding the city, and, as such, prudent, powerful, and patriotic; 412c–e). Philosophers becoming kings, or kings becoming philosophical, was first put forward as the most expeditious way some current actual city could be changed so as to be governed in a manner most closely approximating their imaginary one. The implication would seem to be that any political philosopher would see the wisdom of *all* their arrangements – from the rational division of labour to their warfaring policies – and proceed to reform his own city accordingly insofar as this was practical, and adopt surrogate arrangements insofar as it wasn't. The philosopher's slightly ambiguous answer to the young man's query is the first step in conflating these alternative conceptions of the rulers. The best regime *is* the same as theirs in *other* respects, *and* in the fact that it permanently requires a certain sort of ruler, namely one with the same understanding of the regime as Adeimantos, "the lawgiver", has (497cd). Adeimantos agrees that this had already been prescribed. Yes and no. Earlier, the permanent "overseer" (*epistatēs*) was specified for Glaukon in terms of a candidate's enjoying "the finest mixture of gymnastic with music", with the result that he is "the most perfectly musical and well-harmonized" (412a). The reader who has himself not noticed the possible discrepancy can be counted upon to excuse Adeimantos his similar failure to do so. Sokrates glosses it over in saying that the point, while made clear, wasn't made "sufficiently" clear out of fear of what is now becoming altogether too clear: that its demonstration would be long and hard (497d). This proves to be the understatement of the night.

The philosopher begins by alluding to the risk of destruction entailed in a city's taking up philosophy, but adds that all great things carry risks (cf. 467b). As for *proving* his point, he avows no lack of willingness, but warns he may lack the requisite power (497e; cf. 506d–a). Be that as it may, he ventures that the proper way, and presumably the risk-minimizing way, for philosophy to be practised in a city is just the opposite of the way it is currently practised. For as it is now, callow youths take up the hardest part first, that which has to do with *logoi* (speeches, arguments). And as a matter of fact, such giving and receiving of arguments – dialectics – will be the *culmination* of the novel curriculum Sokrates later outlines for the proper training of philosopher-kings (531e–b). For now, he more briefly sketches the re-

The War Lover

gime of education and experience that would produce lifelong commitment to philosophy. Youths should start with an "education and philosophy" suitable for youths, while at the same time they properly develop their bodies so as to secure "a helper for philosophy". Only when their souls approach maturity should they be subjected to that "more intense gymnastic" of arguments (498b; cf. 539d).

Adeimantos notes the eagerness with which Sokrates speaks of these matters, but adds that the Many are not apt to be persuaded by this, and will be even more eager in opposing than he is in proposing. And as if to prove that the philosopher's "apology" has not been lost on him, the young man here expressly affiliates Thrasymachos with the Many (498c). Sokrates neither agrees nor disagrees with this, but warns against calumniating either him or his new-made friend, whom he intends to help if he can. Perhaps he hopes the sophist rhetorician will return the favour. As for the Many not being persuaded by the philosopher's extemporaneous plain speaking about a true philosopher in charge of a fitting city (accustomed as they are to sophisticated rhetoric), the root of the problem is the same as that which earlier bothered Adeimantos himself: they've never seen anything in deed that matches his speeches (498ea). Nor for that matter are they truly acquainted with truthful speech, speech that strains for truth and knowledge, and that eschews all those subtleties and eristical tricks which strain only for opinion and strife. Sokrates' explicit application of this disclaimer to private gatherings (*idiais synousiais*) as well as to public confrontations reminds us of how natural, and consequently how pervasive, an eristical posture towards argument is (499a).

The philosopher well appreciates the practical problems posed by the Many's prejudices concerning philosophers, but the truth remains: neither city nor regime, nor similarly a man, will ever become perfect (*teleos*) until either some chance necessity compels those few philosophers who aren't vicious to take charge of a city, "whether they are willing or not"; or those who at present are in charge, or their sons, become inspired with a true love (*erōs*) of true philosophy. And while anyone would concede that the chances of this happening are slim, there seems no reason to conclude that it is in principle impossible.[10] For that matter, it may already have happened somewhere unbeknownst to us (499cd). Adeimantos affirms that this, too, is *his* opinion, but Sokrates senses that the young man retains reservations about the Many. And that while he may have contempt for their opinions, he still respects their power. The philosopher gently scolds him for thinking too harshly of the Many, and for his eristical inclination to quarrel with them, rather than aiming at what would be more efficacious, thus more useful: gentle persuasion. The fact that Sokrates says nothing, and need say nothing, about how to persuade unwilling philosophers to rule reveals the extent to which Adeimantos remains a captive to the common view that anyone *would* be willing to rule given a suitable opportunity (cf. 346e–c, 489bc, 517c–d). Nor is there any mention now of preventing the unworthy from practising philosophy; or rather, the political problem posed by false or imitation philosophers has been silently superseded by the political problem posed by true or real philosophers (cf. 519d–c).

As for persuading the Many to be ruled, Sokrates assures Adeimantos that if he will simply distinguish for them whom he means by philosophers – as opposed to those impolite, quarrelsome, boisterous, defamatory practitioners of eristics whom they suppose he means – he will surely soothe away their animosity (500a–b). For once they understand that someone whose mind is preoccupied with the well-ordered things that truly are, and who endeavours to be like such things himself, is necessarily gentle and unenvious, most people will respond likewise. Anyone acquainted with the fate of Sokrates, or even just more broadly experienced with life, might not accept this presumption as readily as would a fair-minded but rather young man. Be that as it may, Adeimantos entirely agrees that the philosopher, consorting with what is divine and orderly (*theiō kai kosmiō*), himself becomes divine and orderly, at least to the extent that this is within human power (500cd). And that were there some necessity for him to mould the character (*ēthē*) of other humans as well as himself, he would not prove a bad craftsman "of moderation, justice, and popular [*dēmotikēs*] virtue as a whole" (500d). A craftsman, of course, is always limited by his material; accordingly, there is no mention of his instilling courage throughout the citizenry, much less wisdom or prudence. Even so, who could object to a city outlined by a "painter" who looks to "the divine pattern" he sees in his mind, and faithfully attempts to imitate *that*, rather than even the best of what he sees with his eyes? Surely no one of good will would object – provided that the imagined pattern derives from this higher reality, and not solely from the painter's own wish-driven fancy (cf. 458a). Thus one would want to know a good deal more about this higher reality so revered by a philosophical regime-painter, and how someone might gain access to it.

For now, however, we are simply assured that such divinely inspired

The War Lover

craftsmen would be immediately distinguishable from other shapers of cities and souls by the fact that they are willing to work only with a clean slate; if necessary, they would first wipe it clean themselves (501a; cf. 540ea). Next, they would sketch not the *form* but "the *shape* of the *regime*" (*to schēma tēs politeias*). (Perhaps more or less as demonstrated in this dialogue entitled "Regime"?) And then in their "filling it out" or "colouring it in" (*apergazomenoi*), they would frequently look both "at what by nature is just and fair [*kalon*] and moderate and everything of the sort, and at what is being produced in human beings." By a judicious blending of practices – and to some extent, apparently, this is a matter of trial and error (cf. 501bc) – they would produce a "flesh-coloured man-image" (*andreikelon*),[11] taking their hints from that which Homer also called "god-formed [or god-like] and god-image" (*theo-eides kai theo-eikelon*; 501b).

Sokrates suggests that merely portraying the philosopher as just such a "painter of regimes" would go far towards pacifying that spirited opposition to his taking charge of a city. Adeimantos retains a trace of skepticism, but the philosopher insists on the point, making it even stronger: their opponents would be altogether gentled and persuaded, if only out of shame (501ea). In the absence of any rational grounds for their opposition, the selfish motivation of such opponents would presumably be transparent to everyone. Similarly, no one could contend that it is simply *impossible* that the descendants of kings, or of those holding power, could be born with philosophical natures; or that they would *necessarily* be corrupted; or that it's impossible their citizens would abide by the laws and practices such rulers would establish. Nor would it be all that wonderful, much less impossible, were some others to come to these same opinions, including the opinion that such an arrangement of political life would be best, presuming only it were possible, and that it *is* possible, albeit difficult (502a–c). And thus Adeimantos is persuaded that their city in *logos* is not irrelevant to actual political life.

But a crucial issue has been uncovered in the course of his instruction. The regime they have in mind has a *permanent* need for such a philosopher-king to rule it, lest it pass out of existence as abruptly as it arrived. This is not something that one would leave to chance, provided there were any alternative: if the fortunate arising of an approximation of this regime is but a remote possibility, how much more remote the likelihood of lightning striking twice, as it were? And given that the always rare philosophical nature even more rarely turns out well unless it receives an appropriate (and apparently very special) nurture, even a workable selective breeding program is not sufficient in itself to guarantee a natural succession of the required rulers. So if the regime's chance actualization were not to be a wasted opportunity, the first responsibility of a philosopher come to power would be to ensure a suitable successor. The original recognition of this permanent need for a specific kind of overseer posed no novel problems; the rulers were simply to be the most respected and patriotic elders of the warrior class (412a–414a) – and of these, their city's reformed but none the less traditional education could be expected to produce a steady supply. But there is no reason to believe that its careful blend of traditional music and gymnastic would produce a steady supply of philosophers both willing and able to rule as kings (indeed, the possibility that it might is later expressly ruled out; 521d–b).

So, having finished with the "difficulty" (or "trouble"; *dyschereia*) concerning women and children, and having raised the question of what "studies and practices" *will* produce the requisite "saviours" (*sōtēres*) of the regime, Sokrates announces that everything concerning the rulers must now be gone through again from the beginning (502c–e). Their first step is to confirm the only previous requirement they had actually discussed: that by all the outward evidence provided by all practical tests, potential rulers must appear to be "lovers of the city" (i.e., patriots; *philopolidas*, 503a; cf. 412c–d). And now that he has dared to say clearly what he earlier shrank from saying at all: that if one wishes to establish the "most precise guardians", one must choose philosophers (503b; cf. 414b), it is now also clear that, even with the best education man could ever hope to devise, such guardians will always be in short supply. Apparently this point – that true philosophers are rare – bears repeating, at least to Adeimantos (cf. 491ab, 495b, 496a, 496c). In any case, Sokrates once more emphasizes that the full constellation of qualities constituting the philosophical nature rarely occurs (503b–d). And its presence is revealed only in action. So each prospective guardian whose convictions survive those other tests in pleasures and pains, labours and fears, must be further exercised (*gymnazein*) in "many studies" in order to determine whether he has the power to endure "the greatest studies", or whether he will instead prove cowardly in this, as others do in other things (503ea; cf. 498b, 535b).

When, as could only be expected, Adeimantos asks what studies the philosopher means by "the greatest", Sokrates indicates that they result in a finer, more precise understanding of what justice, moderation, courage, and wisdom truly *are*, and that this presumes the "longer, fuller way" of understanding the human soul which he had spoken of earlier (504a–b; cf. 435cd). The philosopher's warning here that nothing incomplete (or imperfect, *ateles*; 504c) can be the measure of *anything* has implications for much besides the previous account of the virtues, and "the forms of the soul" to which the virtues are keyed (cf. 369b, 495d, 423e, 509c, 530e, 532d–a, 548cd). Be that as it doubtless is, Sokrates further warns that anyone not willing to go that longer way in pursuit of the fuller, more precise understanding of the soul, "and toil no less at studies than gymnastic", will never "come to the end [*telos*] of the greatest and most fitting study" (504cd). Adeimantos reacts with surprise to the suggestion that there is something greater than justice and the other things mentioned. The philosopher replies that not only is there something still greater, nothing less than the most perfect elaboration of the virtues will suffice – for surely the greatest things are the most worthy of the greatest precision (504de). As for this very greatest and most fitting study, towards which all other great and worthy studies point, it is, as we've so often heard, "the idea of the Good" (505a).

The Sun-Good Analogy, the Divided Line, and the Allegory of the Cave are among the most famous images – not merely of this dialogue, or of the Platonic corpus – but of our entire philosophical tradition. Along with the Myth of the Metals, the Ring of Gyges, the Ship of State, and the Harmony of the Spheres, these images are the property of their creator in the sense that no subsequent philosopher would speak of such things without conscious regard for Plato's original use of them. But the central images are not only celebrated for their richness, they are notorious for the perplexity and controversy occasioned by the myriad efforts over the centuries to interpret them. I do not intend to offer here anything that would qualify as still another interpretation *per se*, believing as I do that this would require a book unto itself – and one, moreover, I'm scarcely qualified to write. I wish, however, to make some observations about them and the revolutionary educational program they preface, especially as they bear on the problem with which this chapter is primarily concerned: pride serving prejudice at the expense of learning. Or, to express the problem in practical terms, how the proud victory-loving timocrat can be transformed from

Pride and Prejudice

an eristical guardian of his own opinions into a dialectical hunter of knowledge, and his love of war sublimated into a love of wisdom.

Let me begin by reiterating an earlier point. The central images are introduced in such a way as to suggest that pursuing the matters they supposedly elucidate leads to, or perhaps presumes or otherwise entails, that fuller, more profound understanding of the distinctly human soul – indeed, that the study of the rational soul and its virtue is itself among those "greatest studies" that potential guardians must bravely endure (503e). This impression is subsequently confirmed by the fact that the philosopher's analysis of the basic categories and relations of existence is explicitly matched with the distinguishable powers and workings of the mind (511de; cf. 478a, 490b, 533ea). So, too, by his later singling out the intellectual virtue of prudence as seemingly more divine, and as manifesting a more durable potency, than the other so-called virtues of the soul (518de) – judgments which surely imply a deeper, more refined psychology than that provided in Book Four. Nor should one overlook what can be learned about one's own soul in the course of its labouring to understand whatever the images themselves convey. But presuming the suitability of the erotic language he uses to introduce and discuss the images (506d–a, 508b, 509a), the more precise understanding of the soul must also require an expanded conception of *erōs*. If there is a lust for *theoretical* knowledge (something a reader confronted with theoretical problems must determine for himself), a psychology that confines *erōs* to the sub-rational parts of the soul most definitely falls short of the truth (cf. 439d).

Moreover, this finer account of the soul may in its own way help one to see why the finest kind of soul, the truly philosophical soul, is so rare. It is not simply that the philosophical life requires an abnormal conjunction of seemingly contrary psychic qualities (as per 503b–d; cf. 375c) – a soul, consequently whose precise configuration rarely occurs. It also requires exceptional psychic *strength* of certain kinds: mental strength, of course, but what is even more basic, exceptional *spiritual* strength. That is, the philosophical life presupposes not only a specific *form* of soul, but one of requisite *size*: a "large" and thus strong soul – a soul of "befitting greatness" (*megaloprepeia*, "magnificent"; 487a, 490c, 494b, 536a), with "an understanding [*dianoia*] endowed with befitting greatness" (486a), thus presumably "great-minded" (*megalaphrōn*; cf. 567b), but "great-spirited" for sure (*megalathumos*; 375c). The challenge of understanding the philosopher's

The War Lover

"daimonic" ontology *cum* psychology (509c) is no doubt a test of such strength: a test both of the mind's ability to recognize its truth and of the spirit's willingness to make the attempt. Successive attempts are but so much exercise whereby one cultivates the intellectual strength required to grasp what is admittedly so very hard to grasp, virtually impossible at first – for it is, as Glaukon perceives, an "enormous task" (*suchnon ergon*; 511c), and one moreover that must be returned to again and again (532d). But cultivating this requisite strength of mind presupposes the *spiritual* strength to persevere, and to overcome certain deep-rooted fears: of the unknown, of failure, of having to confront one's present – and perhaps permanent – inadequacies, of the possibly tragic character of truth itself.

Another general point: from virtually the beginning to the end of his explanation of these matters, Sokrates acknowledges – even emphasizes – that he does not claim to *know* whether what he says about them is true. He allows himself to be prevailed upon to express his opinions or suppositions about the Good and related matters, but only after a similar show of resistance and with as many cautions and disclaimers as when earlier "compelled" to elaborate on that "troublesome" business of the women and children (506b-a; cf. 509c, 450a–451b, 368bc, 472a). He affirms at the outset that "the idea of the Good" *is* the "greatest study", but in the same breath he concedes it is *not* something we "know sufficiently" (505a), and that consequently it is the subject of profound controversy and confusion (505b-d). And in the middle of his exposition he suggests that only some god knows whether all he has expounded is true, but in any case this is how it looks to him (517b). And when finally reaching what would seem to be the culmination of his account, the point at which they would leave images behind and by means of dialectics look directly on the truth, Sokrates once again warns against accepting it all as gospel, but adds that one *can* insist that *something* like it *must* be true (533a). He might also have added what his own account suggests: that any stronger assurances on his part should be both ineffective and unnecessary inasmuch as true knowing is self-confirming.

But the philosopher's acknowledging that we do not know the Good "sufficiently" (*hikanōs*) invites further comment, implying as it does that we do somehow intuit (or "divine"; cf. 505e1) enough about it to ratify several further observations he makes.[12] And while they are all rather formal, they are by no means inconsequential. First, that it *is* the "greatest study" (*megiston mathēma*), since it is in light of one's own idea of the Good that all things are evaluated, even justice itself (cf. 506a). Assessments as to the utility or benefit of anything, including all lesser knowledge, are only as sound as one's *opinion* about the Good. Similarly, prudential judgment takes its bearings from one's conception of the Good: indeed, in the ordinary sense this is what "being prudent" or "sensible" means: acting so as to secure what is "really good" in life (505b). Thus, we can readily see that an inadequate understanding of what truly *is* good renders problematic everything we think we know and try to do. And consequently, *knowledge* of the Good would itself be unqualifiedly good – quite possibly the only thing that is so for human beings. This is reflected in the fact that no one is satisfied with possessing what merely appears or is reputed to be good (as many doubtless are with respect to being just or noble), but everyone desires the reality for himself and accordingly despises what he believes to be mere opinions about it (505d; cf. 382b). Alternatively expressed, most people regard morality as something "idealistic", but everyone is by nature a "realist" when it comes to happiness.

So, perplexing and disputatious as we find the idea whenever we think or talk about it, we do none the less regard goodness as something real – not, that is, as something utterly subjective, without any basis in the nature of things. And we perceive, be it ever so dimly, that this reality of the Good is somehow ultimately responsible for, and thus is somehow foreshadowed in, whatever *seems* good to us (which in turn, as noted, governs all that we pursue and do, all our discriminations and evaluations; 505de). Something real accounts for the fact that our natural posture towards our world is not one of studied neutrality. The psychic experience of pleasure and pain readily suggests itself as such a real "something", and so it is not surprising that the idea of the Good being Pleasure has perennial appeal – it squares with so much of what so many people do, if not always with what they say (cf. 505b).[13] But not with everything that everybody does. And in fact almost anyone can be "compelled to agree that there are bad pleasures"(505c), and to do so moreover without any recourse to speculations based on some (ultimately impractical) hedonistic calculus. For almost anyone can be compelled to agree that there are some inherently ignoble, shameful, ugly pleasures, pleasures in the face of which one's honour-loving, beauty-loving spirit simply revolts.

Given that Sokrates expressly admonishes Glaukon to connect the image of the Cave to the preceding images of the Sun-Good and the Divided Line (517ab), it is both legitimate and useful to discuss these central images together. The Sun-Good analogy adumbrates a cosmology, the Divided Line defines a basic ontological taxonomy coordinate with that of a basic psycho-epistemology, and the Cave Allegory relates all of this to human life as normally experienced. However, we are meant to see an especially close connection between the first two images (the second begins as but a refinement of the first; 509d), and thus appreciate the appropriateness of their being set apart from the other by the division between the books. Book Seven, then, begins with our being invited to contemplate still a third image, one which will portray "our nature in its education [*paideia*] and lack of education" (514a). The resulting Cave Allegory not only depicts the natural day-to-day environment of all human souls, the *study* of it initiates one's *descent* back down to actual political life (a "return" which becomes fully evident only in Book Eight; cf. 516e). But all three images must be integrated with the *non*-imagistic ontic-epistemic taxonomy expressed in the Proportion (at 533e–a). The ability to do so concretely, however, presumes the philosophical education described in the interval (521d–533d).[14]

Both the "Visible Region" (*horatos topos*) ruled by the Sun and the "Intelligible Region" (*noētos topos*) ruled by the Good must themselves be understood in terms of *forms* (*eidē*; 509d, 511a). Noting this is sufficient for rejecting some if not most of the common interpretations of Plato's supposed "theory of forms" (e.g., that forms are to be understood as "ideals", or equated with what modern philosophers call 'universals'[15]). The former region is the domain of the "many things" and is thus what opinion pertains to (cf. 476c–479e); the latter, of all the singular beings instantiated by these various "many's", and thus what intellection and knowledge pertain to (507b, 534a). And much as we need to distinguish sight itself (what sight *is*) from the *power* of sight (which is something variable from person to person and time to time) as well as from actual seeing, so we need to distinguish intellect (its essential elements and activities) from both (variable) intelligence and actual knowing.

However, to get beyond the sketchy account of the Good provided by analogizing from its "offspring" the Sun, one must also bear in mind certain well-known facts, as well as ask some obvious questions. We know, for example, that staring continuously at the sun is not only *painful* (cf. 515c–e, 518a, 532bc), but leads to permanent blindness (the total *loss* of vision). And consequently, that the sun is best studied indirectly: in reflections, or through clouds which dampen its power; in shadows which reveal its absence; in its effects on other things

Pride and Prejudice

(e.g., on plants, one's own skin, dyed cloth, and so on). As for the midday sun itself, we settle for occasional glances at it. What might all this suggest about the Good? Moreover, we know that the eye cannot see itself except by reflection in mirrors and other smooth surfaces (cf. 510a, 596d–e). What might this imply about the mind? We are explicitly told that the sun is somehow responsible for both the succession of seasons and the repetition of the years (516b). Is there anything comparable due to the Good (cf. 619c–d)? And we are reminded that the sun is the "finest" light, but that there *are* inferior kinds of light, presumably related to it somehow (e.g., fire, moon, stars). Are there such analogues with respect to the Good? Pleasure, for example, or reputation? And what, if anything, is to be made of the fact that the sun is a source of heat as well as a source of light (cf. 380e)?

In any case, trying to form a clearer idea of the Good may well entail a full explication of the analogy between it and the sun – which requires attending to *all* references to the sun itself (*hēlios*; e.g., 422c, 473e, 515e, 517b, 532a, 596e; cf. 498a, 556d), to the "sun's heat" (*heilēsis*; 380e, 404b), and to "judged by sunlight" (thus "tested", "distinct", "unmixed", "pure"; *heilikrinēs*; e.g., 478d, 479d, 549b) – with a special concern to see both knowledge and truth as being each in its own way "good-formed" (or "good-like"; *agatho-eidē*, 509a), taking one's guidance from the sense in which sight and light are variously "sun-formed" (or "sun-like", *hēlio-eidē*) – as the *eye* is also said to be (508b), again implying something analogous about the *mind*. Suffice it to say, these are matters hard to grasp. And lest one underestimate the difficulty of comprehending it all, the philosopher's explicit schedule for the education of the guardians, who are not expected to see the Good itself before the age of fifty (and then only if they have lived right and are "in every way best in everything"; 540a), should serve as fair warning (cf. 517bc).

The discussion of the proportionally Divided Line reminds us that it is itself but a perceptible *image* of something that we are to intellect. It is not used, however, the way geometers use images – for the problem it illustrates is *not* about *lines*. The relationships that it posits among the four ontological categories (to which correspond four psycho-epistemological categories, or "affections" [*pathēmata*] of the soul; 511de) are all based on one's understanding of the relationship of dependence between images and the things of which they are images, that is, between "likeness" and "likened" (*homoiōthen, hōmoiōthē*; 510a). This relationship is most readily understood with reference to the visible realm (e.g., a man and his shadow, or his reflection in a mirror). There is a *kind* of reality to, and thus truth about, such two-dimensional shadows and reflections; their existence, however, is clearly dependent upon something "more real", more "substantial": the three-dimensional solid that casts them (though only in suitably lighted circumstances, we should not forget; 507de). This, Sokrates contends, is the nature of the relationship that pertains to *all* unequal segments of the line.[16] The relative length of each segment represents something intelligible but imperceptible, namely, the degree to which it partakes of truth (510a – the precise ratio relating the segments is left indefinite, as establishing it, he observes later, would involve much longer arguments; 534a). Thus, the man who sees his image in a mirror (the very epitome of mere appearance) must think himself as, likewise, but an image of something still higher and more real, whose mode of being is represented by the longest segment.

And thus, it would be a complete mistake to imagine this higher thing – call it, provisionally, a *form* – as simply a "beautified" or "purified" or "idealized" version of something perceptible (rather as the perfect circle of the geometer's imagination stands to the actual circles he might draw). Nor is it something *common* to all particular manifestations of it (something "universal"). For these notions are *not at all* analogous to the relationship between a single man and the many images he casts, that practically infinite multiplicity of two-dimensional "looks", his countless succession of shadows and reflections. Clearly, then, the *eidos* of human being is not something that can be "pictured", any more than can one's own *idea* of human nature; it can only be intellected. Or, to take a simpler example, consider one's idea of *dog*: a single conception that accommodates all actual, perceptible dogs of whatever age, size, sex, breed, colour, texture, smell, sound, mode of behaviour, and so on. Whatever one perceives or otherwise learns about dogs is integrated into one's idea of dog (or "doghood"). And that idea will be more or less *true* as it corresponds to the reality of the *eidos* of dog (cf. 380d, 544cd). Such an *eidos* is not an "abstraction" of something common to all actual dogs, past, present, and future – a sort of distilled "essence of dog", as it were. This mistaken notion results from confusing the ontological problem with the epistemological process whereby one apprehends the family of characteristics (some variable, some essential, some accidental) that one's mind synthesizes into an *idea* of dog. Rather, the relationship of a *form* to its perceptible instantiation is the *reverse* of this: the moment-by-moment existence of any actual dog must be understood as but an (ontological) abstraction of its ruling form, a panaesthetic "phantom" of its *eidos*, and no more a *complete* likeness of this form than its shadow is of it. Moreover, the relationship of the entire perceptual realm to that reality accessible only to the intellect must be understood as analogous to that between a man and his image in a mirror, or his shadow on a wall.

It is, of course, essential to notice that *whatever* the precise ratio employed in dividing and subdividing the Line, the middle two segments – the (presumably) "lower", representing perceptible objects and anything else which might cast "images" of itself; and the "higher", representing (for example) the intelligible objects and principles which mathematicians and physiologists hypothesize in order to reason out their implications – are necessarily *equal* in length. Thus we are tacitly challenged to discern some sense in which each kind of thing partakes of truth and reality to the same extent, if not in the same way. And the awkwardness of the preceding statement accentuates a curious fact about Sokrates' account of his Divided Line: he does not *name* any of his ontological categories save that represented by the shortest segment, those "least real" things he calls "images" (*eikones*). All three "higher", "more real", or "more truthful" modes of being are simply described and illustrated by example. From that, one is tempted to equate the second category (the "likened", of which images are "likenesses") with "empirical objects" ("animals ... , everything that grows, ... artefacts"; 510a). Subsequently, however, he refers to those things that cast shadows in the Cave as "phantoms" (*eidōla*, 532b; cf. 516a, 520c). Such phantoms, as noted, are *of* something still higher and more real. But his use of the term 'phantom' throughout the dialogue is not consistent with his confining the term to empirical – that is, directly perceptible – things. For instance, he refers to the lie in speech as but a phantom of the "true lie" in the soul about the things that are (382b). And similarly, the principle of political justice of the city in *logos* is referred to "as a kind of phantom of justice" (443c) – not so surprising, perhaps, since it was found in a dark and "overshadowed" place (432c). He speaks of a phantom of the Good (534c), but also of a phantom pleasure (586b, 587c, d). And the poet-as-imitator is charged with being no more than a maker of phantoms (598b, 599a, 599d, 600e, 601b, 605bc).

To be sure, such things all exist within the perceptible realm, but neither they nor their "reflections" in and "shadows" on other things

The War Lover

are necessarily themselves directly perceptible. Recurring to the first example, one does not *perceive* the lie itself in speech, but only the sounds or sights used to express it; recognizing a lie as a *lie* can be done only by the intellect. Might there be, then, two kinds of phantoms of reality, perceptible ones (*aisthēta eidōla*, represented by the second line segment) and intelligible ones to which hypothetical reasoning pertains (*noēta eidōla*, represented by the third, and equally long segment)? No other general term is ever suggested for the things which, say, a geometrician grasps with thought and then reasons about, using perceptible illustrations only as aids to his thinking (e.g., "perfect" squares, triangles, circles, lines, and points). Nor for the various ideas of justice particular lawgivers conceive, in light of which they fashion their respective codes of law, as Solon did for Athens and Lykourgos for Sparta (599de). Mistaking such *eidola* of justice for justice itself may result in a kind of parochial "idolatry", not unlike that of worshipping as gods what are at best mere statues of gods. In this connection, note especially Sokrates' reference to contesting in court over "shadows of the just *or* over the statues (*agalmata*) which cast shadows", and the special difficulty one faces in having to dispute about such things with those who have not seen justice itself (517de; this, incidentally, is the sole use of *agalma* in the dialogue; cf. 514b-a).

Initially, with the two upper segments of the Line representing subdivisions of the intelligible region, we are invited to regard both kinds of objects as "intelligibles" (*noēta*; cf. 510b, 511b), much as both dogs and their shadows are "sensibles" (or "perceptibles", *aisthēta*; cf. 507c, 511c, 529b). But according to Glaukon's exposition of Sokrates' imagery, which the philosopher approves as "quite sufficient" (*hikanōtata*), the objects of mathematical thinking (based as they are on "suppositions", *hypotheseis*) are not truly intelligible in themselves, but become such only if "given a beginning [or, foundation; *archē*]" (511d). As for these *archai*, which must be counted among those things represented by the longest line segment as being most real and true – "that which *logos* itself grasps with the power of dialectic, ... the non-hypothesized beginning of the whole" (511b) – one presumes this highest, and it would seem the only *fully* intelligible class of "intelligibles", to be that of the *forms* (*eidē*), and perhaps of the Good itself (although the Good is said to be the *source* of all existence and being [*to einai kai tēn ousian*], but "beyond Being in dignity and power"; 509b; but cf. 379b, 608e). The account of these highest ruling powers, however, actually begins where the guardians' education begins: with a correct account of the gods (377e–383c; cf. 508a, 517c). And it is not completed until the philosopher presents his critique of poetry, and "what imitation in general is" (595c ff).

Unlike the four ontological categories, the corresponding psycho-epistemological categories – the four distinct kinds of *pathēmata* that come to be in the soul's rational parts – *are* all given names. But, alas, not always the *same* names. This would seem an open invitation to endless eristical wrangling. When they are first introduced in conjunction with the Divided Line, we are told to relate "intellection" (*noēsis*) to the longest and highest segment; "thought" (*dianoia*) to the second; "trust" (or "faith", *pistis*) to the third; and "imagination" (*eikasia*) to the last (511de). And after discussing the five mathematical disciplines that, properly studied, help turn the soul around (allowing it to proceed dialectically upward to the first causes of things, the *archai*, presumably forms), Sokrates reaffirms that these lower, preparatory *mathemata* epitomize "thought", being "brighter than opinion but dimmer than knowledge [*epistēmē*]" (533d; cf. 508e, 510d). He immediately, however, depreciates the importance of "disputing about a name" when considering such great matters, thereby discounting in advance merely eristical objections, tacitly exhorting us to concentrate instead on the phenomena themselves. Whereupon he suggests it is acceptable, "just as before [!], to call the first and longest part, '*knowledge*', the second '*thought*', the third '*trust*', and the fourth '*imagination*'; and the latter two taken together '*opinion*', and the former two '*intellection*' (533ea). Having further stipulated that opinion has to do with Becoming (*genesis*) and intellection with Being (*ousia*), he establishes a basic proportion among these eight things: as Being is to Becoming, so are Intellection to Opinion, Knowledge to Trust, and Thought to Imagination (534a) – thereby conveying in non-imagistic fashion some of what was earlier imparted through the image of the Divided Line.[17]

As to quite *how* the *pathēmata* relate to the ontological categories, those four distinct modes of Being and degrees of Reality and Truth, suffice it to say that this is *not* the straightforward matter the Line image might at first seem to suggest. For while it makes sense to speak of "intellecting" the forms, or of "thinking" one's way through mathematical problems, it is not plausible to suggest that an analogous relationship obtains between imagination (*eikasia*) and perceptible images (*eikones*), much less between trust and perceptible phantoms. We don't apprehend shadows on walls and reflections in mirrors by means of our imagination. We perceive them just as we perceive the more substantial objects that cause them. It is tempting to suggest that the things "pictured" in one's imagination none the less have the same ontological status as those perceptible images, but this is not obviously so. For while the physics of light ensures that perceived images are always less distinct than the objects which cast them, what one imagines is *not* always less clear than what one perceives (cf. 509de), nor is it always less true (cf. 510a). It may be so in imagining an absent friend, but what about those perfect mathematical objects imagined in geometrical reasoning? Or perhaps more to the point, what about the city in *logos*? Or Sokrates' god-like conception of a perfected philosopher (487a; cf. 383c, 589cd, 611e, 613ab)? Indeed, is not the imagination involved in both conceiving and understanding the Divided Line itself? After all, Sokrates merely described such a line: he did not actually draw it.

Nor is the relationship between trust and things perceived analogous to that between intellection and intelligibles.[18] It would seem that trust (*pistis*) must pertain to perception as such: we necessarily have faith that when we perceive whatever – be it shadow or substance, reflection or illusion – we do in fact perceive *something*. We cannot offer ourselves an explanation of *why* a stick placed in water merely *appears* to bend without trusting implicitly that we do see what we see. Thus, recognizing the fallibility of perception as a means of disclosing Reality none the less presupposes trusting perception as revealing the (sometimes contradictory) *appearance* of Reality. And likewise we implicitly trust in our ability to recognize an image as an image; for it is only thereby that we distinguish between actually perceiving and merely imagining (or dreaming) perceptible things – which may be why the Line obliges us to regard trust as of higher standing than imagination. And although we do not, indeed cannot, trust implicitly in all opinions (any more than we can all perceptions), we must and do rely on many opinions, while trusting in our ability to recognize grounds for doubting some, much as we trust in our ability to distinguish opinion from knowledge (always in principle, and often in practice; cf. 601e). Thus, it is in the nature of trust to be a variable thing: each of us trusts only to the extent we believe it warranted, and our speech about it reflects that fact (cf. 368ab, 439e, 442de). Furthermore, we trust in there being reasons why people hold the opinions they do, including many that are false, while recognizing that the appropriateness with which they bestow their trust is a major respect in which people differ:

some are "too trusting", while others are mistrustful to a fault (cf. 409a–d). Speaking more broadly, the fact that we feel at home in the perceptible world testifies to the power of trust. We encounter novelties and contradictions in our workaday life, but always within an embracing framework of familiar experience normally treated as unproblematic. And since our trust in this world is repaid daily in terms of survival (at the least), we may see it as a self-sustaining power whereby we resist universal doubt (a disposition that would leave one believing nothing, and practically paralysed).

As noted, though, anomalies do arise in this familiar world: we encounter novelties, but, even more commonly, contradictions in both perceptions and opinions. Dealing with them is the normal work of thought (*dianoia*). Out of this ordinary thinking grow all the disciplines, the various arts and sciences that serve our common needs and wants, and through which natural thinking becomes systematic, or methodical (to the point that certain methods of technical thinking become paradigms of thinking *per se*, e.g., geometry). Through thinking, we discover objects of thought ("intelligibles", *noēta*) whose relative clarity illuminates the relative obscurity of perceptible things; whatever the limitations inherent in its first principles, geometry proves to us the existence of intelligibles, and hence obliges us to recognize the existence of an intelligible realm.

But because the normal work of thought is to remedy the defects of the perceptual realm – the various problems and confusions that arise naturally in the course of practical life – the mind is normally turned towards that realm. Thus the domains of trust and thought are coextensive (and thus the line segments that represent them are of equal length). Thought is perpetually engaged, then, in providing intelligible foundations for the perceptual realm, foundations whose actual status is that of hypotheses. The various *technae* that employ hypothetical thinking necessarily reason "downwards", back down towards the perceived world they are meant to explain and manipulate. And so far as their conclusions square with our experience of that world, we continue to accept the hypotheses upon which they are based (an acceptance that rests ultimately on our trust in our own powers, including the evidence of our senses; cf. 603a). This suffices for all practical purposes, of course, and it is the best one can do given that orientation. But such thinking remains Cave-bound, and can never be intellectually satisfying, for it can never truly clarify its own obscure beginnings. It renders the perceptual world intelligible, but without giving an intelligible account of intelligibility. And thus intelligibility remains circumscribed by unintelligibility. Transcending the limitations of such dianoetic thinking is the task of dialectical thinking that culminates in knowledge (*epistēmē*), a kind of thinking that can lead one out of one's Cave to a fully intelligible world.[19]

If we provisionally equate the Cave with the perceptual realm (as suggested by Sokrates' likening its fire to the sun; 517b, 529cd), the dialogue as a whole suggests that this realm as such – indeed the entirety of political life – is not intelligible on its own terms, and perhaps not *fully* intelligible *at all* (cf. 529bc, 530e). One can labour to clarify one's opinions about the many opinable things encountered there, but this activity, if tenaciously pursued, ends only in "perplexity" (*aporia*; cf. 515b, 556d, 405b). Granted, well-considered opinions are usually sufficient for everyday practicalities, given an awareness that they are no more than that (and thus a healthy respect for the mysterious and unforeseen; cf. 516cd, 584d–a). But so long as discussion remains bounded by ordinary observation of the world, it necessarily will also remain inconclusive, plagued by the impossibility of reconciling the conflicting manyness of things: the plural manifestations of virtually every thing and every quality and relationship, compounded by the plurality of (possibly incommensurate) perspectives from which things are viewed.

The only hope of escaping this indeterminate (and intellectually unsatisfying) situation entails cutting loose from the familiar world and its familiar modes of thinking, letting speculation range in a different direction. For example, one might leave off counting things in order to reflect back on counting itself – what counting (or number) *is*, and what counting presumes (525d). And what is that? A self-ordering sequence of numbers, all made up of perfectly homogeneous "units" having no nature other than to *be*, with which we can analogize whatever we count? In counting, we tacitly acknowledge the "oneness" of each instance of that which we count; having recognized something as an instance of whatever, we "abstract" from all of its identifying characteristics everything but its oneness. We thereby acknowledge only that it too *is*, that it too in some sense reflects Being, however partially, imperfectly, and temporarily. But what about the numbers themselves that constitute this ordered sequence, each being "one more" than another (thus all seemingly composed of "ones")? How is it that in holding up, say, three fingers – a liberating experience available even to someone shackled in a Cave (514a, 523c) – the observer confronts simultaneously three "ones" and one "three"?[20] (The dialogue's countless triads, triplets, trios, and trinities remind us of the oneness of three itself, ... as does our language, apparently.) Whoever can grasp the nature of three should be the better prepared to grasp the form of justice, how it too is simultaneously one thing and three things, either in the sense made explicit by Sokrates (where in being just, a city or a soul is necessarily also wise, courageous, and moderate; 433a–d, 441d–c); or in the sense implicit in his usage (whereby the principle of each thing performing well its own work is united in a single "solid" idea with those other facets of justice having to do with regard for the truth and the recognition of one's debts). In any case, to think about the eternal order of numbers redirects the soul from the perceptible realm of perishable things we count, the realm of Becoming, to the intelligible realm of eternal Being.

But if in the more immediate, practical sense the Cave is everyday political life, an existence based on trust in perception and opinion, in a more profound sense the Cave is the body, from which the divine part of the soul – that which is pure soul – longs to escape (611e). For it is the Cave of the Body that is shackled, and hence shackles us, to the Cave of the City (514a). All of us are born, and most of us live out our lives, preoccupied with bodies, our own and other people's: with bodily health, strength, beauty, and pleasure. And as noted, ordinary science and technical knowledge are aimed primarily at working effects on bodies in general, the better to cater to those bodies most people care most about. Sensation and perception guide thought, but our sense organs are bodily instruments that exist first of all to serve the needs and wants of the body, not those of the mind. And they mislead us most of all about bodies, about the nature of matter, enticing us to regard it as something solid, real, and literally *elemental* – and, as such, the basis of whatever is true about our world. More than anything else, it is this naïve trust in the fundamental reality of matter that closes us off from true reality.[21] Man's experience of his own embodiment suggests that it is embodiment *per se* (as well as the individuation that necessarily results) that is the root of what is called evil, or bad (cf. 611bc) – something confined to the perceptual realm, it should be noted: geometers *qua* geometers need never address the problem of evil, which fact may itself indicate the inadequacy of purely mathematical thought for understanding human life in its fulness.

Be that as it may, Sokrates warns that it is especially pleasures of the body which attach the soul to the realm of Becoming, and deflect its vision downwards (519ab; cf. 586a–b). This would seem to imply that the relationship between philosophy and asceticism is not merely incidental, but essential.[22] Still, however rigorous one's mastery of the carnal pleasures, the truth remains that we are each and all mortal individuals – embodied souls, not pure soul – and are thus incapable of dwelling exclusively in the intelligible realm, with minds engaged in nothing but contemplation of the eternal forms of Being (cf. 500b–d, 519c). Time and again, various facets of bodily necessity (to say nothing of an inescapable dependence on acquiring ever more refined and complete perceptual evidence) draw the philosopher back down to his bodily determined place in some Cave of political life (516e), compelling him to dwell at least part-time among the chronically squabbling, opinionated multitude. Thus required by nature to return and become rehabituated to the dusky, dreamy world constituted by the more or less common consciousness of its permanent residents, he will eventually understand it, truly understand it, as no mere Cave-dweller ever can (517b–d, 520b–c). So, to combine philosophy with the highest kind of political life, that of a kingly man, king of oneself, with an inner regime patterned after that laid up in heaven (580bc, 592b) – to live as a *political* philosopher, a philosopher king – is the best that human conditions allow. In actual practice, the philosophical life consists of a perpetual commuting between the Visible and the Intelligible realms: conveyed by the power of dialectic from the subterranean conditions of ordinary human existence to a higher world accessible only through the rational imagination (532b), and back down again to where one's body may be muted by rest and material nourishment, where one's spirit may be recreated, and one's mind supplied with fresh food for thought.

Having portrayed the human intellectual condition in terms of the Cave Allegory; and having confirmed that their task as founders of the city in *logos* is "to compel the best natures to go to the study previously said to be the greatest to see the Good [*idein to agathon*] and to ascend that ascent [*anabēnai ekeinēn tēn anabasin*]" out of the Cave, "and when they have ascended and seen sufficiently", to compel them to return again to the Cave, there to rule as clear-sighted, fully awake kings (519cd ff) – that done, Sokrates leads Glaukon in a consideration of the "way such [philosophical rulers] will come into being and how

Pride and Prejudice

one will lead them up to the light, just as some are said to have gone from Hades up to the gods" (521c; cf. 516d). In his account of what is intended to be truly (and literally) a *revolutionary* education (cf. 518d, 532b), we are to see the means whereby the eristical lover of victory may be transmuted into a dialectical lover of wisdom, and a warlover such as Er be reborn as a wisdomlover (cf. 614b ff). The account virtually begins with Sokrates' reminder of the *necessity* that candidates for such an education be "champions of war when they are young" (521d).

The sequence of five studies, however, is *not* simply and exclusively an *anabasis* ("ascent"), although rhetorically that is the dominant impression created. Partly this is a carry-over from the Cave Allegory, wherein the release from bonds is followed by a slow, laborious, difficult, step-by-step ascent from the dim firelit twilight of Becoming to the full glaring daylight of Being (517b). This impression is reinforced by the natural pedagogic progression of the studies themselves: one *must* learn arithmetic before plane geometry (cf. 522c), that before solid geometry, that before astronomy (or more generally, kinematics, "solids in motion"[23]), and finally harmony (the study of which originates in the cordant and discordant sounds made by solids in motion, e.g., plucked strings). This is the order in which they are learned in the Cave, and for good reason (cf. 587d). While Sokrates emphasizes that each would be studied in an unconventional way (primarily for the sake of knowing, rather than doing or using – cf. 525c-d, 527ab, 530bc), this does not affect the natural relationships of the studies themselves. Moreover, contemplation of the heavens and Nature's manifold harmonies can hardly fail to arouse a person's curiosity, and deepen a sense of wonder about the world and one's place in it (cf. 604bc, 608cd).

But the progression of study from arithmetic to harmony doesn't bring one ever closer to Being, nor is it said to. The whole curriculum is described, rather, as a "prelude" (*prooimia*) to *dialectics*, a training all the more useful if inquiry into these several subjects culminates in an understanding of "their community and kinship with one another" (531cd; cf. 534e, 536d, 537bc). Indeed, there are several indications that it is the *first* subject, the study of number (of the One and the Many), that best prepares a person to grasp Being as such and its relationship to Becoming. The philosopher spends almost as much time discussing arithmetic as the other four subjects put together, and in the midst of doing so gives his fullest exposition of the relation be-

The War Lover

tween perception and intellection (523a–525a). Moreover, when he speaks of those subjects which do lay hold of *something* of what *is*, he mentions "geometry and the arts *following* on it", adding that of themselves, however, these arts but dream about what is (533b). We should notice that arithmetic is exempt from this qualification.

So, while this (pre)philosophical education is in one sense an *anabasis* from the simple contemplation of number to a mastery of dialectics, in another sense it is a *katabasis, a descent* from Being (immanent in the timeless, motionless, harmonious perfection of numbers) back to the realm of Becoming: to the perceptible world of generation and decay, of "solids in motion" and sounds both harmonious and not. A descent, that is, back down into one or another Cave of actual political life. And thus it returns us to those four archetypal forms of variously unjust regimes that were to be spoken of at the beginning of Book Five before, that is, the Revolt of the Auxiliaries compelled the philosopher to turn away from such all-too-human regimes, and look first to providing a fuller account of erotic matters (culminating in his triad of erotic images that justify the philosophical life, and render ordinary life intelligible). A kind of confirmation that progression through the *mathēmata* is simultaneously a descent back to the turbulent realm of political actuality is provided by the repeated references to war (e.g., 522e, 525b,c, 526d, 527d), by the insistence that the curriculum selected "mustn't be useless to warlike men" (521d), and by the reaffirmation that the guardian being so trained "is both warrior and philosopher" (525b).

The various studies, properly pursued, facilitate that "turning around" (*periagōgē*) from the domain of dark shadows to the source of light. The way they are ordinarily pursued, however, with one eye on utility and the other on empirical confirmation (on "saving the appearances", to use the traditional expression), implicitly requires that their practitioners be oriented towards the perceptual realm, and hence remain captivated by Becoming – as the very names 'geometry' ("earth-measuring") and 'astronomy' ("star-classifying") remind us. For example, people normally study number and calculation for the sake of commerce or other technical applications, and not for the purpose of redirecting the soul through the purely intellectual contemplation of the nature of numbers themselves (525c; cf. 526d–e, 529c–e, 531bc). Properly studied, however, the mathematical sciences can introduce a suitable student to the intelligible realm, purifying and strengthening the instrument of soul (*organon psychēs*) whereby purely intelligible truth can be grasped (527de).

But it is genuine philosophizing that is itself the "upward way" (*epanodos*) to what *is* (521c, 532b). And the "method" of true philosophy is dialectics (533c–d). Only through skill in *dialektikē* does one acquire the power to both give and receive a rational account of what can be known, this being the means whereby human beings can pool their variously inadequate intellectual resources, and so reject or ratify, refine and amplify each other's efforts, and share in the common good – the knowledge – that results. Proceeding purely through *logos*, having "released oneself" from dependence upon the senses (537d; cf. 582d), one mates one's mind with what can only be intellected, not seen (531e–b; cf. 511bc). The method is *demonstrated* before it is announced, however, for it is on display throughout the dialogue, but especially in the discussion of the five *mathēmata* that would best prepare one for acquiring the dialectical art. Notice how that discussion begins, with Sokrates concerned to make plain his "opinion": "Of that which I distinguish [*diairoumai*] for myself as leading or not [leading] to what we were speaking about, become a fellow-observer and concur or dissent, in order that we may see more clearly whether that which I divine is so" (523a). And notice especially the role of various kinds of *mistakes* in his and Glaukon's arriving at a correct understanding of this curriculum (cf. 523b, 524de, 526de, 527d–b, 528e–c). Perhaps more puzzling are the repeated references to laughing and what is laughable ("ridiculous"; 525d, 527a, 528d, 529ea, 531a: cf. 388ea, 451a–b, 452d, 604bc, 606c). In any event, the ultimate goal of dialectical thought is a comprehensive overview (*synopsis*) of the whole world. Only he who can integrate *everything* – perceptible images and things, intelligible phantoms and forms – and not merely as so many formal categories, but in all their heterogeneous substantiality – into a single, coherent synoptic view is a dialectician. And he who can't, isn't (537c).

However, precisely because exercising the great power of dialectics presumes the recognition of the Cave for what it is, and entails the rejection of all conventional restraints on thought and a questioning of all opinions and convictions, even those most sacred and salutary – thereby imparting a kind of "lawlessness" (*paranomia*) to its practitioners (537e; cf. 539a) – because, that is, of its disintegrating effect on the foundation of everyday life, dialectics is inherently a very dangerous power (cf. 608e). The creation of an adequate synoptic account necessarily involves the destruction of inadequate accounts; indeed, their destructibility is what proves them inadequate. But as it is easier to destroy than to create, the destructive power of dialectics comes more readily, hence sooner and to more people, than does the power of dialectical re-creation. Not able, or not yet able, to replace what they destroy with something more solid, novice "dialecticians" are often left with nothing but their vanity and taste for pleasure. Therein lies the danger to oneself, to one's polity, and to philosophy (538c–539c). And so the introduction of dialectics is properly confined to natures who have become sufficiently serious and mature, hence stable and orderly, to be trusted to exercise this power responsibly right from their first acquisition of any part of it (539c–d). But stability and orderliness, seriousness and maturity are not themselves the qualities of soul that constitute the potential for dialectical *achievement*. One must have, along with a multiplicity of intellectual talents, an enormous, overwhelming drive to excel and succeed, such as can come only from greatness of spirit. Ultimately, the full power of dialectics is reserved by nature for that select few who by virtue of mind and spirit are truly capable of self-rule, of being "most kingly and a king over oneself" (580bc).

It is the very *power* of dialectics, however, that makes it so attractive to a great-spirited lover of victory. For a skilled dialectician can easily defeat opponents in argument should he wish to – and any timocrat worthy of the name could only wish to. Given his naturally eristical inclinations, a timocrat is not to be trusted with such power unless and until he has been turned towards Being, and has thus turned his back on the realm where ephemeral victories over merely human opponents are won and admired. Virtually by definition, the *honour*-loving timocrat is incapable of this. Incapable of renouncing the means of satisfying his deepest desire, he is doomed like almost everyone else to remain a perpetual prisoner of his Cave, shackled by love and duty. But as has been noted and discussed in the preceding chapters, the *victory*-loving timocrat, free to choose among whatever challenges appeal to him, has a potential for independence and self-command.[24] His primary love, unlike that of his honour-loving brother, does not wed him to the crowd. He has only to see the pursuit of wisdom as the greatest of contests, and the self-sufficiency of philosophy as

Pride and Prejudice

the most powerful, masterful, free, and beautiful of lives, and he is thereby poised to be turned around.

The pre-dialectical curriculum is for him, designed to do just that.

Epilogue

On Reading Plato's Republic

When I was a boy, there was a program on television called *The Naked City*. As have so many of like genre since, it garnished its viewers' humdrum existence with a weekly dose of vicarious adventure, usually some dark and violent drama set against the seamy side of metropolitan life. The most memorable feature of the series – its aural logo, as it were – was a *basso profondo* narrator who concluded each episode by intoning something to the effect that 'there are seven million stories in the naked city: this has been one of them.'

With similar allowance made for poetic hyperbole, I might say as much for Plato's *Politeia* in relation to the particular interpretation of it offered here. I observed at the outset of this study that each reading of a dialogue is a personal encounter with the text, guided by one's penultimate purpose of reconstituting for oneself the author's own understanding of it. Of course, what actually results from all such efforts are but so many interpretations, more or less adequate in proportion to the interpreter's present ability to imitate Plato. And while most of the countless readings of this dialogue that have occurred over the centuries are apt to be as undistinguished as the vast majority of those 'seven million stories' that people the naked city, I evidently hope and believe that mine is one worth retelling.

The *Republic* is a labyrinthine book, and a three-dimensional one at that. I have endeavoured to lay bare, partially at least, a deeper level of teaching than is usually to be found in textbook accounts of "Plato's philosophy". I have not, to my own mind, answered any important questions with finality; all my conclusions are rendered provisional by their pointing beyond themselves to still more questions, the whole perplexing array originating with that seemingly simple and innocent,

Epilogue

yet in truth dangerous and most comprehensive question: what is justice? I fancy I know more about the dialogue than I've made explicit, however, and have tried to indicate – but without spoiling the adventure for those for whom mere hints are sufficient – lines of investigation that I already have reason to believe are worth exploring. Indeed, only because doing so gives access to even more interesting, profounder, more challenging puzzles and mysteries can one justify partially revealing what Plato so artfully concealed. Some of my rhetorical questions and other enigmatic musings are meant to serve this philosophical purpose, although more often I have been content to provide conjunctions of textual references that I hope others will find as intriguing as I did upon first juxtaposing them. These numbers point to what I think of as subterranean stories: there are surely not seven million of them, or even 729, but I would imagine there are enough to occupy a person for the better part of his life.

This brings me to a final reflection. While I naturally would prefer that each and every reader who labours this far finds that it has been worth his while, in writing this book I have had in mind especially younger readers. Not that it is a book for beginners – quite the contrary: it presupposes some considerable first-hand acquaintance with the *Republic*, and in fact its effect is bound to be proportional to the reader's antecedent familiarity with the dialogue. The essential point is that the reader who is most apt to derive real advantage from my book is one who is not so firmly wedded to a particular interpretation as to be closed to new considerations inconsonant with his prior commitments. Thus those who, like Sokrates, somehow manage to remain at heart ever "young and fair" scarcely need encouragement from me to include themselves among the book's preferred readership.

I believe that the interpretation of the dialogue that I offer here *is* a novel one – sufficiently so to justify my contributing still another testimonial to what must be the most written-about work in our philosophical tradition. And even to present my view of it in the way that, according to Wilhelm Kempff, d'Albert played the *Appassionata*: "as if all before him had been deaf to its message". But if I am right in thinking that I truly have said something new about something so old and much belaboured, my doing so has a broader significance. For it suggests that the fecundity of the *Republic* is virtually inexhaustible, that it has not been and cannot be "studied to death", and that despite its author's vitality being muffled by centuries of scholarly excrescences (cf. 611d), it will none the less reward – amply reward – any serious reader's attempt to look upon it with fresh eyes. One

The War Lover

can say of Plato's dialogues what Artur Schnabel once said of Beethoven's sonatas, that they were better than they could ever be played. Doubtless the *Politeia* still contains within it many untold stories worth telling. I hope the one that I have told inspires younger readers to set out upon a hunt for them.

Notes

PROLOGUE

1 Obviously, this statement requires some qualification. In written personal correspondence, one may both interrogate and reply, and some such arrangement may be extended even to published writings (consider, for example, the invitation Descartes included when initially – and anonymously – publishing his *Discourse on Method* part VI par. 9). Yet as a practical arrangement, this is a clumsy surrogate for the supple, immediate, and persistent questioning, and resultant clarity of understanding, which is possible in live dialogue. But the main point is that, with respect to questions addressed to them, writings seem not to be self-sufficient, but require the further intervention of their authors, who may not be, and ultimately will not be, available.

2 This discussion of the comparative advantages of written over oral speech may require some qualifications in light of modern electronic technology. I shall leave it to my readers to determine for themselves in what respects video tape recordings, for example, are akin to live oral speech, and in what akin to writings. For my own part, I remain skeptical as to their being an altogether satisfactory replacement for either books or lectures, much less for live discussion.

3 Even such a celebrated defence of freedom of publication as Milton's *Areopagitica* is carefully restricted to such views as do not challenge religio-political fundamentals:

Note to page xviii

> Yet if all cannot be of one mind – as who looks they should be? – this doubtless is more wholesome, more prudent, and more Christian: that many be tolerated rather than all compelled. I mean not tolerated popery and open superstition, which as it extirpates all religions and civil supremacies, so itself should be extirpate, provided first that all charitable and compassionate means be used to win and regain the weak and the misled: that also which is impious or evil absolutely, either against faith or manners, no law can possibly permit that intends not to unlaw itself: but those neighboring differences, or rather indifferences, are what I speak of, whether in some point of doctrine or of discipline, which though they may be many, yet need not interrupt the unity of spirit, if we could but find among us the bond of peace. (7th par. from end)

And lest the issue of censorship be thought a concern long since confined to the benighted past, thus of interest only to those desiring to understand that past (including literature produced therein), consider a report of how things stood in the former Soviet Union, from Hedrick Smith's *The Russians*:

> Nowhere else in the world is poetry accorded such religious reverence or the poet so celebrated as priest and oracle as in Russia. If ordinary people escape into alcoholism, intellectuals flee into books, especially poetry, finding there the spiritual compensation for the ennui of ordinary life. ... For daring poetry – or daring art of any kind – teeters on the line of confrontation between tyranny and talent, where censorship and creativity inevitably collide. People come to a poetry reading to see how far the poet dares defy the political laws of gravity and whether he will keep his balance on the high wire or lose it and suffer the political consequences. This becomes a cat-and-mouse game between Authority and the intelligentsia, natural enemies throughout Russian history. For Russian audiences this game provides the main source of tension and flavor and amusement in the otherwise muted and muffled Soviet cultural scene.
>
> It is, of course, an unequal game, just as it was in Pushkin's day or Dostoyevsky's, in which the state and its cultural watchdogs have the ultimate sanctions of approval or punishment and the intelligentsia can arm themselves only with wit, courage and imagination. It is a game of cunning played with ruses and subterfuges, allegories and Aesopian language, hidden meanings and significant inflections, with dramas performed one way to soothe the censors and another way to excite live audiences. (508–9)

> More than one writer observed to me, however, that it was the attractions of big royalties, large editions and big audiences, or of country dachas, and the chance to travel abroad and other perquisites – as much as censorship – that has bought off many would-be 'liberals.' Ideological stalwarts who write patriotic themes are usually the most richly rewarded. (525-7)

Similarly, imagine the current situation in Iran. Doubtless, one could find individuals there who, despite the popular atavistic fervour, still think about the abiding political and cosmological questions, and do not simply accept the regnant orthodoxies. But if they choose to speak publicly about such matters, much less commit their views to writing, one can be equally sure that they employ the greatest discretion in doing so, bridled by a quite proper concern for the present religio-political authorities.

According to David Lamb in *The Africans* the situation is not essentially different throughout most of so-called black Africa. He quotes a Somali official as typical: "Truth is whatever promotes your government. If something is not favourable to your country, then it isn't true and you should not publish falsehoods" (243). The president of that country, Mohamed Siad Barré, ostensibly in order to improve the situation of Somali women, "declared in 1975 that henceforth men and women were equal. Many Moslem scholars in Somalia protested, contending that the Koran held women inferior. Barré settled the argument by executing ten of the scholars and sentencing twenty-three others to prison for up to thirty years. The executions did not provide any new opportunities for women, but no one debates the merits of sexual equality in Somalia anymore" (41).

Indeed, innumerable reports from observers of life in many Asian, Latin American, Middle East, African, and eastern European countries confirm that the preponderance of the world's population continues to live with some considerable degree of official or quasi-official censorship of public communication, and that various kinds of persecution (ranging from social ostracism to torture and execution) remain staples of political life.

Even in the great English-speaking democracies, regimes offering unrivalled freedom of expression, it can be professionally hazardous to take issue publicly with certain fashionable causes. Tocqueville may have exaggerated to make his point (he concedes as much in advising his first English translator, "I felt it my duty to stress particularly the bad tendencies which equality may bring about in order to prevent my contemporaries surrendering to them"), but he had a point worth making:

Notes to pages xviii–xix

> It is when one comes to look into the use made of thought in the United States that one sees most clearly how far the power of the majority goes beyond all powers known to us in Europe. ...
>
> Moreover, a king's power is physical only, controlling actions but not influencing desires, whereas the majority is invested with both physical and moral authority, which acts as much upon the will as upon behavior and at the same moment prevents both the act and the desire to do it.
>
> I know no country in which, speaking generally, there is less independence of mind and true freedom of discussion than in America. (*Democracy in America* 235)

A fuller understanding of the issues involved with censorship is impossible apart from some appreciation of the inherent tension between politics and philosophy. And with respect to that matter, Leo Strauss's *Persecution and the Art of Writing* is essential reading. See also the same author's "On a Forgotten Kind of Writing" in his *What Is Political Philosophy?* 221–32.

4 Precisely because its ubiquitous official censorship was neither restrained nor intelligent, but instead capricious and often vicious to an unprecedented degree, one would hardly expect the former Soviet Union to have been distinguished by great art and literature. Even so, however, there is evidence that some of its better writers wrote with more finesse and subtlety and considered purpose than writers virtually anywhere else in the contemporary world, and that their readers read accordingly.

George Steiner, speaking of the decay of Western culture as reflected in our declining ability to read, much less write, serious books, also notes the contrast between the status of such activities in the democratic West and totalitarian East:

> Even where it has reached the public surface, through censor's oversight, from abroad, or in brief spells of bureaucratic condescension, Russian literature, from Pushkin and Turgenev to Pasternak and Solzhenitsyn, has always been *samizdat*. The cost in personal suffering, in the eradication of personal talent, has been vast; nothing can make up for the psychological hounding to destruction of a Gogol, for the liquidation of a Mandelstam. But the paradoxical gain has also been eminent. No society reads more vehemently, to none is the writer a more indispensable presence. No oppression has ever felt more threatened by the poet's image, none has ever paid to the written

Notes to page xix

word, to the text, the tribute of a more savage vigilance. ("Text and Context" in *On Difficulty and Other Essays* 6–7)

5 In this, as in most of the other devices to be catalogued, Machiavelli was most adept. Consider, for example, his account of the education of Achilles by Chiron, as well as the interpretation he placed on it (*The Prince* chap. 18). Francis Bacon seems to have devoted an entire book to this sort of thing, ironically entitled *Wisdom of the Ancients*. Moreover, as Montaigne observes, even the oldest and most familiar fables are amenable to a variety of allegorical interpretations: "Most of Aesop's Fables have many meanings and interpretations. Those who take them allegorically choose some aspect that squares with the fables, but for the most part this is only the first and superficial aspect; there are others more living, more essential and internal, to which they have not known how to penetrate; this is how I read them" (*Essays* II 10 in Donald M. Frame's translation in *The Complete Essays of Montaigne* 298).

In the Preface that Pope supplied to his translation of Homer's *Iliad*, he has this to say à propos of the *"allegorical fable"*:

> If we reflect upon those innumerable knowledges, those secrets of nature and physical philosophy, which Homer is generally supposed to have wrapped up in his *allegories*, what a new and ample scene of wonder may this consideration afford us? How fertile will that imagination appear, which was able to clothe all the properties of elements, the qualifications of the mind, the virtues and vices, in forms and persons; and to introduce them into actions agreeable to the nature of the things they shadowed? This is a field in which no succeeding poets could dispute with Homer; and whatever commendations have been allowed them on this head, are by no means for their invention in having enlarged his circle. ...

With respect to parable and allegory, it is also worth bearing in mind the observation of Erasmus: "Allegory not infrequently results in enigma. Nor will that be unfortunate, if you are speaking to the learned, or if you are writing. ... For things should not be so written that every-one perceives, but rather so that they are compelled to investigate certain things and learn" (*Opera omnia 1* 19 as quoted by Joel Altman in *The Tudor Play of Mind* 206).

6 It is useful in reading political histories, including Hobbes's own *Behemoth*, to consider the several shrewd observations about the reading and writing

of history that he incorporated in the prefatory material to his translation of Thucydides (who, according to Hobbes, is to be generally acknowledged the "most politic historiographer that ever writ"). Having denominated "history and civil knowledge" as "that kind of learning which best deserveth the pains and hours of great persons", Hobbes emphasizes the advantages of presenting a political teaching in the form of a history (as opposed to, say, a treatise):

> [Thucydides] filleth his narrations with that choice of matter, and ordereth them with that judgment, and with such perspicuity and efficacy expresseth himself, that, as Plutarch saith, he maketh his auditor a spectator. ... So that look how much a man of understanding might have added to his experience, if he had then lived a beholder of their proceedings, and familiar with the men and business of the time: so much almost may he profit now, by attentive reading of the same here written. He may from the narrations draw out lessons to himself, and of himself be able to trace the drifts and counsels of the actors to their seat.
>
> Digressions for instruction's cause, and other such open conveyances of precepts, (which is the philosopher's part), [Thucydides] never useth; as having so clearly set before men's eyes the ways and events of good and evil counsels, that the narration itself doth secretly instruct the reader, and more effectually than can possibly be done by precept.

"More effectually", inasmuch as what a person discovers for himself makes a deeper and more lasting impression than what he is told. As Toqueville put it: "The books that have made men reflect the most and have had the most influence on their opinions and actions are not those in which the author has sought to tell them dogmatically what is suitable to think, but those in which he has set their minds on the road leading to truths and has made them find these truths for themselves" (letter to Corcelle dated 17 September 1853).

Thus, for both rhetorical and pedagogical reasons, an author with something important to say may prefer a form of writing, such as an artfully constructed historical – or apparently historical – narration, which stimulates this self-teaching. For, as Lord Bolingbroke observes, "history, true or false, speaks to our passions. ... " He goes on to contend that history, rightly used,

> is philosophy teaching by examples. We need but cast our eyes on the world, and we shall see the daily force of example: we need but turn

them inward, and we shall soon discover why example has this force. ... Such is the imperfection of human understanding, such is the frail temper of our minds, that abstract or general propositions, though ever so true, appear obscure or doubtful to us very often, till they are explained by examples; and that the wisest lessons in favor of virtue go but a little way to convince the judgment, and determine the will, unless they are enforced by the same means; and we are obliged to apply to ourselves what we see happen to other men.
(*Letters on the Study and Use of History* no. 2 in Isaac Kramnick, ed. *Lord Bolingbroke: Historical Writings* 8–9)

The ranks of those who have subordinated strictly factual reporting to a higher purpose include some of our greatest "historians", beginning with Herodotus; cf. Seth Benardete *Herodotean Inquiries* 6.

Fully examining the uses and abuses of history is a book unto itself, and would be germane to much literature besides scholarly histories. With such a larger conception of history in mind, I suspect that the one who has exploited it best is Shakespeare. In reading him, however, I take for granted the view of John Vyvyan: "The Renaissance was an age of mysterious philosophies; and it delighted to express them in a veiled way, so that they should be published and not published. ... At least it would be unwise to assume, in studying Shakespeare, that what shows on the surface is all that he intends" (*Shakespeare and Platonic Beauty* 14).

7 Machiavelli provides a fertile source of both duplicitous chapter titles and historical examples which, when carefully considered, actually illustrate something other than he suggests they do. As instances of the former, I would submit chap. 4 of *The Prince* and chap. 27 of Book I of *The Discourses*; and of the latter, the example of David and Saul (*The Prince* chap. 13). Nor can one rely upon the individual titles of Bacon's *Essays* to indicate where to find his most important – much less, his complete – thoughts on a titled subject. For example, compare what is said about atheism in the essay of that name with what is said about it in "On Superstition". In his *Joseph Andrews*, Fielding includes a serio-comic discussion of the "secret" and "mysterious" art of dividing one's work into books and chapters, complete with inscriptions indicating each chapter's contents: "And in these inscriptions, I have been as faithful as possible, not imitating the celebrated Montaigne, who promises you one thing, and gives you another. ... " Nonetheless, Fielding recommends that the reader use the chapter breaks to pause and consider the terrain he has passed through. "[F]or howsoever swift his capacity may be, I would not advise him to travel through these pages

too fast: for if he doth, he may probably miss the seeing some curious productions of Nature which will be observed by the slower and more accurate reader." Fielding concludes his revelation about "the Science of *Authoring*" with the observation, "That it becomes an author generally to divide a book, as it does a butcher to joint his meat, for such assistance is of great help to both the reader and the carver" (Book II chap. 1; cf. *Phaedrus* 265e).

8 Once again, Machiavelli is a prime suspect: he apparently departs in at least two important respects from the scheme of "weaving" which he outlines in chap. 1 of *The Prince*: he neglects to mention a certain kind of principate ("elected") of which he subsequently adduces a rather provocative pair of examples (cf. chaps. 11 and 19); and he similarly omits two other ways in which states may be acquired (if, that is, one agrees with him that acquiring a principate through either "popularity" or through "wickedness" is not to be conflated with either "one's own arms and virtue" or "the arms of others and fortune"; cf. chap. 8).

The master of the technique of failing to adhere to one's announced plans, however, is Francis Bacon. He managed this in various ways, but his favourite seems to have been through incompleteness. He was for ever outlining some (usually vast) intellectual project which he then "failed" to carry through, but which he published nevertheless, complete with apologies for doing so despite its incompleteness. *The Great Instauration*, of which the *New Organon* is a part, provides the perfect example. In its "Proem", Bacon claims that "because he knew not how long it might be before these things would occur to anyone else ... , he resolved to publish at once so much as he has been able to complete. The cause of which haste was not ambition for himself, but solicitude for the work; that in case of his death there might remain some outline and project of that which he had conceived, and some evidence likewise of his honest mind and inclination toward the benefit of the human race." Plausible enough – and yet his able and devoted private secretary and chaplain (and subsequent biographer and literary executor), Dr William Rawley, attests that Bacon had already put the work through at least twelve drafts over the space of seventeen years. One can scarce avoid suspecting that the work as published was pretty much the way Bacon intended it to be, and that "incompleteness" was a consciously adopted literary device. As to why he used it, one can only speculate. But is it not emblematic of the modern scientific project, a project which, as Bacon recognized, is inherently open-ended, and fated to remain perpetually incomplete?

Notes to pages xix–xx

Melville begins the chapter of *Moby Dick* entitled "The Honor and Glory of Whaling", wherein he abruptly returns to some historical and legendary observations about this greatest of all kinds of fishing (for, as Ishmael states in chap. 32, "Be it known that, waiving all argument, I take the good old fashioned ground that the whale is a fish, and call upon holy Jonah to back me") thusly: "There are some enterprizes in which a careful disorderliness is the true method." Whatever else, this maxim must be presumed to pertain to that assortment of some eighty-one or so "Extracts (supplied by a sub-sub-librarian)" which preface this great philosophical novel. It might also be noted that his impromptu return to such "extracts" comes immediately after the chapter numbered 81 (i.e., $3^3 \times 3$, or 3^4); the entire book consists of 135 chapters (i.e., $3^3 \times 5$).

That he lacks any order or plan is a complaint one frequently hears directed at Montesquieu, especially in regard to his *L'Esprit des lois*. And this despite his warning in its Preface that the "design of the work" is something one must "search" for (cf. Anne M. Cohler's "Montesquieu's Perception of His Audience for the *Spirit of the Laws*." And in some ironic "Reflections" on *The Persian Letters* which he added thirty-three years after the book's initial (and anonymous) publication – and six years after publication of *L'Esprit* in 1748 – Montesquieu observes: "Nothing in *The Persian Letters* has given more pleasure than the unexpected discovery of a kind of story in them. It can be seen to have a beginning, a development, and an end, and its various characters are linked in a chain." He goes on to speak of the special advantages that accrue from casting this story in the form of a series of letters, and concludes: "But in the epistolary form, where accident selects the characters and where the subjects treated are not dependent upon any preconceived design or plan, the author permits himself to join philosophy, politics, and ethics to the story, and to bind the whole with a secret and, in some respects, hitherto unknown chain" (trans.; George R. Healy), The "letters" themselves present some interesting thoughts about the writing of books (cf. especially nos. 108, 133-7, and 145). And given that they are filled with so many arresting maxims, aphorisms, and epigrams, it is of special interest that Montesquieu has one of his characters express the judgment, "Of all the authors we have seen, these here are the most dangerous: the makers of epigrams – little, sharp darts which make deep and incurable wounds" (no. 137).

9 Melville, himself a self-conscious master of allegory and all manner of veiled speech, contends that a favourite device of his is also one of Shakespeare's:

301

> Certain it is ... that this great power of blackness in [Hawthorne] derives its force from its appeals to that Calvinistic sense of Innate Depravity and Original Sin, from whose visitations, in some shape or other, no deeply thinking mind is always and wholly free. For in certain moods, no man can weigh this world, without throwing in something, somehow like Original Sin, to strike the uneven balance. ... [T]his blackness it is that furnishes the infinite obscure of his backround, – that backround against which Shakespeare plays his grandest conceits, the things that have made for Shakespeare his loftiest, but most circumscribed renown, as the profoundest of thinkers. For by philosophers Shakespeare is not adored as the great man of tragedy and comedy. ... But it is those deep faraway things in him; those occasional flashings-forth of the intuitive truth in him; those short, quick probings at the very axis of reality; – these are the things that make Shakespeare, Shakespeare. Through the mouths of the dark characters of Hamlet, Timon, Lear, and Iago, he craftily says, or sometimes insinuates the things, which we feel to be so terrifically true, that it were all but madness for any good man, in his own proper character, to utter, or even hint of them. Tormented into desperation, Lear the frantic King, tears off the mask, and speaks the sane madness of vital truth. ... And if I magnify Shakespeare, it is not so much for what he did do, as for what he did not do, or refrained from doing. For in this world of lies, Truth is forced to fly like a scared white doe in the woodlands; and only by cunning glimpses will she reveal herself, as in Shakespeare and other masters of the great Art of Telling the Truth, – even though it be covertly, and by snatches. "Hawthorne and His Mosses" 1159–60

10 Consider, for example, Hobbes's clever variations of the "golden rule" in *Leviathan* (i.e., chap. 14 par. 5; chap. 15 par. 35; chap. 17 par. 2; chap. 26 par. 13; chap. 27 par. 4; and chap. 42 par. 11). In a similar vein, notice the reflexive effect of the narrator's subtle replacement of 'ship' with 'craft' in Melville's *White-Jacket*: "Outwardly regarded, our craft is a lie; for all that is outwardly seen of it is the clean-swept deck, and oft-painted planks comprised above the waterline; whereas the vast mass of our fabric, with all its storerooms of secrets, forever slides along far under the surface" (from the unnumbered final chapter, "The End").

11 An especially amusing instance of departing from literary principles in the very course of espousing them is to be found in the chapter "Of Speech"

Notes to page xx

in Hobbes's *Leviathan*. Having presented four "Speciall uses of Speech" to which there are "foure correspondent Abuses", including that of using words "metaphorically" and that of using words "to grieve one another", he promptly "abuses" speech in these very ways, castigating those who "spend time fluttering over their books", and admonishing one and all that "words are wise mens counters, they do but reckon by them: but they are the mony of fooles, that value them by the authority of an *Aristotle*, a *Cicero*, or a *Thomas*, or any other Doctor whatsoever, if but a man." I am satisfied that Hobbes is among the very greatest masters of exploiting language in every conceivable way, including especially those he enjoins; moreover, that he means to show by example how and why doing so is inherent in political life and speech, and thus essential to the persuasive power of a book such as his (consider, for example, the radical contrast he draws between "books of Geometry" and those conveying a "doctrine of Right and Wrong"; chap. 11 par. 21).

12 The "Notice on the Notes" prefacing Rousseau's *Second Discourse* is a nice example of subtle allusion to another text, in this case Plato's *Republic*. For in addition to suggesting that he is a "natural" as opposed to a "civilized" man (having the former's attitude towards work: cf. part I par. 13; part II par. 19; and notes 10 and 11), and distinguishing two broad classes of readers (those who are satisfied with the short account and those "who have the courage to begin again" and who are amused by exploring and hunting around in texts; cf. *Republic* 435d, 451bc, 504b–d), Rousseau's reference to "beating the bushes" alerts the latter kind of reader that, in addition to certain essential refinements in his account of the human soul, one will find in the notes his basic account of justice (cf. *Republic* 432b–d). Thus, his "Notice" incidentally reminds us that merely placing more challenging material among long endnotes or appendices will often suffice for ensuring that it is not read by the majority of readers.

13 I would go so far as to suggest that often philosophers provide some of their most important interpretive clues numerically. To make this more than a suggestion would require a book unto itself, so let the simplest of examples suffice: Locke has evidently taken pains in his *Two Treatises on Government* to distance himself – at least in the eyes of casual readers – from Hobbes, and especially from his blasphemous teaching that the State of Nature is in fact a condition of universal war (Nature itself being, according to the first line of *Leviathan*, "the Art whereby God hath made and governes the World"). Now, Hobbes presents his teaching about the

State of Nature in chap. 13, whereas Locke ostensibly deals with the same subject in chap. 2 of his second treatise (wherein we are told, "And here we have the plain *difference between the State of Nature, and the State of War*, which however some Men have confounded, are as far distant, as a State of Peace, Good Will, Mutual Assistance, and Preservation, and a State of Enmity, Malice, Violence, and Mutual Destruction are from one another"). But if one renumbers the chapters consecutively from the beginning of the *Two Treatises*, chap. 2 of the second becomes chap. 13 of the entire book. Moreover, to gain access to Locke's complete account on the State of Nature, one has to consider the radically different impression of it one finds in chap. 9 (wherein we learn that, men being pretty much as Hobbes describes them, "and the greater part no strict Observors of Equity and Justice", the natural state is "very unsafe, very unsecure. This makes [a person] willing to quit a Condition, which however free, is full of fears and continual dangers"). To this might be added the fact that the first treatise, devoted to demolishing Filmer's thesis of divine right traced back to the scriptural account of the State of Nature (i.e., the Garden of Eden), just happens to have 13 × 13 numbered sections.

Since antiquity, certain numbers have been endowed with symbolic, mystical, and even physical significance, and most of the great philosophers show more than a casual acquaintance with this tradition of numerology. For example, since Pythagoras, four has been associated with – among other important things, such as the Elements and Time (the four seasons) – *justice* (four being the first square, it symbolizes reciprocity). Three, in addition to representing space, often stands for the harmonic synthesis of opposites. Twelve, as well as being the product of three and four, is the number of the signs of the Zodiac, hence is symbolic of cosmic order and salvation – indeed, of all perfection (thus Sebastianus Regulus, speaking of the greatest and most influential of the Latin poets: "I think Virgil wished to divide his poem into 12 books, so that it would seem an absolute, perfect, and complete work, even in its numerical aspect"). Seven, the fourth prime and sum of threeness and fourness, represents the basic notes of music, the seven basic colours (each of which, in turn, has its own distinct associations), the virtues, and the planets (thus also order and completeness). Thirteen, of course, has long been associated with luck or fortune. The fuller meanings of numbers, alone or in various combinations (according to the rules of not only ordinary but also "mystical" arithmetic), occasioned a rich – but now largely forgotten – literature. According to J.E. Cirlot, "In symbolism, numbers are not merely the expressions of quantities, but idea-forces, each with a particular character of its own. The actual digits

Note to page xx

are, as it were, only the outer garments" ("Numbers" in *A Dictionary of Symbols* 220).

A useful survey of numerology in the Western literary tradition (deriving from two distinct but interwoven strands, Pythagorean-Platonic philosophy and biblical exegesis) is Christopher Butler's *Number Symbolism*. He contends:

> We can safely conclude that numerological exegesis as practiced from Philo on, must have made some knowledge of number symbolism the possession of every educated Christian in those centuries, well up to the close of the Renaissance, in which an allegorical mode of understanding a literary text was intellectually respectable. (30)

> Attempts to trace with any exactitude the features of numerological Pythagoreanism and Platonism are further complicated by the Renaissance liking for the occult. For it is extremely important to remember (especially when we look for evidence of numerological influences on works of art), that the Pythagorean doctrines were secret ones. Bongo, for example, says that we have to be careful in our dissemination of the divine and rational knowledge of number, 'nec margaritas mitti ante porcas' ('not casting pearls before swine') ... , and continues 'occulta enim non debant communicari omnibus' ('occult things are not to be communicated to everyone'). (53)

This book, along with complementary writings by Douglas Brooks, Alastair Fowler, Maren-Sofie Rostvig, and others, signals a rediscovery of the importance of number symbolism and numerical-geometrical organization for adequate critical analyses and interpretations of such authors as Virgil, Chaucer, Dante, Boccaccio, Petrarch, Sydney, Spencer, Jonson, Dryden, Shakespeare, Milton, Marvell, Herrick, Cowley, Donne, Chapman, Drayton, Pope, Fielding, and many others. In fact, as Fowler suggests, "It is probably no exaggeration to say that most good literary works – indeed, most craftsmanlike works – were organized [numerologically] from antiquity to the eighteenth century at least" (*Silent Poetry: Essays in Numerological Analysis* Alastair Fowler, ed., xi; the essays' various authors provide detailed evidence supporting Fowler's claim, as does his own *Triumphal Forms: Structural Patterns in Elizabethan Poetry*).

A writer can, to be sure, establish certain numerical associations in the context of his own work, as well as avail himself of such as are extant. One can hardly fail to notice the "threeness" which pervades the Platonic corpus (both *Republic* and *Apology of Sokrates* so abound in triads that one naturally associates the number three with the Platonic Sokrates); or the even more conspicuous "fourness" in Nietzsche's writings. As a matter of fact, four has a special prominence in the writings of quite a few moderns (e.g., Machiavelli, Bacon, Hobbes, Descartes, Locke, Rousseau), as does the number thirteen; cf. Leo Strauss's *Thoughts on Machiavelli* especially chap. 1. The first four of the seven mentions of Plato in *Beyond Good and Evil* confirm that Nietzsche regards seven as 'Plato's number', and a variety of evidence in the Platonic corpus itself supports this judgment. Suffice it to say, whenever a philosopher numbers things – and even when he does not, but his reader easily can – there may be a deeper significance to be discovered in his quantitative distribution of material than is first apparent, and especially in what he has given arithmetical centrality.

14 Radical in the literal sense (from *radix*, 'root'; thus, 'foundation', 'origin', 'basis'). A truly radical investigation is one that attempts to go to the very root of things, and hence is necessarily philosophical in its aspirations. Inasmuch as most people have not themselves established their ethical or other standards on a wholly rational basis, their confidence in them is vulnerable. Consequently, a radical challenge to these beliefs may easily damage or destroy them, without there being any assurance that such people can or will replace them with something better (cf. *Republic* 537e–539a). And so a just writer, aware of this danger and concerned to "benefit friends while harming no one", will show the greatest care in subjecting these beliefs to radical scrutiny.

15 Indeed, Aristotle may be credited with the first explicit employment of the distinction. He uses the expression *exōterikoi logoi* (the first term of which originates as the comparative form of the adverb *exō*, "from without", "on the outside") in *Politics* (1323 a 23), although he also employs other locutions (e.g., "in ordinary discussions", "discourses given in public"; cf. *Eth. Nich.* 1096 a 4, *Physica* 209 b 15, *De Caelo* 279 a 30, *De Anima* 407 b 29). By calling attention to the fact that Aristotle characterized whole speeches and writings as exoteric, I do not mean to preclude the possibility that he also applied the distinction within a given piece of writing. Plutarch, in his *Alexander*, reports:

> It would appear that Alexander not only received [from Aristotle] his ethical and political reasoning [*logon*], but also the more secret and profound teachings, which men privately designate 'acroamatic' and 'epoptic', and do not impart to many. For having already crossed into Asia, and learning that Aristotle had published in books certain dis-

courses [*logous*] on these matters, he wrote him a plainly expressed letter on behalf of philosophy, of which this is a copy: 'Alexander to Aristotle, greetings – you have not done rightly in publishing the acroamatic of your discourses; for in what shall I surpass others if these discourses in which I have been trained are to be common to everyone? I had rather excel in my experience of the best things than in my powers. Farewell.' Speaking with due regard for [Alexander's] love of honour, Aristotle defended himself, saying about these discourses that they have been both published and not published; for truly, the study of the metaphysics [*hē meta ta physica*] is of no benefit for teaching and learning, but is written as a reminder for those already instructed in the basic principles. (VII, 4–9; my translation)

16 As late as the debate over Darwin's theories, one finds references to the conviction that certain views, even some having to do with natural science – and quite apart from their truth or falsity – are not suitable for explicit public discussion; see, for example, the excellent reconstruction of this debate by Gertrude Himmelfarb in her *Darwin and the Darwinian Revolution*, especially her discussion (185–94) of Lyell's part in the evolutionary controversy, explained thus (192): "If Lyell is to be judged by his private rather than public sentiments, he must be accounted among Darwin's predecessors. His misfortune, it may be hazarded, was that if his views of species were in advance of his age, his faith in tradition and his notion of the philosopher as one who avoids unsettling established beliefs and institutions were behind the times. He must have been one of the last to carry over the aristocratic idea that a thinker has not only the right but also the obligation to conceal his true thoughts from the public. He was as consciously an esoteric philosopher as most of the sages of antiquity." Evolutionary biology provides a particularly apt example of a topic that deserves discretionary treatment. Some prudent people recognized from the outset that this ostensibly "factual" matter has enormous implications for so-called value questions. Indeed, evolutionary theory, requiring as it does a radical revision in the very conception of Nature, may well be, as Nietzsche regarded it, "true but deadly"; see the second of his *Untimely Meditations*, "On the Uses and Disadvantages of History for Life" especially chaps. 4 and 9.

17 Not only classical authors, but those of post-classical times, provide a wealth of examples; perhaps the following sample will suffice for the purpose at hand.

Note to page xxii

Averroes, arguably the most eminent of the Islamic philosophers, distinguishes three classes of human beings in terms of their differing intellectual requirements, and discusses certain implications of this taxonomy in *The Decisive Treatise, Determining What the Connection Is between Religion and Philosophy*. And while his discussion focuses on religious convictions – an important enough concern, to be sure – his conclusions clearly have a more general applicability:

> For the natures of men are on different levels with respect to assent. One of them comes to assent through demonstration; another comes to assent through dialectical arguments, just as firmly as the demonstrative man through demonstration, since his nature does not contain any greater capacity; while another comes to assent through rhetorical arguments, again just as firmly as the demonstrative man through demonstrative arguments.
>
> The reason why the Law came down containing both an apparent and an inner meaning lies in the diversity of people's natural capacities and the difference of their innate dispositions with regard to assent. The reason the Law came down with apparent meanings that contradict each other is in order to draw the attention of those who are *well grounded in science* to the interpretation that reconciles them.
>
> Therefore interpretations ought to be set down only in demonstrative books, because if they are in demonstrative books they are encountered by no one but men of the demonstrative class. But if they are set down in other than demonstrative books and one deals with them by poetical, rhetorical, or dialectical methods, as Abû Hâmid does, then he commits an offense against the Law and against philosophy, even though the fellow intended nothing but good. For by this procedure he wanted to increase the number of learned men. But this increased the number of the mischievous, although not without some increase in the number of the learned. As a result, one group came to slander philosophy, another to slander the Law, and another to reconcile the two. (trans. George F. Hourani, as reprinted in *Medieval Political Philosophy* Ralph Lerner and Muhsin Mahdi, eds., 169, 170, 178)

Copernicus, when he was at last persuaded to publish his *Revolutions of the Heavenly Spheres* ("a work which I had kept hidden among my things not merely for nine years, but for almost four times nine years"), he prudently dedicated it to Pope Paul III, and in the course of doing so observed:

Note to page xxii

And although I realize that the conceptions of a philosopher are placed beyond the judgment of the crowd, because it is his loving duty to seek the truth in all things, in so far as God has granted that to human reason; nevertheless I think we ought to avoid opinions utterly foreign to rightness. And when I considered how absurd this 'lecture' would be held ... , for a long time I was in great difficulty as to whether I should bring to light my commentaries written to demonstrate the Earth's movement, or whether it would not be better to follow the example of the Pythagoreans and certain others who used to hand down the mysteries of their philosophy not in writing but by word of mouth and only to their relatives and friends. ... They however seem to me to have done that not, as some judge, out of a jealous unwillingness to communicate their doctrines but in order that things of very great beauty which have been investigated by the loving care of great men should not be scorned by those who find it a bother to expend any great energy on letters – except on the money-making variety – or who are provoked by the exhortations and examples of others to the liberal study of philosophy but on account of their natural stupidity hold the position among philosophers that drones hold among bees. ...

And I have no doubt that talented and learned mathematicians will agree with me, if – as philosophy demands in the first place – they are willing to give not superficial but profound thought and effort to what I bring forward in this work. ... (Trans. Charles Glenn Wallis, 506, 508–9)

Machiavelli might be thought to disagree with Averroes's intellectual typology, for he apparently strikes most modern readers of *The Prince* as someone who frankly and boldly – and indiscriminately – "just tells it like it is". Still, when assessing his style one must bear in mind his assertion that there are at least "three kinds of brains: one understands on its own, the other discerns that which others understand, the third neither understands on its own nor through others" (chap. 22; cf. Hesiod's *Works and Days* 293–7). And it may be germane to this assessment that he privately assured a friend, if with obvious comic exaggeration, "As to the lies of the Carpigiani, I should like a contest in that matter with all of them, ... because for a long time I have not said what I believed, nor do I ever believe what I say, and if indeed sometimes I do happen to tell the truth, I hide it among so many lies that it is hard to find" (letter no. 179, to Francesco Guicciardini, dated 17 May 1521; trans. Allan Gilbert in

Note to page xxii

Machiavelli: The Chief Works and Others II 973; cf. also letter no. 144, p. 939, wherein Machiavelli speaks of why he prefers to tell about an incident partly "hidden under allegories").

Francis Bacon, chancellor of England, "and the greatest, perhaps, of philosophers" (according to Rousseau), whose politico-philosophical mission was nothing less than the refashioning of civil society through the reformation of science, speaks in several of his writings about the need for circumspection in communicating various kinds of knowledge, especially that of politics: "Concerning government, it is part of knowledge secret and retired in both these respects in which things are deemed secret; for some things are secret because they are hard to know, and some because they are not fit to utter" (*The Advancement of Learning* 197). The means of and reasons for discretion in writing are treated at unusual length in his *De augmentis scientiarum*:

> Let the first difference of Method then be this: it is either Magistral or Initiative. Observe however that in using the word 'initiative', I do not mean that the business of the latter is to transmit the beginnings only of sciences, of the former to transmit the entire doctrine. On the contrary, I call that doctrine initiative (borrowing the term from the sacred ceremonies) which discloses and lays bare the very mysteries of the sciences. The magistral method teaches; the initiative intimates. The magistral requires that what is told should be believed; the initiative that it should be examined. The one transmits knowledge to the crowd of learners; the other to the sons, as it were, of science. The end of the one is the use of the knowledges, as they now are; of the other the continuation and further progression of them.
>
> Another diversity of Method there is, which in intention has an affinity with the former, but is in reality almost contrary. For both methods agree in aiming to separate the vulgar among the auditors from the select; but then they are opposed in this, that the former makes use of a way of delivery more open than the common, the latter (of which I am now going to speak) of one more secret. Let the one then be distinguished as the *Exoteric* method, the other as the *Acroamatic*; a distinction observed by the ancients principally in the publication of books, but which I transfer to the method of delivery. Indeed this acroamatic or enigmatical method was itself used among the ancients, and employed with judgment and discretion. ... The intention of it however seems to be by obscurity of delivery to exclude the vulgar

Note to page xxii

(that is the profane vulgar) from the secrets of knowledges, and to admit those only who have either received the interpretation of the enigmas through the hands of the teachers, or have wits of such sharpness and discernment as can pierce the veil." Spedding and Ellis, eds., *The Works of Francis Bacon* IX (122-7)

> But Parabolical Poesy is of a higher character than the others, and appears to be something sacred and venerable; especially as religion itself commonly uses its aid as a means of communication between divinity and humanity. But this too is corrupted by the levity and idleness of wits in dealing with allegory. It is of double use and serves for contrary purposes; for it serves as an infoldment; and it likewise serves for illustration. In the latter case the object is a certain method of teaching, in the former an artifice for concealment. Now this method of teaching, used for illustration, was very much in use in the ancient times. ... In a word, as hieroglyphics were before letters, so parables were before arguments. And even now, and at all times, the force of parables is and has been excellent; because arguments can not be made so perspicuous nor true examples so apt.
>
> But there remains yet another use of Poesy Parabolical, opposite to the former; wherein it serves (as I said) for an infoldment; for such things, I mean, the dignity whereof requires that they should be seen as it were through a veil; that is when the secrets and mysteries of religion, policy, and philosophy are involved in fables or parables. ... (Ibid VIII 442-3)

As for openness in one's political conduct generally, Bacon has this to say in "Of Simulation and Dissimulation": (no. 6 in his *Essayes or Counsels, Civill and Morall*):

> For if a man have that penetration of judgment as he can discern what things are to be laid open, and what to be secreted, and what to be shewed at half lights, and to whom and when, (which indeed are arts of state and arts of life, as Tacitus well calleth them,) to him a habit of dissimulation is a hindrance and a poorness. But if a man cannot obtain to that judgment, then it is left to him generally to be close, and a dissembler. For where a man cannot choose or vary in particulars, there it is good to take the safest and wariest way in general; like the going softly, by one that cannot well see. Certainly the ablest men that ever were have had all an openness and frankness of dealing; and a name of certainty and veracity; but then they were like horses well

managed; for they could tell passing well when to stop or turn; and at such times when they thought the case indeed required dissimulation, if then they used it, it came to pass that the former opinion [already] spread abroad of their good faith and clearness of dealing made them almost invisible.

There be three degrees of this hiding and veiling of a man's self. The first, Closeness, Reservation, and Secrecy; when a man leaveth himself without observation, or without hold to be taken, what he is. The second, Dissimulation, in the negative; when a man lets fall signs and arguments, that he is not that [which] he is. And the third, Simulation, in the affirmative; when a man industriously and expressly feigns and pretends to be that [which] he is not. ...

In few words, mysteries are due to secrecy. Besides (to say truth) nakedness is uncomely, as well in mind as body; and it addeth no small reverence to men's manners and actions, if they be not altogether open. ... Therefore set it down, *that an habit of secrecy is both politic and moral*. ...

The best composition and temperature is to have openness in fame and opinion; secrecy in habit; dissimulation in seasonable use; and a power to feign, if there be no remedy.

Sir Walter Raleigh (Ralegh), with reasons reflective more of political than philosophical considerations, explains to the reader of his *History of the World* why he chose to write about remote antiquity rather than recent events of which he was witness and participant: "I know that it will be said by many that I might have been more pleasing to the reader if I had written the story of mine own times, having been permitted to draw water as near the well-head as another. To this I answer, that whosoever in writing a modern history shall follow truth too near the heels it may happily strike out his teeth." Still, he managed to suggest a contemporary pertinence to his history in the very course of disclaiming it had any: "It is enough for me (being in that state I am) to write of the eldest times; wherein also why may it not be said that in speaking of the past I point at the present and tax the vices of those that are yet living, in their persons that are long since dead? And have it laid to my charge? But this I cannot help, though innocent" (*Sir Walter Raleigh – Selected Prose and Poetry* Agnes M.C. Latham, ed., 199–200). Evidently, however, Raleigh's literary caution was still inadequate, for according to G.P.V. Akrigg: "Raleigh had confidently counted upon the *History* to win favour from the scholarly King

Note to page xxii

James, but when it was finally published in 1614 it was 'called in by the Kinges commaundement, for divers exceptions, but specially for being too sawcie in censuring princes'" (*Jacobean Pageant* 328).

Thomas Hobbes deserves to be acknowledged one of "the most politic philosophers that ever writ", for he has apparently managed to impress the vast majority of modern readers as being the very model of candour, despite his candidly admitting:

> The secret thoughts of a man run over all things, holy, prophane, clean, obscene, grave, and light, without shame or blame; which verbal discourse cannot do, farther than the judgment shall approve of the Time, Place, and Persons. An Anatomist, or a Physician may speak, or write his judgment of unclean things; because it is not to please, but profit: but for another man to write his extravagant, and pleasant fancies of the same, is as if a man, from being tumbled in the dirt, should come and present himselfe before good company. And 'tis the want of Discretion that makes the difference. Again, in profest remissnesse of mind, and familiar company, a man may play with the sounds, and aequivocal signification of words; and that many times with encounters of extraordinary Fancy: but in a Sermon, or in publique, or before persons unknown, or whom we ought to reverence, there is no Gingling of words that will not be accounted folly: and the difference is only in the want of discretion. So that where Wit is wanting, it is not Fancy that is wanting, but Discretion. (*Leviathan* chap. 8 par. 10)

This immediately precedes his rather oblique definition of 'prudence': "When the thoughts of a man, that has a designe in hand, running over a multitude of things, observes how they conduce to that designe; or what designe they may conduce unto; if his observations be such as are not easie, or usuall, This wit of his is called PRUDENCE. ... " One should also bear in mind, when reading Hobbes's own works, his defence of the obscurity of Thucydides: "If then one cannot penetrate into [Thucydides' sentences] without much meditation, we are not to expect a man should understand them at first speaking. Marcellinus saith, he was obscure on purpose; that the common people might not understand him. And not unlikely: for a wise man should so write, (though in words understood by all men), that wise men only should be able to commend him." As for Thucydides' rhetoric: "But yet was this his eloquence not at all fit for the bar; but proper for history, and rather to be read than heard. For words that pass away (as in public orations they must) without pause, ought to be understood with ease, and are lost else: though words that remain in writing for the reader to meditate on, ought rather to be pithy and full" (*Hobbes's Thucydides* Richard Schlatter, ed., 16, 25, 27).

Descartes in Discourse on Method (arguably his most important work, offering as it does a synoptic view of his entire politico-scientific project) is a *tour de force* of literary subtlety. For example, every reader can be relied upon to recognize the intellectual egalitarianism with which he begins: "Good sense is the most evenly distributed commodity in the world, for each of us considers himself so well endowed therewith that even those who are most difficult to please in other matters are not wont to desire more of it than they have. It is not likely that everyone is mistaken about this fact. Rather it provides evidence that the power of judging rightly and of distinguishing the true from the false (which, properly speaking, is what people call good sense or reason) is naturally equal in all men." Not every reader notices, however, that in the very next paragraph Descartes in effect declares himself an exception to his opening generalization (alleging that he has "often longed to have as quick a wit or as precise and distinct an imagination or as full and responsive a memory as certain other people"). As for the "likelihood" of people's being *correct* in their self-flattering assumption about their own share of good sense, Descartes (some few hundred words later) observes that there is "nothing that is not doubtful", and that he "took to be virtually false everything that was merely probable" (i.e., likely). One must conclude that Descartes is an ironist. Consider what he says in part II with respect to his famous "method for rightly conducting one's reason". There (par. 3) he explicitly distinguishes several natural classes of people, most of whom he judges are *not* suitable for using his method:

> This is why I could not approve of all those trouble-making and quarrelsome types who, called neither by birth nor by fortune to manage public affairs, never cease in their imagination to effect some new reformation. And if I thought there was the slightest thing in this essay by means of which one might suspect me of such folly, I would be very sorry to permit its publication. My plan has never been more than to try to reform my own thoughts and to build upon a foundation which is completely my own. And if, my work having sufficiently pleased me, I show it to you here as a model, it is not for the reason that I wish to advise anyone to imitate it. Perhaps those with whom God has better shared his graces have more lofty plans; but I fear that

Note to page xxii

> this plan of mine may already be too arduous for many. The single resolution to detach oneself from all beliefs one has once accepted as true is not an example that everyone ought to follow; and the world consists almost completely of but two kinds of people and for these two kinds it is not at all suitable: namely those who, believing themselves more capable than they really are, cannot help making premature judgments and do not have enough patience to conduct their thoughts in an orderly manner; thus, if they once take the liberty to doubt the principles they have accepted and to keep away from the common path, they could never keep to the path one must take in order to go in a more forward direction – they would remain lost all their lives. Now as for those people who have enough reason or modesty to judge that they are less capable to distinguish the true from the false than are others by whom they can be instructed, they ought to content themselves more with following the opinion of these others than to look for better opinions on their own. (*Discourse on Method and Meditations on First Philosophy* Donald A. Cress, trans., 8)

But given that normal intellectual *hubris* of people (to which Descartes alluded at the very beginning), is it at all likely that such a warning will be taken to heart by those two kinds of readers for whom it would be most pertinent? What is its real purpose, then, and for whose benefit is it really meant?

Descartes's sensitivity to the differing capabilities of his readers is reaffirmed in the "Preface" to his famous *Meditations*. He observes that "the judgments of most people are so preposterous and silly that they are more likely to be persuaded by the first opinions that come along, however false and alien to reason they may be, than by a true and firm, though subsequently received refutation of them." Referring to his earlier, abbreviated treatment of "the question of God and the human mind" in the *Discourse*, he explains: "And the path I follow in order to explicate these questions is so little trodden and so far removed from everyday use that I did not believe it useful to profess at greater length in a work written in French and read indiscriminately by all sorts of people, lest weaker minds be in position to believe that they too are to set out on this path." In the sixth paragraph of his "Preface", Descartes subtly forewarns the readers of these six "meditations" that his teaching is only for those who can grasp it as a whole:

> But now, after having once and for all put to the test the judgments of men, I here again approach these same questions regarding God

and the human mind, and at the same time treat the beginnings of the whole of first philosophy, but in such a way that I have no expectation of approval from the vulgar and no wide audience of readers. Rather, I am an author to none who read these things but those who seriously meditate with me, who have the ability and the desire to withdraw their mind from the senses and at the same time from all prejudices. Such people I know all too well to be few and far between. As to those who do not care to comprehend the order and series of my reasons but eagerly dispute over single conclusions by themselves, as is the custom for many – those, I say, will derive little benefit from the reading of this treatise. ... (*Meditations* 50)

Spinoza, with perhaps more disingenuity than sincerity, professed great indignation at the charge of a certain Lambert de Velthuysen that in his *Tractatus Theologico-Politicus* "with covert and disguised arguments I teach atheism", and that "I have knowingly and cunningly with evil intent argued for the cause of the deists, in order to discredit it", and goes on to say to his correspondent (with whom he does not seem to be closely acquainted): "This contention sufficiently shows that he has not understood my reasons. For who could be so cunning and clever, as to be able to advance under false pretenses so many and such good reasons for a doctrine which he did not believe in? Who will pass for an honest writer in the eyes of a man, that thinks one may argue as soundly for fiction as for truth? But after all I am not astonished. Descartes was formerly served in the same way by Voët, and the most honourable writers are constantly thus treated" (Ltr 49 in *Correspondence* in *On the Improvement of the Understanding, The Ethics, Correspondence* R.H.M. Elwes, trans., 365).

It is not clear that Spinoza's excellent questions ought to be regarded as altogether rhetorical, rather than ironical. Be that as it may, his discussion in that treatise of the different ways of persuading different kinds of men, though applied by him to the understanding of Holy Scripture, clearly has a broader pertinence:

> If anyone wishes to persuade his fellows for or against anything which is not self-evident, he must deduce his contention from their admissions, and convince them either by experience or by ratiocination; either by appealing to facts of natural experience, or to self-evident intellectual axioms. ...
>
> But the deduction of conclusions from general truths *a priori*, usually requires a long chain of arguments, and, moreover, very great caution, acuteness, and self-restraint – qualities which are not often

Note to page xxii

met with; therefore people prefer to be taught by experience rather than deduce their conclusion from a few axioms, and set them out in logical order. Whence it follows, that if anyone wishes to teach a doctrine to a whole nation (not to speak of the whole human race), and to be understood by all men in every particular, he will seek to support his teaching with experience, and will endeavor to suit his reasonings and the definitions of his doctrines as far as possible to the understanding of the common people, who form the majority of mankind, and he will not set them forth in logical sequence nor adduce the definitions which serve to establish them. Otherwise he writes only for the learned – that is, he will be understood by only a small portion of the human race.

All Scripture was written primarily for an entire people, and secondarily for the whole human race; therefore its contents must necessarily be adapted as far as possible to the understanding of the masses, and proved only by examples drawn from experience. We will explain ourselves more clearly. The chief speculative doctrines taught in Scripture are the existence of God, or a Being Who made all things, and Who directs and sustains the world with consummate wisdom; furthermore, that God takes the greatest thought for men, or such of them as live piously and honourably, while He punishes, with various penalties, those who do evil, separating them from the good. All this is proved in Scripture entirely through experience – that is, through the narratives there related. No definitions of doctrine are given, but all the sayings and reasonings are adapted to the understanding of the masses. Although experience can give no clear knowledge of these things, nor explain the nature of God, nor how He directs and sustains all things, it can nevertheless teach and enlighten men sufficiently to impress obedience and devotion on their minds.

It is now, I think, sufficiently clear what persons are bound to believe in the Scripture narratives, and in what degree they are so bound, for it evidently follows from what has been said that knowledge of and belief in them is particularly necessary to the masses whose intellect is not capable of perceiving things clearly and distinctly. ...

However, the masses are not sufficiently skilled to draw conclusions from what they read, they take more delight in the actual stories, and in the strange and unlooked-for issues of events than in the doctrines

Note to page xxii

implied; therefore, besides reading these narratives, they are always in need of pastors or church ministers to explain them to their feeble intelligence. (*A Theological-Political Treatise* R.H.M. Elwes, trans., chap. 5, "Of the Ceremonial Law", 76-8, 79)

Isaac Walton's dialogical allegory on fishing and philosophy (*The Compleat Angler, or the Contemplative Man's Recreation*) has enjoyed a small but steady popularity since its first publication in 1653, and especially with those who, like its dedicatee, can be counted upon to understand "(though there be ignorant men of another belief) that *angling* is an *art*", and moreover, not one which is equally accessible to all: "[I]f *common Anglers* should attend you, and be eye-witnesses of the success, not of your *fortune* but your *skill*, it would doubtless beget in them an emulation to be like you, and that emulation might beget an industrious diligence to be so; but I know it is not attainable by common capacities. And there be now many men of great *wisdom, learning,* and *experience*, which love and practice this *art*, that know I speak the truth" (Dedication). That there may be more to fishing than meets the eye, and thus also to this book about *"fish* and *fishing"*, is subtly indicated in the seventh paragraph of its preface "TO THE READER OF THIS DISCOURSE, but especially, TO THE HONEST ANGLER":

> *Now for the art of* catching *fish, that is to say, how to make a man – that was none – to be an angler by a book; he that undertakes it shall undertake a harder task than* Mr Hales *(a most valiant and excellent fencer) who, in a printed book called* A Private School of Defence, *undertook to teach that art or science and was laughed at for his labour. Not but that many useful things might be learnt by that book, but he was laughed at because that art was not to be taught by words but practice; and so must angling. And note also, that in this Discourse, I do not undertake to say all that is known, or may be said of it, but I undertake to acquaint the reader with many things that are not usually known to every angler; and I shall leave gleanings and observations enough to be made out of the experience of all that love and practice this recreation, to which I shall encourage them. For angling may be said to be so like the* mathematics, *that it can never be fully learnt; at least not so fully, but that there will still be more new experiments left for the trial of other men that succeed us.*

Hobbes, incidentally, chooses this very example of fencing to illustrate the difference between Prudence (based on experience) and Sapience (based on science); see *Leviathan* chap. 5 par. 21.

Locke, in chap. 9 of *An Essay Concerning Human Nature* ("Of the Imperfection of Words"), distinguishes the civil, or political, use of language from its

318

Note to page xxii

philosophical use: "First, by their *civil* use, I mean such a communication of thoughts and ideas as may serve for the upholding common conversation and commerce, about the ordinary affairs and conveniences of civil life, in societies of men, one amongst another. Secondly, by the *philosophical* use of words, I mean such a use of them as may serve to convey the precise notions of things, and to express in general propositions certain and undoubted truths, which the mind may rest upon and be satisfied with in its search after true knowledge. These two uses are very distinct; and a great deal less exactness will serve in the one than in the other."

Locke chooses not to elaborate on either the reasons for his conclusion or on its implications, but they would seem worth thinking about, especially with respect to those writings of his that would seem to combine both uses of speech (e.g., *Two Treatises of Government* and *A Letter Concerning Toleration*). Locke does, however, specify four "Natural causes" of the "imperfection of words", all of which have a special pertinence to things political (there being few ideas more "complex" than that of the well-ordered regime, or whose "connexion in nature" is less certain, or the "standard" of which is harder to know). Chap. 9 virtually concludes with the warning that "discourses of religion, law, and morality, as they are matters of the highest concernment", also pose the "greatest difficulty" of being understood in the same way as their author understood them.

In this connection, it should not be forgotten that Locke never publicly admitted writing either of the two overtly political works named above. They were published anonymously, Locke dealing with the publisher through a trusted intermediary and destroying all draft copies; only in a codicil to his will made but weeks before he died did he acknowledge that these works were indeed his. For the remarkable lengths Locke went to in order to preserve his anonymity and thereby protect himself, see Peter Laslett's "Introduction" to his critical edition of the *Two Treatises* and Maurice Cranston's *John Locke: A Biography* wherein the author laments (xiii): "Locke is an elusive subject for a biographer because he was an extremely secretive man. He modified a system of shorthand for the purpose of concealment; he employed all sorts of curious little cyphers; he cut signatures and other identifiable names from letters he preserved; at one time he used invisible ink."

Rousseau contends that people's differing intellectual capacities pose *the* central difficulty in establishing a well-ordered republic:

> Laws are properly only the conditions of the civil association. The people that is subject to the laws ought to be their author. ... [But]

Note to page xxii

how will a blind multitude, which often does not know what it wants because it rarely knows what is good for it, carry out by itself an undertaking as vast and as difficult as a system of legislation? By itself, the people always wants the good, but by itself it does not always see it. The general will is always right, but the judgment that guides it is not always enlightened. It must be made to see objects as they are, or sometimes as they should appear to be. ... From this arises the necessity for a legislator. ...

Another difficulty deserves attention. Wise men who want to use their own language, rather than that of the common people, cannot be understood by the people. Now there are a thousand kinds of ideas that are impossible to translate into the language of the people. Overly general views and overly remote objects are equally beyond its grasp. ... Since the legislator is therefore unable to use either force or reasoning, he must necessarily have recourse to another order of authority, which can win over without violence and persuade without convincing.

This is what has always forced the fathers of nations to have recourse to the intervention of heaven and to attribute their own wisdom to the Gods. ...

It is this sublime reason, which rises above the grasp of common men, whose decisions the legislator places in the mouths of the immortals in order to convince by divine authority those who can not be moved by human prudence. But it is not every man who can make the Gods speak, or be believed when he declares himself their interpreter. The legislator's great soul is the true miracle that should prove his mission. ... And whereas proud philosophy or blind partisan spirit regards [such men] merely as lucky impostors, the true political theorist admires in their institutions that great and powerful genius which presides over lasting establishments. (*On the Social Contract* Roger D. Masters, trans., Book II chaps. 6 and 7, 67–70)

It should not go unnoticed, however, that the problems of thought and language which both necessitate and perplex the great legislator are continuing ones in political life, and to some extent confront anyone who endeavours to publish a profound teaching about it. Not surprisingly, then, at the centre of his essay Rousseau feels obliged to warn his reader to read carefully, "as [he does] not know the art of being clear for those who are not willing to be attentive" (Book III chap. 1 line 1). Similarly, his *Second Discourse* is salted with indications that he expects to be read

Note to page xxii

variously (see, for example, the concluding sentence of "Part One": "It is enough for me to offer these objects to the consideration of my judges; it is enough for me to have arranged it so that vulgar readers would have no need to consider them." And see especially the central note Rousseau appends to the discourse where he speaks of the "philosophizing rabble", and observes, "to study men, talents are necessary that God is not obligated to give anyone"; thus he wonders, "Shall we never see reborn those happy times when the people did not dabble in philosophy ... ?").

Incidentally, nothing better displays the intellectual gulf – chasm, actually – separating the true political theorist Rousseau from that prophet of the Enlightenment, Voltaire, than the latter's judgment that "Every profane legislator who dared to feign that the Divinity had dictated to him his laws, was a palpable blasphemer and a traitor; a blasphemer, because he calumniated the gods; a traitor, because he subjected his country to his own opinions" (*The Philosophy of History* trans. anon. chap. 53).

Goethe, in *Conversations with Eckermann*, speaks of how both the diversity of people's intellectual capacities and the vagaries of historical circumstances constrain what an intelligent poet is willing to say:

> Could intellect and high cultivation ... become the property of all, the poet would have fair play; he could be always thoroughly true, and would not be compelled to fear uttering his best thoughts. But, as it is, he must always keep on a certain level; must remember that his works will fall into the hands of a mixed society, and must therefore take care lest by over-great openness he may give offense to the majority of good men. Then, Time is a whimsical tyrant, which in every century has a different face for all that one says and does. We cannot with propriety say things that were permitted to the ancient Greeks; and the Englishmen of 1820 cannot endure what suited the vigorous contemporaries of Shakespeare, so that at the present day it is found necessary to have a Family Shakespeare. (J. Oxenford, trans.)

Also pertinent here is his observation about the artistry of Mozart, especially since Goethe knew how well it applied to Shakespeare: "Even when the mass of the audience enjoys a piece simply as a spectacle, the higher meaning will not escape the initiated, as we can see with *The Magic Flute* and some other things."

S.T. Coleridge's 1817 *Biographia Literaria* (the great poet and polymath was "without question the most philosophically oriented and informed critic in the English-speaking world" – Engell and Bate, eds., lxvii) sets a daunting standard of informed literary investigation, ranging as it does over the entire terrain of poetry and politics, philosophy and theology. Having in preceding chapters examined the doctrines of Locke, Berkeley, Leibniz, Descartes, and Spinoza (among others), he says in chap. 9: "Whoever is acquainted with the history of philosophy, during the two or three last centuries, cannot but admit, that there appears to have existed a sort of secret and tacit compact among the learned, not to pass beyond a certain limit in speculative science. The privilege of free thought, so highly extolled, has at no time been held valid in actual practice, except within this limit; and not a single stride beyond it has ever been ventured without bringing obloquy on the transgressor. The few men of genius among the learned class, who actually did overstep this boundary, anxiously avoided the appearance of having done so" (147-8).

Nietzsche it is, however, who can perhaps best teach *us* the permanent significance of discretion and multivocality in writing, our age being so thoroughly saturated with an historicism which derives its plausibility from reading superficially, and which deprives its adherents of any incentive to read otherwise. He returns to the theme repeatedly. In addition to the aphorism on esotericism quoted in the text, one must consider his various references to "masks" (e.g., aph. 40 of *Beyond Good and Evil*: "Whatever is profound loves masks ... "), as well as passages such as the following:

> *On the question of being understandable* – One does not only wish to be understood when one writes: one wishes just as surely *not* to be understood. It is not by any means necessarily an objection to a book when anyone finds it impossible to understand: perhaps that was part of the author's intention – he did not want to be understood by just 'anyone'. All the nobler spirits and tastes select their audience when they wish to communicate; and choosing that, one at the same time erects barriers against 'the others'. All the more subtle laws of any style have their origin at this point: they at the same time keep away, create a distance, forbid 'entrance', understanding, as said above – while they open the ears of those whose ears are related to ours. ...
>
> Finally, my brevity has yet another value: given such questions as concern me, I must say many things briefly in order that they may be heard still more briefly. For, being an immoralist, one has to take steps against corrupting innocents – I mean asses and old maids of both sexes whom life offers nothing but their innocence. Even more, my writings should inspire, elevate, and encourage them to be virtuous. (*The Gay Science* Walter Kaufmann, ed. and trans., aph. 381)

> If this book is incomprehensible to anyone and jars on his ears, the fault, it seems to me, is not necessarily mine. It is clear enough, assuming, as I do assume, that one has first read my earlier writings and has not spared some trouble in doing so: for they are, indeed, not easy to penetrate. Regarding my *Zarathustra*, for example, I do not allow that anyone knows the book who has not at some time been profoundly wounded and at some time profoundly delighted by every word in it; for only then may he enjoy the privilege of reverentially sharing in the halcyon element out of which that book was born and in its sunlight clarity, remoteness, breadth, and certainty. In other cases, people find difficulty with the aphoristic form: this arises from the fact that today this form is *not taken seriously enough*. An aphorism, properly stamped and molded, has not been "deciphered" when it has simply been read; rather, one has then to begin its *exegesis*, for which is required an art of exegesis. ... To be sure, one thing is necessary above all if one is to practice reading as an *art* in this way, something that has been unlearned most thoroughly nowadays – and therefore it will be some time before my writings are "readable" – something for which one has almost to be a cow and in any case *not* a "modern man": *rumination*. (*Genealogy of Morals* Walter Kaufmann, trans., "Preface" aph. 8)

> – Finally, however: why should we have to say what we are and what we want and do not want so loudly and with such fervour? Let us view it more coldly, more distantly, more prudently, from a greater height; let us say it, as it is fitting it should be said between ourselves, so secretly that no one hears it, that no one hears *us*! Above all, let us say it *slowly*. ... It is not for nothing that I have been a philologist, perhaps I am a philologist still, that is to say, a teacher of slow reading: – in the end I also write slowly. ... For philology is that venerable art that demands of its votaries one thing above all: to go aside, to take time, to become still, to become slow – it is a goldsmith's art and connoisseurship of the *word* which has nothing but delicate, cautious work to do and achieves nothing if it does not achieve it *lento*.
> (*Daybreak* R.J. Hollingdale, trans., "Preface" [1886] aph. 5)

18 The failure to understand the dialogues as invitations or provocations to philosophy in the primary rather than secondary sense of the word partly explains the superficiality of much contemporary scholarship on Plato, and

thus partly justifies this present overlong introduction on how to read dialogues for maximum enjoyment and profit.

One consequence of this failure has been the pursuit of issues that are without either political or philosophical relevance. Consider, for example, how many forests have been laid waste so that we may have learned speculations concerning the order in which Plato's dialogues were written. But beyond that, consider the tissue of doubtful assumptions upon which such irrelevant speculations rest, for it helps "put into historical perspective" that easy-going superiority so many contemporary scholars unwittingly presume towards thinkers denied the benefits of a modern education. To begin with, it is assumed that it is possible, as well as valid and useful, to categorize the dialogues in terms of "early", "middle", and "late", as reflecting discernible stages in Plato's intellectual "progress" (i.e., what modern scholars using their own standards judge to be his deepening profundity) – something about which Plato himself gave not the slightest indication. Nonetheless, legions of professional philosophers simply accept this as established fact. But in order to establish it, think what would be required. First, that one has thoroughly and profoundly understood each and every dialogue on its own terms alone – not disregarding as spurious any of the traditional thirty-five without a thorough and unprejudiced attempt to understand it, however strange or inadequate it might seem to those who are somehow sure they already comprehend Plato's authentic thought and style (and for anyone who has ever seriously tried to master even three or four dialogues, this would seem a mind-boggling achievement such as might well consume several lifetimes). Next, that one has systematically compared and analysed them all, and clearly if only roughly discerned *the* natural course of intellectual development implicit in them. Next, that one has somehow seen some indication that Plato in fact followed that natural line of intellectual evolution (and that he didn't ever, for example, temporarily exchange a stronger position for a weaker one, something which – lacking perfect wisdom – could happen to the best of us; for example, by his own admission it happened to Nietzsche – see his "Preface" [1886] to *Human, All Too Human*). Finally, that one has somehow established that whatever Plato wrote necessarily reflected what he thought at the time, and moreover was never revised in light of any subsequent thinking (some have carried this so far as to argue that the *Republic* – which I should have thought would impress even a superficial reader as one of the most beautifully harmonized works ever written – actually consists of unrevised parts from two, or even all three supposed stages. Friedländer's hapless arguments supposedly showing Book One to be an

Note to page xxvi

"early" dialogue and the other nine books as belonging to the "middle" period are representative of such thinking; see his *Plato* III (63-7).

But all of this ignores what would seem undeniable from the kind of careful craftsmanship Plato lavished on his dialogues: that they are not primarily reminders to himself of his own philosophical investigations, much less a public documentation of his progress, but writings designed to serve the educational needs of others. Seen in light of that purpose, then any or all of the dialogues may be products of their author's intellectual maturity, written as his experience with life and pedagogy revealed a need for them. One can not presume that Plato, in the fulness of his wisdom, saw no value in having a more youthful reader explore what he himself regarded as a useful preliminary, or even wrongheaded, view of something. For any number of reasons, *Krito* might well be the last dialogue Plato saw a need to write. We shall never know, and there is little reason to care. But there is every reason to guard against the presumption that one knows what one does not, and in the very nature of the case, cannot know, lest it bias one's own interpretive efforts.

Similar remarks apply to another accepted practice of modern scholars, that of ruling on the authenticity of the dialogues which constitute the canon as it was established in antiquity (with utmost care and rigour, it should be added, and in circumstances far more advantageous for the purpose; after all, Plato's Academy remained in existence for almost nine centuries). The collective result of recent authentication efforts, however, is that several of the less familiar and more puzzling dialogues – the very ones, that is, which might be potentially most useful to us, causing us to rethink our understanding of the others – have come to be widely regarded as spurious, and as a consequence are almost totally neglected today. The web of blithe assumptions and dubious judgments that sustain the current view is neatly dispersed by Thomas Pangle in his "Editor's Introduction" to a collection of new translations and commentaries aptly entitled *The Roots of Political Philosophy: Ten Forgotten Socratic Dialogues*; see also the beginning of Allan Bloom's interpretive essay on the *Hipparchus* in that same volume, 32-5.

However, while an under-appreciation of the political and philosophic significance of Plato's dialogic form of writing is widespread, it is by no means universal. Some students of the dialogues have provided excellent advice on how to read them, and I, for one, am deeply and permanently in their debt. I can only pray that my efforts here reflect favourably on them. Heading the list is Leo Strauss, a man it was never my good fortune to set eyes upon, but whose soul, invested in his books, has served and

Note to page xxvi

continues to serve as the midwife of my philosophical education. I have never read anything of his that was not worth reading several times over, but especially to be recommended for the present purpose is his essay "On Plato's Republic" in *The City and Man*. Intelligent reading is discussed in its first twelve pages and exemplified in the remainder; see as well the book's "Introduction", and an earlier review essay, "On a New Interpretation of Plato's Political Philosophy". Also to be recommended is Allan Bloom's "Preface" and "Interpretive Essay" which accompany his fine translation in *The Republic of Plato*. Jacob Klein has left several helpful statements (e.g., in *A Commentary on Plato's Meno* 3-31; and in "About the *Philebus*" 157-8). So, too, has Stanley Rosen in *Plato's Symposium* xi-xxix and in the "Prologue" to his *Plato's Sophist* 1-57. This last-named source presents a powerful elaboration and defence of what Rosen calls "dramatic phenomenology", which he critically contrasts with the other approaches to the dialogues one commonly encounters today (inspired variously by either Heideggerean phenomenology or some sort of logico-linguistic analysis). Charles L. Griswold, Jr, has edited a valuable collection of essays entitled *Platonic Writings, Platonic Readings* in which several of the interpretive issues I raise are addressed from a variety of perspectives (the contributions by Alan C. Bowen, Rosemary Desjardins, Jürgen Mittelstrass, and Griswold himself are especially noteworthy). Cf. also David Bolotin's *Plato's Dialogue on Friendship* 12-13; Thomas Pangle's *The Laws of Plato* 375-9; Rudolph H. Weingartner's *The Unity of the Platonic Dialogue* 1-12; and Ronna Burger's *The Phaedo: A Platonic Labyrinth* 1-12. Burger has an excellent book exploring the dialogue in which Sokrates expressly raises the political and philosophical issues posed by writing: *Plato's Phaedrus: A Defense of the Philosophical Art of Writing*. See also Cropsey *Political Philosophy* 230-51.

19 This ability to recognize disparate evidence, to weigh its relative importance and reliability, and synthesize it into a single, coherent view is vital to practical and theoretical life alike. Whether one is attempting to integrate the various findings of palaeontologists, biochemists, ethologists, physiologists, and anatomists in an effort to produce a plausible theory of the origin and diversity of life on earth; or bring an ordered understanding of sexuality out of the chaos of evidence presented by comparative mythology, ancient historians, modern anthropologists, studies of early childhood behaviour and learning, primate ethology, clinical psychiatry, and everyday life – success or failure will turn on one's power of synthetic judgment. But recognizing its central importance to all efforts at making sense of the world has a special pertinence for transcending what seems

Note to page xxvi

to me the most dreadful intellectual mistake of modern times: the so-called fact-value distinction, a chimaerical distinction of profound and pervasive consequences for practical life, all of them bad.

Roughly stated, this distinction is based on the view that there are some things called 'values' which are to be understood as ontologically different from everything strictly factual. The latter, but not the former, are evident to one or more kinds of perception and thus can be determined simply by empirical observation and rational analysis. Being based on the perception of qualities and quantities and relations of things (or 'objects') apparently outside and independent of any observer's consciousness, the factual may be thought of as "objective"; this is reflected in the normally broad range of intersubjective agreement one may expect as to "what the facts are". Values, in contrast, are things one tacitly appeals to in making judgments as to what is right or wrong, good or bad, beautiful or ugly, noble or base. Quite what these touchstones of evaluation actually are, and what, if anything, they are supposed to be grounded in, remain mysterious. It seems people not only frequently disagree in their innumerable "value judgments", but the few who have thought enough about the doctrine to espouse it publicly disagree as to how values are to be conceived: some see them as reflections of one's passions or dispositions, others as revelations of God's Will, or of an inexplicable intuition, or as expressions of one's own will or wishes, or as creations of personal "commitments" and "leaps of faith" – but in any case, they are *not* to be understood as derived from a strictly rational analysis of what is factually true concerning an objective reality. Rather, value judgments are profoundly "subjective", essentially – and to that extent, incorrigibly – reflections of the judging subject (a view nicely captured in the popular saying, "Beauty's in the eye of the beholder"). On this view, then, facts and values are regarded as radically different kinds of things, and the one no more bears rational implications for the other than does gold for virtue.

Moreover, a failure to recognize this (factual?) difference is tantamount to gross irresponsibility – if not something worse – on the part of anyone charged with educating others. As Max Weber states in his celebrated essay "Science as a Vocation":

> Now one cannot demonstrate scientifically what the duty of an academic teacher is. One can only demand of the teacher that he have the intellectual integrity to see that it is one thing to state facts, to determine mathematical or logical relations or the internal structure of cultural values, while it is another thing to answer questions of the

Note to page xxvi

value of culture and its individual contents and the question of how one should act in the cultural community and in political associations. These are quite heterogeneous problems. If he asks further why he should not deal with both types of problems in the lecture-room, the answer is: because the prophet and the demagogue do not belong on the academic platform.

... In the lecture-room we stand opposite our audience, and it has to remain silent. I deem it irresponsible to exploit the circumstance that for the sake of their career the students have to attend a teacher's course while there is nobody present to oppose him with criticism. The task of the teacher is to serve the students with his knowledge and scientific experience and not to imprint upon them his personal political views. It is certainly possible that the individual teacher will not entirely succeed in eliminating his personal sympathies. He is then exposed to the sharpest criticism in the forum of his own conscience. And this deficiency does not prove anything; other errors are also possible, for instance, erroneous statements of fact, and yet they prove nothing against the duty of searching for the truth. (*From Max Weber* H.H. Gerth and C.W. Mills, trans., 146)

As to the basis (factual? authoritative? conventional?) upon which Weber can speak about *"the* task of the teacher", or employ such value-laden notions as "integrity" and "responsibility", or justify his or anyone else's "demands", while disclaiming the legitimacy of anyone's speaking "scientifically" (*i.e.*, factually and logically?) about the "duty" of either teacher or scholar – or why everyone who accepts his radical disjunction between "facts" and "values" shouldn't promptly disregard Weber's entire exhortation as merely expressing his own subjective preference, and thus no more rationally defensible than that of the most brazen, unscrupulous demagogue – is never made clear. And is there nothing on the spectrum of human types *between* "value-neutral" scientist at the one end, and prophet or demagogue at the other? Still, no doubt most people today would endorse not only his desire to discourage indoctrination masked as education, but also the basic pedagogical strategy whereby one accomplishes this.

So, in the names of logical consistency and theoretical clarity and practical honesty and pedagogical responsibility, we are all enjoined to recognize that an ontological gulf of unspannable proportions separates the realm of the Is (the factual, the rationally objective, and thus scientifically respectable) from the realm of what anyone imagines Ought To Be. To purport to derive one's "values" from the facts as one sees them is to commit

Note to page xxvi

the "naturalistic fallacy", for as the meanest student of logic will attest, one cannot deduce a conclusion that wasn't already implicit in one's premisses. The fact that for over two millennia the most estimable philosophers proceeded in grand indifference to this view of things should be taken not as counting against it, but rather as evidence that there has been progress in mankind's understanding of such matters. And if we must now admit that no one can rationally demonstrate the superiority of a preference for consistency over inconsistency, for clarity rather than confusion, or for honesty and integrity over fraud and betrayal – and in general, for truth over falsehood – one ought frankly and courageously to admit this fact, and be governed by it accordingly.

As implied above, the distinction in question is of comparatively recent vintage. Although an incipient form of it may be detected as far back as Bacon's "Preface" to *The Great Instauration* (wherein he distinguished the "uncorrupted" knowledge of nature from the "proud" knowledge of good and evil), it gained ascendance only in this century, mainly through a since-discredited view of physical science propagated by the movement known as Logical Positivism (later Logical Empiricism), and to the view of social science so ably advocated by Max Weber, aided and abetted along the way by various philosophical schools giving pride of place to linguistic analysis. (A useful, if incomplete and somewhat superficial history of the emergence of the distinction can be found in Arnold Brecht's *Political Theory* chap. 5; cf. also chaps. 3 and 7. A profound critique of Weber's "scientific value relativism" is that of Leo Strauss, *Natural Right and History* chap. 2.) From its various sources, the distinction entered the mainstream of modern intellectual life – usually *sans* arguments pro or con, and usually in company with modern scientism – whence it has percolated down to grammar schools and permeated outwards to infect virtually all sectors of life.

The widespread, and increasingly dogmatic acceptance of this view that there are some things called 'values' – supposedly "non-cognitive", not rationally grounded in "objective" reality but rather irremediably subjective and irrational (or a-rational) in character – is a potentially devastating development, presenting what can be described without exaggeration as a crisis for Western civilization, manifested in more ways than anyone can count. For the acceptance of this view undermines all confidence in the principles that have guided Western life for almost three millennia, while it precludes our discovering any that are better (denying as it does a rational basis for judging better and worse). The fact-value distinction represents nothing less than a rejection of reason as adequate for disclosing how one ought to live. One is left with only the narrow, crabbed conception of

Note to page xxvi

instrumental reason, seeing it as a mere means of analysis and calculation, thus ultimately in the service of a greater, more embracive unreason. But why even concern oneself with this instrumental, "if-then" rationality, given the presumption that all one's points of departure (the "ifs") are equally unsusceptible to rational establishment? Or if it is impossible to rationally justify to any degree whatsoever a preference for being rational, for "valuing" reason (or any of its subordinate ideas, such as conceptual clarity or logical rigour)? Truly, retail sanity, wholesale madness.

On this view, then, a "taste" for reason, and for "being rational" to whatever extent, is itself no more truly *rational* than a taste for truffles. That it facilitates survival is neither here nor there, since an interest in surviving is no more rational than a preference for perishing, or for destroying. (Is it altogether coincidental that ours is the most destructive century mankind has ever lived through? ... and we aren't through it yet.) That no one actually lives consistent and consistently with this view is neither here nor there, unless one happens to "value" consistency for some non-reason. Needless to say, anyone committed to the fact-value distinction would see no point in seriously studying Plato or any other philosopher, since (insofar as can be *known*) there is nothing intrinsically important to learn, nothing worthy of the name wisdom to be had – or is it that everything is equally worthy of the name, and everything counts as philosophy? ... after all, are not judgments of worth and importance "value judgments"? and who's to say that things learned with the mind are any more worthwhile than things the body learns? maybe riding a bicycle is philosophy ... or, for that matter, maybe falling off is (why prefer success?) – although one should probably add that there's no point in concerning oneself with whether or not anything has a point, since in the final analysis nothing does. And the fact that the great philosophers apparently thought otherwise simply compounds the irrationality of consulting them ... if anyone still retains a "reason" for caring whether his irrationality be simple rather than complex.

I hope I've made my point several times over that, applied reflexively to itself, the "reasoning" behind the fact-value distinction dissolves into incoherence. Now admittedly, this will carry weight only with those who, like me, prefer rational coherence to intellectual chaos and its resulting enslavement to the animal part of one's soul. And in all fairness, one couldn't say that the absurdity of the position is self-evident; one does have to give the matter a lot more thought than most people do. But it is the widespread, unquestioning acceptance of this distinction in the face of all common sense – and most dogmatically among the very people who supposedly think for a living – that speaks volumes about the quality of education in our time. For adopting it is the farthest thing from skepticism about the possibility of ascertaining rational standards and principles: it closes the book on the question. One needn't try, for they don't exist. Ignore the fact that one has to turn massive amounts of everyday experience upside down and inside out in an effort to compress it into this procrustaean bed of modern nihilism – and still it won't fit. Out of belated respect for an utterly abstract distinction required by a defunct misunderstanding of modern science, one must believe that milk's being good for children is incomparably less true to the facts than its being white and rich in calcium. One could fill a fat, boring volume with arguments and evidence showing the innumerable ways this distinction misrepresents the world as we know it, both pre- and post-scientifically, but let the following suffice for present purposes.

Begin with what no sane adult could deny: ought implies can. That is, no one, on pain of being dismissed as a frivolous eristic, would contend that someone ought to do such-and-such while acknowledging that it is physically impossible for him to do it. So much for the yawning chasm between facts and values, for the claim that matters of fact have no implications whatsoever for questions of "value", for the notion that they are of such radically different ontological status that never the twain shall meet, and so on. For surely standards of right and wrong, principles of justice and morality, are limited by what is physically and psychologically and politically possible, and these are matters of fact, difficult as they may sometimes be to determine (thus leaving ample room for intersubjective *dis*agreement).

Second, is there anyone who seriously doubts whether health is something both real and good, *really* good? The natural standards of health may vary with one's race, sex, age, physique, occupation, or even the climate of the place and the season of the year, but no one doubts that there is such a thing. Nor that living things naturally tend towards it: bones mend, wounds heal, immunities are both inherited and acquired, infections are resisted; the senses of smell and taste and touch are biased towards the nutritious. Indeed, the scientific theory of evolution is *founded* on the principle that each surviving lifeform naturally seeks its own comprehensive good health, its "fitness", and furthermore seeks to propagate that good through maximizing its progeny; and that only those most successful at doing so persist. Which is to say (regardless of whether modern biologists acknowledge it), the resulting natural order is not "neutral" with respect to good and bad. Were there no "objective standards" for determining such fitness, evolutionary theory would be incoherent. And I submit that no one truly doubts that living at the peak of one's natural powers is something intrinsically good, and rationally preferable to a life of unremitting pain and debilitating illness. The present massive investment of public and private resources in medical practice and research, enjoying widespread popular approval, merely emphasizes the point. Whatever qualms one may have about the accelerating increase in this investment derive from broader political concerns, not from a belief that it is all in pursuit of something utterly ephemeral or subjective. For while good health is undoubtedly something real, it is by no means the case that one knows precisely what it is, much less how it is best produced, maintained, or restored. If one is to have substantial *knowledge* of this good, as opposed to merely a formal definition of it and opinions about it and an instinct for it, one must actively seek such knowledge.

But this good thing, health, is it solely a matter of body? We know enough about it to know better. As the very term 'psychosomatic' indicates, not only can the condition of one's body affect that of one's soul (i.e., that by means of which one is sentient, conscious, self-sustaining, self-regulating, self-reproducing, and in the absence of which one is a corpse), but vice versa as well. Going without food for the body may leave one feeling surly ("low blood sugar", I'm told); but recognizing an action to be barbarously cruel or grotesquely unjust may cause one to regurgitate a perfectly delicious and nutritious lunch. Virtually all passions have somatic manifestations, some of which count as illness: a grieving person may sicken in body, and even die; the variety of possible physical consequences of living with fear (whether justified or groundless) warrants a generous chapter in medical texts; apparently neither hate nor anxiety is good for the stomach; and what has not been laid at the doorstep of love? And despite all the difficulties, theoretical and practical, with the concept of mental illness, we are none the less pretty sure there are examples of it, ranging from the mildly deranged to the raving mad.

So it is sensible, indeed necessary, to expand one's concept of good health to include a sound mind – better still, soul – as well as a sound body. And since the degree of health one enjoys in both body and soul is a consequence largely of how one lives, one may speak realistically and knowingly of a healthy way of life, one which is to that extent a good way of life, one productive of comprehensive good health. Now, at what point in the course of this expanding orbit of what may be regarded as good does one leave the realm of "facts" and – like Alice falling down the rabbit hole – suddenly find oneself in a radically different kind of place, the imaginary wonderland of "values"? One might add here that, other things being equal, Beauty also seems an intrinsically good thing. And surely it's not altogether in the eye of the beholder. There may not be any rational way of determining who truly is the very most beautiful man or woman in the world, but let's admit this much: most of us are not in the running, and I can't help suspecting it has something to do with how we look (i.e., our perceptible properties).

Third, does one not treat one's own good as if it were something objective, and occasionally attempt to advise others as if theirs was too? People often wonder what would *really* be best for themselves – which career, which mate, which place, and a host of lesser matters – knowing the world or themselves not very well and the distant future not at all. But even granting full marks for the power of positive thinking, virtually everyone actually treats their own good not as something purely subjective, a mere "matter of opinion" (meaning "one view is as good as another"), but rather as something real, about which some views are decidedly better than others. It is often difficult to choose between attractive alternatives, but one shouldn't allow the apparent indeterminacy of that situation to blind one to the fact that we easily eliminate many other repugnant alternatives, and do so in light of objective evidence suggesting it would be prejudicial to our health and happiness. We have every confidence in the world, and justifiably so, that whatever the very best life is, it is *not* one lived in chains. And from the other side of the question, does anyone actually believe that there are never real grounds for regretting that which one chooses, or rejects? The fact that these grounds of regret, and sometimes of shame, are often clear only in hindsight does not alter their "objective facticity"; it is simply one more reason for always proceeding with prudence, and thus for acquiring prudence. True enough, what one is apt to end up being guided by is but an opinion about what is really and truly best, but that opinion is apt to be closer to the truth the better one's understanding of oneself and the world and the possibilities it affords – real things, one and all – and so the pursuit of that better understanding in the interests of a better life makes perfectly good sense.

Finally, consider virtue. Is it really the case that there are no "objective" grounds for rationally preferring and admiring certain qualities of body and soul, while rejecting and despising others? I do not for a moment wish to minimize the problem of finally determining what these are in their rank order, for it is one that taxes the greatest power of synthetic judgment (requiring as it may a comprehensive view of human life under all realistic circumstances, and requiring as it surely does a profound understanding of human nature in both its basic commonality and its significant diversity). The contrast between pagan and Christian conceptions of virtue is sufficient reminder of both the theoretical difficulty and the practical importance of the problem. Still, one should not overlook the fact that certain character traits have nothing to recommend them, whatever one's way of life. Who would wish to be without any power to resist his every desire, however paltry, mean, cruel, or self-destructive? Or to be prey to a host of childish fears, regarding the dark with terror, say, or turning pale and trembling at the mere mention of a snake? Who could want to be so attached to his possessions that he never experienced a sound night's sleep for fear of losing them? Or does anyone long to be downright stupid? ... it doesn't seem so from most people's reaction to the least suggestion that they might be. Is it not simply *true* that some degree of self-control, of mastery over fear, of ability to endure pain, or detachment from one's property, and a basic mental competence are both generally useful and intrinsically enjoyable – and thus *rationally* desirable – whatever one's chosen or allotted way of life? Is not the resulting freedom to act as one's own reason directs innately attractive, and precisely because it is inherently valuable? Is this really just an irrational (or a-rational, or non-rational, or non-cognitive) "value" judgment?

Or is it just a judgment, plain and simple: the application of one's rational power for synthesizing a variety of evidence and considerations and possibilities, for seeing a coherent pattern therein, and drawing a summative conclusion? For is this not what principles and standards – what are today commonly called 'values' – properly represent: summary judgments as to what is right and wrong, good and bad, noble and base, rationally induced from the variety of factors one recognizes to be relevant? One does not *deduce* "values" from "facts"; the rational movement involved is not from the more general to the more particular, wherein one purchases the certainty of one's conclusion at the price of not going beyond what was strictly implicit in one's premises. Rather, the reasoning whereby one arrives at principles and standards is *inductive* and synoptic in character, one of synthesis rather than analysis, integrating a finite heterogeneous plurality of particulars into something general, and potentially unlimited in scope.

This application of inductive reasoning is just as valid and just as fallible as any other; there is no way to guarantee that every relevant factor has been noticed, impartially judged, and properly weighted, or that one's inductive power has been equal to the task. One can do only one's best, and then only if one tries one's best. I think it's fair to add that most people don't even come close, and this itself accounts for much of their

Note to page xxvi

endless disagreeing over questions of "value". Recognition of this fact, along with a fair appreciation of the difficulties such questions pose and of the frailty of even the best human equipment for solving them, amounts to rational grounds for encouraging a due measure of mutual tolerance in political life – whereas, according to the doctrine here in dispute, such tolerance is a "value", neither less nor more rationally defensible than the narrowest, most illiberal fanaticism. (And speaking of fanaticism, I suspect its prevalence in our time is due in no small part to this view of "values" as freely chosen things that are only as "solid" as the intensity of one's "passionate commitment" has rendered them impervious to questioning.)

A recognition of the scale of the problems, seen in light of the limitations of ordinary human reasoning, would suggest that perhaps no one, barring divine assistance, is entitled to hold his induced conclusions about what is right and good and noble other than provisionally, for such summarizing judgments remain ever subject to revision in light of new experience and information, greater clarity, deeper insight. And so, however practically confident one may become as a consequence of sustained effort to refine one's rational judgments about these matters, I suppose one could not finally claim to *know* them. Thus one may have to go to one's grave admitting that, strictly speaking, one knows nothing concerning the matters of greatest importance to a human being, lacking certain knowledge of how best to live. But one has to live none the less in the mean time, winnowing the known possibilities while remaining open to new ones, patiently and persistently endeavouring to bring one's considered opinions ever closer to the truth one seeks.

While much more could be said, I trust the foregoing is sufficient for showing why I believe the problem with the alleged fact-value distinction is *not* primarily that it is "difficult, if not impossible to apply in practice". These difficulties of practical application stem from its being totally fallacious. There are no such things as "values". One may use the word as a sort of omnibus term for standards and principles, and even preferences and tastes, but in the present, confused state of affairs it is dangerous to do so, and we would probably all be better off pretending we'd never heard of such a thing. For plenty of serious questions remain. One may, for example, be thoroughly convinced of the reality, and even of a (partial) knowability of one's own good, but still be highly skeptical about the existence of a *common* good, or of anything else whence a standard of communal justice can take its bearings. These are difficult issues, but one will engage them with the vigour and tenacity they require only if one remains open to the possibility that there is a truth to be known about them.

The great philosophers of our tradition, beginning with Sokrates, all did so. Perhaps it would be best to learn philosophy from them, from men who believed in it, believed in the life of reason, life lived in accordance with the full power and beauty of reason, and who were sympathetic to the possibility that it *is* adequate for dealing with all questions of importance to human beings. Perhaps it would be best to return to Plato.

20 In the weightier words of Leo Strauss:

> Plato's work consists of many dialogues because it imitates the manyness, the variety, the heterogeneity of being. The many dialogues form a *kosmos* which mysteriously imitates the mysterious *kosmos*. The Platonic *kosmos* imitates or reproduces its model in order to awaken us to the mystery of the model and to assist us in articulating that mystery. There are many dialogues because the whole consists of many parts. But the individual dialogue is not a chapter from an encyclopaedia of the philosophic sciences or from a system of philosophy, and still less a relic of a stage of Plato's development. Each dialogue deals with one part; it reveals the truth about that part. But the truth about a part is a partial truth, a half truth. (*The City and Man* 61-2)

21 Though not always so in the dialogues, for occasionally the reader is informed that a particular person who does not speak is none the less present (e.g., in *Protagoras, Phaedo, Republic*). The fact that Plato chose to name someone who simply observes the conversation must be presumed to have some significance, for when he wished to include anonymous onlookers, he did so (e.g., in *Protagoras, Gorgias, Republic, Lesser Hippias*). Indeed, it is only in the capacity of a virtually silent spectator that Plato himself ever makes a personal appearance in the dialogues, and then just once (*Apology of Sokrates*). The importance of this matter could be said to be further emphasized by his expressly noting, again but once, his own *absence* (*Phaedo* 59b; cf. 118a). In any case, the silence of such participants should not be regarded as evidence that their presence is of no consequence, for they are at least witnesses (recall the old maxim of courtship, "two's company, three's a crowd"; cf. *Theages* 123b and *Symposium* 217b). Nor should their silence be unthinkingly interpreted to mean they are merely passive, not active, participants, any more than would a thoughtful reader so interpret his own silence. A bit more conspicuous, if only a bit, is the prolonged silence of a character who earlier had spoken (as in *Gorgias, Kleitophon, Sophist, Statesman, Republic*); his continuing presence should not be forgotten, although

it easily is. In four dialogues, the principal interlocutor is given no name, but rather pointedly identified as a "stranger", either from Elea (*Sophist, Statesman*) or from Athens (*Laws, Epinomis*). And in a related vein, it is remarkable how often Plato elected to present whole discussions as if being recounted by Sokrates, or someone else, to unnamed companions.

22 Leo Strauss *The City and Man* 55. The same cannot be said, of course, about the traditionally accepted subtitles of the dialogues; although they were affixed in antiquity, we do not know by whom.

23 On that assumption I can agree with both Henry James: "No good novel will ever proceed from a superficial mind. ... " ("The Art of Fiction" in *Literary Criticism, Vol 1* 64), and with Ezra Pound: "Great literature is simply language charged with meaning to the utmost possible degree." Equally to my purpose, however, is Pound's observing that the special problem in introducing great literature is that of devising "a system for getting directly and expeditiously at such works, despite the smokescreens erected by half-knowing and half-thinking critics. To get at them, despite the mass of dead matter that these people have heaped up and conserved round about them in the proportion: one barrel of sawdust to each half-bunch of grapes" ("How to Read" in *Literary Essays of Ezra Pound* T.S. Eliot, ed., 23).

But to my mind, few modern writers can speak with more deserved authority about the philosophical basis of great literature than can Joseph Conrad:

> A work that aspires, however humbly, to the condition of art should carry its justification in every line. And art itself may be defined as a single-minded attempt to render the highest kind of justice to the visible universe, by bringing to light the truth, manifold and one, underlying its every aspect. It is an attempt to find in its forms, in its colours, in its light, in its shadows, in the aspects of matter and the facts of life, what of each is fundamental, what is enduring and essential – their one illuminating and convincing quality – the truth of their existence. The artist, then, like the thinker or the scientist, seeks the truth and makes his appeal. ...
>
> Confronted with the same enigmatical spectacle [as confronts the thinker or the scientist] the artist descends within himself, and in that lonely region of stress and strife, if he is deserving and fortunate, he finds the terms of his appeal. His appeal is made to our less

obvious capacities: to the part of our nature which, because of the warlike conditions of existence, is necessarily kept out of sight within the more resisting and hard qualities – like the vulnerable body within a steel armour. His appeal is less loud, more profound, less distinct, more stirring – and sooner forgotten. Yet its effect endures forever. The changing wisdom of successive generations discards ideas, questions facts, demolishes theories. But the artist appeals to that part of our being which is not dependent on wisdom: to that in us which is a gift and not an acquisition – and, therefore, more permanently enduring. He speaks to our capacity for delight and wonder, to the sense of mystery surrounding our lives; to our sense of pity, and beauty, and pain; to the latent feeling of fellowship with all creation – to the subtle but invincible conviction of solidarity that knits together the loneliness of innumerable hearts, to the solidarity in dreams, in joy, in sorrow, in aspirations, in illusions, in hope, in fear, which binds men to each other, which binds together all humanity – the dead to the living, the living to the unborn. ...

The sincere endeavor to accomplish that creative task, to go as far on that road as his strength will carry him, to go undeterred by faltering, weariness, or reproach, is the only valid justification for the worker in prose. And if his conscience is clear, his answer to those who in the fullness of a wisdom which looks for immediate profit, demand specifically to be edified, consoled, amused; who demand to be promptly improved, or encouraged, or frightened, or shocked, or charmed, must run thus: – My task which I am trying to achieve is, by the power of the written word, to make you hear, to make you feel – it is, before all, to make you *see*. That – and no more, and it is everything. If I succeed, you shall find there, according to your deserts, encouragement, consolation, fear, charm, all you demand – and, perhaps, also that glimpse of truth for which you have forgotten to ask. (*The Nigger of the Narcissus* [1897] "Preface")

Clearly, here Conrad was of a mind with his friend and colleague Ford Madox Ford, who has one of his characters observe, "But the fellow talked like a cheap novelist. – Or like a very good novelist for the matter of that, if it's the business of a novelist to make you see things clearly" (*The Good Soldier* part III chap. 1).

24 Ronna Burger, in "Socratic *Eirōneia*", provides an interesting analysis of the perspectives of the three characters who accuse Sokrates of being ironic

(Thrasymachos, Kallikles, and Alkibiades), and of the significance of Sokrates' self-attribution in his *Apology*.

25 In my opinion, many of the finer comic moments of the dialogues often go unrecognized. Doubtless this is due in part to a not-unbecoming piety towards these time-honoured classics, and the evident seriousness of their themes. But as Jacob Klein, himself no stranger to irony, puts it, " ... however serious the purpose and the content of a Platonic dialogue, its seriousness is permeated by playfulness; indeed, ... seriousness and play are *sisters*. ... " ("About the *Philebus*" 157). Unfortunately, readers today are unlikely to be familiar with the more transparently comic of the dialogues, such as the two named after Hippias (a sophist as obtuse and pompous as he was rich and famous), or the still more preposterous *Ion*. Even an ironic masterpiece such as *Protagoras*, containing one of the most amusing satires on intellectual vanity ever created, is seldom recognized for what it is. Hence the typical modern reader, ill-prepared to recognize levity in the dialogues (much less outright wackiness), readily misinterprets the deadpan style of the Platonic Sokrates and his light-hearted manner of treating inherently portentous, even fateful, material (the encounter between Sokrates and Anytus in *Meno* is a *tour de force* of "black humour"). As joyfully as his mentor ever did, Plato makes it his regular business to deflate the pretensions of "the wise", while with equal seriousness he encourages the endeavour to become truly so. In short, whatever respect and talent Plato may have had for tragedy (a lot, I would say; consider the ending of *Phaedo*), one suspects he *loved* comedy. He certainly had the genius for it; but, like Jane Austen, he employed it with much tact and subtlety.

And if I might be permitted a somewhat cryptic assessment here, I would suggest that Plato's capacity for high humour derives from his superior insight into the truth of things, into reality, which he playfully juxtaposes with a world as people wish or imagine it to be. To love the truth – the *whole* truth, including the truth about human aspirations – is necessarily to love comedy. Which is to say, his refined sense of the truly comic is intrinsic to his wisdom. I suspect he would approve of the old uncle in Isak Dinesen's "Sorrow-acre" teaching his nephew, "Tragedy should remain the right of human beings, subject, in their conditions or in their own nature, to the dire law of necessity. To them it is salvation and beatification". But "the true art of the gods is the comic. The comic is a condescension of the divine to the world of man ... " (*Winter's Tales* 51). Plato's apparent strictures against comedy (e.g., *Republic* 388e-a; cf. 451a-b, 452a-e) amount to a warning against letting one's sense of humour corrupt one's judgment (for to laugh at something is to declare it comical, whether or not it truly and justly is so). He who would be a king over himself must learn to think before he laughs. The ironic mode of comedy manifest in the dialogues trains one to do so.

And that my own crypticity might be seen for the tame thing it is, let me add the following pair of observations:

> Plato's political theory is as rigorously musicalized as his astronomy. His legislation on men, women, children, armies, elections, governing bodies, fines, fees, and a host of other problems is grounded, in each political dialogue, on the relevant musical-mathematical model. Beneath every noble sentiment lurks a mathematical jest. Yet his abstract models, despite his humor, remain very beautiful examples of 'communities' with varying degrees of internal complexity and various solutions to the problem of limitation. Plato the writer, however, has fused the sublime and the ridiculous so perfectly that we are not likely ever to separate them successfully. (Ernest G. McClain *The Pythagorean Plato: Prelude to the Song Itself* 130)

> If it remains true that even on the highest level the alternation between gravity and levity is according to nature, one must say that whereas gravity belongs with knowledge of the truth, levity comes into play in the communication of the truth. The same man who is the teacher of founders or princes and who discovers the true character of 'the world' communicates this truth to the young. In the former capacity he is half-man half-beast or alternates between humanity and inhumanity. In the latter capacity he alternates between gravity and levity. For in the latter capacity he is the bringer of a light which illumines things that can not be illumined by the sun. The unity of knowledge and communication of knowledge can also be compared to the combination of man and horse, although not to a centaur. (Leo Strauss *Thoughts on Machiavelli* 290)

26 Cf. Alexandre Kojève "Philosophy and Wisdom" in *Introduction to the Reading of Hegel* Allan Bloom, ed., James H. Nichols, Jr, trans.

CHAPTER ONE

1 This name is one of those explained in *Cratylus*, and moreover in a context that bears directly on the present study. There Sokrates discusses what is most important about names:

> "Does not the same reasoning apply to 'king'? A king will sometimes come from a king, a good man from a good man, a noble one from a noble one, also many others likewise, the offspring of each race (*genos*) being like the others, if nothing monstrous is born. So they should be called by the same names. But there can be a variety of syllables, so that names which are the same [none the less] *seem* otherwise to an individual, ... [whereas] one who knows about names observes their power and is not astounded if some letter is added or transposed, or subtracted, or even if the power of the name is in some entirely different letters. Just as we were now discussing, *Astyanax* and *Hektōr* have none of the same letters in common except 't', but they mean the same thing. And what letters does *Archepolis* [ruler of the city] have in common? Yet it means the same thing; and there are many others which simply mean 'king'. And others mean 'general' [*strategos*], such as *Agis* and *Polemarchos* and *Eupolemos* [good warrior]." (393e-394c, my translation; also, see *Phaedrus*, 257b).

We glean most of what we know about Polemarchos and his family from what is generally acknowledged to be among the finest surviving examples of Attic rhetoric, the speech "Against Erastosthenes" composed by his rhetorician brother, Lysias. There he briefly sketches the family history up to the night he and Polemarchos were set upon by agents of the Thirty Tyrants for having the misfortune of being both prodemocratic and wealthy (cf. *Apology* 32c-d). Lysias escaped, but Polemarchos was taken and executed (by hemlock). Nikeratos suffered the same fate and for the same reasons, as did his paternal uncle, Eukrates (referred to in the remnants of another speech attributed to Lysias, "On the Confiscation of the Property of the Brother of Nikias"). Thus the special poignancy of portraying these particular young men as participants in history's most celebrated discussion of justice and tyranny.

2 While I have consulted and examined many translations of the dialogue during the twenty-odd years I've studied it, I prefer and generally follow Allan Bloom's fine rendition – *The Republic of Plato*. My frequent departures

from it, usually minor, are not explicity noted. In examining the original text, I generally find the Loeb edition (Paul Shorey, ed. and trans., London: Heineman 1937) convenient, but defer to the 1902 Oxford text (John Burnet, ed.), and rely for philological guidance on the critical commentary of James Adam *The Republic of Plato*. Leonard Brandwood's *A Word Index to Plato* is simply invaluable for a serious study of this and all the dialogues. An especially useful discussion of the problem of translating the *Republic*, with a comparison of the merits of some of the readily available English versions, is Joel B. Lidov "Justice in Translation".

The secondary literature on the *Republic* is, of course, enormous. No one could read but a small part of it. I'm sure that I am unaware of many works that are well worth consulting, and if I highlight but a few that I have found especially valuable, no invidious implications are intended. And but for a very few exceptions, I see no point in citing scholarship with which I disagree (the list would be very long indeed); and as for works (or parts thereof) that I regard as noteworthy, I have limited my citations to those which actually serve a purpose in the context of what I have written. At the outset, however, I must acknowledge that my deepest debts are to Leo Strauss's "On Plato's Republic" (in *The City and Man*) and Allan Bloom's "Interpretive Essay" (which accompanies his translation, noted above). Another essay that I found especially interesting is Eva Brann's "The Music of the *Republic*". One other work, although it came to my attention only after my own study was largely completed, did stimulate fresh thinking on several aspects of my interpretation: Seth Bernadete *Socrates' Second Sailing*.

3 As Machiavelli observes, "It is a thing truly very natural and ordinary to desire to acquire; and when men who are able to do so do it, they are always praised, or [at least] not blamed. ... " *The Prince* chap. 3, Leo Paul S. de Alvarez, ed. and trans. 17–18; cf. 101, 111.

4 The primacy of the spirit is a doctrine perenially favoured by men of martial temper. Admiral Nagumo, for example, made it the cornerstone of his exhortation to the flight crews who were to attack Pearl Harbor: "However difficult the situation you may face, don't lose your confidence in victory. Cope with it with calmness and composure. ... Is there anything, no matter how difficult it may be, that can not be done by an intrepid spirit and a burning loyalty?" Quoted by Gordon W. Prange in *At Dawn We Slept* 387.

5 Here, of course, 'music' refers to that which falls within the jurisdiction of the Muses, those nine daughters of Zeus and Mnemosyne ("Memory") who are understood to be divine sources of inspiration for all literature, inquiry, and fine art (cf. Hesiod's *Theogony* 25-115). But whereas in times past it was poetry that primarily constituted the conscious horizon of people, the dominant form of "music" in our time – at least with respect to presenting an intelligible view of the world – is the novel. Stendhal's observation that "a novel is a mirror carried along the high road" (*The Red and the Black* chap. 49) could be said to reflect a Platonic assessment of the novel's essentially "poetic" character. Ezra Pound, incidentally, credits Stendhal with being the first to realize poetry had come to be "greatly inferior to prose for conveying a clear idea of the diverse states of our consciousness ('les mouvements du coeur'). And at that moment the serious art of writing 'went over to prose', ... " ("How to Read" in Eliot, ed., *Literary Essays* 31).

These claims are perhaps substantiated best through critical work such as that of F.R. Leavis, whose essay on *Hard Times* in the journal *Scrutiny* initiated a series entitled "The Novel as Dramatic Poem" (reprinted in his *The Great Tradition* and *Dickens the Novelist*, cf. xi). It is with Henry James's own enlarged conception of poet as including novelists such as himself that Leavis refers to James as an "intellectual poet-novelist of 'high civilization'" (*The Great Tradition* 12). "In calling him 'poet-novelist' I myself was intending to convey that the determining and controlling interests in his art engage what is 'deepest in him' (he being a man of exceptional capacity for experience), and appeal to what is deepest in us" (ibid. 128). James himself contends that what gives the novelist "a great character [is] the fact that he has at once so much in common with the philosopher and the painter; this double analogy is a magnificent heritage" ("The Art of Fiction" in *Literary Criticism*, Vol. I 47).

Moreover, James's conception of the novelist is distinctly "dialogical": "In every novel the work is divided between the writer and the reader; but the writer makes the reader very much as he makes his characters. When he makes him ill, that is, makes him indifferent, he does no work; the writer does all. When he makes him well, that is, makes him interested, then the reader does quite half the labor" ("The Novels of George Eliot" in *Literary Criticism*, Vol. I, 922). In his serio-comic *Tristram Shandy*, Laurence Sterne expresses his dialogical assumptions somewhat differently: "Writing, when properly managed (as you may be sure I think mine is) is but a different name for conversation. As no one, who knows what he is about in good company, would venture to talk all; – so no author, who understands the just bounds of decorum, would presume to think all: The truest respect which you can pay to the reader's understanding, is to halve this matter amicably, and leave him something to imagine, in his turn as well as yourself" (Book II chap. 11).

Nietzsche contends that it is the Platonic dialogue which provides "the model of a new art form, the model of the *novel* – which may be described as an infinitely enhanced Aesopian fable, in which poetry holds the same rank in relation to dialectical philosophy as this same philosophy held for many centuries in relation to theology: namely, the rank of *ancilla*" (*The Birth of Tragedy* Walter Kaufmann, trans., sec. 14). This view, implausible at first, is ratified by no less an authority than D.H. Lawrence: "If you wish to look into the past for what-next books, you can go back to the Greek philosophers. Plato's dialogues are queer little novels. It seems to me it was the greatest pity in the world, when philosophy and fiction got split. They used to be one, right from the days of myth. Then they went and parted, like a nagging married couple, with Aristotle and Thomas Aquinas and that beastly Kant. So the novel went sloppy, and philosophy went abstract-dry. The two should come together again – in the novel" ("Surgery for the Novel – or a Bomb" *Phoenix: The Posthumous Papers of D.H. Lawrence* Edward D. McDonald, ed., 520).

Persuaded, then, that Plato's dialogues provide the prototype for this modern musical form – as simply browsing the pages of, say, Austen or Turgenev or Balzac might itself suggest – I have borrowed the titles of my chapters from some novelists I admire, though not in all cases from those I most admire, nor do I mean to imply that these are their most estimable works. My first criterion of choice is that the title itself be suitably descriptive of the chapter's content in at least one sense, if only ironically. I do not mean to suggest that the chapter offers much insight into the book whence its title was drawn, or vice versa (although I suppose that such possibilities are not to be utterly excluded). Apart from the titles, however, the various references to novels which augment this study of the *Republic* are intended to exemplify my understanding of Plato's teaching concerning the relationship between poetry and philosophy.

But for now, let a master poet-novelist have a final word on this subject:

> Nothing is important but life. And for myself, I can absolutely see life nowhere but in the living. Life with a capital L is only man alive. Even a cabbage in the rain is cabbage alive. All things that are living are amazing. And all things that are dead are subsidiary to the living. Better a live dog than a dead lion. But better a live lion than a live dog. *C'est la vie!*

Note to page 8

It seems impossible to get a saint, or a philosopher, or a scientist, to stick to this simple truth. They are all, in a sense, renegades. The saint wishes to offer himself up as spiritual food for the multitude. Even Francis of Assisi turns himself into a sort of angel-cake, of which anyone may take a slice. But an angel-cake is rather less than man alive. ...

The philosopher, on the other hand, because he can think, decides that nothing but thoughts matter. It is as if a rabbit, because he can make little pills, should decide that nothing but little pills matter. As for the scientist, he has absolutely no use for me so long as I am man alive. To the scientist, I am dead. He puts under the microscope a bit of dead me, and calls it me. He takes me to pieces, and says first one piece, and then another piece, is me. My heart, my liver, my stomach, have all been scientifically me, according to the scientist; and nowadays I am either a brain, or nerves, or glands, or something more up-to-date in the tissue line.

Now I absolutely flatly deny that I am a soul, or a body, or a mind, or an intelligence, or a nervous system, or a bunch of glands, or any of the rest of these bits of me. The whole is greater than the part. And therefore, I, who am man alive, am greater than my soul, or spirit, or body, or mind, or consciousness, or anything else that is merely a part of me. I am a man, and alive. I am man alive, and as long as I can, I intend to go on being man alive.

For this reason I am a novelist. And being a novelist, I consider myself superior to the saint, the scientist, the philosopher, and the poet, who are all great masters of different bits of man alive, but never get the whole hog.

The novel is the one bright book of life. Books are not life. They are only tremulations in the ether. But the novel as a tremulation can make the whole man alive tremble. Which is more than poetry, philosophy, science, or any other book-tremulation can do.

The novel is the book of life. In this sense, the Bible is a great confused novel. You may say, it is about God. But it is really about man alive. Adam, Eve, Sara, Abraham, Isaac, Jacob, Samuel, David, Bath-Sheba, Ruth, Esther, Solomon, Job, Isaiah, Jesus, Mark, Judas, Paul, Peter: what is it but man alive, from start to finish? Man alive, not mere bits. Even the Lord is another man alive, in a burning bush, throwing the tablets of stone at Moses's head.

I hope you begin to get my idea, why the novel is supremely important, as a tremulation on the ether. Plato makes the perfect ideal being tremble in me. But that's only a bit of me. Perfection is only a bit, in the strange make-up of man alive. The Sermon on the Mount makes the selfless spirit of me quiver. But that, too, is only a bit of me. The Ten Commandments set the old Adam shivering in me, warning me that I am a thief and a murderer, unless I watch it. But even the old Adam is only a bit of me.

I very much like all these bits of me to be set trembling with life and the wisdom of life. But I do ask that the whole of me shall tremble in its wholeness, some time or other.

And this, of course, must happen in me, living.

But as far as it can happen from a communication, it can only happen when a whole novel communicates itself to me. The Bible – but all the Bible – and Homer, and Shakespeare: these are the supreme old novels. These are all things to all men. Which means that in their wholeness they affect the whole man alive, which is the man himself, beyond any part of him. They set the whole tree trembling with a new access of life, they do not just stimulate growth in one direction. (D.H. Lawrence "Why the Novel Matters" *Phoenix* McDonald, ed., 534–6)

6 Machiavelli admonishes a prince to

exercise more in peace than in war, which he can do in two modes: one with works, and the other with the intellect. And as for works, besides keeping his own arms well-ordered and exercised, he ought to be always out on the chase, and by that means to accustom his body to hardships and also in part to learn the nature of sites – to know how the mountains rise, how valleys open, how the plains lie, and to understand the nature of rivers and marshes – and in this to put the greatest of care. This knowledge is useful in two modes: first, he learns to know his own country, and he can better understand how to defend it; and then, by means of his knowledge and experience of these sites, he will comprehend easily any other site that he may necessarily have to examine for the first time. ... And that prince who lacks this ability lacks the first requirement of a captain ... (*The Prince* chap. 14: p. 89)

That there is more to such 'topological' expertise than first meets the eye is indicated in numerous ways. *The Prince* virtually begins with a geo-

Notes to pages 9–10

graphical analogy: "for, just as those who sketch the countryside place themselves below in the plain to consider the nature of mountains and high places, and in order to consider the low places they put themselves high on the mountains, similarly, to come to know well the nature of the people one needs to be a prince and to know well that of princes one needs to be of the people." Inasmuch as Machiavelli has a lot to say about both, he presumably has a comprehensive familiarity with both kinds of "sites" and perspectives. And the book virtually ends with his likening Fortune to a river. There can be little doubt but that Machiavelli intended his book to itself be a suitable "exercise" for the intellect.

7 Probably no one more cogently articulates the inner rationale of such matters than Machiavelli: "For between someone who is armed and someone who is unarmed, there is no proportion whatsoever; and it is not reasonable that he who is armed willingly obeys him who is unarmed, nor that the unarmed be secure among armed servants. Since there is disdain on the one side, and suspicion on the other, it is impossible that they work well together" (*The Prince* chap. 14 pp 88–9). He earlier observes in the same work (chap. 6) that "Moses, Cyrus, Theseus, and Romulus, had they been unarmed, would have been unable to make [their people] long observe their constitutions, as in our times happened to Fra Girolamo Savonarola, who was ruined in his new orders when the multitude began not to believe them; and he had no way to hold firm those who had believed nor to make the unbelievers believe." (See also Machiavelli's *The Art of War* "Dedicatory Preface")

8 That Book Five is a comedy is indicated by various textual clues, beginning with the many references to laughter and ridicule and the ridiculous (literally, the laughable) – for example, 445a–b, 451a, 452a, 452c, 452d, 455cd, 457ab. Given its themes, developed in obvious counterpoint to *Lysistrata* and *Ecclesiazusae* and *Clouds*, Allan Bloom is amply justified in characterizing the book as "preposterous", judging it to be "Socrates' response to his most dangerous accuser, Aristophanes, and his contest with him" ("Interpretive Essay" 380). It should be noted, however, that the philosopher's ironic proposals are ridiculous only at the level of the city. As I endeavour to show in chap. 6 ("Portrait of a Lady"), their analogues at the level of the soul – an understanding of which is ostensibly the main epistemic purpose for describing the city (cf. 358b, 366e, 367b, d, e, 368e, 472c) – are serious enough. But one must first allow for the fact that today the politically ridiculous has become many people's ideal, and that accordingly

they experience great difficulty seeing much that is funny about the book. In the first of his Appendices on Book Five, Adam has a useful survey of some of the evidence and arguments pertaining to this being a "contest with Aristophanes", although in confining his attention to a comparison between it and *Ecclesiazusae*, he overlooks a major portion of the relevant material (I, 345-55).

Zdravko Planinc shows another dimension to Book Five, that it in effect plays variations on themes from Homer's *Odyssey*; see his *Plato's Political Philosophy* 275-85.

9 This is the only mention of 'unwarlike' (*apolemos*, 456a) in the dialogue. But the term is used elsewhere in the corpus, most notably in the dialogue *Statesman*. There, the Stranger from Elea is discussing natures with the younger Sokrates while the older Sokrates looks on. The Stranger speaks of "an illness resulting for cities that becomes the most hateful of all", namely:

> It's likely to be the whole arrangement of life. Those who are especially well-ordered are ever prepared to live the quiet life, minding their own business alone with themselves, associating with everyone at home on these terms, and likewise with respect to other cities they are prepared on every issue to be at peace in some sense. And because of just this love [*erōs*], which is often inopportune, whenever they have their own way they become unwarlike without realizing it, and so make their youths the same way, and they are always the prey of aggressors. And thus in not many years, they themselves and their children and the entire city, instead of being free, often become slaves without realizing that it's happening. (307d-a; cf. *Laws* 815d; translation based on Seth Benardete's in *The Being of the Beautiful*)

10 As Leo Strauss observes, "Polemarchus' first mistake in the conversation was his failure to stick to the identification of justice with the art of war: justice in 'peace' is the allied individuals' conduct towards neutrals; there is never simple peace." And "The art of arts is not money-making but the art of war" (*The City and Man* 72, 82). But who better to quote on the subject than Machiavelli? To wit: "A prince, then, ought to have no other object, nor any other thought, nor take anything else for his art, but war, its orders and its discipline; for this is the only art awaiting one who commands. And it is of such virtue, that not only does it maintain those who are born princes, but many times men of private fortune rise

Note to page 17

to that degree by it; and one sees, on the contrary, that princes, when they have thought more of the niceties of life than of arms, have lost their state." This passage, which begins chap. 14, is at the virtual centre of *The Prince* (88).

That these judgments remain true even in The Age of Democracy is best exemplified by the career of arguably its greatest statesman, Winston Churchill. A natural-born prince, his speeches and deeds alike attest that he thought constantly of war, that he was a man eminently suited for it, and that (as his many critics suspected) he loved war – the many-faceted challenge of it, that is, not the pain and suffering and loss it causes. Indeed, to his mind part of the challenge of war is in minimizing its destructiveness, though not at the risk of defeat. "Domestic" politics was for him but a pallid surrogate for the great politics of war, any aspect of which he always found easier to pursue with gusto. He was as adamant as Machiavelli about planning for war in times of peace, a problem greatly aggravated for modern democracies by their treasured distinction – and resulting division of labour – between civil and military authority, and its companion doctrine of subordinating the latter to the former. In *The World Crisis: 1911–1918*, Churchill observes:

> In time of war there is great uncertainty as to what the enemy will do and what will happen next. But still, once you are at war, the task is definite and all-dominating. ... But suppose the whole process of war is transported out of the region of reality and into that of the imagination. Suppose you have to assume to begin with that there will be a war at all: secondly, that your country will be in it when it comes: thirdly, that you will go in as a united nation and that the nation will be united and convinced *in time*, and that the necessary measures will be taken before it is *too late*, – then the processes of thought become speculative indeed. Every set of assumptions which it is necessary to make, draws new veils of varying density in front of the dark curtain of the future. The life of the thoughtful soldier or sailor in time of peace is made up of these experiences – intense effort, amid every conceivable distraction, to pick out across and among a swarm of confusing hypotheses what actually will happen on a given day and what actually must be done to meet it before that day is ended. Meanwhile, all around people, greatly superior in authority and often in intelligence, regard him as a plotting knave, or at best an overgrown child playing with toys, and dangerous toys at that. (99)

11 Aristotle's *Politics* is worth reviewing on this point, for he goes well beyond the familiar observation that humans are the only animals endowed with rational speech (*logos*). He regards this fact as conclusive evidence that the human being is by nature a *political* animal (*ho anthrōpos physei politikon zō-on*; 1253 a 4) – which means much more than simply a "social" animal – and that the political association is both natural and unique to man. The literally dumb (*alogos*) beasts, gregarious or not, are inwardly ruled by pleasure and pain, and thus outwardly by the external causes of pleasure and pain (one reason brute strength figures so prominently in determining their behaviour). Mere sounds are adequate for expressing pleasure and pain, and other passionate states. But *logos* allows communication about the hypothetical, thus about the advantageous and harmful, therefore about the just and unjust, and it is a sharing of these things that makes a polity much more than simply a herd or a pack of gregarious animals. Aristotle, however, further contends that he who is citiless (*apolis*) by nature (rather than by chance) is either something wretched (*phaulos*), or something stronger (*kreitton*) than human, and is – in Homer's words – "clanless, lawless, heartless", as well as by nature "desirous of war" (1253 a 2-8). Aristotle subsequently suggests he must be either a beast or a god (1253 a 29).

Strictly read, then, Aristotle virtually begins his *Politics* with the observation that the whole natural hierarchy environing man is an order of war, with things higher than mere humans as well as things lower being animated by the spirit of war. (And what could account for man's being an exception to this otherwise universal order of war? Is not man a piece of nature, too – as Aristotle would be the first to insist?) His image here is especially interesting: he likens the citiless human to an isolated piece in draughts. I see only one plausible interpretation of this image. For what happens to such "isolated pieces"? They don't expire of hunger or thirst, or perish from exposure or fatigue, much less pine away from lack of love. They are, as we say, "captured" or "destroyed" by the better-deployed pieces of an opponent. Draughts and chess and other such board games have often been likened to stylized warfare, war of purely logical and psychological strategy and tactics – war games for the mind. Quite naturally, they have been favourites of military men throughout the ages.

12 Obviously, a claim of this scope cannot be adequately documented, much less defended, in an endnote. And it involves more than explicit claims, arguments, doctrines. Dramatic features and contexts figure as well. A few indications will have to suffice. The dialogue *Charmides*, which teaches the

Note to page 21

moderation that results from self-knowledge, is set in a wrestling school, and begins with the philosopher freshly returned from war and being importuned to recount the fierce battle he has just survived, although many others perished. Against this backdrop, he in turn asks about philosophy and the virtue of young men. The first words of the *Gorgias*, which teaches about high and low kinds of rhetoric and which shows Sokrates at his most combative, are especially interesting: "War and Battle, they say, must be partaken of this way." The polite skirmishing with old Gorgias and his lightly armed protégé gives way to a real slugfest once the politically ambitious Kallikles squares off with the philosopher. In his *Apology*, Sokrates tacitly likens himself to the greatest of heroes – the adventurous Heracles (22a); and the high-spirited, most warlike Achilles (28b-d) – and he justifies his own way of life as being akin to military service (28de; cf. 38ea). In *Phaedrus*, Sokrates teaches that a base kind of lover will out of jealousy keep his beloved "from experiencing much beneficial intercourse, especially such as would make him become a man, the greatest being that which would make him prudent. This happens to be divine philosophy. ... " Instead, he will contrive to keep the beloved ignorant in mind, and in body "effeminate, not virile, not brought up in the sun, but under mingled [or, common; *summiges*] shadows, inexperienced in manly labours and the sweat of exertion. ... One with such a body, in war and all great crises, gives comfort to his enemies, and fills his friends and even his lovers with fear" (239b-d). In the *Symposium*, in which praise of *erōs* becomes praise of a philosopher, what he is praised *for* is his conduct in love and war, and whom he is praised *by* is reputedly the most erotic and warlike man in the city, Alkibiades (215a-222c). The philosopher's own encomium of Love, which stresses its "power and courage/manliness [*andreia*]", also bears reflecting upon (212bc; cf. 203d). The *Meno* portrays a discussion between Sokrates and a young man on his way to join the same ill-fated expedition of conquest that occasioned Xenophon's *Anabasis*. In it, the philosopher counters a paralysing sophistical puzzle (since known as 'Meno's Paradox') with a puzzling doctrine of his own which teaches that all learning is actually a kind of "recollection" (*anamnēsis*). After supposedly demonstrating its validity by helping Meno's slave to "recollect" the Pythagorean theorem, Sokrates admits that he does not have complete confidence in all that he has argued, but that he is "determined to do battle, in both word and deed" in defence of the belief that we have a duty to inquire after what we do not know, and that doing so will make us "better and more courageous and less lazy" (86bc). The *Greater Hippias* is ostensibly structured by Sok-

Notes to page 21

rates' ironic preparations to "do battle" in an argument concerning the Beautiful (286d; cf. 294d, 299a). See also *Theaetetus* 180a–b, *Philebus* 22c–23a, *Timaeus* 88a, and *Laches* 194a.

13 The disclaimer which begins the preceding note applies equally here. Again, the merest sampling will have to do. The prominence of war in the writings of Machiavelli presumably needs no documentation. What might be worth adding, however, is that his various discussions about arms and citadels and hunting and exploring terrain may also be an esoteric teaching about philosophy. For a clear enough indication of this, consider Book III chap. 39 of his *Discourses* in light of commentaries on it by Leo Strauss in *Thoughts on Machiavelli* 154–5 and Harvey Mansfield *Machiavelli's New Modes and Orders* 421–4.

The heart of Descartes's *Discourse on Method* is chap. 2 (in which are presented four fundamentals of philosophic method) and chap. 3 (which explains and recommends four maxims of provisional morality). This two-chapter section – which advances the basic rules supposedly governing all of his thoughts and actions – *begins* with Descartes's informing his reader that he discovered his method during a brief interlude in a long war; and it *ends* with his explaining why he chose as the suitable locale in which to pursue his philosophic investigations a country that had been made well-ordered by long war. So, according to his own account, war brackets, or surrounds, his philosophic activity. And near the end of the *Discourse*, he likens the problems encountered in the pursuit of truth to those of someone pursuing wealth:

> Or one might well compare them to the leaders of an army whose forces regularly grow in proportion to their victories; they need more leadership to maintain themselves after the loss of a battle than they do after they have succeeded in taking cities or provinces. For one truly engages in battles when one tries to overcome all the difficulties and mistakes that keep us from arriving at knowledge of the truth; and it is really the loss of a battle to accept a false opinion touching on a rather general and important matter. ... For myself, if I have already found any truths in the sciences ... , I can say that these are only results and offshoots of five or six major difficulties that I have surmounted; and I count them as so many battles in which luck was on my side. (Cress, trans., 36)

But the philosopher who is most explicit concerning the relationship between philosophy and war is Nietzsche. He is also, in my opinion, one of Plato's most insightful readers (strange as this might seem at first blush – the seeming strangeness is of Nietzsche's own contriving). Among his many statements on struggle and courage, cruelty and mastery, danger in the alley and in the heart, is this from part I chap. 7 of *Ecce Homo* (the part purporting to explain, or illustrate, why he is " ... So Wise"):

> War is another thing. I am warlike by nature. To attack is among my instincts. *Being able* to be an enemy, *being* an enemy – that perhaps presupposes a strong nature; in any case, it belongs to every strong nature. A strong nature needs resistances, hence it seeks resistances: the *aggressive* pathos belongs as necessarily to strength as the feeling of vengefulness and vindictiveness does to weakness. Woman, for example, is vengeful: that is due to her weakness, just as is her susceptibility to others' distress. – The strength of one who attacks has in the opposition he needs a kind of *gauge*; every growth reveals itself by the search for a powerful opponent – or problem: for a warlike philosopher challenges problems, too, to a duel. The task is *not* simply to master whatever resistances happen to present themselves, but to master those against which one has to bring all one's strength, suppleness, and skill with weapons – to master *equal* opponents ... Equality in the face of the enemy – first supposition of an *honest* duel.

He goes on to reduce his practice of philosophical warfare to four cardinal principles. Let me suggest that Nietzsche's "warlike" posture and policy must always be borne in mind when one is assessing his lifelong preoccupation with the Platonic Sokrates. One might also consider *Ecce Homo's* retrospective appraisal of *Beyond Good and Evil*; it is characterized as a baited hook to be used in "the slow search for those related to me, those who, out of strength", would volunteer to participate in "the great war" (translation based on R.J. Hollingdale's, 47, 112).

CHAPTER TWO

1 Allan Bloom "Interpretive Essay" 380. Even a superficial reading of Xenophon's *Lakedaimoniōn Politeia* ("Constitution of the Lacedaemonions") suffices to prove Bloom's point.

2 The issue of the two names for the cities in *logos* is even a bit more complicated than I have so far indicated, for there are senses in which *both*

Notes to page 25

names are applicable to both cities. When Sokrates first makes his binomial proposal, we have before us a single city in *logos*, and what he says – that it would make little difference in the character of such a city were it ruled by a single best elder or by a small council of such men – seems correct. Apart from the ironical allusion to the philosophical dog (375e–c), there is nothing to indicate that its rulers are *philosophers*. And as most of his references to its ruling class are in the plural, it is natural to think of this regime as Aristocracy. Moreover, with the idea of *philosopher*-kings being introduced as the logical culmination of the radical innovations of Book Five, and tending to dominate attention thereafter – repeated references being made to philosophers becoming kings, or kings philosophers (473cd, 474bc, 499bc, 502a, 543a; cf. 487e, 498ea, 501b, 503b, 540d; also 580bc and 592a–b) – it is natural to associate 'Kingship' with the second and higher city in *logos*, reserving 'Aristocracy' for the first (and sole practical) city in *logos*. But since the only "wage" that can be plausibly offered philosophical rulers is the prospect of being relieved of political responsibilities "in turn" and left free to philosophize "the greater part of the time with one another", even the pretext of this being a workable scheme presupposes a multiplicity of such rulers. Thus, it too could be regarded as an Aristocracy, a small group of philosopher-kings, each ruling in turn, and so – once again – "none of the city's laws worth mentioning would be changed".

3 Hobbes provides us with an alternative explanation as to why two names are used for the same regime: they reflect the difference in perspectives of the subjects who view it. Those who find it pleasing, thus "good", call it something respectable, whereas those who are pained by it use a pejorative appellation:

> When the Representative is One man, then is the Common-wealth a MONARCHY: when an Assembly of All that will come together, then it is a DEMOCRACY, or Popular Common-wealth: when an Assembly of a Part onely, then it is called an ARISTOCRACY. Other kind of Common-wealth there can be none: for either One, or More, or All must have the Sovraign Power (which I have shewn to be indivisible) entire.
>
> There be other names of Government in the Histories, and books of Policy; as *Tyranny*, and *Oligarchy*: But they are not the names of other Formes of Government, but of the same Formes misliked. For they that are discontented under *Monarchy*, call it *Tyranny*; and they

354

that are displeased with *Aristocracy*, call it *Oligarchy*: So also, they that find themselves grieved under a *Democracy*, call it *Anarchy*, (which signifies want of Government;) and yet I think that no man believes, that want of Government, is any new kind of Government: nor by the same reason ought they to believe, that the Government is of one kind when they like it, and another, when they mislike it, or are oppressed by the Governours. (*Leviathan* chap. 19)

It is remarkable that Hobbes in his science of politics devoted so little attention (or, at least, so few words) to differences among regimes. The question that occupies over three-fourths of Aristotle's *Politics* is dealt with (supposedly) in a couple of pages of one chapter of the forty-seven that (along with an "Introduction" and a "Review and Conclusion") compose *Leviathan*. Ostensibly, this is because the distinction that Aristotle regards as fundamental to both the theory and the practice of politics, Right Rule (rule in the common interest) *versus* Wrong Rule (rule in the interest of the rulers), is trivial for Hobbes: all *effective* rule is "right rule", necessarily serving the only interest truly *common* to rulers and ruled: mere life. He, of course, contends that the distinction which is really fundamental to a correct understanding of politics is that between the State of Nature and Civil Society *per se* – an issue Aristotle disposed of in a few pages of the first book of an eight-book treatise (arguing, for a variety of weighty reasons, that the natural state for man *is* civil society).

Hobbes, however, is no one's fool; he is, in fact, a far more discerning reader of Plato than seems to be generally recognized. His apparent slighting of the question of regimes is partly rhetorical. He knows that the distinction between Kingship and Tyranny is not merely a verbal dispute involving names of "inconstant signification" because of the incorrigible subjectivity of their use (see, for example, the concluding phrase of the passage quoted above). Fully three-fourths of *his* book is, in effect, advice on how to be a good king, or prince. *Leviathan* has a very different flavour when read from the perspective of a ruler than it does when read by someone who thinks of himself only as one of the ruled (which is the perspective Hobbes's rhetoric entices most of his readers to adopt).

I am indebted to William Mathie for insight into the importance of this question about regimes for an understanding of both Ancients and Moderns. See his "Justice and the Question of Regimes in Ancient and Modern Political Philosophy: Aristotle and Hobbes."

4 *If* the forms (*eidē*) of regimes are forms in the strict sense, and *if* these very forms – and not merely actual instances or incarnations of them –

are "flawed" inasmuch as the shapes they impart to political life are *inherently* unstable, thus mutable, this is a very interesting tidbit of information about the nature of forms, or the forms of nature, bearing on how forms relate both to each other and to the perceptible realm they supposedly rule (which is itself in some sense a form; 509d). But the 'ifs' here are worthy of double emphasis. For the problem may (rather) be in the defects of the "matter" upon which the forms are imposed (i.e., human beings). Reflection on the account of the oligarchic city seems to point to a defect in the form itself (that it incorporates, much as Marx argued, an "internal contradiction" which will over time destroy it, unless some distinctly political action supervenes – such as the kind Sokrates recommends [556a–b] – action based on a principle transcending that which orders the regime). Thinking about the description of the democratic city, however, suggests that its failing is the result of the normal inclinations of normal people to develop a certain way in the circumstances created by democracy.

The broader problems involved with understanding forms are discussed more fully in chapter 7.

5 The four stages of political decay apparently mirror the four ascending stages in the generation of the best regime:

First, the simple, healthy, "true" (or "truthful") city, a peaceful anarchy that Glaukon calls a "city of pigs" (cf. 575a, 560e, 562e, 558c).

Second, the luxuriated (and consequently) fevered city that matches rather nicely with Sokrates' parti-coloured portrait of Democracy (cf. 557c–e).

Third, the purified city (399e) of austere beauty ('Aristocracy') whose description is completed by the middle of Book Four – notice, 'Oligarchy' is also characterized by a kind of austerity (cf. 554a, 554e–a).

Fourth, the paradoxical city of the philosopher king, to which corresponds the timocratic city ruled by warrior-kings.

It is not clear to what extent, if any, the distinguishable stages in the trajectory of political decay are meant to constitute an incipient "theory of history".

6 This, according to Nietzsche, is what constitutes an authentic *culture*: "unity of artistic style in all outward expressions of a people's life". It is an integrated environment that truly *cultivates* in the old agricultural sense of

the word, tending and nourishing something in an effort to have it grow into the best of its kind (cf. *Euthyphro* 2c–a, *Theages* 121b–c, *Phaedrus* 276b–a, *Republic* 380e and 491d–a). As such, genuine culture is not just any kind of nurture or "way of life" (as modern "cultural" anthropology would have us believe), but that which offers the nourishment best suited to the requirements of a specific nature, in this case that of human beings. It is a nurture that – because of conscious design, or chance, or divine favour, or some combination thereof – happens to perfect human nature. Admittedly, such a conception is a far cry from what people today commonly mean by the honorific terms 'culture' and 'cultivated'. The contemporary view stresses (rather) the broadest – and hence, shallowest – acquaintance with the artefacts of *other people's* "cultures". Our principal "cultural" institution is the museum (of art, of history, of science and technology, of sports, of "everyday life", or whatever), where such artefacts are conveniently gathered and displayed, and where only the cleverness of its floor plan and his own lack of any definite taste protect the modern culture voyeur from the ruder shocks of artistic dissonance.

Probably no one in recent times has given "the problem of culture" more sustained thought, nor was better prepared to do so, than Nietzsche. Intimately familiar with the real thing, as manifested in the culture of Ancient Greece and Renaissance Italy, he had little sympathy with the "ecumenical culture" of the modern, history-obsessed age:

> Let us now picture the spiritual occurrence introduced into the soul of modern man. ... Historical knowledge streams in unceasingly from inexhaustible wells, the strange and incoherent forces its way forward, memory opens all its gates and yet is not open wide enough, nature travails in an effort to receive, arrange, and honor these strange guests, but they themselves are in conflict with one another and it seems necessary to constrain and control them if one is not oneself to perish in their conflict. Habituation to such a disorderly, stormy, and conflict-ridden household gradually becomes a second nature, though this second nature is beyond question much weaker, much more restless, and thoroughly less sound than the first. In the end, modern man drags around within him a huge quantity of indigestible stones of knowledge, which then, as in the fairy tale, can sometimes be heard rumbling about inside him. And in this rumbling there is betrayed the most characteristic quality of modern man: the remarkable antithesis between an interior which fails to correspond to any exterior and an exterior which fails to correspond to any inte-

rior – an antithesis unknown to people of earlier times. Knowledge, consumed for the greater part without any hunger for it and even counter to one's needs, now no longer acts as an agent for transforming the outside world but remains concealed within a chaotic inner world which modern man describes with curious pride as his uniquely characteristic 'subjectivity'. It is then said that one possesses content and only form is lacking; but such antithesis is quite improper when applied to living things. That is precisely why our modern culture is not a living thing: it is incomprehensible without recourse to this antithesis; it is not a real culture at all but only a kind of knowledge of culture; it has an idea of and feeling for culture but no true cultural achievement emerges from them. ... That celebrated little nation of a not so distant past – I mean [the] Greeks – during the period of their greatest strength kept a tenacious hold on their unhistorical sense; If a present day man were magically transported back to that world he would probably consider the Greeks very 'uncultured' – whereby, to be sure, the secret of modern culture, so scrupulously hidden, would be exposed to public ridicule: for we moderns have nothing whatever of our own; only by replenishing and cramming ourselves with the ages, customs, arts, philosophies, religions, discoveries of others do we become anything worthy of notice, that is to say, walking encyclopedias, which is what an ancient Greek transported into our time would perhaps take us for. *On the Uses and Disadvantages of History for Life (Untimely Meditations)* 78–9

The hybrid European – a tolerably ugly plebian, all in all – definitely requires a costume: he needs history as his storeroom for costumes. He realizes, to be sure that none of them fits him properly – so he changes and changes. ... Notice too the moments of despair because 'nothing suits' us – . It is in vain that we parade ourselves as romantic or classical or Christian or Florentine or baroque or 'national', *in moribus et artibus*: the 'cap doesn't fit'! But the 'spirit', especially the 'historical spirit', perceives an advantage even in this despair: again and again another piece of the past and of foreignness is tried out, tried on, taken off, packed away, above all *studied* – we are the first studious age *in puncto* of 'costumes', I mean those of morality, articles of faith, artistic tastes and religions, prepared as no other age has been for the carnival in the grand style, for the most spiritual Shrovetide laughter and wild spirits, for the transcendental heights of the most absolute nonsense and Aristophanic universal mockery. Perhaps it is precisely here that we are discovering the realm of our *invention*, that realm where we too can still be original, perhaps as parodists of world history and God's buffoons. ... (*Beyond Good and Evil* aph. 233 p. 133)

7 Some exponents of "historical materialism" come perilously close to the view that ultimately regimes *do* come from "oaks and rocks", with humans playing but a mediating role. And while most of the problems having to do with bodies affecting bodies are treated with benign neglect in this dialogue, Sokrates himself is not utterly inattentive to the bearing of "material circumstances" on political life (cf. 370e, 373d, 406c–e, 435ea). But there is a basic problem common to all materialistic explanations, having to do with what "matter" *is* and how it is causally efficacious: we never encounter pure "matter", but only *formed* matter (all of whose characteristics are due to its form, not its matter). This problem can be addressed only through ontological – *not* historical – argument (see chap. 7 note 21). Suffice it for now to observe that, upon closer examination, all "materialistic" explanations simply favour certain kinds of formed matter over others (and usually without any convincing rationale for the favouritism).

8 As Leo Strauss observes, "Philosophy as distinguished from myth came into being when nature was discovered, or the first philosopher was the first man who discovered nature. The whole history of philosophy is nothing but the record of the ever repeated attempts to grasp fully what was implied in that crucial discovery. ... " He goes on to say: "The purport of the discovery of nature cannot be grasped if one understands by nature 'the totality of phenomena.' For the discovery of nature consists precisely in the splitting-up of that totality into phenomena which are natural and phenomena which are not natural: 'nature' is a term of distinction. Prior to the discovery of nature, the characteristic behavior of anything or any class of things was conceived of as its custom or its way. That is to say, no fundamental distinction was made between customs or ways which are always and everywhere the same and customs or ways which differ from tribe to tribe"; *Natural Right and History* 82. I would add only that the conceptions and distinctions in which philosophy *originates* are not necessarily adequate for all subsequent philosophizing. For example, if upon further reflection one concludes that customs and conventions as such are *natural* in that any distinctly human way of life (i.e., one in which *human* nature finds adequate expression) is impossible without them, one can no longer believe in a *radical* distinction between nature and convention. Similarly,

one may begin with a conception of nature that is distinct from the divine, but supersedes it with a conception that preserves what is valid in that distinction while none the less encompassing "the totality of phenomena".

9 Aristotle's treatment of slavery in his *Politics* makes it clear that the subject is controversial. Some people think no slavery is justified, whereas others think that some slavery is justified, namely that involving natural slaves (e.g., the mentally incompetent, who must be ruled for their good). Virtually no one whose opinion Aristotle regards worth considering believes that all slavery actually practised (howsoever "legal") is justified (1253 b 15-23). Aristotle's own analysis of the issue has a certain subtlety, dictated in part by rhetorical (i.e., political) considerations. For example, he notes that there are also people whose nurture has been so barbarous and slavish that they lack familiarity with anything other than despotic rule (revealed in how they treat their women; 1252 b 5-9); as a result, they are little better off than those who by some miscarriage of nature or accident of life are rendered mentally incompetent. These slavish barbarians differ, however, in that a remedial "Greek" nurture may eventually make good the deficiencies of the earlier, stunting nurture; at which point they should be emancipated. And there is still another kind of natural slave: those without the will or capacity to defend themselves will become the slaves of anyone who marches against them; for that, too, is grounded in the nature of things (1291 a 6-10; cf. 1327 b 26-9).

When Aristotle turns to his own account of a good regime, he subtly undercuts still further the conventional views about slavery, observing that much so-called slavish work is quite suitable for young freeborn people, and simply leaves the reader wondering what isn't (1333 a 7-11). For some useful discussions of Aristotle's treatment of this issue, which perhaps more than any other tends to incapacitate modern readers for sympathetically understanding the ancient thinkers, see Mary P. Nichols "The Good Life, Slavery, and Acquisition: Aristotle's Introduction to Politics" and Catherine Zuckert "Aristotle on the Limits and Satisfactions of Political Life."

That the views on slavery of both Plato and Aristotle depart markedly from those upon which the entire ancient "political economy" was *based* is sufficient to put the lie to that precious dogma of historicists that these philosophers merely "idealized" the form of polity of their own day. As R.G. Collingwood, one of the more sophisticated historicist writers, puts it in *The Idea of History*:

Now in human affairs, as historical research had clearly demonstrated by the eighteenth century, there is no such fixed repertory of specific

Notes to pages 30-2

forms. Here, the process of becoming was already by that time recognized as involving not only the instances or quasi-instances of the forms, but the forms themselves. The political philosophy of Plato and Aristotle teaches in effect that the city-states come and go, but the idea of the city-state remains forever as the one social and political form towards whose realization human intellect, so far as it is really intelligent, strives. According to modern ideas, the city-state itself is as transitory a thing as Miletus or Sybaris. It is not an eternal ideal, it is merely the political ideal of the ancient Greeks. Other civilizations have had before them other political ideals, and human history shows a change not only in the individual cases in which these ideals are realized, but in the ideals themselves. Specific types of human organization, the city-state, the feudal system, representative government, capitalistic industry, are characteristic of certain historical ages. (210-11)

The *Republic* of Plato is an account, not of the unchanging ideal of political life, but the Greek ideal as Plato received it and reinterpreted it. The *Ethics* of Aristotle describes not an eternal morality but the morality of the Greek gentleman. Hobbes's *Leviathan* expounds the political ideas of seventeenth century absolutism in their English form. Kant's ethical theory ... [etc.] (229)

That holding such a view makes hash of his insistence that the "historian of philosophy" must endeavour to rethink a philosopher's thoughts just as he himself thought them as the price of correct understanding (215) – his having done this very thing supposedly providing the grounds for the historicist's superior insight into the "historicity" of all thought (including historicism itself perchance?) – was unfortunately overlooked by Collingwood. So, too, were the radical *differences* between the city in *logos* and all actual Greek cities (epitomized by this silent, and thereby scarcely noticed – as Collingwood unwittingly proves – abolition of slavery). Cf. Leo Strauss "On Collingwood's Philosophy of History" and "Political Philosophy and History" in *What Is Political Philosophy?* 56-77.

All this is not meant to suggest that Plato, in rejecting by deed institutionalized slavery in his Republic (cf. 579a), was naïve about the slavish nature of many people (cf. 493a-c, 516ea, 590c-d; also Nietzsche's *Beyond Good and Evil* aphs. 44, 61, 207, 257-60).

10 It may be of importance to note that Sokrates' asking Glaukon whether he has "some other idea of a regime that lies within some distinct form"

361

(544d) is one of only two instances in the dialogue of the use of *idea* and *eidos* ("form") in the same sentence (cf. 380d). But these two uses are sufficient to render suspect the view (frequently encountered among scholars) that Plato uses these terms interchangeably.

11 Sokrates' reference to "Hesiod's races and yours: gold and silver and bronze and iron" (546ea) suggests a number of nuances and complications to his science of regimes – if, that is, one accepts the philosopher's tacit invitation to compare what he says with Hesiod's cautionary tale in *Works and Days* (108–201; translation below based on H.G. Evelyn-White in the Loeb Classical Library edition, altered extensively in light of my own examination of the text).

First of all, however, Hesiod describes *five* races, not four; Sokrates leaves out "the race of Hero-men" (*genos andrōn hērōōn*) that Hesiod placed between the races of Bronze and Iron. This has some interesting consequences. "If we count the aristocratic and the kingly [man] as the same" (as we are several times invited to do; e.g., 587cd, 580b, 544e), and refer simply to the guardians ("those competent to rule") as the golden race, the soldier-auxiliaries as the silver race, and the producing class as made up of both bronze and iron men (as per 415a), then one may match Sokrates' account with Hesiod's as follows:

> *Aristocracy* rule by humans of the Golden race, who "lived like gods without sorrow of heart, remote from toil and grief. ... When they died, it was as though they were overcome by sleep, ... and they were called 'daimons' dwelling on earth, kindly, deliverers from evil, guardians of mortal humans; for they roam everywhere over the earth, clothed in mist, keeping watch on judgments and cruel deeds. ... "
>
> *Timocracy* rule by men of the Silver race who "are far less noble" but who are none the less immortalized in death, "and are called blessed spirits of the underworld and, though they are second, honour attends them also" (cf. 615e).
>
> *Oligarchy* rule by men of the Bronze race.
>
> *Democracy* rule by the race of iron.

However, if we add what Sokrates rather conspicuously omits, Democracy matches up with "the race of Hero-men, who are called demi-gods", some of whom are destroyed by war, but the survivors live "untouched by sorrow on the Isles of the Blessed" (cf. 519c). Inasmuch as Democracy is not only the regime ruled by the toiling masses, but also the only actual regime allowing philosophy and the emergence of all kinds of individual excellence, there is a sense in which it fits the race of Demi-gods and Heroes as well as it does the race of Iron (cf. 561d; 590cd, 611e, 613ab). And if we simply continue to match things one to one, we then couple *Tyranny* with the race of Iron, about which Hesiod tells: "there is no rest from labour and sorrow by day and perishing by night. ... Offspring will dishonour parents growing old, mocking and chiding them harshly, knowing not fear of the gods. They will not repay their aged parents the cost of their nurture, for might shall be their right. And one will sack another's city. Nor will there be favour for an oath-keeping or a just or a good man, but they will praise the bad and arrogant. Strength will determine the just, and shame will not exist" (cf. 574a–e).

But it is also interesting to note that of the races Hesiod describes, it is the Bronze race (i.e., the *third* race, with both Gold and Silver above it – to which can be matched *two* better regimes!) that best fits Sokrates' description of the timocratic regime: it was a race "terrible and strong. The lamented works of Ares were theirs, and arrogance. They ate no bread, but had an adamant and indomitable spirit. Great was their strength, and irresistible the arms which grew from their great shoulders. ... These were destroyed by their own hands and passed down to the dark domain of cold Hades, nameless. Formidable though they were, black death seized them, and they left the shining sunlight" (cf. 615e).

A final complication arises from the fact that bronze is not a simple metal, but an amalgam of tin and copper (roughly in proportion of one to nine). This fact fits neatly in a couple of respects with the description of the Timocratic man. But it also has implications for the producing class of the city in *logos*, made up of bronze-souled and iron-souled men, which the "Well-born Lie" invites us to identify with craftsmen and farmers, respectively (415a). In a more important sense, however, this producing class contains within it potentially *three* classes of men, and they are the three principal classes composing Democracy on the verge of Tyranny (564c–a): the few rich (Tin), the many working-class poor (Copper), and the class of "drones" (Iron).

12 Nietzsche's response to his own Sokratic question that titles part IX of *Beyond Good and Evil*, "*Was Ist Vornehm?*" ("What Is Noble/Wellbred?"), offers some insights on this topic, especially the first eight aphorisms, which begin:

Every elevation of the type 'man' [*Mensch*; that is, 'human'] has hitherto been the work of an aristocratic society – and so it will always be: a society which believes in a long scale of orders of rank and differences of worth between man and man and needs slavery in some sense or other. ... As to the origin of an aristocratic society (that is to say, the precondition of the elevation of this type 'man'), one ought not to yield to any humanitarian illusions: truth is hard. Let us admit to ourselves unflinchingly how every higher culture on earth has hitherto *begun*! Men of a still natural nature, barbarians in every terrible sense of the word, men of prey [*Raubmenschen*] still in possession of an unbroken strength of will and lust for power, hurled themselves upon weaker, more civilized, more peaceful races, perhaps trading or cattle-raising races, or upon old mellow cultures, the last vital forces in which were even then flaring out in a glittering pyrotechnic display of spirit and corruption. The noble caste was always in the beginning the barbarian caste: their superiority lay, not primarily in their physical but in their psychical strength – they were *more whole* human beings (which, on every level, also means 'more whole beasts' –). (*Beyond Good and Evil* trans. based on Hollingdale, 173)

Also consider in this connection his observations about the mixing of races (e.g., aphs. 200, 208, 221, 242) and about the races themselves (e.g., aphs. 61, 189, 251, 252), which reflect in interesting ways on the matters of the metals discussed in the note above.

13 As his *Second Discourse* shows, Rousseau sees this clearly. If the issue is that of enjoying an independent and self-sufficient life, and thus a life of natural freedom wherein one is subject to no man's rule but one's own, then one must be satisfied with a simple, rustic existence sustained by a few basic arts that each man and wife can learn and practise themselves and pass on to their children. This vision of independent self-sufficiency is the basis of the natural rhetorical appeal of the so-called Noble Savage, whose healthy and independent and free way of life, eliciting a full development of natural *physical* powers, contrasts so favourably with the sick, weak, decadent dependence of modern Civilized Man. Doubtless, Rousseau well knows most of his readers can't really appreciate how it is the harsh necessity of circumstances that accounts for primitive men's health and strength. Existing to a considerable extent under the same pressures as do the rest of animal life, where there is no compromise between vigour and annihilation, the *survivors* are robust; the rest are dead. Thus one can

argue that political life as such, which allows to varying degrees for the survival of the physically weak (cf. *Republic* 405a–408c, 409e–b, 496bc), constitutes an attempt to subjugate nature.

But as part I of his discourse so convincingly shows, a *rigorous* adherence to the individualistic premises of modern political thought (such as is exemplified in the political teachings of Hobbes and Locke) yields an ethological monograph about – not a noble savage – but a naked ape, from which everything recognizably human is absent; it is a story that goes nowhere. Whereas part II tells a story of man's rise from primitive beginnings to a golden age – in which men are blood-thirsty and cruel, but none the less free and happy – and his subsequent decline to the corrupt social life of modernity. This second story, only superficially continuous with the first, treats as the atom of human life not the solitary individual but the family, bound into a stable unit by the woman, and ruled by the man. Heading a self-sufficient family is as close as a man can get to perfect self-sufficiency. And through the free association of such independent, self-sufficient families, people might be said to have the best of both worlds: natural freedom, yet also the basic benefits of social life, beginning with mutual security. Thus the natural "nobility" of anarchic savage life, lived by people healthy and strong, with bodily powers fully developed, eating simple foods, ornamenting themselves as they please, sharing a few simple pleasures (mainly music and dance and each other's company) – the life more or less as lived, for example, by the Plains Indians of North America. Whereas a division of labour transcending the family renders people interdependent, in need not merely of arts but of each other, and to that extent mutually enslaved. Men who have lost all possibility of self-sufficiency (which is virtually everyone) have also lost all hope of natural freedom. Their only proper aspiration is for the civil freedom of a true citizen, who as a member of a Republic founded on the General Will rules himself by laws he freely gives himself. But being a citizen in this full, ancient sense of the word requires that one divest oneself of all individualistic aspirations, and become as thoroughly and profoundly dependent as possible, identifying so totally with the whole that one is meaningless divorced from it – rather in the manner of the Guardians of the first city in *logos*. While the main features of such a Republic are sketched in the "Dedicatory Letter" of Rousseau's *Second Discourse*, the full articulation of its formal structure is the task addressed in his *On the Social Contract*.

14 Again, it is useful to think of Hobbes, who would have us regard each other as equal in the most significant pre-political sense: equally dangerous.

That is, we are to presume that everyone in the state of nature would be sufficiently equal in natural faculties of body and mind to be equally threatening to what is the sole common denominator of all varieties of good lives, mere life – the loss of which should be each person's greatest fear. And thus he would have us see that the mutual need for physical security is the true foundation of the political association. Of course, he understands as well as anyone that several different kinds of building can be erected on the same foundation, and that men no sooner secure mere life than they begin to dream of the good life. The problem (at least as Hobbes sees it) is they don't all dream alike. Thus, he argues – with some considerable plausibility, I would say – that the best building is one designed with that fact in mind, one that is "low but solid", with a minimum of interior articulation, hence amenable to a variety of non-conflicting uses.

15 Although 'Oligarchy' means literally "Rule of the Few", and thus could refer to the virtuous few, or to the honour-loving few (hence Adeimantos' confusion, 550c), or to the few real men (as in Herodotus' honest formula: *polloi men anthropoi, oligoi de andres*), for some reason it just naturally comes to mean "the few rich". Aristotle's discussion is to the point: *Politics* 1279 b 10–1280 a 7.

16 Patronage of the Arts has been a favourite expression of power for autocrats throughout the ages, be they Ming or Medici, tsar or Sun King. The willingness (and publicity!) with which a despot sponsors pleasing works of spiritual expression – and curries the vanity of their creators – may earn him the title 'Benevolent', 'Enlightened', even 'Wise' (cf. 568a). And to that extent, 'legitimate'. It is a shrewd policy, and perhaps partly explains certain intellectuals' strange infatuation with (and apologetics for) some of history's most infamous tyrannies. For an interesting collection of case studies, see Paul Johnson's *Intellectuals*; while not every person pilloried there is equally deserving – in particular, he has misjudged Rousseau, not understanding the real purpose of that philosopher's "autobiographical" writings – Johnson's book none the less reveals a disturbing tendency in a certain class of mind.

17 According to Homer, Minos, the legendary king and lawgiver of Crete, was a son of Zeus and Europa. And though no favourite of the Athenians because of the tribute he imposed on their ancestors (and from which Theseus liberated them in slaying the Minotaur), Plato memorializes him in a dialogue "On Law". It portrays Sokrates discussing the question with

an unnamed sociologist of law who, true to form, knows next to nothing about the great poetry of his own cultural tradition. In the dialogue, the philosopher defends the name of Minos against the popular slander that he was "savage and harsh and unjust", calling this a "myth, attic and tragic", concocted by Athenian tragedians out of resentment of his waging a victorious war against Athens (320e). Sokrates endorses instead an interpretation of Homer's account to the effect that Minos alone, of all the heroes, was personally educated by "Zeus the sophist", and insists that this is unsurpassable praise: being educated by the god his father (319b-d). The laws he laid down, then, may be regarded as divine (320b), and are the source of "the best of the customs" of the Lacedaemonians (318cd, 320b; cf. *Republic* 452cd). It is interesting, however, that the only example Sokrates provides of these divinely good laws is one which restricts *symposia* and intoxication by wine, with all its consequent playing around (320a; cf. *Republic* 403e). For a penetrating treatment of the dialogue, see Leo Strauss "On the Minos" in *Liberalism Ancient and Modern* 65-75. This essay, along with a new, more accurate translation of the dialogue by Thomas Pangle, is reprinted in Pangle's *The Roots of Political Philosophy*.

CHAPTER THREE

1 And here one must especially beware of temptations to superficiality. Whatever fraternal feelings Ariston's third son may have had towards his two brothers, there are countless ways (including many other dialogues) in which he could have chosen to memorialize them, presuming he saw a need to do so (cf. Apology of Sokrates 34a). The only prudent assumption is that the characters portrayed in the dialogue (and whose relationship to Plato's actual brothers is unknown and unknowable) first of all serve his literary, that is, his politico-philosophical purpose as perfectly as he was capable of making them.

2 The one major exception to this in its way confirms the rule: the essential natures of most of the inferior kinds of cities and men are discussed with Adeimantos. In what is his longest stint of "duty" in the dialogue, he becomes the philosopher's respondent at the moment the conversation turns to the timocrat's nature (548d), and remains such until that point in the discussion of the tyrannical nature when Sokrates speaks of such a person actually taking over a monarchy, whereupon Glaukon "relieves" him (*diadexomai*) in the argument (576b).

3 Their challenge receives detailed examination in chap. 5.

4 As Conrad has one of his protagonists declare: "To slay, to love – the greatest enterprizes upon the life of a man" (*Victory* 200). For an insightful portrayal of the psychic elements common to love and war, one could hardly do better than Stendhal's *The Red and the Black*. And in this connection, one may wish to consider "the only definition of love worthy of a philosopher", namely Nietzsche's: "In its means, war; at bottom, the mortal hatred of the sexes" (*Ecce Homo* Part III aph. 5). Appropriately, it is a "definition" that is open to more than one interpretation.

5 The original story in Homer (*Odyssey* Book 8 266-369) to which Sokrates' comment refers – ambiguously, it should be added, for it's not clear whether it is Ares' overpowering passion for Aphrodite that is censored in the name of moderation, or Hephaestus' passion for revenge – bears in other interesting ways on matters timocratic. As the minstrel Demodocus sings it, the Warrior God not only secretly lay with the Love Goddess, he also plied her with many gifts (cf. 548ab, 420a). And the Artisan God's scheme to humiliate the pair might be said to have backfired. For while it is true that when the two had been cunningly ensnared, the gods called to witness the sight laughed mightily (the goddesses remaining at home in shame), and marvelled at the craft of Hephaestus as they remarked to each other that bad deeds do not succeed; but it is also true that when Apollo turned to Hermes, asking whether he would be willing to change places with Ares, the Soul-Conductor God replied with alacrity: "Would that this might be so, Lord Apollo, Archer; let thrice as many inextricable bonds clasp me, and all you gods, and goddesses too, look on, if I might sleep by the side of Golden Aphrodite" (my translation). Some loves may be worth the price of ridicule.

With respect to the association of love and war, it is also of interest to note that in the Spartan tradition the Aphrodite worshipped is an armed goddess (*Aphroditē Hoplismenē*); see, for example, *The Oxford Classical Dictionary* H.G.L. Hammond and H.H. Scullard, eds., 80.

6 Such seems to be Lord Bacon's view, for he says in his essay 'Of Love': "I know not how, but martial men are given to love: I think it is but as they are given to wine; for perils commonly ask to be paid in pleasures." The essay as a whole seems to echo the perspective on *erōs* one finds in the *Republic*. It begins: "The stage is more beholding to Love, than the life of man. For as to the stage, love is ever matter of comedies, and now

and then of tragedies; but in life it doth much mischief; sometimes like a syren, sometimes like a fury." And as to its effects on one's power of judgment, Bacon observes in the middle of his essay: "For there was never proud man thought so absurdly well of himself as the lover does of the person loved; and therefore it was well said, *That it is impossible to love and to be wise.*"

In criticising Sparta, Aristotle argues that certain of its faults were the result of the disproportionate influence of its women, something he notes is common among "military and warlike races". And here he cites approvingly the mythical association of Ares and Aphrodite (*Politics* 1269 b 24-9). Aristotle's teaching that it is primarily the spirited part of the soul whereby we love is helpful in understanding much that is otherwise puzzling here: "It is obvious that those who are intelligent and spirited by nature are those most readily led to virtue by the lawgiver. As for what is said by some – that to become guardians, they should be friendly [*philetikous*] towards those they know and be harsh towards those unknown – it is the spirit which makes one friendly [*philētikon*], for it is the power of the soul whereby we love [*philoumen*]. A sign of this is that the spirit when slighted is more aroused against associates and friends than against those unknown. ... And all rule and being free come to be through this power; for the spirit is fitted for ruling and is indomitable" (ibid, 1327 b 39-1328 a 8, my translation; cf. *Republic* 440c-d, 375ab).

7 It is worth noting that in its genitive form ($\bar{E}ros$) – and this is the only form in which it appears in the dialogue (i.e., in referring to the story, *apologos*, as that *of* Er, son of Armenios; 614b) – the warrior's name, which means "Spring, son of Suitable", appears as a quasi-homonym of *erōs*.

8 As a measure of the density and importance of the philosopher's brief conversation with old Kephalos, note that all the following topics first arise therein: pleasure, money-making, punishment, fatherhood, desire, the holy, speech, fear, death, man, the polity, wealth, body, tales (or fables; *mythos*), poetry, soul, discussion, woman, family, laughter, peace, freedom, lying, hope, friendship, truth, sleep, children, the Many, prayer, and madness. As a general rule, one should pay special attention to the context in which Plato chooses to have something make its first appearance in a dialogue.

9 In the *Republic*, it is the dark side of *erōs* that receives the lion's share of attention, and perhaps even this is distorted by a righteous passion infusing certain interlocutors. To do *erōs* justice, one would have to complement

what is taught about it here with what Plato has Sokrates and others say in *praise* of *Erōs* in the companion dialogue, *Symposium*. The apparent difference in the respective treatments is accounted for at least partially by the different status of the philosopher's fellow participants: mainly youths and young men in the one case; accomplished and experienced, fully mature men in the other. And whereas in the *Republic* Sokrates professes himself unequal to the task of defending justice (368b), in the *Symposium* he boldly avows himself an expert in nothing but "erotic things" (*ta erōtika*; 177e – a claim he makes elsewhere as well: *Theages* 128b). In fact, he even presents an intriguing account of how he came by such expertise, having been educated by an otherwise unknown woman of prophetic power named Diotima ("Honour of Zeus"), also referred to as a "Mantinean stranger" (211d) and likened to a "perfect sophist" (208c).

10 Cf. Xenophon's *Lakedaimoniōn Politeia* ("Constitution of the Lacedaemonians") II 12–14.

11 This is the sole reference to the "lover of falsehood" (or, "lover of the lie"), not merely in this dialogue, but in the entire Platonic corpus. And it is more than a bit curious, for it is in the feminine gender. What the philosopher literally asks is, "Then, is it within the power of the same nature to be both a lover of wisdom [in the abstract] and a [female] lover of falsehood [*philosophon kai philopsuedē*]?" (485cd). This can be seen as reflecting a large – not to say, monstrous – issue concerning the "androgynous" nature of the philosopher, a matter which will be pursued below (chap. 6). For now, suffice it to note that it would seem to bear on the philosopher's distinctive mode of speech: irony. Inasmuch as irony is at once true and false, comic while none the less serious, frank yet dissembling – arguably the only manner of speech that can do justice to both the equivocal character of reality and the heterogeneous natures of human beings – perhaps the accomplished ironist must be a lover both of the truth and of the lie. So too must the person who loves both wisdom and poetry (cf. 376ea, 377d, 378c, 598d, 607b).

Still, the "femaleness" of loving falsehood needs explaining, and one could do worse by way of beginning than to consult Nietzsche, whose keen senses may be relied upon to catch a dialogue's every subtlety and nuance. He certainly noticed that strange gender ending – as well as the fact that the only mention of a "hater of wisdom" is in connection with women (456a) – and he agreed. Among his truths about "woman as such", one finds, " ... she does not *want* truth: what is truth to a woman! From the beginning, nothing has been more alien, repugnant, inimical to woman than truth – her great art is the lie, her supreme concern is appearance and beauty" (*Beyond Good and Evil* aph. 232; cf. aphs. 86, 127, 144, 145, 148; also aphs. 85 and 131).

Conrad, too, regards this to be an essential ingredient of woman as such. He has the strange hero of *Victory*, Heyst, observe regarding the unfortunate young woman he befriends: "She obeyed with unexpected readiness; and as she had a set of very good white teeth, the effect of the mechanical, ordered smile was joyous, radiant. It astonished Heyst. No wonder, it flashed through his mind, women can deceive men so completely. The faculty was inherent in them; they seemed to be created with a special aptitude." And about another thoroughly doomed female character: " ... Mrs Schomberg sat enthroned as usual, swallowing her sobs, concealing her tortures of abject humiliation and terror under her stupid, set, everlasting grin, which, having been provided for her by nature, was an excellent mask, inasmuch as nothing – not even death itself, perhaps – could tear it away" (77–8, 92).

12 Again, the conspicuous omission of *philalēthia* was not lost on Nietzsche. Whether the motive force empowering philosophy is fundamentally a love of truth is the *question* with which he begins *Beyond Good and Evil* (note especially the first seven aphorisms). As for that "new species of philosophers" he sees emerging: "Are these coming philosophers new friends of 'truth'? That is probable enough, for all philosophers so far have loved *their* truths" (aph. 43, my emphasis).

As for hating lies, the account Conrad has Marlow give of his own distaste for lying is worth considering here: "I would not have gone so far as to fight for Kurtz, but I went for him near enough to a lie. You know I hate, detest, and can't bear a lie, not because I am straighter than the rest of us, but simply because it appalls me. There is a taint of death, a flavor of mortality in lies – which is exactly what I hate and detest in the world – what I want to forget. It makes me miserable and sick, like biting something rotten would do. Temperament, I suppose"; *Heart of Darkness* chap. 1. Rousseau's conception of a "truthful man" pertains directly to the *Republic*, careful as he is to distinguish lies from fictions. He contends that truthfulness is a virtue only insofar as it derives from the love of justice, and that, for the truthful man, "Justice and truth are two synonymous words in his mind, and he takes the one for the other indifferently. The holy truth his heart adores does not consist in indifferent deeds and useless names, but in faithfully rendering to each what is owed in things which are truly his own, in imputing good and bad, in making retributions of honor or blame, praise and disapproval" ("*Fourth Walk*" In *The Reveries of the Solitary Walker* Charles E. Butterworth, trans., 51).

Nietzsche voices a similar view in his second "Untimely Meditation", *On the Uses and Disadvantages of History for Life*, part VI 89:

> Only insofar as the truthful man possesses the unconditional will to justice is there anything great in that striving for truth which is everywhere so thoughtlessly glorified: a whole host of the most various drives – curiosity, flight from boredom, envy, vanity, the desire for amusement, for example – can be involved in the striving for truth, which has its roots in justice. Thus the world seems to be full of those who 'serve truth', yet the virtue of justice is rarely present, even more rarely recognized and almost always mortally hated: while on the other hand the horde of those who only appear virtuous is at all times received with pomp and honour. The truth is that few serve truth because few possess the pure will to justice, and of these few only a few also possess the strength actually to be just.

13 *Beyond Good and Evil* aph. 9. Nietzsche prefaces these claims with an acknowledgment that it is "an ancient, eternal story". Could be.

CHAPTER FOUR

1 This, of course, is not the only enigmatical mathematical to be found in the *Republic*. There is the scarcely less bewildering "inexplicable calculation" (*amechanon logismon*) purporting to show what only a Benthamite could appreciate, that the kingly man "lives 729 times more pleasantly" than the tyrant (587b–e). And there is the convoluted harmony of the celestial spheres in the so-called Myth of Er (616b–617b). It is ludicrous to suppose that Plato was unaware of how baffling most people would find these passages (Glaukon's reactions are sufficient evidence to the contrary). So this becomes the first interpretive question: why have these particular matters been treated in such an overtly mysterious, thereby provocative, way? Throughout the centuries, they have naturally been the subjects of much speculation, and have contributed to the traditions of alchemy, numerology, and astrology. There is considerable evidence that these, in turn, have been – whatever else – traditions of esoteric philosophy. Insofar as we have lost contact with these traditions, we are the more poorly prepared to interpret intelligently what we now are rather inclined to dismiss as "mathematical

mysticism". However, as I discussed in my Prologue (note 13), there has been a revival of scholarly interest in numerology, and eventually this may help restore our interpretive capacities.

Moreover, there is some literature available from a period still in touch with those traditions, such as *Mathematics Useful for Understanding Plato* by the self-described Platonic philosopher of the second century AD, Theon of Smyrna. More recently, Adam has critically surveyed various modern views on this so-called nuptial number in an Appendix to Book Eight of his critical edition of the dialogue (II 264–312). For a particularly interesting and serious contemporary effort at interpreting these passages in the *Republic*, as well as some related ones in *Timaeus*, *Critias*, and the *Laws*, relying primarily on the mathematics of musical harmonies, see Ernest G. McClain *The Pythagorean Plato: Prelude to the Song Itself*.

2 Hobbes, searching for some human absolute upon which to ground a universal science of politics, couldn't find one. Thus he, like Machiavelli, settled for the closest surrogate: the widespread – but hardly universal – fear of violent death. Understanding well enough the normal human inclination to make a virtue of presumed necessity, he endeavoured to convince us that self-preservation is the fundamental law of all nature, approved by reason and instinct alike; and to discredit any authorities, especially those of religion and ancient philosophy, who might persuade a person otherwise. Moreover, it is no accident that an account of the spirit – indeed, any mention of it – is conspicuously absent from his materialistic-mechanistic description "Of Man". But he himself certainly knew that the fear of death, even augmented by the love of mere life, neither did nor could be made to operate with anything like the inexorable necessity of that occult force we call gravity: "On the contrary, needy men, and hardy, not contented with their present position; as also, all men that are ambitious of military command, are inclined to continue the causes of warre; and to stir up trouble and sedition: for there is no honor Military but by warre; nor any such hope to mend an ill game, as by causing a new shuffle" (*Leviathan* chap. 11 par 4).

Despite such subtle indications that there is more to man than desire and calculation, it would seem that Hobbes and other like-minded thinkers have been quite successful in persuading most moderns to accept a spiritless psychology as the basis for a new science of politics, radically different in kind from the ancient teaching which regards the spirit as "the psychic origin of distinctly political action", as Catherine Zuckert puts it in her introduction to a recent collection of essays on the subject, *Understanding the Political Spirit: Philosophical Investigations from Socrates to Nietzsche* 2. While all these essays are valuable, the contributions of Arlene W. Saxonhouse and Werner Dannhauser have a special pertinence to the present study, as does that of Mary P. Nichols, who provides an account of the relationship between philosophy and spiritedness in the *Republic* that differs markedly from mine.

3 To these might be added the highly stylized exercise routines of the classical martial arts of the East, such as the callisthenics of Chinese boxing and the *kata* of karate. Also, it is interesting to note how naturally those who would dramatize a battle for stage or screen speak of "choreographing" the fight.

In the *Republic*, the philosopher contends that as he has given "the models [*typoi*] of education and rearing", there is no need to go through the dances, hunts, chases, athletic contests, and horse races of their Guardians, since those that fit with such models would not be difficult to discover (412b). This exemplifies his general tendency, noticeable throughout the dialogue, to ignore the body when not explicitly denigrating it. Whatever else, this reflects the fact that the bodily desires, summarily represented by the unlimited desire for wealth whereby to supply pleasure and comfort for the body, are the principal cause of injustice in the majority of men, and thus what is most in need of moderation. And diminishing one's respect for these desires (for their importance, that is, not their power) is both logically and psychologically the first step towards cultivating that moderation. But beyond this, men, especially young men, have an exaggerated regard for the body as such, for bodily strength and bodily beauty. And so the philosopher's depreciation of the body may also be intended as a pedagogical counterpoise to this natural tendency in men (or natural weakness, to speak more precisely).

Dance, being the bodily, thus visible interpretation of something immaterial and aural, has long been regarded as a most effective way of introducing grace into the body. The near silence with respect to dance in the *Republic* contrasts markedly with the extensive discussion of it in the *Laws*, one growing immediately out of a much briefer discussion of the martial art of wrestling (814e–816d). There, the philosopher describes in detail the two principal forms of noble dancing: the warlike dances mimicking both offensive and defensive actions; and the peaceful modes of a moderate soul. The frenzied mode of dance associated with Bacchic rites, and filled with shameful motions, is outlawed. But since neither the Platonic Sokrates nor the Athenian Stranger is as forthcoming as one might wish with respect to understanding the deeper significance of dance, one may wish to consult the spirit of Nietzsche:

> Perhaps all of us philosophers are in a bad position nowadays regarding knowledge: science keeps growing, and the most scholarly among us are close to discovering that they know too little. But it would be still worse if it were different – and we knew *too much*; our task is and remains above all not to mistake ourselves for others. We *are* something different from scholars, although it is unavoidable for us to be also, among other things, scholarly. We have different needs, grow differently, and also have a different digestion: we need more, we also need less. How much a spirit [*Geist*] needs for its nourishment, for this there is no formula; but if its taste is for independence, for quick coming and going, for roaming, perhaps for adventures for which only the swiftest are a match, it is better for such a spirit to live in freedom with little to eat, rather than unfree and stuffed. It is not fat, but the greatest possible suppleness and strength that a good dancer desires from his nourishment – and I would not know what the spirit of a philosopher might wish more to be than a good dancer. For the dance is his ideal, also his art, and finally also his piety, his 'service to god'. (*The Gay Science* Walter Kaufmann, trans., aph. 38 pp. 345–6)

It has been argued, quite convincingly to my mind, that "The Dancing Song" of Zarathustra – dealing as it does with Life and Wisdom, Being and Will to Power – is of central importance to an understanding of Nietzsche's greatest book. See Laurence Lampert "Zarathustra's Dancing Song." See also the same author's later treatment in his superb book-length commentary on *Thus Spoke Zarathustra – Nietzsche's Teaching* 100–20. Waller R. Newell uses the same "Dancing Song" episode to explore (among other important issues) the adequacy of the Heideggerean interpretation of Nietzsche – "Zarathustra's Dancing Dialectic."

4 An especially illuminating study of the Japanese timocratic tradition as represented in its great literature captures the point here nicely in its very title: Ivan Morris's *The Nobility of Failure*. Admiral Yamamoto, in a speech intended both to inspire and to sober those who would carry out his attack on Pearl Harbor, reminded his warriors, "It is the custom of *Bushido* to select an equal or stronger opponent" (quoted in Gordon Prange *At Dawn We Slept* 344).

I shouldn't think there are many finer or more poignant expressions of tragic fatalism in English literature than one finds in the poetry of Sir

Walter Raleigh, a great-spirited man whose experiences as warrior, general, governor, explorer, statesman, colonizer, and courtier establish the authority with which he speaks as scholar, poet, and lover (see, for example, his "Farewell to the Court", "Ocean to Cynthia", "The Lie", or "The Nimphs Reply to the Sheepheard").

But to my mind, it is Joseph Conrad who best captures in words what might be called tragic wisdom:

> Droll thing life is – that mysterious arrangement of merciless logic for a futile purpose. The most you can hope from it is some knowledge of yourself – that comes too late – a crop of unextinguishable regrets. I have wrestled with death. It is the most unexciting contest you can imagine. It takes place in an impalpable grayness, with nothing underfoot, with nothing around, without spectators, without clamour, without glory, without the great desire of victory, without the great fear of defeat, in a sickly atmosphere of tepid scepticism, without much belief in your own right, and still less in that of your adversary. If such is the form of ultimate wisdom, then life is a greater riddle than some of us think it to be. I was in a hair's breadth of the last opportunity for pronouncement, and I found with humiliation that probably I would have nothing to say. This is the reason why I affirm that Kurtz was a remarkable man. He had something to say. He said it. Since I had peeped over the edge myself, I understood better the meaning of his stare, that could not see the flame of the candle, but was wide enough to embrace the whole universe, piercing enough to penetrate all the hearts that beat in the darkness. He had summed up – he had judged. 'The horror!' He was a remarkable man. After all, this was the expression of some sort of belief; it had candour, it had conviction, it had a vibrating note of revolt in its whisper, it had the appalling face of a glimpsed truth – the strange commingling of desire and hate (*Heart of Darkness* chap. 3).

5 In aph. 45 of *Beyond Good and Evil*, Nietzsche illumines the possible significance of distinguishing between the two kinds of hunting. Bearing in mind his judgment that "psychology is now once again the path to the fundamental problems" (aph. 23), consider:

> The human soul and its limits, the range of inner human experience reached so far, the heights, depths, distances of these experiences, the entire history of the soul *so far* and its as yet unexhausted possibilities:

Note to page 71

that is the predestined hunting ground for a born psychologist and lover of the 'great hunt'. But how often must he say despairingly to himself: 'one individual, alas, but one individual! and this great forest, this jungle!' And then he wishes he had a few hundred beaters, and subtle, well-trained tracker dogs whom he could send into the history of the human soul to round up *his* game. In vain: he discovers, again and again, thoroughly and bitterly, how hard it is to find beaters and hounds for all the things that excite his curiosity. What is wrong with sending scholars into new and dangerous hunting grounds, where courage and prudence and subtlety are needed in every way, is that they cease to be of any use precisely where the 'great hunt', but also the great danger, begins – precisely there they lose their keen eye and keen nose. (Walter Kaufmann translation)

If one requires further confirmation of there being a natural connection between philosophy and hunting, one might consult Ortega y Gasset's *Meditation on Hunting* (and a most "untimely" meditation it is for an age in which one hears people speak of "animal rights" and "animal liberation" in tones of utmost serious; cf. *Republic* 563c):

And this is what concerns us: what does man do when, and in the extent that, he is free to do what he pleases. Now, this greatly liberated man, the aristocrat, has always done the same things: raced horses or competed in physical exercises, gathered at parties, the feature of which is usually dancing, and engaged in conversation. But before any of these, and consistently more important than all of them has been ... hunting. (27)

These inherent qualities of effort and exploit which comprise hunting at its best have meant that it has always been considered a great education, one of the preferred methods of training character. Only in the contemporary period and, within that, only in the most demoralized regions of Europe has an affinity for hunting been held in disesteem. (35)

The hunter is the alert man.
But this itself – life as complete alertness – is the attitude in which the animal exists in the jungle. ... Only the hunter, imitating the perpetual alertness of the wild animal, for whom everything is danger, sees everything and sees each thing functioning as facility or difficulty, as risk or protection.

And this is how we can understand the extraordinary fact that, with maximum frequency, when a philosopher wanted to name the attitude in which he operated when musing, he compared himself with the hunter. (130-1)

> Like the hunter in the absolute *outside* of the country, the philosopher is the alert man in the absolute *inside* of ideas, which are also an unconquerable and dangerous jungle. As problematic a task as hunting, meditation always runs the risk of returning empty-handed. Hardly anyone can fail to know the probability of this result, if he has tried, as I have in these pages, to hunt down the hunt.(132)

6 In his *Seventh Letter*, Plato speaks of the ability to endure hard labour as a practically sufficient test for separating out from all those who *profess* to be philosophical the few who truly *are*:

> To such persons, one must show what the whole business is, how it is done, and how much labour is involved. On hearing this, if one is akin to the philosopher and divinely worthy, he believes he has been shown a wondrous road and braces himself to follow it, there being no life otherwise. ... But those who are not really philosophers, but merely anointed with opinions like men whose bodies have been superficially burnt by the sun, upon seeing how many studies there are and how great the labour and the ordering of one's practices so as to suit the business, they regard it as hard or impossible for themselves, and so lack the power of pursuing it; while some persuade themselves that they have been sufficiently instructed in the whole, and no longer require any further effort.
>
> Now, this test proves the clearest and most infallible with respect to those who are soft and lack the power to endure labour ... (340b-341a; my translation)

To this might be added the observations of Dostoevsky's narrator in *The Brothers Karamazov* concerning Alyosha:

> [H]e was to some extent a youth of our own time – that is, honest in nature, demanding the truth, seeking it and believing in it, and seeking to serve it at once with all the strength of his soul, demanding immediate action, and ready to sacrifice everything, life itself, for it. Though these young men unhappily fail to understand that the sacrifice of life is, in many cases, the easiest of all sacrifices, and that to

sacrifice, for instance, five or six years of their seething youth to hard and tedious study, if only to multiply ten-fold their powers of serving the truth and the cause they have set before them as a goal – such a sacrifice is utterly beyond the strength of many of them. (Constance Garnett, trans. rev. by Avrahm Yarmolinsky, part I Book I chap. 5)

7 With respect to the psychology of the *Republic* (upon which everything else rests), the common causes of superficiality that infect much modern scholarship – the implicit condescension of historicism, which vitiates any serious effort of interpretation; the failure to recognize a pedagogical purpose informing the whole dialogue, or a natural pedagogical trajectory within it; the emphasis on analysis of its parts, without a complementary concern to synthesize the parts into a coherent whole; the too slight regard for, and understanding of, dramatic context; the inappreciation of political considerations that might affect writing about political matters – are augmented by a prejudice against "old-fashioned" philosophical psychology in favour of some supposedly more scientific, thus superior approach to understanding the human "organism". Refuting this prejudice in detail would be a long story, but to make it short: the view in question involves misconceptions of both science and the problem posed by the human soul. I would hope that my exposition of the psychology presented in this dialogue, grounded as it is on experience familiar to any normal adult – experience that is necessarily presupposed in any attempt to provide a more sophisticated psychology – sufficiently demonstrates the value of the philosophical approach. Strictly speaking, 'psychology' ("rational speech about the soul") is a misnomer for a school such as behaviourism that is premissed upon a materialistic empiricism (long since abandoned by contemporary physics), and which attempts to explain human behaviour without any recourse to such allegedly metaphysical notions as soul. That it cannot give an adequate account of *any* human use of speech, much less its own use, says all that needs saying about the prospects of such an approach.

Some discussions of the *Republic's* psychology that I have found helpful include essays 3–6 in H.W.B. Joseph's *Ancient and Modern Philosophy*, the entirety of Allan Bloom's "Interpretive Essay" in *The Republic of Plato*, and chap. 2 of N.R. Murphy's *The Interpretation of Plato's Republic* (despite suffering somewhat from the limitations mentioned above, this book is an always respectful and sensible – and thus frequently insightful – treatment of the dialogue).

8 Perhaps the most glaring "omission" in the dialogue's treatment of the soul is the absence of any explicit discussion concerning the nature of its connection with the body. The philosopher speaks of some "so-called pleasures stretched through the body to the soul" (584c), and of the soul's being "maimed by community with body and other evils" (611bc), and of certain of the soul's virtues being "probably close to those of the body" (518d) – yet nowhere does he address the question of how that two-way threshold between "matter" and "consciousness" is crossed in either direction. But his silence may in fact be his solution to this problem. Any relevance the body has to an adequate understanding of the soul is already represented in one's awareness of the interaction of the parts of the soul: it's not the body that "feels," "desires," or "does" anything, but only the soul.

9 Hobbes well appreciates the significance (better still, the "cause") of the "impartiality" of geometrical reasoning compared with reasoning about anything that touches what people regard as their vital interests (and surely Hobbes would acknowledge that their erotic interests are included here, although if all one knew about humans was what could be gleaned from *Leviathan*, one would scarcely be aware that we are sexual beings). In any event, Hobbes certainly had no illusions that casting his political teaching in quasi-geometrical *form* would place it beyond controversy, given most men's less-than-absolute respect for reason:

> Ignorance of the causes, and originall constitution of Right, Equity, Law, and Justice, disposeth a man to make Custome and Example the rule of his actions; in such manner, as to think that Unjust which it hath been the custome to punish: and that Just, of the impunity and approbation whereof they can produce an Example, or (as the lawyers which onely use the false measure of Justice barbarously call it) a Precedent; like little children, that have no other rule of good and evil manners, but the correction they receive from their Parents, and Masters; save that children are constant to their rule, whereas men are not so; because grown strong, and stubborn, they appeal from custome to reason, and from reason to custome, as it serves their turn; receding from custome when their interest requires it, and setting themselves against reason, as often as reason is against them: Which is the cause, that the doctrine of Right and Wrong, is perpetually disputed, both by the Pen and the Sword: Whereas the doctrine of Lines, and Figures, is not so; because men care not, in that subject what be truth, as a thing that crosses no mans ambition, profit, or

lust. For I doubt not, but if it had been a thing contrary to any mans right of dominion, or to the interest of men that have dominion, *That the three Angles of a Triangle should be equall to two Angles of a Square*; that doctrine should have been, if not disputed, yet by the burning of all books of Geometry, suppressed, as farre as he whom it concerned was able. (*Leviathan* chap. 11 par. 21)

10 These philological matters warrant still further comment. The term (*thumoeidēs*) is used only three other times in the Platonic corpus. One of these occurs near the beginning of *Timaeus*, where Sokrates appears to be recapitulating the most important conclusions of the preceding day's conversation – a discussion strikingly similar (but only similar) to that recounted in the *Republic*: "For the nature of the soul of the Guardians, I think we said, must be distinguished as being highly spirited [*hama thumoeidē*] and highly philosophic [*hama philosophon*], in order that they have the power correctly to become both gentle and harsh" (18a; my translation). The other two occur in a passage in the *Laws*, which because of its peculiar pertinence is worth quoting in full:

> Let us all be lovers of victory when it comes to virtue, but without envy. He of this sort – always competing himself but never thwarting others with slander – makes cities great. But the envious one, who fancies he must gain superiority by slandering the others, both lessens his own efforts to attain true virtue and makes his competitors dispirited [*athumian*] by getting them unjustly blamed, and through that he makes the whole city ill-trained in the contest for virtue, and does what he can do to diminish its fame.
>
> Every *man* should be spirited [*thumoeidēs*], but yet also as gentle as possible. For there is no way to avoid those injustices done by others that are both cruel and difficult to remedy, or even impossible to remedy, except by fighting and defending oneself victoriously, and not at all slackening punishment; this every soul is powerless to do without a well-bred spirit [*thumos*]. However, with regard to the curable injustices that are committed, one must first understand that no one unjust is ever unjust voluntarily. For no one anywhere would ever voluntarily acquire any of the greatest evils – least of all when the evil afflicts his most honoured possessions. Now the soul, as we asserted, is truly the most honourable thing for everyone; therefore no one would ever voluntarily take the greatest evil into his most honourable possession and keep it for the rest of his life. So the unjust one, like

the one who possesses bad things, is pitiable in every way, and it is permissible to pity such when his illness is curable, in this case becoming gentle by restraining the spirit [*thumos*] and not keeping up that bitter, womanish scolding. But against the one who is totally and incorrigibly perverse and wicked, one must give anger free rein. This is why we declare that it is fitting for the good to be spirited [*thumoeidēs*] and also gentle, as appropriate. (731a–d; translation based on Thomas Pangle's in *The Laws of Plato*)

The other, more ordinary term for spirit (*thumos*) is scattered a bit more widely, but only a bit. In addition to its extensive employment in the *Laws*, the *Republic*, and *Timaeus*, it appears in four other dialogues. In *Philebus*, Sokrates speaks of there being false manifestations of spirit (along with false pleasures, false fears, and false opinions; 40e). In *Protagoras*, Sokrates asks this famous sophist whether he agrees with the common view that knowledge is but a servant of other psychic forces, mentioning spirit, pleasure, pain, love (*erōta*), and ("often") fear (352b–c; cf. 351a3, b1). In *Cratylus*, *thumos* figures in two of Sokrates' sometimes suspect etymologies; he links its power to "desire" (*epithumia*), and its name to the "raging and boiling of the soul" (*thuseōs kai zeseōs tēs psychēs*; 419de). And in *Sophist*, the stranger claims that the souls of "the worthless" are filled with oppositions, mentioning in particular the oppositions between opinion and desire, between spirit and pleasure, and between reason and pain (228b).

Neither term for spirit appears in the other twenty-eight dialogues – including, most importantly, *Phaedrus*, despite its centrepiece being an elaborate mytho-poetic account of the soul that fairly begs comparison (and integration) with what one can learn about the soul from the *Republic* (see the following note). Indeed, more than eleven-twelfths of Plato's explicit references to the spirit are confined to the *Laws*, the *Republic*, and *Timaeus*.

The last-named dialogue, in particular, augments and confirms the account of the soul given in the *Republic*. Timaeus's teaching about the spirit requires a detailed analysis in light of the entire discussion which he leads, something which cannot be provided here. But the mere surface of his account includes the following relevant points. That the immortal beginning or foundation (*archē*) of soul is framed within a mortal body along with another form of soul that is mortal, and is the seat of passions both terrible (or clever; *deina*) and necessary: first, pleasure, the greatest lure to evil; next, pains, from which good things flee; besides these, rashness and fear, foolish counsellors both; spirit (*thumos*), which is "hard to appease" (*dysparamythēton*); and hope, ever ready to seduce. All these, along with irrational sensation (*aisthēsei alogō*) and all-daring love (*erōti*), are necessarily blended in the mortal species (*genos*). But so that the divine element (located in the head) would not be polluted, unless through absolute necessity, the mortal elements were set apart in the body, with only the "isthmus" of the neck connecting them. And within the body cavity, the mortal species of soul (*to tēs psychēs thnēton genos*) is divided into two parts, the better being "the courageous and spirited part which loves victory"; it is placed nearer the head so that it might hearken to reason, using its strength in common with reason's to subdue the species of desires whenever they are not willing to obey reason (69c–a; cf. 42ab, 70b–72d).

11 Alas, this image so naturally suggests itself that something like it seems to have been used before (cf. *Phaedrus* 246a–249d ff; note especially 248d and 252c).

Because the simultaneous "oneness" and "manyness" of the soul and its relationship with the body are so perplexing, one suspects its nature can be captured *only* in poetic images. Be that as it may, Plato resorts to a variety of such imagery in order to express what seems otherwise inexpressible. In one context, the soul may be likened to a lyre which needs skilful tuning (*Republic* 411ea, 584c; cf. *Phaedo* 73d, 92a–c); another time, to an illustrated book wherein memory, sensation, and passion record opinions (*Philebus* 38e ff).

It should be noted, however, that the same problem which arises in connection with the primary divisions of the soul (i.e., that of conceiving at once the soul's unity and its plurality) pertains as well to each part's respective subdivisions. So, in one sense the spirit is a unified thing, but in another equally important sense, it can be further divided into discernible "parts", and *must* be so divided if one's analysis is to remain faithful to the soul as we experience it. Still, in attempting to analyse those parts, their relationship to each other, and the phenomena their action and interaction cause, one finds that an overly mechanistic or schematic portrayal (and thus misunderstanding) inevitably result.

By contrast, contemplation of a carefully wrought image – such as Plato's conception of the embodied soul as a chariot, charioteer, and team – affords a more subtle intuitive or "noetic" grasp of things. For while the parts of the image are distinguishable, they resist the oversimplification inherent in discursive analysis. As noted, the two horses, representing (I would argue) the two halves of the spirit, remain a common form of thing (horse), *in* each instance of which is replicated a larger portion of the problem than what each itself represents: for each horse (in order to be seen as

Note to page 104

a *horse*) has its own spirited part and its own desiring part, both of which are similar to yet different than that of the other horse. The whole image is necessarily replicated within the human charioteer, whose own soul is presumably elucidated by the very image in which he is but a part (cf. *Republic* 588cd). The reflexive (and thus reflective) possibilities afforded by such rich imagery seem practically inexhaustible.

So, it is an oversimplification to "locate" strictly on one "side" of the human spirit a person's sensitivity to, for example, beauty or nobility (and thus to the ugly or shameful as well). The normally different reactions of men and women to beautiful examples of their own and the opposite sex is sufficient reminder that the soul's taste for beauty is not due exclusively to the higher side of the spirit – that which finds order, precision, proportion, coherence, harmony, symmetry, completeness, and so on pleasing (thus its natural affinity for reason). Rather, one's sense of human beauty is a compound thing, manifesting not only these formal qualities, but also considerable traces of the animalistic desires for self-preservation and self-reproduction served by the spirit's lower half (which thus is sensitive not only to what makes for a suitable sexual partner, but also to signs of a physically wholesome environment; even the sense of "appropriate scale" intrinsic to our judgments of human beauty – so humorously, and revealingly, violated by Swift in *Gulliver's Travels* – may be *partly* attributable to this side of the spirit). Yet, our very educability with respect to higher standards and conceptions of beauty and nobility clearly bespeaks a side of the spirit that can be rationally led.

Similarly, the human desire for honour should not be *equated* with the animal's instinctive pursuit of higher "status" (which in beasts serves strictly utilitarian purposes, as it results in enhanced access to food, protective sleeping and nesting places, "breeding privileges", and so on; even if a high-status animal "feels better", the presence of such a feeling is presumed to have survival value). True enough, the love of honour could be understood as having evolved *primarily* out of that impulse, but it none the less does *not* fall exclusively within the domain of the lower, animal-like half of the spirit. For humans both distinguish and rank various *kinds* of honours, and do so at least partly on the basis of rational considerations. A sensitivity to such ranking, then, would seem to reflect the influence of that upper, reason-allied part of the spirit. Consequently, the presence in humans of a concern for *honour* – inseparable from judgments of what is *truly* honourable (e.g., victories *fairly* won) – remains beyond the capacity of contemporary biology to explain.

Note to page 104

As they are typically experienced, human emotions also seem to be compound mediations synthesized in the spirit, one side of which faces up towards that part of the soul which recognizes, analyses, compares, judges, and so on; the other side of which is allied to those needs and wants we share with lower animals. There is much more to human grief, for instance, than can ever be manifested by a devoted dog over a lost master, but one wouldn't want to ignore utterly the component of simple brute attachment to some degree present in the vast majority of cases. Similarly, the cowed demeanour of a scolded dog shows some "ingredients" of genuine shame, but virtually all rationality being absent, it is much more akin to the simple embarassment that a child might display upon being introduced to a strange adult. The child's discomfort, however, is an incipient form of the real thing, into which it will develop with his growing powers of rational understanding and judgment. Anger, like any emotion, is an expression of the whole spirit, but the differing occasions of its manifestation often show the greater prominence of one or the other side. As an immediate response to frustrated desire, involving as this does little if any rational contribution, it is the lower, animalistic facet of the spirit that is primarily being expressed. Whereas, in indignation on behalf of perceived injustice to others, it is the upper, rationality-allied (indeed, rationality-dependent) part that has set in motion the whole spirit, and thereby the whole soul (cf. 436b1).

I believe that Nietzsche is right in contending that "Courage wants to laugh" (*Zarathustra* 7th parable, "On Reading and Writing"). An adequate analysis of the higher spiritual basis of our sense both of the comic and of the tragic would doubtless require a book unto itself. It seems clear enough, however, that in addition to one's having an eye and ear for beauty, an appreciation of tragedy is dependent upon such spirit-seated phenomena as pity, fear, a sense of the noble, and a will to justice. And it seems almost as clear that our sense of humour – as uniquely human as our sense of beauty – is some psychic synthesis of passionate and rational reactions, the spirit reacting with joy and delight to certain surprising recognitions and understandings. That the surprise is often a surprisingly fitting violation of what is "fitting" suggests that our capacity to experience comedy may proceed from the same spiritual root as our capacity to experience beauty: the passionate sensitivity to what is altogether fitting. Be that as it may, humour's special appeal to the spirit is clearly evident in the fact that few things are as effective in defusing anger.

As for why comedy is inherently *higher* than tragedy (contrary to popular estimates), it must here suffice to say that a conscious recognition of this truth is simply a manifestation of wisdom (cf. 500bc, 602b, 604bc, 608cd). But a full acceptance of this truth (entailing as it does a depreciation of all human, only-too-human concerns) would seem to depend on the balance of one's spirit. A person with a lively sense of humour, by nature more readily inclined to laugh at life than to rebel at its endless frustrations, disappointments, injustices, and misfortunes – one who is capable of looking down on life from an Olympian perspective, as it were – has a natural advantage so far as loving truth is concerned.

12 There can't be many more amusing and convincing portrayals of how ignobling are the vices of spite and envy (or how their absence in a given character enhances his attractiveness) than one finds in Fielding's *Tom Jones*. Speaking as the narrator of that "History", Fielding observes: "To say the truth, want of compassion is not to be numbered among our general faults. The black ingredient which fouls our disposition is envy. Hence our eye is seldom, I am afraid, turned upward to those who are manifestly greater, better, wiser, or happier than ourselves, without some degree of malignity; while we commonly look downwards on the mean and miserable with sufficient benevolence and pity. In fact, I have remarked, that most of the defects which have discovered themselves in the friendships within my observation have arisen from envy only: A hellish vice; and yet one from which I have known very few absolutely exempt" (Book XVII chap. 5). Hobbes finds resentment and ingratitude so personally offensive and politically pernicious that he passed a natural law against them (his fourth, to be precise), although true to his form he gives the issue a mercenary twist:

> As Justice dependeth on Antecedent Covenant; so does GRATITUDE depend on Antecedent Grace; that is to say, on Antecedent Free-gift: and is the fourth Law of Nature; which may be conceived in this Forme, *that a man which receiveth Benefit from another of mere Grace, Endeavour that he which giveth it, have no reasonable cause to repent him of his good will.* For no man giveth, but with intention of Good to himselfe; because Gift is Voluntary; and of all Voluntary Acts, the Object is to every man his own Good; of which if men see they shall be frustrated, there will be no beginning of benevolence, or trust; nor consequently of mutuall help; nor of reconciliation of one man to another; and therefore they are to remain still in the condition of *War*; which is contrary to the first and Fundamentall Law of Nature, which commandeth men to

Seek Peace. The breach of this Law, is called *Ingratitude*; and hath the same relation to Grace, that Injustice hath to Obligation by Covenant. (*Leviathan* chap. 15 par. 16)

This has several interesting implications, not the least of these being that Rulers, having received benefits from the ruled, *do* have obligations to them, despite the fact that they can never be truly charged with injustice.

CHAPTER FIVE

1 The glory and the misery of such men are a frequent theme of Shakespeare's plays. As John Alvis, in "Shakespearean Poetry and Politics", observes about the spirited, honour-loving class in general:

> Shakespeare's plebs, servants, and citizens display the liveliness of vigorous senses rather than the spirited dispositions of men who live for honor. Spiritedness requires the persistent self-awareness that dominates the consciousness of minds who enjoy or aspire to privileges of rank. Shakespeare's nobles constitute a second order of human character distributed across the lines demarking specific political arrangements, a perennial estate of the soul comprised of men and women whose conduct brings to prominence the soul in its spirited, we may say, its self-determined aspect. If the commoner inhabits a world of immediate satisfactions, the Shakespearean notable lives by and for his aspirations. He desires more amply than the commoner, and the good he most intensely desires is almost beyond the comprehension, certainly beyond the reach, of the populace. ...
>
> In his quest for honor the spirited man will espouse virtually any means to win admiration. The usual paths to celebrity are conspicuous wealth, birth, position, beauty, valor, or services rendered to the state. These may be combined with more peculiar claims to distinction; a noble may want to be known as a lover, a subtle diplomat, a mirror of fashion and manners. Whatever their accomplishments, Shakespeare's nobles expect that virtue will be ratified by fame. (In *Shakespeare as Political Thinker* John Alvis and Thomas G. West, eds., 15)

The problems inherent in living for a good that depends on the judgment of others – on both the competence and the justness of that judgment – can amount to tragedy in the case of the highest kind of honour-loving man: he who wishes to be honoured for his virtue. One such is Coriolanus, about whom Allan Bloom observes:

Note to page 113

In reading his great diatribes against the people, one cannot help but be impressed with the reasonableness of the substance, if not the style. All the accusations are accurate descriptions of the actions and thoughts of the people as Shakespeare describes them. But there is a difference in tone, if one can compare Shakespeare's presentation to that of Coriolanus. The latter is full of hatred and bitterness; there is almost what one would today call a reformer's spirit in Coriolanus' approach. Shakespeare indicates that he himself possesses a spirit of acceptance. That is the way things are, and there is no hope of reforming humanity. In this, Shakespeare, I believe, takes his cue from Plutarch. Plutarch blames Coriolanus, not for his opinion of the people, but for caring about them. He brings in as witness the gentle Aristides, who largely shared Coriolanus' estimation of the many, but who, for that very reason, expected nothing of them. He accepted with the same equanimity the archonship and ostracism. The difference between the two men is that Coriolanus is hungry for honor; that is his deepest urge. He wishes to prove himself best. A man only knows himself best on the witness of others; he, as a Roman, must follow the *cursus honorum*, success in which is the sign of virtue.

However, this success now depends on the people, who vote according to their understanding and taste. To be attached to them is contemptible; they are not worthy judges. There is a myth that the man who obeys the laws and is courageous in war will be rewarded; actually, the man who is best adapted to the popular temper of his nation is the one who succeeds. Coriolanus' spirited nobility will not permit him to accept this fact. If easy deception is the road to honor, why should he engage in the difficult enterprises that made him famous? He wants competent judges of his merit; he wants Aufidius to be great so that he can defeat him; he needs a world of heroes to fight so that he can be approved the hero among heroes. He does not want to win a cheating election that covers the true quality of things; he wants others to admire him for what he really is. Coriolanus wants his virtue to be independent. But, in the decisive sense, he is dependent on the city, which is not virtuous, but is a composite of good and bad. All the honor that comes from it is tainted. This is Coriolanus' tragedy. ("The Morality of the Pagan Hero" in Allan Bloom with Harry V. Jaffa *Shakespeare's Politics* 84–5)

Brutus in *Julius Caesar* is another example. In this case, however, Shakespeare is concerned to show somewhat different consequences of the radical contradiction in the character of the man who would be honoured for his virtue. Brutus appears – even to himself, it often seems – as a man who lives for his idea of virtue (i.e., Stoic virtue), who truly regards virtue as its own reward. But Shakespeare has scattered clues throughout the play (the most obvious being Brutus's pretending to first learn of Portia's death from Messala; IV 3 180–94) that Brutus actually cares more for the honour that comes from appearing virtuous than for the virtue itself (and those actions which virtue dictates, irrespective of appearances). This fact both gains him the leadership of the anti-Caesar conspiracy and utterly subverts its purpose. But the problem of portraying this truth is complicated by Shakespeare's wish to preserve for the majority of his audience the apparent nobility of Brutus, especially the nobility of his effort to defend freedom and the Republican regime. On the surface, then, Brutus is portrayed as a tragical hero – so successfully, it seems, that many regard the play as misnamed, that it would more properly be called "The Tragedy of Marcus Brutus". But beneath that surface is a withering critique of Brutus, and especially of why the kind of virtue Brutus wishes to be seen as exemplifying is politically pernicious.

There are several excellent analyses of this play, including the essay by Bloom noted above, David Lowenthal's "Shakespeare's Caesar's Plan," Michael Platt's "Julius Caesar" in his *Rome and Romans According to Shakespeare*, and Jan Blits's *The End of the Ancient Republic*.

2 On this point and several others pertinent to the present study, the testimony of Field Marshal Sir William Slim (based on his World War II experiences in Burma) is worth quoting:

> In preparation, in execution, in strategy, and in tactics we had been worsted, and we had paid the penalty – defeat. Defeat is bitter. Bitter to the common soldier, but trebly bitter to his general. The soldier may comfort himself with the thought that, whatever the result, he has done his duty faithfully and steadfastly, but the commander has failed in *his* duty if he has not won victory – for that *is* his duty. He has no other comparable to it. He will go over in his mind the events of the campaign. 'Here,' he will think, 'I went wrong; here I took counsel of my fears when I should have been bold; there I should have waited to gather strength, not struck piecemeal; at such a moment I failed to grasp opportunity when it was presented to me.' He will remember the soldiers he sent into the attack that failed and who did not come back. He will recall the look in the eyes of the men that

trusted him. 'I have failed them,' he will say to himself, 'and failed my country!' He will see himself for what he is – a defeated general. In a dark hour he will turn in upon himself and question the very foundations of his leadership and his manhood.

And then he must stop! For, if he is ever to command in battle again, he must shake off these regrets, and stamp on them, as they claw at his will and his self-confidence. He must beat off those attacks he delivers against himself, and cast out the doubts born of failure. Forget them, and remember only the lessons to be learned from defeat – they are more than from victory. (*Defeat into Victory* 121)

3 Something of the difference between Glaukon and Adeimantos in this as well as other respects is reflected also in Plato's portrayal of Laches and Nikias in the dialogue "On Courage" (appropriately named *Laches*). There is a good translation and useful commentary by James H. Nichols, Jr, in Thomas Pangle *The Roots of Political Philosophy: Ten Forgotten Socratic Dialogues* 240-80.

4 The twenty-six aphorisms of Zarathustra's seventh parable ("On Reading and Writing") and the twenty-four of his tenth ("On War and Warriors") are helpful in understanding the contrast between the two brothers, and the subtle differences in Sokrates' way of speaking to them – to say nothing of the differential effects of Plato's dialogues on his various readers (cf. Lampert's *Nietzsche's Teaching* 44-7, 50-3). Especially pertinent here are the following:

> You look up when you desire elevation, and I look down because I am elevated.
> Who among you can at the same time laugh and be elevated?
> He who climbs the highest mountains laughs at all tragic plays and tragic seriousnesses [*Trauer-Spiele und Trauer-Ernste*].
> Courageous, carefree, scornful [or, mocking; *spöttisch*], violent – so wisdom wants us: she is a woman and loves always only a warrior.
> You say to me, 'Life is hard to bear [literally, heavy; *schwer*].' But why have your pride in the morning and your resignation in the evening?
> Life is hard to bear: but do not presume to be so tender. We are all fair asses and assesses of burden.
> I should believe only in a god who understood how to dance.

And when I saw my devil, I found him serious, thorough, profound, solemn: it was the Spirit [*Geist*] of Gravity – through him all things fall.

Not by anger, but by laughter one kills. Come, let us kill the Spirit of Gravity.

From our best adversaries [*Feinden*] we do not wish to be spared, and also not from those whom we love thoroughly from the depths [*Grund*]. So let me tell you the truth!

My brothers in war! I love you thoroughly from the depths; I am and always have been of your kind. And I am also your best adversary. So let me tell you the truth!

I know the hatred and envy of your hearts. You are not great enough not to know hatred and envy. So then be great enough not to be ashamed of them!

And if you cannot be saints of knowledge, at least be its warriors. They are the companions and forerunners of such sainthood. (Translations based on Kaufmann's)

5 This is a recurrent theme in Conrad, a man profoundly familiar with both modes of life, the "active" as well as the contemplative. As he observes in *Nostromo*: "Action is consolatory. It is the enemy of thought and the friend of flattering illusion. Only in the conduct of our action can we find the sense of mastery over the Fates" (part I chap. 6). And as he has Marlow muse in "Youth": " ... I remember my youth and the feeling that will never come back anymore – the feeling that I could last forever, outlast the sea, the earth, and all men; the deceitful feeling that lures us on to joys, to perils, to love, to vain effort – to death; the triumphant conviction of strength, the heat of life in the handful of dust, the glow in the heart that with every year grows dim, grows cold, grows small, and expires – and expires too soon, too soon – before life itself".

The antipathy between action and thought is especially prominent in the perspective of Heyst, the son of a pessimistic philosopher, and the main protagonist in Conrad's *Victory*: "The young man learned to reflect, which is a destructive process, a reckoning of the cost. It is not the clearsighted who lead the world. Great achievements are accomplished in a blessed, warm mental fog, which the pitiless blasts of the father's analysis had blown away from the son" (88–9). The author later reveals, perhaps, the reasoning behind this general view as to the futility of action:

Note to page 121

[Heyst] stirred impatiently in his chair, and raised the book to his eyes with both hands. It was one of his father's. He opened it haphazard, and his eyes fell on the middle of the page. The elder Heyst had written of everything in many books – of space and of time, of animals and of stars; analysing ideas and actions, the laughter and the frowns of men, and the grimaces of their agony. ...

And Heyst, the son, read:

Of the stratagems of life the most cruel is the consolation of love – the most subtle, too; for the desire is the bed of dreams.

He turned the pages of the little volume, "Storm and Dust", glancing here and there at the broken text of reflections, maxims, short phrases, enigmatical sometimes and sometimes eloquent. It seemed to him that he was hearing his father's voice, speaking and ceasing to speak again. He abandoned himself to the half-belief that something of his father dwelt yet on earth – a ghostly voice, audible to the ear of his own flesh and blood. With what strange serenity, mingled with terrors, had that man considered the universal nothingness! He had plunged into it headlong, perhaps to render death, the answer that faced one at every inquiry, more supportable.

Heyst stirred, and the ghostly voice ceased; but his eyes followed the words on the last page of the book:

Men of tormented conscience, or of a criminal imagination, are aware of much that minds of a peaceful, resigned cast do not even suspect. It is not poets alone who dare descend into the abyss of infernal regions, or even who dream of such a descent. The most inexpressive of human beings must have said to himself, at one time or another: "Anything but this!" ...

We all have our instants of clairvoyance. They are not very helpful. The character of the scheme does not permit that or anything else to be helpful. Properly speaking its character, judged by the standards established by its victims, is infamous. It excuses every violence of protest and at the same time never fails to crush it, just as it crushes the blindest assent. The so-called wickedness must be, like the so-called virtue, its own reward – to be anything at all ...

Clairvoyance or no clairvoyance, men love their captivity. To the unknown force of negation they prefer the miserably tumbled bed of their servitude. Man alone can give one the disgust of pity; yet I find it easier to believe in the misfortune of mankind than in its wickedness.

These were the last words. (206-7; part III chap. 5)

6 The antecedents of both the Platonic and the Herodotean versions of this story (which themselves make for a most interesting comparison; the latter's *Histories* virtually begin with his "rationalized" account of Gyges) are skilfully ferreted out by Kirby Flower Smith in a two-part essay, "The Tale of Gyges and the King of Lydia." He contends: "Gyges, whose commanding yet curiously complex personality is still clearly felt in the tradition of him, was the first great 'barbarian' with whom the Hellenic world had come in close contact. He was associated with the early traditions of art as well as other inventions much less creditable to himself. In the time of Archilocus his wealth was a by-word" (261). Smith also provides some clues helpful in interpreting both Glaukon's supernatural version (for example, concerning the sacred and magical significance of bronze, the Titanic stature of the corpse, and the ring), and Herodotus' more overtly erotic version. Cf. Cicero *De Officiis* III 38-9.

Rousseau claims to have thought often about the ring of Gyges and what use he would have made of its power. And although he is sure that he would have employed it almost entirely in benevolent ways, he mysteriously confesses to one weakness that he judges would have been enough to have done him in. Thus he concludes, "All things considered, I believe I will do better to throw away my magic ring before it makes me commit some folly" ("Sixth Walk" in *The Reveries of a Solitary Walker* 82-3).

7 Thus, Rousseau refers to Plato's *Republic* as "not at all a political work, as think those who judge books only by their titles. It is the most beautiful educational treatise ever written" (*Emile, or, On Education*, Allan Bloom, trans., 40). Of course – as the very context from which this statement is drawn makes clear – no one understands better than Rousseau the deeper congruence of the issues of politics and education. It is precisely because the regimes characteristic of the modern age no longer permit of citizenship in the full and original sense that another kind of education than the "public education" described in the *Republic* may be necessary, one such as that depicted in *Emile*. In his *Second Discourse*, Rousseau excepts "Sparta alone" from his generalization about the inadequacy of laws and the inevitable abuse of social institutions, because in Sparta "the law attended principally to the education of children" (173).

Notes to pages 135–7

Leo Strauss suggests that "the *Republic*, whose subject is precisely the relation between education and politics," deals with the priority between the two "by distinguishing two kinds of education (522a2–b3), the education of all, and the education of potential philosophers" ("On a New Interpretation of Plato's Political Philosophy" 360 note 44).

8 The whole of Nietzsche's "Untimely Meditation", *Schopenhauer as Educator*, rests on the same principle: that it is not his *doctrines* that are of primary importance (and about which Nietzsche says almost nothing), but rather the man himself, who proved by his example that the philosophical life, as conceived and lived in antiquity, is still possible in modernity. It is this example that can liberate a youthful soul that today "lies fettered by the chains of fear and convention" (127). Virtually every feature of Nietzsche's account of Schopenhauer as philosopher begs to be compared with the portrait of the philosopher in the *Republic*:

> [He is a] true thinker [who] always cheers and refreshes, whether he is being serious or humorous, expressing his human insight or his divine forbearance; without peevish gesturing, trembling hands, tear-filled eyes, but with certainty and simplicity, courage and strength, perhaps somewhat gallantly and stiffly [literally, knightly and hard; *ritterlich und hart*] but in any case as a victor: and this it is – to behold the victorious god with all the monsters he has combated – that cheers one most profoundly. ... For at bottom there is cheerfulness only where there is a victory; and this applies to the works of true thinkers just as much as it does to any work of art. (135)

Late in his essay, Nietzsche speaks of "the conditions with the assistance of which a born philosopher can, in the most favourable case at least, avoid being crushed by the perversity of our times ... " (cf. *Republic* 492a–496c). According to Nietzsche, Schopenhauer had the good fortune to enjoy these conditions most felicitous to philosophy: "There is no lack of contrary conditions, to be sure: the perversity of the age came fearfully close to him, for example, in the person of his vain and culturally pretentious mother. But the proud and republican-like free character [*stolz und republikanisch freie Charakter*] of his father as it were saved him from his mother and bestowed upon him the first thing a philosopher needs: inflexible and rugged manliness" (180; cf. *Republic* 549c–d).

The entire concluding section of Nietzsche's essay, distinguishing genuine philosophers from all those emasculated pretenders who so demean the dignity of philosophy (thereby destroying its appeal for superior youths), is modelled on Sokrates' discussion of the same problem in Book Six. Nietzsche begins:

> These, then, are some of the conditions under which the philosophical genius can at any rate come into existence in our time despite the forces working against it: free manliness of character, early knowledge of humankind, no scholarly education, no narrow patriotism, no necessity for bread-winning, no ties with the State – in short, freedom and again freedom: that wonderful and perilous element in which the Greek philosophers were able to grow up. Whoever wants to reproach him, as Niebuhr reproached Plato, with being a bad citizen, let him do so and be a good citizen himself: thus he will be in the right and so will Plato. Another will see this great freedom as a piece of presumption: he too is right, for he himself would do nothing with it and it would be very presumptuous in him to claim it for himself. That freedom is in fact a heavy debt which can be discharged only by means of great deeds. (182–3)

The test of whether genuine philosophy is being promoted, rather than sophistry and tepid, timid scholarliness (for example, in today's state-supported institutions of 'higher learning'), is whether the conception of philosophy is understood "*Platonically*, which is to say as seriously and honestly as though its highest objective were to produce new Platos" (183). It is worth noting that in this final part of his essay, Nietzsche mentions Plato more often than he does Schopenhauer.

Nietzsche insists that he can "profit from a philosopher only insofar as he can be an example ... , capable of drawing whole nations after him through his example" – as did the philosophers of India and Greece (136-7). And this was the power of Schopenhauer's example for young Nietzsche, or so he would have us believe: "this pure and truly antique attitude towards philosophy" (139). What should perhaps be emphasized, however, is that Nietzsche never laid eyes on Schopenhauer. He speaks of his "joy and amazement" upon first discovering Schopenhauer: "I sensed that in him I had discovered that educator and philosopher I had sought for so long. But I had discovered him only in the form of a book, and that was a great deficiency. So I strove all the harder to see through the book and to imagine the living man whose great testament I had read and who promised to make his heirs only those who would and could be more than merely his readers: namely his sons and pupils" (136). In this respect, of course, Plato's Sokrates and Nietzsche's Schopenhauer are on a par – as indeed are the books of all true philosophers.

9 Cf. Leo Strauss *Thoughts on Machiavelli* 288-9.

10 These two generalizations, bespeaking an all-too-human tendency to be less than just in one's judgments, are fundamental to Machiavelli's view of political life, and go far towards justifying it. See, for example, the fourth and central paragraph of chap. 17 of *The Prince* and the first sentence of Book I of his *Discourses*.

11 Hobbes, for instance, derives some of these principles from his first and fundamental law of nature; see chap. 14 par. 30 of *Leviathan*. Of course, if one accepts Hobbes's reasoning as correct, it might serve to justify Sokrates' referral of such issues to the discretion of well-educated gentlemen rulers, on the assumption they could reason as well as Hobbes.

12 Over the centuries, much of course has been written about Plato's "theory of justice", but *not* a lot proportional to the entirety of literature generated by this dialogue. Despite its traditionally being regarded as "On the Just", it's my impression that more attention has been paid to other aspects of it, such as its critique of poetry, its portrayal of philosophy, some presumed "theory of forms", its account of the soul, and its critique of democracy. Even discussions of its "ideal regime" are not usually focused on the supposed *justness* of the city or cities in *logos*. Most of the more recent literature that does attend to the dialogue's teaching about justice is critical and condescending, but not much of it is truly well-informed, either about the whole problem of justice as Plato reveals it, or (consequently) about the character of his response to it. Gregory Vlastos's attempt to defend Plato's account of justice from some of the common criticisms made against it offers a convenient survey of several prominent views of the day, and an equally convenient contrast to the interpretation offered here ("Justice and Happiness in the *Republic*" in *Plato II* G. Vlastos, ed., 66-95).

13 This would seem to be the "moral" of what is probably the most memorable vignette in Machiavelli's *The Prince*: the use and abuse by Cesare Borgia of "Messer Remirro de Orco, a cruel and expeditious man" (recounted in the eighth and central paragraph of chap. 7). It is also the initiating political theme of Shakespeare's *Measure for Measure*.

14 In this, as in so many respects, *Utopia* reveals Thomas More to be an insightful student of the *Republic*; see the fourth chapter of part II ("Of Sciences, Crafts, and Occupations").

15 As hinted above, one might think of these divergent goals as being exemplified by Sparta and Athens, the two great and accordingly dominant regimes of the Hellenic age. The attractiveness of Athens needs no more defence today than that which Thucydides has Pericles give it then. As for those who cannot truly understand why the regime of Lykourgos was so highly respected in antiquity, and by political philosophers throughout the ages, they might wish to read more of Thucydides than just this famous "Funeral Oration". Xenophon provides a complementary, if somewhat beautified, in any case more systematic account in his *Regime of the Lakediamonians*. As noted in chap. 2, this small work is of no small importance for our better understanding not only the dialogue's account of Timocracy but both regimes in *logos* as well. Xenophon begins by admitting that he too "wondered" why Sparta, despite its sparse population, was the most powerful and renowned *polis* in Greece: "But when I considered the practices [*epitēdeumata*] of the Spartans, I no longer wondered." Instead, he wondered at the "uttermost wisdom" of Lykourgos, who gave them laws unlike those of any other *polis* (cf. *Minos* 320a–b).

16 According to Caesar, whose writings show him to be in no wise superstitious, but (rather) as steadfastly inclined to a naturalistic explanation of everything as Herodotus or Aristotle, "the Druids attach particular importance to the belief that the soul does not perish but passes after death from one body to another; they think that this belief is the most effective way to encourage bravery because it removes the fear of death. They hold long discussions about the heavenly bodies and their movements, about the size of the universe and the earth, about the nature of the physical world, and about the power and properties of the immortal gods, subjects in which they also give instruction to their pupils." As for the character of that instruction, "It is said that during their training they learn by heart a great many verses, so many that some people spend twenty years studying the doctrine. They do not think it right to commit their teachings to writing, although for almost all other purposes, for example, for public and private accounts, they use the Greek alphabet. I suppose this practice began originally for two reasons: they did not want their doctrines to be accessible to the ordinary people, and they did not want their pupils to rely on the written word and so neglect to train their memories" (*The Gallic Wars* VI 14, Anne and Peter Wiseman, trans.).

It is of some interest that the man whom many military historians regard as one of the greatest American battlefield commanders, General George S. Patton, Jr, also apparently believed in reincarnation. As he once wrote his wife after reading about the Norman conquest of Sicily, "I feel that I may be either William Fer-a-Beas or Roger of Sicily, probably the former, as he fought his last battle at 71" (*The Patton Papers: 1940-1945* Martin Blumenson, ed., 382).

CHAPTER SIX

1 Bloom consistently translates *epieikēs* as 'decent' – more in the sense of "that's a decent approximation" than of "that's an indecent proposal". This may be the best compromise term available in English for the range of meanings associated with the dialogue's some thirty uses of the term and its cognates. In everyday use, meanings of *epieikēs* would run from 'fitting', 'meet', and 'suitable' through 'plausible', 'reasonable', and 'fair' to 'fair-minded' and 'equitable' (the adverbial form, *epieikōs*, is used rather like our 'pretty' or 'fairly', as in "pretty near" or "fairly far"). I, however, prefer 'reasonable' or 'equitable' for two reasons: the term 'decent' carries moral overtones for us that frequently do not seem indicated in the original text; and *epieikēs* (in the sense of 'equitable') is often used in contradistinction to *dikaios* (i.e., strictly just). Aristotle, for example, teaches that judgments of *epieikeia*, being adapted to the particulars of a given case, are a sort of higher justice whereby one rectifies what sometimes amounts to a miscarriage of justice through strict application of the law (see *Eth. Nich.* 1137 a 31–b 34). A decent, equitable, *epieikēs* man does not always insist on the letter of the law.

2 Sokrates' rhetorical efforts here are akin to Mark Antony's pleadings to the crowd that they not make him read Caesar's will.

3 Especially for someone great-spirited (hence prideful), the threat of ridicule may constitute a higher test of courage than most of the dangers encountered on the battlefield. As Stendhal's Julien observes in *The Red and the Black* (C.K. Scott-Moncrieff's translation), "He is brave, and there is no more to be said, she tells me. And even then, brave in facing the swords of the Spaniards. In Paris everything alarms him, he sees everywhere the danger of ridicule. He has not an idea which ventures to depart from the fashion" (chap. 40). The "she" refers to the high-born but independently minded Mathilde, about whom Stendhal writes (chap. 44):

> She abhorred want of character, it was her sole objection to the handsome young men among whom she lived. The more gracefully they

mocked at everything which departed from the fashion, or which followed it wrongly when intending to follow it, the more they condemned themselves in her eyes. They were brave, and that was all. 'And besides, how are they brave?' she asked herself: 'in a duel. But the duel is nothing more now than a formality. Everything is known beforehand, even what a man is to say when he falls. ...

A man will face danger at the head of a squadron all glittering with steel, but a danger that is solitary, strange, sudden, truly ugly?'

And if the philosophical life will always seem ridiculous to most people, it will remain closed to the man who cannot master his "childish" fear of being laughed at.

4 As Hardy expresses the point in *Tess of the d'Urbervilles* (chap. 53): "'Oh, my boy, my boy – home again at last!' cried Mrs. Clare, who cared no more at that moment for the stains of heterodoxy which had caused all this separation than for the dust upon his clothes. What woman, indeed, among the most faithful adherents of the truth believes the promises and threats of the Word in the sense in which she believes in her own children, or would not throw her theology to the wind if it weighed against their happiness?"

5 Can one find this view better expressed than in the words Jane Austen provided for her heroine in *Persuasion*? Anne Elliot is conversing with a retired naval officer, Captain Harville, concerning the relative constancy of men and women in their loving:

'Yes. We certainly do not forget you, so soon as you forget us. It is, perhaps, our fate rather than our merit. We cannot help ourselves. We live at home, quiet, confined, and our feelings prey upon us. You are forced on exertion. You have always a profession, pursuits, business of some sort or other, to take you back into the world immediately, and continual occupation and change soon weaken impressions.'

'Granting your assertion that the world does all this so soon for men, (which, however, I do not think I shall grant) it does not apply to Benwick. He has not been forced upon any exertion. The peace turned him on shore at the very moment, and he has been living with us, in our little family-circle, ever since.'

'True,' said Anne, 'very true; I did not recollect; but what shall we say now, Captain Harville? If the change be not from outward circumstances, it must be from within; it must be nature, man's nature, which has done the business for Captain Benwick.'

'No, no, it is not man's nature. I will not allow it to be more man's nature than woman's to be inconstant and forget those they do love, or have loved. I believe the reverse, I believe in a true analogy between our bodily frames and our mental; and that as our bodies are the strongest, so are our feelings; capable of bearing most rough usage, and riding out the heaviest weather.'

'Your feelings may be the strongest,' replied Anne, 'but the same spirit of analogy will authorize me to assert that ours are the most tender. Man is more robust than woman, but he is not longer-lived; which exactly explains my view of the nature of their attachments. Nay, it would be too hard upon you, if it were otherwise. You have difficulties, and privations, and dangers enough to struggle with. You are always labouring and toiling, exposed to every risk and hardship. Your home, country, friends, all quitted. Neither time, nor health, nor life, to be called your own. It would be too hard indeed' (with a faltering voice) 'if woman's feelings were to be added to all this.'

'We shall never agree upon this question' – Captain Harville was beginning to say, when a slight noise called their attention to Captain Wentworth's hitherto perfectly quiet division of the room. ...

' ... Well, Miss Elliot,' (lowering his voice) 'as I was saying, we shall never agree I suppose upon this point. No man and woman would, probably. But let me observe that all histories are against you, all stories, prose and verse. If I had such a memory as Benwick, I could bring you fifty quotations in a moment on my side the argument, and I do not think I ever opened a book in my life which had not something to say upon woman's inconstancy. Songs and proverbs, all talk of woman's fickleness. But perhaps you will say, these were all written by men.'

'Perhaps I shall. Yes, yes, if you please, no reference to examples in books. Men have had every advantage of us in telling their own story. Education has been theirs in so much higher a degree; the pen has been in their hands. I will not allow books to prove anything.'

'But how shall we prove anything?'

'We never shall. We never can expect to prove anything upon such a point. It is a difference of opinion which does not admit of proof. We each begin probably with a little bias towards our own sex, and upon that bias build every circumstance in favour of it which has occurred within our circle; many of which circumstances (perhaps those very cases which strike us the most) may be precisely such as cannot be brought forward without betraying a confidence, or in some respect saying what should not be said.' (II chap. 11)

Of course, the novel as a whole proves that the incomparable Jane does not always agree with her heroine.

6 That is, responses which do not beg the question. One which would is the argument that Plato was prevented from including women by the requirements of "dramatic realism", since free-born Greek ladies simply did not meet with men in conversations such as those portrayed in the dialogues. While this is doubtless true, it clearly fails to address the issue of the resulting (in)adequacy of the conversation as created. Moreover, other of his dialogues prove that he *did* have a "realistic" way of introducing a female interlocutor when he wished to do so. In the *Symposium*, for example, Sokrates' speech in praise of *erōs* (201d-212c) takes the form of a recapitulation of conversations he allegedly had with a certain priestess of love, a "Mantinean woman named Diotima", who made him an expert in *erōtika* (177de; cf. *Theages* 128b). It is interesting to note that such "love matters" are the *only* thing he ever claims to be knowledgeable in, and that according to his own account he learned it all from a woman (it is not clear whether the instruction was exclusively verbal) – whereas all the *other* praisers of *erōs* portrayed in the dialogue had eulogized love between males as being the highest kind. Also, in *Menexenos* Sokrates recounts how he was allegedly taught rhetoric by Pericles' mistress, Aspasia (cf. *Meno* 81a). The point is, Plato could in similar fashion have introduced a woman indirectly into his *Politeia*, but chose not to do so.

7 I suppose one should add a qualification to this position, for there are no doubt people who believe fervently in its basic premiss (the substantial sameness of men and women, with a consequent requirement for complete and unqualified political equality), but who would none the less be deeply offended – not to say, revolted – were some latter-day Plato to create a dialogue about justice with an all-male cast. Insofar as one can offer a rational defence of such feelings, it would seem necessarily to be based on an assumption that this "sexual-sameness" premiss, while true, is not sufficiently *known* to be true ... for some reason (and here the defender must be very careful in specifying what that reason is, lest he give the whole game away). Therefore, in the interest of dispelling darkness and

furthering people's education into the truth, one is obliged on every occasion and in every decent way to ratify this basic premiss. And, moreover, it is doubly important that works intended to serve a pedagogical purpose provide appropriate "role models" for students of both sexes.

But this is no sooner said than perplexing questions arise. Had Plato somehow managed to include a Lysistrata or a Praxagora among the interlocutors of *Politeia*, why should we believe that such female characters provide the appropriate role models for female students of the dialogue? Or rather, how is such a belief compatible with the basic premiss? *Why*, if the the sexes *are* substantially the same, should a young woman more readily "identify" with a Praxagora than with a Polemarchos? And even more to the point, why should we right-thinking people *want* them to? I feel obliged to add that, based on a couple of decades of teaching experience with all sorts of students, I find the claims for the importance of sexual (and for that matter, racial) "role models" to be much as Mark Twain did the rumours of his death: "greatly exaggerated".

8 Teiresias (or Tiresias) is the legendary character referred to in the fourth and central of the seven quotations from Homer that begin Book Three ("'He alone possesses understanding; the others are fluttering shadows"; *Odyssey* X 495). Teiresias was the blind Theban seer of great longevity who, in addition to advising Odysseus when he visited Hades for that very purpose (referred to in the line quoted), played a prominent role in the Oedipus affair and in that of the so-called Seven against Thebes. Of the various stories told about him, one is especially pertinent to the dialogue:

> ... Tiresias once saw two snakes coupling on Mount Cyllene in Arcadia. He wounded them or, as some say, killed the female, and instantly he was transformed from a man into a woman. For seven years he lived as a woman and was notorious for his love affairs. At the end of that time he again saw two snakes coupling and, as some say, killed the male and was transformed once more into a man. Hera and Zeus, being engaged in an argument about which sex enjoys the physical aspects of love more, decided to consult Tiresias, who had experienced these aspects as both a man and a woman. Hera maintained that the male derived the most pleasure from love-making, and contended that this was why Zeus was so often unfaithful to her. Zeus mocked her and claimed that it was the female who enjoyed it most. On being appealed to, Tiresias agreed with Zeus. If the parts of the pleasure of love were counted as ten, he said, women got nine

Notes to pages 211-12

parts and men only one. This infuriated Hera and she struck Tiresias blind. Zeus, to make up for this, gave him long life and the art of soothsaying. ('Tiresias' in *The New Century Classical Handbook* Catherine B. Avery, ed., 1105)

9 The nature, extent, and development of observable sexual differences and their aetiology are among the most intensely studied subjects in modern scientific psychology. A recent effort to summarize and synthesize the results so far includes an annotated bibliography of some fourteen hundred items published in English during just the years from 1965 to 1973 (Eleanor Emmons Maccoby and Carol Nagy Jacklin *The Psychology of Sex Differences*). This work, incidentally, is a particularly valuable survey, not only for the breadth of its authors' acquaintance with modern efforts to investigate systematically the subject, but also because of their intelligent appreciation of the various reasons for the limited validity of so much work in this field, and the caution with which they interpret its results. Their concluding chapter ("Summary and Commentary", 348-74) offers a concise overview of their interpretation of the findings; they suggest that the following generalizations are "fairly well established": that girls have greater verbal ability than boys, that boys excel in visual-spatial ability, that boys excel in mathematical ability, and that males are more aggressive (and that "the primary victims of male aggression are other males"). On another range of questions (e.g., fearfulness, activity levels, compliance, and inclinations "to behave nurturantly"), they find the formal research evidence either too sparse or too ambiguous for confident conclusions. About relative competitiveness, they say: "When sex differences are found, they usually show boys to be more competitive, but there are many studies finding sex similarity. ... [However,] almost all the research on competition has involved situations in which competition is maladaptive. ... It appears probable that in situations in which competitiveness produces increased individual rewards, males would be more competitive, but this is a guess based on commonsense considerations, such as the male interest in competitive sports, not upon research in controlled settings." Most such research, as they note, has been based upon only three age groups: new-born infants, nursery-school children, and college-age youths. About "dominance", they remark that it "appears to be more of an issue within boys' groups than girls' groups. Boys make more dominance attempts (both successful and unsuccessful) toward one another than do girls. They also more often attempt to dominate adults."

Note to page 212

Another, slightly more recent work that is particularly useful in providing food for thought on this matter is Robert May's *Sex and Fantasy: Patterns of Male and Female Development*. May's analysis draws on evidence from modern psychoanalytic practice. Moreover, he directly addresses the highly politicized atmosphere in which all research and discussion of sexual differences currently take place (and which has rather obviously compromised so much of the past couple of decades' research in this field; today, even primate ethology shows the distorting effects of fashionable ideology):

> Is it legitimate and allowable for a man to write about women? There is a current separatist position that would say no, would say that any man's understanding of women is bound to be so defective as to be useless if not actively destructive. Obviously I do not agree. One of the disturbing trends in our cultural and intellectual life is a kind of Balkanization that is ultimately based on the narcissistic assumption that only like can understand like. We have not only the right, but the positive obligation to follow our imagination across these boundaries and try to understand the nature of others' experience.
>
> One theme of this book is that there *are* significant psychological differences between the sexes, and that these differences are worth thinking about; a mild point, it would seem. In fact there is a tendency, at least in America these days, to think that anyone who raises the question of sex differences is at best mean-spirited and at worst a reactionary bigot. We are eager to talk as if there were a level of humanness that is independent of gender. I think this is a mistaken way to put it. I would rather say that each of us comes to a level of humanness *through* our maleness or femaleness. From the moment of conception we are either female or male; from early in life we are psychologically *both* male and female, and we are so by a complex inner structure, not an amorphous mixture in which black and white make grey. (xi)

Included in May's account is an especially useful chapter ("The Case for Sex Differences", 71-103) summarizing the major findings in a variety of fields that bear on the question (animal ethology, especially involving primates; physiological studies of hormonal effects; neonatal studies; cross-"cultural" comparisons; observations of the "seemingly insignificant" details of life). In no one place or approach does one find decisive and unproblematic evidence on any issue of importance, but if one cares to look for it there *is* a pattern of coherent regularities sufficient for reaching some practical conclusions.

And, of course, one must never lose sight of the fact that the truth about masculinity and femininity is necessarily going to be a matter of broad generalities, whereas the practice of justice is often (but by no means exclusively) a matter of how particular individuals are dealt with. "Statistically significant" differences between boys and girls, men and women, strictly pertain only to that statistical abstraction called a 'norm', whereas the *distribution range* of actual individuals with respect to a given quality or ability can be fairly similar for both males and females. However, in thinking about just political arrangements and the nurturing of children, it is not difficult to see that some reliance on normal expectations is not only unavoidable in practice, but perfectly appropriate (despite its resulting in those much maligned bogeymen of modern democracies, "prejudices" and "stereotypes"). Moreover, it hardly seems prudent to become so preoccupied with individual qualifications that no attention whatsoever is paid to group dynamics. For example, no one who really cared about the fighting qualities of his army would decide the issue of whether women should be included in combat units simply on the basis of whether some women can meet all the same individual requirements as do the men.

10 There are exactly twice as many mentions of 'woman' (*gynē*) and 'womanish' (or, 'feminine'; *gynaikeios*) in Book Five as in the entirety of the rest of the dialogue (sixty and thirty references, respectively). There are seven references to mothers in Book five, seven precede it (if we include *dysaristotokeia* at 388c), and seven follow it. Of the thirteen references to 'daughter' (*thygatēr*), five are in Book Five, as are all seven references to 'female' (*thēlys*).

11 Thus all reference to women of any kind is avoided until the philosopher agrees to consider for Glaukon "a feverish city", the better to see "how justice and injustice naturally grow in cities" (372e); whereupon the first women, specifically "courtesans" (*hetairai*, literally, "female companions"), are introduced into their city in *logos*, along with a broad range of feminine concerns (perfume, embroidery, jewellery, hairdressers and cosmeticians, craftsmen who specialize in "feminine adornment", and so on). It is clearly suggested that a love of luxury is especially characteristic of women (and thus that men ought to regard it as a feminine trait). But it is not made equally clear whether this concern for luxury proceeds more from women's having a greater desire for bodily comfort than do men, or more from a concern with their status (and first of all, with particular men; cf. 420a, 548ab).

Notes to pages 214–21

12 An anthropologist, studying the primitive Yanomamo tribe of the Venezuelan-Brazilian borderlands, recently reported:

> I have gradually come to realize that a chronic shortage of women determines much of these Indians' social structure. One theory in anthropology is that warfare among primitive peoples can usually be traced to conflicts over land or water or some other inanimate strategic resource. Another view holds that blood relatives do not war against each other. The Yanomamo refute both these theses by their actions. ...
>
> No village with fewer than forty inhabitants can last long, since it would have too few men for adequate defense. And that is the main reason Kaobawa and Bahimi want the potential warriors that male infants represent. Yet, as a village grows larger it becomes more difficult for the Yanomamo to hold it together through kinship and marriage ties, or by the charisma of a headman.
>
> 'When we are many,' explained Kaobawa, 'we fight among ourselves all the time – it is always over some woman.' Such fights flare-up, subside, and break out again, pitting close relatives against each other in skull-cracking club fights. Most villages break apart before they reach 125 people.
>
> Alliances enable each village to call on friends for help in raiding other villages, or for temporary refuge from the raids of enemies. Yet allies can not be trusted, for they are tempted to abduct the women of visiting friends. (N.A. Chagnon "Yanomamo, the True People" 212)

13 And thus an account more akin to that with which Aristotle begins the first book of his *Politics*, wherein families group together to form villages which grow into towns.

14 I rather incline to Nietzsche's view: "The struggle for *equal* rights is actually a symptom of disease: every physician knows that. – The more a woman is a woman, the more she fights tooth and nail against rights in general: for the state of nature, the eternal *war* between the sexes, accedes to her by far the first rank" (*Ecce Homo* "Why I Write Such Good Books" aph. 5, Walter Kaufmann translation in *Basic Writings*).

15 As Arlene Saxonhouse puts it ("The Philosopher and the Female in the Political Thought of Plato"), "In order to establish this equation [between male and female], Socrates ... must de-sex the female, make her void of

any special erotic attraction or function" (198). He abstracts from her true specialty (motherhood) and introduces her into political life, "which is historically, at least, alien to her – only through a perversion of her nature. In order to become political, she must sacrifice her role as the female of the species" (202).

16 Cf. *Phaedrus* 246d-c, 248c-a. Or consider what may be simply a modern version of that ancient teaching:

> What we experience in our dreams, if we experience it often, is in the end just as much a part of the total economy of our soul as anything experienced 'actually': we are on account of it richer or poorer, feel one need more or one need less, and finally are led a little in broad daylight and even in the most cheerful moments of our awake spirit by the habits of our dreams. Suppose someone has flown often in his dreams and finally, as soon as he dreams, is conscious of a power and art of flight as if it were his privilege, also his personal and enviable happiness: such a man as he believes he can realize any arc and angle with the slightest impulse, knows the feeling of a certain divine frivolity, an 'ascension' without tension or constraint, a 'descent' with condescension or degradation – without *gravity*. – How could a human being who has had such dream-experiences and dream-habits not at last find the word 'happiness' had a different color and definition in his waking life too! How could he fail to have a *different* kind of – desire for happiness. 'Soaring' as described by the poets must seem to him, compared with this 'flying', too earthly, muscular, forced, too 'grave'. (*Beyond Good and Evil* aph. 193; translation based on Walter Kaufmann's)

17 Hobbes does a neat job of both explicating and resolving a version of this basic problem at the beginning of part III of *Leviathan*.

18 For those so confused by the carnival of life in modern democracies as to be utterly at a loss concerning what these differences might be, they could turn for guidance to the great tradition of English novels, generated in times when both ordinary and extraordinary men and women had a more solid sense of who and what they are, if not necessarily always why. In this respect, Jane Austen probably has few peers, though the names George Eliot, Henry James, and D. H. Lawrence come immediately to mind. For that matter, one could do a lot worse than read Anthony Trollope. And because her excellence is not so widely acknowledged, I would make

Note to page 226

special mention of Isak Dinesen; in tale after marvellous tale, she proves what she has one of her characters say: "man and woman are two locked caskets, of which each contains the key to the other" ("A Consolatory Tale" in *Winter's Tales*). And according to no less an authority than Lawrence:

> The great relationship, for humanity, will always be the relation between man and woman. The relation between man and man, woman and woman, parent and child, will always be subsidiary.
>
> And the relation between man and woman will change for ever, and will for ever be the central clue to human life. It is the *relation itself* which is the quick and central clue to life, not the man, nor the woman, nor the children that result from the relationship, as a contingency.
>
> It is no use thinking you can put a stamp on the relation between man and woman, to keep it in the *status quo*. You can't. You might as well try to put a stamp on the rainbow or the rain. ("Morality and the Novel" *Phoenix*, McDonald, ed., 531)

Of course, a moment's reflection suffices to confirm that changes in the *relation* between man and woman in no way imply changes in their respective natures. And the well-proven fact that there are various modes of their relating simply raises the age-old question, which way is best.

It is only against a background of some common understanding of natural sexual differences that Hardy could sensibly write: "The sun, on account of the mist, had a curious sentient, personal look, demanding the masculine pronoun for its adequate expression. His present aspect, coupled with the lack of all human forms in the scene, explained the old-time heliolatries in a moment. One could feel that a saner religion had never prevailed under the sky. The luminary was a golden-haired, beaming, mild-eyed, God-like creature, gazing down in the vigour and intentness of youth upon an earth that was brimming with interest for him" (*Tess of the d'Urbervilles* beginning of chap. 14).

Or that Melville could allegorize:

> It was a clear steel-blue day. The firmaments of air and sea were hardly separable in that all-pervading azure; only, the pensive air was transparently pure and soft, with a woman's look, and the robust and man-like sea heaved with long, strong, lingering swells, as Sampson's chest in his sleep.
>
> Hither, and thither, on high, glided the snow-white wings of small unspeckled birds; these were the gentle thoughts of the feminine air;

but to and fro in the deeps, far down in the bottomless blue, rushed mighty leviathans, sword-fish, and sharks; and these were the strong, troubled, murderous thinkings of the masculine sea.

But though thus contrasting within, the contrast was only in shades and shadows without; those two seemed one; it was only the sex, as it were, that distinguished them.

Aloft, like a royal czar and king, the sun seemed giving this gentle air to this bold and rolling sea; even as bride to groom. And at the girdling line of the horizon, a soft and tremulous motion – most seen here at the equator – denoted the fond, throbbing trust, the loving alarms, with which the poor bride gave her bosom away. (*Moby Dick* first paragraphs of chap. 132, "The Symphony")

19 As Rousseau exhorts Republican women in the final paragraph of the "Dedicatory Letter" to his *Discourse on Inequality*: "Could I forget that precious half of the Republic which creates the happiness of the other and whose gentleness and wisdom maintain peace and good morals? Amiable and virtuous countrywomen, the fate of your sex will always be to govern ours. It is fortunate when your chaste power, exercised solely in conjugal union, makes itself felt only for the glory of the state and the public happiness." Or as George Eliot put it in her *Scenes from Clerical Life*: "Every man who is not a monster, a mathematician, or a mad philosopher, is the slave of some woman or other" ("The Sad Fortunes of Amos Barton", chap. 4).

20 It is just this sort of philosophizing that Aristophanes lampoons so beautifully in *The Clouds*. I have more to say about it and other inadequate kinds of philosophy and pseudo-philosophy in the next chapter.

21 Nietzsche begins *Beyond Good and Evil* by challenging his readers to "suppose" that "truth is a woman", in which case (he suggests) certain things follow with respect to all philosophers, at least "insofar as they were dogmatists". He subsequently confirms that "in the end she is a woman: she ought not to be violated" (aph. 220).

22 In this connection, one does well to consider Bacon's teachings about all "four classes of idols which beset men's mind" (*New Organon* Book I aphs. 39–68), but especially about those he calls 'Idols of the Cave' (which "take their rise in the peculiar constitution, mental or bodily, of each individual"). The second of the four aphorisms devoted to discussing this class (no.

Note to page 235

55) reads as follows: "There is one principal and as it were radical distinction between different minds, in respect of philosophy and the sciences, which is this: that some minds are stronger and apter to mark the differences of things, others to mark their resemblances. The steady and acute mind can fix its contemplations and dwell and fasten on the subtlest distinctions; the lofty and discursive mind recognizes and puts together the finest and most general resemblances. Both kinds, however, easily err in excess, by catching the one at gradations, the other at shadows."

In his *Emile*, Rousseau speaks explicitly of the respective mental strengths and weaknesses of each sex:

> Women's reason is practical and makes them very skillful at finding means for getting to a known end, but not at finding that end itself. The social relationship of the sexes is an admirable thing. This partnership produces a moral person of which the woman is the eye and the man is the arm, but they have such a dependence on one another that the women learns from the man what must be seen and the man learns from the woman what must be done. If woman could ascend to general principles as well as man can, and if man had as good a mind for details as woman does, they would always be independent of one another, they would live in eternal discord, and their partnership could not exist. But in the harmony which reigns between them, everything tends to the common end; they do not know who contributes more. Each follows the promptings of the other; each obeys, and both are masters. (377)

Or, consider Tolstoy's comparison in *Anna Karenina*:

> 'Thou hast hid these things from the wise and prudent, and hast revealed them unto babes,' thought Levin while talking with his wife that night.
>
> He thought of the Gospel text not because he considered himself wise – he did not – but because he could not help knowing that he was more intelligent than his wife and Agatha Mikhaylovna; he could not help knowing that when he thought about death he thought with all the powers of his soul. He knew too that many great and virile minds, whose thoughts on that subject he had read, had pondered it, and yet did not know a hundredth part of what his wife and Agatha Mikhaylovna knew on the subject. Different as were those two women, ... in that respect they were exactly alike. Both knew with certainty what Life was and what Death was, and though they would

Note to page 235

have been quite unable not only to answer but even to understand the questions that confronted Levin, neither doubted the importance of those phenomena, and they both had exactly the same outlook upon them – an outlook shared not only by them but by millions of others. The proof that they knew surely what death was, lay in the fact that they knew without a minute's hesitation how to behave with the dying and did not fear them. But Levin and others, though they were able to say a great deal about death, evidently did not know anything, for they feared it and had no notion what to do when people were dying. ...

She ordered supper to be brought, unpacked their things herself, helped to make the beds, and did not forget to sprinkle insect powder on them. She was in that highly-wrought state when the reasoning powers act with great rapidity: the state a man is in before a battle or a struggle, in danger, and at the decisive moments of life – those moments when a man shows once for all what he is worth, that his past was not lived in vain but was a preparation for these moments. (Part V chap. 19, Louise and Aylmer Maude, trans.)

H.L. Mencken gives a rather different twist to the sexual distinction of minds, and thus is also worth quoting here:

Women, in truth, are not only intelligent; they have almost a monopoly of certain of the subtler and more utile forms of intelligence. The thing itself, indeed, might be reasonably described as a special feminine character; there is in it, in more than one of its manifestations, a femaleness as palpable as the femaleness of cruelty, masochism, or rouge. Men are strong. Men are brave in physical combat. Men have sentiment. Men are romantic, and love what they conceive to be virtue and beauty. Men incline to faith, hope and charity. Men know how to sweat and endure. Men are amiable and fond. But in so far as they show the true fundamentals of intelligence – in so far as they reveal a capacity for discovering the kernel of eternal verity in the husk of delusion and hallucination and a passion for bringing it forth – to that extent, at least, they are feminine, and still nourished by the milk of their mothers. ... Find me an obviously intelligent man, a man free from sentimentality and delusion, a man hard to deceive, a man of the first class, and I'll show you a man with a wide streak of woman in him. Bonaparte had it; Goethe had it; Schopenhauer had it; Bismarck and Lincoln had it; in Shakespeare, if the Freudians are to be believed, it amounted to downright homosexuality. ...

It would be an easy matter, indeed, to demonstrate that superior talent in man is practically always accompanied by this feminine flavor – that complete masculinity and stupidity are often indistinguishable. Lest I be misunderstood I hasten to add that I do not mean to say that masculinity contributes nothing to the complex of chemico-physiological reactions which produces what we call talent; all I mean to say is that this complex is impossible without the feminine contribution – that it is the product of the interplay of the two elements. In women of genius we see the opposite picture. They are commonly distinctly mannish, and shave as well as shine. Think of George Sand, Catherine the Great, Elizabeth of England, Rosa Bonheur, Teresa Carreño or Cosima Wagner. The truth is that neither sex, without some fertilization by the complementary characters of the other, is capable of the highest reaches of human endeavor. Man, without a saving touch of woman in him, is too doltish, too naive and romantic, too easily deluded and lulled to sleep by his imagination to be anything above a cavalryman, a theologian or a bank director. And woman, without some trace of that divine innocence which is masculine, is too harshly the realist for those vast projections of the fancy which lie at the heart of what we call genius. Here, as elsewhere in the universe, the best effects are obtained by a mingling of the elements. The wholly manly man lacks the wit necessary to give objective form to his soaring and secret dreams, and the wholly womanly woman is apt to be too cynical a creature to dream at all. ("The Feminine Mind" *In Defense of Women* chap. 2)

23 Or, as Nietzsche puts it in *Beyond Good and Evil* (aph. 26):

Every choice [or chosen; *auserlesene*] person strives instinctively for a citadel and a secrecy where he is *set free* from the crowd, the many, the majority, where he may forget 'people who are the rule', being their exception – barring only the one case in which he is pushed straight towards this rule by a still stronger instinct, as a seeker after knowledge in the great and exceptional sense. Anyone who, in dealing [or trafficking, communicating, having intercourse; *Verkehr*] with people, does not occasionally glisten in all the colors of distress, green and grey with disgust, satiety, sympathy, gloominess, and loneliness, is certainly not a person of elevated tastes; supposing, however, that he does not take all this burden and disgust upon himself voluntarily, that he persistently avoids it, and remains, as I said, quietly and proudly hidden in his citadel, then one thing is certain: he was not made, he was not predestined, for knowledge. If he were, he would one day have to say to himself, 'The devil take my good taste! but the rule is more interesting than the exception – than I, the exception!' And he would *go down*, and above all, he would go 'inside'. The study of the *average* human being, protracted, serious, and with much dissembling, self-overcoming, intimacy, and bad company – all company is bad company except with one's equals – this constitutes a necessary part of the life-story of every philosopher, perhaps the most unpleasant and malodorous part, that most filled with disappointment. (Translation based on Kaufmann's)

CHAPTER SEVEN

1 Hobbes well understands the perspective of such men: "To agree with in opinion, is to Honour; as being a sign of approving his judgement, and wisdom. To dissent, is Dishonour. ... " And he would have us further understand that "Honour consisteth onely in the opinion of Power" (*Leviathan* chap. 10 par. 30 and 48). This, of course, is of a piece with his teaching that "Love of Vertue [is] from love of Praise" (chap. 11 par. 6).

Montaigne, ironically, depreciates reading books while fairly celebrating an eristical approach to dialogue:

> The study of books is a languishing and feeble activity that gives no heat, whereas discussion teaches and exercises us at the same time. If I discuss with a strong mind and a stiff jouster, he presses on my flanks, prods me right and left; his ideas launch mine. Rivalry, glory, competition, push me and lift me above myself. And unison is an altogether boring quality in discussion.
>
> As our mind is strengthened by communication with orderly and vigorous minds, so it is impossible to say how much it loses and degenerates by our continual association and frequentation with mean and sickly minds. There is no contagion that spreads like that one. ... I love to argue and discuss, but in a small group and for my own sake. For to serve as a spectacle to the great and make a competitive parade of one's wit and chatter is an occupation that I find very unbecoming to a man of honor. ("On the Art of Discussion" *Essays* Book III, Donald M. Frame, ed. and trans., 704; cf. D.L. Schaefer, "Montaigne's Intention and His Rhetoric.")

2 Leo Strauss's distinction between a philosopher and a sophist is pertinent here: "The sophist is a man who is unconcerned with the truth, or does not love wisdom, although he knows better than most other men that wisdom or science is the highest excellence of man. Being aware of the unique character of wisdom, he knows that honor deriving from wisdom is the highest honor. He is concerned with wisdom, not for its own sake, not because he hates the lie in the soul more than anything else, but for the sake of the honor or prestige that attends wisdom. He lives or acts on the principle that prestige or superiority to others or having more than others is the highest good" (*Natural Right and History* 116).

3 Cf. John Locke *An Essay Concerning Human Understanding* Book III chap. 9 par. 3.

4 And it apparently *is* a *single* basic power of reason, for to distinguish (all) the respects in which two things *differ* is simultaneously to recognize those in which they *don't*, thereby tacitly disclosing the basis of their being collected together, i.e., the respects in which they are the same. One's *conscious focus* shifts according to whether one is seeking differences in order to "differentiate" or discriminate ("divide"), or seeking likenesses in order to generalize ("collect"), but it would seem to be necessarily the same rational power at work in either case.

5 Leo Strauss *The City and Man* 119.

6 It is interesting to note in this connection that Nietzsche confesses, "until a very mature age I always ate *badly*" (*Ecce Homo* part II aph. 1).

7 This is somewhat amended in the immediately ensuing discussion, but on the doubly suspect basis of Sokrates' arguing that the dog is a lover of learning and therefore a philosopher (cf. 376c).

8 The word 'strange' here (*atopos*; literally, "out of place") is the same term Glaukon uses to describe the Cave image and its prisoners (515a).

9 This is but one of several obvious parallels between Sokrates' "apology" for himself in *Apology of Sokrates* and his apology for philosophy in *Republic* (cf. *Apology* 31d–a, 32ea).

10 Similarly, Rousseau sees the coming into being of a good republic as a matter of chance – specifically, the timely appearance of that unique, transpolitical man he calls a "Legislator". His discussion of what the role requires makes it clear that it could be perfectly fulfilled only by a political philosopher, whose aura of divinity derives from what is truly miraculous: his greatness of soul (*On the Social Contract* Book II chap. 7).

11 James Adam's extensive textual note on this passage is especially helpful for appreciating the multivocality of the term *andreikelon* (*The Republic of Plato* II 42).

12 Tolstoy's Levin (in *Anna Karenina*) presents his own version of this. Having learned of an old and respected peasant named Plato who "lives for his soul and remembers God", Levin now "went along the high-road with long strides", and experienced the sudden integration of "a whole group of disjointed impotent separate ideas that had always interested him". As he expresses it to himself:

> 'Theodore says that Kirilov, the innkeeper, lives for his belly. That is intelligible and reasonable. We all, as reasoning creatures, cannot live otherwise. And then that same Theodore says that it is wrong to live for one's belly, and that we must live for Truth, for God, and at the first hint I understand him! I and millions of men who lived centuries ago and those who are living now: peasants, the poor in spirit, and sages, who have thought and written about it, saying the same thing in their obscure words – we all agree on that one thing: what we should live for, and what is good. I, and all other men, know only one thing firmly, and clearly, and certainly, and this knowledge cannot be explained by reason: it is outside reason, has no cause, and can have no consequences.
>
> 'If goodness has a cause, it is no longer goodness; if it has a consequence – a reward, it is also not goodness. Therefore goodness is beyond the chain of cause and effect.
>
> 'It is exactly *this* that I know, and that we all know.
>
> 'What greater miracle could there be than that?' (Louise and Aylmer Maude, trans., part VIII chap. 12)

13 The predominance of this view is tacitly confirmed by Sokrates' taxonomy of actual, "human" regimes (cf. 497c), all of which are ruled by the pursuit of pleasure, and differentiated only by the partiality (or impartiality) which

each shows for the various *kinds* of pleasures. Timocracy favours pleasures of the spirit, especially those that attend victory and honour, whereas natural oligarchs take a peculiar pleasure in restricting the satisfaction of desire to what is strictly necessary for sustaining life – and in accumulating the wealth (and power) that would otherwise be expended on unnecessary desires. Democracy refuses on principle to rank desires or pleasures in order that freedom, understood as the liberty to do whatever one desires, might so far as possible be justified; and that everyone, reduced to the common denominator of pleasure-seeker, can the more plausibly be regarded as equal. Tyranny in the profoundest sense is being enslaved to the pursuit of those pleasures most inimical to both law and reason.

14 The analysis from this point on owes much to insights gained from Jacob Klein's *A Commentary on Plato's Meno* and Robert B. Williamson's "*Eidos* and *Agathon* in Plato's *Republic*".

15 The term 'universal', a staple of English-speaking philosophy since the times of the first Elizabeth, is adapted from the *universalia* of mediaeval philosophers, who equated it with Aristotle's *ta katholou* (cf. *On Interpretation* 17 a 36–17 b 1). Ironically, Hobbes may be correct in maintaining that there is "nothing in the world Universall but Names ... " (*Leviathan* chap. 4 par. 6).

Much of the mistaken and/or irrelevant analysis centred on this portion of the dialogue seems the result of two general causes. One is simply insufficient respect for Plato as a thinker and a writer. This scholarly condescension manifests itself in innumerable ways, but these are among the most common: that for all of his natural abilities (which even his most vituperative critics must concede), his understanding of basic problems and possible responses to them remained fairly primitive; that his thinking was subject to influences of which he was unaware, but which we – beneficiaries of so much philosophical progress – can readily detect (true, his Cave Allegory seems to address this very point, but he scarcely could have appreciated *all* the ramifications of socio-historical circumstances, or of the prejudices implicit in the Greek language, to say nothing of his own unconscious, and so on); that his views were not sufficiently clear even to himself, with the consequence that his use of terms betrays confused and contradictory conceptions (e.g., that he uses *eidos* ["form"] to mean many different, and not altogether compatible things).

The other cause is that discussed in the Prologue to this volume: the failure to understand the purpose of the dialogical form of writing. Many scholars, as a consequence, attempt to analyse dialogues as if they really are no different than treatises (in which doctrines are presented in a more or less geometric, step-by-step manner), but which Plato has carved up to suit his dramatic or memorial predilections. The work of R.C. Cross and A.D. Woozley is fairly typical of the kind of scholarship that results – *Plato's Republic: A Philosophical Commentary* and "Knowledge, Belief, and the Forms" in *Plato I*. Gregory Vlastos, ed., 70–96.

16 His contention might seem suspect because it is based on a perceptible relationship between two kinds of perceptible things, whose separate existence as well as the relationship between them is unproblematic. Whereas the primary issue posed by the Line concerns an alleged relationship between the perceptible things of the material world and (*per hypothesis*) a radically different kind of thing, something intelligible but whose (presumedly immaterial, eternal, unchanging) existence *independent of* the conceiving intellect is precisely what *is* problematic. As anyone familiar with our philosophical tradition is aware, the problem has exercised (and divided) philosophers for millennia. Two modest points here will have to suffice.

First, the existence of material objects is *not* as unproblematic as it seems to the unreflective consciousness. For to exist materially is to exist as something *definite* (i.e., not merely as a "thing" or as a "material object", or even as "a rock", but as quartz, or as granite; not merely as "a tree", or "deciduous tree", but as an oak rather than an elm; not as some "flying creature", or as just "a bird", but as an eagle, not an owl, much less a sparrow). One might be able to imagine a world made up exclusively of idiosyncratic things, but in any case it's not the world we live in. And here one must take care not to be misled by language, in particular by the existence of so-called universal terms, which for all their utility do not always reflect reality; some may refer to *natural* groups of related species of things (e.g., rock, bird), whereas others may not (e.g., flying creature). But what accounts for a particular thing's specificity, making it but one of many such *kind* of thing? Certainly not the matter out of which it is composed, which is simply what makes it particular (and which is itself but some *kind* or *kinds* of matter, posing the problem all over again). And while the notion of existence *per se* is useful for purposes of analysis, it may be no more than an intellectual abstraction. Why should one think that the *actual* existence of a material thing is somehow separate from the kind of thing it is? What *a priori* grounds are there for simply assuming that its material existence is *not* inherent in its species? This question, of course, returns one to the problem of accounting for the fact that the perceptible world is made up of *species* of things, not merely of things – the problem, that is, to which the Divided Line is meant to suggest a solution. In short, the existence of perceptible objects is no less problematic than that of purely intelligible things; indeed, both may be facets of the *same* problem, much as the Line image implies.

Second, the *relationship* between a perceptible thing and its perceptible images – its various shadows and reflections – is not all that straightforward either. To begin with, strictly speaking the relationship itself is *not* perceptible. It only *seems* so, so easily and naturally do humans "see" the rational connection between the two things, and come to *understand* at least this much of how the world works. Whereas dogs also see their shadows, and have sense enough to seek shade from the summer sun, but they give no indication that they recognize which shadows are "theirs", or what causes what. Once one appreciates that even this most simple relationship can only be intellected, not seen – that it is a rational *interpretation* of the perceptual evidence – a broader conception of the "image-to-original" or "likeness-to-likened" relationship is readily accommodated. The script of a play bears no perceptual likeness to an actual performance of it, but it may still be usefully thought of as an image. Similar remarks apply to "sheet music" in relation to that which is actually played, or to a diagram of the solar system (complete with perceptible "orbits") *vis-à-vis* the real thing, or to the blueprint of a building relative to the finished structure. In each of these cases, it is the intellect which translates the image into another, quite different medium. Thus work all analogies, similes, and metaphorical language (whereby we communicate, e.g., about regimes and souls; cf. 487e-a, 588b). *How* this process works – how the mind transfers meaning across the great divide between perceptual and intellectual experience – is deeply mysterious. But *that* it does so we cannot doubt. When Sokrates speaks of the luxuriated city as "feverish", or likens suitable guardians to well-bred dogs, we are neither bewildered nor the least tempted to treat his words literally.

17 Applying the terminology of the Proportion (533ea) to the Divided Line (509d-511e), and supplying convenient terms for the described but unnamed ontological categories that correspond to the four psycho-epistemological categories (those distinct kinds of *pathēmata* we experience in our souls), allow one to fill out the Line image and expand upon Sokrates' non-imagistic *analogon*:

Note to page 279

	BECOMING (*genesis*) [visible realm]		BEING (*ousia*) [intelligible realm]	
IMAGES (*eikones*)	EMPIRICALS (perceptible "phantoms", *aistheta eidōla?*)	HYPOTHET'LS (intelligible "phantoms", *noēta eidōla?*)	FORMS (*eidē*)
IMAGINATION (*eikasia*)	TRUST (*pistis*)	THOUGHT (*dianoia*)	KNOWLEDGE (*epistēmē*)
	OPINION (*doxa*)		INTELLECTION (*noēsis*)

[Note: above the line, linear proportions represent relative truthfulness (*alētheia*); below the line, relative clarity (*saphēneia*) – 510a, 511e.]

The Proportion that Sokrates establishes among four pairs:

$$\frac{\text{BEING}}{\text{BECOMING}} :: \frac{\text{INTELLECTION}}{\text{OPINION}} :: \frac{\text{KNOWLEDGE}}{\text{TRUST}} :: \frac{\text{THOUGHT}}{\text{IMAGINATION}}$$

is an inversion of that which he had specified earlier (510a), and obviously extends to six more pairs:

$$\frac{\text{KNOWLEDGE}}{\text{THOUGHT}} :: \frac{\text{TRUST}}{\text{IMAGINA}} :: \frac{\text{FORMS}}{\text{EMPIRICLS}} :: \frac{\text{HYPOTHETS}}{\text{IMAGES}} :: \frac{\text{FORMS}}{\text{HYPOTHETS}} :: \frac{\text{EMPIRICLS}}{\text{IMAGES}}$$

Moreover, the Line is amenable to further non-imagistic interpretation in terms of six more proportions. Four of these involve only two analogical pairs:

$$\frac{\text{HYPOTHETS}}{\text{EMPIRICLS}} :: \frac{\text{THOUGHT}}{\text{TRUST}}$$

[Note: as these always involve equals, this proportion is numerically 1, and is the only proportion to which we can assign a precise numerical value. The challenge, as noted, is in seeing *why* we should regard the first pair as partaking equally in truth, the second equally in clarity.]

$$\frac{\text{FORMS}}{\text{IMAGES}} :: \frac{\text{KNOWLEDGE}}{\text{IMAGINATION}}$$

[Note: whatever the basic ratio used for dividing and subdividing the line, this proportion will reduplicate that ratio. E.g., if the basic ratio is 2:1, this will be 4:1; if 3:1, 9:1.

And of these four, the following two – while geometrically valid – do not have such clear ontological or epistemological implications:

$$\frac{\text{BEING}}{\text{IMAGES}} :: \frac{\text{INTELLECTION}}{\text{IMAGINATION}} \qquad \frac{\text{FORMS}}{\text{BECOMING}} :: \frac{\text{KNOWLEDGE}}{\text{OPINION}}$$

But presuming that there is sense to be seen in comparing a *part* of one realm to the *whole* of another (e.g., Images to Being, or Knowledge to the

Note to page 279

whole realm of Opinion), then the precise ratio used for dividing and subdividing the Line takes on added importance. For example, if the ratio is at least 1.618034, then Forms partake more of truth than does the whole realm of Becoming (as does Knowledge partake of clarity compared to all Opinion) – rather as we would expect from the general tenor of Sokrates' presentation. Whereas if it is 1.618033 or less, then Becoming has more truthfulness than the part of Being constituted by Forms; and Opinion as a whole (comprising both Imagination and Trust) more clarity than true Knowledge! If upon due reflection one concludes that acceptance of the latter alternative would reduce the entire schema to gibberish, then either one has taken a step towards the more precise determination of the Proportion; or one must reject the initial assumption that such comparisons are legitimate (which would seem to have further implications concerning the adequacy of purely formal geometrical reasoning for capturing with full fidelity the natural relations among the respective parts of Being, Becoming, Intellection, and Opinion).

There is a further possibility, however, and an intriguing – but very perplexing – one it is. Suppose the line to be divided and subdivided according to the "Golden Ratio" – namely, such that the proportion between the longer and the shorter sections is the same as that between the whole line and the longer section; this proportion is the irrational number traditionally designated 'phi' (Φ):

$$\Phi = \frac{\sqrt{5} + 1}{2}; \text{ approximately} = 1.6180339. \ldots$$

According to tradition, fascination with Φ and the Golden Ratio – to the point of regarding it as the basis of all harmony in Nature – goes back at least as far as Pythagoras. This fact alone lends credence to the speculation that Plato has it in mind as *the* correct division of the line, despite his having Sokrates expressly decline to specify it because of the length of the argument it would involve (534a). And despite the irrationality of Φ, one can readily illustrate its consequences by dividing the line according to three sequential numbers from the additive sequence named after the mediaeval mathematician Fibonacci (where each "Fibonacci number" is the sum of its two predecessors; as the sequence proceeds, the ratio between adjacent numbers ever more closely approximates Φ). So, using, for example, the eleventh, twelfth, and thirteenth Fibonacci numbers to assign numerical values to the line segments:

89	144	144	233
A	B	C	D

As is readily seen, the segment representing Forms (D) is *equal* to that of Becoming (A+B) (the same holds, of course, for their correspondents on the epistemological side of the Line – Knowledge and Opinion); and the relation between Being (C+D) and Images (A), like that between Intellection and Imagination, will retriplicate the basic ratio (i.e., Φ^3, or approximately 4.2360673). What any of this might mean is far from clear, but to repeat, dividing according to the Golden Ratio (Φ) *does* suggest interesting "possibilities". And there are still more suggested by the amazing properties of Φ itself, e.g., that its inverse is (approximately) 0.6180339 ... ; that $\Phi^2 - \Phi = 1$, and $\Phi + \Phi^2 = \Phi \times \Phi^2$. Thus, the successive powers of Φ themselves constitute an additive sequence (with Φ the proportion between sequential numbers); and thus, if $A = 1/\Phi$, B and $C = 1$, and $D = \Phi$.

Two more geometrically valid proportions each involve six pairs, but once again it is not clear what sense (if any) is to be made of the comparisons:

$$\frac{\text{BEING}}{\text{HYPOTHETS}} :: \frac{\text{BEING}}{\text{EMPIRICLS}} :: \frac{\text{INTELLECT}}{\text{THOUGHT}} :: \frac{\text{INTELLECT}}{\text{TRUST}} :: \frac{\text{BECOMING}}{\text{IMAGES}} :: \frac{\text{OPINION}}{\text{IMAGINAT}}$$

and

$$\frac{\text{BEING}}{\text{FORMS}} :: \frac{\text{INTELLECT}}{\text{KNOWLEDGE}} :: \frac{\text{BECOMING}}{\text{EMPIRICLS}} :: \frac{\text{BECOMING}}{\text{HYPOTHETS}} :: \frac{\text{OPINION}}{\text{TRUST}} :: \frac{\text{OPINION}}{\text{THOUGHT}}$$

Treated purely in terms of this mathematical reasoning, the entirety of Being, including as it does not only the (hypothesized) axioms of (for example) mathematics but also the even more truthful Forms in which all correct hypotheses are grounded, must as a whole be accorded more truth than the class of Hypotheticals alone (this is the case whether one conceives of Being's truthfulness as the "average" or the "sum" of its parts' truthfulness). But the second proportion dictates that Being as a whole must *also* be accorded more truthfulness than the class of Forms alone. This may be so, but it is not nearly so self-evident (and would seem to require the "summative" interpretation). One must not overlook the possibility, however, that reflection on the entire family of proportions is meant to reveal the *limitations* on mathematical reasoning: that not all the possibilities of formal mathematics are necessarily *natural* possibilities, nor can the fulness of the world as humans experience it be reduced without loss or distortion to the colourless, passionless ideas of mathematics.

18 As Nietzsche observes in his *Antichrist*, "Truth and the *faith* that something is true: two completely separate realms of interest – almost diametrically

opposite realms – they are reached by utterly different paths. Having knowledge of this – that is almost the definition of the wise man in the Orient: the Brahmins understand this; Plato understands this; and so does every student of esoteric wisdom" (*Antichrist* aph. 23 in *Portable Nietzsche* 590-1).

19 Integrating the Divided Line in an interpretation of the Cave image suggests that human beings can be divided into four intellectual classes: the opinion-shackled Many who mistake the shadows of phantoms for reality itself; the unshackled Few who make and carry about the Cave the various phantoms of beings (and who could rightly be called 'opinion leaders'; cf. 514b8, 517a, 584de); those "Theoreticians" who employ hypothetical reasoning in an effort to explain and exploit Cave phenomena; and the minuscule group of genuine philosophers.

20 In his exposé of the "prejudices" of previous philosophers, Nietzsche makes a very interesting – and, it seems to me, valid – point about this "three-finger exercise" of Sokrates: "After I have looked long enough between the lines of the philosophers and at their fingers, I say to myself: one must still count [*rechnen*] the greater part of conscious thinking among the instinctive activities, and even in the case of philosophical thinking. ... " *Beyond Good and Evil* aph. 3; my translation.

Passing over Nietzsche's reference to the most famous "lines" in philosophical literature (and his simultaneous allusion to Plato's esotericism), what has he "seen" as a consequence of reflecting on the not-nearly-so-famous image of holding up one's hand, with thumb and forefinger touching and the other three fingers extended upwards? Why, having contemplated this illustration from Sokrates' discussion of *arithmetic*, does Nietzsche now "count" even the most self-conscious thinking – philosophical thinking – "among the instinctive activities"? He does not explain. But consider: when one looks at a hand held up as Sokrates describes, does one not naturally – that is, "instinctively" – focus on the *fingers*, ... and *not* on the vee-shaped *spaces* in between (which are every bit as much a part of the total visual field, as is immediately evident when one directs attention to them)? This familiar experience, along with a plenitude of similar ones it evokes, rather strongly suggests that man has an eye for significant form, an *innate* predilection to search for it, and that his mind works naturally and for the most part unconsciously to order the chaos of "sense data" into recognizable patterns in space, ... and *time* (e.g., words in speech, tunes in music).

Notes to page 283

Here it is useful to recall that the original meaning of *eidos* ("form") is the visual "look" of a thing, derived from the verb for seeing (*eidō*, etymologically related to the Latin *video*). Only when a pattern or form is not immediately recognizable do we become *conscious* of searching for one. Or when invited to look for something hidden behind or beneath closer, more obvious forms, as in those children's picture games that challenge them to see something else in cleverly drawn foliage or clouds.

21 Modern physics confirms that Aristotle is essentially correct in his analysis of matter: that it must be conceived as something passive, not active (*On Generation and Corruption* 324 b 18); as something potential, not actual (*Metaphysics* 1050 a 15); that Nature (including the distinctive natures of all materials) inheres in form, not matter (*Physics* 194 a 30); and that matter is perceptible not as pure matter, but only in some determinate form (all of whose characteristics are due to the form in which the more "elementary" particles – molecules, atoms, protons, neutrons, electrons, quarks, superstrings, whatever – are configured). Thus, what is thought of as *material*, the "matter" of which something is made, is always relative to a given level of analysis (*Physics* 194 b 9; for example, steel is "matter" for a sword-maker, but it is "form" for a steel-maker imposing it on iron, carbon, chromium, whatever). As expressed by the Nobel laureate Werner Heisenberg:

> [E]xperiments have shown the complete mutability of matter. All the elementary particles can, at sufficiently high energies, be transmuted into other particles, or they can simply be created from kinetic energy and can be eliminated into energy, for instance into radiation. Therefore, we have here actually the final proof for the unity of matter. All the elementary particles are made of the same substance, which we may call energy or universal matter; they are just different forms in which matter can appear.
>
> If we compare this situation with the Aristotelian concepts of matter and form, we can say that the matter of Aristotle, which is mere 'potentia', should be compared to our concept of energy, which gets into 'actuality' by means of the form, when the elementary particle is created." ("Quantum Theory and the Structure of Matter" in *Physics and Philosophy: the Revolution in Modern Science* 160)

Speaking to the same subject on a later occasion, Heisenberg compared the views of the ancient Atomists and of Plato with the findings of modern physicists:

Note to page 283

The best description of these collision phenomena is therefore not to assert that the colliding particles have been broken up but to speak of the emergence of new particles from the collision energy, in accordance with the laws of the theory of relativity. We can say that all particles are made of the same fundamental substance, which can be designated energy or matter; or we can put things as follows: the basic substance 'energy' becomes 'matter' by assuming the form of an elementary particle. In this way the new experiments have taught us that we can combine the two seemingly conflicting statements: 'Matter is infinitely divisible' and 'There are smallest units of matter,' without running into logical difficulties. This surprising result again underlines the fact that our ordinary concepts cannot be applied unambiguously to these smallest units.

During the coming years, the high-energy accelerators will bring to light many further interesting details about the behaviour of elementary particles. But I am inclined to think that the answer just considered to the old philosophical problems will turn out to be final. If this is so, does this answer confirm the views of Democritus or Plato?

I think that on this point modern physics has definitely decided for Plato. For the smallest units of matter are in fact not physical objects in the ordinary sense of the word; they are forms, structures or – in Plato's sense – Ideas, which can be unambiguously spoken of only in the language of mathematics. ... " ("Natural Law and the Structure of Matter" in *Across the Frontiers* Peter Heath, trans., 115–16)

There are any number of accessible, non-technical books offering cogent summaries of where such thinking has led contemporary physicists and "scientific" cosmologists. Paul Davies has written several – for example, *The Edge of Infinity* and *God and the New Physics*. Roger Penrose presents an account in conjunction with his analysis of the prospects of so-called artificial intelligence – *The Emperor's New Mind* chaps. 5 through 8. For an account that challenges some elements of the dominant cosmological interpretation of the day, see Lawrence M. Krauss *The Fifth Essence: The Search for Dark Matter in the Universe*.

If one accepts the findings and speculations regnant in modern physics, the immaterial "solids" of solid geometry are scarcely less solid than the most solid matter, which has next to no material substance to it, being almost entirely space. We're told that when completely concentrated in those most powerful gravitational fields called "black holes", matter that would weigh *twenty billion tons* on earth fits into a *tablespoon* – which is to say, the bodies of the entire human population of the earth, and of *fifty more* earths just like it, would make up but one tablespoon of truly *solid* matter! This "too too solid flesh", it would seem, ... ain't. So much for the self-evidency of ever-popular sensual materialism, and all nominalistic views based thereon.

22 For an apparently contrasting view concerning the relationship between philosophy and asceticism, one that argues the latter is but a mask, "the *philosopher's pose par excellence*", see Nietzsche's *Genealogy of Morals* "Third Essay" (especially aph. 10).

23 Sokrates' "mistake" of proceeding straight from plane geometry to astronomy (addressing what are presumably the most important "solids in motion") without having first considered solids themselves (528ab) is, of course, ironic. For the mistake has nothing to do with the fact that the heavenly bodies are presumed to be (spherical) *solids* – after all, they *appear*, and thus are actually studied as, but points and planes of light – but has to do, rather, with how one conceives their *motions* (528de): in terms of cross-sectional cuts of regular solids (e.g., spherical or conic sections; cf. 529de, 616b–617b).

The discussion of solid geometry (the account of things having "depth", *bathys*, and in the perceptible realm also "weight", as shadows and reflections do not; cf. 602d), rather pointedly suggests that it is a metaphor for philosophy. No city honours it; the Many despise it because it seems to have no utility; it is feebly sought because of its difficulty; fitting teachers are hard to come by; potential students are hubristic, and do not follow it through to its natural completion; despite its ridiculous condition, however, it still has its charm, and so on (528b–d). This identifying of philosophy with solid geometry has potentially more implications than I would venture to specify. But I am reasonably sure that the philosopher sees justice, the soul, and the city as each having three dimensions – and not just the one or two that he makes explicit (cf. 587d–e).

In this connection, one might adapt to the interpreting of Plato's dialogues what Strauss advised with respect to Aristophanes' plays: "One must transform the specific two-dimensionality of his comedy into a transcomic three-dimensionality. Transcomic does not mean tragic" (*Socrates and Aristophanes* 51).

24 Nietzsche's variation on this theme is worth quoting at length:

> One may conjecture that a spirit in whom the type 'free spirit' will one day become ripe and sweet to the point of perfection has had its decisive experience in a *great liberation*, and that previously it was all the more a fettered spirit and seemed to be chained forever to its pillar and corner. What fetters the fastest? What bonds are all but unbreakable? In the case of men of a high and select kind they will be their duties: that reverence proper to youth, that reserve and delicacy before all that is honoured and revered from of old, that gratitude for the soil out of which they have grown, for the hand which led them, for the holy places where they learned to worship – their supreme moments themselves will fetter them the fastest, lay upon them the most enduring obligation. The great liberation for those who are thus fettered comes suddenly, like the shock of an earthquake: the youthful soul is all at once convulsed, torn loose, torn away – it itself does not know what is happening. A drive and impulse masters it like a command; a will and desire to go off, anywhere, at any cost; a vehement dangerous curiosity for an undiscovered world flames and flickers in all its senses. 'Better to die than go on living *here*' – thus responds the imperious voice and temptation: and this 'here', this 'at home' is everything it had hitherto loved! A sudden terror and suspicion of what is loved, a lightning bolt of contempt for what is called 'duty', a rebellious, arbitrary, volcanically erupting desire for travel, strange places, estrangement, coldness, soberness, frost, a hatred of love, perhaps a desecrating blow and glance *backwards* to where it formerly loved and worshipped, perhaps a hot blush of shame at what it had just done and at the same time an exaltation *that* it has done it, a drunken, inwardly exultant shudder which betrays that a victory has been won – a victory? over what? over whom? an enigmatic, question-packed, questionable victory, but the *first* victory nonetheless. ... (*Human, All Too Human* R.J. Hollingdale, trans., 6–7)

Also especially pertinent is aph. 41 of *Beyond Good and Evil*, which begins: "One must test oneself to see whether one is destined for independence and command; and do so at the right time. One should not evade one's tests, although they are perhaps the most dangerous game one could play, and are in the end tests which are taken before no witness but ourselves and before no other judge" (my translation).

Bibliography

The following is a list of works cited. It does not include, however, literary classics (such as the dialogues of Plato, treatises of Aristotle or Hobbes, plays of Shakespeare, novels of Austen, Conrad, Fielding, Melville, and so on) unless a specific edition has been referred to.

Adam, James. *The Republic of Plato*. Cambridge: Cambridge University Press 1902

Akrigg, G.P.V. *Jacobean Pageant*. Cambridge, Mass.: Harvard University Press 1963

Altman, Joel. *The Tudor Play of Mind*. Berkeley: University of California Press 1978

Alvis, John, and Thomas West, eds. *Shakespeare as Political Thinker*. Durham, NC: Carolina Academic Press 1981

Avery, C.B., ed. *The New Century Classical Handbook*. New York: Appleton-Century-Croft 1962

Bacon, Francis. *The Advancement of Learning*. Oxford: Oxford University Press 1974

– *The Works of Francis Bacon*. James Spedding and Robert Ellis, eds. London: Longmans & Co. 1857–74

Benardete, Seth. *The Being of the Beautiful*. Chicago: University of Chicago Press 1984

– *Herodotean Inquiries*. The Hague: Martinus Nijhoff 1969

– *Socrates' Second Sailing*. Chicago: University of Chicago Press 1989

Blits, Jan. *The End of the Ancient Republic*. Durham, NC: Carolina Academic Press 1982

Bibliography

Bloom, Allan. *The Republic of Plato*. New York: Basic Books 1968

Bloom, Allan, with Harry Jaffa. *Shakespeare's Politics*. New York: Basic Books 1964

Blumenson, Martin, ed. *The Patton Papers: 1940–1945*. Boston: Houghton Mifflin 1974

Bolotin, David. *Plato's Dialogue on Friendship*. Ithaca, NY: Cornell University Press 1979

Brandwood, Leonard. *A Word Index to Plato*. Leeds: Maney & Son 1976

Brann, Eva. "The Music of Plato's Republic" *Agon* 1 no. 1 (April 1967) 1–117; reprinted Annapolis: St John's College Press

Brecht, Arnold. *Political Theory*. Princeton, NJ: Princeton University Press 1959

Burger, Ronna. *The Phaedo: A Platonic Labyrinth*. New Haven, Conn.: Yale University Press 1984

– *Plato's Phaedrus: A Defense of the Philosophical Art of Writing*. Birmingham: University of Alabama Press 1980

– "Socratic Eironeia" *Interpretation* 13 no. 2 (1985) 143–9

Burnet, John, ed. *Platonis Opera*. Oxford: Oxford University Press 1900–7

Butler, Christopher. *Number Symbolism*. London: Routledge & Kegan Paul 1970

Caesar, Julius. *The Gallic Wars* Anne and Peter Wiseman, trans. London: Chatto and Windus 1980

Chagnon, N.A. "Yanomamo, the True People" *National Geographic* 150 no. 2 (August 1976) 211–23

Churchill, Winston. *The World Crisis: 1911–1918*. London: Macmillan 1941

Cirlot, J.E. *A Dictionary of Symbols*. Jack Sage, trans. London: Routledge & Kegan Paul 1962

Cohler, Anne M. "Montesquieu's Perception of His Audience for the *Spirit of the Laws*" *Interpretation* 11 no. 3 (1983) 317–32

Coleridge, S.T. *Biographia Literaria*. James Engel and W. Jackson Bate, eds. Princeton, NJ: Princeton University Press 1983

Collingwood, R.G. *The Idea of History*. Oxford: Oxford University Press 1956

Conrad, Joseph. *Victory*. New York: Modern Library n.d.

Copernicus, Nicholaus. *Revolutions of the Heavenly Spheres* Charles Glenn Wallis, trans. *Great Books of the Western World* XVI Chicago: Encyclopedia Britannica 1952

Cranston, Maurice. *John Locke: A Biography*. Oxford: Oxford University Press 1985

Cropsey, Joseph. *Political Philosophy and the Issues of Politics*. Chicago: University of Chicago Press 1977

Cross, R.C., and A.D. Woozley. *Plato's Republic: A Philosophical Commentary*. London: Macmillan 1964

Davies, Paul. *The Edge of Infinity*. New York: Simon and Schuster 1981

Bibliography

- *God and the New Physics*. New York: Simon and Schuster 1983
Descartes, René. *Discourse on Method and Meditations on First Philosophy*. Donald A. Cress, trans. Indianapolis: Hackett 1980
Dinesen, Isak. *Winter's Tales*. New York: Book-of-the-Month Club 1985
Eliot, T.S., ed. *Literary Essays of Ezra Pound*. London: Faber & Faber 1954
Fowler, Alastair, ed. *Silent Poetry: Essays in Numerological Analysis*. London: Routledge & Kegan Paul 1970
- *Triumphal Forms: Structural Patterns in Elizabethan Poetry*. Cambridge: Cambridge University Press 1970
Frame, Donald M., ed. and trans. *The Complete Essays of Montaigne*. Stanford, Calif.: Standford University Press 1958
Friedländler, Paul. *Plato*. Vol. III. Princeton, NJ: Princeton University Press 1969
Gerth, H.H., and C.W. Mills. *From Max Weber*. New York: Oxford University Press 1946
Gilbert, Allan, ed. and trans. *Machiavelli: The Chief Works and Others*. Durham, NC: Duke University Press 1965
Goethe. *Conversations with Eckermann*. J. Oxenford, trans. London: J.M. Dent 1930
Griswold, Charles L., Jr. *Platonic Writings, Platonic Readings*. New York: Routledge 1988
Hammond, N.G.L., and H.H. Scullard, eds. *The Oxford Classical Dictionary*. Oxford: Oxford University Press 1970
Heisenberg, Werner. *Across the Frontiers*. Peter Heath, trans. New York: Harper & Row 1974
- *Physics and Philosophy: The Revolution in Modern Science*. New York: Harper & Row 1958
Himmelfarb, Gertrude. *Darwin and the Darwinian Revolution*. New York: W.W. Norton 1968
James, Henry. *Literary Criticism, Vol. I*. New York: Library of America 1984
Johnson, Paul. *Intellectuals*. New York: Harper and Row 1988
Joseph, H.W.B. *Ancient and Modern Philosophy*. Oxford: Oxford University Press 1935
Kaufmann, Walter. *The Basic Writings of Nietzsche*. New York: Modern Library 1968
- *The Portable Nietzsche*. New York: Viking 1954
Klein, Jacob. "About the *Philebus*" Interpretation no.3 (1972) 157–82
- *A Commentary on Plato's Meno*. Chapel Hill: University of North Carolina Press 1965
Kojève, Alexandre. *Introduction to the Reading of Hegel*. A. Bloom, ed., J.H. Nichols, trans. New York: Basic Books 1969

Bibliography

Kramnick, Isaac, ed. *Lord Bolingbroke: Historical Writings.* Chicago: University of Chicago Press 1972

Krauss, Lawrence M. *The Fifth Essence: The Search for Dark Matter in the Universe.* New York: Basic Books 1989

Lamb, David. *The Africans.* New York: Vintage 1987

Lampert, Laurence. *Nietzsche's Teaching.* New Haven, Conn.: Yale University Press 1986

– "Zarathustra's Dancing Song" *Interpretation* 8 no. 2/3 (1980) 141–55

Leavis, F.R. *Dickens the Novelist.* New Brunswick, NJ: Rutgers University Press 1979

– *The Great Tradition.* New York: New York University Press 1973

Lerner, Ralph, and Muhsin Mahdi, ed. *Medieval Political Philosophy.* Ithaca, NY: Cornell University Press 1972

Lidov, Joel. "Justice in Translation" *Interpretation* 12 no. 1 (1984) 83–106

Locke, John. *Two Treatises of Government* P. Laslett, ed. Cambridge: Cambridge University Press 1960

Lowenthal, David. "Shakespeare's Caesar's Plan" *Interpretation* 10 no. 2/3 (1982) 223–50

Maccoby, Eleanor Emmons, and Carol Nagy Jacklin. *The Psychology of Sex Differences.* Stanford, Calif.: Stanford University Press 1974

Machiavelli, Niccolo. *The Prince.* Leo Paul S. de Alvarez, ed. and trans. Irving: University of Dallas Press 1980

Mansfield, Harvey. *Machiavelli's New Modes and Orders.* Ithaca, NY: Cornell University Press 1979

Mathie, William. "Justice and the Question of Regimes in Ancient and Modern Political Philosophy: Aristotle and Hobbes" *Canadian Journal of Political Science* 9 no. 3 (1976) 449–63

May, Robert. *Sex and Fantasy: Patterns of Male and Female Development.* New York: W.W. Norton 1980

McClain, Ernest G., *The Pythagorean Plato: Prelude to the Song Itself.* Stony Brook: Nicholas Hays 1978

McDonald, Edward D., ed. *Phoenix: The Posthumous Papers of D.H. Lawrence.* New York: Viking 1936

Melville, Herman. "Hawthorne and His Mosses" in *Pierre, Israel Potter, The Piazza Tales, The Confidence-Man, Uncollected Prose, Billy Budd.* New York: Library of America 1984

Montesquieu. *The Persian Letters.* George R. Healy, trans. Indianapolis: Bobbs-Merrill 1964

Morris, Ivan. *The Nobility of Failure.* New York: Holt-Rinehart-Winston 1975

Bibliography

Murphy, N.R. *The Interpretation of Plato's Republic*. Oxford: Oxford University Press 1951

Newell, Waller. "Zarathustra's Dancing Dialectic" *Interpretation* 17 no. 3 (1990) 415-32

Nichols, Mary P. "The Good Life, Slavery, and Acquisition: Aristotle's Introduction to Politics" *Interpretation* 11 no. 2 (1983) 171-83

Nietzsche, F., *Beyond Good and Evil*. R.J. Hollingdale, trans. Harmondsworth: Penguin 1973

- *Beyond Good and Evil*. Walter Kaufmann, trans., in *The Basic Writings of Nietzsche*. New York: Modern Library 1968
- *The Birth of Tragedy*. Walter Kaufmann, trans., in *The Basic Writings of Nietzsche*. New York: Modern Library 1968
- *Daybreak*. R.J. Hollingdale, trans. Cambridge: Cambridge University Press 1983
- *Ecce Homo*. R.J. Hollingdale, trans. Harmondsworth: Penguin 1979
- *Genealogy of Morals*. Walter Kaufmann, trans., in *The Basic Writings of Nietzsche*. New York: Modern Library 1968
- *Human, All Too Human*. R.J. Hollingdale, trans. Cambridge: Cambridge University Press 1986
- *Untimely Meditations*. R.J. Hollingdale, trans. Cambridge: Cambridge University Press 1983

Ortega y Gasset, José. *Meditations on Hunting*. Howard B. Wescott, trans. New York: Charles Scribner's Sons 1972

Pangle, Thomas. *The Laws of Plato*. New York: Basic Books 1980

- *The Roots of Political Philosophy; Ten Forgotten Socratic Dialogues*. Ithaca, NY: Cornell University Press 1987

Penrose, Roger. *The Emperor's New Mind*. Oxford: Oxford University Press 1989

Planinc, Zdravko. *Plato's Political Philosophy*. Columbia: University of Missouri Press 1991

Platt, Michael. *Rome and the Romans According to Shakespeare*. Salzburg Studies 1976

Prange, Gordon W. *At Dawn We Slept*. New York: McGraw-Hill 1981

Rosen, Stanley. *Plato's Sophist*. New Haven, Conn.: Yale University Press 1983

- *Plato's Symposium*. New Haven, Conn.: Yale University Press 1968

Rousseau, J.J. *Emile, or, On Education*. Allan Bloom, trans. New York: Basic Books 1979

- *On the Social Contract*. Roger D. Masters, trans. New York: St Martins 1978
- *The Reveries of a Solitary Walker*. Charles E. Butterworth, trans. New York: New York University Press 1979

Bibliography

Sallis, John. *Being and Logos: The Way of Platonic Dialogue.* Pittsburgh: Duquesne University Press 1975

Saxenhouse, Arlene W. "The Philosopher and the Female in the Political Thought of Plato" *Political Theory* 4 no. 2 (1976) 195–212

- "An Unspoken Theme in Plato's *Gorgias*: War" *Interpretation* 11 no. 2 (1983) 139–69

Schaefer, David L. "Montaigne's Intention and His Rhetoric" *Interpretation* 5 no. 1 (1975) 57–90

Schlatter, Richard, ed. *Hobbes's Thucydides.* New Brunswick, NJ: Rutgers University Press 1975

Shorey, Paul, ed. and trans. *Plato: The Republic.* London: Heinemann 1937

Slim, Sir William. *Defeat into Victory.* London: Cassell & Co. 1956

Smith, Hedrick. *The Russians.* New York: Ballantine 1977

Smith, Kirby Flower. "The Tale of Gyges and the King of Lydia" *American Journal of Philology* 23 no. 3 (1895) 261–82 and no. 4 (1895) 361–87

Spinoza, B. *On the Improvement of the Understanding, The Ethics, Correspondence.* R.H.M. Elwes, trans. New York: Dover 1955

- *A Theological-Political Treatise.* R.H.M. Elwes, trans. New York: Dover 1955

Steiner, George. *On Difficulty and Other Essays.* Oxford: Oxford University Press 1978

Strauss, Leo. *The City and Man.* New York: Rand McNally 1964; reprinted Chicago: University of Chicago Press 1977

- *Liberalism Ancient and Modern.* New York: Basic Books 1968
- *Natural Right and History.* Chicago: University of Chicago Press 1953
- "On a New Interpretation of Plato's Political Philosophy" *Social Research* 13 no. 3 (1946) 326–67
- "On Collingwood's Philosophy of History" *Review of Metaphysics* 5 no. 4 (1952) 559–86
- *Persecution and the Art of Writing.* Glencoe, NY: Free Press 1952
- *Socrates and Aristophanes.* New York: Basic Books 1966
- *Thoughts on Machiavelli.* New York: Free Press 1958
- *What Is Political Philosophy?* New York: Free Press 1959

Theon of Smyrna. *Mathematics Useful for Understanding Plato.* Robert and Deborah Lawlor, trans. San Diego: Wizard Bookshelf 1979

Tocqueville, Alexis de. *Democracy in America.* J.P. Mayer and Max Lerner, eds., G. Lawrence, trans. New York: Harper & Row 1964

Vlastos, Gregory, ed. *Plato I: Metaphysics and Epistemology.* Garden City, NY: Anchor Books 1971

Bibliography

- *Plato II: Ethics, Politics, and Philosophy of Art and Religion*. Garden City, NY: Anchor Books 1971

Voltaire. *The Philosophy of History*. trans. anon. New York: Citadel 1965

Vyvyan, John. *Shakespeare and Platonic Beauty*. New York: Barnes & Noble 1961

Weingartner, Rudolph H. *The Unity of the Platonic Dialogues*. Indianapolis: Bobbs-Merrill 1973

Williamson, Robert B. "*Eidos and Agathon* in Plato's *Republic*". *Essays in Honor of Jacob Klein*. Annapolis, MD.: St John's College Press 1976

Zuckert, Catherine. "Aristotle on the Limits and Satisfactions of Political Life". *Interpretation* 11 no. 2 (1983) 185–206

- *Understanding the Political Spirit: Philosophical Investigations from Socrates to Nietzsche*. New Haven, Conn.: Yale University Press 1988

Index of Names

Abû Hâmid 308
Adam, James 342n2, 348n8, 373n1, 415n11, 427
Aesop 297n5, 344
Akrigg, G.P.V. 312-13, 427
Alexander the Great 306-7n15
Alfonso X ("The Wise") 177
Altman, Joel 297n5, 427
Alvarez, Leo P.S. de 342n3, 430
Alvis, John 387n1, 427
Aquinas, St Thomas 303n11, 344
Aristophanes 347-8n8, 358, 409n20, 425n23, 432
Aristotle 142, 145, 303n11, 306-7n15, 344, 350n11, 355n3, 360-1n9, 366-1n9, 366n15, 369n6, 397n16, 398n1, 406n13, 416n15, 423n21, 427, 430, 433
Aspasia 401n6
Austen, Jane 339n25, 344, 399-401n5, 407n18, 427
Averroes 308, 309
Avery, C.B. 403n8, 427

Bacon, Francis 297n5, 299n7, 300n8, 306n13, 310-12, 368-9n6, 409-10n10, 427

Balzac, Honoré de 344
Barré, Mohamed Siad 295
Bate, W. Jackson 321, 428
Beethoven, Ludwig van 292
Benardete, Seth 299n6, 342n2, 348n9, 427
Berkeley, George 322
Bismarck, Otto von 411
Blits, Jan 389n1, 427
Bloom, Allan 325, 326n18, 340n26, 341-2n2, 347n8, 353n1, 379n7, 387-8n1, 393n7, 398n1, 427-8, 429, 431
Blumenson, Martin 398n16, 428
Boccaccio, Giovanni 305
Bolingbroke, Henry St John, Viscount 298-9, 430
Bolotin, David 326n18, 428
Bonaparte, Napoleon 411
Bonheur, Rosa 412n22
Borgia, Cesare 396n13
Bowen, Alan C. 326n18
Brandwood, Leonard 342n2, 428
Brann, Eva 342n2, 428
Brecht, Arnold 329, 428
Brooks, Douglas 305

Index of Names

Burger, Ronna 326n18, 338n24, 428
Burnet, John 342n2, 428
Butler, Christopher 305, 428
Butterworth, Charles 372n12, 431

Caesar, Julius 397n16, 428
Carreño, Teresa 412n22
Catherine the Great 412n22
Chagnon, N.A. 406n12, 428
Chapman, George 305
Chaucer, Geoffrey 305
Churchill, Winston 349, 428
Cicero 303n11, 393n6
Cirlot, J.E. 304, 428
Cohler, Anne M. 301n8, 428
Coleridge, S.T. 321-2, 428
Collingwood, R.G. 360-1n9, 428, 432
Conrad, Joseph 337-8n23, 368n4, 371n11, 371n12, 376n4, 391-3n5, 427, 428
Copernicus, Nicholaus 308-9, 428
Cowley, Abraham 305
Cranston, Maurice 319, 428
Cress, Donald A. 315, 429
Cropsey, Joseph 326, 428
Cross, R.C. 417n15, 428

Dannhauser, Werner 374n2
Dante 305
Darwin, Charles 307n16
Davies, Paul 424, 428-9
Democritus 424
Descartes, René 293n1, 306n13, 314-16, 322, 352n13, 429
Desjardins, Rosemary 326n18
Dinesen, Isak 339n25, 408, 429
Donne, John 305
Dostoyevsky, Fyodor 294, 378-9n16

Drako 155
Drayton, Michael 305
Dryden, John 305

Eliot, George 343, 407n18, 409n19
Eliot, T.S. 337n23, 343, 429
Elizabeth I of England 412n22, 416n15
Ellis, Robert 311, 427
Elwes, R.H.M. 316, 318, 432
Engel, J. 321, 428
Erasmus 297n5
Evelyn-White, H.G. 362n11

Fibonacci, Leonardo 420
Fielding, Henry 299-300n7, 305, 386n12, 427
Filmer, Robert 304
Ford, Ford Madox 338n23
Fowler, Alastair 305, 429
Frame, Donald M. 297n5, 413n1, 429
Friedländer, Paul 324, 429

Garnett, Constance 379n6
Gerth, H.H. 328, 429
Gilbert, Allan 309, 429
Goethe 321, 411, 429
Gogol, Nikolai 296n4
Griswold, Charles, Jr 326n18, 429
Guicciardini, Francesco 309

Hammond, N.G.L. 368n5, 429
Hardy, Thomas 399n4, 408
Hawthorne, Nathaniel 302n9, 430
Healy, George R. 301n8, 430
Heath, Peter 424
Heisenberg, Werner 423-4n21, 429
Herodotus 299n6, 366n15, 393n5, 396n16

Index of Names

Herrick, Robert 305
Hesiod 309, 343, 362-3n11
Himmelfarb, Gertrude 307n16, 429
Hobbes, Thomas 297-8n6, 302n10, 302-3n11, 303-4n13, 306, 313-14, 318, 354-5n3, 361n9, 365n13, 365-6n14, 373n2, 380-1n9, 386-7n12, 396n11, 407n17, 413n1, 416n15, 427, 430, 432
Hollingdale, R.J. xxiii, 323n17, 353n13, 364n12, 426, 431
Homer xxv, 14, 48, 53, 100, 123, 268, 297n5, 346n5, 350n11, 366-7n17, 368n5, 402n8
Hourani, George F. 308

Jacklin, Carol N. 403n9, 430
Jaffa, Harry 388, 428
James, Henry 337n23, 343, 407n18, 429
James I of England 312-13
Johnson, Paul 366n16, 429
Johnson, Samuel 206
Jonson, Ben 305
Joseph, H.W.B. 379n7, 429

Kant, Immanuel 344, 361n9
Kaufmann, Walter 322, 323n17, 344, 375n3, 391n4, 407n16, 413n23, 429, 431
Kempff, Wilhelm 291
Klein, Jacob 326n18, 339n25, 416n14, 429, 433
Kojève, Alexandre 340n26, 429
Kramnick, Isaac 299n6, 430
Krauss, Lawrence M. 424, 430

Lamb, David 295, 430

Lampert, Laurence 375n3, 390n4, 430
Laslett, Peter 319
Latham, Agnes M.C. 312
Lawlor, Robert and Deborah 432
Lawrence, D.H. 344-6, 407-8n18, 430
Lawrence, G. 432
Leavis, F.R. 343, 430
Leibnitz, G.W. 322
Lerner, Max 432
Lerner, Ralph 308, 430
Lidov, Joel 342n2, 430
Lincoln, Abraham 411
Locke, John 303n13, 306n13, 318-19, 322, 365n13, 413n3, 428, 430
Lowenthal, David 389n1, 430
Lyell, Charles 307n16
Lykourgos 41, 397n15

McClain, Ernest G. 340n25, 373n1, 430
Maccoby, Eleanor E. 403n9, 430
McDonald, Edward D. 344, 346, 408
Machiavelli, Niccolo 297n5, 299n7, 300n8, 306n13, 309-10, 342n3, 346-7n6, 347n7, 348-9n10, 352n13, 373n2, 396n10, 396n13, 429, 430, 432
Mahdi, Muhsin 308, 430
Mandelstam, Osip 296n4
Mansfield, Harvey 352n13, 430
Marcellinus 313
Marvell, Andrew 305
Marx, Karl 356
Masters, Roger 320, 431
Mathie, William 355n3, 430
Maude, Louise and Aylmer 411, 415n12

437

Index of Names

May, Robert 404, 430
Mayer, J.P. 432
Melville, Herman 301n8, 301-2n9, 302n10, 408-9, 427, 430
Mencken, H.L. 411-12
Mills, C. Wright 328, 429
Milton, John 135, 293-4n3, 305
Minos 41, 367n17
Mittelstrass, Jürgen 326n18
Montaigne 297n5, 299n7, 413n1, 429, 432
Montesquieu 301n8, 430
More, Thomas 396n14
Morris, Ivan 375n4, 430
Mozart, W.A. 321
Murphy, N.R. 379n7, 431

Nagumo, Adm. Chuichi 342n4
Newell, Waller 375n3, 431
Nichols, J.H. 340n26, 390n3, 429
Nichols, Mary P. 360n9, 374n2, 431
Nietzsche, Friedrich xxii-xxiii, 306n13, 307n16, 322-3, 324, 343, 353n13, 356-9n6, 361n9, 363-4n12, 368n4, 370-1n11, 371n12, 372n13, 374n2, 375n3, 376-7n5, 385, 390-1n4, 394-5n8, 406n14, 407n16, 409n21, 412n23, 414n6, 421-2n18, 422n20, 425n22, 430, 431, 433

Ortega y Gasset, José 377-8, 431
Oxenford, J. 321

Pangle, Thomas 325, 326n18, 367n17, 390n3, 431
Pasternak, Boris 296

Patton, Gen. George S. 397-8n16, 428
Penrose, Roger 424, 431
Pericles 397n15, 401n6
Petrarch 305
Philo 305
Planinc, Zdravko 348n8, 431
Platt, Michael 389n1, 431
Plutarch 298, 306-7n15
Pope, Alexander 297n5, 305
Pound, Ezra 337n23, 343, 429
Prange, Gordon 342n4, 431
Pushkin, Aleksandr 294, 296n4
Pythagoras 48, 99, 304, 305, 309, 351, 420

Raleigh, Sir Walter 312-13, 375-6n4
Rawley, Dr William 300n8
Regulus, Sebastianus 304
Rosen, Stanley 326n18, 431
Rostvig, Maren-Sofie 305
Rousseau, J.-J. 303n12, 306n13, 310, 319-21, 364-5n13, 366n16, 371-2n12, 393n6, 393n7, 409n19, 410, 415n10, 431

Sallis, John 431
Sand, George 412n22
Saxenhouse, Arlene W. 374n2, 406-7n15, 432
Schaefer, David L. 413, 432
Schlatter, Richard 314, 432
Schnabel, Artur 292
Schopenhauer, Artur 394-5n8, 411
Scott-Moncrieff, C.K. 398n3
Scullard, H.H. 368n5, 429
Shakespeare, William 299n6, 301-2n9, 305, 321, 346n5,

Index of Names

387–9n1, 396n13, 411, 427, 430, 433
Slim, Field Marshal Sir William 389–90n2, 432
Smith, Hedrick 294–5, 432
Smith, Kirby Flower 393n6, 432
Solzhenitsyn, Alexander 296n4
Sophocles 16
Spedding, James 311, 427
Spenser, Edmund 305
Spinoza, B. 316–18, 322, 432
Steiner, George 296–7n4, 432
Stendhal 343, 368n4, 398–9n3
Sterne, Laurence 343–4
Strauss, Leo xxix, xxx, xxxii, 296n3, 306n13, 325–6, 329, 336n20, 337n22, 340n25, 342n2, 348n10, 352n13, 359n8, 361n9, 367n17, 394n7, 396n9, 414n2, 414n5, 425n23, 426, 432
Swift, Jonathan 384
Sydney, Sir Phillip 305

Tacitus 311
Theon of Smyrna 373n1, 432
Thucydides 298, 313–14, 397n15
Tocqueville, Alexis de 295–6, 298, 432
Tolstoy, Leo 410–11, 415n12
Trollope, Anthony 407n18

Turgenev, Ivan 296n4, 344

Velthuysen, Lambert de 316
Virgil 304, 305
Vlastos, Gregory 396n12, 417n15, 432
Voltaire 321, 433
Vyvyan, John 299n6, 433

Wagner, Cosima 412n22
Wallis, Charles Glenn 309, 428
Walton, Isaac 318
Weber, Max 327–8, 329, 429
Weingartner, Rudolph H. 326n18, 433
Wescott, Howard B. 431
West, Thomas 387n1, 427
Williamson, Robert B. 416n14, 433
Wiseman, Anne and Peter 397n16, 428
Woozley, A.D. 417n15, 428

Xenophon 351, 353n1, 370n10, 397n15

Yamamoto, Adm. Isoroku 375n4
Yarmolinsky, Avrahm 379n6

Zuckert, Catherine 360n9, 373–4n2, 433